WITHDRAWN

WITHDRAWN

MAKING SENSE
OF
SOCIAL
STUDIES

COMMISSION MEMBERS

MAKING SENSE OF SOCIAL STUDIES

DAVID JENNESS

A Publication of the
National Commission on Social Studies in the Schools

A Joint Project of the
American Historical Association
Carnegie Foundation for the Advancement of Teaching
National Council for the Social Studies
Organization of American Historians

MACMILLAN PUBLISHING COMPANY
NEW YORK

Collier Macmillan Canada
TORONTO

Maxwell Macmillan International
NEW YORK   OXFORD   SINGAPORE   SYDNEY

373

Macmillan Publishing Company
A Division of Macmillan, Inc.
866 Third Avenue, New York, N. Y. 10022

Collier Macmillan Canada, Inc.
1200 Eglinton Avenue East, Suite 200
Don Mills, Ontario M3C 3N1

Library of Congress Catalog Card Number: 90-41565

Printed in the United States of America

printing number
1   2   3   4   5   6   7   8   9   10

Library of Congress Cataloging in Publication Data

Jenness, David.
  Making sense of social studies / David Jenness.
    p. cm.
  "A publication of the National Commission on Social Studies in the Schools."
  "A joint project of the American Historical Association . . . . [et al.]."
  Includes bibliographical references and indexes.
  ISBN 0-02-921155-7 : $34.95
  1. Social sciences—Study and teaching (Secondary)—United States.
  2. History—Study and teaching (Secondary)—United States.
  3. Geography—Study and teaching (Secondary)—United States.
  I. National Commission on Social Studies in the Schools (U.S.)
  II. American Historical Association.   III. Title.
  H62.5.U5J46   1990
  300'.71'073—dc20
                                                                90-41565
                                                                CIP

This book is dedicated
to
Eleanor Collins Isbell,
good colleague and friend

Contents

PART
ONE

The Scope of Social Studies
1

PART
TWO

History of the Curriculum
51

PART
THREE

The Subject Matters
165

PART
FOUR

Conflicts and Concerns
319

PART
FIVE

Conclusion: After a Century of Social Studies
387

Foreword

Concern over the lack of clarity and agreement in social studies, the lack of coherence in history, geography, and the social sciences at all educational levels, and the multitude and complexity of the challenges faced by the schools led the governing bodies of the American Historical Association, in 1984, and the National Council for the Social Studies, in 1985, to call for a national commission to determine goals and priorities and to recommend ways and means for reordering and strengthening the curriculum and the teaching of social studies in the schools. In December 1985 these two organizations agreed to join forces in a combined effort, and inaugurated a project to establish the National Commission on Social Studies in the Schools. The Carnegie Foundation for the Advancement of Teaching and the Organization of American Historians joined the coalition a few months later.

Because social studies draws on many disciplines, the founding organizations extended invitations to all the relevant professional organizations to join in the enterprise. In addition, invitations were issued to school administrators, teachers, and members of the concerned public. Since 1985, over 80 organizations concerned with education have been consulted, and have offered advice and encouragement to the Commission in its work.

The Commission both reflected and built upon a widespread current interest in educational reform. There has been much evidence in recent years of public concern that substantial numbers of the graduates of our schools fail to identify basic facts and issues of local, state, national, and world history, of political traditions, institutions, and processes, and of geography. However, while rightly documenting what they perceive as deficient achievement, most reform reports, with some exceptions, do not address themselves to the heart of the matter: what teachers should teach and children should learn.

Most of the reports also have neglected to deal with the goals to which schooling should be addressed. What should be the goals and vision of social studies as we set about to prepare young people for citizenship and leadership in the next century? What historical, geographic, political, social, and cultural knowledge is indispensable for good citizenship and a rich cultural life?

In many school systems, a pattern of borrowing from discrete social science and humanistic disciplines, without considering their relationships to the whole curriculum, and the introduction of subjects and skills that are unrelated to each other or only remotely related to a central purpose, have fragmented and sometimes marginalized the field of social studies. It is not surprising, therefore, that attempts to provide a unifying synthesis have failed.

Some of the present social studies in the schools took form in 1916 as a result of the effort of a subcommittee of a National Education Association Commission on the Reorganization of Secondary Education to establish the goals that social studies education should attempt to achieve. In the 1930s a commission under the aegis of the American Historical Association attempted to realign the goals and programs of social studies away from ethnocentrism and an exclusive concern with the United States and Western Europe toward a larger world orientation and modern social studies synthesis. However, this Commission on the Social Studies, as it was named, stopped short of recommendations on the framework of the actual curriculum, and its impact was thereby dissipated. Attempts beginning in the late 1950s to produce a new synthesis and to define the nature of the relationships of the social science and humanities disciplines also produced limited results. The "reform" upheavals of the 1960s and early 1970s focused on the educational community's attention on how to teach and involved a zeroing-in on process and content, but without sufficient concern for the overall question of what interrelated content young people should learn, and why.

Three other developments have had significant impact on school social studies. First, special interest groups have pushed for the inclusion of their own projects into the school curriculum. More often than not, such courses (career education, ethnic studies, consumer education, or, more recently, environmental, peace, nuclear, or drug education) became part of the social studies mosaic. Although most social studies teachers have indeed thought that the goals of the new courses were worthy, the effect of their inclusion in the social studies curriculum has been to further complicate the attainment of coherence.

Second, coexisting with an attempt in the "new social studies," beginning about 1960, to foster "inquiry" and "discovery," which rested on critical thinking and greater attention to scholarly processes of investigation, there were increasing cries for "relevance" and "self-realization," reflective of the societal upheavals of the time.

Third, even while pressures were beginning to mount for rigorous attention to content in the social studies, teachers were losing the support and involvement of their traditional allies. In the 1960s and later, academic historians and social scientists, like academics in other fields, faced rapid growth in their graduate schools, responded to a trend toward increasing specialization within their disciplines, and experienced more intense pressure to publish articles and monographs. Academic scholars evinced less interest in classroom teachers than had once been the case. This development in universities resulted in the failure of efforts to maintain or effect improvement in school programs: that failure remains today as a legacy of the period.

The inauguration of the National Commission on Social Studies in the Schools meant that, for the first time in more than fifty years, all major relevant educational organizations, together with representatives of the broader public concerned with the vitality and soundness of social studies, were united in a coalition dedicated to the reform of that vital portion of the education of young Americans.

The executive committee organized itself in early 1986 and took steps to organize the full commission and its staff. The Commission held its first plenary meeting in November 1987. The Commission has been notable for a strong sense of collaboration between those who, on the one hand, teach social studies and influence its curricular guidelines and goal statements in the schools and, on the other hand, university historians and social scientists concerned about the content, relevance, and coherence of social studies.

During the past three years, the National Commission has examined the content and effectiveness of instruction in the social studies in our elementary and secondary schools, the goals of such studies, and the priorities in the field. It charged its Curriculum Task Force to make recommendations for reform. The Task Force responded with its November 1989 recharting report, Charting a Course: Social Studies for the 21st Century, which has now been distributed in some 50,000 copies across the United States. The report takes a bold stand on what actually needs to be taught in K–12 social studies courses.

As the Commission undertook its task, it realized that reform of the social studies was hindered not only by a lack of agreement on what should be done in the classroom, but also by a failure to understand what been recommended, and accomplished or not accomplished, in the past. All too little was known from the cumulative experience of the various social studies reform movements during the past seventy-five years.

The executive committee of the Commission therefore called upon their fellow Commissioner David Jenness to prepare a book-length study of the history of the social studies movement, with particular attention to the efforts of the disciplines at various stages to influence the process. The volume at hand is the remarkable result of that request. We believe that this analysis of the history of attempts to influence and shape social studies in the schools is an essential pre-requisite to an understanding of where we are today—and where we can reasonably aspire to go.

The views expressed in this book are those of the author, and not necessarily of the signers of this Foreword or the Commission's sponsoring organizations. They reflect independent analysis and judgment. In a field inevitably fraught with conflict between disciplines, political points of view, and institutional interests, a careful and disinterested map of the terrain creates the condition precedent to common action. Jenness has given us a shrewd, fair, and honest account of how we got here. It will be up to teachers, scholars, administrators, and citizens of goodwill to take the next steps in the fuller understanding of the historical dynamic of social studies reform.

The Commission extends its heartfelt thanks to David Jenness for undertaking this necessary and difficult task, and for concluding it with such dispatch and skill. We also wish, once again, to thank our dedicated Executive Director, Fay D. Metcalf, for her selfless, efficient, and able assistance in this, as in all other tasks, of the National Commission on Social Studies in the Schools.

Support for the research and writing phases of this publication, as well as for much of the work of the Commission itself and the development of its other publications (see p. ii), was made possible by grants from the Rockefeller Foundation, the Carnegie Corporation of New York, the National Geographic Society, the John D. and Catherine T. MacArthur Foundation, and by the four founding organizations. We appreciate their confidence and generosity.

ARTHUR S. LINK—President of the Commission; George Henry Davis '86 Professor of History, Princeton University; former President of the American Historical Association, the Organization of American Historians, and the Southern Historical Association

ERNEST L. BOYER—Vice-President of the Commission; President of the Carnegie Foundation for the Advancement of Teaching; former U.S. Commissioner of Education

STANLEY N. KATZ—Executive Committee Liaison for the Commission; President of the American Council of Learned Societies; former President of the Organization of American Historians

Preface

One measure of what could be the timeliness of this book is that, when I told friends and colleagues that I was going to write it, they often seemed taken aback. To some of those professionally involved with higher scholarship and research, the very name 'social studies' evidently indicates a suspect, perhaps a hypothetical entity—which some other term would make more real. This is puzzling. I remember almost nothing of my early schooling, except the personality of two or three teachers, and it is true that I had not paid attention to the school curriculum for many years; but it still seems to me that most of my contemporaries have 'taken' social studies, as have their children. Why should there be a problem with the label, and what it labels?

Elsewhere, for example in England, 'social studies' is used in a matter-of-fact fashion, but not so as to refer specifically to precollegiate education. That, it appears, is half the answer. School subjects are thought of by those long since out of school, especially perhaps by those who deal with intellectual matters, as not actual subjectmatters but, instead, as a kind of shorthand for a segment or a stage of an educational process that consists, concretely, of time in the school day, lesson plans, teaching strategies, textbooks—and, to be sure, rudiments of knowledge.

Moreover, it seems, 'social studies' rudiments are not structured in ways that correspond closely to university subjects, as may be the case with English or chemistry. There is some Augustinian doctrine at work which holds that the redemptive act of studying 'real' subjects later in life acts backward to purify the simple and approximate forms encountered in school, thus stabilizing and reaffirming in each educational generation the eternal essence of the field. This is clear enough in the remarks voiced by academics, who say, first, that they very much want 'their' subject to be represented in the curriculum; but, second, that if it can't be *real* chemistry (or sociology, or whatever), better not to have it at all. It sometimes appears, by this argument, that nothing would be left in the school curriculum but the vocational subjectmatters and moral instruction.

We all, of course, suffer from professional deformations—definitional, ethical, and procedural assumptions that predispose us to distorted views of fields in our purview, but not under our control. What, however, accounts for the puzzlement expressed by ordinary folks—parents, taxpayers, those with everyday pursuits distant from education—when one says that he is going to look into social studies? There is often the admission, meant condolingly, that the person one is discussing this with has never been clear what social studies *is* or *are*. (In fact, laypersons often use 'social studies' and 'sociology' as equivalent terms, a synechdochical confusion whose origin can be traced in recent social and intellectual history.) There is often the suggestion that insofar as social studies deal with 'social reality,' they do so in a remote and artificial way, since how the social world works is largely self-evident. (A similar suggestion is made by those, beginning with M. Jourdain, who find it odd that persons who live in a world of talk or written messages should study language; but is never made, analogously, about studying science or math.) Finally, it is sometimes suggested that the social *sciences* as research and professional fields are so arcane and whimsical an endeavor that few grown-ups will ever engage in them; hence, social studies must prove a waste of time for many youngsters.

Although I was educated in the humanities and trained in the biobehavioral sciences, most of my professional life has been spent in the social sciences. It seems to me that the educated American public (and it is a well-educated public, relatively speaking) have had a distinctly provisional and ambivalent understanding of and respect for these fields in society and in the culture. The objective indicators—enrollments, research funding, rate of creation of departments and institutes, and the like—suggest that the 'age of the social sciences,' if it existed in the midcentury, as many claimed it did, has ended: not that the fields themselves are under attack, but that the action is elsewhere. I value these fields and wish for their further development, but I believe that they have a difficult future unless they are better understood by more people, and less taken for granted in a discounting or dismissive way. (In another sense, being taken for granted would be beneficial.) That, of course, seems to imply that they possess at least a stable, if not more commanding, presence in public education. It was for these reasons that in 1987 I accepted membership in a commission then being formed, the National Commission on Social Studies in the Schools, which was intended to set distinguished and wise individuals to work on some of these problems and confusions, and enable them to recommend how the situation could be bettered. It was for these reasons that I also accepted the unexpected invitation by the leadership of the Commission to write this study. Initially my study was to survey the ground for the Commission's tilling. However, I made it clear that my study would be an independent piece of work, not guided by the Commission's particular agenda and only incidentally a report to it. I hoped that it would prove useful not only to the Commission but to all those who care, or have a genuine curiosity, about the topic. Thus, in the end, the book is written for that same general educated public whose puzzlement I found so puzzling.

I hope that the title of this book is taken, not as a claim that someone at last has written a user's handbook, but to convey two general notions: First, that social studies are aimed at *making* sense of what is not, in fact, a self-evident realm. Second, that we all should be sensible about how far such a program can go, how different it can be from other branches of knowledge in education, even how important it is in some ultimate sense. Social studies should be rich, various, realistic, idealistic—and tentative and rough-and-ready.

The hallmark of good social studies in the schools, it seems to me now, after a period of reflection, is a kind of creative and critical (that is, an evaluative) thoughtfulness. This thoughtfulness is partly personal and private, taking shape in one student's mind, and partly transpersonal and public, involving negotiation and validation among several or many dealing with or aware of each other. In the first mode, the teacher-student relationship is focal, and the teacher can model, in many ways, the processes and attributes of thoughtfulness. In the second mode, the teacher can to a degree guide and rehearse the process, but there are more parties involved than teacher and student (for example, student and student, student and parents, and so on), and more stakeholders in the outcome of the process. Social studies have both a cognitive and a constructivist facet, and a political and cultural, even a rhetorical, character.

In its exploration of both facets, this book has definite limitations. With regard to learning and understanding in individual minds, I have not attempted to review or argue from recent research on learning, cognition, and pedagogy. These research fields are lively and productive these days, in flux, and in any case too technical to be covered here. It is also well to remember that the processes being studied are *not* entirely contained within (and between) individual minds. Today's research still underattends to the complex interplay, especially over time, of group processes, social learning, modelling, social and affective development, and the dynamics of classrooms and related milieus.

With regard to the political and cultural character of social studies as fields, and social studies education as a public enterprise, I have not been able to discuss in any depth the ways in which social studies and social studies education function as *systems*, contained within education as a system, all such systems being marked off conceptually from other systems, each with its own set of goals, resources, and concerns. Part of this limitation is my inability—unwillingness might be a more honest term—to analyze in this book directly what I refer to elsewhere as "crudely speaking, the sociological and demographic aspects of schooling." There are, to be sure, frequent glancing views and comments in what follows. I regret the episodic and laconic nature of my treatment here, on both intellectual and ethical grounds, because I believe that all too many commentators on education willfully give only glancing and uncritical attention to these aspects. The general topic of the cultural forms and political purpose of education, however, goes far beyond the analysis of how many and who attend, and how schooling reflects their origins and characteristics and affects (or does not affect) their lives. What is involved, finally, is the social study *of* education, not books on social studies *in* education. This too is an established field of scholarship and research, but it is underfunded and its results often downplayed, if not buried. In addition, we may have reached a stage where the various subdisciplines that put *of education* at the end of their names—sociology, history, economics, ethnography, and the like—need to transcend rather than perpetuate conceptual and methodological divisions if they are to make substantial further progress.

Other obvious limitations of my book are the absence of much sustained discussion about textbooks, what textbooks can and cannot do, and how textbooks and tests and curriculum decisions affect each other; and the lack of any serious attempt to describe or explain regional differences. I had intended to cover the first topic, but time and space did not permit. Save for some brilliant work in American educational history, the second topic is for the most part unexplored.

In the course of my observation of, research on, and thinking about the schools—which actually began about 1977, when I became professionally involved for a time in music education—I have observed in myself and others some rather prevalent misconceptions or unfortunate tendencies that are hard to overcome. One is that we all tend to misremember our own early educations, and generally draw conclusions from personal educational experience that are not veridical. What we experienced at early stages is overlaid with, and distorted by, what we experienced later, or what our neighbors' kids are said to have experienced recently, or how we think about education now as taxpayers (as distinct from how we thought about it when we were younger), or what we read in the papers. A number of keen observers have pointed out that most of us judge that our local schools are relatively untroubled and doing fairly well, considering how much of a disaster "the schools" are known to be. The illogic of this hardly needs to be dwelt upon. But our tendency to forget, edit, and draw illogical inferences leads to a certain petulance. *We* did it, why can't they? If kids aren't learning something, give them *more* of it. I was drilled on the facts, and I learned to think: *ergo*, drilling leads to thinking.

Not only do those outside education blame educators for many sins, largely of omission, to a grossly unfair degree, but many teachers fail to see beyond their immediate fields of operation. (Not surprisingly, since there are few opportunities for those involved in day-to-day work in the schools to step outside the system, or to one side in it.) Some teachers really think that other teachers or other schools are pretty bad, and that tougher standards or policing by tests would improve matters—but are not needed for themselves or in their schools. More typically, teachers believe that their own work and that of their colleagues is pretty good, and that their students are happy—and thus that repeated careful studies of educational practice that find serious problems must be wrong or malicious. The inability—which all of us share—deeply to grasp the idea that most practice, in any arena, must necessarily lie *at the average* (and that the average is taken over all cases, not just familiar ones) leads us to false pessimism or optimism, depending on our points of view or temperaments. It is especially sad to see teachers making these errors if one believes, as I do from considerable direct observation, that teachers taken as a group are among the most hardworking, benignly motivated, and underappreciated of all working adults.

The root of these misconceptions and faulty inferences may be that we confuse what happens during schooling with what schooling itself brings into being or determines. Many things happen in schools because that is where most children of certain ages are. Many things happen to young people in the course of attending school that would happen anyhow; and many things follow in a given sequence, in the lives of school-goers, not because educational 'treatment *x*' leads to 'outcome *y*,' but because that is how human lives in our society, or universally, unroll.

Reading, for example, is certainly a crucial activity that takes place in school, and is there practiced, potentiated, and carried into new realms. But few if any children are taught to read, uniquely and sufficiently, through schooling. It may make sense to test reading proficiency in the school environment, not only for reasons of monitoring this proficiency for the sake of internal decisions about pedagogy and sequences of instruction, but for the simple reason that that is where those who are moving from nonreading to proficiency in reading are located. It seems to be almost impossible, however, to conduct testing in schools to assess the course of *any* process of human growth or development without that testing being taken as a direct index of how good the schools are. The notion that teaching bears a rather modest relationship to learning (and to the accumulation and distribution of knowledge in general in society) is a radical one to most people, but one that deserves close scrutiny.

Schools, of course, are about far more than just teaching. In all of their aspects, however, those who work in the schools need to protect themselves, and be protected, from assuming responsibilities by proxy. Schools should be spared being the locus of assessments that are more properly made in other sectors, or at later ages. How fluently a person speaks, across a range of situations; how far she achieves in scientific research; whether he becomes a successful artist; whether she engages in active and responsible activity as a citizen—all these have something important to do with schools, and are appropriate goals to be kept in view in schools, but perhaps are less the sovereign concerns of the schools than is commonly assumed. I hope that those who today are contributing with a renewed vigor and ingenuity to ethical, political, and pragmatic philosophy will attend to this dimension of sectoral responsibility more ably than I can do. Schools have little to be ashamed of. But they can be helped to be more vibrant, less defensive, more productive, and more confident than they are today.

Acknowledgments

As the Foreword and Preface have made clear, I wrote this book at the invitation of the National Commission on Social Studies in the Schools, but as an independent scholar rather than as a member of the Commission. The chance to participate in meetings of the Commission and its committees was of course of great benefit, since those involved in the Commission's work have much wisdom and interestingly diverse points of view. (For the list of members of the Commission, see p. ii of this volume.) I am grateful to the members of the Commission's executive committee—Ernest Boyer, Donald H. Bragaw, Stanley N. Katz, and Arthur S. Link—for their personal encouragement, their patience and tact, and their firm but friendly insistence that the research had to come to an end and the writing begin (and later, stop).

Many members of the Commission have had a discernible effect on the book from my reading of their work on the social studies, the social sciences, history as a field and as a school subject, and education as a domain. But that work is of a stature and importance that guaranteed that I would have located and used it in any case. Certain members did take the initiative to introduce me to crucial sources and informants, to issues and philosophical questions, and to research opportunities early in the process; I am grateful for their guidance, and for their tolerance of my sometimes opportunistic way of using their leads in following up their suggestions. Those whose influence counted for much early in the process included the late Hazel Hertzberg, Paul Bohannon, Thomas Cronin, Lee Hansen, Donald Bragaw, and Fred Newmann. Donald Bragaw, Jean Craven, and Howard Mehlinger not only spent time explaining basic aspects of the educational system and procedures, but made it possible for me to observe this firsthand.

At an early stage, as I was trying to organize research, reading, and school visits to take the most advantage of limited time and funds, a number of those involved in or familiar with social studies and the schools shared their thoughts and background knowledge generously with me by letter and phone. These include James Marran, Denis Doyle, Howard Gardner, Salvatore Natoli, Carla Howery, James Gardner, Carl Kaestle, William Kruskal, Steven Buckles, Robert Highsmith, Thomas Dynneson, Mary Jane Turner, Mary Soley, Carolee Bush, Frances Bolin, Mary Fishler, William Walstad, Frances Haley, David Hill, Wayne Herman, Freeman Butts, Lawrence Stedman, Mary Hepburn, David Harris, the late Jean Grambs, Myron Marty, Richard Gross, Vic Bunderson, John Harrold, Al Short, Fred Risinger, Jane Lowrie Bacon, Phillip Bacon, Lee

Cronbach, Stephen Thornton, Brewster Smith, Janet Spence, and James Barth. As I review my early correspondence and notes from telephone calls, I realize with some astonishment how many leads, direct or indirect, and how many generative thoughts and comments they provided, through a tortuous process of which only I can have any real sense.

Early in the process also, Thomas Peet, Patricia Thévenet, Joe Dunbar, Lawrence Stedman, James Marran and Lucia Dunn, John Patrick, Mary Jane Turner, Sheila Mann, Ira Cohen, Gail Burrill, Jerry Knowland, Freeman Butts, Salvatore Natoli, James Giese, Thomas Dynneson, Jean Craven, Isabel Beck, and Jerry Brophy provided me with important data or materials to which I would otherwise not have had access easily, if at all. Throughout the research phase, Jeanne Griffith and others on the staff of the National Center for Education Statistics and Larry Long and Paul Siegel of the Census Bureau were most helpful. All the staff of the Department of Education Library were lavish with their time and pertinacious beyond the call of duty. Without the presence of this specialized library in Washington (and certain collections of the Library of Congress) I could not have done this study in more or less the form I wanted. Other scholars will not be so fortunate in the future if the budget of the Education Library is not protected.

At a later stage of work, I held conversations with a number of persons, often in the course of field trips, which had important consequences with regard to how I organized my thoughts, materials, and lines of argument. These included Thomas James, Shirley Brice Heath, Jerome Kagan, Vito Perrone, Donald Oliver, Charles Willie, Hugh Mehan, Roy D'Andrade, John Patrick, Jerome Bruner, Judith Tanur, Judith Torney-Purta, Russell Farnen, Jere Brophy, David Tyack, Richard Snow, Shirley Engle, Anna Ochoa, Judith Wooster, Fred Risinger, Gerald Marker, Fred Newmann, Robert Stake, Charlotte Crabtree, Michael Hartoonian, William O. Baker, Christine Bennett, Lee Ehman, Jesus Garcia, Norman Overly, and Sam Wineburg.

A writer needs good readers of drafts, those who will be generous with time and attention, and knowledgeable and tough-minded too. Those who read large parts of my book in draft included Stanley Katz, Carl Kaestle, Donald Bragaw, Hugh Mehan, Dell Hymes, Howard Gardner, and Harold Raynolds and George Perry. Each paid me the courtesy of reading carefully, questioning sharply, clarifying muddles and preventing mistakes with a few words, a fact, or a reference. Others read shorter units of the draft, and saved me from unproductive bush-beating. That I have been unable to deal adequately with all the suggestions of these readers is my own loss, and should not indicate to them anything less on my part than trust, respect, and gratitude.

With all of this guidance, stimulation, and generosity on the part of others I still would have nothing of importance to say had I not been able, over the years, to get a sense of schools, how they work, and how it feels to be in them. The willingness of superintendents and principals, curriculum specialists, practice teaching supervisors, and department chairs to explain patiently what the salient aspects of their schools are, how they became that, and what might be in the process of change; their generosity in sharing lessons plans, curriculum guides, administrative documents, and the like—this willingness and generosity is remarkable, given the pressure of their working lives. The willingness of teachers to be observed and questioned by an essentially anonymous outsider is incredible, going far beyond what other professionals tolerate. The reason, of course, is that administrators and teachers care so deeply about making education a success, about helping to establish on a moral and informed basis what Thomas Jefferson called the sovereignty of each succeeding generation. I particularly have to express gratitude to, among administrators, Jean Craven in Albuquerque, Victor Smith in Indianapolis, and Clarence Hoover and George Perry in Massachusetts, and to their counterparts in other school systems. The teachers must go unnamed, among other reasons because there have been many whose full names I never knew. But my abiding thanks and admiration go to the teachers in Boston and surrounding towns; Hartford and New Haven and their suburbs; Albuquerque and nearby communities; San Francisco, Berkeley, Oakland, and Palo Alto; and Indianapolis. There the teachers and the students I have observed and talked to have given me some of the most treasurable moments of my life.

Finally, over a period of eighteen months, my working life has been made easier and more productive through the hard work and solicitude of members of the staff of the National Commission, especially Mary Kennedy Ward, Ned Hartfiel, Joe Hartlaub, and research assistant Tony Hake. Fay Metcalf, the Commission's executive director—whether instructing me in word processing, introducing me to valuable sources, or explaining how history lessons work—has been the ideal colleague, and a helpful critic and friend at every step. My most personal affection and gratitude go to her.

DAVID JENNESS
Washington, DC

Other Publications of the
National Commission on Social Studies in the Schools

Charting a Course: Social Studies for the 21st Century.
   A report of the Curriculum Task Force of the National Commission on Social Studies in the Schools. 1989. 84 pages. $9.00 per copy (including postage and handling) from:

   American Historical Association
   400 A Street, S.E.
   Washington, DC 20003
   202/544-2422

   National Council for the Social Studies
   3501 Newark Street, NW
   Washington DC 20016
   202/966-7840

   Organization of American Historians
   112 N. Bryan Street
   Bloomington, IN 47408-4199
   812/855-7311

Voices of Teachers: Report of a Survey on Social Studies.
   Prepared by the staff of the National Commission on Social Studies in the Schools. 1990. About 64 pages. Available November 1990 from:

   National Council for the Social Studies
   3501 Newark Street, NW
   Washington, DC 20016
   202/966-7840

Note to Readers

In this book I have adopted certain conventions that I hope will contribute to clarity and ease of understanding.

I have used quotation marks to indicate something that has actually been said or written. I use single quotation marks to indicate a special meaning, tone of voice, or usage: for example, ideologically loaded terms, cultural shibboleths, specialized concepts, or other phraseology of my own or someone else's that should be registered or scrutinized.

The name for an intellectual field may refer at one and the same time to an educational discipline; some broader surround in which research, scholarship, or specialized practice takes place; a conceptual or procedural attitude common to those in the general culture who think about things in a particular way; and certain processes or elements that are thought of as taking place or existing in the world. With regard to the fields most discussed here, *political science* is the narrowest, since it refers specifically to disciplinary and closely related activity, and *history* is the broadest. The other fields fall between—as shown, for example, in such phrases as "sociology of poverty," "anthropology of the classroom," "international economics," which are likely to refer, respectively, to certain dimensions of a set of problems, a way of looking at an arena of activity, and actual processes involving trade, payments, and the like. I have tried to make these distinctions clear in context, but urge readers to be aware of them, since otherwise much discussion is at cross-purposes. I have used one special device, however, for clarifying what is often confusing. When the name of a field is used with an initial capital letter, it always indicates a named *course* present in the curriculum (at any level). Thus it becomes possible to say, for example, that teachers trained in history teach considerable economics in History, or that some students are exposed to instruction in world geography in World Cultures, or that some teachers trained in anthropology teach no Anthropology but are able to introduce anthropological concepts here and there, or that Economics is not taught in the elementary school, though elements of economics may be. Similarly, a teacher trained in History is one who has taken courses so named; other teachers may of course know much history.

For related reasons, I use the compound term *subjectmatter* to indicate what is normally dealt with in a formal educational exposition. The subject matter of history is infinite. Historians have treated some portions of that material; and scholars writing monographs, graduate students working on dissertations, and

xxvii

amateurs collecting and organizing local evidence may all be enlarging that portion which comprises historical scholarship. But curriculum specialists, textbook publishers, school boards, and teachers create, select, or determine the subjectmatter in History; it is that which one finds, and expects to find covered, in lectures, texts and readings, class discussion, and tests. My usage here may be needlessly self-conscious, in which case I ask the reader's pardon. On the other hand, much debate is directed precisely at the question of scope and emphasis in History or Economics or the other areas of the curriculum: that is, *which* facts, *what* models, and *where* boundaries and the minima and maxima of exposition lie, ideally or by convention.

Readers will observe that footnotes on the page deal with substantive matters, while endnotes deal largely with sources. Inevitably, there is some overlapping between the two.

PART I

The Scope of Social Studies

1.0   A Nation at Risk?
Excellence in the 1980s

Early in the 1980s a spate of widely publicized reports warned that American society was in danger from the accumulating, perhaps accelerating, inadequacies of public education. *A Nation at Risk* was the blunt title of one report, in 1983—that of the National Commission on Excellence in Education, which, Secretary of Education Terrel Bell reported, was a front-page story on virtually every newspaper of any size in the country. One of the commission's statements, in particular, provided a dramatic and memorable lead: "If an unfriendly foreign power had attempted to impose on America the mediocre educational performance that exists today, we might well have viewed it as an act of war.... We have, in effect, been committing an act of unthinking, unilateral educational disarmament."[1]

Those with some knowledge of educational and social history knew, of course, that denunciations of the schools have been a feature of American public education since the beginning. At each era there have been some who found the schools grossly inadequate in terms either of what they were trying to do, how they were attempting to do it, or the resulting educational achievement. It is because education has been viewed as so important, Richard Hofstadter has pointed out, that the "educational jeremiad" has been a constant feature of American public comment.

But impending *failure*, with serious national consequences, has not been the normal prediction. During the 1970s, for example, the dominant message in comparable reports had been that the schools were attempting to do too many, and incompatible, things: pursue academic mastery and vocational preparation, emphasize cognitive skills and social relevance, provide courses that every student needed and an additional range of courses that particular students might want. With the schools trying to do so much, energies were scattered and goals occluded. Some observers concluded that a unitary system of mass precollegiate education had become impossible, and that a differentiation of types of schools might serve us better, in the way that higher education had become differentiated into research universities, liberal arts colleges, technical schools, two-year and community colleges, corporate and adult education programs, and the like.[2] Even those who did not favor that solution still wanted the schools to focus in, and do what they did better. The watchword of the era was *accountability*. Were the schools achieving what they claimed to accomplish?

3

The Tone of the 1980s

The calls for reform in the 1980s were quite different in tone and in their premises. The criteria cited were largely external ones, having to do with demonstrable outcomes judged by noneducational consequences. There was little regard, in the most publicized reports, for what the schools on their own were trying to accomplish, and how well they were succeeding in their own terms. To the contrary: there was present subliminally the notion that the partial reorienting of the schools in the 1960s and 1970s—toward helping to solve the social ills and internal problems of America—had not only proven unfeasible but may have contributed to a sense of stasis and impotence in the society. Nor was there much consideration of qualitative aspects, such as how students experienced the process of education, for good or bad, and how this predisposed them toward or away from serious engagement as individuals in society; or how teachers and administrators dealt with problems and negotiated priorities, and whether they believed that they were making progress. Reflecting their nature as assessments by citizens, these reports took a peremptory tack: either the schools were meeting societal needs adequately, or they were not.*[3]

The consensus was that they were not. The 'American century' appeared to be drawing to a close, the American cynosure to be fading. The entering work force was unqualified. American productivity was declining. American goods were not competitive, in quality or price, with those of Japan, West Germany, or Korea. In mathematics and the natural sciences, test scores among those completing high school were abysmal, and achieved literacy was merely 'functional'—meaning hardly sufficient for the new information age. The rhetoric was minatory and militant: the United States would not become a 'third-world' nation.

In keeping with the corporate and competitive tone of the most publicized of the reports and commissions, the demands placed on the schools amounted to more product and better output. The 'minimal competency' that educators had sought in the 1970s—that is, the notion that every student would achieve to a level that would enable her or him to move on, in a relatively unproblematical fashion, into higher education or the world of work—was outmoded. *Minimal competency* was no longer enough. The judgment was that the aggregation of an assortment of diverse competences did not equal the maximum that could be

---

*In what follows, I distinguish between reports that challenge the schools and those that call for reform. The challenge tendency was evident in those reports by panels and commissions created by foundations, national panels, or citizens' groups, such as the Commission on Excellence, the Education Commission of the States, or a Task Force of the National Governors' Association; less so in reports issued by those professionally engaged in education. Thus, the report on *High School*, issued by the Carnegie Foundation for the Advancement of Teaching, and the books by John Goodlad and Theodore Sizer, which appeared at about the same time, gave considerable attention to the morale of teachers and administrators, the experience of students, and the various forces operating within, and impinging upon, 'the system.'

achieved in the system if *excellence* were truly the end goal. Unlike practice in the 1970s, the schools should emphasize rigorous intellectual mastery in a more circumscribed, more 'basic,' set of subjects. What was needed was longer school days and school years: more science and math, more foreign language; more (that is, additional) teacher training and retraining; fewer curriculum alternatives and variations; more mandated requirements; better scores, and more tests to demonstrate them. The legal school-leaving age should be increased, and students should be prevented, if necessary, from dropping out. Since the challenges to the schools originated externally, it followed that they could be implemented from the top down—that is, by regulation.

The note of crisis, in these calls in the early 1980s for better performance, was not unlike that of the late 1950s, when, after Sputnik, the schools were charged with achieving a rapid quantal improvement, especially in the sciences. Then the overriding concern had been national security in military and geopolitical terms. In the 1980s, the concern was for national security in terms of economic efficiency and standard of living. There were, to be sure, differences between the two eras. The late 1950s called for a kind of focused mobilization of effort on the part of those students with most to offer. If science was needed, those who could do science should get lots of science; those who were without much ability in these fields could receive less (and perhaps should be 'tracked' out of the more advanced courses lest they impede others' achievements). Students, in general, should be grouped by IQ and area of most efficient achievement, so that those most ready to progress in each field would do so most rapidly. In the 1950s, the presence of a rather large number of students with only modest scientific and technical competence did not endanger the republic—so long as *some* students were high achievers. Students of a nonscientific bent might not contribute much, but they did not represent a negative input. Specialization in education, as in industry, implied that production needs were finite.

The emphasis in the 1980s implied a far broader base for achievement. Now the challenge was that the young adult population *in general* become more productive and competent—and technologically up-to-date, so as to be able to adapt to future change. Sustained growth in GNP and a recapturing of American leadership in the international economy could not rest on the accomplishments of a narrow elite. An expanding economy and power in the world would require more than breakthroughs in rocketry or communications.

Thus, in the 1980s, *excellence for all* became the slogan. The overtly elitist strategy of the Sputnik era was rejected. At the same time it was pointed out that the pluralistic, laissez-faire (some said 'cafeteria-style') public education of the late 1960s and 1970s—which had aimed at ensuring equity by offering something for everybody—had proven to be a delusion. Something-for-everybody had meant, in practice, that students simply made their ways through the system without the schools' providing much that was distinctively school-based, much that was value-added. Students who found, in that system, courses and teachers that suited them and that produced marketable skills would come out in a favorable position; those who did not, would not. (Obviously, those who entered school already in a favorable position were most likely to find their way.) Thus, in the name of fair treatment, the schools perpetuated the status quo.

Who Shall Benefit, and How?

What the panels and reports of the 1980s did not clarify was how, in this era, excellence and equity could be balanced, how *everyone* (or nearly so) could be guided toward true proficiency.* How could raising the height of the bar help those who could not get off the ground? If the panels and reports did not attempt the kind of philosophical analysis that might illuminate such questions, they nevertheless had the great benefit of making it clear what they wanted. In a system in which educational goals and priorities are negotiated politically, rather than centrally imposed, it is vital that those who advocate change be candid and tough-minded about what it is they want to achieve. Otherwise the mixed chorus of dissatisfaction that accompanies the work of the schools will amount only to another peal of school-bashing.

In some respects, the economic rationale and corporate management tone of the calls for reform in the 1980s was more like those of the 1920s than like those of the era of Sputnik. In the 1920s, the business community took it as a routine procedure to specify what intellectual and practical skills were needed for an era of industrial change and expansion—at a time in the Western world, at any rate, where the costs of the World War to other nations guaranteed American hegemony in the international economy, and where under- or miseducation in the populace (much of it of foreign origin) might breed a failure of appreciation of American values.[4] In the 1920s, however, the corporate community felt quite confident about the technocratic dimensions of the future, and about the subject matters and skills that would be needed. The rather modest level of formal education in the general population and the lack of any widespread commitment, across classes, to a liberal, rather than a utilitarian, education meant that parents were willing enough to accept that their children needed to be educated in a new and 'modern' way. Thus science and social studies, for example, found acceptance as new fields in the secondary schools.

Even while demanding more and better performance in the schools, the reports of the 1980s made few specific recommendations and outlined few hard choices. States were urged to set higher requirements—but which requirements was unstated.[5] There was to be more math, but there was no stipulation as to whether calculus, vector algebra, or analytic geometry would serve: more

---

*In this respect—that of excellence for all—the national reports of the educational reformers were consonant with the reports of the citizen-leader groups. By no means do all those who put equity in education first believe in a widely diversified curriculum, with something for everyone. They may insist on a core curriculum, but with the significant condition that all or nearly all students genuinely benefit from it.

science—but no analysis of whether course-hours in geology or evolutionary biology or biochemistry would be appropriate, or whether these would substitute for course-hours in physics and inorganic chemistry. America's position in the world required more knowledge of foreign societies and languages, but which societies and which languages?* Besides emphasizing the familiar subjects of English, math, science, and social studies, the Commission on Excellence broke fresh ground only in recommending at least one course in computer science.

The relatively unspecific nature of the recommendations probably reflected a democratic reluctance to prescribe lock-step measures, together with a defensiveness with regard to sensitive political and ideological conflicts. Such conflicts were readily apparent. The emphasis on a high-tech society and an up-to-date managerial elite comported uneasily with the recognition that technological change was now so rapid that it was useless to *train* for technical competence (as opposed to *educating* for basic understanding). Which would be better for the society of the future: some hundreds of thousands more trained scientists or engineers, or some millions more educated persons who were scientifically literate and could participate in decision-making involving technical issues? And why the emphasis on advanced, or even expert, achievement—whether in science, the utilization of verbal and written language, or the understanding of human relations—when experts predicted that the bulk of the growth in new jobs in the 1990s would come largely in relatively undemanding roles in such areas as data processing, retail service, repair and maintenance of technical systems, health care and care for the aged?† Why an emphasis on skills for the 'information age' if most of the new jobs in the electronic industries involved piecework? Who needs to understand how computers work in order to place chips in control boards? Would millions of individual Americans, seemingly facing limits to growth, an aging society, and lowered expectations as to their real standard of living, be willing to invest massively in a sharply 'better' educational system—especially if the reclaiming of American superiority would be accomplished by the few, and enjoyed by the few?

Questions about the base *for* excellence, the distribution *of* excellence, and the pattern of benefits *from* excellence had to be faced. Some critics maintained that present divisions in society between the educational and occupational haves and have-nots was already an internal threat equal to any posed by a slipping of America's relative position in the world. In the 1980s in America, the rich were getting richer, and the poor poorer. Minorities had shared relatively little in

---

*The 1983 Commission on Excellence recommended two years of foreign language in high school *for the college bound*—a reasonable recommendation, perhaps, but one which showed a rather limited commitment either to Excellence or to Excellence for All.

†To be sure, there was and is considerable controversy among labor economists and other experts on these projections. Roughly speaking, high-tech occupations have in this decade experienced high *rates* of growth, but from a small base. The *number* of new jobs created in the near future may be far larger for cashiers and fast-food workers than for computer programmers.

economic advances. Ill health and human misery were becoming concentrated in certain age groups, regions, classes, and ethnic communities. For example, analysts of the test scores that had set off alarms contended that it was not so much that the schools in general had slipped as that *some* schools were now unequivocal failures. Poor test scores were coming from certain states, from large urban systems, and from schools populated by the nonwhite and the poor.

Moreover, the reports of the earlier 1980s focused almost entirely on the high schools, and gave markedly little attention to the early grades and to the social and economic status of children coming into the schools, or the experience of those passing through the grades. How could a ratcheting-up of accomplishment in the secondary grades suffice, without the protection, let alone improvement, of human capital—talent, dignity, trust, motivation—at earlier stages of life? Then, too, immigration and demographic patterns in the United States meant that the foreign-born would become increasingly numerous in the decades ahead. In San Francisco, for example, fully a third of those now enrolled in the public schools do not have English as their native language, and in this sense may adapt less easily to formal schooling (and schooling to them). Finally, in at least half the states the public school population is predominantly nonwhite.

'Non-native'; 'minority'; 'poor.' These are distinct statuses, but they often intersect in socially explosive, humanly painful ways. Insisting that the educational system produce more and produce better could be like expecting ever more spectacular cures from biomedical science while failing to protect the basic health of the population. The claim that weaknesses in American education put a nation at risk did nothing to help improve the performance of students at risk in education.

In fact, some progress had been made even before the various reports of the 1980s were released. Beginning in the later 1970s, many states had revised, clarified, and upgraded their curriculum requirements, had explored more sensitive and variegated forms of testing, and had revised their standards for teacher education. More hours of 'the basics' were already being taught. Test scores nationally had begun to show small gains. It was also encouraging that SAT scores climbed *more* for minority students between 1978 and 1988 than for whites. But the gains were small, and the scores of whites remained far in advance of those for minorities.[6] At the very same time, the drop-out rates for urban minorities soared. Apparently, only some of the 'disadvantaged' were making progress educationally. And what did rather small gains in test scores mean, at any rate, when international comparisons showed that in math and science Americans students were performing poorly?[*] As always, when challenges are set and expectations raised, the achievement of only modest gains can seem derisory. Then there may be an insistence on still more achievement—

---

[*]International comparisons are often misleading. Certainly, a national education system that attempts to educate only a portion of its young people will produce 'better' scores on achieved knowledge than a system of mass education in a more heterogeneous society.

from a system that has improved as much as is possible without more sweeping change—or, worse, a blaming of the system itself.

The difference between change *within* a system and change *of* a system is salient in secondary education especially. The tremendous enlargement of American secondary education from about 1890 to 1950 altered the high schools from a preparatory milieu for the elite—those headed for further academic or professional study (or lifelong personal commitment to humanistic reflection and leisure)—to a mass system in which most persons were provided with the various skills and knowledge sufficient to making a living. The reports of the 1980s suggested that what was needed now was a system in which *every student* is provided with a broad set of fairly high-level competences with which to function in society—that is, a mass 'preparatory' system.

Avenues Toward Change

Those who believe in this coming transformation must, however, face decisions that involve considerable risk. The basic dimensions of industrialization and professionalization in the United States were seemingly obvious to educators in the 1910s and 1920s. A similar perception of a coming shift in the division of labor and resources, of functions and 'slots' for individuals in society, is less clear today. Why then invest massively in a *new* form of mass education when the older form is seen as having yielded a disappointing return on investment?

Moreover, there is another abiding theme in educational philosophy in the Western democracies—the expression of humanistic values and personal fulfillment, the pillars of liberal culture. Surely there is more to education than societal efficiency, than fitting abilities to 'slots'? Need greatness in a society be a matter of national hegemony? Cannot a nation be proud without being at the forefront of invention and productivity? Cannot a nation be great by virtue of having a great—which is to say, an educated and civic-minded—citizenry, regardless of trends in per capita GNP?

Finally, there is a third conviction, largely professional and academic in origin—that education could in fact be better if it were guided by more knowledgeable and experienced persons, particularly those expert in the psychology of learning and in the structure of the disciplines.

Those who give primacy in education to cultural consensus and continuity tend to want to prune, shape, and refigure the curriculum. Education need not be new (that is, 'modern' in its technical aspects) so much as culturally integrative and self-renewing. The central assumption here is that the core curriculum of schools will be those subjects that provide all students with a common frame of meaning, experience, and value. It is a form of philosophical essentialism: in the core lies the essence. Specialized and practical knowledge can be acquired elsewhere, and later in life.

Some professional educators, on the other hand, especially those who work in the disciplines in higher education, care less about the accumulation of specific items of knowledge-in-common and more about knowledge and intellective procedures that generate curiosity, and enable further learning to go deeper and to ramify. There is no essential knowledge that does not seek to go beyond itself. What is needed, in their view, is not just more science, more history, but the *principles* of science or history, well taught and deeply understood. Here a degree of methodological awareness is the key: not that one know facts (though of course in any subject the rudiments must be achieved by any student), but that the student possess disciplined and productive habits of mind. Finally, the argument runs, a person learns how to learn, in a process far broader than that centering in instruction. Since structures of knowledge are not fully revealed by the mere exposure of facts and terms to students—for example, in a core curriculum—disciplinary scholars tend to want a degree of specialization, which in the high schools typically means the provision of electives.

All may agree that American education today is less than it should be. But there will be disagreement about next steps. None of the reformers of the 1980s, whether inside or outside education professionally, recommended a sweeping sociopolitical rethinking of schooling (as had, for example, been proposed in the 1930s).* The national reports of the 1980s were quite silent on what may be crudely summarized as the sociological and demographic aspects of the system of public education, and silent also on the matter of educational finance. Thus, after the first expressions of alarm, 'next steps' came almost by default to center in choices about the curriculum, and to a lesser extent pedagogy.

Even here there were many cross-currents of values and strategic calculations. Foreign-language education, for example, might be recommended by liberal arts advocates, on the grounds that an educated person should be able to travel abroad and read easily in foreign literatures, or promoted on more immediately practical grounds by those concerned with the management of transnational corporations and the techniques of global marketing. Professionals in English and the language arts recommended sustained study of language in all its aspects—not just grammar, but style, rhetoric, and discourse. Professionals in science education recommended that the organizing ideas of modern science be explored in a way that cuts across fields and disciplines, and strongly suggested that the wrong modes of thinking in science were being advanced in the schools.[7] 'Back-to-basics' reformers, however, considered such recommendations highfalutin and academic in the worst sense. Let students in school master correct English usage, and know the table of elements and the basic calculations of Newtonian physics. (Indeed, they argued that an overemphasis

---

*An exception here might be the recommendation by Ernest Boyer and his colleagues at the Carnegie Foundation that all graduating students have spent considerable time in school-based community service. This was not a new idea, but not a widely accepted one either The general notion continued to be discussed as the decade proceeded.

on idiosyncratic approaches to defined subjectmatters and an overly theoretical cast to sequentially mastered facts and skills were partly the cause behind declining scores on national tests.)

The National Governors' Association emphasized the need for deeper knowledge of foreign societies and cultures, and a familiarity with world history and with the language and literatures of other peoples. Indeed, it said that "international education must become part of the basic education of all students." But the assistant secretary for research and improvement in the U.S. Department of Education was indignant at those who stressed "one-worldism" and the "global orientation of today's reformers, who would have youngsters start by understanding the oneness of all humankind before turning to matters more specific to themselves and their nations."[8]

As noted earlier, the overarching message of the Commission on Excellence and similar groups that found schooling inadequate by external criteria—that is, in terms of what the society would need—took the form of a challenge, which is not precisely the same as the call to *reform*. The challenge tended to focus on science and math, of which there is not enough, and on efficiency of output relative to input. It was reasonable, given that the typical high school student took a total of only four to five semesters of work in science and math (in 1982), to demand more. It was realistic, in a system where students took on the average one semester of foreign language instruction, to expect that some students might well take two years.[9]

Reform in the Social Studies

In English and in social studies, however, the demand was not for *more*, but for *better*. English and social studies together already accounted for half the high-school requirements, so that *more*, while it might be welcome, was not the crux of the matter. Here, if anywhere, reform was evidently in order. Reformers of the curriculum are inclined to qualitative distinctions, are concerned to distill what is good, strip away the inessential, and elevate and purify the language and habits of the tribe. With regard to the social studies, however, the reports of the 1980s were vague. Clearly, "functional literacy"—linguistic competence sufficient for modern life, employability, and participation in civic processes—was of high priority. Since experts agree, for the most part, that "literacy" is a moving target, and that in the American population as a whole functional literacy had steadily increased, the implication was that certain *kinds* of "literacy" were lagging (hence, the recommendation for computer science work) or that certain *groups* were lagging.

Although the justification for the reports was heavily economic, there was no evident insistence on more economics in the schools, perhaps because of a general awareness that economics had for some years been the social studies subject showing the most rapid growth (in terms of state requirements).*[10] The call for a more comprehensive awareness of foreign societies, economies, cultures, and systems was unmistakable but nonspecific. The reports did recommend "more" history and geography, but in a largely pro forma fashion. Equally superficial was the justification for a continued commitment to the study of government and civics, on the unexceptionable reasoning that modern youth should become loyal and active participants in the democratic process.

As of about 1985, then, those charged with responsibility for social studies in the schools might have regarded their fields as generally exempted from challenge on the part of national leaders. These fields, however, were not free from the dynamics of reform. Those dynamics were generated primarily within the field of education, but gained resonance from the concerns of the public—who had so recently, and so forcefully, been told that "the system" as a whole was failing.

In 1987 Diane Ravitch, a historian, and Chester Finn, a federal education officer, reported national test results indicating that factual knowledge of American history was unsatisfactory. Similar results were reported at about the same time with regard to students' geographical knowledge, in terms of recognizing place-names and locating places on maps.[11] These were assessments at one moment in time, and in rather imprecise terms. They did not ask, Compared to what?† They could not determine whether knowledge of dates, persons, and events, among those with secondary-level education, had steadily fallen over time or had recently plummeted. They could not enlighten us as to *which* students were weakest, and they could not go very far toward determining on which *aspects* or *forms* of historical and geographical knowledge students performed worst or best. These reports, however, had set out not to answer such comparative or analytical questions, but to give a rough estimate of present performance—and, as it turned out, an early warning. The reports sounded credible; indeed, many parents reported that their children seemed to know (and to be asked to know) fewer specific names, places, or terms than parents recalled as required in their own educations. The conclusion, in brief, was that today's students were weak on facts. If this finally implied that today's students would not be able to function in the modern, competitive world, or would not understand the rules and procedures of American citizenship so as to contribute productively to civic life, then reform in the social studies was clearly indicated.‡

Although this was an assessment offered primarily from within the educa-

---

*Economists concerned with secondary education, however, reported that students were less than impressive in basic economic knowledge.

†In fact, in contrast to international comparisons in science and mathematics, recent testing in history, geography, and knowledge of governmental institutions and procedures has shown unimpressive results in most 'developed' nations in all parts of the world.

‡Researchers have suggested, however, that students themselves (and their parents), when not faced with the yes/no question Are things good enough? may be relatively satisfied with the nature and level of school performance. Parents want their children to feel positive about school, and confident about their intrinsic abilities.

tional realm, others professionally engaged in that realm disagreed with the diagnosis. For many years, for example, there had been debates among experts and thoughtful critics about whether place-name geography was the crux. Perhaps, in the same way that adults had learned the names of 48 state capitals, today's students should learn the names and locations of 150 national capitals around the world. If so, this was feasible: drill still works. But perhaps contemporary geography should focus not so much on places as on processes—economic, demographic, agronomic, climatic, industrial, ecological, historical, cultural—in a more comprehensive, more systematic fashion, if students were to understand the complexities of the study of occupied space, especially now that the globe could be viewed more as a whole, from a vantagepoint hundreds of miles out in space.

Similarly, a debate had been in process since the beginning of serious study of history in the schools, eighty or ninety years ago now, over *how* to treat history. How much American history should be taught, relative to the history of other nations, or the history of the world or its major regions and epochs? Within American history, how important was it to bring that history up to the present: was historical knowledge useful *only* if it enlightened present dilemmas, or on the contrary most useful when it provided students of any era with a stable understanding of the founding principles and institutions of the American nation? If the latter was the case, what were these fundamental conceptions? Did students taught history in the earlier grades comprehend little more than its mythic and narrative appeal; and, if so, was this good or bad for later instruction in history? Did good citizenship follow naturally from historical understanding, perhaps rendering the detailed study of government and politics less vital? Did the unease with which many Americans today regard their place in the world imply that American history should take pains to convey that the national experience was unique and exceptional, and that the system that has evolved throughout that history is clearly the best in the world; or had one of the problems with history in the schools been an overemphasis on parochial complacency?

Not only had history and geography and civics changed over the decades as school subjects—as the result of reform and change initiated by historians, geographers, and political scientists—but the general development of 'the social studies' *other* than the traditional triad had inevitably allocated time to other topics, and had introduced approaches deviating from the learning of names and dates, places, or 'functions' of government in favor of more conceptual and less factual understanding. The fundamental difference between traditional approaches and the more recent 'scientific' ones can be understood by considering the difference between datum, an element to be used in inquiry, and factum, an entity to be grasped and recalled. These trends over time in social studies education had reflected the rapidly growing influence of academic social science in twentieth-century American universities. Had this process gone too far *in the schools*? Assistant Secretary of Education Chester Finn found it shocking that, as he put it (quoting with scorn a social studies educator), "Transmission of knowledge is not the overriding goal of social studies . . . [which is, rather] to prepare young people to identify, understand and work to solve the problems that face our increasingly diverse nation and interdependent world.[12] Finn charged that factual knowledge was being shortchanged, arguing further that "eight- and fifteen-year-olds . . . are apt to know little save what they learn in school" (a claim disputed by many laypersons and experts). Some historians charged that 'social studies' had ruined history, by emphasizing how to think about history rather than what history to know.

When one adds to these largely intramural controversies—*datum* versus *factum*, configurational versus analytical approaches, the traditional school curriculum versus that curriculum expanded by social-science subjects—the fact that public expectations of the social studies are multiple and to some extent contradictory (a topic discussed in Section 15 of this book), it is not surprising that the field of social studies has been perceived, in this decade, as in conflict, or adrift. Other fields may show acute conflict—for example, grammar-based versus discourse-centered English—but the debates in social studies are more complex and longer-lived. The issues in social studies almost never center in the sequence of material (the order in which what facts or concepts should follow), since the subjectmatters are not seen as essentially hierarchical in degree of difficulty, logical entailment, and so on. They rarely involve absolute choices between pedagogical approaches. Although it is true that the long-standing goal of 'going beyond the facts' has proven elusive, this reflects more the practical decision to make sure 'the facts' are covered than a principled reluctance to go beyond them. The debates in social studies tend to be about scope (what *kinds of topics* should modern, or sound, or American social studies emphasize?) and, even more, *tone* (how is the discussion carried out, and why?).* One inference that could be drawn from this state of affairs is that in social studies goals and priorities *must* be set outside the schools, since goal consensus within the schools generally proves impossible to achieve. For professionals in the field of social studies, this may involve the strategic calculation of whether enough freedom can be won from the public, through the political process, to permit internal reforms and readjustments to proceed, or whether the mood of the 1980s will result in the public's deciding that educational practice is too important to be left to the educators.

Any student of curriculum history knows that the social studies have long been contentious. The branch of the school curriculum known as the social studies took shape about 1900. It has been expected, within the broader framework of schooling, to provide useful knowledge about the conditioning realities (in Charles Beard's phrase) of modern life, a sense of continuity and change in the world's societies—our own and others—and a level of civic awareness and commitment that will perpetuate the basis for democratic

---

*It is of course possible that the constant disagreement about scope and tone prevent ever 'going beyond the facts.'

processes and participation. At different eras, social studies have taken on distinctive tones or agenda. In the Progressive era, a kind of broad descriptive sociology was sought, largely with a domestic range of reference. Around the middle of the century, social studies were partly reoriented so as to include newly relevant kinds of knowledge about foreign nations and areas. In the 1960s, two trends—a movement toward 'relevance' and the attempt to raise the quality of discipline-based thinking and learning in the schools—overlapped, and to some extent conflicted.

Inherent in social studies, thus far in their history, are goals both for factual learning and for effective decision-making in individuals' own lives and in society at large. Hence there is always some tension between those who wish to see more 'content' imparted and those who believe that, since much of the established content at any point will become obsolete, it is more important to develop reliable ways of thinking socially and acting responsibly. While the two are not intrinsically in conflict, the schools find it difficult to balance these, and still other, objectives. The public, civic leaders, university scholars, educationalists, and students themselves assign quite different priorities to the various goals of social studies. The agitation in the 1980s for change and reform in social studies, an agitation not greater than that at earlier periods, may have nevertheless reinforced the tendency of various actors—state school officers, local school boards, professional groups, advocacy organizations, parents—to revise curricula and to mandate subject matters and pedagogical approaches without taking fully into account these multiple goals and somewhat conflicting expectations. A confusion between *change* and *reform* may also prove troublesome. An emphasis on change can deflect or override feasible reforms, while energy spent on reform can prevent confronting the need for change.

The tensions between various traditions and groups within history and the social studies, as voiced in the 1980s and sketched in here, originated largely within the field. The national reports and studies of the 1980s did not subject these tensions to close scrutiny. But recognizing the national mood for challenge, reform, and reexamination in public education, social studies experts, critics, and observers have tended, naturally enough and in a fashion that is appropriate within the rules of our open society, to 'go public' with their concerns and preferences. If Finn's basic charge—"simply put, what most 'experts' in the field want students to learn is not what most parents and citizens expect them to know"—is accurate, then it is likely that these school fields will become, sooner or later, the focus of more acute and urgent attention.

This should hardly be prevented, or deplored. As Americans sense the coming of a new and challenging era in their history, they reexamine, as they have done before at similar moments, the role of public education in providing the knowledge that society needs, in making more possible a degree of personal fulfillment for individuals, and in forming and expressing shared experience and common agenda for the nation's citizens. During all of this century, social studies have had a prominent place in public education. In the chapters that follow, I try to describe what social studies have been, why they have developed in the way that they have, and what some of the directions or alternatives for the future—intellectual, institutional, and moral—may be.

2.0 Organization of the Curriculum

The term 'social studies' or 'the social studies' was introduced about 1916, and was intended to impart a particular meaning in curriculum thinking (section 4.4). Today, it is used, for the most part, as a generic or an administrative term, referring to a set of subjectmatters or a segment of the school curriculum—comparable, for example, to 'language arts' or 'science.' 'Social studies' indicates the study of history, government, geography, economics, civics, sociology, and related subjectmatters.

2.1   Social Studies' Share

In terms of that summarizing usage, we may look at the number of credits required for graduation in the public high school districts of the country as a whole.

The ideal distribution of credits to be earned in four years of high school attendance, offered as the 'New Basics' by the National Commission on Excellence in Education,[1] is a goal reflecting what is feasible, given the existing pattern of public high schools, and the temper of the reform movement of the 1980s. Responding to the latter, most states have specified requirements more tightly, with a lessening of freedom for variation at the district or school level. It is evident that the social studies retain their share of the high-school curriculum—a share, relative to English and the language arts, that dates back to the 1950s or earlier. Mathematics in high school has come closer to the ideal laid down by the 1983 commission, while science lags behind—a lag generally ascribed to the lack of trained teachers in the sciences at the high school level. In social studies, the

17

Table 2-1 Mean Number of Credits Required for Graduation 1982 to 1988[1]

Subject and Year	NCEE[2] recommendations	All Districts with High Schools	North Atlantic	Great Lakes and Plains	Southeast	West and Southwest
English	4.0					
1982		3.6	4.0	3.4	3.9	3.6
1985		3.8	4.0	3.6	3.9	3.8
1988		3.9	4.0	3.7	4.0	3.9
Mathematics	3.0					
1982		1.6	1.7	1.4	1.8	1.8
1985		1.9	1.9	1.7	2.2	2.1
1988		2.3	2.4	2.0	2.6	2.2
Science	3.0					
1982		1.5	1.5	1.4	1.6	1.7
1985		1.8	1.7	1.6	1.8	2.0
1988		2.0	2.2	1.8	2.2	2.2
Social Studies	3.0					
1982		2.6	3.1	2.5	2.4	2.6
1985		2.8	3.1	2.7	2.5	2.8
1988		2.9	3.2	2.8	2.7	2.9

[1]U.S. public high schools. Credits represent year-long courses.

[2]National Commission on Excellence in Education

SOURCE: U.S. Department of Education, Center for Educational Statistics, Fast Response Survey System, No. 23, *Academic Requirement.*

regional differences are longstanding; the two coasts have taken the lead in social studies requirements since World War II, at least in terms of quantity expected for graduation.

Some 'academic' high schools have more rigorous course requirements in the college preparatory sequence than in that leading to the regular or general diploma, even though the number of total credit hours required is the same across 'tracks.' It is interesting to note that 'tracking' is markedly *less* for English (language arts, etc.) and social studies than for science or mathematics. This illustrates the commitment all schools have to literacy and to citizenship, goals that have been nearly universal in the schools since the expansion of high school education early in this century. It also, of course, raises questions: whether science and math are considered inherently more difficult for the 'average' student than English and social studies, and whether schools should or should not provide the same required core of courses and credits for all.

At other levels of schooling, requirements take a different form. At grades

K through 6, instruction is not organized in course units, especially in K–3. Instead, states may specify number of minutes of instruction in different curriculum areas on a weekly basis. In 1977 a careful national study[2] showed that in grades K–3, on the average, reading instruction occupied about 100 minutes per day, mathematics about 45, social studies a little more than 20, and science a little less than 20. Since 1977, most experts agree, the 'back to basics' movement has resulted in relatively less time given to science and social studies, more to math and reading.

In grades 4–6, course-like titles become more common, although there may still be a pattern of instruction that involves brief periods during the day and short instructional units, of days or weeks. Much depends on whether students stay primarily in one room with a homeroom teacher, during the school day, or move from class to class. The same 1977 survey showed that in grades 4–6 fewer minutes than in grades K–3 were given to instruction in reading and more to social studies and science; but the relative allocation of time across subject areas was about the same—50 minutes to math, 35 to social studies, and 30 to science.

In junior high schools (grades 7–8 or 7–9) and in middle schools (usually grades 5–8 or 6–8), the pattern is more mixed.* Junior high schools may tend to use high school–like subjectmatter titles, while middle schools may use more generic labels, such as general science or social studies, as content descriptions.† Good national data are lacking on requirements at this level. Exact state requirements as to *courses* to be taken are infrequent, nor are minutes of instruction commonly specified. Thus, patterns at the district level are quite variable. However, language arts and social studies are the leading areas of instruction.

Across all school levels, then, social studies is a long-established part of the curriculum. There is no evidence that recent emphasis on competing content areas such as math and science has resulted in their diminution. Some social studies teaching occurs in most schools for most students nearly every year—or is at least available.

---

*The labels given to levels of public education are a source of confusion. The public tends to think in terms of 'primary' and 'secondary' education, the latter indicating high school. This makes less sense today than in the past, since today the completion of 12 grades is expected of the typical young adult. Nor is it common usage in the schools. About 20 or 30 years ago, a 4-4-4 grade pattern seemed to have been established; these sets of grades corresponded to elementary, middle, and high school. Recently, fifth-graders have been considered too immature to be grouped with older children, or to have different interests; a 6-3-3 pattern has emerged in many districts, corresponding to elementary, junior high, and senior high school. (Both the junior-senior pattern and the four-year high school pattern are called 'secondary education.') In other districts, a 5-3-4 pattern is recognized: elementary, middle, and high school. In social studies, the structure and tone of instruction tend to change noticeably between grades 3 and 4. In the present volume, we try to indicate specific grade levels, as needed. We also use 'early elementary' to refer to grades K–3, and sometimes 'the middle grades' to refer loosely to grades 5 or 6 through 7 or 8.

†That is, in elementary schools 'social studies' denotes a portion of instructional time, whose content is largely determined by the individual teacher. In some (but only some) middle schools there is a named subjectmatter, 'social studies,' with a text or workbook similarly named.

2.2   The Modal Curriculum Pattern

What is studied in twelve years of schooling, and in what order? Many close investigations during the last ten years converge on the following as the *modal* pattern.

In this idealized, but widely recognizable, scheme, the first four to seven years may be designed to follow a pattern known as *expanding horizons* (or expanding environments, developing horizons, and so on), in which the student focuses on successively wider or more complex environments, up through the first exposure to national history and to a selection of contemporary societies in other parts of the world (world cultures). If the Western/Eastern hemisphere pattern is followed in grades 6 and 7 (and they are sometimes reversed, where followed), the expansion of focus levels off at this half-a-world scope. If, on the other hand, world study in grade 7 has a solidly geographic or a fused geography and history emphasis, then this grade marks the beginning of a less purely descriptive approach: for example, the basic concepts of physical and human geography are provided, together with an outline, at least, of relevant aspects of ancient, medieval, and modern history. The scope may be wide, but the approach is less that of the *tour d'horizon*, and more systematic in nature.

If Western Hemisphere studies are given in grade 7, or if a World History

Table 2-2 Typical Progression of Courses Throughout Twelve Grades*

Grade	Subjectmatter
K	Self-school-home
1	Families
2	Neighborhoods
3	Communities
4	State History; Regional Study
5	U.S. History
6	World Cultures • World Cultures, Western Hemisphere
7	World Geography (and/or History) • World Cultures, Eastern Hemisphere
8	American History
9	Civics *or* American Government • World Cultures
10	World History *or* World Studies
11	American History
12	American Government (year)
	or Government; Economics
	or Semester Electives, such as
	Economics
	Political Science
	Sociology
	Psychology

*In grades 6–7 and 9–10, one common pattern lies toward the left of the chart, the other to the right.

course is organized primarily around political history (with geography having a lesser role), the underlying rationale *may* be to provide a preparatory framework for the second cycle of American History. (That is, the emphasis may be on the European parts of Eurasia and on modern European history since 1600 or so, in order that the origins of and main influences on American history be more clearly discerned at grade 8.) When offered, World Cultures at grade 9 tends to be contemporary in emphasis and to involve material from around the globe. Correspondingly, World History at grade 10 often centers on Western Europe, once again in relation to what is intended to be the deepest examination of American history in the following year.

In general, then, the right-branching pattern of the diagram in grades 6–9 represents a tendency toward global studies as the underlying rationale, while the left-branching pattern represents the tradition of geography and history as subjectmatters, both (or the latter) being oriented toward what is salient in American history.

State history, though required for graduation by many states, is often taught in connection with an American History course at a higher grade level. Many districts offer an American Government course at grade 9 in place of Civics (see section 6.2), together with an elective course at grade 12 in Political Science, with the former meeting what is often a statutory requirement for the study of national (and state) constitutions and the basic structure and functions of government at various levels. On the other hand, a number of districts now urge that American Government and Economics be taken in two successive semesters in the twelfth year. Finally, yet another world-study course is gaining ground in some states at the twelfth grade; it is either a World History course, with a non-European or broader-than-European emphasis, or a course in World Systems (economic, political, sociological) that is more rigorous than that at grade 10, but also contemporary in tone or with a focus on America in the world.

Obviously, choices—or even curricular fine-tuning—at one level strongly constrain emphases and selection at other levels. For example, the multiplicity of courses in table 2-2 with 'world' elements in their titles reflects existing variation around different overall goals and emphases; few students would be offered or avail themselves of all the alternatives listed somewhere in the table.

How the subjectmatter of American History is apportioned across the three cycles varies widely. While American History texts generally present the entire sweep from precolonial times to post–World War II, some systems tend to focus on the eighteenth century at grade 5, the nineteenth century at grade 8, and the twentieth at grade 11 (see section 11.1). This in turn affects how Civics or American Government is taught at grade 9 or what the emphasis is in a twelfth-grade World History or World Systems course.*

---

*The grade 5 course has tended over the years to be called U.S. History, while the other two tend to be called American History. The explanation may be that the first cycle tends to focus on national founding and development, while the courses at grades 8 and 11 often includes more material about the Americas and about U.S. foreign policy and relationships.

There are many other sources of variation, some codified and some implicit. A large school system may guide college-bound students into a different sequence of courses from a 'general diploma' student. Thus the former will take a Government course at grade 9, in order to leave room for more than one elective at grade 12. Some schools provide acceleration options for students by 'testing out' or other means. Transfer students, of course, may need to take courses out of order so as to meet district or state graduation requirements.

Many city systems or districts impose additional requirements for graduation or promotion on top of state requirements: a course in economics is a common example. Some states are moving explicitly toward grade-level standardization, recognizing that electives taken will be few or nonexistent. Other states have few *course* requirements, but mandate 'coverage' of many topics—national and state constitutions, free-enterprise economics, law-related studies, global studies, and the like. This may result in familiarly named courses having, in fact, nonobvious content (for example, free enterprise economics may be covered in Civics, rather than in Economics. For a fuller discussion of labeling problems and oddities, see section 2.4).

2.2.1 The problem of enrollments

Above all, what is offered in the way of courses (beginning about grade 9) is not necessarily what is taken. Lists of course titles and tallies of enrollments do not correspond well. Just as we do not have, in the United States, a set national curriculum, we also do not have (except in a few states) reliable data on how many take what. Adequate data have to be built up from a complete census or systematic survey at the district, if not the school, level—and there are close to 16,000 public school districts nationally. Setting down typical curriculum patterns (as in table 2-2, or for any state or, indeed, a given district) is a crude means of rising above variations in course content and course sequences, as experienced by individual students. There is so much ambiguity—so much reliance on familiarity and judgment within systems—that even frequency counts of course titles cannot lead to valid comparisons across systems or across time. The federal government does gather enrollment statistics, using established titles or content areas, but here again the sorting of numbers of persons into curriculum categories is very uncertain.*

Many observers report, for example, that World History courses at grade 10 tend to have relatively low enrollments. The explanation may be that this is not typically a required course; it sometimes represents a holdover from an earlier tradition in college-preparatory curricula of offering a kind of European history or Western civilization option for the college-bound. On the other hand, in some

---

*Federal surveys of enrollments are conducted less frequently than once a decade, during which time the frames of reference may shift.

surveys the category 'history' may not differentiate successfully among U.S. History, World History, Latin American History, and so on. In grade 12, psychology, sociology, and anthropology are elective courses that owe much of their prevalence in the curriculum to an emphasis in the 1960s and early 1970s on 'social *science*' offerings; today, the latter two are sometimes in the curriculum but underenrolled (or not offered every year).

As suggested, data on enrollments in subject areas, as provided by the federal statistics office or other sources, are generally hard to interpret. First of all, in compiling the data, someone has to interpret the essential content of courses whose titles may be extremely variable or misleading. A sometimes meaningful distinction between Civics and American Government may be overlooked, or a nondifference distorted (e.g., American Government at grade 9, which may be essentially 'civics'). Second, enrollment figures directly reflect a more fundamental dimension: which courses are *required* and which *elective*. Enrollments in the former will obviously tend to be larger, but one cannot always be sure that this factor outweighs that of popularity. Third, totals showing how many students *ever* took a course or courses in a subject area—for example, once or more between grade 7 and 12, or prior to graduation—may undercount or overcount (depending on how the tally is done) coursework that is repeated across grade levels, the clearest example being American History. Such cumulative totals (i.e., 'ever-taken' counts) also do not reveal at what grade levels courses tend to be found. Fourth, national enrollment figures that *are* shown by grade level tend, for the casual observer at least, to discount or conceal enrollments in courses that are taught at various levels. For example, many students take state history at some point, but they may take it at grade 4, 7, or 9, or some other level, so that the data entry for any single grade-level is not impressively large. Fifth, enrollment figures for a given year or half-decade will reflect subjectmatters, especially electives, that are popular briefly but lack staying power. In sum, however, the main data problem is still, here as in other respects, the ambiguity of course titles and the variability inherent in grouping them into broad subject matter areas.

A 1980 national survey[3] provided useful data from some 500 social studies teachers, in that the data were expressed in terms of number of *sections* taught. This tends to weight course titles by some factor of enrollment. Table 2-3 shows that Geography was predominantly a seventh-grade course, that Civics and Political Science do occupy separate niches at grades 9 and 12, that the 'social science' electives are not restricted to grade 12, and that American History is fairly common at grade 10 as well as grade 11.[4] Since 1980, as a result of additional or tighter state and district mandates, Economics has gained in prevalence nationally at grades 9 and 12, world studies have become more common at grade 12, and disciplinary electives have become more localized to the senior year.

A careful state-by-state survey reported by Morrisset[5] revealed considerable change in emphasis from the mid-1970s to the mid-1980s. The majority of states

Table 2-3 Number of Sections of Social Studies Courses Taught, by Grade Level

Course	7	8	9	10	11	12	Total
American History	67	329	65	121	321	23	926
American Government/ Civics/Political Science	36	25	80	14	42	134	331
World History/Cultures	96	6	104	116	43	19	384
Sociology/Psychology/ Anthropology	5	0	4	10	44	56	119
Geography	107	21	37	16	14	13	208
Economics	12	2	4	9	9	33	69
Other Social Studies	27	39	40	21	50	41	268*
							2305

N = 552 teachers

*These secondary social studies teachers also reported teaching 165 non–social studies courses.

SOURCE: Lynn Fontana, *Perspectives on the Social Studies* (Bloomington, IN: Agency for Instructional Television). Research Report 78, p. 35.

responding found their own patterns basically similar to the modal curriculum. However, state social studies specialists found that curriculum changes in their own states were in the direction of greater prescriptiveness; they approved of this direction of change for their own states—but, curiously, not so much for the nation as a whole. Geography (at the middle school and elementary level) was reported as the focus of increased attention, as were world studies and Economics (especially free-enterprise economics) in the middle and high schools.

Cutting in at the more precise level of districts, Herman[6] also looked at change from the 1970s to the 1980s. The study involved only 77 districts, spread around nationally, too small a number of districts for firm conclusions on the national level. He found that about half the districts continued to follow the expanding horizons scope and sequence pattern in K–6, but that 'skills' rather than 'content' were being emphasized in recent years—no doubt a reflection of the 'back to basics' movement. In the elementary program, increased emphasis was being put on geography and history.* In grades 7–12, it appeared that both state history and geography were tending to move downward in terms of grade level: that is, an increased emphasis on geography in the upper elementary grades with some corresponding decline at grade 7 or above, while by the 1980s state history

*There is a possibility here of confusion. The general 'back to basics' movement of the 1970s tended to emphasize minimum standards of literacy, numeracy, and the like. The 'excellence' movement of the 1980s has tended to take this as a given, and emphasize a strong factual or content approach. Thus, for example, with regard to Herman's elementary-grade findings, it is quite possible that history and geography and social studies in general were diminishing in terms of instructional time (as many observers reported), but that factual history and geography were being emphasized in whatever social studies were taught.

was clearly less common at grade 7 or above than previously. World history was showing up at grades 9 and 10 more clearly than at grade 7.

An exhaustive compilation of social studies course titles in all the public high schools of Bergen County, New Jersey, in 1985–86[7] produced the following course frequencies, countywide: History (U.S. and World), 236; Government (and Political Science), 28; Psychology, 28; Sociology, 24; Economics, 20; Law, 11; Anthropology, 9; Geography, 4. Knowing that New Jersey mandates the study of American government in high school (as well as U.S. history) would suggest that it is often 'covered' in history courses.*

2.3   Modified State Patterns

While the modal curriculum is recognizable nationally, the degree of variation from state to state and district to district is very considerable. Michigan, for example, in its state-level plan† omits U.S. history at grade 5, dividing American history into two sweeps: exploration to Civil War at grade 8, and Reconstruction to the present at grade 11. The state suggests two consecutive years of Western Hemisphere studies, at grades 5 and 6: the U.S. and Canada at 5; Mexico, Central, and South America at 6. Texas requires Texas History and Geography at grade 7, building on grade 4 Texas History. It calls for U.S. History and Citizenship at grade 8, meaning that the Constitution and the basic structure of the American government are emphasized in that year. It requires a semester course in Economics with Emphasis on the Free Enterprise System and its Benefits, and either a year of World History or World Geography in high school.

New York State calls for the following pattern:

Table 2-4

Grade	Subjectmatter
K	Self and Others
1	Self, Family, School
2	Communities (U.S.)
3	World Communities
4	Local History and Government in the Context of American History
5	U.S./Canada/Latin America (especially Geographic, Economic)
6	Western Europe/Eastern Europe/Middle East
7 and 8	U.S. and State History (Foundations of Government)
9 and 10	Global Studies (by region)/The World Today
11	U.S. History and Government (Chronological)
12	Economics/Participation in Government

*The number of districts for which courses were counted was 35, and some districts had more than one high school. Thus it is clear that American government as such was not offered in every school. This is a case where year-by-year enrollments in subjectmatter areas would help to clarify the situation.

†This is not a mandate; it is not known how many districts follow the plan.

It is often readily apparent why a departure from the modal curriculum of the social studies makes sense for a particular state. Texas has an unusual history and constitutional-legal legacy, which would not be easy to teach in one year at grade 4, or within a conventional U.S. History framework. On the other hand, New York State's relationship to the Union was such that it is feasible to teach the rudiments of state together with national history at grade 4, and again at grades 7–8 where both levels of government systems are covered in detail. History and government are once again related closely at grade 11, this time in a large chronological presentation. New York places special attention on global, regional, and international content, with a geography-and-economics integration in the middle grades and a more political-and-cultural focus at grades 9 and 10. This state also chooses to emphasize community service or involvement in the last year of high school, either through supervised service or through special projects and study units in school.

If New York tends to use history in correlation with or as an organizing framework for a broader range of topics, by contrast California, in its 1988 framework,[8] goes in the other direction, emphasizing history cum geography as the core of the course of study. The new California framework is as follows:

Table 2-5

Grade	Subjectmatter
K	Learning and Working Now and Long Ago
1	A Child's Place in Time and Space
2	People Who Make a Difference
3	Continuity and Change
4	California: A Changing State
5	U.S. History and Geography: Making a New Nation
6	World History and Geography: Ancient Civilizations
7	World History and Geography: Medieval and Early Modern Times
8	U.S. History and Geography: Growth and Conflict
9	Elective Courses in History-Social Science
10	World History, Culture, and Geography: The Modern World
11	U.S. History and Geography: Continuity and Change in the Twentieth Century
12	Principles of American Democracy (One Semester) and Economics (One Semester)

The early grades program minimizes (though it need not eliminate) an expanding environments sequence, emphasizing instead the twin dimensions of time and space, the contrast between then and now, and the theme of continuity and change, explicitly. Despite the implied contemporaneity of its title, the grade 4 California course is historically organized. In principle, each level of history from grade 7 to grade 11 builds on the last, with provision for review and linkage at the beginning of each new level. History and geography are intended to be closely interwoven in the study of all epochs. Although 'citizenship' is an element woven through the entire curriculum, according to the California plan, it is only at grade 12 that American governmental and civic processes (that is, the Constitution, legal processes, the three branches of government, federalism, and comparative political systems) are explicitly addressed. A semester of main-stream economics is provided for at grade 12, but the curriculum plan permits other discipline-based elective courses only at the grade 9 level, and necessarily makes them a rather more rudimentary *introduction to* anthropology or sociology or psychology than 'social science' electives at grade 12 might otherwise be.*

All in all, California has responded most overtly to calls in the 1980s nationally for a 'core' of history and geography at nearly every grade level. It seems to be steering away from another main theme in calls for reform in the decade, that of global/international study, and departs sharply from a pattern of offering 'social science' electives at the twelfth grade. The history/geography armature will necessitate extensive revision of textbooks; it will be interesting to see how quickly, or whether, this comes about.

Some states or districts do not use course mandates so much as set graduation requirements in terms of coursework at a particular level. For example, Indiana requires that U.S. History and Government be taken at the secondary level; Indianapolis adds an Economics requirement to the state mandate (as do the schools of Albuquerque, and many others). But Massachusetts simply requires the study of American history and government for graduation; Boston, for example, 'handles' the government requirement within the history syllabus.[9]

2.4   Terminological Confusions

We have pointed out that the generic term 'social studies' is used pervasively and without self-consciousness in the schools generally, to refer to a broad federation of subjectmatters. This federation always includes history, government, and geography; the last two of these are not always treated as distinct courses. We have used the term 'social *science* electives' to refer to subjects that are considered as discipline-based or discipline-oriented and as fields, both in the university (and the world of scholarship) and in the schools. That is, sociology, psychology, anthropology, and economics were organized as separate fields of formal study in the later nineteenth century, and made their way into the school curriculum in the mid-twentieth century. For good or ill, they have been called

---

*The plan for grade 9 does include possible choice by the student of semester courses in area studies (selected world cultures or culture regions), the role of women in U.S. history, ethnic studies, or law-related studies, all of which are familiar enough at the grade 9 level and may have a multidisciplinary social science basis. The ninth-grade electives include physical and regional geography, which may permit a more sophisticated study of the subjectmatter than is normally provided in sixth and seventh grade 'world' amalgams. The California framework also allows the study of world religions and of a humanities unit at this level. However, few students are likely to take these courses in addition to an expanded history-geography sequence.

'sciences' partly to reflect this more recent development, and to distinguish them from subjects such as history and government (or politics) that have been part of a liberal education in the West for much longer. In the schools, the distinction is not epistemological or a reflection of intellectual history, but a shorthand way of acknowledging that such courses are intended to serve as introductions to college-level first courses in the corresponding disciplines, or, following other educational goals, as distillations of these subjectmatters for those whose education ends with high school.

A much-quoted *definition* of 'social studies,' that of Wesley,[10] was that Social Studies were the subjectmatters of the social sciences simplified for pedagogical purposes.* The broad questions of how well the school subjects correspond to or lead toward university-level subjectmatters will be discussed at more length in Part III of this book. Here it may suffice to say that the statement applies best to the social science electives, where practice and usage imply some relationship to university-level content. A telling instance is that Political Science in the school curriculum always implies that, whereas Government may or may not. There are still many difficulties. Economics may be organized like a college-level introductory course, or it may be a strongly normative course in the principles of free enterprise. Sociology may be largely social problems; Anthropology is unlikely to go as deeply into the rudiments of archaeology or linguistics as does the typical introductory college course. Psychology in the schools may be found as a course in the science department, or under a broad rubric of health, adjustment, or problems of living, in which case the content tends to reflect that emphasis.†

The Wesley definition does not apply neatly to the traditional school 'core subjects.' Here it can be argued that history and government and geography are substantially different in tone, organization, and purpose from university-level subjects.‡ The Wesley formulation applies least well to certain inherently nondisciplinary subject areas in the schools, notably Civics, Law-Related Edu-

---

*Wronski[11] has shown clearly that Wesley meant his phrase descriptively, not definitively. He simply intended to indicate that the social sciences in the university and the social studies in the schools address a common large subject area: that of human relations, behaviors, and institutions. It is certainly understandable that those outside the schools assumed more than this.

†When it is included in the Social Studies 'department,' as it most often is, it generally consists of elements of the study of personality, motivation, human learning, abnormal behavior, child development—that is, the most familiar topics of 'general psychology'—omitting animal studies, physiological and neurological functioning, sensation and perception, and a whole range of quantitative and experimental subject matter. (Curiously enough, the school course title is sometimes Social Psychology, which simply indicates the range suggested above; it does not often go deeply into academic social psychology per se.)

‡Sometimes this may reflect a time-lag. For example, Government, still a common title in the schools, is no longer evident as a course title in many universities, but once was. World History in the university was supplanted for a time in many institutions by the title Western Civilization (or the equivalent). This was seldom true in the schools. Extending the school-university comparison further, there are those who believe that 'social studies' inherently indicates a low level of pedagogy or learning ability, divorced from scholarship and the accumulation and revision of knowledge. In Britain and France, at least, 'studies' does not convey this meaning.

cation (seldom organized into separate courses but widely represented in the high school curriculum), and Global/World/International Studies. The lack of fit with university-level subjects is not inadvertent. For the last seventy-five years or so, the schools have designed subjects such as these, or courses carrying titles like Problems of Democracy, Social Issues, or Life Adjustment, which the schools consider to be essential parts of primary or secondary education— necessary for the education of all (or most) students, whether or not college-bound. (This is, of course, the basis for a fundamental controversy over the integrity of the school curriculum.) In that sense, the term Social Studies may be used by some to refer to a nondisciplinary, to some degree nonacademic, residuum in the curriculum of the schools.

Finally, as has been mentioned, the term 'Social Studies' is used administratively in the schools to refer to a department or a group of subjectmatters; is used in the elementary schools to refer to a segment of the time budget for instruction of students who do not move from class to class; and is sometimes used in the middle or junior high schools to refer to courses organized in multidisciplinary ways.

All of this is readily understandable if one looks carefully at the system and its development. It is easy enough to see why Social Psychology in the schools may not be what a university student or professor might expect. Some persistent labeling problems, however, cause serious misunderstanding. Take, for example, the question of whether or to what degree history should be the core of the Social Studies.

2.4.1   THE POSITION OF HISTORY

The very form of that question is vexing to some. In considering it, those inside and outside the schools often talk at cross-purposes, whatever their position. School people assume, unless there is some special usage indicated, that Social Studies includes history (in fact, centers on history). Outside observers may not. They may cite the fact that the distinction can be an important one in determining how teachers are educated and certified; here, indeed, History and Social Studies backgrounds may imply quite different preparations. They may also know that the term 'social studies' was first used some eighty years ago to usher in a school curriculum that would go beyond history, though not leaving history out (see section 13.0). Finally, some members of the lay public may be generally confused about what 'Social Studies' means, as they are about what 'social science' may be: for them, the term *history* will simply be more familiar.

Such misunderstandings are not trivial. In particular, all tallies of the prevalence of history *versus* that of social studies should be regarded as highly suspect, unless specific course content has been examined in the assignment of each datum. In the same way that Social Studies is not always understood to include History, so the course title History in a school syllabus may be misleading. For instance, a course in an unusually sophisticated academically oriented high school in the mid-1970s was titled World History. This was its stated syllabus content: "The first semester constitutes a survey of the social studies, including the interests, processes, and subject matter of such fields as history, geography, sociology, anthropology, and economics. In each of the two remaining quarters ... students may elect ... unit course offerings [such as] Man and His Buildings, Interesting Women in World History, the American Indian, and a Glimpse of West Africa."*

In a Berkeley, California, junior high school in the fall of 1988, a class labeled History in the school schedule used a world geography textbook and compared present-day agriculture in China and India. In Boston, a magnet high school specializing in international studies had a sequence of richly interesting courses involving foreign policy and diplomacy, regional studies, and contemporary world leaders—all called History in the school schedule. On the other hand, several upper elementary classes in Geography observed in 1988 were actually taught as exploration or westward expansion within a U.S. history framework. Historians of the curriculum[12] have pointed out that the customary label History was common in the schools during the 1920s and 1930s, while, in fact, new subject matter from the social sciences, aimed generally at training in citizenship, was introduced. On the other hand, though the term Social Studies was officially promulgated about 1916 to indicate a particular direction of reform, Tryon, the most meticulous historian of the social studies curriculum prior to 1934,[13] cites examples of the term being used that early as "an encyclopedic term to include history, civics, commercial geography, economics, politics, and sociology."

There are two general conclusions to be drawn here. First, it is not possible to know exactly what content is implied by course labels such as History, Geography—or Social Studies (which may or may not in a given instance be exactly history or geography). To gain a reliable impression, one must look at syllabi, texts, and materials used; must visit the class; or must have an informant for that school's practice. This pervasive ambiguity of usage is, of course, functional within the system. It permits a district to maintain the curriculum it prefers, or sometimes simply the labeling it prefers; it permits a state to achieve an educational profile or public allegiance that it deems most philosophically or politically appropriate; it allows individual teachers to teach to their own strengths and use texts and other materials selectively—all of these without altering the label (or, sometimes, by changing the label without altering the content). In Georgia, for example, the state guidelines show World Studies in the required core curriculum; college-bound students, however, actually take World History. The ambiguities and complexities of the actual course of study, class by class, protects the schools from premature judgment by parents, academics, or the business community. To those who question why the educa-

---

*The date of the course is not insignificant; the 1970s saw a trend toward the inclusion of 'mini-units' within courses and the integration of disciplinary approaches and methodologies into broad multidisciplinary overviews.

tional system of the United States cannot yield reliable, simple data on precisely what is taught, when, and to whom, the question can be turned back on the questioners. We could have such data if we had a centralized, national curriculum and a thorough monitoring or data-gathering system; if, for example, detailed, actually implemented, lesson plans were deposited automatically at the end of each day by each teacher in some central data bank. Would such a state of affairs be desirable—or worth it?

The second conclusion is that people might as well accept the *term* 'social studies.' Serious questions about whether social studies and history are inimical, or whether social studies is inherently a multidisciplinary undertaking or the sum of disciplined understandings, should be considered on their merits. There is no way to clarify such questions *simply* by redrawing terminological boundaries or changing usage by fiat. The problem affects interested groups in different ways. For example, geographers who claim that "geography is taught only at the seventh-grade level" and "is required for high school graduation in only about four states"[14] do so to argue for more geography. But by doing so, they may fall into category errors (that is, only that labeled Geography is geographical in nature) or, by failing to capture what is taught, but unlabelled, sell their own fields short.

3.0   Curriculum Control

By provision of the Tenth Amendment, control over public schooling is a function of the states which has, at certain eras, been forwarded downward to the level of communities. Differences across schools have always been apparent at the local level and at the level of states and regions. Histories of education have traced such differences throughout the history of the United States in terms of the influence of individuals (for example, Horace Mann and the inauguration of the common school in New England), the actions of state legislatures in imposing standards or patterns above the level of the community, and the more general influence of regional culture and traditions in the history of schooling.[1] In general, as with so many aspects of public institutions and culture, the overall trend has been rationalization of the system across locales, which may be seen more as the layering of controlling influences, each on top of the last, than as the replacement of local responsibilities by higher-order institutions.[2]

During the entire post–World War II period, state educational bureaucracies grew, giving rise to such roles and offices as chief state school officers or state curriculum specialists. As operating funds for school districts began to come more and more from the state (albeit for specific purposes, such as funds for special instructional programs or for textbook purchase), most states moved to exert greater influence on the system. Legislatures took more initiative in mandating specific procedures and standards, partly because political pressures on the schools in a given state came to be more and more directed at state legislatures and partly in recognition of widespread reform anxieties and imperatives to which legislatures did not wish to appear indifferent. State education officers and departments also reacted to national and local concerns—in part to restrain local diversity and the challenges that might arise from some districts being very different from others, in part to avert legislative action that might prove infeasible or misguided. A significant recent turning point was reached in 1979, when for the first time the proportion of public school revenues contributed by the states exceeded that contributed by local authorities.[3][*]

Earlier in this century, change in the curriculum tended to follow general intellectual and social trends, often marked or seized upon by the deliberations and recommendations of national commissions (sections 4.2–4.6). In more recent years, the ability of such nonofficial bodies to effect change has been limited, given the degree of initiative taken within the states. In most educational domains, what was once recommended for the schools, and then adopted slowly, to a greater or lesser extent, within them, has now become in one sense or another legislated: the preparation and licensing of teachers, the length and pattern of the school day and school year, standards and mechanisms for the education of the handicapped or the gifted, credits and test results needed for graduation, and the like. Not only did states (and districts and, indeed, local school officials) come to feel positively, that is, proactively, responsible for achieving equitable and effective education, but legal challenges posed to such authorities by citizen groups and special interests led them to be concerned defensively with 'accountability.'

3.1 Mandates and Legal Language

Since early in the century, in some cases since the last century, most states have required that students be instructed in the rudiments of American history and the national and state constitutions. (The force of such requirements has varied, of course, as a function of how long students were legally bound to attend school, or as a function of whether students were simply to be exposed to instruction or had to achieve a certain level of demonstrated knowledge for promotion or graduation.) By no means are all state requirements enforceable. Careful studies of laws on the books and practices codified by state authorities show that most states 'require' practices, attitudes, or observances that are grossly antiquated or meaningless. (Few obsolete statutes are ever revoked.) In addition, many states have education law that permits the state education department or agency considerable freedom to act unless the legislature intervenes. A very thorough review of state laws and procedures in 1979, under the joint auspices of the American Bar Association and the Social Science Education Consortium,[4] concluded that this delegated authority was typical of the states, that school systems are less than completely responsive to state-level mandates (for a number of good reasons), and that much that is done by curriculum designers and teachers at the local level is driven by myths or misunderstandings: for example, by the presumption that 'the law requires it' when that is not the case.

[*]As the proportion of state revenues climbs, education becomes a major budget item for the state, and thus highly political. As local governments are prevented, by supervening legal means, from establishing greatly disparate funding levels across schools, state control becomes even more crucial.

A comparable study, if done today, would no doubt find more legislatively stipulated aspects of the curriculum and less slippage between what is 'on the books' and what is practiced. In other words, the system is tightening up.*

Bearing in mind that *changes* in a system of requirements are more attended to than stable longstanding patterns, virtually all in the public schools report a trend toward increasing statutory specification. This has immediate effects, for good or ill, upon the curriculum as a whole, in terms of its coherence as a pattern and in terms of its degree of flexibility (for example, choice among electives, or the ability of a student to take coursework out of grade level). For example, about half the states have had some economics requirement for some time. Recently, there has been a discernible trend toward specifying a separate course in addition to whatever economics may be 'infused' into U.S. History and Government. If such a course is located at grade 12, choice among electives is reduced. (In an already crowded curriculum, few students can take more than one social studies—or language, or science—course in a given semester or even a given year.) Such a course, required at grade 12, is likely to be an academic, social science–oriented course covering the basic concepts of the discipline. That may, in turn, suggest to other interest groups that a need for consumer economics or business economics (or free enterprise economics) is not being met; they observe that the twelfth grade text is mainstream economics, not normative or civics-oriented. There is then pressure to require a course turned toward consumer economics at the ninth or tenth grade—which further reduces the chance for electives there, and further constrains the curriculum pattern as a whole.

It may (or may not) be desirable for students to have some economic history and basic economic terminology and concepts (markets, economic growth, etc.) in U.S. History, some consumer or business economics in grade 9, and an introduction to the discipline at grade 12. The point is that each decision not only adds to curricular pressure but helps determine what the particular slant or emphasis will be—which may then be found inadequate on other grounds.

Similar pressures, rather in a direction away from courses, are being experienced with geography. In the last few years more and more states have been specifying that 'geography' be included at all levels of the schools; and texts, correspondingly, are including more geographic material in history and world cultures texts. Much the same is true of 'global' content. This is all to the good, from one point of view, but it may allow curriculum officers to claim they are doing more and more geography or global education—albeit not in courses with such titles. (It is, of course, harder for outsiders to monitor what is supposed to be 'infused' into existing courses than the presence or absence of a separately labeled course in a curriculum.)

Thus, to ask what is required by law becomes almost meaningless. State

*In the 1970s the tightening-up process was due mainly to federal regulations and financing incentives, which tended to prevent states from independent actions. With the receding of federal initiative, the states began to take more initiative. Federal funds, however, have never been a major source of mainstream instructional or operating costs in schools.

education laws are replete with wording requiring the schools to foster students' allegiance to the principles of democracy, knowledge of the Constitution, and a commitment to American procedures. Most states have such citizenship goals stated in their education legislation. Many states will also call for instruction in consumer education, or will require that due attention be paid in the curriculum to the particular history and culture of minorities, women, and so forth, or that instruction proceed with due attention to global issues and interests of the United States. Without an action plan for implementation and without stated or established sanctions, such legislative language is of little consequence unless an interest group cites it in appealing for concrete new action. Similarly, certain stated requirements—for example, that 'commercial geography' be taught— have been on the books for so long, and have been ignored or superseded for so many years, that they have probably lost their legal force.

Ambiguity as to specific enforceable legislative requirements does not always lead in practice toward a simplification of the required curriculum. Since in most states the state education agency has broad discretionary powers, there have developed various nonlegislative means for curriculum tightening; and these have been employed widely in recent years. The power of financing means that state education agencies can decline to accredit a school that does not follow its curriculum plan, or decline to provide state monies to such a school. In Michigan, for example, education law calls only (within social studies) for instruction in civics and elements of government, but the education agency acknowledges that the study of American history is in effect required.[5] Such prescriptive procedures have been more marked in recent years. State requirements for competency or proficiency tests, either in connection with graduation requirements or for rankings of school performance (section 3.2), can cause virtually all schools to fall into line.

Since about 1980, a number of states have moved from requiring economics instruction to mandating an economics course somewhere between grades 8 and 12. About 25 states require economics instruction;[6] 15 call for a course or major unit in high school, and another 15 or so call for 'infusion' of economics in other courses. (Some states call for both.) Recent tightening of stated requirements in economics tends to involve mention of free enterprise or the American system; as mentioned above, how this is implemented in a course syllabus depends partly on the grade level involved.

Several states have recently required or are currently moving to require courses in global or international education. It is not always clear whether existing courses in world or hemisphere studies meet the requirement; in New Mexico, for example, new courses at grade 12 are being designed. Reflecting similar concerns, but preferring a different emphasis, other states have tightened their requirements for the study of world geography and world history.*

---

*Some states are sharply increasing their requirements in this area for graduation, which may not involve new courses at specific grade levels but does imply that the school be able to show substantial instruction in these subjects at some point, generally between grade 7 and 12.

Finally, a number of states are placing renewed emphasis on 'citizenship,' typically with no more specific prescription than using that term. In sum, there is reason for state social studies specialists* to report that the "dominant characteristic of social studies in the U.S. today—as is probably true of other areas of pre-college education—is *prescriptive.*" The general conclusion is clear: the required curriculum, across the states, is becoming tighter and more crowded. There is less room for electives or for experimentation and variation on the part of districts or schools.

Bearing in mind the different degrees and interpretations of 'required,' and acknowledging also that at any given time about a quarter or a third of the states are revising or at least reexamining their requirements, we summarize the states' required curriculum as follows. As of 1988, of the 51 states (including the District of Columbia), 48 states require U.S. history.[†]

Almost all these 48 states require the course at either the secondary level or at two or even three levels (among elementary, middle, and secondary, always including the secondary). One state does not specify the level, and one state requires the course at junior high school; in both cases, American History is also taught in high school.

As stated above, most states require that there be instruction in state history and the state constitution or government. The *modal* location is grade 4. In recent years, some states have amplified (or complicated) the requirement. Now some 13 states require that 'state history' be taught at grades 9–12, and another 13 at grades 6–8. In practice, this means a substantial unit or element of state history within, typically, U.S. History courses, in addition to what may be taught at grade 4.

Geography, as noted, is one of the traditional triad of subjectmatters in the social studies (together with American history and civics or government), but for many years it has had a problem of identity, being taught at many points throughout the curriculum in conjunction with other subjectmatters as well as (often) at grade 7. Our 1988 analysis shows that when geography is specifically *required* by the state, the grade level specified is more often in high school (eight states, with grade 9 being the most common grade location). Five states *require* geography to be taught between grades 4 and 8. Government/civics, like geography, is widely required, but not always as a separate course, since it is sometimes 'covered' in U.S. History.[‡]

---

*Cited in an analysis of some states' requirements by Morrissett, *Status*. Morrissett also concludes, with reference to the nine most common subjectmatters of the social studies, that "Nine of the states formerly had requirements or recommendations of more than half of these subjects; now 18 of the 27 have more than half."

[†]The exceptions are Alaska and Hawaii and, recently, Wyoming. In these and the following data, we take "required" to mean called for by law or by published standards of the board or department of education. I thank the staff of the National Commission on Social Studies in the Schools for analyzing state documents and clarifying ambiguities by telephone calls to state officials.

[‡]We continue to make the distinction between the required study of American government or civics, and the study of government or political science as a 'social science elective.'

Table 3-1 Number of States Following Three Basic Patterns of Social Studies

Pattern A: Traditional

(A1) U.S. History	(A2) U.S. History	(A3) U.S. History
—	—	World History
Civics/Government	Civics/Government	Civics/Government
—	World Geography	World Geography
—	—	—
N = 12	N = 2	N = 5

Pattern B: Comprehensive

(B1) U.S. History	(B2) U.S. History
World History	World History*
Civics/Government	Civics/Government
World Geography	World Geography*
Economics	Economics
N = 8	N = 3

Pattern C: Recent

(C1) U.S. History	(C2) U.S. History	(C3) U.S. History
—	World History	—
Civics/Government	Civics/Government	Civics/Government
—	—	World Geography
Economics	Economics	Economics
N = 6	N = 3	N = 4

N = Number of states
*Students must take either, but not both.

In table 3-1 we show data that speak to the question of the configuration of the 'core' social studies; that is, whether the traditional triad of courses holds or some other modal set now dominates. The table shows the required or 'strongly recommended' course patterns (grades 7 or 8 through 12) as of 1988, for 43 states where in the present author's analysis such a pattern is clear. The five most common subjectmatters in the social studies in general are listed in the same order, so that the absence as well as the presence of particular content can be easily discerned. The table attempts to capture certain subjectmatter dependencies: for example, *given* that U.S. History is almost universally required, what then is the pattern? Where Economics is required, which of the older-established subjects go with it?*

Clearly the most frequent single pattern (A1) is U.S. History and Civics/Government, with the latter sometimes taught within the former. Two addi-

---

*In counting Geography, we consider courses in World Regions, Hemisphere Studies, and the like to be heavily geographic. Courses in World Studies or World Cultures or Area Studies are excluded from the count, although there may be considerable geographic content.

tional states add Geography, thus achieving the putative traditional triad (A2). Five states (A3) include World History and Geography: in effect, these states show the traditional triad *and* are especially rich in history. (An alternative interpretation is that these states keep the triad, but now put special emphasis on non-U.S. material.)

The second most prevalent pattern (B1), involving all five of the most common required subjectmatters, reflects the fact that some states are deliberately comprehensive: either they actively endorse these five, or they emulate what they perceive to be the basic set in American social studies today. (If the latter, they are less 'prescriptive' than simply taking pains to enumerate, administratively, what 'Social Studies' means.) These eight states may be set somewhat aside in an analysis of choices, on the grounds that they have 'chosen' all.* Thus they are shown in the figure as intermediate between those states that center on History and Civics/Government and those that also have Economics as a common element.

In pattern C, six states require Economics along with the 'basics' of History and Government, while a total of seven other states include Economics in a set including either World History or Geography. Three additional states (B2) require that *each* student choose *either* World History or Geography; the pattern is almost indistinguishable from B1 or from C2/C3.

A reasonable summary of current patterns is as follows: 12 or 14 states appear to retain the traditional U.S. History-Civics-(Geography) configuration; 5 states continue a History-enriched pattern long typical of 'better' academic schools; while some 24 states have by now moved to a pattern of U.S. History-Civics/Government-Economics (plus World History and/or Geography). Given the recent rapid increase in Economics requirements, it seems plausible to consider, across the states, that a traditional two- or three-subject pattern now coexists with a newer, four- or five-subject pattern. If so, in addition to the traditional dyad or triad, Economics is here, and World may be coming.

Any way one views it, the additive process, the cumulative 'requiring' (in some fairly strong sense) of social studies courses in grades 7 to 12, has gone about as far as it can go, given the 'share of the curriculum' historically allotted to the social studies (in terms of credits for graduation; table 2-1). Bear in mind that U.S. and World History courses are normally two semesters in length, and that Hemisphere and World Studies also typically involve paired semesters. Looking at the national picture, one is forced to conclude, in fact, that while most schools will continue to innovate and/or offer an array of social science elec-

---

*In the words of the 1979 ABA/SSEC study: "Teachers ... generally agree on what constitutes the mandated social studies. American History is the core of the national social studies, government an important satellite that is sometimes spun off on its own and other times brought back into history, and the constitutions, civics, and culture are often synonyms for history and government. Other subjects exist on the peripheries. Fad and fortune periodically draw attention to these shooting stars" (p. 88). The question now is whether teachers are coming to accept a basic pentad.

tives,* it is unrealistic to expect substantial enrollments in them, except in special circumstances.†

Does this mean that, as many have warned, we have reached what is in effect a national curriculum in the social studies? Not quite. So long as subject coverage is not mandated in terms of specific courses at particular grade levels, schools and districts retain considerable freedom to make adjustments in their overall curricula. They have always shown great ingenuity in doing so: teaching civics/government within U.S. History, doing history (or geography or cultural anthropology) in World Studies, distributing law-related studies or human geography throughout the middle-school years. They also may arrive at locally desirable patterns and sequences of courses: splitting U.S. history into two rather than three sweeps, or permitting motivated and qualified students to take certain required courses earlier than normal in order to free up time in grade 12 for Advanced Placement courses or electives.

Some flexibility along these lines must always remain, not only to accommodate community needs and preferences but to handle students who transfer from other districts or states. Moreover, states that lay down too rigid requirements may be subject to legal challenge, either because they cannot then meet the needs or rights of particular students or communities; or because in the process they fail concretely to implement legislative language on the books; or, more subtly, because they leave themselves open to the challenge: If my child did all that was required of her, why is she not being promoted (or receiving a diploma)? The more every choice, on the part of the school and the student, is specified, the more the system, operating by the book, becomes unable to adopt or to accommodate valid exceptions.

3.2   Accountability Through Testing

Mandating is not the only important influence in the tightening process. The curriculum has recently been driven, at a rapidly increasing pace, by the instituting or the wider use of competency or proficiency tests.‡

---

*The reasons for keeping such an array include prestige for the school, principled pedagogical considerations that demand a variety of offerings, the recognition of the preferences and educational strengths of particular teachers, implicit or explicit 'tracking,' or simply the accommodation, where possible, of individual preferences.

†The obvious exception is Psychology, which appears to maintain relatively high enrollments. However, Psychology is more prevalent in certain regions and states, and in larger schools. Moreover, it is not always classified as part of social studies.

‡These, for the purposes of this discussion, are standardized tests used to assess how much subject matter knowledge is possessed by students who have reached particular grade levels or who have been through a particular sequence of courses or portion of the curriculum. Typically they are 'objective' tests, probing for multiple-choice, true/false, or completion responses, and thus easily and reliably scored; and they are given at the same time to all students at the specific grade level (perhaps constrained by 'tracking') in districts or across the state.

There are of course other kinds of tests of proficiency—for example, in reasoning or inference or deeper textual understanding—that require 'higher level' responses and more evaluative scoring. Such approaches to in-school testing are being developed by the Educational Testing Service, the Harvard Project Zero group headed by Howard Gardner, the National Center on Effective Secondary Schools at the University of Wisconsin led by Fred Newmann, a group working on testing and evaluation headed by George Madaus at Boston College, and a number of other researchers. This enterprise is important, since social studies are intended to produce more than rote or factual knowledge on the part of students (section 17.0). There are also standardized 'knowledge tests' that may be administered to some general population without special reference to educational attainment or processes (section 14.0)—although the results of such tests are often used to make judgments about the 'state of education.' In this section we deal only with in-school tests used for gauging what content is being taught or what students have learned—that is, evidence on the basis of which curriculum decisions may be made.

Standardized achievement testing in American schools has a long and contentious history. The original social and educational purpose of such testing was to provide a means of assessment that would cancel teacher bias, be blind to social origins, ignore previous performance by the students, and bar consideration of a student's (imputed) degree of motivation, cooperation in the classroom, and other factors that may enter in to grading and promotion. These tests are in principle summative in nature—different in kind from aptitude tests, which are meant to measure native abilities. However, the summary scores from a period of performance, while it may have a specially dramatic meaning for a student's self-image or parental satisfaction, are usually no more conclusive as to achievement than are cumulative grade point average, teacher recommendations, and other measures accumulated throughout the educational experience.

In fact, results from achievement tests have seldom had much summative meaning, and have generally been used for forward-looking decisions like occupational choice or application to certain colleges.* The main exception to

---

*That is, the results have some predictive value, for which test-makers strive. To predict whether the student will do well in college, or trade school, or an apprenticeship, knowing her score on an achievement test is better than nothing (though it may not be so good as some other predictor). The problem is that students or parents may take such scores as an exact representation of what is known and/or what has been learned in school, whereas what was specifically 'known' (i.e., answered correctly, which is hardly the same as 'known') was a very small sample of a domain of possible knowledge, only a small portion of which is contained in the school curriculum, not all of even that portion being learned there. An exceptionally clear discussion of some of these problems and misperceptions is given by Robert E. Stake of the Center for Instructional Research and Curriculum Evaluation, University of Illinois at Urbana-Champaign, in an unpublished paper, "Quality Control and Deceptive Packaging" (1989); and by George F. Madaus, "The Influence of Testing on the Curriculum," in Laurel N. Tanner, ed., *Critical Issues in Curriculum* [87th Yearbook of the National Society, Part I] (Chicago: National Society for the Study of Education [University of Chicago Press], 1988), 83–121. The paradox is that students, parents, advisors, and others may use scores for forward-looking choices (thus, predictions), while misinterpreting such scores as true summations of achieved school knowledge at a point in time. Thus, the reasoning goes, a student 'knows English' and therefore is 'college material'; if not, not.

this is in the case of such tests of long standing as the New York State Regents Exam, or similar tests given late in high school that determine whether a student, in effect, graduates with a general or an honors diploma. In certain states, the crucial result will be to entitle a student to attend the first tier of the state university system or to be eligible for state aid—or to bar such possibilities. It could affect entry level in the job market for students not proceeding to college. But the important effect is in the path onward, the determination or accessibility of the next step. While such an effect is important in individuals' lives, proficiency test results are seldom the single crucial factor in this 'gatekeeping' process, and seldom cancel prior processes in a do-or-die fashion. At least until recently, few students have been denied graduation from school owing to the results of one test, nor is an entire school record expunged because of a scored lack of achievement. Tests of achieved knowledge do not ratify exits so much as condition further progress.

Similarly, although educational policy at the various levels of schooling has varied over the years, relatively few students have been denied promotion from one grade to the next on the basis of one set of test results. Of course, subject-specific proficiency tests, 'reading readiness' tests, and so on have many real and important consequences at many points in a student's career, especially at the earlier levels: they affect how quickly she moves from one class to another, or which class section or pedagogical track she enters, or the sequence or pace of the material she encounters. The general point, however, is that the major irrevocable decisions about a student's progress are not made on the basis of an achievement test score, but on the basis of a composite of indicators of achievement, effort expended, educational process, and experience. In a non-lockstep system, this is necessitated for practical and legal as well as ethical reasons.

Moreover, the exact knowledge possessed by individual students cannot be determined absolutely on the basis of such test scores.* Tests are imperfect in the way they sample and represent knowledge. There is no agreement on all the items of knowledge that an individual should possess. Perhaps most important, the degree to which schooling itself produces discrete bits of 'knowledge' relative to a prior baseline of ignorance is impossible to determine. What a student knows may come from the general culture, parents, independent reading, peers in and out of school, time spent on the task or in reflection (which may occur in school, but need not), reading ahead in the text, or many other avenues. It is generally impossible to ascribe the change from ignorance to knowledge of a given datum to the specific process of teaching and learning. Thus, tests of competence or proficiency are, in educational lingo, used for 'diagnostic' purposes—to suggest to the student, and those concerned with him, next steps or directions.

*It can of course be argued that such an absolutist system—involving attainment or nonattainment of sets of specific 'outcomes' on tests—would ultimately be fairer than the present system of multiple, sequential, complexly interrelated judgments. Tests of technical skills, in occupational or military settings for example, may indeed involve getting the entire fixed set of 'items' right.

These generalizations describe a situation in which the public is content with the schools. In recent years, however, the public has been taking a closer and more skeptical look at the public schools, and educational professionals have become more and more conflicted about achievement testing. Both groups, with reason, doubt the continued viability of the view described, in principle, immediately above: that tests are useful, but not to be depended upon too much. This skepticism may imply less testing or more testing, depending on the nature of the challenge and the nature of the educational goal.

There is also apparent the curious assumption (unsupported in test theory and illogical on the face of it) that while achievement scores for an individual student mean little, and should not form the basis for crucial decisions, sets and distributions of scores for schools and school systems have compelling face validity. Every year, parents and educators and taxpayers look at reading and math achievement scores published in the newspapers for the various schools in their community, and discover that some schools fare well, others poorly. It is striking how, year after year, schools known in the local culture as 'good schools' seem to attract 'good' students and yield 'good scores.' When there is change across schools or school districts, students begin to apply for transfers, corporations alter plant investment decisions, home prices are driven up or down, teachers do or do not get hired or upgraded in pay. State education funds flow unequally to local districts, either to the poor-scoring ones (to improve matters) or to higher-scoring ones (to reward and institutionalize accomplishment). In some cases, the details of the curriculum and the nature of teacher-student interaction are directly affected: for example, a course syllabus will be revised, or a teacher will decide privately to 'teach to the test.'

As for the states themselves, the direction of change is clear: where states are changing, it is toward a greater reliance on achievement tests. A state must be concerned about its educational reputation and about equity: it must know, relatively speaking, how many poor schools there are, where these stand in terms of resources and financing relative to the 'good schools,' who attends them, and so on. The recognition that low scores in a district may not be the *fault*, causally, of the schools themselves does not obviate the need to know. The states also must have data for dealing with widespread, if diffuse and internally contradictory, charges by interest groups, taxpayers, and parents that public education in general is not as good as it used to be, or should be. Leaving aside for the moment the question of how one compares 'the quality' of education today to quality at another time, or to an ideal or even a better hypothetical situation, states still need to know what the present situation is.*

---

*This remains true even though the states, in the process of testing, sometimes suffer from that knowledge. In Florida, for example, in the late 1970s, the state rather abruptly introduced tests of basic skills and functional literacy as a requirement for high school graduation. The intention was to assess and improve schools. A result, at first, was that parents sued the state: After twelve years of dutiful attendance, my child can't graduate?

3.2.1   IMPACT ON THE CURRICULUM

What does the general trend (it has not been felt in all states) toward more achievement testing across grades and schools mean for the social studies? At the K–3 level, the preponderance of teachers with social studies backgrounds report that the 'back to basics' trend of the 1980s has meant sharply increased classroom time on reading and calculation. No one questions that the elementary schools should have these subjectmatters as basics; nor, in these two areas, do experts worry much about whether it is entirely, and strictly speaking, only the school's job to ensure these competencies. All further learning depends on their being in place. Although there is widespread dissatisfaction with 'testing mania'—with the cumbersomeness, expense, and disruptiveness of the testing process, with test anxiety on the part of the children, or with using teachers as test administrators, and so on—the results of such tests are indeed used, for the most part, for individually diagnostic purposes. Further, since 'basic skills' are being assessed, and no one fully understands the ways in which children, individually and in classrooms, master those skills (though it is obvious that nearly all children do), teachers and schools *at this level* are relatively protected from charges of malfeasance or inefficiency. If the reading score for some second graders is poor, it is not the teacher's fault. (By sixth grade, the situation may have changed.) The remaining concern, felt particularly by teachers, is whether instructional time and effort is so consumed by basic skills and their testing that there is no time for children to be exposed to the elements of, specifically, social studies and the sciences. Teachers report that while classroom readers (that is, instructional books) contain science and social studies material, placed there in order to interest students in these subjectmatters, teachers driven to produce reading no longer use this material to teach—build, develop, point to, illustrate, enlarge, comment upon—the foundations of social study.

Thus it is no surprise that self-reports by teachers and observers show that the number of minutes per day or per week spent 'doing' social studies has declined in the first few grades. This may be of concern, since the number of minutes devoted to such purposes has never been great (section 2.1). On the other hand, both lay assumptions and educational lore hold that students in K–3 are not expected to *do* anything much with content knowledge (language and calculation being considered 'skills'), and that students' potential interests in the different subjectmatters are, at this level, nurtured through reading, stories, games, discussion, the use of informative materials, guests in the classroom, and so on. Thus the crucial question with regard to the trend toward more instruction in 'the basics' is not likely to be Is social studies caused to suffer? but rather Does the *additional* emphasis on reading and math produce the expected *increment* in competency? If this proves to be the case, everyone gains, since whatever social studies teaching does occur is likely to be more successful.

At the middle-school, junior high school, and high school levels the effects of 'accountability'-driven knowledge testing are more clear cut with regard to both the curriculum and teacher-student transactions in the classroom. In 1986, social studies supervisors in nineteen states reported recently added forms of state-wide testing,[7] and several states have announced elaborate testing plans since then. Some such schemes simply sharpen grade promotion procedures; others are more end-loaded, aimed at the approach to graduation (or promotion from one major level to another) or other summative assessments of student outcomes. Let us look at several instances of change.

Here is a minimal instance. Michigan has had explicit 'curricular objectives,' written by teachers and specialists for students at the end of grades 3, 6, and 9 in the areas of social studies and science. Accordingly, it is administering knowledge-achievement tests at the beginning of grades 4, 7, and 10. (The tests are voluntary, which means that a school need not make irrevocable decisions based on the results.) This is a rational procedure: why have knowledge objectives unless there can be some assessment of to what extent they are being achieved?*

Here is a more complex example, also from Michigan, which has only a civics requirement in its formal education law. As of 1989, the state education department has been urging schools to put in place a ninth-grade civics course with emphasis on economics and law as well as the traditional structure of government. The placement of such a course works well, in principle, for Detroit and other urban areas, where the drop-out rate climbs after grade 9. Nonurban districts, however, prefer a government- and-economics sequence at grade 12. If a state civics achievement test is eventually written (for administration early in grade 10), will the state also devise a different test appropriate for administration toward the end of grade 12? (Why? What could be done with the results of such a test?) As long as the tests are voluntary, nonurban schools may opt not to test at all. Will they keep to that plan if high-achieving urban students offer their test scores, for example, in applying to the state university system—and no such scores are available to nonurban students? Michigan is in the process of designing a comprehensive advisory social studies scope and sequence, and offers districts extra funds to try it out. Districts have been slow to comply. A state proficiency test was written for U.S. History, for administration at the end of tenth grade; lo and behold, districts began to shift their traditional eleventh grade course to grade 10.

Massachusetts, also a state without elaborate legal mandates, has developed a new Curriculum Framework.[8] A primary reason for its development now is that the Commonwealth is instituting statewide achievement testing at grades 4,

*The writing of curricular goals and objectives within school systems is a laborious and, in some districts, seemingly continual process. If such objectives are imposed from above, by a subjectmatter specialist in the state capital or a department chair, the teachers ignore them. If the teachers are involved, enormous amounts of discussion and released or after-school time are involved—and many teachers still ignore them. Discrete objectives in a syllabus or lesson plan are in practice often overridden by what is in the textbooks, or how material is arranged there. In systems where textbook choice is up to the teacher, her choice in principle should reflect prior objectives. In systems where textbook 'adoption' is systemwide, writing objectives becomes superfluous, except when a new adoption cycle is on the horizon.

8, and 12—in the case of social studies, for the first time. The framework itself is interesting, admirable, well-argued, and has many reasons for being other than the new tests. However, it is couched at a level that is clearly intended to build orderly course patterns—that is, at the level of a syllabus and progression of lessons—appropriate for testing.*

Massachusetts is not using standardized national subject-area tests, but is involving teachers themselves in constructing the tests. The process will not be easy. In Boston, for example, 'geography' is taught as a course only in 3 out of 17 high schools; otherwise it is 'infused' into History and Global Studies. If a geography test is written, what kinds of items will be chosen? Will teachers with Geography degrees want to test for conceptual competence, History teachers for history-related specific proficiency, Global Studies teachers for regional knowledge? What will an excellent magnet school in Boston, whose curriculum is entirely organized around world studies, do when achievement tests are fully deployed? Will that change the nature of the school? (The principal's answer: "I don't know. I worry about it.") In Massachusetts, the stated aim in instituting such tests is to improve poor schools, and to pay nonpunitive attention to individuals who score in the lowest quartile. The magnet school is unlikely to have many such scorers, if any. Why then administer the test? But is it wise, or possible, to exempt entire schools from statewide testing?

For an even more far-reaching instance, let us look at the recent history of the accountability movement in Indiana. Ten years ago, the state had no official mandated curriculum for the social studies, except for a requirement that all students take U.S. History and Civics-Government. There was much variety within the state. Indianapolis, for example, has mandated grade 12 Economics since the mid-1950s, but on a statewide basis probably no more than 50 percent of students take economics (including consumer or business economics). In the late 1970s accountability pressures arose, especially among the business community. The state education department considered how to be responsive to such concerns. Local school districts were required to document goals and objectives, and to use appropriate subject-area achievement tests at various grade levels. Many districts began to administer the Iowa Tests of Basic Skills, which despite its name is largely an achievement-oriented set of tests. The state department pooled and analyzed comparable results from the districts (for example, for grade 8 History) and concluded that, in general, Indiana students were doing better than the national norms for the ITBS, particularly in elementary grades. Those who were naive about tests could not understand the score distributions.

---

*Massachusetts involved its teachers integrally in the development of the framework, and continues to stress a high degree of curricular choice for teachers and schools. The Department of Education points out, for example, that if a school's goal is *only* to increase achievement test scores, following this or any other overall framework may not be the most efficient means: that is, a stronger form of 'teaching to the test' would work better. Massachusetts also emphasizes the way courses are taught and the way students are treated, and the importance of developing critical thinking skills, over and above content coverage.

More important, those who believed that public education was slipping (or that in one way or another the Indiana system needed reforms) refused to believe the results.

In 1987 the state decided to move to common testing in all districts and adopted a different set of tests, more thoroughly achievement-based in nature, to be given at four grade levels about March 1. In reading and math, low-scoring students would be required to take summer remedial work in order to be promoted to the next grade in the fall. Overall, the students still did better than expected; fewer of them went to summer school than anticipated. In some quarters the response—once again—was not to salute the apparent level of educational achievement, but to say, We'd better get a tougher test.

In social studies, because of intense agitation within the education system, state achievement tests were not administered. Instead, much briefer criterion-referenced tests were written and administered. That is, specific knowledge items were drawn from the actual curriculum in several subjectmatters (as identified by teachers and department heads)—for example, at a given grade level, four items of geography, four items of American history, and so on, the items to be rotated or replaced from one year to the next in the testing scheme. Indiana social studies teachers appear to be comfortable with this testing scheme, although some observers believe that there is a discernible difference in what is taught, and how instruction is done, prior to March 1 and subsequently. Not to put too fine a point on it, classroom instruction seems a lot more variegated and interesting in the last three months of the year.

It is easy to be hyperskeptical about standardized, conventional knowledge testing. By showing that statewide grade-level testing has problems and dangers, one could be led to the position that tests within classrooms, administered and scored by the teacher, are defective. Then one is back to the situation where a student 'passes' because she has good attendance, meets the teacher's eye, and can write acceptable short-essay answers on midterms and finals. There are many profoundly important benefits, socially and educationally, to achievement testing. Further, as many commentators have shown, testing has deep roots in the history of 'efficiency' in schooling.[9] Finally, Americans traditionally dislike mystical, priestly, or personal authority in schooling as much as they do for employment remuneration, fees for service, guild membership, and the like.

3.2.2 ARE SOCIAL STUDIES EXEMPT?

However, with regard to the testing movement, there may be special problems for curriculum areas such as social studies or science. The main reason Massachusetts is involving its social studies teachers in writing its new achievement tests, the main reason Indiana at the eleventh hour excluded social studies from national tests, is that in this subject area it is difficult to find or develop test items that fairly reflect the *actual* curriculum—what the teachers actually teach, let alone what the students actually learn.

Why this should be so is not mysterious. An eleventh-grade U.S. History test may be valid for a course of study that is a traditional, chronological 'sweep' from 1607 to the present. The same knowledge test would be inappropriate for a course that concentrated on the period Reconstruction to the present; or one that included a substantial unit of state history and a special focus on economic history and labor relations, the Progressive era, and turn-of-the-century immigration; or one that covered the entire period but concentrated on constitutional issues from the federal period through the Twenty-sixth Amendment. Moreover, there are important subjects in social studies that are inherently non- or multidisciplinary: two obvious examples are citizenship and global education. The development of national standardized multiple-item tests in these areas that would be both fair (that is, reflect actual variations in practice) and related in rational ways to some independently valid standard of knowledge (such as the disciplinary content of political science or international economics) seems unlikely on both technical and practical grounds. There is also the question of whether, in subject areas such as these, the aim of education should be to transmit a known body of 'facts' or provide a basic orientation and analytical capacity toward a limitless conceptual field.

Attempts to deal with these problems tend to go in one of two directions. One is into the actual classroom. Administering tests whose items will correspond to what is concretely taught—in a particular track of a particular course at a particular grade level of a particular school in a particular year—quite quickly reduces to what teachers' quizzes or tests supplied by the textbook publisher tap. The validity of achievement testing depends on the presence of variability: that *some* students will know *some* items, but that not all items will be known (or not known) by all students. Validity also rests on the notion that test items themselves are a sample of *kinds* of knowledge, not the exact knowledge itself.

The other direction is into the general culture. Administering tests that deal with those facts that, indeed, everyone should learn and never forget—1776, the location of the Soviet Union, the definition of GNP, and how east relates to north—is feasible; but such knowledge could be produced without schools, or at least the schools we have created.

How to reach reasonable agreement in the social studies on standardized knowledge testing depends on substantial agreement on the curriculum, on what knowledge is worth testing for, and on the essential dimensions of the teaching-learning transaction. But this is exactly what the debate is about, and always has been.

At present, it is probably advisable for those in charge of social studies to resist the kind of achievement testing that may be appropriate for reading or mathematics or mastery of the basic vocabulary of a foreign language. In fact, teachers and scholars in these areas, too, are allies. There is far more to reading and mastery of a foreign language than simple decoding, pronouncing, and vocabulary skills—as proponents of the 'writing throughout the curriculum' movement are quick to point out. Mathematics teachers, for their part, debate the extent to which calculation skills and algorithms of various kinds are sufficient, even at the lowest grade levels. On the other hand, if the social studies are viewed as inherently untestable, or their practitioners as hostile to testing, very serious dangers arise. That position will reinforce the notion that social studies are 'fuzzy' and unstructured, and that social studies experts cannot agree on what to teach and toward what goals. For students, it will send the message that studying, or not studying, social studies has no consequences; or, more realistically, that when you 'take' history or geography you needn't do more than remember a few facts and concepts for a few weeks, until the end-of-the-chapter test. Social studies experts, in sum, may need to decide not whether but *how* their fields are to be included in statewide testing, and try to arrive at principled positions on how far and in what direction statewide testing should go.

It is easy to say that, in general, testing should be tied to course syllabi. The testing and accountability debate, however, cannot be pursued without reference to other parts of the system. Movements toward tougher curriculum mandates and toward testing for accountability are obviously closely interrelated. Once a state has 'set' its curriculum, it only makes sense to test. But what if a state sets a curriculum (and specifies pedagogical goals) that are not adaptable to existing tests? For example, California, in instituting its new, nonmandatory social studies framework, built around a history cum geography core, recognizes that new tests will have to be written. Much will depend on whether textbook publishers respond to the revised California Framework, by producing new texts for the new scope and sequence in this very large market. If they do, matters are simpler: the most reliable way for tests to be tied to syllabi in a textbook adoption state is for the texts to be taken as the source of most test items. If new texts are provided by the publishers and adopted by the state, it will become exceedingly difficult for individual districts not to come into line with the new framework. (If a district uses the same texts as neighboring districts but attempts to follow a somewhat different detailed course of study, it is likely that its scores will go down: the 'alignment' of instruction to texts to tests will be less exact.)

On the other hand, if states write their own tests, invidious comparisons may still ensue. What if the Indiana scores had, for any number of technical reasons, appeared poorer than comparable test scores in, say, Illinois? Might there not have been a move, on the part of the state education authorities or the governor, to use Illinois tests? That is, to try another test in the hope that more favorable scores would result? Or to move the Indiana curriculum into accord with that of Illinois, in the hope that more testable learning would thus take place?*

It is impossible to predict, today, the end result of 'reform' at the state level (or for that matter, within states) toward a more uniform and 'rational' curriculum, mandated in terms of specific courses at specific grade level; with 'rationally' related testing schemes; and with 'rationally' selected textbooks as the

---

*The recent decision to report test results from the National Assessment of Educational Progress on a state-by-state basis (see section 14.3) may well aggravate such tendencies.

primary purveyors of bodies of knowledge.* A possible result is something close to a national curriculum, in social studies as in other curricular areas. The other possibility is a sharpening of alternative subnational models: a New York State model coexisting with a California and a Texas model and a few others, with smaller states almost inevitably driven into one or another camp. Either possibility should receive the most cautious consideration by those concerned with educational reform.

*The general tendency toward 'hyperrationality' in the American school system has been incisively noted by Wise in *Legislated Learning*, among others. It is, of course, a matter of concern to those who study bureaucratic systems and professional communities generally.[10]

PART II

History of the Curriculum

4.0 Description of the Curriculum

4.0.1   DIFFICULTIES IN DESCRIPTION

To write about curriculum history is fascinating but frustrating. Ideally, one would want data over time bearing on specific units of instruction—how they were arranged and what they contained, in some detail. Such data are rare; either components are missing or the data are misleading because unrepresentative. Generally speaking, schools do not have a record of departmental syllabi, teachers' lesson plans, or tests. Those detailed records that do exist are the recent files of particular teachers or departments, covering only the past few years. The lack of centralized records, ordered across time, reflects the fact that in most schools teachers are free, within guidelines, to work in the classroom on a day-to-day basis as they think best. Daily lesson plans, if prepared, are soon discarded (or, worse, never discarded and used for years); at best they are plans for instruction rather than reports of what actually occurred.

Few observers or critics of the schools seriously propose that things should be different. The job of the department chair or the curriculum specialist is to guide a continual process of adjustment in the curriculum, semester to semester or year to year. That such adjustments are continually being made, that the curriculum is always in a state of at least minor revision, is a sign of vitality and flexibility—as well as an indicator of professional activity. In a sense, it is not realistic for 'the system' to measure too carefully how much change is occurring or not occurring over the years, or to limit change to certain periods. Since the reality of instruction in the classroom cannot be written down, elaborate records spelling out unit titles, pedagogical objectives from week to week, and all the rest could lead only to highly misleading indicators.*

There is one natural measure, at least in some districts. About half the states now follow a state-level textbook adoption system, as do many large city systems; moreover, in some other states where state funds are used to purchase teaching materials, good records are kept of the number of texts purchased for specific courses in individual schools. Analysts can then get a reasonably objective idea of the range and emphasis of content *possibly* involved in the various courses, although they cannot be sure that all the content was covered (and how) or what additional material teachers may have used. However, only if records of comparative 'shares of the market' (i.e., adoptions) are kept on a comprehensive basis will such analyses be fruitful. Conclusions about what the curriculum was 'really' like in earlier decades, based on inspection of popular texts, should be looked upon with some doubt, since the texts that have found their way into educational libraries or archives are unlikely to be representative.†

It may not be reasonable to expect schools to keep archives of actual curriculum materials, plans, rationales, assessments, and the like. Some schools, invariably schools that have been educational cynosures, have such archives;

---

*Concerning what was probably the most thorough research study of alternative high-school curricula in relation to 'outcomes,' in this case achievement in college (a study known as the Eight-Year Study), Ralph W. Tyler, one of the leading figures in education of the past fifty years, wrote: "In my experience with investigations of such educational programs as activity schools, core curriculum, open classrooms, and alternative schools, I found the definitions used by different practitioners and researchers so widely varying and the secondhand data so undependable that the information reported was often meaningless."[1]

†There is room here for useful cooperation among state and local educational bodies, book publishers, and professional groups. For example, educational authorities might keep the adoption records, while professional libraries might archive the actual books. The publishers would need to be more cooperative, severally, than is now the case. For obvious reasons, publishers do not provide detailed sales records freely. And in their printed books, they are often vague as to which revision, year of publication, or what has been revised. Such vagueness reflects the fact that publishers continually alter their texts, and wish to suggest that each edition is simultaneously up-to-date yet not a radical departure from an earlier, familiar standard.

they are enormously useful to researchers (see section 5.4). Most schools do prepare, each year, descriptions of the courses (sections, alternative sequences, and so forth) to enable students and parents to make choices or know how the school year is to be organized. At a minimum, schools might retain such publicly disclosed, externally oriented explanatory materials. They are an indicator, over time, of a school's profile and philosophy (as well as its course offerings), and as such they should be part of the social and intellectual history of the community.*

Ideally also, in sketching in 'curriculum history' for a portion of the curriculum, one would want to embed an interpretation of changes or continuities in that part of the curriculum (for example, social studies) within the context of changes and continuities in the public school curriculum as a whole; and all of this should be related to general educational history in the context of the greater society and its national history. This is a tall order, hardly ever attempted. The post–World War II period has seen brilliant accomplishment in the history of American public education, such as that of Cremin, Bailyn, Kaestle, Tyack, Ravitch, Curti, and a number of others. Generally speaking, these treatments deal both with very broad curriculum change (for example, academic versus vocational courses, or the change from a classical to a liberal to a 'modern' curriculum) and with the ups and downs and ins and outs of specific subjectmatters (for example, the relative strengths over time of ancient or medieval versus modern European history, or the dwindling of Latin and the rise of Spanish). Typically the latter are taken as examples of the former—but without any sustained attempt to gauge how a general change in attitude or goals brings about more specific curriculum adjustments, or how a number of local adjustments may in fact accumulate and amount to a general shift. Curriculum history tends to follow an externalist model, by which factors at the societal level affect the curriculum at the level of either broad social orientations, trends in the various branches of knowledge (for example, in universities), or specific school courses.† The relationships of particular course patterns and pedagogy to slower, broader trends *in the curriculum as a whole* are treated, often in minute detail, in the textbooks of educational methodology courses, especially for the elementary level where the question of how to allot time and attention is always uppermost. But such books seldom refer to larger societal trends—political, social, intellectual—except in a perfunctory way: as something that is evident and needs no analysis.

Conversely, the volumes of commentary and recommendations produced by national commissions and study groups tend to move directly from societal to

---

*The prognosis is not good. In most American communities it is no longer possible to find telephone directories from previous decades. An invaluable research resource for local history is being lost.

†One study that examines the direction of flow of changes across levels (and the rapidity of change) is Kliebard.[2]

curricular specifics, as if the educational system were not an intervening reality.* In these analyses, the specific curriculum patterns of interest in the recent past are examined for trends (gains, losses, alterations in emphasis, and so forth), without substantial reference to the rest of the curriculum or the structure of schooling. The situation of the field under inspection is then evaluated with reference to a set of intellectual and pedagogical or social ideals that tend to be derived philosophically and accepted as givens (intellectual rigor, relevance to the needs of the society, considerations of educational opportunity and social equity, and the like). It is, of course, not surprising that the critics of any age let the assumptions and pertinent aspects of the time go undescribed. No one can see his own present in perspective. What is more surprising is that the societal contexts shaping *earlier* developments, the spirit of *past* ages, are not analyzed. The studies by commissions and professional groups tend thus to be more 'internalist' than is really intended: it is as if change in a particular curriculum area in the past had been largely undirected, self-generating—with consideration of what should be, or could be, different left until now.†

In the treatment of the development of social studies that follows, I shall proceed across the various decades and eras, synthesizing the voluminous work of others and trying to point out where there are important disagreements or what seem to be errors of interpretations. With regard to the latter, the errors of the 'internalists,' those who begin from the detailed patterns of the social studies and work outwards, are largely those of omission: for perfectly good reasons, they have not always moved to the larger picture, or could not have at the time they were writing. The errors of the 'externalists,' those who see societal-level events or trends as closely coupled to change in the curriculum in general (or portions of it), are perhaps more important to identify, since they may misrepresent the intentions or perceptions of those actually in the schools and may assume the schools were more consciously responsive to calls for change than was the case.

In the period covered, approximately 1890 to date, there were two eras of

---

*This is true at least in the social studies. It is this kind of unreality that Davis[3] describes: "Commission reports, assertions by prominent social studies figures, and pronouncements by professional societies have been seen as the principal realities of the field.... The prominent statements of the field serve as landmarks. By themselves, however, they do not serve it well enough. Examination of discourse about curriculum reveals that much of the language does not describe the world as it is; rather, it portrays an invented world, one that should be. This rhetoric is persuasive in nature, combining both exaggerated claims with understatement. Focused on success and change, as most of these statements are, evidence of routine practices, even failure, seems studiously avoided; it is identified only for the purpose of convincing individuals to alter present or conventional practice [p. 29].... Understanding of the social studies during any time must reconcile impressions from the available discourse and the commonplace of schooling. Each enlightens the other. Neither is a faithful reflection of the other" [p. 34].

†There are, of course, treatments of the history of social studies, to be referred to in what follows, that *do* interrelate the three levels—the particular subject matter, the general curriculum, and broader educational history—but these are not of book length; thus they are either nondetailed or noncomprehensive. The most useful and dependable such treatment is Hertzberg, *Social Studies Reform.*[4] This was intended by the author as a first version of a longer and more thorough book, on which the author was working at her untimely death.

change or pressure for reform in social studies that were of widespread and long-lasting importance, in terms of both contemporary perception and subsequent impact. The first, around the 1910s, saw the creation, as it were, of that segment of the curriculum to be called Social Studies. This was an era when change was rapid, obvious, and synchronous across all three levels—the nature and goals of the schools, the design of a comprehensive curriculum for the 'modern' age, and the invention of a set of courses for social studies that would go beyond, without dislodging, history. The second distinctive era, around the 1960s, is known in the field as the era of the New Social Studies, when a sweeping pedagogical alteration took place, at least in terms of enunciated principles. This coincided with pressure for reform in the curriculum in general, and with an anxiety among the public about the quality of schooling in terms of national achievement and self-image. It now appears that the actual changes at the lower two levels—the social studies and the general curriculum—were roughly consonant with each other, but that these changes within the schools did not well match or fulfill societal expectations.

Curriculum change is by no means simply a matter of intellectual and pedagogical choices. In constructing any form of educational history, among the most basic data are the size, structure, and dynamics of the system under examination. The following pages provide data on some of these factors. This information will be referred to in the historical treatment of the social studies curriculum that occupies the rest of Part II of this volume.

4.1   Size and Composition of the Educational System

Between 1900 and the 1980s the nation underwent enormous population growth, clearly evident in the school-age population, those aged 5 to 17.* Slowing in the growth of the population at these ages is attributable to alteration in fertility rates owing to the Depression and World War II, and to the secular trend toward lower fertility in the recent period. These rescissions in growth are seen also in the population of the schools, with the predictable lags. For example, the number of students in high school continued to grow in the 1930s while the number of students in elementary school declined, the latter in part reflecting the dropping birth rates of the 1920s and 1930s. Figure 4-1 cannot capture the age *structure* of the population. For example, the rise between 1950

---

*When U.S. educational statistics were developed as a separate system, a process completed in the 1940s, 5 and 17 were the typical boundary ages. In earlier decades of the century children entering the system late simply skipped a grade or two (kindergarten was not prevalent) and then progressed normally; and those who stayed in the system far enough to enter high school tended to complete high school in four years and graduate at 17. Later, entrance into grades depended in some eras on cognitive and social readiness, promotion policies were revised, and relatively more students took additional time to progress through high school. For reasons of standardization, educational statistics still use the 5–17 'window,' while Census Bureau and other federal statistics provide data on those attending school at higher ages. The methods of counting are also very different; there is apparently no good solution.

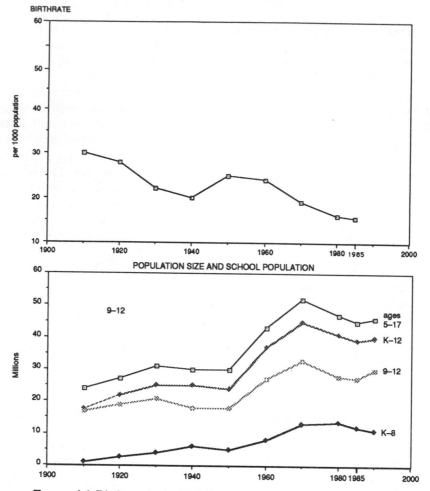

FIGURE 4-1 Birthrate in the U.S. Population; Size of the School-age
Population; and Enrollments in the Schools

SOURCES: (birthrate) U.S. Dept. of Health and Human Services, *Vital Statistics of
the U.S.*, 1986, vol. 1, section 1; (school-age population and enrollment levels) U.S.
Dept. of Education, National Center for Education Statistics, *Digest of Education
Statistics, 1988* (CS 88-600), table 30; U.S. Dept. of Commerce, Bureau of the
Census, *Statistical Abstract of the United States 1988*, 25; U.S. Dept. of Education,
National Center for Education Statistics, *Projections of Education Statistics to
1997–98* (CS 88-607), 1988, 22–23.

and 1970 for ages 5–17 and grades K–8 is not due to change in the current birth
rate, but to fertility dynamics—that is, the accumulation of young adults having
children, the so-called baby boom.

In 1900, over 70 percent of the appropriately aged persons in the population
attended public school at least for a few of the earlier grades; by 1930, a little over
80 percent; and by 1970, about 86 percent (the balance, since about the 1930s,
being those attending private schools). This means, of course, that the K–8 curve

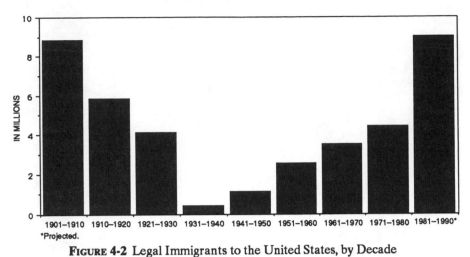

FIGURE 4-2 Legal Immigrants to the United States, by Decade

SOURCE: John B. Kellogg, "Forces of Change," *Phi Delta Kappan* 70 (November 1988): 200.

in the figure will track the curve for age 5–17 in the population quite closely, and that the prior fertility rate will be a major factor.

The growth in attendance, grades K through 8, that occurred in the first three decades of the century is attributable partly to increased fertility before the turn of the century and to immigration, but also to social changes that made primary schooling inevitable for almost all children. Immigration was high in the first two decades, and again in the 1970s and 1980s, with illegal immigration also being an important factor in the latter period. The currently high rate of immigration, concentrated in urban areas, will itself increase K–8 attendance in the 1990s and probably beyond, since immigrants tend to be of child-bearing age.

The *rate* of growth in high-school attendance was, in the early decades of this century, built on a far smaller base, in terms of the proportion of those in a given age range attending school. This rate increase was more gradual and lasted longer; a higher and higher *proportion* went to school, notably in the 1970s. (Figure 4-1 shows the absolute *number* of grade 9–12 students diminishing.) The K–8 attendance *rate* 'topped out' around 1950 at about 98 percent in attendance at *some* grade level (today the figure is about 99 percent). Attendance at high school (at *some* level), ages 14 to 17, reached about 90 percent by 1960 and has fluctuated between about 93 and 95 percent ever since. (This includes, however, students who stay only for a year or two.)

As is evident in figure 4-3, only 6.4 percent of those younger than 18 were high-school graduates in 1900 (and relatively few completed high school thereafter, at later ages). The highwater mark in terms of *proportion* of the population completing high school 'on time' occurred about 1970: it has fallen since then, although recently there has been a slight reversal upward. If the age boundary is raised to 19, the percentage completing high school increases for the population as a whole by one or two percentage points (excluding high school diploma

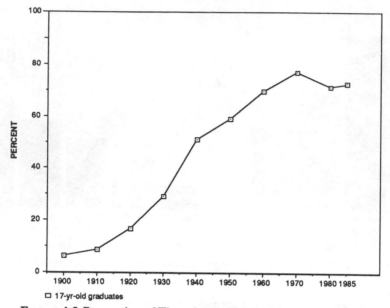

FIGURE 4-3 Proportion of Those in the U.S. Population Who Have
Graduated from High School by Age 17

SOURCE: U.S. Dept. of Education, National Center for Education Statistics,
Digest of Education Statistics 1988, table 77.

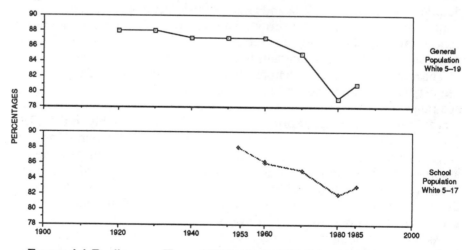

FIGURE 4-4 Decline over Time of Whites in the U.S. School-age Population, in
Relation to Proportion of Whites in Actual School Population, Ages 5–17. (The latter
statistic is not reliable prior to 1953.)

SOURCE: (upper curve) U.S. Dept. of Commerce, Bureau of the Census, 1980 *Census of
Population. General Population Characteristics* (Publication PC80-1-B1), table 45, and *Current
Population Reports*, Series P-25, no. 1022, table 2; (lower curve) U.S. Dept. of Commerce,
Bureau of the Census, *Statistical Abstract of the United States 1988*, 25.

equivalencies). Looking at the proportion of graduates at age 19 rather than at 17 increases the rate for blacks, especially since 1983,* but not for Hispanics, for whom the rate of completion of high school by age 19 has not altered much since the early 1970s. Taken at age 19, the completion rate for whites is about 77 percent, for blacks about 65 percent, and for Hispanics about 55 percent (including diploma equivalencies). (See table 4-1.)

Figure 4-4 shows the proportion of the U.S. population *at school age* between 1920 and 1985 who were white, together with the proportion of those *in school* who were white, from 1953 to date.† During the last thirty-five years or so, the relative participation in schools by nonwhites has varied. In the 1950s and 1980s nonwhites increased their rate of school attendance relative to their representation in the age 5–19 population, while in the 1960s and 1970s the age-specific general population became nonwhite more rapidly than the school-going population.

The expansion in size of the system of schooling over the past eighty years or more, together with the steady increase in the proportion of participation in education (albeit with marked regional and racial differences), is a signal characteristic of American society, much remarked and recently emulated, to some extent, elsewhere. This is also taken (together with evidence of periodic curriculum reform) as an indicator of what educationalists call the 'holding power of the schools,' a curiously penal-sounding phrase. Here again, there may be a confusion of levels, or a measure that ignores a number of externalities. No one doubts that socially benign school systems with well-motivated teachers and an interesting course of studies serve to keep some students in school, instead of entering the world of work or doing not much of anything with their time. However, especially in recent decades of near-universal participation in schooling, this is a phenomenon at the margin. It is not as if all students actively ponder whether or not to attend, or keep on attending, school. Far more important, it would seem, in any decade, are macroeconomic factors, the size and state of repair of the physical school plant, child labor laws, unemployment levels, the presence or absence of recent immigrants of school age, fertility dynamics, the number of 'caretakers' or mentors available to persons of school age in society generally, and the estimation by the young (and their parents) of their future 'life chances.'‡ It is hard to determine how much 'holding power' schools possess in and of themselves.

Those in charge of schools should not believe that all the important factors are

*Perhaps related to the young black male unemployment rate.

†In these data, those of Asian origin are considered white, and those attending private schools are included.

‡On the matter of the breadth and depth of support for school-age persons in society as a whole, see Coleman.[5] With regard to schooling and economic well-being, it is not necessarily 'rational' for every student, no matter what her or his occupational goal, to complete high school—at least in one unbroken episode. That is, for some intended occupations it is better (statistically speaking) to leave high school before graduation, perhaps to return later.

under their control. They must also concern themselves with the intrinsic human and social worth of the education they offer. In doing so, however, they may unwittingly accept the assumptions and values of idealists who believe that schools must take primary responsibility for the totality of the healthy development of individuals from age five or six to eighteen or more. As we will see, in examining educational reform in the first decades of this century, this assignment to the schools of a very large human task is not recent, but characteristic of American attitudes toward education. The range of choices about curriculum is directly affected by these considerations. Does the curriculum adjust itself continually to societal trends and needs? Do waves of reform come from widespread public dissatisfaction? Or should the curriculum be a conservative institution, not veering and tacking with the perceived needs of each decade but providing students with what is time-tested, intellectually coherent, personally generative? The obvious answer is that both aspects are needed; the curriculum must both follow trends and drag against them. But in looking at the system over time, particularly with regard to the social studies—where the study of these subjectmatters is directly related, in principle, to the wise participation of each upcoming generation in the continuing debates—we need to trace how these two principles have been balanced.

Awareness of these larger, societal factors is useful in deciding, for example, what the implications of the 'drop-out' rate may be. An increase, perceived or documented, in noncompletion rates among different groups or different locales calls into question the 'holding power' of the schools. Alternatively, it can be analyzed as an aspect of labor force participation or the sociology of work, or as an index of alienation on the part of individuals. Careful statistical studies of recent dropping out fail to establish intrinsic school factors as *directly* causal.[6]* The drop-out rate is certainly, to some extent, an artifact of the success of the system as a whole. That is, in earlier decades there were no 'dropouts,' at least from high school: only in the case of those born about 1920 did even a simple majority enter high school, let alone graduate. The instituting of mandatory school attendance laws raised the school-leaving age from below;† the recent pattern of somewhat delayed high school completion alters the upper skirt. Moreover, drop-out rates are hard to define and measure. There can be an increase in 'dropouts', given particular definitions, when individuals are followed longitudinally through the system, even while the gross participation rates are increasing.

Table 4-1 shows some relevant data reaching back to the 1970s. In the early 1980s, the completion rate for blacks, nationally, improved. The high-school noncompletion rate in the South has historically been higher than for other sections of the country, and remains so in recent years. Ages 18–19 are 'risk' ages,

---

*That is, few leave school early because and only because they dislike it. By and large, those who dislike school are 'at risk' otherwise.

†In virtually all states, one may not legally leave school below the age of 14; in many states, before 16.

Table 4-1 High-school Completion by Race and Hispanic Origin, Persons
Ages 18 to 19 and 20 to 24: 1974 to 1986

Year	Age: 18 to 19				Age: 20 to 24			
	Total	White	Black	Hispanic[1]	Total	White	Black	Hispanic[1]
	Percentage of age group				Percentage of age group			
1974	73.4	76.2	55.8	48.9	83.9	85.6	72.5	59.0
1975	73.7	77.0	52.8	50.0	83.9	85.9	70.5	61.3
1976	73.1	75.4	58.2	50.9	83.7	85.4	71.9	58.0
1977	72.9	75.7	54.9	50.7	83.7	85.1	73.4	56.6
1978	73.5	76.3	54.9	48.9	83.7	85.2	73.5	58.7
1979	72.8	75.3	56.4	53.7	83.2	84.9	71.8	55.8
1980	73.7	76.1	59.3	46.1	83.8	85.1	74.3	57.1
1981	72.5	74.8	59.6	47.2	83.7	85.0	75.7	59.3
1982	72.0	74.5	58.2	51.7	84.1	85.4	76.2	60.2
1983	72.7	75.6	59.1	50.3	83.3	84.6	75.8	56.6
1984	73.3	75.5	63.0	58.3	84.6	85.7	79.3	60.7
1985	74.6	76.7	62.8	49.8	85.3	86.0	80.8	67.4
1986	74.6	76.6	64.9	54.7	84.8	85.4	81.0	61.6

[1]Most of the year-to-year differences in completion rates for Hispanics are not statistically significant due to the small size of the Hispanic sample. Hispanics may be of any race.

NOTE: Separate analyses were not done for Asians because they are not identifiable from the October Current Population Survey data tapes.

SOURCES: U.S. Department of Commerce, Bureau of the Census, Current Population Reports, Population Characteristics, Series P-20. *School Enrollment—Social and Economic Characteristics of Students: October* (various years); Current Population Surveys (unpublished tabulations).

especially for males, but some return to school later. The perceived increase in drop-out rates widely discussed in the past few years is largely an urban phenomenon, especially in the larger and older cities, and most marked among some minority students, particularly Hispanics. There are reports that white males are again 'dropping out': this is hard to isolate in the statistics.

Completion rates and particular patterns of school-leaving, to use a neutral and perhaps broader term, are important in curriculum planning for at least two reasons. Current moves for the tightening or intensifying of the curriculum, or for raising educational requirements and graduation standards, *may* inadvertently increase school-leaving exactly among those who would otherwise have completed the last year or two of high school. That is especially likely in instituting competency tests for graduation (section 3.2.1), when students who have been educationally 'disadvantaged' for a number of years in school are confronted with an up-or-out ordeal. Graduation-related competency testing normally occurs in grade 11 or even grade 10, for obvious reasons. Factors in school-leaving that are strongly connected to family background and social class—which are stronger statistically than school quality per se—appear to operate most strongly in the transition *into* high school, rather than toward the end. The same critics who label 'the drop-out rate' as scandalously high sometimes call simultaneously for tougher schools. How to achieve both ends simultaneously is by no means clear. If tests for graduation, for example, are to be meaningful measures of 'excellence,' some must fail, and may then 'drop out.'

Especially in social studies, the curriculum design over the years has been affected by considerations of the timing of school leaving. It is generally held by educational historians that the tradition of U.S. History in grade 5 (emphasizing the U.S. Constitution and form of government), a tradition that goes back to the nineteenth century, was determined jointly by the belief that children at this age could 'handle' the subjectmatter* and that the students would likely end their education by grade 6. It is certain that U.S. History at grade 8 was put in place some decades later to catch those who would be leaving after eighth or ninth grade. In the period from about 1920 to 1940, experts argued over the placement of civics courses on similar grounds.

While school-leaving after grade 8 has been a noticeable phenomenon from about the 1920s to date, by about 1965 an apparent asymptote was reached, where an irreducible 5 or 6 percent of students would leave the system. Otherwise, for many decades and for both sexes, school-leaving has been steeper for the transition from grade 10 to grade 11 and from grade 11 to grade 12 than from grade 9 to 10.[7] Once again, curriculum mandates and testing requirements aimed at graduation may indeed affect the dynamics of school *completion* near the end of high school rather than school *leaving* earlier. Presumably, as the state of Florida discovered (section 3.2), if requirements are to be tightened at or near the outcome point in education, they need to be adjusted all the way through.

With this brief consideration of the size and composition of the public schools as a context, we turn now to the history of the curriculum.

4.2 How the Curriculum Took Shape: 1890 to 1950

4.2.1 PRIOR TO 1900

The history of the curriculum prior to about 1890 may be impossible to write at any authoritatively detailed level. At least, those who have written about it disagree sharply. For example, there is a persistent dispute over the strength, in the public schools, of history as against geography. Hertzberg[8] says that in the 1880s history was not a major subject. Peet and Tryon[9] disagree. The latter writer, looking carefully at very fragmentary data, reports that by 1890 or so American history was likely to be found in a familiar location, grade 5, and that

---

*Note that part of the assumption was that children in school at grade 5 presumptively had shown 'academic' ability, else they would already have left.

geography—in this era, consisting of place names closely tied to history and elements of 'commercial geography'—was taught throughout the upper primary (elementary) grades.* Many writers have pointed out the large number of 'geography' books for grammar school instruction, going back to the early decades of the 1800s. By the later 1800s, grammar schools were 'graded' up to grade 8, at least in the larger communities, and were thus articulated to some degree with the oncoming system of public high schools. There is considerable evidence that in these upper grades, prior to about 1875, geography tended to subsume history, rather than the other way around. History was strung along the thread of geographic expansion from the 1600s to the late 1800s; and while fifth-grade history paid special attention to the founding of the republic and to constitutional and civil government arrangements, it too had the tone of geographical determinism.

Peet's analysis is focused on the 'upper primary' grades, grades 6 and beyond, and on the high school then taking shape. He points out that by 1890 many states required American history at this level, and that a substantial number of students took some American and some European and/or ancient history. It is important to realize that ancient, medieval, and European history were far better established, with regard to course content in the American schools, than U.S. history. The former had been taught in the private academies and the preparatory divisions of colleges for many years. American history was still inchoate. One possible reason for the curious absence of U.S. history books and courses all through the mid-1800s is that the subject could not be 'set' until after the era of dispute over states rights, the Civil War, and Reconstruction; until the mountain states had joined the Union, American Indians in the Great Plains and the western states been pacified (if that is the word), the railroad completed, and industrialization begun.†

Several external factors converged in the 1890s. Public high schools began to surpass the academies in number and enrollment. Both the private colleges and the public universities began to grow in number and size. Some colleges began to enlarge in scope so as to become universities, as those public institutions founded under the Morrill Act already tended to be. This transition involved moving from the classical curriculum to a fuller set of courses, more modern in spirit and more eclectic. By the end of the century, both the colleges and

*Commercial Geography was a sort of rudimentary economic geography, dealing with transportation systems, such as the new railroads and the major rivers that brought goods to market; and with regions in the production of agricultural goods and finished goods.

†This attitude, if present, would have corresponded to German historiography of the time, which held that the study of any national history had to wait for a considerable time until objective, scientific evidence was marshaled. In fact, we know that American history books per se in the early 1800s were limited to the founding of the nation, the break with England, and the structure of civil government. Donald Bragaw has suggested another plausible interpretation: that in the early nineteenth century, literate persons 'read' history rather than studying it, and that most of the readings were original pieces—speeches, essays by prominent figures, and other ephemeral material (personal communication). At the time of Emerson, there was certainly a history-as-literature movement.

universities expected incoming students to have had some American history.

At the same time, the disciplinary professions were organizing during the 1890s and the next two decades.[10] This had the effect of stabilizing, at the university level, the basic scope and structure of each academic discipline. Had this definition of the disciplines in the university not occurred, the question of whether and how 'high school' would lead to college would not have arisen at that time.

The public high school of the 1890s was not, however, an academic, college-preparatory enterprise. Many, knowing the tiny proportion of the appropriately aged population in high schools then, and knowing that the universities began to enlarge enormously at about the same time, assume that high school was created essentially to lead to college.[11] In fact, high schools were thought of as 'people's colleges'.* They were 'academic' in emphasis only in the sense that they did not offer vocational courses.[12] They were charged with providing the substance of a 'higher' education not only to those aimed for college but to the many more numerous persons who would persist through all twelve grades for various personal reasons. This 'secondary' education (since by definition it had to go beyond what the graded grammar schools provided) was inevitably designed, in its subjectmatters, to the template provided by the colleges; no other model was available, save possibly for that of the academies, by then losing popularity.

For their part, the colleges were reorganizing a general education to include modern subjectmatters and reflect new disciplinary patterns and specialties. The common characterization is that the classical gentlemen's education typical of, say, England, gave way to the specialties and empirical concentrations of Germany. At the same time, the colleges were keenly aware that in modernizing they might attract an entire new stratum of students—precisely those who had previously chosen to stay in school through grade 12 but had never planned to go further.

In sum, both high schools and universities were, simultaneously and recipro-cally, dealing with the invention and testing of a general education, broadly available. High schools, in particular, from the outset struggled with the attainment of solid 'academic' instruction, defining that pattern with an eye toward, but not as synonymous with, the requirements of the university. Even in the more academic high schools, there was a division between those who followed a classical and those following a modern (or liberal) course. Thus, the need to include science and a new approach to mathematics. Thus, English as a course of study, the teaching of modern foreign languages, and the inclusion of new modern literature, European and even American, in the 'canon' of literary

---

*Some 'high schools' indeed were 'normal schools,' and thus were vocational in that they prepared their students to be schoolteachers. The term 'normal' is obscure, but seems to indicate that prospective teachers were taught what students of various ages could normally comprehend or benefit from.

study.* And thus, American history and the formal study of American government, at least to some extent.

Toward the end of the 1880s, the National Education Association called for a national commission effort to deal with the rationalization of *both* levels of the curriculum together. I state it this way advisedly. Another interpretation is that the universities sought, through this effort, to align the schools with their own needs—that is, to provide themselves with entrants who would have some coherent pattern of preparation. That may have been the motivation of some individual university academicians who supported the very large effort, which lasted from about 1887 to 1893. But the NEA itself included all levels of those professionally involved in education, from elementary school on up; and the nature of the NEA call for the effort is quite clear.

4.2.2   THE 1893 NEA REPORT

The NEA's Committee of Ten, headed by President Charles Eliot of Harvard, looked at all the major curricular areas, both classical and modern. A subgroup examined History, Civil Government, and Political Economy. Geography was then considered essentially a physical science, at least in the university, and was assigned to a different group. The chair of the subgroup, also (confusingly) a committee of ten, was the president of the University of Wisconsin, Charles Kendall Adams; the membership included university, college, and high school educators.† *This* Committee of Ten (to which I refer as such in what follows) included both Woodrow Wilson, a young professor of political economy and jurisprudence at Princeton, and James Harvey Robinson, an eminent historian and a founder of 'the New History.'

The (subgroup) Committee of Ten reported in 1893. It recommended an eight-year uninterrupted sequence of history, including an extension into college. That sequence was to begin in grades 5 and 6 with a sort of general history based on biography and mythology—that is, great men and great myths. It then proceeded as follows:

Grade 7   American History; Elements of Civil Government
Grade 8   Greek and Roman History
Grade 9   French History
Grade 10   English History

---

*Henry Wadsworth Longfellow may have been the first to design, at Bowdoin, a course in 'modern' European literature.

†Up through the 1930s, professors and administrators in higher education had often, in their earlier years, been teachers or principals or superintendents in the schools. It was expected that each level of education would be well-informed about the others.

Grade 11   American History
Grade 12   "A special period, studied in an intensive manner"; and Civil
            Government

American History in grade 7 was intended to present a more formal chrono-logical study of political history (as opposed to the geography cum history of the grammar school), together with the legal and structural elements of govern-ment. The latter were to be imparted by oral lessons and ancillary materials, not by texts. French and English History were to do several things at once: diminish the sprawling nature of medieval and modern history in the schools by focusing on areas where the evidence was most accessible and where applicability to America was clearest, and at the same time cover French and English material in a wider epochal and geographic framework. The program for grade 11 signaled once again that serious American History was here to stay. The program for grade 12 essentially involved a bow toward historiography, or at least scholarship. Some special aspect of American history or some concept like 'Renaissance' was to be developed, with specific recourse to 'study documents.' Finally, in grade 12, Civil Government was to be a formal, text-based study, examining governmental structures and functions at local, state, and national levels and including the study of foreign systems.

This last course element was important. With the deepening and enrichment of American History, it could no longer adequately cover American govern-ment. This needed to be looked at synchronically, structurally, and (hidden in the phrase 'civil government') functionally, and even to include rudiments of comparative government. By contrast, 'political economy' was deliberately ruled out as a separate subject matter, but 'covered' in American History and Civil Government. The reasoning was not explicit. However, by 1893 the classical model of economics was not thoroughly worked out (at least not so as to seem 'classical'); presumably sensitive aspects of *political* economy, for example, Spencerian determinism versus Progressive thinking, were not high school fare; and comparative economics was positively to be avoided.*

The 1893 report has been seen in later times, especially among those con-cerned with the balance between history and the nonhistorical social studies, as a highwater mark for history. This is a bit misleading. It submerged nothing nonhistorical. It was the tide of *modern*-style history that swept into the curriculum as a whole. The New History was to be German in style, empirical and scholarly, with narrative to be constructed on the basis of research. It was to be professional, not amateur, history, going beyond Ranke, scientific and (we

---

*As benchmark dates, Alfred Marshall lived from 1842 to 1924. Mathematically based economics was not well established until the 1920s, first in England. Karl Marx lived from 1818 to 1883. Moreover, in 1893, the American Economic Association included both economists and sociologists, and reflected a tension between those who emphasized institutional factors in economic processes and those who emphasized individual factors.

would say today) broadly social in emphasis—in the sense of dealing with processes and sets of events in interrelation going far beyond great men and great myths.   Moreover, Government was established as needing its own approach (though not very much time in the curriculum) largely by the decision of historians.

More important, looking ahead toward the history/social studies balancing that would occur episodically in later decades, the Committee of Ten report was clearly in the spirit of a broad general education for all who were intellectually motivated enough to attend high school. This curriculum, especially as implemented by "newer methods," was to "counteract a narrow and provincial spirit . . . prepare the pupil in an eminent degree for enlightenment and intellectual enjoyment in after years; and . . . assist him to exercise a salutary influence upon the affairs of his country."[13]   In other words, to repay that intellectual curiosity, to equip a student for the modern world, and to conduce to mature citizenship.

It has been widely remarked in educational history that commissions do not invent, but shape what is already happening—at least if they have any impact. The 1893 report did a little of both. Tryon[14] reports that in the decade following the number of courses in American History in high schools showed a marked increase, English History a lesser one. French History and special periods or topics did not 'take.' In the same period, however, the teaching of the older style 'general history' (that is, ancient-to-modern, largely of the imperial West) actually increased. Probably the period saw a divergence of patterns, as high schools tried to differentiate their curricula into something approaching an academic (now in the sense of college-bound) and a general course. If so, the larger aim of the NEA effort was not achieved.

4.2.3   THE 1899 AHA REPORT (GRADES 9–12)[15]

In 1899 a Committee of Seven of the American Historical Association ratified, in many ways, the work of the Committee of Ten. Even more sharply than the Ten, the Seven emphasized that a solid sequence of history, taught chronologically, was a hallmark of a good secondary education, when "fashioned with the thought of preparing boys and girls for the duties of daily life and intelligent citizenship." Vis-à-vis the Ten, there are some interesting nuances. One studies history, "not the art of historical investigation." The source-study method was to be used judiciously; that is, secondary sources were at least as important as primary ones. The special-period or topics course recommended in 1893 was dropped. One gathers that no direct reproof of the Ten was intended; the Seven, all historians with experience at both the university and schools levels, were in a sense more focused on the feasibility, tested through experience, of history in the high school and what could practically be achieved. There is discernible, however, a slight tone of correction of what may have been seen as a German-style scientism in the 1893 report. With regard to Civil Government, the Seven acknowledged that it needed separate study, but that was not sufficient; otherwise it would be too presentist and static. Unlike that of the Ten, the report of the Seven spent no time endorsing the inclusion of sociological and economic material in history; neither did it inveigh against it.

The report of 1899 had greater tangible impact than that of 1893, primarily because it recommended a simpler course pattern—and one which was close to some established practice, in the better high schools. It did not concern itself with lower levels, which was probably strategic. Its pattern was

Grade 9   Ancient History
Grade 10   European History: Medieval to Modern
Grade 11   English History
Grade 12   American History/Civil Government

It is a simpler pattern, free from any attempt to emphasize some European history (as in 1893) against a broader background. In fact, in this scheme, the entire grade 10–11–12 sequence is a kind of focusing down toward the American subjectmatter. Greek and Roman history, the vestige of a classical emphasis, were to recede into Ancient History, which was to have a broad European–Near Eastern approach, continuing to the fourth century A.D. or even 800, with the end of the Holy Roman Empire.

4.2.4   The 1909 AHA report (the lower grades)[16]

An AHA committee in 1909 reported on the earlier grades, in effect recommending history throughout grades 1 through 8. No doubt reflecting the increasing richness of the subjectmatter in graded grammar schools, the study of myths and national holidays was restricted to the earliest grades; the biographical approach was recommended at grades 4 and 5, with a European-to-America chronological sweep for grades 6, 7, and 8. Thus, in 1899 and 1909, the 1893 pattern was extended downward, which permitted simpler and more sequentially logical patterns in both grades 1–8 and 9–12.

One further trend is worthy of study. The 1909 AHA committee, in sketching out a complete grades 1 to 8 history sequence, firmly separated the study of civics, even more than the 1899 Seven. It did so by suggesting that in grades 5 and 6 students take what later came to be known as 'community civics,' that is, a diverse approach to participation in public life, emphasizing the different groups and sodalities visible in the public arena and how these mediate between individual action and civic experience. The prescription is generally sociological in tone: this civics was to be socially complex and socially realistic. In grades 7 and 8, students would address the state and national governments from a structural-legal point of view.* The importance of this aspect of the 1909 report is that 'civics' was identified as a complex subject matter, with at least two aspects (the structural/legal and the processual/functional). The former aspect might (with difficulty) be covered by history; the latter aspect could not be.

It took, then, two or three commissions (and an already receptive milieu), but by 1910 the pattern of courses in the schools had definitely changed. Peet [17] says that high-school-text publishers adopted the 1899 high school pattern rapidly—always the best sign of real change in the schools. General history died out, and ancient history changed in its breadth and focus. Let us not forget, however, that corresponding changes were taking place in this period in the universities, especially in the core or general education curriculum for the first two years. The same persons concerned themselves with both: it would have been odd had fundamentally different goals obtained.

Simultaneously, a differentiation in the high schools between college-track and general curricula quickened. In this era of well-publicized reform and change, it is likely that the schools not falling into line—schools with regional commitments, rural schools (on the elementary level), poor schools, small schools—declined to respond to surveys or attend NEA conferences. The forefront schools were now requiring American History; other schools may not have been, and probably liked it that way.

Furthermore, the familiar difference between what is required or offered and what is taken, even within a school, shows up again and again. A 1914–15 Department of Education survey of over 7,000 high schools [18] showed that many students were taking Ancient and American, at grades 9 and 12; fewer (but still more than half) were taking European and English. This very pattern should alert one to sampling bias. We know that high-school completion around 1915 was only about 12 percent. If, as in this study, about as many students (in absolute numbers) took American History in grade 12 as Ancient History in grade 9, the schools responding must have been schools with exceptionally high completion rates, or schools with college-bound students, or both.

4.3   The 1916 Watershed

The 1893 and 1899 proposals for the design and purposes of secondary education were widely, if not universally, accepted. How is it then that, around 1916, educational policy took such a different and historic turn?

One answer is certainly the limitation posed by the pervasive formalism of the turn-of-the-century designs. The solutions outlined for the curriculum as a whole and for history 'and its allied subjects' were stated as a fixed course of

---

*The 1909 committee also described 'state history' at grade 4; that subjectmatter was to be the first stage of the grades 4–5 biographical approach to American history. In effect, as early as 1909, state history was lodged where it tends to be today.

study to be followed, subjects to be 'taken.' While the doctrine of mental exercise—the idea that the process of mastering a finite and formally organized subjectmatter improved mental capacities for wider learning—was already widely challenged,[19] the underlying notion that learning was an externally set challenge, a body of knowledge to be assimilated, was hardly open to question. The point of the reforms around the turn of the century was to set that challenge in intellectually and socially modern terms. All the history committees, revealingly, fulminated against the mere imposition, the enforced memorization, of facts. Instead, students were to be taught to understand history organically, to see how one set of conditions or events led to another. Given what we know of the shallowness of teacher preparation at the time, and taking note of the eloquence of such hortatory language, one must conclude that the committees were pointing to a serious pedagogical weakness—and one that was unlikely to vanish by virtue of being denounced. (The colleges were at the same period shifting similarly, from the traditional exposition of subjectmatter to a mode of teaching that would reveal more of how evidence is assembled, how judgments are made, how arguments are justified.)

After 1900, as suggested above (p. 71), a process of gradual bifurcation in secondary schooling was discernible. Part of this was regionally based; for example, the General Education Board was begun with Rockefeller funds in 1903 precisely to help the South create public high schools. More important, both 'academic' and 'general' high schools were increasing in number very rapidly. The better schools became coldly academic (though not necessarily college preparatory in aim), while the less-good schools floundered or became sterile imitations. It was not just that some schools, inevitably, would fall behind in quality, but rather that, increasingly, numerous high schools unable or unwilling to be 'academic' would have *no* rational program.

At the elementary level, beginning about 1900, the child study movement associated with the study of child development in psychology and with the influence of G. Stanley Hall[20] had far-reaching effects. The basic philosophy of the normal-school approach—that students were led like sheep through a series of gates and conduits, with the leaders kept in line and the stragglers brought up—began to give way to the idea that each child was an individual. The teacher, while not expected to provide individualized instruction per se, was expected to bring along each mind and personality in flexible ways, respecting individuality and recognizing that students could be deflected from learning, not as a function of their native abilities but as a function of how they were treated in school.

The diversity of students' backgrounds, at all levels of the schools, broadened dramatically after 1900. More male students came to the high school; prior to 1900, most high-school students had been female. Industrial reforms and child labor laws, in concert with compulsory school laws, brought working-class children into the upper elementary grades and the high schools in large numbers. Immigrant children also appeared in the schools in large numbers (figure 4-2), not only lacking some basic skills for schooling but bringing with them new interests and experiences and allegiances. Thus, some found it odd to teach European history with predominantly northern European content to children of southern European origin.

4.3.1   PROGRESSIVISM AND THE INFLUENCE OF DEWEY

These social trends and aspects, and others associated with industrialism, technology, the creation of huge corporations, the growth of cities, the founding of state universities in the Midwest (and elsewhere), agrarian reform, a progressive income tax, and so on, combined to create a new national agenda known as Progressivism. Many have written at length about how the social *reform* aspect of Progressivism underlay the sweeping educational change that occurred after about 1910.[21] Dealing with rapid economic and demographic growth and its consequences, helping the children of the urban slums, and simply preparing them to face a technologically and socially changed world obviously required that the schools impart a 'modern' set of knowledge and attitudes far beyond what 'liberal education' might mean to the president of Harvard.*

More important, the intention of the Progressives to bring the power of the corporations to heel, to form the basis for an industrial democracy, to break the power of the big-city bosses, and to use the federal government and courts to prevent at least some extremes of human disaster, meant an enlargement of the polity and a degree of participation in civil action—in unions and other associations, through churches, and at the ballot box—that was unprecedented. Since the founding of common schools in the early 1800s, an abiding and central purpose of the schools had been to train citizens in civic participation and to ensure an enlightened, periodically reratified, consent of the governed. The Founders had said over and over that without that capacity democracy would be lost, either to autocracy or to mob rule. However, as many have pointed out, the working assumption had been that only a portion of the people would participate: men of property or (for Tocqueville) those who could rise above bourgeois self-interest and devote themselves to reflective civic judgment. By 1910, progressive reformers believed that further progress would be made, and the system itself preserved, only with something approaching universal suffrage and the active involvement in public affairs, at various levels, of millions rather than thousands. Thus the depth and extent of active, enlightened citizenship became a more urgent and self-conscious goal of the schools. Where else could widespread literacy be achieved, democratic values formed, and modern knowledge promoted?

In addition to political and social reform and to the broadening of democratic process, there was a third aspect of progressivism, a philosophical aspect, less

---

*That is, as the chief executive of an Ivy League college. Many Harvard spokesmen over the decades have, of course, served effectively as social critics and reformers in education.

studied but important to educational change. This version of 'progress' implied graduation, change built on small steps, coordinated human action that could be adjusted to balance many interests and needs. This sense of sequence, of process, of forward steps (as the word implies in its Latin base) was a counter-force to the other conception of 'progress' in the nineteenth century, vulgar evolutionism or social Darwinism. Progress, to the Progressives, was not inexorable, but the result of deliberate and authentic human actions. That, of course, is the essence of John Dewey. Goals are approached pragmatically, experimentally, on the basis of experience. In this endeavor, specialized knowledge, including scientific knowledge, is useful, but in a particular purposeful mode: in the words of another American pragmatist, a fact is something that makes a difference.[22]   In education, knowledge is something that persons experience, rather than simply acquire. Gaining knowledge is an active transaction with the surrounding world, a form of problem-solving—including defining what needs to be known and discovering how to encounter it.

In educational and social history, of course, Dewey stands for many things: One who believed that institutions can and must be altered, but a proponent of orderly change. One who believed in the study of child development and the uniqueness of each individual, but who put little faith in therapeutic intervention or the building of autonomous motivation, turning instead to the design of social environments where individuals would thrive severally and cooperatively. One who believed that the acme of intellectual understanding was 'science,' but that a mind possesses scientific understanding through approximation and discovery rather than through an expert's appreciation of its logic. In all realms—political, social, psychological, epistemological, philosophical—Dewey was an enemy of absolutism, formalism, and a priori concepts.

Dewey lived a long life, which spanned enormous alteration in the realms with which he was concerned. He had many followers, and many claimed to follow him. While there has been renewed attention in recent years to Dewey as a philosopher, owing to the reemergence of pragmatism and 'practical philosophy,'[23] a thorough modern study of Dewey as an educationalist would be welcome. Careful commentators point out that Dewey was not responsible for, indeed was critical of, the excesses of the Progressive Education Association (1919–1955), from which he assiduously kept his distance. If some who belonged to the PEA in fact created schools that were vast kindergartens (at all grades), where children expressed themselves and engaged in little learning, the schools that Dewey and his associates created were exempt from these judgments. If Dewey believed that ingesting precooked bits of knowledge led to nothing but the ability to continue doing so, if indeed he regarded critical judgment and self-motivation as the hallmark of true learning, he still regarded disciplined learning, that is, learning based on established, transpersonal methods and standards, as the mode of mature scholarship. If Dewey believed that a new, broader public education would, in fact must, reform society, he did not believe, as did the Social Reconstructionists of the 1930s,[24] that those who managed American schools could create a new social order in one generation. If Dewey believed that authoritarian and teacher-dominated schools stifled inquiry and blocked true learning, he did not say that no school could be 'good' to any degree if as an institution it was not governed democratically—that is, with the full assent and participation of the students. If Dewey hoped, as he did, that schools would train socially effective persons, able not only to earn a living but to create, as it were, a surplus of practical knowledge for the betterment of society, he was nevertheless a foe of those who believed in the extremes of Social Efficiency, with its reliance on tests and routines and input-output functions.*

The judicious commentators say all this. Then, like Cremin and Hofstadter, they go on to say that Dewey is *indirectly* responsible for many excesses. He lived so long that he said contradictory things; he failed to denounce those who misunderstood him; he wrote badly. Such judgments are matters of balance and perspective in intellectual and social history. It is difficult to place Dewey, once and for all, against the backdrop of Progressivism and industrial democracy, and in the context of American pragmatism; difficult to separate his intentions from the inferences of those who followed him.

The same is true, of course, of our valuation, over time, of the ideas of thinkers on education like Arnold or Rousseau, or, for that matter, Plato. Mischief results, however, when contemporary educational partisans admit that they have not read or do not understand Dewey. For example, Kieran Egan,[26] who says "I acknowledge that throughout [a discussion of Dewey's supposed intention to base the entire curriculum on children's experience] I probably do not interpret Dewey's meanings adequately," but goes on to point out that "nearly every professional educator in North America accepts that Dewey has been profoundly misunderstood . . . (yet) seems confident of his or her own interpretation of Dewey." What is understood quite well, thanks to historians such as Cremin,[27] is what Dewey's Laboratory School and other such prototype schools were like. Briefly, they were intensely intellectual, with a curriculum centered in history; they were unrepresentative in terms of the student body, tending to attract academically oriented middle-class children, and they were extremely labor-intensive, in terms of the preparation and supervision of teaching and other activities.

*The similarity of terms should not lead one to assume that the social efficiency movement in schools reflected any special influence from, or had any particular influence on, the social studies. 'Social efficiency' was a part of the agenda of many institutions in society, and closely connected to professionalization, bureaucratization, and 'rationalization.' In the first two decades of the century, in schools, the sciences, for example, also took it as part of their agenda to establish their relevance to social concerns (as in the term of that time, 'social biology') and to be, above all, practical. The whole movement toward General Science in the curriculum reflected these goals, together with the desire to make science accessible again to the lay public, as it had been in the previous century. A New York City high school principal wrote in 1907: "Let it remain for the college to make biologists; our effort should be to make intelligent citizens."[25]

4.4   The NEA 'Social Studies' Report

To those in the field, the 1916 Report of the Committee on Social Studies of the Commission on the Reorganization of Secondary Education of the NEA marks a great transition. It is variously thought of as the occasion on which the term 'social studies' became officially recognized by a national overviewing body; relatedly, as the moment at which something more than history was pronounced necessary for secondary schooling; relatedly, as the first proposal of its kind actually to reduce the time given to history in the curriculum, relative to then-current practice; as the occasion on which civics was defined as a necessarily multidisciplinary subjectmatter; and as first establishing social issues and problems as a focus of study at the high school level. None of these perceptions is incorrect, but they all need careful interpretation.

As in 1893, the Committee on Social Studies was part of a much larger commission, looking at (primarily) secondary education in an even more comprehensive fashion than the NEA enterprise of 1893. The commission itself did not report until 1918 (see section 4.4.1). Much of the supposedly revolutionary import ascribed to the 1916 Report reflects, retrospectively, the accumulating significance, developing from 1918 onward for many years, of the parent commission's broad, revisionist view of the purpose and goals of public education. Conversely, what the committee had to say about civics in 1916 directly reflects and reinforces a somewhat separate prior investigation of 'civics' by a smaller group of experts from the various levels of education, which in 1915 published a bulletin titled "The Teaching of Community Civics."[28] We take up these various reports in chronological order.

The civics study group concluded that current practices did not work. The conclusion was probably foreordained. In 1899 (section 4.2.3), a similar group of experts had in effect said that there was more to civic knowledge than history; but that all that could be captured in a book and studied directly was the structure of government; and that the rest of the richness and variety of the description of contemporary sociopolitical life was to be conveyed in an impromptu manner by the twelfth-grade teacher as time permitted. The 1915 study group and the 1916 committee found both solutions flawed. The Civil Government course that had become standard at grade 12 was found to be a "simplification of political science" and, moreover, unsatisfactory to economists and sociologists.* At lower grade levels, the problem with 'civics' was that the largely historical framework for its teaching omitted economic and 'vocational' aspects.

The 1916 solution to the civics problem *as a part of the curriculum* was to create Community Civics, a triune course at grade 9 that would combine

---

*In contrast to 1893, when 'political economy' was ruled out of the high-school curriculum, the spirit of 1899 had been to found Civil Government on some amalgam of government, economics, and sociology. By 1916, sociology as a separate field of study, rather than as the institutional aspect of economics, was established in the university. The American Sociological Society was formed in 1907.

elements of government, economics (largely, recent economic history explaining the transformations of the economy since about 1880), and the analysis of social structures and processes justifying the term 'community' in the course title. That would legitimate serious study of civics at the opening of high school. In effect, this was the 1899 solution for grade 12, moved forward by four years and 'enriched' by more sociology. In its report, the committee followed two steps of reasoning. First, Civics is the study of the constitution and the structure of government and legal institutions, plus x: solve for x. Second, if the obtained x is not to be of a college-level character (that is, by not being disciplinary in nature), move it downward in the sequence.

With Civics now refigured and located firmly at the beginning of high school, what should happen to the uneasy grade 12 study of Civil Government? Here the reasoning needs to be quoted directly.[29]

> The traditional courses in civil government are almost as inadequate for the last as for the first year of the high school. Efforts to improve them have usually consisted of only slight modifications of the traditional courses or of an attempted simplification of political science. . . . The only feasible way the committee can see by which to satisfy in reasonable measure the demands of several social sciences, while maintaining due regard for the requirements of secondary education, is to organize instruction, not on the basis of the formal social sciences, but on the basis of concrete problems of vital importance to society and of immediate interest to the pupil. . . . In other words, the suggestion is not to discard one social science in favor of another, nor attempt to crowd the several social sciences into this year in abridged forms; but to study actual problems, or issues, or conditions, as they occur in life.*

The committee's new course at grade 12 was designated Problems of American Democracy. The language of the report makes it clear that 'problems' were a fact of life, and that students, having studied history and civics and the rest, should be able to face societal problems realistically. The report is neutral as to whether such problems are transitory or recurring or inherent in American democracy. Given a later attempt to charge 1916 and the social studies generally with premature Social Reconstructionism (see section 4.5.1), it is noteworthy that the committee refers matter-of-factly to problems, issues, matters of social importance, and matters of student interest. It is hard to see any provocative doctrine of social criticism here.

It was significant that for the first time a synthetic, that is to say, nondiscipli-

---

*The appearance here, as elsewhere in the 1916 report, of such terms as "political science" (rather than "government"), "the formal social sciences," and the like, reflects two factors. First, growing usage in the university: The University of Chicago had a famous Social Science building, in effect a superdepartment, by the late 1920s; the Social Science Research Council was founded in 1923. Second, faith in the scientific method, which was a part of progressivism in its educational aspect.

nary course title appeared in a curriculum forum of this national scope. The report makes it clear that the committee was not attempting a social science methods course, or a systematic multidisciplinary explanation of selected phenomena. Instead, they felt that students about to enter the larger world ought to be able to analyze its complexity using knowledge gained in school. The fact that—some decades later, as the Problems of Democracy course waned—its 'slot' in grade 12 became the locus for social science electives does not mean that the 1916 committee intended the course as a stalking horse or holding action toward that end.*

The emphasis on civics and social problems inevitably implied the inadequacy of history as the single, sufficient subject for knowledge of the social world and its institutions and forms.† However, the proposals for alteration within history were not extreme (not more so, for example, than the recommendations of the 1899 Seven relative to those of the 1893 Ten). Here was the total curriculum scheme, including grades 7 and 8 as precursors.

Grade 7	Geography; European History
Grade 8	American History, Including Civics
Grade 9	Civics
Grade 10	European History to about 1700, Including the Discovery and Settling of America
Grade 11	American History since about 1700, with Inclusion of More Recent European History
Grade 12	Problems of American Democracy

Geography at grade 7 was to be *either* taught with European history, in which case its content is obvious, *or* it was to be a separate year-long strand. In the latter case, it was to address the geography of non-European countries as well as European, and it was to be 'thoroughly socialized.' This meant simply that it was to be human geography, not physical or strictly economic geography.

In its European History sequence, the committee explicitly attempted to retain a good deal of classical, which is to say largely ancient European, history: at grade 10, this was to occupy the first half year or so. It also attempted to retain an emphasis on English history as the central figure in the tapestry of recent European history. Finally, it anticipated a flexibility between European and American history—where, for example, to do justice to both ancient and

---

*Hertzberg, *Social Studies Reform*, 28, states that the Problems course was an "answer to rival claims of the social sciences, none of which, in the committee's view, was adapted to the requirements of secondary education." This may be anachronistic, in that the sciences, as disciplines, made no such claims (rival or otherwise) on time in the curriculum until several decades later. The important point, in the present writer's view, is that at least some of the high-school social studies were not to be disciplinarily based.

†The Committee's definition of 'social studies' was subject matters relating "directly to the organization and development of human society, and to man as a member of social groups."

medieval periods within the European framework, American history on a national basis might not begin until midway through the eleventh year. The committee defended itself against the possible charge of shortchanging formal American history; it said that grades 7–8–9 should be seen as one cycle, Europe to America to the United States in the modern world, and grades 10–11–12 as a deeper repetition of that cycle.* The committee report is internally consistent in this regard. For example, it describes how civics in grade 8 could emphasize the relationship among local, state, and national structures and processes, that is, all within a U.S. History framework, while Civics at grade 9 should explicitly consider America in relation to its allies and America in the world. Similarly, grade 11 American history was to study the constitutional period and subsequent constitutional/legal adjustments in depth, while Problems of Democracy should typically attempt to include international linkages and relations.†

Most analysts agree that the 1916 design *as implemented in the schools* (section 4.5) jettisoned much of the overlapping and the complexities of the report, so that the actual curriculum pattern was as follows:

Grade 7	Geography; European History
Grade 8	American History
Grade 9	(Community) Civics
Grade 10	European History
Grade 11	American History
Grade 12	Problems of Democracy

This is the scheme we intend henceforth, when we refer to *the 1916 pattern*.

Thus, relative to the 1899 high-school pattern, the 1916 report recommended a cutting back of history from about three and a half years to two years, including a reduction (in practice) of ancient and medieval history in favor of European History, the latter to be broader than English (or for that matter, English plus French). American History, however, was not diminished. It is important to realize that the readjustments of emphasis in history (over and above the need to find time for Civics and the Problems course) were the product of historians' thinking, and were widely accepted by historians. While the chair of the 1916 committee was a sociologist, Thomas Jesse Jones, from Hampton Institute,‡ the

---

*The committee observed that repeating cycles of instruction were justified because large numbers of students complete their schooling with grade 6 and then grade 8 and 9. This reasoning seemed self-evident then and until well after World War II (at least as regards leaving at grade 8 or 9). It was carried over into the design of the middle school when that was devised, about the 1950s, in part to keep students in school by providing a richer curriculum in the transition between 'the grades' and 'high school.'

†This is probably the first appearance of an extended citizenship model in the curriculum, whereby the civic duty and interests of the educated citizen, having historically been extended from the city, state, or comparable level to the national level, now should be extended to the international arena.

‡Where he taught 'social studies.'

leading intellectual influence on the Committee was James Harvey Robinson, one of the progenitors of the (then) New History. Robinson had been a member of the NEA Committee in 1893.

Robinson, like his colleagues Frederick Jackson Turner and Charles Beard, advocated a history that would draw directly on recorded evidence and a broad range of documentation, and which would illuminate above all the ongoing processes and dynamics of historical change. History was not to be the record of events and precedents, arranged seriatim from the beginning of recorded time forward, but a dense interpretation of change, including change in the broad conditions of life, the habits of thought in societies, and long-lasting cultural forms and arrangements. In retrospect, the New History contained the seeds of social history, intellectual history and *mentalités*, and to some degree the rapprochement of narrative history with social science methods. It rejected what now (and then) seemed the spurious scientism of some nineteenth-century European history, but endorsed a benign positivism of the twentieth. It was thus not surprising—least of all to historians—that ancient and medieval history, where 'the evidence' was not dense, should be pared back in favor of more recent periods, or that European history should be studied in terms of a Continental synthesis or culture (as opposed to English, French, Dutch, and others).

Most of all, what Robinson and his colleagues wanted to elicit or train was 'historical-mindedness.' This phrase, used in the report, entailed the view that history was not to be taught as if "it had meaning or value in itself," but instead to "show its relation or contribution to the present." It can be argued, then, that the 1916 realignment of history in the schools, including the ceding of curriculum time, involved the clearing away of some deadwood. Needless to say, Dewey, who was friendly with Robinson, agreed. Dewey thought of history and geography, closely interwoven, as one of the crucial strands in any education (the other strand being a knowledge-based, but reality-tested, participation in the ongoing business of society). He simply observed, as a first principle, that "The true starting point of history is always some present situation with its problems."[30]

4.4.1   THE CARDINAL PRINCIPLES OF 1918

Although Dewey was not a member of the larger parent commission that reported in 1918, and was not, as far as is known, a direct influence upon it, that commission's central emphasis, the center of gravity for all its deliberations, was precisely the "present situation with its problems." (As has been suggested, Progressivism took 'problems' as opportunities.) The 1916 social studies committee's recommendations for curriculum change were substantial though hardly revolutionary: inevitably, school curricula did not automatically fall into line. The commission's report of 1918 *was* revolutionary in its restatement of the *purpose* of public education, and thus its intended character. Individual schools might or might not adopt curricular change, but they could hardly fail to be affected by the newly stated philosophy of the National Education Association as to what schools were for.

In its comprehensive report,[31] issued in 1918 and distributed in at least 130,000 copies, the commission promulgated a set of Cardinal Principles of Secondary Education. The seven goals of public schooling were health, command of fundamental processes, worthy home membership, vocation, citizenship, worthy use of leisure, and ethical character.

Of these, "command of fundamental processes" was the academic purpose (though the processes were largely the basic skills, the three R's). "Ethical character" and "worthy use of leisure" were inherent in the goals of Western classical and liberal education. "Citizenship" had been a purpose of American education since the invention of the common school, and had been clearly enunciated as an overriding goal in the 1893 statement. As for the others, the 1918 Cardinal Principles were intended, and perceived, as a message that Charles Eliot and his colleagues in 1893 had been, not wrong, but narrowly academic. Ultimately, all of the purposes of schooling were aimed at some area of personal welfare and preparation for life. Contemporaneous with the 1918 statement, the kindergarten came into prominence about the time of World War I in part to deal with the health of the young, especially the urban young. "Worthy home membership" referred to the charging of schools to deal with immigration (at a historic high about 1910), as well as to the general movement known as social meliorism.

"Vocation" seemed new, although rural grammar schools had not been insensitive to vocational needs in teaching computation and literacy for retail trade, or general science and geography for agriculture and commerce. With children now channeled into the schools rather than into child labor, with the growth of unions and the beginning of unemployment or occupational injury insurance, with the scientific management of industry, it seemed obvious to the commission that spending eight or ten or twelve years in schools was a luxury, and an iniquitous one, if students were not then prepared to make a living. The motivation behind the inclusion of vocationalism was not simply practical. With the disappearance of the 'mental discipline' assumptions about learning in schools and with the rapid growth of intelligence testing (stimulated by wartime needs), what was really being assumed was the idea that native intelligence was distributed so that the majority of students would not benefit from or wish to engage in an 'academic' course. This was philosophically very different from Dewey's idea that there was nothing more practical than the mastery of organized intellectual subjectmatters (in fact, that without that there was no true 'mastery').

It was also, in the name of modern social meliorism, more sociologically deterministic than the kind of democratic elitism of Eliot and 1893, where it was assumed that those who could attend high school deserved a good academic education. The statement of 1918, born of the spirit of progressive reform, was a mixture of social meliorism, social determinism, social efficiency, social enrichment (in terms of lifelong adjustment), social reform—that is, all the early twentieth-century mixings of the shades of meaning of 'social,' confusing and inchoate as they were. In the name of democratic education, 1918 set 'tracking' in motion.[32] The idea may be paradoxical, but it is not sinister or even illogical. All those who believe in a widely inclusive public educational system must balance the attempt to give everyone a flavor of the 'best,' defined by some official standard or canon, and the attempt to give everyone a 'good,' defined more pluralistically.

In the words of James and Tyack,[33] "In all of this planning, educators showed little appreciation of ethnic differences, for they were convinced of the appropriateness of their middle-class 'American' values and unconscious of the bias in their supposedly universal science of education. Their confidence in the 'science,' their optimism about the power of education to correct social ills, and their search for professional autonomy led them to intervene, with an arrogance that was typically unwitting, in the lives of people different from themselves." It is well to remember, however, that *at the time* the 1918 report was criticized mostly for not going far enough, for being too residually humanistic and academic. An excellent discussion of the tenor of the general response is given by Kliebard,[34] who further points out the significance of professionalization in education. With (in principle) a scientifically, test-validated, differentiated curriculum, which would sift and sort students into their best trajectories and lead to a multiple set of humanly cost-effective outcomes, the authority of both parents (and laypersons) and university educators directly to affect the design and character of the schools began to recede.* In the case of academics, this trend would continue until about 1960; in the case of the citizenry, it would wax and wane.

As we have suggested, the degree of change inherent in the 1916 social studies curriculum report was far less than the corresponding shift, which really did approach a sea-change, in the rhetoric and philosophy of the larger, 1918 report on the goals of schooling. This was inevitable, since practice in the schools always represents a negotiation among interests, and between what is currently feasible and what might be attempted. There is, however, a more important discontinuity between the two reports. The 1918 Cardinal Principles shift has been seen, with some justice, as an example of social engineering and social reform carried to extremes; its component, the social studies report, might be expected to show the same pattern: anti-intellectualism, vocationalism, and the like. The language of the 1916 report does not do so, however.

---

*We have in mind here some presumptive plurality of discipline-based academics in the universities. Clearly, many or most education and psychology professors fully endorsed the principles of 1918 on reasoned professional grounds. Many of those in higher education held broad social views deeply in consonance with this complex expression of social rationalism and reform. Many others always have assumed that only some few students can truly benefit from 'academic' work.

The discussion of the recommended curriculum is in no way anti-intellectual or nonhumane in tone. The justification for the study of history, for example, is eloquent, referring fundamentally to the "community" (a favorite word) of humankind that history reveals. Even while the time recommended for ancient and medieval history is reduced, the report says that all students have an instinct for beauty and order to which the history of Greece will always speak, and a sensitivity to religion which guarantees that medieval history will always be relevant.

The 1916 committee deals with vocationalism in a straightforward manner, appealing to a duality of levels:

> The committee on social studies believes that education as a whole should take account of vocational needs. . . . As for the (course of study) now under consideration, the committee is here interested in its vocational guidance aspect *only* as an incident to the broader social and civic training of the youth. If it can be made to contribute anything to his guidance toward a wise choice of vocation and intelligent preparation for it, it is that much gain.[35]

In brief, social studies is not vocational education. (The committee does comment that a good citizen is self-supporting, and that one cannot be either without an informed and intelligent grasp of the contemporary social world and how it developed.)

The conception of practical citizenship, of informed participation, as *inherently* part of social learning is of crucial importance. In fact, the committee discusses this first:

> The social studies differ from other studies by reason of their social content rather than their social aim [since all education has a social aim]... from the nature of their content, the social studies afford peculiar opportunities for the training of the individual as a member of society. They should accomplish this end through the development of an appreciation of the nature and laws of social life, a sense of the responsibility of the individual as a member of social groups, and the intelligence and the will to participate effectively in the promotion of social well-being.

Here, for the first time, the substantive core of a social studies curriculum *aimed at citizenship* is clearly enunciated. Unlike the 1893 committee, which asserted that a decent academic education in high school will conduce to good citizenship, what is being said here is that fulfilling one's social responsibilities at various levels requires knowledge of history (especially historical-mindedness), a broad and rich grasp of civic processes, and (more implicitly) a moderately sophisticated social awareness or social realism. The report several times alludes to the recent development of sociology as an intellectual resource. And it describes the content of civics—community civics—over the space of many pages. For a fuller discussion see section 6.1.4; here we summarize by saying that the report describes in detail a broad, fused knowledge of local, regional, national, and international structures and processes—from how the courts work, to the presence of interest groups, to how goods get to market, to how legislation is made, to the functioning of international markets. Over and over again, it is stated that the 'community' does not refer simply to the local surround, but that persons are members of interpenetrating circles of involvement and responsibility, and thus are members of a complex community, defined as the extent of *actual social action*.* No one who reads the 1916 report could miss the main point: that the social studies should enable one to know and to act in the real world.

4.5   Implementing 1916

In its report, the 1916 social studies committee refers frequently and in detail to specific good practices in the curriculum, for example, those of Philadelphia or Indianapolis. Thus, as with most such committees, what was being recommended was in part already at hand. With regard to history, the committee refers to a widespread dissatisfaction with the 'fourfold history' approach (that is, the 1899 pattern) and remarks that there is wide agreement that civics involves more than government.†

The rapidity and extent of the spread of effect of the 1916 report is difficult to gauge. For one thing, the school system was in the midst of an enormous expansion. From 1890 to 1920 alone, the number of high schools rose from 2,500 to over 14,000, and this rate of expansion lasted until the late 1920s.[36] For another thing, the entrance of the United States into the European war meant that curriculum reform was hardly front-page news.

Hertzberg[37] points out that the professional teaching journals in history briefly reported the 1916 recommendations without any sense of confrontation of a landmark having been reached; and that they then concentrated on recent European history, political and military, in connection with the war. Peet[38] points out that not until 1921 did there appear any critical examination of the 1916 pattern in *The History Teacher's Magazine*. War issues courses proliferated both in the high schools (what more urgent 'problem of democracy' could there have been?) and in the colleges. In the latter, for example, the famous Contemporary Civilization course at Columbia was created about 1919, as a historically

---

*This is, conceptually, a basis for Paul Hanna's development in the 1940s and 1950s of an 'expanding horizons' scheme for the early grades (see p. 107). The report does not say that the world and all its people are *inherently* one community. For a discussion of this conception today, see section 12.3.

†The 1899 nothing-but-(dead)history pattern may have been especially difficult for big city schools to adopt. In 1911, a member of an American Historical Association curriculum committee wrote: "it seemed absurd that a pupil should have to know who Cleon was in order to be graduated from high school, but . . . he might be densely ignorant of [Chancellor] Bismarck." Quoted in Peet, *Selective History*, 130.

organized collaboration among the departments of history, philosophy, government, and economics.* That course may be seen as an intermediate stage in the evolution of European History to Western Civilization.

In the schools, it seems clear that Problems of Democracy courses at grade 12 became common, sometimes by state-level edict, while Civil Government courses became somewhat passé. With the waning of the 1899 pattern of American History and Civil Government, a full-year pattern of American History at grade 11 became easier to accomplish, and contemporary textbooks show the change. It is probable, paradoxically, that with history now contained in two (rather than three-plus) years in high school, European History (and its subsequent modification, Western Civilization) became more coherent—since after 1899 many high schools had waffled on European and English history.

Curriculum changes addressed primarily to the junior and (now) senior high school affected the lower grades. According to Tryon,[39] large-scale surveys of grades 6 through 8, conducted about 1911 and 1931, showed that in this twenty-year period Roman and Greek history virtually disappeared; that state and local history continued to gain at grade 4; and, most interestingly, that 'early' and 'later' American history qua history had obliterated "biographical stories of leading Americans." By 1930, in other words, sequential American History was established at grades 5, 8, and 11—the pattern persisting to this day. Geography was firmly lodged at grade 7.

Against the simplicity of this pattern, Tryon[40] points out that by 1930 the junior high school had become the main locus of 'fused' or integrated social studies.† What this means concretely is hard to determine. History-cum-geography and history-cum-civics were nothing new. On the other hand, junior high school covered grade 9, where the 1916 committee had strongly recommended a year-long, dense, rather sociological Civics. Now, although Civics was still dominant there, many traditional schools were teaching ancient or world history (which is to say, not Western Civilization but a broader course beginning with the ancient world). 'Fused' courses often used nontextbook materials. We probably see in these data the tendency toward 'fused' courses that has always been, at least in principle, attractive to junior high and middle schools; a certain confusion about exactly what ninth-grade civics should be; and the coexistence of several approaches to history.

An American Historical Association national survey of 1924[41] showed that Civics was by now about even with Ancient History (the 1899 pattern) at grade 9, but that Problems of Democracy was only beginning to appear at grade 12. There are very few good data for the 1930s. In the mid-1940s, one fairly large study[42] showed Geography and American History vying for dominance at grade

*Hertzberg, *Reform*, 30, says, "The chief influences were James Harvey Robinson and John Dewey."
†To be sure, social studies were 'fused' in the elementary grades, but in a different pedagogical sense. In junior high schools, which were primarily located in cities, beginning about 1910, the course syllabi showed a deliberate attempt to correlate systematic expositions of history, geography, and civics.

7, American History firm at grade 8, Civics at grade 9, World History at 10, U.S. History at 11, and Problems of Democracy at 12. Other surveys found economics frequently taught at grade 12.

With reference to the stipulated 1916 course pattern, and bearing in mind the expansion of the system and the resulting variability across schools, we may conclude the following, as of about 1945. *Upper elementary*: state history at grade 4 and U.S. History at grade 5 were more or less fixed. *Middle/junior high*: a variety of history, geography, and civics, often 'fused' in approach, but with World Geography tending to be at grade 7 and American History common at grade 8. The 1916 recommendation for European History at grade 7 had clearly failed, perhaps because its relationship to Geography at that level was never clear. *High school*: more or less the 1916 pattern. Grade 10 European History was not exactly what 1916 had ordered, but close: a World History with a western civilization flavor. Civics was under some pressure at grade 9, and Problems of Democracy even more unstable at grade 12. In this last regard, the absence of good data from the 1930s is unfortunate, since, given the Depression, the level of governmental and social experimentation of the New Deal, and the desire within some in the education establishment for a Social Reconstruction imperative for the schools, it is almost certain that the Problems of Democracy course reached its zenith then.*

Edgar Wesley, in his introductory overview volume of 1944 for the Committee on American History in Schools and Colleges,[143] identifies the mid-1940s modal social studies pattern as approximately that summarized in the preceding paragraph. In that volume, Wesley presents a chart showing the Social Studies curriculum in Urbana, Illinois, from before the 1893 reform to a good twenty-five years after the 1916 'change.' The striking thing—in a 'good' academic high school—is the lack of abrupt change and the continuity of specific courses and grade levels over time. (See table 4-2.)

We suspend this across-decades review at about 1945, to make several general observations. First, on the level of the curriculum and the philosophy of the schools, important changes were about to occur, as they were in American society as a whole. Second, the mid-1940s social studies curriculum as described above does look quite like the 1916 pattern—and quite like the modal pattern of 1980 (section 2.2)—in terms of the course pattern. This is what permits observers to say that 1916 ushered in a dominant pattern that has lasted for seventy-five years. But it is equally appropriate to point out that change inaugurated by the 1916 report was *less* abrupt than that following 1893, reflecting both a transition already under way before 1916 and a persisting

---

*There is no evidence that the POD course ever had much of an international orientation, as intended by the 1916 Committee. This may also be ascribed to the domestic tenor of the 1930s.

[†]Of the American Historical Association, the Mississippi Valley Historical Association (the forerunner to the present Organization of American Historians), and the National Council for the Social Studies. See section 4.7.

Table 4-2 Social Studies Offerings in the Urbana, Illinois, Public Schools

Grade Level	1885	1899	1920	1943
MIDDLE GRADES	U.S. History Geography	5: U.S.History : Geography 6: European Background /U.S. History : Geography	5: U.S. History : Geography 6: European Background/ U.S. History Geography	5: U.S. History : Geography 6: European Background/ U.S. History : Geography
UPPER GRADES	U.S. History Geography	U.S. History Geography	7: U.S. History Geography 8: U.S. History : Illinois History : Geography : Civics	7: U.S. History Geography 8: U.S. History : Geography : Civics
HIGH SCHOOL	U.S. History* English History* Civil Government*	Civics* General History* Greek History Roman History Egyptian and Scripture History English History	U.S. History* Civics* Ancient History Modern History	U.S. History* Civics* Ancient History Modern History World History Economics Industrial Geography

*Required for graduation
Simplified from Wesley, *American History*, 1944, 28.

gradualness thereafter. Equally important to note, between about 1950 and 1970 a major period of perturbation occurred (section 5.3). The modal pattern of about 1980 may show a *resumption* of the older norm, but it is misleading to hold that 1916 had an uninterrupted run.

Course patterns in social studies seem to turn toward a central tendency, and never fully reflect ideological and pedagogical differences that authorities see as crucial matters in the description and the evaluation of this branch of the curriculum. To explain this inertia, we must look at such patterns in a wider and more dynamic context.

4.5.1   THE SPIRIT OF 1918 IN CURRICULUM HISTORY

If educational policy in 1918, as enunciated in the Cardinal Principles, had been less oriented toward multiple, probably inconsistent, goals, and had the personnel of the schools themselves been able to agree on a ranking of priorities to address within the principles,* educational history would have been distinctly different. The same would be true of the social studies branch of the curriculum—and perhaps even more so, since, as we have seen, the 1916 committee recommendations were nowhere near so philosophically radical as the 1918 report, and did not in fact call for sweeping curriculum revision.

For a time, the tide seemed to flow in one direction. From the end of World War I until 1929, there were powerful factors and trends working toward consensus and compromise. It was a period of extremely rapid economic growth and increasing urbanization. School finance, in terms of per capita expenditure, was stable. The birth rate continued in its longterm decline, which meant that relatively more resources for relatively fewer students could be anticipated. Immigration slowed sharply after about 1923. The need for teenage labor in society diminished, and expectations as to median level of education increased. Political life was stable, at least in terms of perceived national experience; the more urgent of the Progressive Era reforms had been accommodated, at least to some extent. International pressures were minimal, and economic opportunities abroad favorable. The universities were themselves in a period of rapid growth. The marked improvement of the schools between about 1890 and 1920, combined with an increasingly large cohort of students, allowed colleges and universities not to worry about 'supply,' in terms of either quantity or quality (in principle), but to concentrate on devising their own general education curriculum for grades 13–16 and on, rapidly enlarging their discipline-based research capabilities. In 1893, and again in 1916, a bargain had been struck: high schools should (and could) be 'good' but not exclusively 'academic.' Citizenship was almost universally accepted as a central aim of schooling.

---

*Which is to say, had the public schools been under centralized political and professional control, which of course they were not.

In sum, it was an era that assumed social progress, with the broadening of education as one of the engines of that progress. A rising per capita GNP and favorable circumstances within and external to the society suggested that conflict between the Hamiltonian and Jeffersonian goals, between elite and popular participation, between societal productivity and democratic inclusion, could be steadily allayed. James and Tyack catch the spirit of the era neatly, when they write: "[Schools] reflected a popular desire to reform society without changing its basic structure or restricting the freedom of action of adults.... Few educators were alert to the serious inequities, both in the social order and in the secondary schools, that made basic reform through education an implausible dream."[44]

A certain unreality, as far as education is concerned, is evident in retrospect. The high schools were now expected to encompass high-quality preparation for the university, solid 'academic' learning for those leaving school about 17, and serious, involving, and practical vocational education for non-academic-minded students. Already the high school was perceived to be fully developed, with a full set of courses in the two tracks—academic and vocational. Junior high schools were instituted to ease the transition from the more individually oriented grammar schools, provide room for life adjustment training (the health and home membership aspects of 1918), and permit subjectmatters to be taught in a flexible and 'fused' fashion.

All accounts agree that the new flavor of progressive education was felt throughout the elementary schools. That spirit, together with the fact that the populace as a whole was becoming gradually more 'learned' in terms of subjectmatter knowledge, meant that the lockstep recitation mode of the classroom in the early grades had to give way. Child development ideas worked in this direction; equally important, probably, the growth of the testing movement reassured parents that a child's intellectual (or vocational) aptitude would be scientifically uncovered at the appropriate age or grade, so that rote learning and mental discipline could be de-emphasized.

At the higher school levels, there was a differentiation of the curriculum within and across high schools, made possible by the growing number and size of high schools in the society and, evidently, by a degree of tacit understanding that variety in actual goals and practices could be maintained within an inclusive official rhetoric. In the context of the social studies, for example, we have seen that while new courses called Civics and Problems of Democracy could be *added* into the high schools, the thorough *revision* of the rest of the curriculum called for by the 1916 committee—that is, the rethinking of the purposes and intellectual emphases of history—was far less easy to accomplish.

In many schools, the older history persisted. The College Entrance Examination Board was founded in 1903. One of its most important subject areas was History, specifically the fourfold history pattern of 1899, which was by then the pattern expected by the colleges. Despite all the alterations of course titles and emphases that may have followed 1916, in History the CEEB in 1943 still examined college applicants essentially on the 1899 fourfold curriculum. There must, then, have been a kind of coevolution throughout the entire period: in one strand, the New History, new courses, new texts; in the other strand, the retention in practice of the traditional pattern. (No doubt the actual test items changed somewhat, with a gradual 'modernizing' of the questions.) The point is that the CEEB could not have been testing according to the older pattern, to any substantial degree, had not that pattern perdured, and had not many college-bound students been directed into it.

The Lynds' famous study of 'Middletown' (Muncie, IN) in the mid-1920s[45] found that the high schools had *two* 'academic'-content tracks, the college preparatory and the general, and *in addition* a number of vocational programs. The latter were the "darling of Middletown's eyes," partly because they provided students with exposure to the extracurricular realm: afterschool clubs, sports teams, business-sponsored activities, and the like. Middletown, in other words, fully understood and supported the idea of the schools as a microcosm of the town, as an institution rehearsing the whole range of adult civic functions—occupational, recreational, and commercial as well as professional and intellectual. The mediating spirit between school and community was boosterism; beyond this, and permitting some broadening of horizons, was an intense American patriotism. The Lynds found many avenues by which a conservative community re-created itself through the schools—many ways in which the students, with diverse abilities and interests, were led to their predestined, socially reduplicating roles.*

The Progressive Education Association was founded in 1919. As has been mentioned, John Dewey, in whose name 'progressive education' proliferated, was never an officer of the PEA and kept his distance from it. While the number of schools modeled on Dewey's Laboratory School prototype waxed and waned as a function of local circumstances over the next thirty or more years,† the PEA had very considerable effects on teacher education (in that the NEA became largely 'progressive' in its own professional orientation) and on the invention, for public schools generally, of such exemplary forms in the classroom as cooperative teaching, group learning, the 'project method,' and the like.

Finally, at the university level, the social sciences were strengthening themselves in disciplinary terms throughout the 1920s, with the founding of departments and building of a research base, and the term 'social sciences' was coming into broad use. The disciplines were still very small. Reliable statistics for the number of social science 'majors' or undergraduate degrees are lacking. But about 1920, no American social science discipline turned out more than one

---

*If this was true in Muncie (and some sociologists have felt that the Lynds were too schematic in their analysis of this sorting and sifting process), it was certainly even truer in communities with wider ethnic divisions or with a higher proportion of young adults who moved away.

†The extreme examples of 'progressive' schools always tended to be private elementary or middle schools, often operated in close association with an academic institution.

hundred Ph.D.s; by 1930, only history, economics, and psychology (in that order) did so (and few historians counted themselves as 'social scientists'). Only history produced any sizable number of undergraduates who might staff the schools (as it had since the 1890s).   Such statistics are beside the point, anyhow, and anachronistic, since it was not until the late 1930s that most public school teachers in city schools had a bachelor's degree of any kind.[46]

The period of consensus and perhaps complacency, of confident expectations about the progress of ever-more-inclusive schooling, of quantity and quality combined, lasted until the Great Depression. We have suggested that the contradictions among the schools' purposes, visible in retrospect within the Principles of 1918, might logically have ended that consensus eventually; but 1929 and what followed after brought the era to an abrupt end.

In the 1920s, politics were absent from the schools—in theory. Growth, inclusion, and 'progress' meant that public schooling was a way to mitigate politics. In the 1930s, schools became as problematical as the rest of American society, with the crash and the long, obdurate depression; negative growth in the economy; the collapse of financing for cities and transportation systems; ecodis-asters in agricultural regions; internal migration; and all the stresses that this era brings to mind. Schools had become major items in the budgets of municipali-ties, which now found themselves unable to finance their schools from local revenues. Special programs in the schools—afterhours activities, the arts, field trips, enriched vocational units—were cut; the more expensive academic courses, commanding lower enrollments and expensive instructional materials (either for the very able or the underachieving), were also reduced. Schoolteachers took substantial cuts in pay, and in some districts more highly educated but inexperienced teachers were hired instead of, or displacing, those already in the pipeline. While elementary enrollments declined, as a function of processes under way since about 1920s together with a more recent lowered fertility, the size of high schools tended to increase, as schools were combined for efficiency and as unemployable teenagers remained in school.[47]

Internally, there is no evidence that educational quality suffered; it is possible, in fact, that the effects of crisis were tonic, at least in the earlier years. Teachers and administrators in the 1930s became far more active politically in terms of the institutional needs of the schools and of teaching; they joined the NEA and other national organizations in large numbers, lobbied state legislatures for increased state funding for the schools, and urged improvement of teacher certification, tenure, and preparation procedures (as a self-protective measure).[*]

In external forums, however, educators were politically more cautious, and tried to keep a low profile. The tough questions about the role and achievement

[*]Experts agree that the 1930s saw the rapid professionalization of educators in the schools, in part responding to and in part trying to limit the ramifications of crisis in the system. In addition, the larger 'output' of the universities, combined with the stringencies of the job market in the schools, meant that by the end of the decade most teachers had college degrees.[48]

of schools in American society came from outside. The Lynds, restudying "Middletown," found teachers in the classroom even more careful than before not to offend the sociopolitical mores of the community; many other observers found the same pattern. Neutrality as regards partisan political action went hand in hand with the professionalization movement. Tyler[49] and others report that in the early 1930s school people spent considerable time in citizens' forums devoted to questions like, Can the schools survive? The educators' answer, of course, was two-fold: Schools have to survive, if society is to hold together—and educators can be trusted to make the right decisions.

The political caution of school educators was not universal. It is true that most educators, in the early 1930s, promoted changes from within to meet external demands. In this sense they continued the progressive tradition. The PEA, particularly, was active in analyzing ways to make schools work better—for example, by aligning the high-school curriculum and practices with social welfare inventions such as the Civilian Conservation Corps or the Works Progress Administration, via work-study and other school-and-society relationships. Some educators, however, speaking as social philosophers rather than as those involved in the management of the system, challenged the system not to cooperate, but to provide a basis for more sweeping change. In 1932, George Counts, an influential professor at Teachers College, published his widely noted book, *Dare the School Build a New Social Order?*

Counts, and other social reconstructionists, pointed to the economic weaknesses of American capitalism, the apparent severe social costs of laissez-faire, the growing popularity of Father Coughlin and right-wing extremists, the eight million unemployed, the soup kitchens. They pointed out that the Principles of 1918 called for the optimal education for full social participation of each individual, and proposed, therefore, that the schools launch a process of social criticism and examination of how such a meshing of individual and society could occur. It was, intellectually speaking, a collectivist proposal: schools as a system should suspend their normal procedures of transmission of existing values, should assume a critical stance in order to find a new direction, and should, if necessary, indoctrinate students toward these revisionist ends.

Briefly put, the schools declined the dare, though school leaders were deeply shaken by it.* In the years just following Counts' book, the radical change wing of the New Deal lost ground,† blocked not only by political counterforces but by the courts. By the mid-1930s, the most dramatic decline in school financing (with school closings, and so forth) was over. But the question of how the schools could *serve* a changing social order remained, and was addressed by many educators

---

*Kliebard, *Struggle*, 193, quotes a nice description of the "stunned silence" at the PEA meeting where Counts flung out his challenge.

†That is, the Tugwell-Berle-Ickes faction. A widely used text by Tugwell, *Our Economic Society and Its Problems*, lost one-third of its annual sales in the high schools after being denounced as seditious by the superintendent of the Gary, IN, schools.[50]

in various ways for the rest of the decade. How, after all, could the schools express the 'social efficiency' goals of the 1920s, the intent to fit each person to his or her best position in society, given the reality of the Depression? How could the vocational aspect of the high schools be realized when a sizable proportion of students were in school because they could not find work and did not expect to be able to do so? How could the college preparatory course continue to be built on the high-cultural consensus of English literature and history in an era of social unrest and radical institutional reform (and with a new orientation of the social sciences in universities toward structural analysis of society)? How, in good conscience, could progressive education's commitment to education for life adjustment (among other goals) be sustained in a time when many questioned the soundness of American society? Perhaps most of all, how could the overriding goal of citizenship training be formulated so as to be accepted by all, when some saw citizenship as based on critical thinking, and others on passive loyalty?

The obvious answer was a redoubling of effort with respect to, and a rebalancing of, the multiple goals of the Principles of 1918. Unlike the 1920s, the contradictions and tensions within these principles were clearly recognized—but now they had to be faced. The schools could not be reoriented toward largely academic ends. Already, 'academic' high schools were roundly criticized as elitist and luxury items. Furthermore, the colleges and universities were still small. About 13 percent of high-school graduates went on to college, and those who completed high school were already a relatively privileged group. On the other hand, the schools could hardly be reoriented to strictly vocational ends—not while economic growth and employment were stalled and while business funds were not available for cooperative programs with and around the schools.

A number of state commissions and studies concluded, in effect, that high schools were full of students who did not want to be there and were being ill served—and urged that high schools attract and 'hold' more of them, and do better with them. The so-called Regents Inquiry in New York State, for example, called once again (as such groups had done since before the turn of the century) for a successful *Education for American Life*.[51] The title itself expressed the perduring desire for good schools for all. This commission, however, groped toward a tighter differentiation of programs, some sense of fewer but clearer (that is, more candidly acknowledged) 'tracks.' It called, "in addition to the college preparatory program, which has been so much overemphasized, for more specific courses and work to fit boys and girls for useful citizenship, for self-support, and for a growing individual life." Secondary—that is, subject-centered—instruction should begin in the seventh grade; junior high school was to be serious business. The curriculum should include more mathematics and science, human relations and community life, and the arts; most of all, broad fields of knowledge were to be presented "in the ways in which they are generally encountered in life and work, and not as semester hours for college entrance."

In the work of the regents, as in that of other influential commissions and organizations,[52] one clearly sees that the multiple goals of the schools were reaffirmed, but in a spirit of facing rather than papering over the contradictions and tensions involved. Scientific management of the training of individuals to fit the needs of society; life adjustment and self-realization; schools as, not the basis for a new order, but for the further development of American democracy— all these ends were consciously sought among school leaders, even while, given the difficulties of the era, they seemed further away than ever.

Recognizing this as a period of recalibration as to the purposes of the schools, one is alert for signs of a major proposed curricular solution, or possibly a fundamental pedagogical one. None is evident. This stasis may be an exception to the general rule that when people are dissatisfied with the schools they seek to change the curriculum. More likely, though, is that Americans believed the schools were doing the best they could, in difficult times. By the end of the 1930s, however, changes are latent in the literature of school policy. With regard to the curriculum, the Regents Inquiry speaks of a modestly broader set of subject matters, beginning earlier. Other inquiries refer to the fact that the 'better' colleges now turn college-preparatory applicants away—and remind parents that higher education is becoming more diverse. (That is, that the range of choice is wider than the Ivy League.) In 1940, the American Council on Education and American Youth Commission, in a joint effort, carefully studied the topic "What the High Schools Ought to Teach."[53] The panel reaffirmed that the schools should seek and should teach personal development and social values, but went on to say that the academic program should be reorganized: there should be more emphasis on social studies, on reading, on supervised independent study, on *serious* study of physical and mental health and the problems of family life. New ideas and new content should be made available as subjectmatters *within* the general academic course.

The call for a more modern, variegated substantive content was not new; from the turn of the century, various groups had wanted the schools to be more responsive to the interests of their students. The 1893 solution had been a more intellectually modern history, including a special period of study or research. The 1918 pattern had emphasized heavily the not-strictly-academic content. The foreign language proponents, having won the battle to go beyond classical languages, throughout this period stress the teaching of European languages through means more flexible than dictation, the analysis of grammar, and the reading of preselected excerpts from foreign literatures. But something new was being adumbrated here. The ACE/AYC panel spoke, for example, of the special problem of the ninth grade: "Pupils in this grade come from the general curriculum of the elementary schools or from the liberal curriculum of the junior high school where exploratory courses have opened up many avenues of interest. The ninth grade puts an end to all general studies. It is essentially a period in which every course is designed as preparation for what is to come later, in which every course is seriously lacking in direct appeal to general interests."[54]

By the end of the decade, results had also been obtained from the first systematic and thorough curriculum evaluation study, in which academic achievement was directly related to variation in the preceding course of study. This was the famous Eight-Year Study, sponsored by the Progressive Education Association under the research direction of Ralph W. Tyler. Beginning in 1933, some two hundred colleges were persuaded to waive their normal entrance requirements for students from selected high schools. For their part, about thirty private, university-related, and public high schools, selected from each region of the country, participated. The researchers sought to build on variation across existing schools, so that in these schools normal practices could continue without disruption of the program, the introduction of new teachers, waivers of state requirements, and the like. However, the schools did generally strip down their programs to some extent, to a somewhat more sharply profiled set of elements or strands, so that evaluators could analyze the specific content, texts and materials used, teaching styles, and so on.* As time went on, each school's course of study was further sharpened by asking each participating school class to suggest further modifications toward achieving the essential curriculum of that school. For example, one pattern of change within some schools was reported to be team-teaching and an interrelating of English and social studies courses.

The overall results of the Eight-Year Study were clear enough.[55] Students from innovative or 'progressive' high schools did as well in college, in terms of grades in introductory courses, as students from schools with traditional college-preparatory programs. There are many problems, technical and interpretive, with the study.[†] But what was being called for in the Regents Inquiry and the ACE/AYC report, and described in the Eight-Year Study, was the actual realization in practice (as well as in curriculum planning) of a more variegated set of subjectmatters within the academic program of at least some high schools and junior high schools. In other words, after years of rhetoric, it is likely that— confining our supposition only to the social studies—Geography in the junior high school was indeed more 'social'; Civics did have more discernible economics content and an orientation to something very like descriptive sociology; European History was broader than royal houses and wars. To a limited degree, at least, the piecemeal addition, over the years, of 'units' and 'readings' within the old framework; the accretion of teaching reflecting the intellectual interests of better-educated teachers; the increase in size and comprehensiveness of textbooks—all of these, past a point, stopped being merely experiments or add-ons and began to amount to a different kind of course. In *some* schools.

This is an inference, in one sense an obvious one. With the educational level

---

*This pattern of alteration to fit the experiment resulted in reduced variability within a school, but increased variability across schools.

†Some of the obvious possible flaws—for example, that the participating schools or students were inherently more able academically, or that the admitting colleges gave these students special chances to catch up—are more or less ruled out. Unfortunately, since the report of the study did not appear until 1942, the attention of researchers and educators had shifted elsewhere, and the 'experiment' could not be continued or followed up over a longer timespan.

of the country increasing generally, with universities adopting more complex and wide-ranging programs of study, with 'serious' books and journals for the educated reader proliferating, and with alert citizens focused on questions of major sociopolitical import, it is logical to assume, twenty or more years after the Committee of 1916, that social studies education was at least more 'social' than it had been, and that students' interests (*subjectmatter* interests, not trades or commercial skills) were to some degree accommodated.*

To the extent that this inference is correct, the change must have been put in place, and experienced, at the level of course *sections*. A new teacher, with a new kind of university preparation, would have taught geography or civics or American history in a different way: more economic, or sociological, or technological in emphasis, for example. A teacher with tenure and with the security of knowing a great deal of political history would finally take the chance to conduct her classes in twentieth century U.S. History with a current-issues approach. As established forms evolve, in the schools as elsewhere, and meet new opportunities and fill new needs, they eventually become distinct entities. Civics, if taught in a thoroughly sociological attitude, eventually becomes Social Problems, or Sociology. American History with a strongly economic emphasis becomes Economic History. As more and more students stayed longer and longer in the 'academic' program of American high schools (as they did in the 1930s) and as a range of student interest, reflected in the various subjectmatters, was taken more and more seriously, it is likely, we believe, that what (in the schools of the 1940s) would amount to *electives* were being invented.

What we may see by the end of the 1930s is a pragmatic agreement on the core of the social studies, together with a principled tolerance for a varied set of subjectmatters beyond the core. The alternative interpretation is that what we see is *subversion of the core* by teachers encouraged by a doctrine of playing to student interests. Two versions of this latter view exist: one, that teachers were driven into intellectually indefensible subjectmatters by the facile, often not feasible, preferences of students; two, that teachers preferred to teach new courses for their own reasons, appealing to 'student interest' to rationalize that preference. Both charges were subsequently laid against the high schools. The criticism appeared very sharply in the late 1940s, framed then in terms of the sins of progressive education.

Before turning to the post–World War II period, however, let us look back into the more circumscribed history of the social studies after 1920 but before about 1945. As we have seen (section 4.5), there was only limited formal curricular change, in terms of formally labeled courses; the only entirely new element was the creation of Problems of Democracy for grade 12.

---

*This inference also assumes that merely pointing to a course-title curriculum pattern that changes slowly over the years (see tables 4-2 and 5-1) does not prove that 'the curriculum,' as delivered in classrooms to actual students, has not altered.

4.5.2   HISTORY AND ITS SIBLINGS

Within the social studies as school fields, during all of the 1920s and 1930s, there were few calls for formal revision of the curriculum, but continual internal assessment—first, of what the 1916 committee pattern did mean, and then, as new challenges to the society and the schools came about, what it should mean. Throughout the period, the university-schools relationship, as regards the actual content and tone of the curriculum, was a close one, but complex in form. Major figures and groups within the academic fields of history, political science, sociology, and economics struggled over the directions and emphases of parts of the curriculum. However, internal disagreement—or lack of strong interest— generally prevented the disciplinary associations as official bodies from taking consistent stands on curriculum revisions. (For discussion of the relationships, over the years, between disciplines and school subjects, see Part III of this volume.)

Part of the reason for this continuing but conflicted relationship of the disciplines to the schools reflected the widespread belief, especially in the 1930s, in 'scientific' curriculum-making rather than overt political negotiation. This was more than a recognition of the rapidly growing professionalization of primary and secondary education. It was consonant with efforts in the universities to design modern general education programs, whether under the aegis of liberal arts in some universities or a mixed liberal arts/professional/technical model in others (for example, the state universities). More important, all the social science disciplines, in their own ways, were taking account of wider ranges of empirical material, recognizing new subfields, and at times suspending theoretical agreement on first principles.* Briefly, history itself continued to separate out into various directions of 'new' or deeper or more specialized fields; political science was going beyond political theory, in favor of a more behavioral approach and the study of public administration; economics was becoming more quantitative and less normative; sociology adopted a more micro-level approach to social data, and a more functional, less evolutionary theoretical stance. It was thus natural for both professional curriculum experts in the schools and interested scholars to approach the social studies curriculum piecemeal: a deletion of outdated topics here, the addition of newly worked out material there.

It is not a full description, but it is not inaccurate to say that sociologists and economists were interested in enriching Civics, so as to make it more than the study of formal governmental structures. Political scientists did not necessarily disagree: they tended to find the Civics seconded to them by the historians around 1900 banal and unrealistic, but disagreed among themselves on what else from their field to add.

All fields were aware of the significance of the Problems of Democracy course

---

*One way of viewing this movement, up to about 1940 at least, was in terms of a continuing differentiation of the various fields from history. Ross, "Development of the Social Sciences."

(where it was taught, primarily in the new, larger high schools) as a culmination of the social studies curriculum; and all fields agreed that citizenship should be the central focus of this course, if not indeed the rest of the course of study. In essence, the debates turned on whether the course should focus on current issues or on recurrent tensions in the American system; on the degree of utilization of non-U.S. material; and on important new trends in the social sciences, such as the 'economic interpretation of history' of the 1930s, and newer methods of empirical inquiry, such as community study or the analysis of business cycles.[56]

Many historians were bothered by the specter of presentism in the approach to history in the schools—that is, in a popular phrase of the times, 'history taught backward' from some contemporaneous interest—and by the presence of the POD course, which, whatever it was, was not history. The American Historical Association had 'signed on' to the 1916 committee report. However, its so-called Schafer committee, which in 1918–1920 tried to reach a broad consensus on history in the schools, antagonized both the NEA Committee on the Social Studies, by seeking more history in grade 9 Civics, and important segments of the historical profession, by seeming to recommend world history at the expense of American or European history (and probably by seeming uncritical about what the 1916 aim of "socialized history" might mean in practice to the field). The association did not endorse the Schafer report, waiting for a broader commission in 1934 to sort out matters.[57]

It is important to realize that these conflicts within history and between history and other fields were inevitable, not only for reasons of its own development as a field of scholarship but because history was by far the largest social studies field, training most of the teachers (insofar as they studied distinct subjects in the colleges), generating most of the texts, and necessarily participating in, or organizing, most of the commissions. Fundamental (to a few, fatal) compromises had already been struck. History had accepted citizenship as an overriding goal of public education, had agreed that other subjectmatters should be represented in the curriculum, and had accepted the rather sweeping Principles of 1918. For their part, all the other scholarly fields accepted the primacy, in practice if not in principle, of history in the curriculum. No responsible person believed that history should not be taught: those who wished most sharply to *limit* the teaching of history were the advocates of vocationalism and social engineering through the schools, not other disciplinarians (see 4.4.1).

Thus history, as the overwhelmingly strong and experienced elder sibling (or parent, depending on one's view of the development of disciplines) was the cynosure—and, as such, the target for challenge and complaint. Within the academic realm, how the other fields were to be 'represented' was precisely the question; much hangs on the interpretation of the term. Throughout these post-1918 decades, historians cooperated constructively, at a number of different levels. Most important institutionally, in 1921 the AHA created the National Council for the Social Studies. The NCSS was first organized by a group of predominantly history teachers; its first president was Albert McKinley, the

editor of *The Historical Outlook*, an AHA teaching journal. The AHA helped
to support NCSS in its early years, and in effect endowed the new organization
with its journal, which became *Social Education*. Among its important early
leaders were Leon Marshall and Ross Finney, a well-known economist and
sociologist respectively. The early NCSS was an attempt, well understood as
such, to further or at least prepare for the development of a federation of subject
matters; certainly it signaled the rejection of a view that history teachers in the
schools could 'handle' all other discipline-derived content. The NCSS was also
oriented toward teachers and their support, intellectual and moral, at all levels
(not excluding the colleges); it avoided a close association with school administration interests of the social efficiency type. It was affiliated with the NEA, but
for many years met in conjunction with the AHA annual meeting. The latter
circumstance probably reflects the fact that other disciplinary associations did
not form clear lines of communication with NCSS; an attempt at some kind of
representative governance across the disciplines was apparently abandoned.[58]
For over two decades, the AHA-NCSS relationship waxed and waned, but never
became less than officially cordial. The AHA helped the NCSS financially
during the Depression. However, by the late 1930s, higher education membership in NCSS had dwindled markedly, and the more eminent university-level
historians had become inactive. No other disciplinary group replaced them.

This was not an indication of a breach, but the result of several tendencies.
One was the growing professionalization of 'school people.' Another was the
fading away of a pattern of an earlier day, in which college-educated men
(predominantly) taught school for a time, and then went back to the university
for higher degrees, eventually becoming academics.* Public school teaching
became more and more feminized, unlike university faculties (although most
high school social studies teachers have been male). Moreover, as has been
noted, in the 1930s and into the 1940s the colleges were working on their own
needs for a coherent core in liberal and general education. In a sense, the
principle enunciated by the 1893 Committee of Ten—that all secondary education should be meaningfully 'academic'—and the development of Western
Civilization and Contemporary Civilization core courses in the colleges in the
1930s and 1940s were counterparts, each seeking a principled common course
for the educated person. (However, in the interim, the median number of years
of schooling had risen, so the locus of the search shifted upward, at least for those
in an academic track.)

Finally, as research and scholarship developed in the U.S. universities, as
subfields and methodologically based divisions appeared within the disciplines,
the demands of specialization in the *production* of knowledge, that is, research,

---

*This pattern has been noted for the general period 1880 to 1920 or so, in sociology and economics
as well as history; its disappearance contributed to the growing separation between the schools and
the colleges. Acting against this trend, some high school teachers in the 1930s and 1940s moonlighted
as part-time academics, in the larger cities.

came to dominate: the previous community of interest in teaching that had once spanned the various educational levels became obsolete.

Before turning to the most important intellectual expression of the AHA-NCSS consanguinity, in the 1930s, we should mention a challenge to that spirit of cooperation (and to what we have said above was a general accommodation) that began in the 1920s and had important tangible effects. A disciple of George Counts's at Teachers College was Harold Rugg, probably the most effective of the Social Reconstructionists (section 4.5.1) among those specifically concerning themselves the social studies curriculum. Rugg was energetic, well-known, and had a base as director of the Lincoln School, the Teachers College laboratory school beginning in the 1920s. He saw that much hinged on what the Problems of Democracy course would be. If it was to be the culmination of a larger, more various, more socially realistic, more contemporaneous course of study, earlier units in the curriculum would need to be carefully designed and sequenced. He also knew that teachers could not be expected to do things differently without some clear direction as to what to teach, and how. By 1923 Rugg was arguing that the other broad areas of the curriculum were responding to the spirit of 1918 (the Cardinal Principles), while social studies was not. He scorned the limited approach of groups like the Schafer committee of the AHA. He said that 'correlating' facts and concepts from different disciplines was not sufficient: that it would not do for a history-trained teacher to stud her exposition with bits of sociological insight or geographical reference. Correlation would amount to something only when it was so extensive and pervasive as to be a totally unified content, drawn from the different fields but reconfigured for (upper) elementary and secondary school purposes.

Further, the central principle for what was to be unified had to be consideration of what decision-making problems students would face. Rugg's problem-approach was justified as follows:

> Not the learning of texts, but the solving of problems is what we need. ....
> For the pupil to think, he first must be mentally blocked and thwarted
> until he is obsessed with a desire to clean up the matter; he must also have
> at hand data, the facts on all sides of the issue, before he can think con-
> structively on it; and third, he must be practiced in deliberations on
> situations that are somewhat similar.[59]

He held, further, that one can "scientifically" analyze bodies of research and other organized scholarship and make a kind of concordance of facts and concepts to present to students as, and only as, the students engage in problem-driven inquiry of urgent significance to them. Accordingly, he and his students at Teachers College began to cull such elements from established and 'frontier' thinkers. More practically, he wrote a series of short texts for junior and senior high school under the general series title of *Man and His Changing Society*, which from 1929 on (to the early years of World War II) sold millions of copies. They took social problems—immigration, urban poverty, occupational stratification—and set forth what Rugg considered to be the relevant facts and concepts. Historical material was by no means in short supply, but the approach was an extreme of 'history written backward,' in that first one set the problem and then found the historical 'evidence' that applied (ignoring, among other things, the possibility that the very definition of the problem may be historically obtuse).*

Rugg's is the first full statement of a number of concatenated themes in the assessment of social studies as a curriculum area. Rugg was recommending the problems of society as the 'set text' of social studies. Pedagogically, he emphasized challenging students to want to go beyond what they already knew (and what was in the textbooks). He urged making students think by making them uncomfortable, and then to practice 'decision-making' over and over again. A high degree of open discourse in the classroom was understood, among students and with the teacher, with the specific decision outcome being in some sense negotiated by those present. This was not logical, step-by-step problem-solving that an individual student might do, for example, in geometry. This was politics within the teaching-learning situation.[†]

Finally, though information and insights from the disciplines were to be densely provided, and the latest knowledge imparted, the intended 'fusion' was at the subdisciplinary level. That is, to address a problem, itself inherently nondisciplinary, a student need not have mastered the full sweep and internal logic of history, economics, sociology, and all the rest; instead, he needed to be familiar enough with them to find what he needed. Although Rugg was a disciple of Dewey's in the conviction that one great aim of learning is social and political participation, he seems not to convey the Deweyian idea that organized knowledge is inherently rewarding, and can be led to in any individual in carefully nurtured steps from any starting point. Moreover, while Rugg reads the 1916 committee as wanting to challenge students to reach socially meaningful decisions (or at least practice doing so hypothetically), a more reasonable reading, it seems to me, is that the 1916 committee recommended that the curriculum recognize the changing nature of students' social *interests*, then devise appropriate intellectual means for pursuing them.

The 1934 commission described in section 4.6 would also address the difficult relationships among (and distinctions between) factual knowledge and problem-solving, inquiry and decision-making, logical deduction and political nego-

---

*A fuller, interesting account of Rugg's ideas is contained in Kliebard, *Struggle*, 200–207. It is the availability and evident popularity of these short, problem-oriented works that permit one to conclude that a Problems of Democracy course actually flourished, in some schools, in the 1930s— and that the course, where given, was not just another cycle of civics, perhaps with an occasional class period spent on some current event, or, alternatively, a convenient label for grade 12 social science electives, as taught by appropriately prepared teachers.

†It was inevitable, given this and the underlying Social Reconstruction ideology, that Rugg would be attacked in the later 1930s for anti-Americanism, and his kind of social studies as defeatist and disrespectful of adult authority.

tiation, personal interest and the participation needs of society, the disciplines as sources of knowledge and as structures for further questioning. So would social studies thinkers in the 1960s and 70s. So do we today.

4.6   The 1934 Assessment; The AHA Bows Out

The reports and individual volumes of the AHA's Commission on the Social Studies in the mid-1930s are, intellectually speaking, probably the most cogent brief for a full, various program of discipline-based school studies ever achieved in social studies. This brief took about five years of active committee work and drafting to prepare. The term 'brief' is used to signify a detailed, closely argued rationale for what the social studies should (and could) be: the commission's summary reports do not describe then-current practice in detail, nor on the other hand are they simply philosophical statements of some ideal situation."[60]

The life of the commission involved three phases. About 1925 the AHA council once again felt it useful to survey the situation of history and the allied subjects of the social studies in the schools. As summarized in the foregoing, some historians were comfortable with the 1916 solution (in which they had participated), while others believed that history would be undercut by current tendencies. This internal tension is not alluded to in the introduction to the *Charter* by the chairman, the historian A. C. Krey. He did refer, however, to the "chaotic" situation of social studies curricula, as documented in recent AHA surveys; this undoubtedly reflected the co-presence of the 1893, 1899, and 1916 curriculum patterns in the schools. Krey also says that by 1922, "nearly all of the great national associations had published committee reports suggesting more or less extensive remedial measures," thus delicately indicating that the political scientists (who had gone back and forth on the issue), the economists, and the sociologists, especially, while accepting the primacy of history in the curriculum, no longer believed that history courses could 'cover' all the necessary content.

The AHA planning committee created a commission of academic and professional high-achievers who managed to work hard and cooperatively almost to the end of the enterprise. The chair, A. C. Krey, was a historian; other historians included Henry Johnson, an educational and intellectual historian from Teachers College, and, most influential of all, Charles A. Beard.

Thus, as with 1916, the history 'wing' of the commission was strongly that of the 'new' history. The educational establishment was strongly represented, but with theorists rather than administrators or teachers: the superintendent of schools of Washington, D.C., was the exception. Then-current and recent NCSS

---

*In this discussion, I refer to the Commission's summary reports: first, the initial volume, *A Charter for the Social Sciences in the Schools* (1932), largely the work of Charles Beard and the most influential of all the volumes, then and now, and second, the official summary of the commission, the 1934 *Conclusions and Recommendations*. I use the latter volume to date the Commission and its work in general, for example, in referring to "the 1934 Commission."

leadership was well represented. George Counts was a member, as were others from Teachers College. There were foundation executives and college presidents. Most important was the presence of very strong figures from the other disciplines: the geographer Isaiah Bowman, the economist Leon Marshall, the political scientist Charles E. Merriam, and the sociologist Jesse Steiner. Funding, obviously in a very large amount, was obtained from the Carnegie Corporation of New York.

The very membership of the 1934 commission tells part of the story. The 1893 committee had been composed of historians and leaders of higher education; the 1916 committee of school people, together with historians; the 1934, commission of intellectual leaders from history and the social sciences (a term now accepted without comment in the universities), some of whom had considerable influence in the schools.

The 1932 *Charter* is Beard's work, but the record shows that it expressed the thinking of the commission accurately and eloquently. In terms of social philosophy, the *Charter* is somewhere between progressive and radical, stopping short of the extreme reconstructionism of commission member George Count* or Harold Rugg, but considerably more activist than the 1916 committee report. The spirit is 'radical' only if one considers the early New Deal radical. In terms of educational recommendations, the approach is conceptual and nonspecific, surprisingly so since the AHA charge had included the specification of courses, sequences, and grade levels. As to the *purposes* of the social studies, the 1932 volume is quite conventional. In essence, the *Charter*, which takes up only 117 small pages, establishes a triangular balance among the "conditioning realities" of the American society of the day, the resources and intrinsic limits of the social sciences in relation to education in the schools, and the rights, needs, and responsibilities of young people as participants in society.

In the *Charter*, the overarching purpose of social studies, and of education, is not problematical. The report uses "civic education" interchangeably with "social sciences" and "social education." There is no discussion of using education and the social studies in order to bring more persons into the socio-civic realm, as there had been in 1916, or to forge a basis for a deeper social equity. There is no questioning of how many young people are attending school, and from what origins and strata. In this sense, Beard's volume is 'critical' in that it does not so much ask how to involve more citizens in the sociopolitical process, but rather whether the sociopolitical process that is officially described is, first, accurate, and second, worth participating in.

With regard to the rights, needs, and responsibilities of young people (by implication, recently educated persons), 'citizenship' simply refers to social action. There is no debate about whether rights or responsibilities should dominate in 'citizenship,' no particular focus on voting, access to power, legal safeguards, or how the consent of the governed is conveyed. Civic education

*As expressed in his own 1932 book, *Dare the School Build a New Social Order?*

leads to social action. Social education must lead to an inquiring, rational, realistic mind:

> It is a changing world, accompanied by endless diversity of opinion, for which our instruction in social studies must fit the youth of the schools the best it can, fallibly, of course, and yet with an open-eyed regard for the nature of things [p. 30]. . . . A program of social studies must reassert the significance of criticism and *inventiveness* as a potent force for progress [p. 112, emphasis added]. . . . Social inventiveness is an essential quality of the good citizen (p. 112).

Decisions are of course necessary in social life, but they tend to be choices based on knowledge and critical acumen; the problem-solution emphasis of Rugg is entirely missing.

> Pupils go out of the schools into a pluralistic world of competing allegiances and loyalties . . . the child must become acquainted with this pluralism if he is to deal wisely with competing allegiances and handle them effectively in practical life . . . if civic education does not make clear the demands of these loyalties . . . [children] will not be fortified with the knowledge necessary to make wise choices and the strength of character required to carry them into effect. (pp. 113–114)

The tone throughout is that of informed choice, not that of practiced problem-solving. Likewise, the founding of instruction on current issues and controversies is strongly questioned. The thesis that social studies should be a "presentation and discussion of current issues . . . is supported by high authority . . . [but] burning questions of the hour may be ashes tomorrow . . . [and] partial, one-sided, and perhaps trivial in spots" (pp. 42–43).

Finally, it is a "hasty opinion that the public schools can solve the problems of democracy or at least prepare the way for easy solutions." Formal instruction in civics must, above all, be honest and realistic.

> Instruction in citizenship, if it is not limited to sterile abstractions, cuts into difficult themes and affects powerful interests in society. An attempt to conceal this fact would be futile; an evasion would lead to stultification. It would be better to ignore entirely the subject of government in social studies than to confine it to innocuous generalizations on which people agree in theory and disagree violently in practice. (pp. 37–38)

On the other hand, enduring values and prevailing cultural attitudes must not be avoided.

> Loyalty to America, an appreciation of its achievements, and faith in its powers are indispensable . . . the wise, no doubt, draw upon the wisdom of all lands and all ages . . . but they know that they have a geographical location and a cultural heritage . . . the loyalty which history and the social sciences can instill is, then, the loyalty of reasoned affection. (p. 105)

The recommendation for open-eyed, candid reason is not remarkable, although it was in fact different in tone from other prescriptions of the time for social studies. What is new in the 1932 *Charter* is the approach to a *description* of the reality within which one makes reasoned choices.

A realistic program of social studies cannot be drawn with mathematical precision . . . from the realm of scholarly ideas without reference to actuality—the prosaic world as a going concern . . . . With ruthless might new facts upset the fair pageantry of eternal schemes: Jefferson's America of free and upstanding farmers ruling the country in liberty has been turned upside down by steam and machinery. Ten million teachers singing the praises of agriculture would have been powerless to block that inexorable march [p. 24]. . . . On every hand dissatisfaction is found with our present industrial order—dissatisfaction which ranges from minor proposals relative to unemployment insurance and old age pensions to schemes for fundamental reconstruction. . . . What is potential, as well as what is, must enter into civic instruction if it is to be more than a sterile transmission of acquired customs and habits (pp. 40, 53).

Some of the specific resonances of such passages may now be lost (in 1932 some of these 'minor proposals' were hotly debated). About one-third of the book, however, is devoted to such contemporaneous references, and the message is clear, if only by the weight of its expression: social studies must track social life as well as draw upon organized knowledge.

Organized knowledge, though, is no weak reed. The *Charter* looks at "conditioning realities" and the capacities of the disciplines together, binocularly, fusing them into one compelling image.

A wide knowledge of facts and a discipline in thinking are the prerequisites to a fruitful consideration of controversial questions [p. 46]. . . . The worlds of fact and opinions, parts of the same thing* reflecting perhaps some deeper underlying reality, evolve together [p. 17]. . . . Speaking summarily, we may say that the primary information which social science must supply through the schools to individuals is information concerning the conditioning elements, realities, forces, and ideas of the modern world. . . (p. 98).

It is to be provisional 'information': "Recording long lists of human errors, [social science] conserves a saving sense of fallibility" (p. 116), and it is to be detailed information, "eschewing generalizations that transcend . . . knowledge and experience, abstractions that cannot sink into immature minds" (p. 92). Here, William James is quoted: " 'No one sees farther into a generalization than his own knowledge of details extends' " (p. 92). And by no means is it to be all 'scientific' knowledge about present-day 'conditioning' realities.

---

*Note the antipositivist reference, unusual for its day.

Crowning them all is history. . . . Written history seeks to organize world affairs in their chronological chain according to their inner connections. It attempts to explain, within limits, how things came to be what they are by throwing them into perspective and sequential, if not causal, relations [p. 19]. [History gives the other social disciplines] a patterned background and . . . a dynamic which pertains to the future.*

Thus, to simplify: social studies is civic education that enables one to confront modern-day reality with a range of disciplined knowledge. Social action requires more than this—but it does require this. In the end, after all the rhetoric is examined and the later turmoil surrounding the commission's conclusions is stripped away, the position is quite clear—and not all that routine in 1932. The aim of social studies is not to socialize more people to the existing system, nor to win broader allegiance for it: it is to examine reality Schooling is not the avenue toward radical social revision. Thinking precedes action; schools do not train for solving the problems of democracy. Social studies draw from a set of organized disciplines, a true confederation of knowledge.

The last message was of particular importance. The *Charter* (p. 20) specifically denies that there can be any such thing as a synthetic, fused Social Science (either in the abstract, as a set of overarching and unifying concepts, or for pedagogical purposes, by simplification and recombination for the schools). It assumes that several disciplines are directly relevant, history being the "crown." It says nothing about academic versus nonacademic tracks, about the kinds of knowledge that may be relevant to different educational purposes. And it says nothing about who is to design and write the actual curriculum, or relate the particulars of "information" to selected aspects of "conditioning reality."

Brilliant as it is (and as is much of the corresponding language of the 1934 *Conclusions and Recommendations*), the *Charter* is wildly abstract, perhaps even naive in its assumption that disciplined knowledge and prosaic reality can be brought into relation with each other via the process of education. The entire intervening realm—the *process* of education—is omitted. The 1932 volume describes an object of study, not the means. Every influential prior curriculum report spoke of the problems and importance of the education of teachers; warned against a pedagogy based on facts alone; said that a sequence of courses was a practical necessity. The *Charter* is virtually silent on such matters.

Despite the AHA's original charge, the 1934 *Conclusions* also chose not to recommend a scope and sequence, or give much advice on the educational process. The commission could, of course, point to its series of more specialized, professionally informed volumes as filling this need; but what that meant in practice was that educators would use those volumes on their own merits, or for the users' own purposes, quite uncoupled from the arguments of the summary

---

*This eloquent valuation of history, by a historian, would seem unassailable from within the profession. But the nuances—"sequential, if not causal" and "pertains"—proved troublesome in 1934, when the AHA considered the final report.

reports. The *Conclusions* did refer in a knowledgeable way to the social studies of the time, in their curricular arrangements; it suggested that the 'expanding horizons' organization* of the early grades was sound practice, and that the interests of the student at all grades should be taken into account. It recommended a focus in the primary school on community, nation, and domestic issues; for the secondary school, more attention should be paid to international systems and connections (comparative government and economics being specifically mentioned).

The decision not even to sketch out a sequence of courses or to limn the selection of factual content has been seen either as the consequence of internal dissension in the commission, as it came to issue its final report, or as an example of educational naiveté on the part of the members as to how to be effective. As for the first explanation, it is true that some members dissented from the *Conclusions*, largely because there were references, troublesome or offensive to them, to the impending cessation of laissez-faire management and the approach of 'collectivization.' (It is odd that, in 1934, some term like 'national planning' did not surface in the report.)

It is probably true† that, given this underlying malaise, the commissioners simply could not adjudicate more strictly educational choices that might have been made in their report: that is, ideological suspicion must have colored pragmatic negotiation. In any case, experienced educational leaders on the commission from the important schools of education and large school districts must have warned that a report without specific curriculum recommendations would have little direct influence on the schools, no matter how brilliant the philosophical arguments.

The decision to be vague about a curriculum may, however, have been quite deliberate, either on tactical or ethical grounds. Recall that the AHA planning committee that brought about the commission took as its starting consideration the 'fact' that the then-current curriculum was in 'chaos'—that is, different schools followed different patterns. The commission knew that historians themselves had rejected, in 1920, an attempt to rationalize the history curricula within the general framework of the 1916 pattern; they knew that Beard was a controversial historian; and they knew that by 1934 the New History was being seen as a movement that had fulfilled its promise, and was no longer a risky if fresh approach. They also knew that the disciplinary associations other than history had a consistent record of claiming increments of the curriculum for themselves—even while officially ceding to history the lion's share, and declining to commit themselves to true engagement in the schools on a continuing basis. Finally, even the rather vague curriculum improvements that the commission seemed to espouse would not, it was clear, be easy to put into effect. Thus

*The expanding horizons (or expanding environments) model was formally worked out by Paul Hanna in the 1940s and 1950s. See p. 325.

†As implied by Kliebard, *Struggle*, 197.

one may speculate that the commissioners feared making a bad situation worse: why recommend a fourth history pattern and an array of discipline-based studies for which no one would fight?*

It may have been a miscalculation. It may have been the assumption, partly arrogant, partly modest, by intellectual leaders that their job was to describe what should be, leaving implementation to others. In the event, for all the continuing excellence of the commission's work, there were several probably negative consequences. The work, in schools, of implementing a broad range of social studies was left, not to those with the authority and vision carefully to work out a new curriculum, following the commission's lead, but to teachers or subject specialists designing syllabi, 'units,' and ancillary texts—thereby increasing the curriculum 'chaos' (if that is the fair term).

With the 1934 commission, the AHA ended its distinguished endeavors as the convener of major curriculum reform efforts, coordinating history and the other disciplines and the academic and professional educational worlds. The 1934 commission designed an edifice housing the several academic disciplines, but there were no organizations (and few teachers in the schools) in the disciplines other than history to furnish it.

There is also present, subliminally, in the commission's report a paradox that plagues curriculum planning in all fields. Disciplines constrain inquiry, as well as potentiate it. They foreground some 'problems' and exclude others. How did the commission expect 'conditioning reality' to be confronted directly, so that disciplinary knowledge could be brought to bear on it, when disciplinary knowledge itself conditions reality? If disciplinary learning per se was not the goal—and the commission was clear on this point—would not the knowledge actually used in the process of education in the schools inevitably be a highly reduced, 'received' kind of wisdom, only vaguely related to ongoing social science inquiry? The understated tone of ordinary realism evident in the commission's reports is particularly ironic in the social studies, where the accumulated wisdom of specialists, based at least partly on theory and research, happens to resemble in form and in language that 'common sense' which reflects only lay opinions. Many must have read the *Charter* and *Conclusions* and failed to see that more than 'common sense' was being recommended.

It is also a problem for the social studies in a related way. The commission hung back from recommending a tightly specified content, in part because it laid great stress on independent thinking in students at every stage. Yet it seemed to assume that all students' perceptions of and intellectual reaction to 'constraining social reality' would be more or less the same: without that—and without a set disciplinary frame—how would any curriculum be organized in a given year? Which 'conditioning reality' would be examined? Both Boyd Bode and John Dewey, the two most profound philosophers of progressive education, went on

*In 1934 the professional social studies organization, the NCSS, was in trouble from the Depression, and was losing members and money. It would not have been in a position to wage the battle over the long term.

record in the next few years to question the apparent recommendation by groups like the commission to do without the framework of organized knowledge in the curriculum. As Kliebard points out,[61] Bode, in remarking that "The pupil must acquire some capacity for thinking as the specialist thinks," anticipated the New Social Studies of the 1950s. And Dewey, in his most important book on education, said that, while learning must *begin* with curiosity and the experience of the learner, "The next step is the progressive development of what is already experienced into a fuller and richer and also more organized form, a form that gradually approximates that in which subjectmatter is presented to the skilled, mature person."

4.7   At the End of the 1930s

Building on the interest created by the 1934 AHA commission, but clearly trying to go beyond it to a more specifiable curriculum, several organizations in the 1930s examined alternative course sequences. There were two NCSS year-books, in 1934 and 1936, that did so, and then in 1939 a wide-ranging NCSS bulletin, *The Future of the Social Studies*, whose editor was the not yet best-selling writer James A. Michener.[62] The bulletin offered some fifteen scope and sequence models for consideration, some very specific, some very abstract. The NCSS array showed that there *was* a degree of agreement in the social studies: history, but not only history, and not so much history taught for the sake of history as for the larger understanding of civic education. All of them suggested that there was room for incremental improvement, but that no one sequence ought to be adopted. In 1939 the thinking was that teachers and curriculum specialists would try out various plans and would come to consensus naturally, over the course of time. With the coming of World War II, however, attention shifted elsewhere.

A tally of the models offered in 1939 shows agreement (always with some dissenters) on an expanding environments pattern for grades 1 through 4, and an acceptance of three years of American History at grades 5, 8, and 11 (give or take the shift of a year, here and there, for specific reasons). There was a rather prevalent interest in expanding world studies, based on history and other disciplines, in the junior high school years, and a wide acceptance of the POD course (under some name) at grade 12. (Relatively few of the experts preferred social science electives in grade 12.) Grade 9 Civics was unstable; a number of experts preferred to see more world cultures, world civilization, or Geography at grade 9 or 10, but a single alternate was not clear, nor was the nature of 'world' studies. In summary, in 1939 the weight of recommendations, taken together, was not unlike the 1916 pattern—or the 1980 modal curriculum. Somehow, social studies curriculum thinkers on the one hand worried about 'chaos' (section 4.6), but on the other reinvented the modal pattern.* It is hard to see that

*With the troublesome areas being civics and the constituting of 'world' studies.

these assessments in the later 1930s took account of the 1934 AHA commission in any significant way.

Perhaps that was just as well. After about 1950, the entire spirit of public education changed, with the change proceeding downward from higher education to the schools. The 1940s, in the schools, were deceptively quiet. Owing to the long-declining birth rate in the 1930s and during the war, the size of the school system did not grow (see figure 4-1); the share of school revenues coming from the states continued to grow (relative to local revenues), but school financing in general was tight until the late 1950s. The level of school achievement, however, continued to climb. The proportion of those completing high school rose to nearly 60 percent in 1950; this, combined with other avenues to high-school completion (or equivalency) among servicemen, meant that the median years of schooling among the general population under about age 30 also increased. During the 1940s the teachers left in the system were older, and had been teaching for some years. They were weary of the long struggle to keep the education system viable during the Depression and the war. What Kliebard[63] calls the three curricular traditions of midcentury public education—the academic, the child-developmental, and the social-efficiency—were all still present in the later 1940s in an unstable mixture.

Perhaps most important, there was a change coming in the character of the teaching profession in the schools. Prior to 1950 or so, the 'best' teachers, in the sense both of pedagogical experience and academic preparation, were gentlemen and gentlewomen with a liberal education of their own; as has been pointed out, they were often persons who might as easily have been college teachers, and often became that. But they were very few in number. Most teachers, nationally, were ill-prepared intellectually, and depended almost entirely on the texts. All that means, of course, is that teaching was preprofessional. The war produced a cohort of young men and women whose personal lives had been altered by service in the military or new occupational roles in the economy at home. They were filled with a sense of efficacy and national hopefulness, far different from that in the late 1930s. With the G.I. bill and with their own upgraded occupational goals, they flocked to higher education, which offered them a far wider range of courses in terms of academic majors, preprofessional courses, and the like. Specifically, the schools of education were about to grow enormously.

No doubt for good and bad, school teaching was to become more 'professional,' more homogeneous in nature—certainly less inept at the lower end of the scale, conceivably less imaginative at the upper end. In the fields relevant to social studies, preparation in a wider range of subjectmatters was now possible; in a sense, the social *science* aspect of teaching education could only now begin.* For example, though the need for 'world study' in the schools had repeatedly been voiced, only after World War II did nontraditional foreign languages and

---

*That is, in the fields other than history, where solid preparation had long been possible.

Table 4-3 Education Degrees Conferred by U.S. Universities, 1950–1986

Year	BA	MA	PhD	MA/BA
1949–50	61,472	20,069	953	.33
1955–56	69,926	30,127	1,583	.43
1959–60	89,421	33,512	1,590	.38
1965–66	117,185	50,430	3,063	.43
1970–71	176,614	88,952	6,403	.50
1975–76	154,807	128,417	7,778	.82
1980–81	108,309	98,938	7,900	.91
1985–86	87,221	76,353	7,110	.88

Source: Adapted from U.S. Dept. of Education, National Center for Education Statistics, *Digest of Education Statistics 1988* (CS 88-600), Table 193.

area studies programs take off in the universities, and did anthropology and modern human geography become major disciplines in their own right.*

4.8 After 1945: Modern Times in the Schools

Educational historians remark on the suddenness, about 1950, of the collapse of the progressive education presence.[64] It must have been due in part to the new spirit in higher education and the inevitable decline in power of those school professionals who had charge of public education all through the 1930s and early 1940s. Now, not only did higher education resume its influence over the entire system, but state legislatures once again became active in setting standards and curriculum patterns. The Progressive Education Association itself ceased, quite abruptly, in 1955. Well before then, figures like Dewey and Bode had distanced themselves from the extreme child-orientation and life-adjustment dogmas of the PEA. The social reconstructionist aspect of progressive education, as exemplified in the 1930s by Counts and Rugg, was dead, in the strong surge of national pride and optimism of the postwar period. The vocational movement, however, which as a facet of social efficiency had at least coexisted with more fundamental strands of progressive education since the Cardinal Principles of 1918, was stronger than ever.

Vocational education was the main focus of federal policy in the Office of Education, and also of great concern to the more industrial states. The nation's industrial plant was retooling for domestic production, and agriculture was mechanizing; both sectors now had foreign markets (though initially subsidized for assisting in the rebuilding of Europe) far beyond those of the 1930s. Wartime

*As usual, I use the term social *science* to refer to the presence of strong, separate university-based teaching and research fields, not to comment on whether or not these fields were inherently 'scientific.' When the National Science Foundation was being formed prior to 1950, social science leaders themselves chose not to force a choice on that matter, preferring their fields to be omitted from the organizational structure.

technology, from metallurgy to machine tools to electrical inventions, was altering all aspects of production, as were new methods of management and industrial relations developed in the war. This meant that the *spirit* of vocationalism was quite different. In the 1930s the emphasis on vocational training was largely a moral obligation of the high schools: if much of the now-larger high school population was enrolled because jobs were not available, it was a necessity of citizenship training to help young people adjust as practically as possible to a problematical working world. In the later 1940s, with an industrial boom beginning, with professions proliferating, with universities and trade schools (under the GI bill) offering a wide new variety of applied arts and sciences, vocationalism was simply the cutting edge of adjusting to an expanding economic and technological frontier.

Just as the boom would lead to something like full employment in the occupational sector, so did the universities begin to descry something approaching full enrollment in some form of higher education. The college population virtually doubled by 1946, and the high schools experienced no 'drop-out' problem.* Lazerson[65] holds that higher education was coming now to be viewed as an 'entitlement,' although in this regard one notes the propensity of those in higher education to focus on the 60 percent completing high school, rather than the 40 percent not. In any case, once again, as around the turn of the century, it became a matter of concern to the leaders of higher education to determine how the high schools would feed into the universities, and what the *variety* of pathways between the two levels should be. In the universities, at the undergraduate level, this involved whether or not to opt for general education, a core, versus a wide set of electives leading to a wide range of academic and professional degrees. In the schools, it meant, correspondingly, debating how wide and how homogeneous the 'academic' track should be.

4.8.1 THE HARVARD "RED BOOK"

Once again, a Harvard president took the lead. As with Charles Eliot in 1893, James Conant, leading a Harvard faculty study panel on *General Education in a Free Society*,[66] began from the premise that general education was to be provided in high school *and* college, not simply the latter. In the 1870s Eliot had sought to preserve 'liberal arts' by loosening it and insisting on electives in the undergraduate course. Around 1910, another Harvard president, Lowell, followed the lead of Columbia and moved Harvard's curriculum back toward core courses and with distribution requirements—away from free electives. Now, in 1945, Conant et al. resisted the proliferation of courses offered by some of the public universities, and recommended a general core in college: humani-

---

*In part, see figure 4-1, because the high- school enrollment rate was not yet so high that noncompletion was viewed as 'dropping out.'

ties, social sciences, natural science, and physical science. (Specialization and professional education was highly acceptable in the university—but after the undergraduate program was completed.)

For the schools, however, 'liberal' and 'general' education were indistinguishable. "The general education of the great majority of each generation—not the comparatively small minority who attend our four-year colleges" was the task, according to the 1945 report, and this must include 'modern' knowledge such as science and foreign language. But it must also include history, art, philosophy, literature, and all those subject matters that deal with "our cultural pattern" and the realm of values; else, it will not "provide a sufficient educational background for citizens of a free nation. . . . There is nothing new in such educational goals; what is new in this century in the United States is their application to a system of universal education" (pp. viii–ix). In the secondary schools, the "education which seeks to promote active, responsible, and intelligent citizenship is ordinarily general rather than special education. . . . The social studies have a more immediate relationship to civic education than do the other studies of the secondary-school years, and even though they are concerned with other aspects of general education than training for a life of civic responsibility, *this is their distinctive justification*" (p. 133, emphasis added). The report emphasized the centrality of the study of history, and agreed with Beard's 1932 warning that a "study of immediate problems is ordinarily inadequate."

Thus far, the Harvard report represents familiar reasoning. It breaks new ground in its next steps, however. According to the report, those who expect to continue on to college and those who do not should take essentially the same subject matters. "But differences in background and in intellectual competence will call for variety in materials and teaching methods" (p. 135). Specifically, for those continuing on, the "course dealing with government and economics might be postponed until the college years on the assumption that they could [then] be studied in a more mature way." Thus tracking is needed *within* the general course. But it is not that college-bound students should be able to take 'social science electives'—that is, begin their formal study of disciplinary approaches in high school—as was implicit in the 1934 report and the practice of the better high schools of the late 1930s. Almost the contrary: college-bound students should go deeper into history, leaving 'the sciences' until college.

In the elementary years, instruction should avoid sweeping repetition of the same material at about the same conceptual depth. Instead, geography—political, economic, 'cultural'—should be prominent, as long as it is not an "interminable series of lists of capitals, rivers, and principal products." Assuming an 8-4 grade pattern, the report delicately suggests that Civics and narrative American History be withheld from those going on to college, but provided for those leaving earlier than the twelfth grade (which, since such a decision requires forward planning, means that tracking must start quite early). Again we note the assumption that specialized knowledge, other things being equal, is best acquired later—quite a different approach, within a generally rich 'academic' scheme, from that of 1934, which had included challenging electives within the curriculum so as to keep up the intellectual motivation of students.

The recommended scheme for high school, in the 1945 report, is fundamentally two years of European/World History, Geography, and related cultural study, followed by two years of domestically oriented study: U.S. history at grade 11, "Problems of American Life" at 12. The World History course will inevitably be European in focus, but not formalistically so (that is, it can be tied to other topics): "Its central goal must be kept clearly in mind: to set forth the main tendencies in the development of modern civilization." American history is not to be repeated several times: this "leads neither to mastery of nor to interest in American history." Selected periods and aspects are to be emphasized, while "only the simplest narrative is employed to tie together parts of the whole pattern." Most important is the training of students to weigh evidence: *"Few traits more clearly distinguish good teaching from bad than intelligent use of the principle that interpretation and generalization, though important, are valuable only when based on an understanding of the facts to which they relate"* (pp. 142–143, emphasis added). Once again, "History is studied not for its own sake but because of its relation to the whole of general education." Once again (as in the 1932 Charter; see p. 105) William James is alluded to, in his remark that "we can see into a generalization only so far as our knowledge of detail goes."

In 1945 or today, a hostile critic could say that the Harvard image of 'general education' in the schools was what would lead gracefully to Harvard's freshman- and sophomore-year program—even for those not headed there, and even to the extent of seeming to ask schools not to teach specialized or 'social science' courses. Conversely, one may suspect that certain subjectmatters, by being emphasized in the schools, are being kept out of college. In this regard, Conant believed that geography was not a college-level subject.

In its lengthy and eloquent espousal of history and more history, including training in historiography, the Harvard report even resembles that of the 1893 Committee of Ten. But there are very significant differences between the two in the kinds of history they recommend be offered. Furthermore, in keeping with its view of the goal of history—not for the sake of history but for citizenship—the 1945 report comes out strongly for a grade-12 course on the "nature of contemporary society—a fitting culmination for all the work in the social studies that has preceded it and . . . an invaluable introduction to the task of citizenship which lies just ahead" (p. 143). It is to be some rich blend of government, economics, and sociology, whose mixture will vary with circumstances, it is to go beyond current issues, and it should be a course on 'problems' only insofar as it gets deeply into the "basic structure and processes which go to make up the political, economic, and social system."

Thus the course is consonant with Beard's 1934 recommendation for the study of "conditioning realities." But in clear opposition to Beard's view (and in reference to a controversy within political science during the later 1920s and 1930s), it says that the "realistic" (quotes in the original) study of government and economics can be facile if it neglects historical forces and the "role played by relatively abstract principles of politics and economics" as contained in law and legal-political institutions. Such principles are also to be conveyed by means of statements and documents. Here, however, the details of selection are revealing. According to the report, students in their culminating course—after 12 grades—can understand "certain of the great speeches of Pitt, Burke, Lincoln, Wilson, and Roosevelt," but not Mill's *On Liberty* and only some of *The Federalist Papers*, unless the "teacher has the training and the capacity to explain their place in the growth of American polity" (p. 146). A reader may wonder why it is that after so many years of rich, topically dense history (including intellectual and political history) and so much training in the weighing of evidence and close reading of documents, students about to take up the task of citizenship that lies just ahead should be unable to understand more deeply, and how this aspect of the course has to depend so much on the training of the teacher when the basic processes and structures of political, economic, and social life are to be apprehended. Here and elsewhere the report seems to call for an intellectual depth in the college track, while evincing some doubt as to whether most students in it can master the material.

It is a humane, beautifully written document, but stunningly *parti pris*. By 1950, only three out of ten high school graduates went on to college, and only some fraction of them to small liberal arts institutions (whether espousing 'general education' or not) like Harvard. No wonder President Harry S. Truman's 1948 Commission on Higher Education recommended something entirely different: not only the support of public universities on a broad scale, but the creation of an entire new system of community colleges and other kinds of postsecondary institutions, able to accept any high-school graduate without financial or curricular barriers.* Not for the first time, eminent university leaders were stipulating quality education for all, and an intellectual program justified for democratic ends—without there being the means of accomplishment. Whether Conant did not know the demographic and sociopolitical facts or chose to ignore them—or perhaps believed that wishing would make it so—is not known.

The Harvard report can now be read, and probably was then read, as the first postwar statement by academic leaders—who of course represented a wider set of persons influential in the society—of impatient dismay with the broad agenda of the principles of 1918. The report utterly ignored the possibility of social reconstruction through the schools; this was in keeping with the times, since the war had seemingly brought an end to many of the dilemmas of the 1930s. It did not address the goals of vocationalism in the schools, but assumed an entirely different overriding function for public education. It cautioned against that curriculum aspect of 'life adjustment' which would set students' interests at the heart of decisions about subjectmatters to be covered.

---

*In 1950, for the first time, more students were enrolled in public education than in private. Lazerson, "Introduction," 28.

For social studies, it passionately argued the case for history as the one 'core' subjectmatter in the high school, on two grounds: first, the cultural binding as well as intellectual coherence that such a focus would provide; second, the belief that high school students could not profitably master the specialized approaches and structures of the social science disciplines.* Accordingly, it opposed any serious tendency toward electives and toward including complex material, other than history, in the course of study. It argued that less would be more, in terms both of the avoidance of superficial surveys of knowledge and in terms of the concentration of effort on one centering field. "Too many children have learned too little about too much. The fault has been as much with school authorities and with those responsible for college-entrance requirements as it has been with teachers" (p. 147).

Those who believed, with Conant and his group, that high schools should offer a solidly intellectual, sophisticated, and dense curriculum for all, or most, of their students, might still disagree sharply with the last point. Indeed, by the 1950s, concern over the nation's position in the world led leaders of higher education to recommend, not that high schools do less, better, but that they do more, better. To them, the world was becoming too complex to wait for the colleges to introduce students to the analytic and methodological elements of the disciplines. Technological change in the economy and the demands of national defense required that academic 'standards' in the schools be raised— with 'standards' meaning primarily the range of content mastery. Further, by about 1960, scientists and cognitive psychologists particularly believed that powerful training in the more analytic fields was being delayed far too long, on the mistaken assumption that humanistic knowledge must precede scientific knowledge. Indeed, by 1959 Conant himself,† in his influential study of high schools, argued that the schools must be large enough to offer a full range of electives, especially in languages and all the sciences but also in economics, anthropology, and other areas of social studies. Then too, as academic leaders foresaw high schools becoming college preparatory institutions on a mass scale, many or most tended to reject the general-education program in undergraduate study for the more specialized and variegated pattern of the multiversity, in Clark Kerr's well-known phrase.

In the abstract, the Harvard report posed no insuperable official challenge to social studies. The report endorsed, roughly speaking, the existing curricular pattern, of world study in the middle grades, American and world history in the high school, and some kind of a problem-oriented capstone course. The underlying challenge to the multiple-purpose high school sought by the principles of 1918 had been a sharper challenge. However, in its oblique discounting of formal instruction in civics and related areas, except in the non-college track,

---

*This was not an argument about cognitive capacity so much as one about educational efficiency, of time well spent.

†See section 5.1.

the report had discouraging implications. It was another indication that there was no consensus on what students graduating from high school needed to know to be intelligent, active, participating members of society.

Since the end of the previous century, all the educational reform movements had asserted that something more than historical knowledge was appropriate. Civil Government (1893, 1899) had proven shallow. Community Civics, the 1916 panacea, with its admixture of economics and sociology to government, had proven hard to realize, partly because it was difficult to prepare teachers in it and to agree on texts. The 1934 vision of bringing the organized disciplines of the social sciences to bear on 'social reality' was full of paradoxes, and the 1945 Harvard report seemed to pronounce that approach ill-suited for the schools. It now appeared that rich, topically dense, interpretive history would be sufficient, after all.

That conclusion is not entirely fair to the 1945 report. In its final pages on social studies, the report says that teachers must espouse and demonstrate freedom of thought and speech, must engage in analysis and discussion, "not stump oratory" (p. 149). The report, though cautioning teachers that discussion of controversial topics without a foundation of facts is wrong, also cautions those outside the schools to expect change in politics, as well as in science, and says, "Orderly change, as the founders knew, can proceed only out of free discussion."

Internally, some of the best minds in social studies were, in the 1940s, finally elaborating in some depth the Deweyan notion of reflective inquiry.* This thinking was painstakingly aimed at avoiding the facile excesses of some programmatic thinkers in social studies: those who had recommended 'training in problem-solving' as a school-based means toward social reconstruction, or those who had seemed to push 'critical thinking,' without a factual base, to the point where it became cheaply iconoclastic. The attempt in the 1940s was to develop, and to train teachers in, methods whereby sensitive areas of society could be opened up for responsible, objective analysis; and to establish a kind of patient, dialectical pattern of teacher-student interaction, where students would be encouraged to form inferences and generalizations, which would then be subjected again to the test of factual and conceptual clarity; where ahistorical judgments would be questioned by other students; and where values in and of democracy would be not simply indoctrinated but analyzed as complex and at times incompatible entities.

The 1945 report, in its emphasis on knowledge-based judgment and discussion, was inveighing against the same ills that were opposed by those attempting to develop true reflective inquiry. But, being distant from the schools, the report cautioned more than it supported. It also seemed to imply, in its description of the actual curriculum, that the schools had neither the time nor the capacity on

*Singleton, "Patterns of Democracy," 96–101, is an excellent brief intellectual history of these matters, analyzing the work of Erling Hunt, Lawrence Metcalf, and Shirley Engle, among others, during these years. See section 17.0.

the part of teachers to conduct reflective inquiry and discussion of values. (Both were true, of course, to some extent; but neither was intrinsically true, given the requisite seriousness of purpose and clarity of goal.)

Thus when, beginning around 1950, some influential public figures began to find schools in general a possibly subversive enterprise,[67] social studies were in multiple jeopardy. They had, in the 1920s and 1930s, espoused a widening of democratic inclusion and a degree of social revision that were no longer on the national agenda, and thus were thought of as troublesome. Now they drew much of their content from the social sciences and 'revisionist' history, which were also under attack in the 1950s as inherently subversive. In many quarters, the social studies were charged with meddling in matters that threatened the social order. Simultaneously, some part of the academic world found school social studies too ambitious intellectually, in the sense of trying to deal with too much content, some of which might best be left to higher education. All told, in their particular charge—to educate for citizenship—social studies seemed, to those within the schools, blocked on most fronts. This would not change until the late 1950s, when, with the New Social Studies, a rather different overriding purpose would be assigned them, by academics if not by the general public.

5.0 How the Curriculum Took Shape: 1950 to the Present

5.1 Sputnik and Beyond in Curriculum History

After 1957, when the Soviet spacecraft Sputnik launched a cycle of educational anxiety, the cycles of reform of the schools began to shorten and the co-presence of incompatible elements from previous eras became more obvious. This claim does not just reflect the possibility that we can see recent history in greater detail more easily. Hampel, for example,[1] says that high schools were more 'alike' comparing 1945 to 1965 than comparing 1965 to 1975. Another indicator of rapidity of change is the fact that the pathbreaking National Defense Education Act of 1958 and its legislative follow-up in 1964 had markedly different goals, the former for the rapid intellectual *enrichment* of the subjectmatters in school (by implication, for those able to benefit, with little concern for others), the latter for wider *access* to good education, 'compensatory' education, and other special needs. A new vocational education act in 1963 brought renewed attention and funding to an educational area that in the late 1950s had been downgraded in the federal agenda. Finally, many have commented on the sharp contrast between the 1960s and the 1970s in political and pedagogical thinking about schooling.

Each cycle brought in something new without completely doing away with previous practice. This combination of change and retained complexity was

119

made possible by the very enlargement of the institution of schools, the broad-ened financial base, and American prosperity (generally speaking) over the period from the 1950s to the mid-1970s. These fortunate underlying trends also permitted the inclusiveness and 'holding power' of the schools to grow, despite a number of cross-pressures. Birth rates again declined, and GNP grew; investment per child in public education continued its climb, from $20 in 1920 to $200 in 1970 in *constant* dollars.[2] At the same time, almost as if by providence, the 'baby boom' of the 1960s—more precisely, here, the rapid growth of the school-age population, especially in the elementary grades—within the frame-work of larger-scale slowing of population growth and economic boom justified a sizing up of the schools. When broadly deployed federal funding for public education came into the picture, a national tax base was available for the first time. Local and state bond issues and special funding referenda became more common. Smaller communities could now afford high schools. (And after 1950, the 'output' of BAs in the social studies teaching fields kept pace with the enlargement of the school system.) The labor market did not need teenagers; in fact, economists and sociologists could demonstrate that a high school diploma was becoming almost the necessary minimum for a broad range of employment.* Once again, a set of external circumstances were conducive to the belief that schools could (and must) do everything, without adults and taxpayers being seriously discommoded.

The rapidity of change can be seen also in the figure of James B. Conant. His 1945 Harvard report was academic, broad, and liberal, anticipating a solid 'general education' for students at every level (from the upper elementary grades on through college). The establishment of a core, together with a profusion of electives, would suit all needs, even those primarily vocational in nature.[†] Conant's 1959 book, *The American High School Today*,[3] is very different in emphasis. Conant continued to believe in a comprehensive high school; in fact, he maintained that a high school had to be moderately large to have a respectable program. And Conant personally was committed to the high school as a socially unifying institution, a school in common serving all students' needs. But the burden of the 1959 book is about students' "evident or probable destinies" (not Conant's, but his Harvard predecessor, Eliot's, phrase from sixty years before), about distinct tracks and programs, about a kind of forward sorting—toward liberal arts colleges, state universities, professional schools, vocational colleges, and so on. An evident backing-away from earlier aims of an inclusive general education for all was justified by an appeal to the possibility of social mobility through common schooling—that is, the chance for 'destinies' to be altered. Conant had moved, in terms of his actual recommendations, from a

---

*In these years studies claiming that additional years of schooling 'added' so much additional lifetime earnings became common.

†These values and assumptions are also evident in Arthur Bestor's famous educational polemics of the early 1950s; see below.

liberal-democratic academic stance to a more technocratic/meritocratic position.[*]

5.1.1   EXCELLENCE AND EQUITY

What had happened in the meantime to predispose persons like Conant to this shift? Revilement of the schools throughout the 1950s; the back-to-basics move set off by Sputnik; the collapse of 'progressive education'; a demand for national prestige through the accomplishment of 'excellence' in public education. The demand for 'excellence' in public outcries has always seemed to necessitate tangible outcomes: test results, a better-prepared college entrant, and the like. Earlier insistence on academic achievement, evident throughout the century, might be seen as a forward-to-basics movement, an attempt to reach an ideal modern curriculum that would produce 'excellence.' Here, however, is the first 'back-to-basics' movement, the first time that outsiders insisted that the schools produce better math and science scores, better reading, and so on—quickly and deliberately, by purifying the curriculum and revising pedagogy and, if necessary, by subordinating other educational goals. The school curriculum should become tougher; the gifted should be identified and enabled to shine. Other institutions should take care of preparation for life. Among other implications, the increased emphasis on disciplinary learning and knowledge 'output' meant that the goal of civic education receded, not only for social studies but for schools in general, at least at the junior high and high school level. Foreign language education, for example, was a matter of urgency in this period, but its justification (unlike that in the late 1940s) was for the sake of national security, not the sake of world citizenship.

Already, of course, a countershift was developing. Admiral Hyman Rickover, with his concern for science achievement in the face of Soviet competition, was one cultural hero, but Reverend Martin Luther King, Jr., was another. The Freedom Rides occurred, the implementation of the 1954 Brown v. Board of Education Supreme Court decision was felt, the U.S. involvement in Vietnam began, and an era of activism and rebellion among the young got under way. The tonal agenda of schools in the 1960s communicated relevance, not excellence. That is, the rhetoric altered: in terms of the educational process, the achievement of excellence through 'new' approaches and the stipulation of 'rigor' proceeded. As Lazerson[5] points out, the Great Society's goals for a war on poverty and for the expansion of opportunity were to be realized largely through education; hence, the 1965 Elementary and Secondary Education Act, and the various

---

[*]When the English sociologist Michael Young published his famous book, *The Rise of the Meritocracy*,[4] the title was intended ironically: Young thought 'meritocracy' an absurd neologism. However, the notion that one's life-chances would be largely determined by a set of achievement or aptitude scores came to seem normal.

'titles' in federal education law dealing with minorities, children with special-needs, and other groups. At the same time, the work of the cognitive-developmental psychologists, among them Jean Piaget and Jerome Bruner, took the spotlight away, as regards educational application, from the psychometricians and learning theorists, and emphasized the great importance of early experience, thus providing another foundation for Head Start and similar educational programs. While these were largely preschool programs, especially at first, the general implications for a more demanding and 'productive' early primary school were clear, especially with regard to reading and math.

Some commentators[6] believe that the colleges and universities, in their own response to the emphasis on 'relevance,' reinforced tendencies in the schools to put excellence on the back burner. The argument is that the liberal arts colleges reduced their own entrance and graduation requirements and loosened their own 'core' requirements, and that this signaled the high schools especially that a coherent curriculum pattern was not of the highest priority. This would in part explain the proliferation of experimental programs, minicourses, nonacademic experiential learning, and so on. It is true that such trends were evident, less true that they affected the majority of schools. Certainly the ideas of romantic reformers of education who called for open or alternative education (especially at the early grades) and writers with an intellectual public, such as Paul Goodman and Ivan Illich, received more publicity than actual adoption in public schools. It is also the case that the liberal arts colleges were now attracting a smaller proportion of high school graduates; the state universities and specialized colleges had offered, for some years, a multiplicity of programs leading to diverse educational and professional ends. Moreover, even while the range of high-school electives increased, many of them were discipline-oriented *academic* electives (not the least in social studies); as part of this trend, advanced placement courses became common. In sum, it appears that, while the demand for relevance did sweep through the educational establishment, the specific recommendations of Conant in 1959—essentially, for diversity within comprehensiveness—represent the more fundamental dynamic process. Relevance pulled, but other factors were already pushing.

Common to the two decades, so dissimilar in many respects, was a strong attention to curriculum. As always, everyone's dissatisfaction with the schools, whatever form it might take, seemed to imply that the curriculum should be changed or 'strengthened.'* Federal funds went in large part to studies of the curriculum, at all levels, and to curriculum improvement projects. A national frame of reference was always implicit in such projects. The 'new' math, science, social studies, the new approaches to reading—all were led by national figures anticipating national solutions. The National Assessment of Educational Prog-

---

*An exception would be the educational romantics referred to above, who believed that the real problems lay with the ideological and social conflicts or hypocrisies reflected in the institution of public education.

ress, which began about 1968, was to be the "nation's report card" (section 14.3). For political reasons, it would not report scores on a state-by-state or local basis, but for various subpopulations (ages, sex, and so forth) sampled nationally. Salaries for curriculum specialists in the schools were often paid for by federal funds, indirectly at least. The social studies specialist in Oregon was more likely to be in touch with her counterpart in Illinois than with the language arts specialist in her own state.*

Predictably, the explicit emphasis during the later 1960s and early 1970s in the schools on equality of opportunity and social relevance led to a cultural reaction, a blend of disillusionment and fatigue. Local conflicts broke out over the issue of federal involvement in schooling, on both constitutional and less principled grounds. Suspicion about 'secular humanism' as a supposed school orthodoxy arose. Public opinion polls showed a wide hostility toward young people, especially after the university rebellions of 1968. Psychologists questioned the results of early enrichment programs such as Head Start. Sociologists such as James Coleman (and, initially, Christopher Jencks) suggested that the schools were not effective as avenues toward egalitarianism or even individual social mobility; worse, that movement toward such goals, central to American democratic education, could cause schools to 'tip,' that is, to lose majority support to such an extent that they became worse environments, rather than better. Whereas in the immediate postwar years the schools had been charged by some with breeding disloyalty, they were now charged with social seditiousness, with aggravating tensions and cleavages within the society. The social studies were a focus for such complaints.†

Lazerson remarks: "The politicization of American education between 1965 and 1975 was unprecedented.[7] In part, the political struggles were so intense because the issues were among the most fundamental in American society: the disparities between the ideals of equality, liberty, and justice on the one hand, and the realities of discrimination and lack of opportunity on the other." And as Graham puts it:[8] " 'Equality of opportunity,' however vital a concept ... does not address the internal pedagogical and organizational questions of schooling. If equality of opportunity means that poor black children and rich white ones can both attend a school in which they take courses that will help them adjust to life according to their probable destinies, then the disparities in genuine educational opportunity remain great."

---

*At least in terms of thinking about the curriculum and its reform, if not in day-to-day practice. When a state only has a few such specialists, they tend to be not in English or math but in science, the arts, and the other more specialized areas that seem always to have to justify their existence in ways that the 'basic' subjectmatters do not. In this regard, social studies is interesting, in that it is a major component of all state curricula—but is continually reinventing and justifying itself anyhow.

†As for the social sciences on the university level, the charge that sociology was really socialism was heard, even in Congress. And a number of scholars have pointed out that the social science evidence cited by the Court in *Brown* v. *Board of Education* was not conclusive in terms of research, so those hostile to the social sciences could claim with some justice that 'science' was being used for ideological purposes.

In 1974 a special panel of the President's Science Advisory Committee in effect gave up on comprehensive high schools, urging that smaller, more specialized high schools be organized, that more teenage students should work (and that employers be given incentives to facilitate this), and that lifelong educational vouchers should be used to reduce the pressures on the high schools. As James and Tyack put it,[9] "In essence, the panel responded to the achievement of universal education in comprehensive high schools by suggesting that the result had become a burden, not a triumph." A Kettering Foundation commission also suggested that students should be able to leave school at age fourteen, arguing the case on both practical and humane grounds. For good or ill, the stagnation of the national economy beginning about the mid-1970s did not permit such 'reforms' to be tried.

It is important to remember that the mood of weariness and resistance to politicization of the schools was characteristic primarily of the white middle-class majority.* However, those who had felt themselves to be outsiders in the schools (and in society) did not change their opinions, or become more resigned to the status quo, just because the dominant segment of society was tired of militancy. While rhetoric about democratic education as the solution to social inequity was suspiciously florid in the period of about 1910 to 1940, so long as the schools were growing in size and inclusiveness it was rhetoric without a substantial counter-rhetoric. From the 1970s onward there is more than one rhetoric, which made for a more honest, if more painful, debate. One implicit model evident in some explanations of achievement test score declines in the later 1970s is that the schools now contained a number of educationally alienated youngsters, who quite consciously stayed in school for pragmatic reasons, but who were not interested in majoritarian educational experience and did not bother to learn very much from it.†

It is also important to remember that the excellence movement of the late 1950s and early 1960s—while short-lived as the dominant tonal center of education—did persist at the level of curriculum experiment and pedagogical reform for some time, and did in some areas change things. It can be reasonably asserted that the 'new math' failed, and that the demand for higher standards in science was never fully implemented. The foreign language emphasis stalled, but brought new methods into use. The 'New Social Studies' had an ambiguous effect. To this we turn in section 5.3.

Before doing so, we might mention that a controversy of special relevance to social studies—over how to achieve 'excellence'—was apparent by the 1950s,

---

*The tendency in historical treatments to assign one tone or mood to a decade is evident in recent educational history, and is no doubt true of this present treatment. In general, except for Ravitch, *Troubled Crusade*, detailed, book-length educational histories stop with the 1950s, so this tendency is all the more seductive in dealing with the most recent decades.

†This is difficult to prove or disprove. The recent—that is, since about 1980—improvement in such scores *might* be attributable in part to high-school drop-out rates that have once again been rising. The evidence is not at all compelling. See section 14.4.

and was revived around 1980, after the fading away of New Social Studies and with the onset of a new excellence initiative. Arthur Bestor, a well-known historian who had himself attended the Lincoln School, the progressive lab school at Teachers College, spoke up strongly for a liberal core education of high quality for all students—in this regard agreeing with the Harvard "Red Book" position. Bestor[10] argued that the schools had stopped concentrating on subjectmatter in favor of 'how to think,' thus needlessly trying to pre-empt the work of the universities. Furthermore, what was needed was *traditional* subject-matter, that which was time-tested in pedagogical feasibility and cultural significance. In schools, as in the early years of college, students should acquire bodies of distinct, disciplined knowledge before being encouraged to venture into uncharted, perhaps nondisciplinary, fields. For the social studies, the interest in 'fused' subjectmatter in the middle schools (for example) was inappropriate, since it did not lead to true mastery of basic facts and concepts. In high school, history should be restored to a publicly recognized preeminence, and trendy and presentist courses restrained. Bestor granted that most of 'social studies' was in fact history, and did not recommend the extirpation of other subjects, but held that the significance of history as the unifying and synthesizing discipline had been clouded ever since the reform of 1916.

In an argument quite distinct from that of others who also espoused history over the other social studies, Bestor maintained that in their contemporaneity the social sciences could *only* configure the present moment, could only analyze the overt factors obvious to all—that is, that they were inherently superficial. It was history that focused on change, on the development of society up to and into the present moment. No doubt Bestor was reflecting to some extent the sway of what was called in the 1950s 'consensus history,' which redressed some of the extremes of revisionist reinterpretations of American history offered by Charles Beard and others in the 1930s, and which put a great emphasis on the ability of the American nation to surmount and negotiate internal conflict. Some, like Hertzberg,[11] have evaluated Bestor sharply, for having an uninformed conception of 'social studies' in the schools and for offering the image of a 'golden age of history in the schools' which, if it ever existed, had been found inadequate by historians fifty years before. Other academics, however, have agreed with Bestor's diagnosis.[12]

It was apparent that Bestor clearly found social studies and the entire development of progressive education two interbred aspects of the same regrettable epigenetic process. But it was also true, on narrower grounds, that social studies *had* risen to prominence, following 1916, and *was* widely found wanting by the 1950s. The question of history versus the other social studies—the possibility that 1916 represented a seventy-year-long misunderstanding, an attempt to blend incompatible elements—would recur in the 1980s. In the meantime, the New Social Studies, in the 1960s, reinforced the importance of the disciplines, but in quite a different spirit from Bestor's.

First, however, on the matter of the importance of disciplines and what a 'disciplinary' approach implies (for example, the question of whether a disciplinary approach implies traditionality of subject), there was, in 1962, an attempt to examine some of Bestor's issues and concerns, before the New Social Studies was well under way.

5.2   Turning Toward the Disciplines

The 1962 study, *The Social Studies and the Social Sciences*,[13] jointly sponsored by the NCSS and the American Council of Learned Societies, was not only an examination of some of the issues raised by Bestor but, in effect, a progress report on the promise of the social science disciplines that was so clearly evident in Beard's 1932 *Charter* and in several individual volumes from that AHA commission.

For anyone in the disciplines or interested in the history of the social sciences, the ACLS-NCSS 1962 volume seems a significant and revealing work. The judgments of what, within the fields, is promising, what fundamental, and what marginal or obsolete have in most cases proven accurate. The level of writing and argument is good. All the disciplines are represented, and there are additional chapters of timely interest, for example, "Teaching about Russia and Eastern Europe."

In organizing the volume by disciplinary chapters, the report implicitly responds to Bestor's 1953 charge (though Bestor is never mentioned) that the history/social sciences balance in the schools is wrong. However, there is a tendency throughout the volume to go even beyond disciplines: for example, Bernard Berelson, the distinguished sociologist and foundation consultant who wrote the introductory chapter, says that in the social studies* curriculum, there are four "major segments": world areas (history, geography, cultures), American history and government, political economy (economics, economic geography, governmental relations to the economy), and the behavioral sciences (anthropology, sociology, psychology).† These four, Berelson says, could be assembled in a number of useful, rational ways—into affinity groupings (as his categorization suggests), into interwoven strands, into relationships where one field provides the examples and case material for all the others, and so on. The position here is clearly that social studies are not the separate social science disciplines simplified. Most of the disciplinary authors comment, in one way or another, that in their own fields the school curriculum tries to cover everything, and inevitably fails. The solution is not to revert to one or two subjectmatters, but to select intelligently from a huge range of topics and concepts.

---

*By using the term without comment, Berelson and colleagues shifted the argument away from Bestor's frame of reference.

†Berelson is generally credited with inventing the term 'behavioral science' in the early 1950s, in a planning study for the Ford Foundation.

The historian of the volume, Joseph Strayer, states goals far removed from those of Bestor.

> The teacher of social studies is supposed to draw on all human experience in order to acquaint his pupils with all aspects of human behavior and all forms of social organization. . . . Every human activity is carried on in society. . . . The student is to learn about widely varying systems of belief and patterns of organization. . . . To see how beliefs and institutions interact. . . . To get some idea of the complexity of human society and the widely divergent responses to similar social problems . . . . The broader the vicarious experience gained through social studies, the better prepared the student will be to make intelligent choices later in life. (pp. 22–23)

Here Strayer is admitting that social studies cannot do everything, but is still arguing that the *direction* and nature of the attempt is correct. (All of his desiderata, by the way, apply to history as an integral part of the social studies.) He does hold a special place for history, to give context to the "real situations that students will face," but says that historians must not attempt to do everything through their own subjectmatter; world history, for example, has been badly overloaded with "vast amounts of factual data." History courses will be interesting "if they keep the story in history, if they deal with a limited number of concrete problems, and if they give the student a feeling that understanding these problems is not impossibly difficult." Strayer thus writes as a traditional, rather than a revisionist or analytic, historian.

The book, in and of itself, is a brief for academic, discipline-based but not discipline-bounded, approaches to the curriculum. There were, however, two problems. The ACLS-NCSS report, curiously enough, shows no awareness of the complex, convoluted, and controversial history of social studies, and little knowledge about the schools. The idea that there is more than one 'track' in high school is never broached. Berelson notes that high school graduates take, on the average, about two-and-a-half social studies courses, and then makes the hopeful statement: "The fact remains that, given other claims for attention, the social studies curriculum can at most be allocated a course a year for all high school students and will probably have to do with less" (p. 14). For his part, Lewis Paul Todd, an officer of the NCSS, observes that the "social studies should and must command a *larger* amount of time . . . it is utterly unrealistic to assign the social studies to a marginal place in the curriculum and then to expect them to carry a large share of the burden of educating the whole man and the alert and intelligent citizen" (pp. 299–300, emphasis added). Both writers seem to be obliquely addressing the issue of the share of the curriculum—probably acutely aware of the movement, at the time, to improve math and science education and increase foreign language. Otherwise, the 1962 volume does not address the 'share' for social studies, nor does it give any attention to a sequence or ideal balance of courses. Probably because of this decoupling of substantive material in the book from questions of realization in the schools, and also because the book was not made known widely in the school community, it received very little attention there.

The second problem is that the book waffled on the crucial question of whether the social studies were aimed primarily at intellectual achievement or at preparation for or mastery of citizenship. Todd quotes from an NCSS statement, which puts one point of view very neatly: "The fundamental premise upon which democracy rests is the presumption that men and women can be taught to think for themselves and to measure the right and wrong of the actions against freely accepted standards of conduct." Virtually all the contributors endorse 'thinking for oneself,' in one form or another, but only some relate this ability to the survival or the improvement of democracy. In fact, there is polarized disagreement. Ben Lewis, the economist, wrote: "An economics designed to produce the economic understanding required for responsible citizenship will do nicely across the board." But Gresham M. Sykes[*] wrote that disciplinary learning cannot be a means to an end: "The spirit of free inquiry and objectivity is the foundation of sociology, just as it is the foundation of all other liberal arts and sciences; and it cannot help but be undermined if the study of sociology is curbed or channeled by the demands of an ideology, even a democratic one." Berelson, noting such disagreement, rose Olympian above it, on behalf of all concerned: "My own impression is that this is largely a spurious issue that will go away if it is put in a different frame. As a starter, suppose we were to say that we—all of us involved—want to give high school students the best introduction we can, within limits of practicality, to the best available knowledge from the social science disciplines *as a means to the end* of producing responsible citizens" (pp. 6–7). Berelson, using language at once cajoling and minatory (and rebuking Sykes, it appears), solved nothing: the issue did not go away.

The New Social Studies, which got under way about the time of the ACLS-NCSS volume, reflected its time and provenance in that it focused on essentially intellectual goals and on the curriculum, though in a fashion fundamentally different from that of other thinking of the time. The NSS concerned itself with pedagogy only to the extent that a new style of 'delivery of the curriculum' was implied. It assumed that a federated social studies was the reality, and did not worry about what balance among disciplines should be achieved. Nor did it worry about citizenship, or any other superordinate goal in schooling.[†] Nor did it, fundamentally, concern itself with what kind of 'coverage of knowledge' the schools should attempt. That is, although inevitably the NSS, in developing materials, worked out a partial scope and sequence, this was not in the spirit of ruling on what subjects must be dealt with (as opposed to what could be optional)

---

[*]Perhaps invoking an eponymous Gresham's Law.

[†]Of course, some of those involved in the movement laid particular stress on certain aspects, for example, 'higher order thinking'; some of these emphases, not always compatible with each other, are touched on in what follows.

in the schools, what knowledge 'the modern age' demanded, or what aspects of intellective process should be reserved to higher education. Previously, national commissions and professional study groups had started there, or had taken such a review into account. In this respect, the New Social Studies was unique.

5.3   The New Social Studies

Even before this movement of curriculum reform began, soon after 1960, there was already recognition in part of the social studies community that these subjects lacked analytical depth. This recognition was stimulated not only by critics of the 1950s but also by an awareness of the New Math movement, which sought to change the teaching of mathematics from the learning of rules and routines to a more conceptually based approach. In the 1950s, Lawrence Senesh, at Purdue University, developed an elementary grades curriculum that put economics, rather than history, at the center, relating materials from other fields (including much history) to economic concepts and terminology, all within a general expanding-horizons framework. Edwin Fenton and colleagues at the Carnegie Institute of Technology began to work out an approach to history teaching that would break into a traditional chronological pattern by looking in some depth at the structural aspects of a period or topic or set of events, from a generalizing rather than a particularizing point of view—that is, making a kind of synchronic cut into a diachronic structure. (Fenton also reintroduced the source documents approach to school history.) The High School Geography Project began, about 1960, as an alliance between disciplinary scholars, teachers, and private interests such as the National Geographic Society, all aimed at deepening the comprehension of geography beyond mere place-name learning coincident with history.*

The curriculum reform era of which the New Social Studies was a part, however, is considered to have begun with the Woods Hole conference of 1959. That conference was devoted to the challenge of improving precollegiate science education, was clearly a reaction to Sputnik and critics such as Admiral Rickover, was funded by a range of federal agencies (including the military agencies) and private foundations, and was somewhat dominated by Harvard and M.I.T. scientific figures. Harvard's Jerome Bruner was selected to write the conference report, *The Process of Education*,[15] which is perhaps the most

---

*The dates of publication of NSS materials are some years later than the inception of the projects to which they relate. The term "New Social Studies" was first used some years into the movement by Fenton and Good as an indicator of an ongoing process, not as a manifesto term. Midstream assessments were provided by Fenton, who focused on the transition from curriculum revision by experts to the development of materials and the need for teacher training, and by Morrissett, whose report of a large conference of disciplinary specialists, curriculum experts, teachers, and outsiders such as philosophers of science forms a fascinating slice of intellectual history. A good summary history of the movement is provided by Haas.[14]

influential prescriptive, that is, deliberately reforming, volume in the history of curriculum in this country.*

Bruner was a pivotal figure for the curriculum reform movement as a whole and for the New Social Studies. In the latter frame of reference, he was a Harvard psychologist, an expert on cognitive child development, a proponent of Piagetian and other continental influences just then beginning in academic psychology, a progenitor of a new, semi-naturalistic, semi-experimental, approach to the study of mental structures and processes, and a founder of the Harvard Center for Cognitive Studies, the first such center, in the early 1960s. He was knowledgeable about linguistics, also then beginning an important revolution that was deeply cognitive in nature. At Harvard he had strong ties to both the arts and sciences departments and the School of Education, whose research faculty was first rate. He was a cultivated person, well versed in European humanistic scholarship; and he was an excellent writer. All of this meant that he had stature in the social sciences and social studies, not excluding the world of education, and that his book received rapid and appreciative recognition in academic circles generally (not just in the sciences) and in the media that reported on such circles and on education.†

The selection of Bruner was fortunate in another respect. Some of the physicists at Woods Hole had overtly called for the development of 'teacher-proof' material, on the assumption that science teachers currently in the schools would not be able to master the new approaches. Though Bruner later charged himself and his colleagues with a certain naiveté about the need for cooperation with, rather than cooptation of, teachers, he and educational psychologists never made quite this mistake.

It is on the social sciences and related research that we focus here. The sustained attention to intellectual *process*, to learning and inquiry as shapely, describable procedures, was the first such since the days of progressive education's lab schools. Piaget had provided a description of developmental-cognitive 'stages' in children that could be seen in terms of mentalistic 'structures' of increasingly logical form, and mental 'operations' that permitted specific kinds of thinking. The claim was, not that age and internal processes of development alone brought such structures into being in the mind (since exposure to the cognitive environment was of course necessary), but that all children passed through this development of stages in an invariant sequence. Although this had obvious relevance to educators of the young and had an immediate impact on

---

*That is, in terms of the rapidity and visibility of the response. The more philosophical works of Dewey and others took decades to reach their audiences, and educational implementation proceeded slowly, though broadly. The works of such critics of education as Bestor or Charles Silberman identified problems without suggesting solutions—at least not that were widely adopted.

†As the 1934 AHA Commission was often called 'the Beard commission,' because Beard wrote the *Charter*, so the Woods Hole movement is sometimes misleadingly attributed to Bruner, who wrote the conference report. Bruner was one of the planners, but only one, of the effort. He took no special role in the New Social Studies.

them, Bruner and others quickly pointed out that Piaget's focus on formal logical mental structures and operations applied best to the comprehension of the mathematico-physical realm, not the comprehension of the social world or of humanistic conceptions.

Moreover, Bruner and many others showed that Piaget effectively ignored the importance of language either as a medium of thought or as a shaper of thought: conceivably, this might not be crucial in the learning of math, but it clearly would be in other areas of instruction. On the linguistic side, beginning about 1957, the influence of Noam Chomsky and transformational generative grammar became widely noted in intellectual circles; for example, it was thought that linguistics was becoming 'scientific,' mostly because it developed a seemingly mathematico-logical model. The generative grammar notion led many, quite superficially, to propose analogies to organized knowledge structures generally: that is, a 'field' had a 'deep structure' (of fundamental conceptions or prime ideas) that generated 'surface structures' visible in a particular historical or sociological or intellectual context; those who had mastered a 'field' worked to elaborate and refine matters at the surface-structure level, doing so through their shared understanding of the deeper 'syntax' of the field. It was irresistible for educators at all levels to talk in terms of how, following the Chomskyian metaphor, intellectual 'performance' in any field must rest on a deeper kind of 'competence.' Once a student had the latter, the former followed; or, to some degree contradictorily, teachers must lead students *through* various 'performances' toward the core of competence.

Additionally, the 'master idea' of the 1960s and 1970s was cognitive structuralism, succeeding behaviorism.[16] Part of this was a renewed interest in an earlier aspect of psychology, the study of categorization and concept formation. Here the central notion was that any concept is 'nested' within a larger, broader concept or category, and is itself superordinate to more particular, limited, partial concepts. Any single 'fact' (object, event, conception) is, at the same time, a *kind* of object, event, or conception. This approach was of course appealing to social studies educators who, for at least fifty years, had preached the need to go beyond 'mere factual learning.' The central notion is not the property of psychology, but is found in Alfred North Whitehead and other modern epistemologists.[17]

Given the mid-century history of social studies, and the intellectual currents of the time, it is not hard to see how the *rational structuralism* of Woods Hole would affect the social studies, or how Bruner's famous dictum "Any subject can be taught effectively in some intellectually honest form to any child at any stage of development" would have a hopeful impact. The approach seemed to justify inquiry and discovery methods long advocated in social studies, where a child was seen as behaving to some extent like a scholar in exploring and organizing knowledge, and to support the pedagogical strategy of 'spiraling'—that is, leading students through the same material ever more deeply. At the same time it reassured academicians who balked at 'simplifying' their fields for early instruction, since it was the very 'structure of the disciplines' that was to be taught to learners. It pleased humanistic scholars, who found grubby empiricism distasteful in the social sciences, and reassured physical scientists who had doubted that the social sciences had any 'structure' at all. It sounded rather like Dewey's emphasis on experimental learning, that is, that we learn to think by encountering problems.*

Finally, Bruner pointed out an educationally salient feature of the approach: "Knowing was a canny strategy whereby you could know a great deal about a lot of things while keeping in mind very little."[18] Had historians and humanistic scholars pondered this deeply, they might have had serious qualms (in fact, some did). However, for many, the emphasis on inquiry and discovery was attractive: while most history obviously aims at a rich particularism, it was still possible for students to learn how to uncover and assess evidence—like historians.

By 1965, social studies scholars reviewing recent developments in their field[19] could say: "Most state departments of education have completed or are in the midst of a major revision. . . . All the social science professional organizations in the field have plans and projects for new curricula. . . . [There is] high consensus that new social studies programs should emphasize content from the social sciences, be inquiry centered, utilize social science methodology, and selectively study in depth some eras, areas, or issues." They further conceptualized three 'task-stages': "the clarification of inquiry purposes, the conduct of the inquiry, and the report of the findings. *Elementary* students should be challenged with each of these tasks if they are to approach history, sociology, and anthropology *in a professional way*" (emphases added). A geographer[20] commented: "Children should be exposed to the same kinds of problems that research workers are trying to solve, not to the insignificant questions that are now so common in geography. . . ."

A newspaper description of a Roselle, Indiana, high school reports:[21] "Lake Park (High School) teaches the American Revolution as a revolution†. . . . [The student] will be continually asked to support or refute various opinions by combining historical fact with logical reasoning." The same newspaper account describes an inductive, logical approach to geography and world history. "Each student, or pair of students, is assigned a country, but the outline is disguised so that it is unrecognizable. The student is told only the latitude, longitude, climate, soil, rivers, mountain ranges, and natural resources. From this information he must determine the location of main cities, form a government, decide whether it is an industrial or agricultural state, and who the country will accept or reject foreign aid from. Students are told later what their country is." The former approach may simply be a good example of any form of 'going beyond the facts' in history; the latter is distinctively New Social Studies.

---

*In fact, it was quite different in approach, since Dewey had believed that through everyday interaction with the world one acquired concepts and structures and a motivated curiosity that eventually led, at its most developed, *to* an understanding of the 'structure of disciplines.'

†That is, as an *instance* of a *type* of event in history.

As early as 1962, the California Department of Education had published a new social studies framework consisting of correlated generalizations from geography, history, political science, economics, anthropology, psychology, sociology, and philosophy. Roughly speaking, the 1960s were a period of curriculum design by teams and networks of experts; the 1970s, a period of implementation through the development of materials, often prepared in proto-type with federal funding but published by commercial publishers. When New Social Studies *projects* are spoken of, generally both phases are meant, though the personnel and funding in any one project may have gone through many stages.* The National Science Foundation provided major funding for "Com-paring Political Experiences," the Anthropology Curriculum Study Project, Sociological Resources for the Social Studies (SRSS), "Man: A Course of Study" (MACOS), and the High School Geography Project. The U.S. Office of Education set up curriculum development centers in specific subject areas at universities, as did many private funding sources. A group around Edith West at the University of Minnesota set out to identify the basic 'structure' of all the disciplines, hoping to map them all onto appropriate grade levels (the eventual focus turned out to be anthropology as the armature), and a similar enterprise was undertaken by the well-known curriculum authority in social studies, Hilda Taba, at San Francisco State College. The Social Science Education Consortium was begun in the mid-1960s, headed by an economist, Irving Morrissett.†

5.3.1   THE ANALYTIC STRATEGY

First came model-building, the specification of the concepts of the fields; then was to come the cross-relating of these structures, to fit the realities of grades and course titles (for example, World Cultures, Eastern Hemisphere Studies) and to induce the formation of social science concepts broader than any single disci-pline would permit. (The intention, after all, was never simply to re-create each discipline in its own 'slot' in the precollegiate curriculum.) Disciplinary scholars would lead in the first; curriculum specialists, working with scholars, in the second. Cross-referenced concepts at the subdisciplinary level would lead naturally to cross-disciplinary generalizations, summaries of social knowledge that could be taught toward; they would not be ends in themselves, but ways for students to orient their progress by seeing that different subject matters dealt with similar kinds of phenomena, in similar but still distinct ways. Finally, materials would be developed, and teachers would be trained (either new

*Because of this and because NSS materials tended to take multiple forms—not just texts, but workbooks, displays, films, et al.—bibliographic citation is difficult; also, many of the ancillary materials have been lost. For further information about specific projects, the reader is referred to, for example, Haas, *Era.*

†Unlike the NCSS, a broad professional membership organization, the SSEC was a vehicle for discussion and cooperation on the curriculum between subject experts in the schools and disciplinary scholars, together with interested others. The membership is by election.

teachers or existing ones by means of in-service work) to use these multiplex models of the structure of fields to guide students into and through orderly sequences of 'discovery,' which is to say, inductive learning.

Many historians had difficulty from the beginning in discerning a finite set of concepts in history and a level of cross-disciplinary generalizations to which they could subscribe, except on a trivial level. The historian Edwin Fenton, a prominent contributor to the NSS effort, nevertheless believed that, for history, the point was to give some attention to the structural *properties* of events and situations, that is, through the method known as 'postholing' to tap into a deeper density of evidence, much of it taken from fields other than history, without lodging such structures in the Heraclitean flow of history itself. In Morrissett's judgment[22] historians were not interested in an implicit hierarchy: questions leading to concepts, leading to generalizations, leading to theory. Fenton, Morrissett reported, "denigrated generalizations, found little utility in concepts, and settled on questions as 'the heart of history.'"* The same was true of some political scientists. Turner quotes one as saying, "There remain a substantial number of political scientists who doubt the existence of an underlying unity in human social behavior" (which would permit the comparative-contrastive model across fields).[23]

By contrast, it was inevitable that the contrastive/comparative/correlative programme of the Woods Hole enterprise would put anthropology and, to a lesser extent, sociology at the center of activity. Both of these look at *generic* concepts of human and social life, using a kind of grid of culture-specific or societally significant forms and structures as an organizing template. (Even the very definition of 'culture' or 'society' is loose and relativistic, spanning different realms, historical periods, and kinds of phenomena.) When the NSS set out, as it did, to arrange for students to look at many exemplars of concepts in order to form the concept itself, the distinctively modern and comparative social sciences of anthropology and sociology were entailed. To deal with role, status, class, kinship, ritual, authority, religious or political symbols, and so on, one naturally directs students' attention across a large comparative array. Thus it is not surprising that anthropology came into the curriculum of the schools virtually

---

*Such skepticism toward an intrinsic hierarchy of intellectual procedures would also be appropriate in any of the traditions of social science that descended from various forms of positivism, where 'theory' means, not inductively reached supergeneralizations that summarize established knowledge, but sets of interconnected hypotheses, loosely founded on evidence, that form a provisional structure for *research*, and that are opportunistically revised from time to time on the basis of new evidence. Any structuralist approach to fields of knowledge that maps 'deep' structure onto its various surface manifestations or assumes that the field can be logically specified, to some fairly extreme degree, by a census of its concepts (and methods) has difficulty in explaining the dynamic revision process by which discontinuities and gaps and contradictions are further explored, and the generalizations of a given moment eventually discarded. The static, and in one sense atheoretical nature, of such models is well known. To this day, for example, authorities disagree sharply on whether a 'discipline' is essentially a container of established knowledge useful for the education of new students in a field, or a matrix of *kinds* of questions in relation to *kinds* of methods for research.

for the first time in the NSS era—and even, sometimes, to a large extent as an organizing 'armature,' rather than as a distinct subjectmatter. This was welcomed in some schools. The reason was that schools that aimed at *analytical* forms of learning, rather than *configurational* ones devoted primarily to cultural transmission, could handle external diversity more easily than internal diversity. It may be true that, in David Lowenthal's suggestive phrase, "the past is a foreign country,"[24] in that it is not the here and now, and thus has strangeness built into it. But in another sense the national history, at least, is *not* foreign, but our own—and it is hard to look at it as if it would not matter if it were otherwise, or as if it simply exists to exemplify generic structures. Relativism is an important concept in social studies—but it is easier when relativism begins offshore. The notion that all societies include dominant and subordinate groups, that some roles and statuses are preferred over others, that wars are not always fought for defensive purposes—such lessons come more easily out of anthropology, for example, or comparative sociology than American history, or so many in and out of the schools would argue. All history, some maintain, is unique and *sui generis*—and one's own national history is more unique than others.

This predisposition in the NSS toward the comparative fields was not entirely realized in practice. As is well known, the growing influence of anthropology in the NSS enterprise, and its utilization in the school curriculum, was abruptly slowed by public controversy over the "Man: A Course of Study" project. MACOS dealt with what it means to be human, in both cultural and biological terms. Its materials were rich and dramatic—so much so that they caused distress among parents, who objected to materials that described or referred to infanticide, the abandonment of the elderly, and various seemingly aberrant kinds of group living. To be sure, these traits (and other objectionable ones) were shown in 'exotic' cultures. But some parent and civic groups, far from concluding that 'civilized' cultures were thus a more highly developed form of humanity, complained that that lesson was not being put directly enough, that MACOS was some kind of brief for 'secular humanism' and relativism of values. The controversy, aired in Congress as well as in school districts, had serious negative consequences, not only in education but on the budgets for curriculum work and for social science itself at the National Science Foundation.*

In the first phase of the NSS, the orderly decomposition of social science fields into their constituent concepts and the analysis of each field's hierarchy of concepts (to the extent that such appeared) proceeded, as did the marshalling of such into cross-disciplinary generalizations. This was largely a deductive enterprise. The disciplines were mapped, as for example in 'fundamental ideas' charts such as those shown here for economics and sociology.[26] For their part, curriculum experts recombined the elements into cross-disciplinary generalizations. For example, to cite one set of corresponding concepts across fields, taken from a school's teachers' guide of the time:

*Contrary to what some believe, MACOS materials have continued to this day to be rather widely used and admired in some school districts.[25]

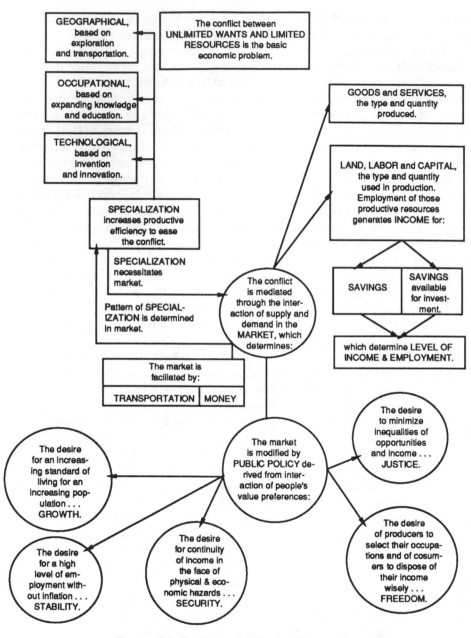

FIGURE 5-1 Fundamental Ideas of Economics

SOURCE: Lawrence Senesh, "Organizing a Curriculum Around Social Science Concepts," in Irving Morrisett, ed., *Concepts and Structures in the New Social Science Curricula* (West Lafayette, IN: Social Science Education Consortium, 1966), 25.

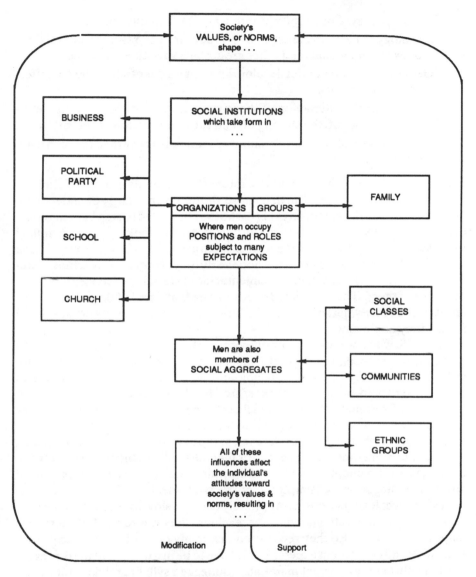

FIGURE 5-2 Fundamental Ideas of Sociology

SOURCE: Lawrence Senesh, "Organizing a Curriculum Around Social Science Concepts," in Irving Morrisett, ed., *Concepts and Structures in the New Social Science Curricula* (West Lafayette, IN: Social Science Education Consortium, 1966), 31.

Anthropology: Community groups adapt to their environment.

Sociology: The characteristics of a group are the result of interactions between individuals and other groups in a specific environment.

Geography: Communities develop different modes of adaptation to different environments.

Economics: the interaction of the various cultures within a group determines the use of, the sharing of, and the conservation of resources.

History-Political Science: Community groups are governed through leadership authority.

In any scholarly field, the attempt to capture the essentials in a tight definition or a structural 'map' is useful, in that it tests the depth and clarity of understanding of that field on the part of an expert, who may be forced to step back and view the field as if from afar. But the ordinary reader looking at such linked propositions as those above is likely to see them as useful, at best, as a way station *toward* a syllabus for teaching—and hopelessly inappropriate as teaching materials themselves. The charts of fundamental ideas are maps of concepts, not expositions of them. The 'correlated concepts' are bland and of doubtful validity, and it is hard to see what sort of meaningful generalization—in any propositional form—they might amount to.

The NSS, which was not a centrally coordinated effort, did not find it easy to move on to the second phase—of marshaling such analyses of 'content' into inductive, discovery-oriented teaching and learning. Summer institutes of teachers were held, but they were expensive, hard to staff, selective, and limited in whom they reached. Worse, the teachers found themselves learning, not how to use these taxonomies and models, but the models themselves. It was as if the analysts forgot what the models were for, as those who teach medical diagnosis, for example, sometimes fail to get across that the medical student is supposed to use diagnostic taxonomies as a universe within which to work out steps toward differential diagnosis, not simply memorize the table.

NSS project leaders were, appropriately enough, slow to commit themselves to developing elaborate materials for teaching; they wanted to field-test such materials first, and also they recognized that many others besides disciplinary specialists and curriculum experts would have to be involved. But hard-pressed teachers always crave actual materials; bootlegged syllabi and denatured versions of summer institute notes soon reached the field, some of them offering nothing much more sophisticated than the cross-field truisms illustrated above. Some teachers had heard that the new materials were intended to be 'teacher-proof,' and were prepared to be skeptical. Others had been oversold on their promise. Whatever their expectations, they were unimpressed. An experienced teacher, shown some of the early products of the NSS, probably would have said: It's always easy to set down goals and objectives—but how do I make a lesson plan to reach them?

5.3.2   THE SCHOOLS AT ARM'S LENGTH

It would be misleading to suggest that examples such as that above were typical, or that premature and partial dissemination of partly formed thinking was the root of the problem. The best of the NSS projects produced valid, superbly interesting materials, and they have had a long, if subterranean, effect.* But it took a decade for most materials to appear, by which time an emphasis in the schools on 'relevance' and the direct study of current issues and problems made them seem obsolete. More important, since materials and texts alone could never have altered the educational process in the classroom, only a tiny proportion of teachers ever were able to receive a just orientation toward the basic spirit and purposes of the NSS.

According to the 1977 NSF study of the field[27] and to other observers, most teachers and curriculum experts in the schools were aware of the movement, but few of the materials were ever used and some of them were abandoned quite quickly. The number of social studies teachers who participated to any significant degree in in-service education aimed at using the new materials was very small, on the order of 5 percent. Specialized studies focusing on one field or grade level produced some revealing patterns. For example, in a study of the adoption of *Inquiries in Sociology*,[28] it was found that teachers with strong sociology backgrounds (or majors) did not adopt the new material to any greater extent than nonspecialists. In fact, there seemed to be a disciplinary resistance. The author wrote:

> This structuring of the content and teaching activities, while perhaps appealing to those with little preparation in sociology, might be less appealing to those well prepared in the subject . . . [who] might indeed see himself or herself as a sociologist and as quite capable of structuring the discipline and preparing his or her own course outline. . . . The rejecters [of the SRSS material] stated that they felt locked in by the course . . . that there was little opportunity for the teacher to deviate. Adopters, however, generally reported that the structure provided by the SRSS course was quite helpful, *especially the first time through the material* [emphasis added].

Marker[29] offers a thoughtful analysis of, not simply the NSS 'inquiry materials,' but a larger issue in the sociology of education. He points out that, not only were NSS materials adopted because teachers crave new and interesting innovations, but they were dropped because they became familiar, and no longer challenging. In addition, the materials were never seen as appropriate to all teachers, with a wide range of abilities and interests. Teachers reported that the

---

*A number of commercial texts emulated aspects of the NSS movement, especially in end-of-chapter analytic questions, tables of related concepts, and the like. This influence is discernible today.

materials were, for their students, more 'complex' but no more interesting (though not less). He emphasizes the problem that achievement tests were not developed for the materials, and that this militated against widespread or sustained teacher adoption. There were comments like "How do you test thinking skills?" or "I knew the stuff was working but I just couldn't prove it."

Many adoptions in schools ceased when the particular teacher left or took on other courses. Some teachers felt that they 'owned' certain courses, and had invested great effort into designing those courses in their own way; they were not eager to try something new. Some teachers found themselves using the materials in inappropriate ways: leaving out the charts and graphs (the structural core of the material) and instead preparing ditto sheets of verbal definitions and terms, thus truncating any 'inquiry' process and providing sets of facts to be learned by rote. None of these responses are distinctive to the NSS materials; they describe a more general pattern in schools—of advocacy, adoption, and revision to the tried and true. However, in concluding, Marker points (without hard data) to what may have been the crucial problem: the students, by and large, never quite 'got the point,' and thus remained uninvolved. "Students rather than administrators and other teachers control one of the most powerful incentives. Teachers really care about their students and want them to be interested in what is being taught."*

5.3.3.   TWO CULTURES

In retrospect, the problems lay deeper than failure of implementation or outreach, or the gap between university scholars and the schools. There was a want of ecological validity in the movement, with respect to both the disciplines themselves and the schools. As for the former, many social scientists were bothered by the presentation of disciplines as fixed structures. They were also doubtful that the presentation of a discipline's internal structure was useful for teaching: at the university level, for example, this kind of meta-analysis is reserved for majors or even graduate students, in Systems courses or Theories of the Field seminars. As David Elkind[30] has observed, "An integrating principle is conceptually simple and integrating only to the expert, not the novice." In other words, definitions come at the end of inquiry, not a priori.

---

*If student lack of interest is in fact a key reason why the NSS failed in the schools, the problem, of course, may not be entirely in the approach or the materials but could be that previous learning experience had turned students away from an appreciation of such learning. This is not to say that 'traditional' methods had dulled native wit, but simply that the cognitive expectations and classroom norms were oriented elsewhere. Many, of course, have found students quite unreactive to what seems to adults or curriculum developers intrinsically exciting materials. Much depends on how these materials are used in the classroom, and how the teachers themselves react to them. Another possibility is suggested in Marker's comments on the lack of tests: from the point of view of many students, why should they work hard in new ways to achieve something that will not count for much?

Further, as we have seen, some disciplines lent themselves to concepts and generalizations more easily than others.   In most disciplines in the social sciences, a perfect finished structure is at any moment a chimera. In any event, 'structures' in disciplines are not equivalent to 'structures' in minds. Even more doubtful to some was the idea that learning through 'discovery' should ultimately serve to discover, or perhaps uncover, preexisting intellectual structures, as if they were fixed by nature.*

As for the benefits in the schools, challenges came quickly and cut deep. Newmann[31] said: "Why should a general lay population be taught to perform intellectual operations of a nature preferred uniquely by the academic profession?" The historian Mark Krug[32] objected early on to the quality of the generalizations arrived at.   "An example of a great idea in history, cited by Bruner, 'A nation must trade in order to live' is so broad and so full of fuzzy implications that its value for classroom instruction may prove to be ... useless." Krug pointed out that Crane Brinton had searched, for example, for the defining characteristics of a 'revolution,' across history, and had been unable to find them.

Others pointed out that drawing generalizations can be highly ideological or at least biased: for example, to offer all instances of 'slavery' as if they belong to a single category may reduce to the implication that slavery is part of the condition of every society. Some objected to the apparent assumption that each field has only one structure, while others objected to the idea that because the various fields deal with sociality or humanness they can be taught as an amalgam. Krug pointed to Bruner's naiveté about the sociopolitical, historical world as seen in such remarks as "Man is constantly seeking to bring reason into his world . . . and that he does so with a striking and fully rational humanity" (p. 403). Finally, the idea that students of the social studies should emulate research scholars struck many as condescending and illogical.   Krug (p. 404) cites Christopher Jencks: "The analogy between physics and history is at bottom misleading. The men who really 'do' history are not, after all, historians. They are politicians, generals, diplomats, philosophers. It is these people whom the young need to understand, far more than they need to understand the historians who judge them."

To these often-cited objections I would suggest two more.   Conceptual 'structures' reside in minds—scholars' or students'—as achieved entities.† Not only is there typically an absence in such a representation of developmental detail—as to how such ideas take shape and are revised and constructed through experience (including interpersonal experience mediated, for example, by language)—but there is also an absence of an *epistemic subject*. Such a model, although not necessarily unproductive, is foreign to the educational process.

---

*This doubt of course reflects modern historicist thinking about the construction of knowledge; the position of Dilthey or Herder as opposed to Descartes.

†Or, revealingly, to some, like Popper or Piaget or Vygotsky, may exist in some transpersonal, transhistorical realm beyond any individual life or lives.

Correspondingly, teachers see themselves as origins of a great part of the educational process, as persons who reveal and lead the young through a rich skein of facts and examples and inferences. While the NSS never questioned this, in fact depended upon it, it tended to see the teacher as one who helps students achieve a full grasp of structure, rather than as someone who himself or herself is also always a student, who continually joins in a learning discourse *with* students, one who points and cajoles and directs attention and debates.* If a teacher does not ever fully master knowledge structures, if she does not consider herself the keeper of some fully specified architectural drawing of a field, why should she emphasize leading students toward such a goal?

In summary, the era of the New Social Studies was an exciting but, finally, troubling one—troubling because, fundamentally, it neither succeeded nor failed unequivocally. If it had fully succeeded—after some period of thorough revision of the approach taken by schools of education and the university departments to training teachers, and after several generations of texts and related materials had been tested in use—there is little doubt that a higher level of intellectual rigor, as seen by the disciplines, would have obtained, especially in the 'elective' subjectmatters. Probably the curriculum would have been angled away from central reliance on history, even in the early grades. (The NSS never had as much impact on the middle grades as, potentially, on the elementary and the high school.) Civic education might have become an obsolete goal, at least as something specifically charged to the social studies. The 1916 curriculum pattern would have been a thing of the past (at least in the plans and descriptions of curriculum experts). The 1970s trend toward a cafeterialike display of not very well-structured special courses and units might have been avoided. Such a turning of social studies might or might not have been beneficial for the field.

As it was, the NSS era exacerbated existing tensions between history (and to a lesser extent government) and the other 'social sciences' within the context of social studies. Henceforth, the economists, notably, would make their own separate place in the curriculum through their own professional curriculum-making and direct interaction with schools. The fields of psychology and geography, which in the NSS era showed interesting signs of achieving a greater degree of 'structure' as school subjects, would to some extent lose this sense of progress. Anthropology would recede and become primarily an ingredient in the teaching of World Cultures; and Sociology would tend to revert to a field, in the schools, which was sometimes social science–based but more often a version of Social Problems.

The disciplinary emphasis of the NSS gave a mandarin tone to curriculum reform in this era, which only served to widen the gap between the university and the schools and also deepened the distance between those fundamentally interested in a richly configured factual exposition of subjectmatter and one based on few facts but much analysis. This discrepancy would affect not only

---

*There is of course the kind of teacher who see herself as the *fons et origo* of all knowledge; but she (or he) too is generally not interested in the 'structure of the discipline.'

those within education but parents, who appeared to find much of the NSS movement, insofar as they knew anything about it, rather rarefied (or subversive of cultural givens). Inevitably, also, those students who were actually exposed to NSS-style teaching tended to be the more able students in the 'better' schools, where curriculum experiments seem always to focus.

On the other hand, a number of academics, through observing or participating in the NSS, became professionally involved in the schools for the first time. In addition, the conceptual clarification of the fields and the genuinely interesting cross-relating of material from different bodies of knowledge continued, and continues, to have great promise for teachers (if not unequivocally for most students). The NSS probably improved textbooks generally, though it seems to have had little effect on methodology texts in teacher education. The level of factual accuracy and methodological sophistication increased noticeably beginning in the late 1960s, according to many.

The NSS was an attempt—and was perceived thus—to raise academic standards of social studies. This was important in an era when there still remained a residual form of progressive education whose main wisdom was 'wait until the children are ready,' and when there had also been ten years or more of ideological attacks, from left and right, on the whole social studies enterprise. While the NSS proved, dramatically, that curriculum revolutions in the schools cannot be accomplished simply by means of new syllabi, it is likely that some teachers today feel that their exposure to developments in this era, when they were entering teaching, was the most important influence on their work—and feel lucky to have had it. Moreover, some states, through participating in systematic reexaminations of their curricula in order to respond to the NSS, inevitably clarified their purposes and procedures in ways that benefited their systems.

One other legacy of the New Social Studies appears to have been the systematizing of 'analytical' approaches to the study of personal and social values in the social studies curriculum. Much of this work was under way before Woods Hole, but the spirit of such projects as the Public Issues Series by Newmann and Oliver[33] or the work on *Decision-Making in a Democracy* by Shaver and colleagues at Utah State University[34] was congenial with that of the more discipline-oriented work. Indeed, these projects drew admirably on a broad comparative framework of evidence and on canons of philosophical logic in the broad context of a deeper approach to civics (see section 6.3). Some view these approaches—values clarification, and the analytical study *of* values—as an essential part of the New Social Studies: certainly they prospered at the same time.*

*Adding to the statement cited by Turner, see p. 134 above, the political scientist who rejected the idea of important commonalities in the study of social life across disciplines, observed: "[Many] political scientists ... are more inclined to hold with the view of Oliver, that central to the political process are a set of values designed to maximize individual choice and to facilitate personal fulfillment." This commentator was saying that values should be studied directly, not overlooked within generalizations.

Not for the first time, in this study of the history of the social studies, we can observe something like geological strata at the end of an epoch of change. By the mid-1970s, the NSS had receded but had left much behind. The modified 1916 pattern reemerged, without much active effort on anyone's part, as if it were the natural topography of the field. Some of the stresses and strains—history versus 'the allied subjects,' teaching for facts versus teaching for understanding, inculcating civic virtue versus value clarification—were, if anything, worse. At the level of educational philosophy there was a kind of benign but not very convincing détente; at the level of the teachers' own work, and perhaps in the consciousness of students in social studies, there was unclarity about goals and, even more important, a confusion about what is legitimate, and how many ways are acceptable, in the classroom.

5.4   Social Studies in One School: 1950 to 1986

With this treatment of the era and character of the New Social Studies, we are now in a position to trace part of the evolution of the social studies curriculum, doubling back to about 1950 and carrying the analysis up to the present. We can do this in satisfactory detail in a particular high school, but only in an unusual high school—New Trier High School in Winnetka, Illinois, an unusually fine school distinguished since the earliest decade of this century for the quality of its program, including history and then social studies.* By also referring to table 4-2, which shows the Social Studies curriculum of a similar school in earlier years, the reader can get some sense of trends in (and the stability of) the curriculum over a one-hundred-year period—representative, at least to a degree, of large 'academic' high schools in the Midwest.

Winnetka, an affluent suburb of Chicago, has a largely academically oriented school population and a solidly middle-class, even professional-class, constituency. The New Trier high school draws from all Winnetka plus several neighboring townships. In 1966 a second large high school, New Trier West, was opened to accommodate the sharply rising high school population (see figure 4-1); it closed in 1981, when enrollments declined. This second high school was equal in educational quality, in its academic course at least, to the older school, and if anything was more venturesome, offering even more, and more specialized, courses. In the analysis that follows we deal only, for the sake of comparability, with the original school.

---

*As mentioned earlier (section 4.0.1), almost no school district can provide year-by-year detail of courses, sections, content descriptions, statements of goals and purposes, and the like, over time. Thus we are deeply indebted to school officials in this system for their cooperation. I thank James F. Marran and Lucia Dunn, of the New Trier Township High School, for their help in making this curriculum material available. Winnetka has been a cynosure among school districts at least since the days of Carleton Washburne, who in the 1920s took seriously a project of working out with his teachers exactly what content was required, grade by grade, for social studies.[35] As Mary Hepburn has pointed out,[36] in some respects Washburne anticipated the recent project of E. D. Hirsch, Jr., in listing concepts, facts, and names that a well-educated high-school student should possess.

Table 5-1 Social Studies Offerings at New Trier High School, Winnetka, Illinois[*]

Grade level	1950–51	1967–68	1973–74	1981–82	1986–87
NINTH	History Community Civics	World History to 1600 World History Survey Civics	World History	World History (Formation of the Western Tradition) World History (and Literature) World Cultures U.S. Politics and Government	World History (Formation of the Western Tradition) World History (and Literature) World Cultures Comparative Political Cultures
TENTH	Ancient/Medieval History Geography	Modern World History Geography	Geography Introduction to Behavioral Science –Modern History –Study of Africa –Modern Africa –Role of Women in History	Geography Introduction to Behavioral Science Urban Studies Modern History –Popular Culture –Study of Africa	World Geography Introduction to Behavioral Science Modern History –Popular Culture –Urban Studies
ELEVENTH	U.S. History English/Modern History –Latin-American History	U.S. History –British History –Asian Studies –Political Science –Russian History	U.S. History –English History –Russian History –Political Science –Sociology –Economics –Geography of Africa-Asia –Far Eastern History –Latin American History –World Conflict and Change	U.S. History American Studies –British History –Russian History –Politics and Government –Sociology –Economics –Modern China –Anthropology –Crime and Justice –International Relations: Areas of Conflict –Future Alternatives –Psychology –Theories of Personality –Internship in Local Government –Independent Study	U.S. History American Studies Internship in Local Government –British History –Russian History –Political Science –Sociology –Economics –Modern China –Anthropology –International Relations: Areas of Conflict –Psychology –Theories of Personality –Independent Study
TWELFTH	Latin-American History –Far East History –Civics –Economics –Sociology	Seminar in U.S. History –Independent Study Seminar	Seminar in U.S. History Advanced Modern European History –English History Seminar –Twentieth-Century United States –Twentieth-Century World	Advanced Modern History Advanced U.S. History Twentieth-Century Issues	Advanced Modern History Advanced U.S. History Twentieth-Century Issues –Crime and Justice

[*]For a similar longterm comparison in an Illinois public-school system, see table 4-2. Courses listed below the solid line could be taken at that grade level or *in later years.* Courses indented, with – preceding, were one-semester courses; if not so listed, they were year courses.

145

A glance at table 5-1 shows an experienced analyst that this has been an academically distinguished, middle-to-large-sized high school in an economically favored community. From the point of view of the social studies curriculum, there are certain distinctive characteristics persisting over time. Civics is present only minimally, even in the early period, and nothing resembling a grade-12 Problems of Democracy course is ever seen. The role of Government or Political Science is relatively modest. Geography has an unusually high presence throughout, at about grade 10. The panoply of history courses is unusually rich, apparently from the outset having been richer than the 1899 history pattern. Some form of world history has consistently been in the program at grade 9, a not unusual feature in 'good' suburban schools. Electives, specialized one-semester courses, and advanced placement courses occur widely beginning at grade 10, not being reserved for the final year; however, enrollment figures on how many students chose them are not available.

Not apparent in the table is the fact that throughout the entire period the New Trier high school has been 'tracked' *within* the basically academic course. That is, in general, the required and more heavily enrolled courses have several sections, aimed at different interests and abilities—all spelled out in candid exactitude. This should be kept in mind throughout the following discussion, since for the most part we omit references to the less academically demanding sections.

A tracing-through of the details of curriculum change in this period reveals many interesting aspects. In 1950–51 the school offered for grade 9 a *general* History course, a huge survey of 'themes' such as religion, citizenship, development of nations, and the growth of natural science from 5,000 B.C. to the present. The audience for the course is specified: those expecting to attend liberal arts or "Eastern" colleges, or art schools, or aiming to become kindergarten teachers (*sic*). Others might take Community Civics, which consisted of one semester of local-state-national government and one semester of international relations. The 1916 design for 'community' civics was not reflected in the course description. Grades 10 and 11 show the persistence of the 1899 history pattern in a relatively pure form—that is, without 'Western Civilization.' The presence of Latin American History at grades 11 and 12 is probably not a reflection of interest at the time in area studies but is, rather, for those concentrating in Commerce or Spanish. Far East History, however, is academic in focus.

Civics at grade 12 is a more sophisticated version of the structure of government, with some 'problems and activities' but without international relations. Sociology is social problems, as close as New Trier comes (not very close) to a Problems of Democracy course. Economics is a curious blend of 'principles' with emphasis on the consumer, money and banking, problems of the farmer and of labor, and "prospects of economic planning and evaluation of sources of information." This appears to combine some of the elements of community civics with concerns of the times, and fulfills an Illinois graduation requirement in consumer education. Finally, Geography is built on the study of climate, and can be seen as a transition between the older physical and the newer human geography.

The New Trier curriculum remained stable for ten or more years after 1950–51. In the mid-1960s, the history pattern shifted to a year of Modern History, now quite overtly Western Civilization, with British History becoming a grade 11 or 12 half-year elective, of a status comparable to that of Far East History.

By the later 1960s, considerable change is apparent, first of all in purpose and philosophy. The earlier New Trier statement of goals for social studies simply listed "an appreciation and understanding of the history of the United States; an explanation of the privileges, duties, and responsibilities of citizenship; a broader and deeper understanding of the roots and growth of Western culture; and an awareness and sensitivity to other cultures in the world." Now, an elaborate explanation is given: "the social sciences [*sic*] are in search of patterns which reflect the human experience.... The Social Studies [*sic*] have been developed to raise questions ... not provide [the student] with solutions ... [but lead] the student on to the questioning which must be the work of his life.... During his studies the student will be directed in the use of primary and secondary source materials, techniques for reading, evaluating, and interpreting ... critical thinking, independent study, and oral and written expression." We see here much of the rhetoric of the New Social Studies, but in its intellectual inquiry aspect rather than its analytical, logic-of-the-disciplines aspect. In fact, a sharp distinction is made between social science and social studies, not along the lines of Wesley's dictum, but reflecting a dual attitude that would have seemed reasonable both to John Dewey, in his concern for reflective inquiry, and the Harvard 1945 report, in its premium on sophisticated intellectual skills.

This statement of mission remains, virtually unaltered in tone though reduced in verbiage, in the New Trier curriculum up to the present. New Trier never adopted an extreme logic-of-the-disciplines approach, but the curriculum as a whole came closer and closer over the years to a college-level, liberal arts, social science array—that is, never emphasizing scientific methodology as such, but offering detailed surveys of the disciplines, comparable to college-level introductory courses, together with an extraordinary variety of history. This is not, of course, the only example of an 'academic' social science content married to a reflective inquiry, independent-thinking rationale. (Nor are the two approaches necessarily antithetical.) It does show how teachers can adopt a basically higher-education slant on content while espousing a distinctly secondary-education philosophical goal. Note also that if citizenship education is implied at all, it is contained within the concepts of curiosity, inquiry, and sensitivity. ("Social studies develop in students a curiosity about and sensitivity to the environment in which they live.")

In 1967–68, New Trier continues its commitment to World History in grade 9 (Civics being downplayed, and Geography being lodged at 10), but now ancient plus medieval has become stretched to World History to 1600. For the less history-minded, but still academic, student the World History Survey offers a rather more anthropological slant, including technological development and a sampling of "religious and social institutions among significant and representative societies of the world's people." Civics remains largely devoid of content other than government and political institutions.

At grade 10, Modern World History has an emphasis on the "cultural, industrial, and philosophical revolutions [of] the world since the seventeenth century." By now, in grades 9 and 10, the 1899 pattern and a brief 1950s fling with Western Civilization have been retired in favor of a fairly thematic broader world focus. (This is in contradistinction to the grade 11 U.S. history approach, which is specifically "narrative and chronological.") Geography as a human science appears for the first time: instead of the focus on climate of 1950–51, the core of the course is now settlement geography, emphasizing cities and urban regions.

Russian History is history; Asian Studies is cultural anthropology. Political Science, interestingly, has become a more detailed version of governmental institutions and processes, but with considerable political theory—principles of democracy; Locke, Rousseau, J. S. Mill, even Cicero; and "precedent-establishing decisions of the U.S. Supreme Court." There is not much sign, if any, of the behavioral trend in university political science of the decade. Independent study is tutorial; topics might range from medieval history to regional planning. The U.S. History seminar (grade 12) is group discussion together with "research"— apparently a counterpoise to the narrative organization of the grade 11 course.

By 1973–74 the program has grown in size and variety. A New Social Studies approach appears clearly in World History at grade 9: it is multidisciplinary and thematic, revolving around the "interaction between human nature and the physical and social world," western and nonwestern, from early man to modern times. The texts are World History texts, apparently chronological in organization. But the framework is analytic—"to show that there are basic needs which all human beings seek to satisfy... to understand the *concepts* of space and time [and] change and continuity ... to *synthesize elements* to form a structure not clearly seen before, to organize and re-organize ideas and statements ... to determine the relationship between factual knowledge and generalizations" (emphasis added)—and includes numerous other issues customarily addressed in graduate seminars. There is also a World History–English variant, with double credit, involving the correlative reading of world literature, and the "interaction, conflict, and diffusion of cultural ideas." Although this is a course for freshmen, the student must have not only the "highest reading skills" but also "some experience in researching, organizing, and writing expository material." The basic reading list is heavily contemporary: William Golding, Pearl Buck, T. H. White, Herman Hesse, James Michener—along with the Bible, Homer, and Shakespeare.

Grade 10 Geography too is more analytical and regional/areal, aiming to "provide a basis for understanding the problems and achievements of people living in various types of environments," as well as special attention to the Soviet Union and Japan. Units from the High School Geography Project are used. A less-rigorous section is open to appropriate students. Modern History is still thematic and materially (and intellectually) oriented,* but with more emphasis on the twentieth century and the West than five years earlier. Modern History, like many other courses now, can be taken in grade 10, 11, or even 12.

The newly introduced Introduction to Behavioral Science is a multidisciplinary course: psychology, anthropology, and sociology, using New Social Studies material,[37] as well as more conventional texts, and a book on psychoanalysis. The course is aimed, among other things, at "helping the student to develop a critical attitude toward sweeping generalizations about behavior." Study of Africa is cultural anthropology, history, and geography focused on traditional Africa, with readings from Chinua Achebe, Jomo Kenyatta, and Amos Tutuola as well as books by anthropologists Paul Bohannan and Colin Turnbull. Modern Africa, on the other hand, is directly related to the impact of African culture on U.S. culture, with readings from Melville J. Herskovits, W. E. B. Du Bois, and Frederick Douglass. The course on women in history is not 1980s-style women's history, but is oriented toward the feminist movement, calling for role-playing, sustained debate, and "small group-within-the-group dynamics."[†]

The grade 11 U.S. History course has by now changed, in its 'honors' section, to the New Social Studies interrupted-narrative approach, with Fenton's text[38] being used. The student should "recognize and be able to develop an historical thesis...be conversant with the dominant social and cultural patterns of the U.S. from the colonial period to the present ... [and] be able to explain with some clarity the major trends of national development." Critical and analytic reading skills, the ability to discuss, the ability to write, familiarity with charts, diagrams, maps, graphs, and so forth—all these are the priorities. Accordingly, the more traditional mastery of grade 11 American history is tactfully downgraded: "The student will be exposed to and recognize the names of dominant political leaders ... as they have been *or are* germane" (Whiggish emphasis in the original). There is also, however, another, lesser history section offered, using a conventional chronological text, as well as a tutorial/remedial section, where test achievement is overtly sought.

Political science has swung back to institutions and professional politics, still with little behavioral flavor and now with political theory apparently minimized as well. The reading ranges from Nelson Polsby to Mike Royko's *Boss* (1970). Sociology has altered from a problems-orientation to a basics-of-the-modern-discipline approach, including mass society, culture, power structure, family, and social movements. Economics remains an odd mixture—learning "how to make

---

*That is, away from the strictly political.

†This is one of the two or three (at most) evidences of 1970s 'relevance' impacting upon the curriculum in Winnetka. Such an impact was more evident in other school systems, often in the form of 'minicourses' within traditional or portmanteau titles.

better economic decisions" by reading *Barrons* and *Forbes* and *Newsweek*, and Heilbroner's *The Worldly Philosophers* (1967)."

Geography of Africa-Asia excludes Soviet Asia, and is focused on human-environment interaction, with stress on underdevelopment and population (not from an economic development but from an environmental point of view). Far Eastern History continues to include much geography and cultural anthropology; rather inconsistently, there are 'units' on Chinese communism and Japanese industrialism—all in all, an area studies, rather than a history, approach. Much the same is true of Latin American History. World Conflict and Change is primarily mass movements and broad-scale conflicts, crises, or supranational developments since 1920 (for example, the Common Market, the Third World). There is no text; students write papers (on the "demands and methods of extremists," among other topics). This appears to be a version of a contemporary world politics course.

On the evidence of the 1973–74 sequence, up through grade 11, one could interpret 'traditional' history, both U.S. and world, as having been repudiated. In grade 12, however, there is an advanced placement Modern European History course ("to impart a solid foundation of the chronology and narration of Modern European History"). On the other hand, the U.S. History Seminar is historiographic and uses only monographs by the "most outstanding American historians,"† and the English History Seminar asks for research papers to be written using the Newberry Library on topics confined to one of three 'post-holing' periods. Finally, moving from the sublimely demanding to a far lesser level, Twentieth-Century United States and Twentieth-Century World are current events courses with *Newsweek* as the main source.

Though the New Trier curriculum will continue to alter and diversify in some respects, the change from the mid-1960s to the mid-1970s is by far the most dramatic change in the entire 35-year period.‡ The mid-1970s is also the time of the extreme reach of the analytic form of New Social Studies; a number of the courses would later become more conventional (in secondary school terms), though no less demanding. (The 1960s–1970s change in the curriculum does not of course prove that all teachers altered the day-to-day content of courses or their teaching styles.)

By 1981–82 the World History course at grade 9—always a significant feature of the New Trier program—had again been revised, toward a concentration on those aspects of Western civilization "which furnish our own cultural heritage"; the new course subtitle clearly indicates the alteration. But an alternative is provided: World Cultures (People and their World), which begins with an introduction to the various social sciences and then focuses on selected cultural areas and topics such as architectural history or comparative economic systems.

*Over the entire period at New Trier, economics is the most idiosyncratic of all the familiar electives.
†The syllabus makes it clear that this is a course *beyond* mere advanced placement American history.
‡cf. Hampel's claim, p. 119 of this volume.

In some respects the course resembles the World History Survey course in 1967–68, but it is contemporaneously oriented.

After a decade or more of interruption, the 1981–82 grade-9 curriculum again includes the more nationally typical civics or government course. The New Trier course is a political science course emphasizing, apparently for the first time, political decision-making, including media impact, polling, special interest lobbying, and other noninstitutional, nonstructural factors. (A Civics alternative is provided at grade 9.) This change probably reflects a new national concern with citizenship in the context of schooling that most observers report in the early 1980s.

At grade 10 all courses are now open to any nonfreshman student. The 1973–74 African courses have been replaced by a media-focused semester course in popular culture and a year-long course called Urban Studies, which is a course not in social problems but on the history of urban settlements from Mesopotamia to urban renewal and planning in the United States.* At grade 11 the U.S. History course has been shorn of all New Social Studies inquiry–styled description; in fact, the rhetoric of New Social Studies is now missing from all course descriptions in the entire program. American Studies is a fused English/ social studies course ranging from the influences of Puritanism to the Black experience. The grade-11 one-semester electives are, taken together, less reflective of a comprehensive world history-geography emphasis than in the 1970s. A number of social science courses like Anthropology and Crime and Justice appear, as do two forms of psychology. This trend does not appear to reflect a sudden surge of interest in social science electives; instead, with the second New Trier high school now closed, some of its innovative courses are shifted to the older school. International Relations: Areas of Conflict picks up the 'world conflict and change' format of 1973–74 (grade 10); in this year, it emphasizes ideological and political aspects of the Middle East.

Internship in Local Government, a double-credit course for juniors and seniors, is an opportunity, pioneered by social studies experts in New York State and adopted elsewhere, for students to work in local government offices and agencies for at least twelve hours a week. Participating students also take part in a school-based seminar and write up their experiences. The approach is, in a sense, a more active, participatory form of the 'community civics' interest of 1916, in that it gets at day-to-day, realistic civic operations and functions across a wide variety of sectors and agencies. (It also is said to offer an introduction to public service careers.)

The most recent course pattern at New Trier shows little change from five years previously. The sheer increase in courses, especially electives and specialized courses, that occurred around 1970 and then again around 1980† is not

---

*Yet another example of how 'counts' of course titles may mislead: this course is stated to be "a topical approach to the study of history."
†The latter reflecting an institutional change, in the closing of the second school.

duplicated here; in fact, some courses have precipitated out of the curriculum. The grade-9 political science course, always (with civics) unstable at New Trier, has a comparative political systems emphasis in the second semester (dealing with communism, socialism, fascism—on the face of it, resembling courses taught in the 1950s in many American schools). The grade-10 geography course is described in terms familiar from previous years, and retains a regional geography focus; the word "World" seems to reflect 1980s concerns for the study of America-in-the-world, rather than a world-systems approach. The Psychology course stresses drugs and alcohol, another timely topic.

Reviewing the New Trier program from 1950 to date, one must be struck by several things. First, in terms of its curriculum and other indicators (test scores, college admissions, and so forth) this is a superb high school academically—the kind of school that spoils many students for the first year or two of higher education. Second, the variety of electives and special courses, and the fact that students can take most courses in one of several grades and entire sequences of specialized courses across grade levels, shows how misleading enrollment counts and summaries of the 'modal' curriculum are on a national level.* Third, in any given year the New Trier curriculum is both 'like' and 'unlike' the modal national curriculum of the time, so far as that can be known. Analysts could reasonably point either to the similarity or dissimilarity, depending on the frame of reference. Fourth, and relatedly, this school shows continual small-scale experimentation and adjustment to local circumstances with respect to social studies 'fashions,' never switching abruptly from one pattern to another. This is characteristic of any school district that is at least moderately large and moderately 'good,' academically. At New Trier, over the years, 'world history' was constantly being revised and refocused in its western/nonwestern balance, multidisciplinary versus history balance, and narrative versus topical approach. (The last of these aspects of debate within history was also apparent, over the years, in U.S. History.)

The New Social Studies movement clearly 'took' for a time at New Trier,† but in a particular form organically linked to the enriched academic ethos established in the school in all eras. Finally, the overall growth and differentiation— efflorescence would not be too strong a word—of the course of study over the decades is the result of a confluence of influences: the internal growth of enrollment in Winnetka; the maturing of various disciplines and subdisciplines in the colleges and universities to which its students were headed; the ever-wider content preparation of teachers, including the trend toward academic majors

---

*For example, U.S. History at grade 11 is consonant with national practice, and enlarges that statistic; geography at grade 10 is unlike the national pattern, and thus would tend to disappear in national data; the ability of students to take economics, anthropology, and other social science electives at almost any grade would increase total high school ever-taken figures for these subjectmatters, but would flatten out any grade-by-grade profile of them (see section 2.2.1).

†Even more markedly so in the second high school, whose existence more or less coincided with the NSS era.

and masters degrees; and, perhaps most of all, the steady accretion of what seems to work. In any system of this kind, fewer courses will ever be dropped than added. Parents and siblings of former students expect to find in the high school what used to be there—plus. New Social Studies content persists, though perhaps under quite a different philosophy of teaching. Electives last. Experimental courses like Internship in Local Government become the norm.

With regard to the curriculum today, an observer would conclude that vestiges of the New Social Studies movement remain, to a greater degree than most other places, but primarily within a context of gradual enlargement and upgrading. Correspondingly, a recent reversion to the (modified) 1916 pattern, often seen elsewhere, is far less apparent—to a considerable degree, because that pattern was never the predominant one at New Trier. Looking at New Trier over the past thirty-five years, one might be struck by the variety and quality of the nonhistory social studies—or by the continual presence of an extraordinarily rich history curriculum. One might even be impressed by the existence of both together. It depends on what one is looking for.*

5.4.1   THE FLOWERING OF MINICOURSES

New Trier, of course, is an unusual high school. It happens to be well known in curriculum history and related circles, and happens to have kept primary records. Despite this, it would be wrong to leave any impression that it is unique in terms of the fullness and quality of its program. There are many other high schools in the country of comparable quality.

In Kokomo, Indiana, for example, it is possible to see one clear shift in the curriculum that is not discernible at New Trier. That is the contrast between the heyday of the minicourse in social studies, about the mid-1970s, and the more conventional coursework format that obtains today. Kokomo, in both the 1970s and the 1980s, has encouraged students to do independent study in the social studies, especially those who are college-bound and/or have a particular interest in this broad curriculum area. The philosophy has been that students should have as various and flexible an education as possible. The main difference between the decades is that in the 1970s the high school established a pattern of some dozens of nine-week 'minicourses' (called 'phase electives'). The school worked out a complicated scheme for how each minicourse would be credited (for example, as history, behavioral science, or government, but with many units being inherently interdisciplinary and thus eligible for credit as history *or*

---

*A number of curriculum historians remark, informally, on the curious skimpiness of primary data from the 1960s and 1970s. I think it can be suggested that the very extent and rapidity of curricular change in this era, together with the statistical oddities produced by cross-sectional counts of courses and enrollments referred to above, overloaded the system, so that even fewer records than normal were retained.

government *or* sociology, and so on). Thus, within the guidelines as to number of hours in each branch of the curriculum, graduation or state requirements, and so forth, Kokomo students could assemble an extraordinary range of personally appealing packages of minicourses. The 'courses' had titles such as the following (more or less randomly cited): Tuning In—How We Perceive and Interpret; Until Death—or Divorce—Do Us Part; My Vote Doesn't Count; Politics, a Dirty Business?; Lure of the Wild Wild West; People, the Bull Moose and the Pride of Princeton; the Lion Roars—Emergence of Africa; When Knighthood Was in Flower; The British Empire—The Sun Never Sets. In order to coordinate all this, there was a special social studies resource center and an instructor detailed to it to help the students pursue their independent study.

By contrast, today Kokomo High School still supports independent study, but in a less cafeteria-style fashion. "Any course or appropriate subject in the Social Studies Program may be taken through independent study." The student proposes the topic, gets faculty approval, does research, and writes a paper. She is restricted ordinarily to one independent course a year.

No firm judgment can be made, obviously, about which format was of higher educational quality, or 'better' for students. The 1970s pattern represents the extreme of 'relevance' built into the high school curriculum, together with the natural tendency of any rich curriculum to exfoliate. It is certain (and widely recognized) that the 1970s-style format of minicourses was expensive, very difficult to administer, hard to credit (both for high school graduation and for college entrance). Occasionally it served as a sop to teachers who were bored or troublesome in the system. On the other hand, something is no doubt lost in settling back to a more standard pattern, perhaps especially for the motivated student who does not go on to college, who does not do so immediately after high school,* or who goes on to an undergraduate curriculum that is highly restricted in its freedom during the first year or two so that a student does not encounter 'electives' again for some time. At Kokomo an important aspect of independent study today in social studies is a Sociology and Government Work Study program for upper grade students, which provides for very significant amounts of community involvement.

There have been a few detailed studies of the minicourse trend in the 1970s.[40] Generally speaking, minicourses were most numerous in medium-sized high schools, and in the already most capacious, well-established curriculum areas, principally American history, world history, and government. To some extent, such courses were used to 'solve' longstanding frustrations within established courses—for example, to provide detail on or room for state or local history within U.S. History or depth on the Constitution within Government. It was often convenient for schools to accommodate state coverage requirements in this way. Minicourses, for example, coincided with the marked growing popu-

---

*Nationally, at present, only about half of those entering higher education do so within the year that they finish high school. There is considerable variation in this percentage, as a function of the employment picture in a given year.[39]

larity of law-related education of the period. They were also popular in certain colorful subject areas, like Civil War military history, that might not otherwise find much room in the regular curriculum.

5.5   At the End of the 1970s

Several studies in the 1960s and 1970s, as summarized by Peet,[41] showed limited but interpretable patterns of change. As late as the 1960s the Problems of Democracy course was still strong in the East, with American Government correspondingly weak at grade 12. By contrast, Civics (at grade 9) was far stronger in the South than elsewhere. This is consonant with the idea that the POD course tended to have a marked industrial democracy flavor, while Civics has tended to be more idealized, less subject to local or temporal coloration. Some version of economics (or economics with sociology) showed up in about half the high schools nationally by the early 1960s—prior to any New Social Studies influence. A number of studies showed World History to be offered in nearly as many high schools throughout the 1960s and early 1970s as American History—which is to say, in most of them. (This at a time when World History as an entry-level course in universities was uncommon.)*

A large 1977 survey by Gross[42] combined data from cooperating schools, federal enrollment statistics, and social studies experts. These data showed Civics and POD rapidly dying out, and Economics, Sociology, and Psychology growing in prevalence. Other data show Psychology growing as an elective very rapidly during the 1960s, less rapidly thereafter (figure 13.1). Surprisingly, Gross's data showed American History and World History as offered by only a little more than 50 percent of the junior and senior high schools. Other sources and knowledgeable observers found the former results familiar, but such a drop in history was met with skepticism.

Gross concluded that the modified 1916 social studies curriculum pattern had been "shattered," a conclusion denied by most others. Gross subsequently conceded that there appeared to have been methodological problems, probably having to do with pervasive alteration in course *titles* in the 1970s. For one thing, Gross's data could only have been correct had a very large proportion of schools been violating state laws as to course requirements. The very broadly based, nationally sampled NSF studies published in 1977 and 1978[43] do not show a major drop in U.S. History enrollments or course offerings, but the status of World History remained clouded; again, terminological unclarity is the most likely cause.†

As this writer has suggested, a reasonable interpretation of curriculum

---

*That is, Western Civilization was the more common introductory course, while specialized histories—Far Eastern, African, and so forth—were also increasing in the undergraduate curriculum.
†Most analysts over the decades have found that world history courses were numerous in the schools, but that enrollments were comparatively low.

change in the period 1950 to the present is that (a) a modified 1916 curriculum was characteristic of the public schools in 1950;* (b) the era of the New Social Studies affected the nominal curriculum in *some* schools, possibly a quarter or a third at the highest point of influence, to some limited degree; (c) in the latter part of this period, the growth of the social science disciplines in the university, in teacher training, and in their general profile in society accounts for the increase in specialized elective courses and for an overall broadening of the curriculum in most schools. The apparent reappearance, about 1980, of a modal curriculum that resembles the 1916 pattern does not indicate a deliberate reversion. At certain grade levels, there has been actual continuity since the 1920s (or before), while at others the familiar course may occupy its 'slot' by the narrowest of pluralities. At all periods, the 'modal' curriculum has concealed a great variability; that is as true in the 1980s as it has ever been.

5.6   The Curriculum at Present

Thanks largely to major studies funded in the mid-to-late 1970s that attempted to assess the national status of 'science education' in the schools, a reasonably consistent, well-supported description of the situation of social studies was available by about 1980. The preliminary report of significant change, by Gross, had proven premature. The nature and pattern of social studies was, in 1980, substantially what it had been about 1950; in the meantime, a cycle of tentative reform had come and gone.

The prevalence among educators of expressed concern for and frustration with social studies was also as it had been for about thirty years. Prior to about 1940, though there were many disagreements about what social studies should ideally be (for example, to what extent it could and should deal with current social issues and problems), the dominant tone of internal discussion was frustration at not making more progress faster. From about 1950 on, the dominant tone was that of deadlock and contradiction with regard to basic goals and 'styles' of social studies instruction.

Summarizing one evaluation—the SPAN project (Social Studies Priorities, Practices, and Needs), funded by the NSF and conducted by the SSEC[44]—the authors, all veteran social studies educators, quoted another educator's claim that "social studies today lacks secure moorings, and is wandering in search of focus" (p. 362) and pointed out that there was little new in such a complaint. They wrote: "The need for [reestablishing a sense of identity and direction] is now familiar and self-evident to many of us. It has something to do with disappointment over the new social studies movement, dissatisfaction with and confusion over the back-to-basics movement, frustration over the many de-

---

*With independent schools likely to be following the 1899 history plan.

mands placed on social studies by special interests ... and concern over social studies not being highly valued by parents and students.'"

The SPAN report continued: "While persons both in and out of the profession have maintained that social studies lacks uniformity and predictability, the data analyzed in SPAN indicate that is not true" (p. 365). The SPAN researchers pointed to the unifying effect of the "central tool used to convey ... content— the textbook," showing that between grades 4 and 12 a good 60 percent of class time was spent in direct use of texts, with another 30 percent or so involving other materials; that New Social Studies materials were not widely used; and that teachers were happy with the texts they employed.   Various studies had also shown that most social studies teachers lectured daily and led class discussions— the latter accounting for more minutes of class time (by teacher self-report) than the former."†

A 1979 study is especially revealing, in that it represented an assessment of American practices by non-Americans and compared what is called for in teacher education with what obtains in the classroom.[45] The authors, experienced social studies educators in Australia, had the chance to observe many U.S. classrooms in the course of supervising student teaching in American schools; in addition, they had built up a definite picture of social studies methodology in this country from studying the leading American methods texts. They wrote of their year-long experience as follows: "The image of the social studies in the U.S. which we developed while [in Australia] ... might be summarized as being conceptually based, interdisciplinary (or multidisciplinary) in nature, concerned with values and valuing processes, emphasizing inquiry learning and inductive teaching, as well as being committed to student-centered learning.... We found a considerable 'lack of fit' between our expectations and the classroom practices we observed" (p. 293). Though they found a number of examples of teaching for concepts, they found more emphasis on the "transmission of factual information," accomplished in an expository fashion. "In talking to students ‡ about the range of teaching strategies which they might employ, we noted that they found it *difficult to accept* the idea that they need not be the primary source of information in the classroom" (p. 294, emphasis added).   Coverage of the material was the operational imperative. Finally, though the material presented virtually always touched on values, there was little exploration of this dimension: much exposition, for example, of how a bill is written and passed, no discussion of what might constitute a 'bad bill.'

Of special interest in the Australians' report is what appears to be a certain discrepancy between their conclusions and their own evidence. For example,

'In the last regard, one might argue that the stability of the share of the curriculum enjoyed by social studies—for example, after a decade or more of agitation about the level of science education— implies at least passive approval by parents.

†Most careful observational studies have shown that 'discussion' itself is teacher-dominated. See section 17.3.

‡i.e., education students.

they imply that a New Social Studies orthodoxy is present in social studies methods texts. Yet in their detailed and helpful table summarizing the characteristics of the most-used texts, very sharp divisions appear: between those recommending the structure of the social sciences as the approach, and those holding that the "content of any act of thought is likely to cut across subject matter boundaries"; and among those urging instruction following a hypothetico-deductive pattern, those urging inductive learning in the interest of problem-solving, and those urging reflection on currently salient issues. This illustrates, one can conclude, that the very identification of what officially counts, at a given moment, as 'good social studies' can conceal—by a pluralist rhetoric so familiar as to be no longer perceived—sharply divergent opinions.

A similar picture of historically developed stability—albeit a stability deplored by some outside the system—appeared in a thoughtful and sensitive "interpretive report" (like the SPAN assessment, based on NSF-funded studies) by Shaver, Davis, and Helburn.*[46] These authors pointed out that the NSF studies rested solidly on combined data from three venues: elaborate and well-designed surveys, exhaustive searches of the educational research literature, and a carefully done observational study, using highly trained observers and reliable instruments in eleven school systems around the country. The several NSF approaches converged on a few important realities. Despite some dissatisfaction on their part, teachers were substantially in control of the 'delivery' of social studies in the classroom. Teachers had a strong voice in text adoption. The textbook, once again, was found to be the "dominant tool of instruction—the basis for *recitation discussions* and for student testing."† Texts tended to be 'traditional'; about 50 percent of teachers used only one text. The subjectmatter was largely history and government (with geography at the elementary level); there was little interdisciplinary teaching, little discussion of controversial issue, and few special topics or minicourses. Inquiry teaching was seldom seen. There was a clear assumption that 'book learning' was the mode and the goal, and that external motivation was necessary for learning to proceed: that is, students work for grades, for promotion, for getting ahead in life (not the least, by graduating). One of the overriding concerns of teachers is to socialize students into this motivational 'set,' and this has far-reaching consequences: classes must be orderly, the texts must be seen as things that contain answers, test-taking is part of the game to be learned and shows that the content has in fact been 'covered,' the classroom 'system' will break down if an adequate degree of 'coverage' is not achieved.‡

*A number of commentators have found this to be the best balanced and most cogent of recent overall assessments, which makes it unfortunate that it was never published in full.

†Emphasis added: 'discussion' is often highly controlled. The student testing referred to here means teacher-made tests. The problem with external achievement tests, of course, is that they may *not* reflect what is actually in the texts or, more important, what text-based content is actually 'covered' in the class.

‡The authors did not offer this characterization in a spirit of denunciation. They point out that some of the pattern, at least, "may reflect desirable responses to legitimate societal needs for the socialization of the young."

This should not be a surprise. Higher levels of education show similar patterns of negotiated order, particularly with regard to mastery of material from books, together with proper methods of research and scholarship. There is, one might suggest, precious little 'inquiry' teaching in the first year or two of most college experiences, although clever students learn to signal, appropriately, to the professor that they possess 'critical' faculties, should these be needed. The focus, in higher education, on academic or professional or vocational socialization may, of course, be one reason why educators at higher levels want the *schools* to provide room for critical thinking and reflection.

One disturbing feature that may be peculiar to social studies instruction in the schools, however, is mentioned in passing by Shaver and his colleagues: that some teachers tend to use text-learning punitively—if a student misbehaves, she must read more, or write another report. Those who behave can relax. Many studies of schooling suggest that when socialization toward learning clashes with socialization toward authority, the latter wins out. As Shaver et al. put it: "Socialization is *preemptive*' [emphasis added]. Correcting behavior such as daydreaming or cheating takes precedence over conceptual learning." Part of this description, of course, applies to the school curriculum generally. But these authors point out that there is a difference between science and social studies: most science is elective, or reserved for the best students, and some attention is paid to field-specific mastery such as laboratory techniques or to independent work. That is true only of senior-high-school electives in the social studies, most of which are taught so that "nonacademically inclined students can obtain a passing grade."

Further, unlike science courses, the *cognitive tone* of the required part of the social studies curriculum tends to remain the same across many grade levels: what seems to be demanded, from the students' point of view, is simply systematic 'coverage' of material, with little recognition that the teaching-learning interaction has now moved onto a different plane, where the nature of the discourse might be new or the spirit of the endeavor changed. (This is not simply a question of whether 'inquiry' techniques are evident, but rather of the relationship of the learner to the teacher-delivered material or the teacher.)

The possibility that students may perceive grade 11 in social studies as 'feeling like' grade 8 may quite directly reflect the persistence of socialization toward civic virtue and socialization toward good studentship, at all levels in social studies. Shaver et al. speculate that the relative absence of inquiry teaching or even occasional 'modeling' of inquiry procedures by teachers reflects the fact that they themselves have not been thus educated. (However, there is some evidence in studies of goals and practices that teachers are aware that they 'should' do more than simply cover the material, and feel uneasy about not doing so. See section 17.0.) Teachers do not seem to feel frustrated about failing to confront controversial issues. "They are quite sensitive to the values of the community . . . it appeared that, in fact, such sensitivity was a common criterion, explicit or not, in the hiring of teachers." A major goal, articulated or not, is to "impart the attitudes that will make the students adjusted, participating citizens. . . . All teachers, except the completely disillusioned or intimidated, indoctrinate—although in different degrees, with different tactics, and stressing different values."

Shaver and his colleagues reported, on the basis of the multiply validated evidence of the NSF studies, that teachers (above the elementary grades) worried about students' indifference toward social studies, and, moreover, about a growing surliness and alienation among students. "Particularly distressing to many teachers . . . is what appears to be a recent increase in the unwillingness of students to accept authority, to accept textbook 'truths,' to do their assignments or even to believe that they are worth doing." However, they "picked up no feeling that [this] moved teachers to examine the basic assumptions from which they teach."

The overriding need for system-maintenance in schooling is not news to sociologists and anthropologists, but it comes as a surprise to reformers, both within education and without. Shaver et al. comment, correctly: "Failure to address such primary concerns has been a consistent failure from the Progressive Education Movement . . . to the competency-based teacher education movement of today. Reform, to be effective, must be based on the recognition that teachers operate with [in] a total system."

This summary statement is important. While the teachers may 'control' the classroom experience to a high degree, there is more in 'the system' than teachers' behavior and attitudes. For one thing, many studies show (and Shaver et al. comment) that teachers genuinely care about their students and that students, generally speaking, perceive this—even if some still count themselves out of the process to some degree. Students also, and parents, are well aware of the *constant* characteristics of the particular 'system' they inhabit: the traditions of that school, the sensitivities of that community, the societal agenda of that era. Teacher behavior is only one 'cell' in an adequate analysis of factors in schooling.

And curriculum is clearly only one dimension. Shaver et al. recognize this: "The same textbooks are used in a course 'sequence' that varies little across the country . . . so that students face few problems of continuity in moving from district to district, no more so than moving from one school to another within a district. Yet, the day-by-day social studies experiences of youngsters often vary dramatically, even in adjacent classrooms." Here is an important clue to the presence of distinct alternative *patterns* in social studies, created by the interaction of a limited number of curriculum options and a few overriding goals, not all of which can be achieved at once (that is, which cannot be collapsed into one inclusive goal). As Shaver et al. also recognize, and as everyone who offers a description of social studies should emphasize, the evidence for the stability of *modal* practices, across various samples and situations, quite misses the experienced reality of these particular interactive patterns themselves.* All observers and researchers in the schools state, with some fervor, that they see a wide range

*On 'patterning' in social studies, relative to other curriculum areas, see sections 15.3 and 18.4.

of styles, practices, climates. They emphasize the brilliant teaching they have seen, the relaxed but vibrant classrooms, the superb lesson plans and materials they have seen used. They then, almost universally, go on to describe what is, overall, a rather bleak and boring central tendency.

This is true of a comprehensive and well-planned study of over a thousand classrooms, conducted in the late 1970s and early 1980s by John Goodlad and associates, and a smaller but richly observed study of about fifteen high schools by Perrone and associates at about the same time; and it as been shown historically by Cuban.[47] These studies document many excellent social studies classes and teachers, but the Goodlad study, because of its very size, tended to put a rather discouraging central tendency into the spotlight. It found an overwhelming preponderance of 'teacher talk' (of various kinds), with little responsiveness to individual students and to activities initiated by them. Even specific feedback from the teacher, guiding students' work, was rare. According to Goodlad, the ways in which teachers steered students toward substantive work and oriented them to their classroom roles were of a low order of cognitive complexity, as was their testing of 'coverage.' That is, most teachers acted like traffic cops—or at best museum guides—rather than inspiring mentors. While the teacher's use of texts was not necessarily the same as the format of the text itself, they were "of the same genre": the "topics of the curriculum . . . were something to be acquired, not something to be explored." Goodlad comments:[48]

> One would expect the teaching of social studies and science in schools to provide ample opportunities for the development of reasoning; deriving concepts from related events, testing in a new situational hypotheses derived from examining other circumstances, drawing conclusions from an array of data, and so on. *Teachers listed those skills and more as intended learnings.* [emphasis added]. We observed little of the activities that their lists implied, and teachers' tests reflected quite different priorities—mainly the recall of information. . . . On the way to the classroom (the natural and social sciences) are apparently transformed into something of limited appeal. (p. 468)

Further, "pedagogy and curricula are geared, it appears, to only a small fraction of [the stated] goals—the lowest common denominators" (p. 470). Perrone and his colleagues put this in an interesting perspective: "Teachers could describe good teaching but did not generally feel that they were performing that role as well as they might. . . . They are not confident, however, that their communities view good teaching as they do" (p. 645).

The Perrone study confirmed that most teachers follow the text, but commented that there was a wider variety now than in previous decades of supplementary materials, guides, and tests—all, however, *keyed to the text,* so that, in effect, independent, locally specific input into a given lesson is further reduced. They found that schools tend to track students more heavily than had been expected, and that grade 9 was a crucial point in this procedure. This was understood by all but seldom remarked upon. Tracking reflected, not only a way to cope with diversity among students, but to attempt to ensure *minimal* levels of achievement for all—yet another demonstration of the minimum becoming the operational goal. The Perrone study suggested that most schools, though hard-pressed, were not in crisis because of external demands or internal diversity. The researchers also reported finding, perhaps contrary to outsiders' impressions, that "teachers, in general, are able to communicate quite effectively with the students" (p. 650). This finding may contradict to some extent the suspicion reported by Shaver, Davis, and Helburn (above) that a growing minority of students are not willing truly to engage themselves in the typical process of the classroom, but it need not. Experienced observers of classrooms almost always find that students in the front of the room (metaphorically speaking, to some extent) pay attention, seek the teacher's recognition, and attempt to participate, while those in the back have forgotten to bring their books, and find what is happening out the window or in the hall more interesting than whatever the teacher may be doing.

In my own observation, it is not so much a matter of expectations that those in the back of the room *never* participate but that 'a good student' is *defined* by consistent engagement. This may also be shown by grading practices, in which a 'good' student who disengages from time to time suffers for it, since it is impolitic for a student 'with potential' not to deploy it. Such findings have been reported back into the prior century, so long as teacher-led and teacher-paced instruction is involved. The exceptions invariably involve classrooms where group work of some sort—peer tutoring, cooperative learning, projects, and so on—is used. Research almost invariably shows that such interaction does not prevent the more able students from learning. On the other hand, *what* they learn under such conditions may well be different. No easy generalizations can be drawn without being specific about the criteria for achievement (see section 17.0).

Other indicators of the stability of social studies instruction as of the early 1980s, in terms of both curriculum and classroom realities, include a study of texts that showed that inquiry-oriented materials had receded, if they ever were common.[49] The authors of this study point out, however: "Substitute the term decision-making for inquiry and you obtain a different picture.... Free enterprise (in economics) is a distinct course ... decision-making is being built in as a goal" (p. 465). This could mean that text publishers include an apparatus in their texts that indicates the 'right kind' of going-beyond-the-facts, even if teachers do not necessarily spend time on it. In the same way that teachers are often seen to rise above the text in terms of variety, flexibility, sensitivity to the different needs of students, and so forth, so texts may tend to be more inclusive of a variety of officially desired goals and styles than what teachers actually draw upon.

A final indicator of a stable social studies, a field that is not in a state of fission, is given by a Delphi-technique study of social studies experts (supervisors, curriculum specialists, and so forth) that revealed a high degree of consensus about the location and sequence of specific academic material or content in the curriculum.[50] The respondents were asked to judge where specific themes or concepts in the various fields, as formulated by disciplinary scholars, should be included in the curriculum. For example, an anthropology concept, to be assessed for its difficulty and its logical place in the curriculum, might be "Categorizes all modern men as Homo Sapiens, explains that type variations are minor, whether races are viewed geographically, topologically, biologically, psychologically." Not only was there general agreement about the placement of such material, but there was little scatter—if the dominant choice was, for example, grade 6, the other choices were grade 5 or grade 7. In general, the basic skills of a field were located in the lower grades, while the more sophisticated content of the same field—that which defines a 'modern' approach to a subject-matter or, significantly, is necessary for decision-making relevant to that field—is located in the highest grades. In other words, the curriculum experts anticipated that certain subjects would be built up following a rational sequence of rudimentary concepts and skills, acquired over a number of grades, with deeper conceptualization being finally sought: this was typical of Economics and Government, for example. Some fields—Social Psychology (that is, the study of interpersonal relations), Geography, Anthropology—were viewed as especially appropriate for the middle grades. In general, the curriculum experts tended to find considerable content in almost every canonical subject appropriate for grades 4 to 9.*

One can, of course, maintain that the experts tended to recommend what was, not what might be; they agreed on present practices. But this alone can be seen as reassuring. In the pooling of much content into the middle grades, they seemed to be expressing a desire for richly conceptual, nondisciplinary learning there. Further, the study turned up at least one mismatching that may indicate a common problem for the field. The university-based experts in history described the following attributes among history learners (p. 97):

- They used a process of inquiry;
- They logically analyzed contemporary circumstances by investigations of origins;
- They identified point of view, bias, and historical interpretation;
- They used analytical reasoning from data-useful methodology;
- They gained skills in reading and writing.

The first four of these were assigned by the experts to the high-school grades, the fifth to the primary grades. The descriptions do not have much to do with chronological comprehension or an appreciation of the ubiquity of change in

---

*Specialized or synthetic subjectmatter—contemporary issues, global education, or behavioral psychology, for example—were confined to the uppermost grades. Legal education was thought appropriate for grades 7–9.

history, which most recent studies show to be the dominant concerns in school history. In essence, judgments on what typifies history *content* in grades 5, 8, and 10 (statistically speaking) were not sought by the university experts—and were not provided. In contrast, the statements by disciplinary experts in political science and geography, for example, showed no particular bias toward analytic goals (as in the New Social Studies approach) but generated a range of content description that the respondents had little trouble placing at gradelevel. In the last few years, some historians and humanistic scholars have called, on general cultural grounds, for a turning back toward 'traditional' history in the schools.[51] In the Herman study, certain professional historians in universities (so far as is known, not consulting each other) generated quite conceptual and abstract instructional elements. In this field, it may be that the main division is not between university and school, but that a three-way conversation is implied— among school historians, university historians qua professionals, and historians speaking to a broader cultural purpose.

PART III

The Subject Matters

6.0   Political Study

The most difficult and problematic of all the fundamental aspects of social studies is the role of citizenship education in the public schools. As we have seen, one purpose of schooling that state education law invariably mandates is the creation through education of good citizens, often stipulating that civics or government or history be taught toward that end.* It is also the case that, while not all teachers or parents rank 'citizenship education' highly in their goals for the schools, virtually all educational leaders, professional organizations, and national commissions that pronounce on public education in the United States explicitly state that the overriding goal of the entire enterprise—not just social studies—is citizenship. Thus, calls for math and science improvement use that justification, as do briefs for the arts in education. Those concerned with the humanities and their revival at various levels in education use the same rhetoric. Those who are working on behalf of vocational education use it, as do those who propose a serious commitment to 'global education.' As one example, Merrill Peterson, speaking at a panel meeting at the American Council of Learned Societies, said: "The humanities are important to the shared reflection, commu-

*In this discussion I use 'civics' to refer to a portion of the curriculum, typically but not necessarily contained in schools (there is, for example, 'civics' taught for adults or new citizens in night school, church-sponsored courses, and the like), and 'citizenship' to refer to an ideal held by society for a role to be played by, and a commitment and set of attitudes to be held by, its members.

167

nication, and participation required of a democratic community. They are essential to reasoned civic discourse."[1] It is, of course, possible to 'read through' such statements and conclude that national economic and political pride of place are of special concern to science and math, while the arts and humanities lay stress on an individualistic goal, that of the fully developed person. But the fact remains that all groups seeking school reform follow the same reasoning: improvement of education is not for the sake of the few, but for all; and the reason for this is the peculiar demand of democratic education, whose binding common purpose is citizenship.

6.1   Education for Democracy and Politics

However, when one turns to the official curriculum statements and descriptions of a state or district or school, one realizes that those who write the sections describing the curriculum 'basics,' primarily English and mathematics, do not seem to feel it necessary to precede these descriptions with any broad rationale. (They may state an approach or pedagogical slant, but that is a different kind of message.) It is the 'enrichment' fields for which rationales are offered and here two curious phenomena can be noted. First, the rationales at this level do *not* invoke citizenship very heavily, but rather modernity, intellectual power in the world, and economic self-sufficiency (science), human breadth and richness (humanities and the arts), the humanistic and instrumental benefits of knowing foreign languages, and so on. It appears that in these areas, 'citizenship' is invoked only at the most official level, that which acknowledges the overriding purposes of schools in general, not at the level of realization at the curricular level. Second, social studies, while often considered an 'enrichment' field in the curriculum,* is not *optional* in schools, as even science may be; the reason is, bluntly, that social studies has special responsibility for citizenship.

This special responsibility laid on social studies is simultaneously the great strength and the great problem in the field. A high-school teacher recently commented to the writer that 'civic training' would be taken care of if only her students could be out in the world, working or apprenticing, as people of that age once were. It is true that civic education takes place far beyond the schools, for both young and older adults. But the comment shows a lack of both current and historical perspective. A very large proportion of high-school students today *do* work (in some states, more than half do so), but for the most part not at true 'entry' jobs—that is, not in positions that lead to a career or occupation but in hourly-paid jobs from which they come and go. Although some must work, many of these students seek such jobs for the sake of social stimulation from their age-mates, because they are more fun (in some cases) than school, and for

*Because it lacks a tightly bounded, sequentially organized subjectmatter. For example, Stodolsky pp. 4–5.[2]

disposable income—the last often encouraged by families with two or more wage-earners who still cannot afford cars and VCRs for their teenagers. Such jobs may have beneficial personal and social aspects, but an introduction to the broad occupational world and an instilling of civic participation are not strong among them. To the extent that they cut into educational achievement, they may ultimately be counterproductive for the individuals involved and for society.

The teacher's statement also ignores the fact that public schooling in America was invented to bring about citizenship in a sense beyond that of simply living and working in the society. Those who created and built the schools believed that without them, and the civic education that the schools would provide, our democratic society would fail—either because the citizenry would be ignorant and apathetic, and thus not enlightened participants in the democratic process, or because the effects of pluralism, without an overriding commitment and common experience, would fragment the polity. The teacher's comment shows an unawareness of the intentions of the Founders of the Republic, as well as the founders of the schools; of the goals of the reformers of 1918, involving the enlargement of civics through the schools; of Dewey and others who sought a socially harmonious and creative purpose in school; and of the goals of later influential groups, such as the back-to-basics proponents of the 1950s, the civil rights and compensatory education advocates of the 1960s, and others up to the present. At every era, 'citizenship' has been reformulated—but reinforced.

This summary is supported by recent superb studies in American educational history, for example by Cremin or Kaestle, which see both these dangers—ignorance and alienation, and divisiveness in a heterogeneous population—as present from the beginning of the republic, certainly from the beginning of schools. A recent interpretation bearing especially on the forms of civic education in schools at various eras is given by J. Freeman Butts. Very thoughtful interpretations of political theory and philosophy relevant to what democratic education must be, or could be, are given by Rush Welter, Amy Gutmann, and Donald Warren.[3]

The problems with citizenship reflect the paradoxes of democracy. Do we educate for freedom or for virtue (Gutmann)? Do we educate for leadership and followership together, or for one or the other, or for a little of both in each person? Which is more important, *pluribus* or *unum* (Butts)? Must the commitment to democratic values precede the educated ability to examine and reform them, or are unexamined values—even 'root' values—ultimately dangerous to society? Where is the essence of the 'American Creed' (Myrdal): in the universal human rights of the Declaration of Independence, the norms and procedures of the Constitution, or the oft-regulated balance of individual rights and societal obligations of the Bill of Rights and later amendments? If the prepotency of majority rule over individual rights, but with the protection of the latter by the former, is the crux of the matter (Tocqueville), will universal education widen or narrow the gap, increase or limit the stakes? Should the designers of education in the society be the already best-educated and powerful, or the most patriotic or wisest? If consent of the governed is the bedrock consideration in democracy, what constitutes informed consent, and what does this imply about the extent and nature of participation?*

6.1.1 CITIZENSHIP THROUGH EDUCATION

Let us go more deeply, though briefly, into these conflicts and paradoxes as they affect public education. At the broad verbal level, they seem like stable paradoxes—built permanently into the design of modern democracy and not threatening to our survival as a society. Thus, Patrick simply points out that "[citizenship] entails *both* obedience and constructive skepticism, respect for authority and constructive criticism of authorities. Good citizens in a free society are both compliant and independent."[4] But Patrick also sees the majority/minority relationship as the central tension, and when we begin to respond *as citizens* to that tension—for if it is not salient, it can hardly be a 'tension'—choices come into play. Is not the realized protection of minority rights largely a means of protecting the majority rule that now obtains? If we know that some minorities are systematically kept at some distance from full participation in society, for whatever reasons, do we not need to strive for something like compensatory citizenship education for such groups? If certain groups are further from power than others, how can we in good faith cite active participation as a hallmark of true citizenship? If a member of a relatively excluded group appears in federal court to sue for her rights in some specific instance, do we withhold this right—to seek redress—because that person has not participated fully as a citizen? Gutmann[5] examines the freedom-versus-virtue paradox in terms of public education in some detail.

> Either we must educate children so that they are free to choose among the widest range of lives (given the constraints of cultural coherence) because freedom of choice is the paramount good, or we must educate children so that they will choose *the* life that we believe is best because leading a virtuous life is the paramount good. . . . Neither alternative is acceptable. [Here Gutmann speaks of the "tyranny of dualisms."] The decision not to teach virtue [she means the view that schools must not indoctrinate] or, more accurately, to teach only the virtues of free choice faces opposition by citizens who can claim, quite reasonably, that freedom of choice is not the only, or even the primary, purpose of education. Why should these citizens be forced to defer to the view that children must be educated for freedom rather than virtue?

---

*cf. James Madison, on knowledge and power: "Knowledge will forever govern ignorance. And a people who mean to be their own governors must arm themselves with the power that knowledge gives." (Quoted in Patrick, below.)

On the issue of leadership and followership in civic education, Turner[6] cites a 1908 American Political Science Association statement of purpose for such education: "The results of the neglect of [American government] in our educational institutions can easily be seen in the general unfitness of men who have entered a political career.... Are the schools perhaps to blame for the lack of interest in politics shown by our educated men? [In the schools] we find the judges, legislators, diplomats, politicians, and office-seekers of the future.... Here are the future citizens *too*." (Emphasis added; the assumption is that citizens are those whom the judges, legislators, and office-holders lead.) This implies that ordinary citizens are educated in order to fulfill their normal roles, while potential leaders are educated *for* a higher form of participation. This distinction is not an obsolete one. The historian Paul Gagnon[7] writes: "Political history thoughtfully presented is indispensable to educating citizens. For what is democracy but that remarkable system in which 'ordinary people' are expected to comprehend, and to judge, the choices made by their elites?"

To escape Gutmann's "tyranny of dualisms" it is helpful to look at dimensions or degrees of citizenship education, with close attention to the subjects to be allotted prominence. If the root value is justice, as it is for Butts, then legal process, 'the rules' of the game (probably as captured in constitutional law), becomes of special importance. If the root value is individual dignity, as it is for Newmann,[8] considerable attention would have to be paid to forms of civil disobedience in a framework broader than established law—that is, to the political history of social movements—and to administrative forms within government that increase or diminish human dignity in their workings. If the root value is consent of the governed, at some point the costs and benefits (as illuminated by history, political science, and the humanities, at the least) of nonsurvival of political systems, such as revolutions or other forms of cancellation of existing political authority, have to be studied. Finally, in a broader framework, that of education as a universal process of enculturation for the young, Engle and Ochoa[9] have written forcefully of the need, especially with regard to political education, for both socialization and 'countersocialization'—the inculcation of skepticism and the critical capacity.

Another way of ordering the aspects of citizenship, beyond simple dualisms, is implicitly developmental. That is, the earliest goal may be attitudinal, to instill obedience, loyalty to, and personal identification with the society and its political forms. The next goal is cognitive, to make 'the system' known in its full variety, contradictions and all. The final stage is pragmatic, to enable an individual to make the system work for her or him. In terms of theories about human development, there is at least a rough accuracy about such a scheme, at least with respect to the necessary order of the first and second (section 6.3.1).* In terms of historical development it is tempting to relate a rough set of stages

---

*Though even here such different thinkers as Rousseau and Dewey drew urgent cautions against rigid 'stage' thinking.

of American citizenship education to such a scheme: the first being characteristic of the 1800s, the second (together with the first) characteristic of the first half of the 1900s, the third (together with the first and second) appearing about midcentury—for example, as an aspect of law-related education or as a facet of a meritocratic/technocratic society in which the vast majority of citizens reach a relatively high degree of education. However, Welter holds that both the first and third were characteristic of the earlier 1800s, in education, and that the third—preparation for a range of differentiated roles in society (that is, multiple empirical forms of citizenship)—was distinctive in the scientific management movement of the first two decades, and beyond, of this century. Many commentators believe that undue emphasis on the first leads to moral ineptitude, such as jingoism, while undue emphasis on the third leads to cynicism or privatism. Almost all give at least formal approval to the second, in education, though many would observe definite limits as to the degree of emphasis.

Leming, for example,[10] maintains that premature rationality and the propensity toward 'criticism' breeds mistrust and lowered sense of political efficacy regarding the political system. He says, "Adults sometimes suffer feelings of political impotence, anger, despair, frustration, and outrage. The adult citizen, however, is typically resilient because his/her years of experience with our political system has enabled him to . . . roll with the punches. . . . Youth however are more impressionable and lack the capacity to view things from a tempered perspective." Thus, within general agreement on the desirability of factual knowledge, there is disagreement based on calculations of whether what you do know is likely to hurt you, or what you don't know.

Complicating the model is the fact that many observers believe that some citizenship education does not so much capture or express the sociopolitical world per se as focus on the microcosm in which the education occurs—the school itself. Thus, as suggested in a well-known and influential treatment:[11] "It seems likely that much of what is called citizenship training in the public schools does not teach about the city, state, or national government, but is an attempt to teach regard for the rules and standards of conduct *of the school*. . . ." For this reason, also, Engle and Ochoa call for 'countersocialization' as one deliberate purpose (within limits) of schools, although others have argued that instruction about freedom and choice conducted within an authoritarian system leads to destructive outcomes.

The existence of paradoxes need not, apparently, mean the experience of conflict. Tocqueville found America inherently more fortunate than European democracies, because America was free of conflictual religious, cultural, and class commitments—or at least could confront conflicts with historically newborn vigor and freshness. In *An American Dilemma* Myrdal found the American Creed "more widely understood and appreciated than similar ideals are anywhere else . . . as principles that *ought* to rule, the Creed has been made conscious to everyone in American society." Others have taken hope from the fact that the binding, bonding effect of shared moral principles and values could proceed free of ultimate commitments to religion in the civil realm. In all these senses, the inclusion of education for public life builds communality and commitment.

6.1.2   SCHOOLING FOR CITIZENSHIP

Such difficult and probably unanswerable questions as those touched on above begin to come into focus, as such questions often do, though historical inspection. Historians generally see the Founders as more concerned with an actively informed and committed citizenry, as a defense against tyranny, than with pluralistic stresses and strains (which would in their era have been allayed by the processes of revolution and nation-building). Their position was a partial rejection of the Platonic idea that those who know are entitled to rule; their argument was more that those who rule—that is, the people—*must* know. It is true that for the purposes of political participation, 'the people' in effect were those with property and the leisure to inform themselves and to deliberate, those poised to take part in the civic experience—that is, well-off white Protestants. Thus the expected form of education was the private academy. By the time the common school movement began, the fissioning potential of immigration was apparent in society, there was fear of Roman Catholicism, and in general the desire to 'Americanize' much of the populace. By the time of Horace Mann, in the 1840s, the influence of the Jacksonian 'rabble' was also a present concern, as was a growing regionalism of South and North.

For Mann, then, schools would be 'common' in several senses—open to the many rather than the few, widespread in number, and nonsectarian. As Warren points out,[12] though state control of the schools was fought for over many decades, the schools themselves were often, in the mid-1800s, called "national schools," meaning that they were to rise above class and regionalism and serve nation-building (and nation-strengthening) ends. All scholars of the early schools report that the curriculum was largely a matter of purveying the official rudiments of 'the American experience': the heroes (some of them), the dates, the places, the inevitability of expansion and progress. The educational method was that of the catechism, memorizing the texts.* Political and social controversy was assiduously avoided. No one knows whether knowledge increased—certainly the sectarian schools and the academies doubted it; but the American memory began to be forged.

During Reconstruction, common schools were imposed on the South, partly in the service of the wider national allegiance and partly because it was believed that an uneducated populace had nearly brought down the Union—exactly what the Founders had feared. One result was that blacks attended the field schools, wishing to be educated. So segregated schools were quietly devised, with poorer

---

*In fact, school books were thoughtfully laid out so that precepts were separated and italicized for easy memorization, with the supporting material, if any, relegated to the small print.

teachers, different educational aims, and lower budgets—devised not by the local authorities alone but by federal offices. This, lasting until 1954 (and later), may be the paradigm case for how educational inclusiveness runs up against political limits, for 'equity' carried only so far. (Urban Catholics, of course, had taken a different course by devising their own schools.) When foreign immigrants came to America in large numbers, beginning in the 1880s, the program of the schools was again one of instilling basic loyalty to the nation and its heritage; but the diversity of the immigrants themselves and their situations led to a more diverse, and more localized, set of solutions.* A rough standard for the instructional goals of the schools (that is, the graded primary, common schools) was mastery of the content called for in the naturalization process, prior to taking the oath of allegiance.

The perpetual conflict over pluralist inclusion in the schools has continued to this day, and is inevitable. It needs also to be said that, for all their failings in this regard, the schools of America have been more inclusive than those of other heterogeneous societies. It is easy enough to see the origin and prevalence of that persistent spirit in citizenship education in the schools that has bothered so many observers—call it chauvinism, boosterism (which repelled the Lynds in Middletown), or cultural myth-making by guardian elites. Less obvious to view is conflict over the other great goal, active informed participation in political life. Here the dimensions of conflict are evidently more subtle.

With regard to 'participation,' Rush Welter[13] held that a key to American educational history is the importance throughout the 1800s of economic independence for individuals, the potential for personal success in economic terms within the framework of a growing and economically thriving nation. While the academy and the lyceum had 'higher' cultural aims, common schooling reflected an increase in the base of those economically involved, those fostering productivity in first the agricultural, then the mercantile, sector. "Anarchy with a schoolmaster" was his summary for this assumption—similar to that of Tocqueville—that a functioning American society, especially in its economic aspect, must bring the populace into complex vigorous interrelationships (not the least, producers to markets). Such an assumption is implicit in the Lockean form of liberalism, which held that individuals followed a classical form of rational self-interest in the economic realm, and established economic 'stakes' in society, while in the political realm representative government and differentiated roles demonstrated supra-individual, institutional constraints. If this is accepted, schooling would facilitate social innovation in the economic sphere (as it certainly did, with regard to technology, invention, continental expansion, and the like), while limiting social innovation in the realm of political conceptualization and processes. 'Political education' would be conservative, veering always toward constitutionalism, legal process, and orderly discussion, while 'social education' in some of its other aspects would be less normative and more liberal.

*Including the toleration of what we would now call transitional bilingualism in instruction.

This is, of course, one of the dominant interpretations of Progressivism, in society and in education (section 4.3.1). One goal of Progressivism was to carry forward reforms and modifications that would permit a growing, industrial, urban society to be realized; these would demand a literate and technologically modern workforce and a complex kind of sociality, built on the division of labor and on cooperation across class and regional lines. The consonance between the ways in which a free enterprise system allocated economic roles and functions and the ways in which the 'social efficiency' and scientific management aspects of educational progressivism handled preparing each person for his or her position in life has often been noted.*

Here, as elsewhere, the period around 1900 to 1914 seems a pivotal one. In the early part of the century, with Frederick Jackson Turner's western frontier closed, a social frontier opened within. The Spencerian mode of inherent societal determination, the 'march of life' through various pathways (including education), which was espoused around 1900 by some early and influential sociologists (section 9.1), lasted from the 1880s or earlier up through 1929. Dewey's emphasis on 'life as it is now,' on the continual testing and refiguring of reality within an established epistemological and social-institutional framework, came into education around 1910 and lasted up to the 1950s. The concern of George Counts and others for life as it should become, for revision and reconstruction, began in the 1920s, and had a short vogue.†

As schools, in part following the management model, became more nearly all-encompassing institutions, at least in the aim of some reformers, citizenship became far more than the memorizing of facts in a civics class. A new kind of participation on the part of students, within school (for example, school government by students) and outside of school (for example, community service), was anticipated.

6.1.3   Beyond 'Civil Government'

Furthermore, a greater degree of factual and conceptual knowledge about the social and economic world was needed. A shorthand way of tracing these changes, using the curriculum as a metaphor and model, is this: Up to about the turn of the century, History and a modicum of Civil Government were adequate to bind together increasingly pluralist schools and to permit individualistic economic competition to proceed. Detailed, nonhistorical investigation of

---

*Often, to be sure, in debates over what was or was not a part of Progressivism, in education and elsewhere. Dewey's view of pragmatic, experiential confrontation *with* society (through education and other means), of testing of knowledge *against* possibilities, was orthogonal to the allocative/ management ideology in schooling; but it was also orthogonal to the social-evolutionary dynamism of the preceding generation, and to the planned reconstructionism of later decades, both of which have been seen as aspects of the progressive movement.

†None of these generalizations should be taken to mean that these elements were restricted to one set of dates, beginning and ending neatly. All these views are with us today, in education and elsewhere.

social problems was not needed in the curriculum. Deep inquiry and reflective thinking was not a goal, except for leaders-to-be in their college education. The dominant 'master idea' at the level of the disciplines—and more or less common across the social science disciplines, including history—was social evolutionism.

In the terms of our curriculum model, the spirit of the committee of 1916 involved adding a tincture of Sociology and Economics to the prescription for citizenship. On the level of the master ideas of the disciplines, structural-functionalism became the dominant mode of social thought. Students could not move toward fixed concepts and norms without understanding how the sociopolitical system works as a system (with inputs and outputs and 'steady states') and why some of its contradictions and tensions are functional. *Why* the market economy is efficient is as important as *what* it is, descriptively. *How* social stratification works is important, not simply that there is such a thing. Historians and nonhistorians alike held that the value of history (among other values) was as a kind of protoscientific approach to present reality—including the American democratic process.

In looking at citizenship at various stages, we will be returning to these paired metaphorical elements, the linking of the master ideas of social thought (on, generally, a transdisciplinary basis) with the additions to (or subtractions from) the school curriculum in terms of subjects—the first affecting the conceptualization of citizenship education, the second thought to be the key to effecting it. In getting closer to actual educational practice, we rely heavily on the comprehensive and insightful dissertation by Mary Jane Nickelson Turner.[14]

We know what Civil Government about 1900 meant: the study of the American and English constitutional traditions, and the detailed and painstaking description of the various levels of government as to their formal structures and normal functioning. At lower grade levels, the 1909 AHA committee[15] (section 4.2.4) concluded that at grade 5, 20 minutes a week (within History) should be spent on Civics, specifically on the "service occupations" (police, fire, libraries, and so forth); in grade 6, 20 minutes a week on water supply, sewage, health services, suffrage, juvenile courts, and other aspects of city government. At grade 7, Civics, 40 minutes a week, was to take up the functions and machinery of local and state governments, using a text; at grade 8, 60 minutes a week was to be spent on the national government, the "function of its parts rather than machinery," but the "machinery to render service to citizens."*

Writing in 1922, Earle Rugg (the brother of Harold) stated that for the preceding ten years or so there had been an "insistent demand that school courses . . . make a more definite contribution to . . . effective citizenship."[17] He

---

*Tracing civics texts, for example *Magruder's American Government*, through all their editions, from the 1890s forward, analysts see constitutional aspects gradually dropping out in the 1940s and 1950s and detailed legal processes and procedures becoming more and more carefully described thereafter. But in any era, controversy and problems are always avoided, and American institutions and ideals are celebrated. See, among others, the evaluation of texts by Barth and Shermis[16] (who also cite some sterling exceptions).

cites the influence of the crisis of the Great War, with its war activities in the schools, and "Americanization work." The latter referred to patriotism and bravery in battle in the military and, in the civil sphere, to messages aimed at German-origin groups in the United States and generally to immigrants.*

Rugg himself emphasized the then-new Cardinal Principles of 1918. He states that in the preceding century civics was the study of state and national constitutions, and that the nineteenth-century spirit of civics reflected the conviction that public education "trained pupils to take their places as citizens." He does not comment on the broader (if still rudimentary) pattern recommended by the historians of 1909, but stresses that historians have tried to keep up with changing needs. "The inclusion by the historians of more political history† to provide for civic instruction and an equal increase of economic topics like banking, manufacturing, agriculture, and transportation in history texts... show that they were aware of the struggles of these new social sciences for a place in the curriculum" (p. 66). Rugg then emphasizes the Spencerian tradition of "descriptive sociology," which he says is drawn from the broad materials of history, economics, political science, sociology, psychology, and anthropology, permitting curriculum designers to "acquaint the pupil with life's crucial social activities and modes of living," as well as "practice in constantly thinking about and drawing conclusions from contemporary problems and issues" (p. 67).‡ Here Rugg reveals an implicit definition of 'social studies' as, not the disciplines simplified for pedagogical purposes (Wesley's 1937 phrase), but an eclectic fused amalgam of "available knowledge and materials." He also clearly distinguishes between two *levels* of the new civics: what would be known as factually based community civics at grade 9 and a "discussion course," Problems of Democracy, at grade 12. Rugg's description serves to show that the 1916 revision was taking hold in the schools.

Rugg identifies Dewey§ as an advocate of 'social efficiency,' contending that Dewey's aim was "to stimulate each pupil to bear his fair share of the load," and then focuses (p. 69ff) on A. W. Dunn, the inventor, as it were, of 'community' civics (see section 4.4). This approach was, indeed, something like descriptive sociology, much in the spirit of the then-popular community studies: maximizing the "socializing value of a first-hand study" of the activities of modern communities (not limited to one's own).[19] Dunn's book was said to have widened the scope of the subject and improved the content of the Civil Government course, and, by its wide adoption, to have caused university-based historians to rethink their needs. Rugg is probably not claiming too much. We know[20] that Dunn's

---

*Michael Kazin[18] remarks that "not until the era of World War I did 'Americanism' become closely bound up with a fealty to the status quo."

†Rugg meant more nearly what we would call social history, or at least non–Great Men history.

‡Rugg does not note that Spencer himself was no advocate of a broad common education, but rather of 'modern' education for an elite.

§Mistakenly, or for his own purposes, I believe.

text was widely used; and of course the 1916 committee did represent, in part, the kind of broadening of subject to which he alludes as the coming thing. Also, inspection of economics books of the 1920s, by Leon Marshall and others (see section 7.1), reveals that a broad descriptive sociology, not neatly disciplinary in style, soon became the style for grade 9 civics.

6.1.4 'CIVIL EDUCATION'

With regard to the grade-9 course, the subject focus was essentially broad sociopolitical competence, a realistic view of 'the system' in considerable empirical detail. One is tempted to call this civics Civil Education, on analogy with civil engineering. That is, first, the subject is those social and human structures that can be seen near at hand, in one's own neighborhood, and then recognized in comparable communities. These are structures built by ordinary people, not by national founders or exceptional leaders. Second, a matter of great emphasis is (a new theme in civics) the balance between private interests and public goods, which are created by social cooperation and compromise.

Welter believes that this latter concern became anathema in the 1920s to American business, which felt that its own entrepreneurial role was to find that balance and create effective social arrangements. That is, business leaders should now occupy the sort of regulating—one could say paternalistic—roles that political leaders filled. Others see the business community as far more concerned with allocating students into their eventual occupational niches, a concept of management rather than entrepreneurial trusteeship. In any event, the distinctive 1918 notion of each student's learning to be his own civil governor probably had a rather short run.

The actual (or even the intended) nature of Problems of Democracy courses is much more difficult to determine. Course frequency data show that the POD course did cut into American Government courses at grade 12, at least to a limited degree, and may well have altered the tone of some 'Government' courses beyond this, especially in the later 1930s. Turner points out (p. 55) that by 1960 or so those schools that for one reason or other retained the POD name in fact offered advanced civics courses, in which, moreover, the emphases were the structure and function of government and the historical background—often with the latter looming larger than the former, perhaps because so many government teachers were history-trained (p. 88). Between the 1920s and the 1960s, there is considerable evidence that what were meant to be POD courses, employing discussion and the analysis of problems and issues, were in fact directed reading courses—that is, courses playing to the special topical interests of students or, often, teachers.

Tryon points out (p. 423ff) that in the 1920s and 1930s some POD syllabi showed a focus on problems *facing* the American democracy, others on problems *in* American democracy, still others on problems of democracy generally. It could be, in other words, a course on current issues, or on the paradoxes of the American democracy (a kind of American political theory course) or a treatment of comparative systems of democratic government. The last two would approximate either a sophisticated sort of advanced civics or a broad political theory/comparative government course. Tryon's analysis of texts, in 1928, convinced him that a focus on the current (or recurrent) problems facing American democracy—that is, an external, perhaps broadly sociological, orientation—was rare: government and politics were the real center of gravity. "Probably because of their inadequate training in sociology, these authors actually constructed a stool with two legs instead of three." In other words, POD had either reverted to Civil Government or had evolved into a proto–Political Science elective. Charles Beard, in 1932,[21] cautioned against making any grade-12 course entirely a forum for issues discussion, saying that "experience, daring, and maturity are necessary to large enterprises in democracy, and the schools have no monopoly in this field."* One can sense Beard yearning for some kind of essentially analytic, multidisciplinary, proseminar in grade 12—that is, something more intellectually structured than issues discussion, and certainly less activist than establishing a base for social action. "A wide knowledge of facts and a discipline in thinking are the prerequisites to a fruitful consideration of controversial questions. Here, it seems, the schools may lay their emphasis, with less danger to their instruction and perhaps more profit to the country."

Singleton,[22] in his trenchant discussion of the POD course, points out that emphasis must have shifted back and forth as a function of the times. A true current-issues format was unlikely to have obtained very often, because it required too much teacher preparation each year. In the 1930s, the perceived societal crisis probably led more schools to adopt the POD course, as if this very label would contribute to crisis resolution; however, there was always the tendency to rest at the factual level and the "imagined obligation to cover everything." Singleton suggests that what the POD was intended to be (in terms of the 1916 prescription) was not adequately specified (hence, could not be implemented) until the 1940s and 1950s—when POD courses as such had largely disappeared from the curriculum.†

If POD courses were often, in fact, directed reading or independent study courses, this is consonant with the appearance, by 1934, of a new positivist, behaviorist, and discipline-oriented spirit in social studies generally, as exemplified by the AHA Commission (section 4.6). The key term may be 'positivist,' since when a similar disciplinary orientation occurred again in the 1960s and 1970s, it expressed quite a different master idea, that of cognitive structuralism.

---

*Compare Leming's view, p. 172.

†He refers here to formulations spelling out with considerable care how to conduct such a course in the style of reflective thought, grounded and tested belief, or the systematic, factually based investigation of 'closed areas' in social life. A still-later implementation of the POD idea may be seen in the 1960s Harvard Public Issues approach of Oliver and Newmann (section 5.3.3).

The positivist spirit in the university social sciences came strongly to the fore in the 1930s and 1940s, reflecting for the most part logical positivism, the ideal of physics, in the period before World War II, and another kind of positivism, that of behavioral/empirical realism, after the war. In these years, political systems came to be seen as, in the end, systems of human relationships and behavior, to the analysis of which all the social sciences contributed. With regard to citizenship, political science took some pains to stand aside from any role as the only relevant discipline.

6.1.5   SOCIAL EDUCATION

In Charles Merriam's 1934 book (for the AHA Commission) on civic educa-tion,[23] it is quite striking how much the growth of the several disciplines, and the access of faith in the social sciences in society generally, undergird his views. Merriam, perhaps the leading political scientist of his generation, put compara-tively little stress on the study of government and political process per se; he assumed that within a reasonable time all the social sciences would elevate the power of social education by some order of magnitude. Progress in these fields was seen to be both empirical and methodological; the implication was that for the first time (other than in the case of history), social studies could be based upon mature bodies of and approaches to knowledge.*

One may recall that the Wesley definition of social studies—the disciplines simplified for pedagogical purposes—was coined in 1937; much prior to that, it would not have made much sense.[†] In terms, once again, of our model of intellectual succession in the curriculum, 1934 marks the moment at which the 1916 amalgam of History, Government, and 'descriptive sociology/economics' adds, *tout court*, the concept 'plus the other social sciences.'

In retrospect, Merriam's confidence seems premature. Today we are aware that the production of Ph.D.'s in the social sciences did not accelerate sharply until after World War II, and that historically most of the growth in these sciences occurred between 1950 and the mid-1970s. Some key methodologies were not available until after the war (for example, survey research), and federal research money did not start to run in significant amounts until about 1960. Merriam, however, viewed change from the very low baseline of the century's early decades, and saw that in his own professional lifetime significant growth was under way; he had no way of knowing that much more rapid growth would ensue later. In the mid-1930s, geography was beginning to be organized as a social or human, not physical, science, and one could reasonably predict that soon it would stand separate from history in school instruction. Anthropology as a research field was enlarging rapidly, in areas beyond ethnology (namely, linguis-

---

*Merriam's own positivist faith in social science was echoed, as we have seen, by his commission colleague, Charles Beard, in the latter's vision of the POD course. Interestingly, however, Beard's overall *goal* for social studies was still that of 1916, the "creation of rich, many-sided personalities."

†See section 2.4 for a caution on the interpretation of Wesley's dictum.

tics and archaeology), and beginning to become a department separate from sociology in research universities. In psychology, a strongly theoretical, well-articulated learning theory was present, moving that field from essentially correlational inquiries (personality, testing, abnormal behavior, and the like) to a causal orientation, physics-like in this respect and in reliance upon quantification.

Merriam may have downplayed the primacy of political science for reasons specific to his own field. Beginning in the 1920s, political thinkers and political scientists like Walter Lippmann and, a little later, Harold Lasswell introduced elements into political science that were non-structural/functional—that is, consideration of the dynamics of public opinion, the role of attitudes and 'psychology' in political decision-making, the force of the irrational, and the cross-pressures of interest groups. An implication was that politics was, to a significant degree, unconditioned by rational training through education or other means. Beyond this a new level of dynamic process and descriptive detail in the field intellectually presaged an impending shift toward a behavioralist rather than a formalist stance. Then, too, as the federal government gradually enlarged its functions, the profession of nonacademic political scientist was also enlarging at all governmental levels. The general field of public administration eventually separated from political science, professionally and to some extent on the campuses; political science tended to take the position that political scientists were scientists, devoted to theory and analysis, not functionaries.

Be that as it may, the participation of political scientists and economists in the New Deal was one of rough-and-tumble maneuvering, not theory and analysis. And the triumph of the New Deal was to find solutions by trial and error, hardly waiting for the play of rational, informed, broadly based and broadly tested democratic decision-making. It represented, in one respect, the de facto agreement of government, business, and the professionals—for example, in the creation and staffing of agencies. To the left of the New Deal lay the collectivists, like George Counts, the radical reformers; to the right of the New Deal lay conservatives who appealed to constitutionalism and laissez-faire principles to restrain the pragmatic bent in Washington. None of this was alluded to in Merriam's book, but it is reasonable to assume that part of his endorsement of the social sciences severally, beyond reflecting his own principled beliefs, was a certain unease about where the field of 'Government' was headed, and what it would distinctively offer in civic education in the schools. In that particular regard, the important point is that in the 1930s and 1940s the promise of *science* in the relevant disciplines was first felt as the wave of the future, conceivably a qualitatively different, pan-disciplinary basis for social studies.*

---

*It is, of course, true that the term 'social science' was used from the 1880s onward, that it was the American Political *Science* Association founded in 1903, and so on. It is also true that 'science' in these fields around the turn of the century meant the gathering of 'facts' that spoke for themselves— a kind of naive empiricism characteristic, for example, of 'scientific history.' The positivist promise of the later decades was to provide theoretical frameworks and methods that would organize facts meaningfully, and generate them as well.

The professional field of political science had been satisfied with the civil government emphasis in the schools, circa 1900, and with being essentially a satellite of history. It had also endorsed the Dunn 1915 community civics pattern (and the 1916 committee report), as APSA reports about this time reveal.[24] The field originally accepted the idea that citizenship was the core of social education.

But by the mid-1930s, leaders such as Merriam were not so sure that citizenship was the central object. Moreover, some political scientists were unhappy with the diffuseness and lack of rigor of POD courses in the schools.[25] On the one hand, many of these courses were intellectually sloppy; on the other hand, to the extent that they were orderly from an intellectual point of view, they tended to be so by virtue of being taught by history-trained teachers. Little wonder that by the 1940s there seemed to be a tacit consensus that, in the end, what was feasible was a solid Advanced Civics/American Government course in high school (that is, at grade 12). Unlike the historians, many of whom put enormous effort into curriculum development and the training of teachers between about 1890 and 1930, political scientists never engaged in this kind of direct effort. To be sure, political science was never, in this era, anywhere near so sizeable a field as history. (See table 16-1.)

Thus, beginning about 1934, one might have seen the several social sciences moving in concert toward a gradually more empirical, critical study of citizenship, at least in spirit.* But the world war intervened, diverting manpower and attention. Then there ensued a touchy national political climate, marked by two opposed sets of pressures. On one side were those, always emerging after a successful war, who cared primarily about American hegemony in the world, the American century, American markets, and American influence in emerging nations. They were not interested in the inherent philosophical problems of citizenship, but in getting on with the job of ruling the world. Reverses, such as the rise of Soviet power or the 'loss' of China, were, they believed, due to disloyalty and faulty training in Americanism. In this era, for the first time overtly, the social sciences were attacked in their university safehouses for being disguised forms of communism. On the other side were those who thought in terms of One World, transnational frameworks, invoking pleasant if infeasible notions of universal citizenship, supranational loyalty, and cultural freedom that would somehow join the first and second worlds. Thus, in one way or another, by 1950 or so all extant approaches to citizenship in social studies seemed blocked: simple allegiance to the nation (too chauvinistic), a dispassionate social scientific analysis (too critical), or a mildly reformist descriptive sociology (too intellectually outmoded).

There were also new concerns in political science as a discipline that, taken together, tended to separate academicians from the schools (and tended conse-

---

*Although the realities of the 'production' and training of teachers makes one doubt that much depth could have been achieved, other than in history.

quently to leave civics largely in the hands of historians). We have mentioned how, first, the goal of the training of elites for government service and then, second, the aspect of public administration had moved away from the core of the academic discipline. Now the notion of active universal participation in affairs of the polity, which had been the most consistent theme in American political theory since the time of Jefferson and Madison, came seriously into question as part of the behavioralist revolution in political science. New research and theory on political participation in American society, as a factual matter and as a philosophical value, meant that, while those in the schools and those in the universities could still agree on one focus of study—the structure and functioning of government—they could no longer agree (without tortuous reasoning) on the assumption that citizenship must mean active, informed participation (section 6.2). A queasiness within the discipline resulted vis-à-vis civics education in the schools. At about the same time, many in the academic profession turned to the study of political socialization, as an empirical rather than a normative enterprise (section 6.3). This had the effect of making the development of citizens' attitudes and knowledge the *object* of study within political science, rather than the *goal* of education as an enterprise.

6.2   The Enlargement of Politics: Government to Political Science

In brief, the behaviorally oriented political science of the 1950s and beyond, which involved sophisticated survey techniques and elaborate case studies of actual political processes such as legislation, referenda, identification of issues, selection of candidates for office, and the like, turned up a mass of evidence showing that most of the citizenry do not participate actively in political action, and when they do participate do so sporadically, in limited contexts with limited impact, and through multiple networks. In a sense this was not news: the arguments by political scientists in the early years of the century for the education of elites implied this—the notion that the citizenry at most ratified the actions of their leaders; and Tocqueville and others, as well as the sociologists of the early decades, had described the importance in American society of sodalities and pressure and issue groups. Research now demonstrated not only how little the citizenry participated, particularly at the level of the national 'system,' but how shallow their interest and knowledge were.

The model of aggregated individual rational decision-making that might be assumed in neoclassical economic theory did not work in political science, as Schumpeter pointed out.[26] Dahl[27] argued that only certain segments of society can be informed about much of anything, that different segments will be informed about different aspects of policy, and that the "making of governmental decisions is not a majestic march of great majorities united upon certain matters of basic policy. It is the steady appeasement of relatively small groups."

The empirical study of competing interests and processes implied more and more that educating large cohorts toward the principles of even classically described representative democracy was not only wasteful but wrong. Specifically, the very *modality* of such education—the provision of facts, practice in weighing the merits of arguments, calculation of self-interest against the public good—was irrelevant to the pragmatic interplay of politics: that is, the enshrining of rational decision-making as the intrinsic discipline of schooling was orthogonal to the larger political reality. Of course all this did not mean that students should not learn the structure and machinery of government, or be instructed in the central values of American democracy. It did mean that it became difficult for political scientists to endorse in good faith the idea that the *purpose* of such education was political participation and efficacy.

What would the alternatives be? One might be a closer study of specific sets of political actors. For example, a new and more empirical study of the behavior of elites took shape in the discipline. V. O. Key, Jr., pointed out: "The longer one frets with the puzzle of how democratic regimes manage to function, the more plausible it appears that a substantial part of the explanation is to be found in the motives that actuate the leadership echelon, the values that it holds, in the rules of the political game to which it adheres."[28] One implication here is that elite actors may be somewhat more 'rational' in their actions than the larger polity, and more perceptive about democratic values. More attention might be paid in advanced civics classes, for example, to the specific interests and styles of action of labor unions, lobbying groups, and various other groups-as-actors. The problem here (foreshadowed by the Middletown studies and others) is that to some degree the actions of such groups, be they elite, popular, or special-interest, are at least partially closed to students. For many reasons—the self-interest of such groups, a fear of skepticism being bred in students, or sheer practicality—most communities do not want students to know a great deal about the situated, that is, local or localized, inner workings of political life.

The repeated documentation, during these decades, of the parlous hold of adults on democratic principles—virtually every study showed that the public believed in the protection of minority rights, but far more so if they were not faced with particular instances[29]—might argue for increased discussion of values and political theory in the schools. After all, a cynical, self-interested, highly negotiated politics was not specific to American democracy, and in fact might be much more true of oligarchies and even totalitarian bureaucracies. Unfortunately, in this era the perceived threat from other nations was high, the suspicion and reality of internal disloyalty in the Western democracies was great, and the spectre of totalitarianism was held up by scholars such as Hannah Arendt as well as journalists and commentators. In fine, at a time of external threat and a crisis mentality, it was difficult to propose a deeper and more candid examination of politics in the schools.*

*Too much weight should not be assigned to such eral interpretations. In the 1960s and 1970s, *internal* stresses and strains—the civil rights movement, student rebellions, and so on—were the reason why many people believed the schools should be circumspect. A general conclusion has to be that the critical function of public education is always limited.

The great growth in the economy and the notably high level of productivity during these decades increased labor force participation and occupational status (and real earnings) for many, even most, groups in society. This coincided with the inclusion of more and more of the young in schools (figure 4-1). One could argue, once again, that the public viewed 'democracy' very much in terms of broad access to opportunity, the possibility of upward social mobility; in that sense, fealty toward the democratic process might depend on a rejection of class and other segmental interests (as had been true, in a different form, in the earlier part of the nineteenth century). The broad acceptance of the 'new industrial state' (as with John Kenneth Galbraith) or the 'end of ideology' (as with Daniel Bell), and familiarity with a government and an economy whose modern functional and institutional complexity and constraints were of an order of magnitude greater than those of the first half of the century—all of these can be cited hypothetically to explain why the central idea of Progressivism, progress through directed political action on the part of an ever-widening segment of the citizenry, became obsolete.

The danger, for a commitment to citizenship, in a too-credulous acceptance of such a bland 'reality' was not overlooked in this period. We know, for example, that school materials were prepared around the issue of control over the military, following the firing of General MacArthur by President Truman and President Eisenhower's warning about the military-industrial complex. But waves of external and internal crises—the possession of the hydrogen bomb, Korea, bomb shelters in the schools, Sputnik, Cuba, assassinations, Vietnam, civil unrest—militated against any thorough revision of a superficial civics (advanced or not, grade 9 or grade 12).*

What we may draw from all this is that civics became a sensitive part of the curriculum, to be given only cautious attention in the schools, and that the discipline of political science became, on theoretical and principled grounds, uneasy about its hitherto special relationship with civics. It is not accidental that law-related education in the schools, begun as an initiative of the American Bar Association, became widely accepted in the 1960s. The understanding of law in its constitutional aspect would, it was seen, serve a bonding and affiliating purpose; and in its criminal and civil law aspects (and, beyond this, its legislative and regulatory aspects) might be a safe avenue toward both realistic understanding of society—in the sense, of how legitimately to 'work' society for one's legitimate interests—and the long-enunciated, ever-elusive goal of actual participation in civil life. The law-related education movement was facilitated by Watergate and its constitutional issues about 1972. Unlike external crises, Watergate was a challenge within our system, rather than to it, and could he examined in traditional constitutional terms.

In higher education, there began to be some movement toward the preparation of teachers to handle civics and government more professionally—that is,

---

*It probably meant also that a wave of interest in international relations and global interconnectedness, evident in the late 1940s and 1950s, was angled markedly in the chauvinistic or defensive direction.

as specialists. One of the AHA commission volumes, published in 1937, had said: "The history teacher should have special preparation in geography, economics, sociology, and political science. No one of these, however, should be regarded as a special field of education."[30] However, beginning in the mid-1940s, there was some attempt on the part of schools of education and in the licensure agencies to encourage 'social studies' majors. In parallel, the BA 'output' of political science began to rise after 1960 (table 16-1). The former movement, which died out with the coming of the New Social Studies era (except for some elementary teachers), involved double majors or distribution of coursework in the academic course spread over several fields—generally, history plus another subject area, but also, to some extent, preparation in sociology-anthropology-psychology (a 'behavior science pattern') or government-sociology-economics (a 'social science' or civics-related pattern). In this volume we do not do more that touch on teacher education patterns over the years. However, Turner, writing in the later 1970s, quotes[31] assessments such as the following of the preparation for civics and government teaching:

> A general downgrading of the importance of politics in our schools, reflected in an inadequate training of government teachers and in the time actually devoted. . . . A majority of teachers actually devote only 10–15% of classroom time to government and the rest to history. Many teachers have training in history, few if any in political science. . . . Most teachers rely almost solely on textbooks, most of which are dull, outdated, one-sided, and reactionary.

Turner reports that most government courses were taught "in a formal, descriptive, and bookish way," and quotes a number of studies that showed that classroom controversy or issues discussion was generally avoided.*

6.2.1   Assessment of Civics

After a period of partial separation from civics and government in the schools (for reasons outlined above) and responding to the promise of the New Social Studies, which had not yet faded, the APSA again, in 1970, reexamined its responsibility to these school subjects, by creating a distinguished committee on precollegiate education. Its first task was a thorough review of texts and teaching materials and prevailing practices.

The committee's report[32] is a fairminded and trenchant assessment not only of its own field but of some of the broader aspects of the situation of the social studies as of the 1970s; in these respects, the situation is little changed today. Had

---

*She also points out a very important aspect of the problem: that the academic coursework of teachers (other than perhaps historians) is likely to be inappropriate to the purpose, since the university-level instruction tends to be given by research-oriented professors or graduate students (in basic-level courses) who dislike a 'survey' approach to their own fields and do not care about pedagogy.

the APSA had the continual identification with the school curriculum that the AHA had (for the most part in earlier decades), and had the APSA chosen the format of a national, multidisciplinary commission (like, for example, the 1934 AHA commission), it is likely that this report would have had notable repercussions in the social studies. As it was, the report was addressed to the disciplinary profession, only some of whom cared about the schools.

The APSA report was quite devastating. It said that political science education in the schools was grossly inadequate, and that this had serious consequences.* Here are some of the summary comments:

- Political science education in elementary and secondary schools should transmit to students a knowledge about the 'realities' of political life as well as exposing them to the cultural ideals of American democracy.†

- Political science education . . . should transmit to students a knowledge about political behavior and processes as well as knowledge about formal governmental institutions and legal structures.

- Political science should develop . . . a capacity to think about political phenomena in conceptually sophisticated ways.

- Political science should develop . . . a capacity to make explicit and analyzed normative judgments about political decisions and policies.

- Political science should develop . . . an understanding of the social psychological sources and historical-cultural origins of their own political attitudes and values.

- Much of current political science instruction transmits a naive, unrealistic and romanticized image of political life which confuses the ideals of democracy with the realities of politics. . . . Elementary materials present a picture of an America where everyone cooperates and no one fails.

- Weakness is found in almost all the widely used secondary level textbooks upon which teachers place strong, almost obsessive, reliance . . . they confuse what *is* with what *ought* to be.

- On the whole, instruction . . . places undue stress upon historical events . . . dreary descriptions . . . ethnocentric preoccupation . . . seldom are students confronted with issues, instructed in the methods of inquiry, or motivated to use facts effectively to substantiate or refute political beliefs. (pp. 434–439)

In the later pages of the report, the committee analyzed the educational system in a way that made plain its recognition that much of the problem of isolation between the discipline and the schools lay with the university teachers

*The 1971 report did not debate what was civics, what government, and what political science but used the last term generally—and preferentially. It thus reflected the academic orientation of the era, rather than the spirit of 1916.

†The phrase "cultural ideals" contains a lot, succinctly.

and researchers, and that certain other aspects of the general problem were aspects of 'the system.' The committee recognized its ongoing responsibility for constructive criticism and for the improvement of teacher training, texts, and materials—and indeed the enlightened governance and financing of schools as institutions. However, there was to the casual reader of the diagnostic part of the report an apparent tone of teacher-bashing. Teachers, already under pressure from academics to adopt a new style of instruction, in the New Social Studies, were being told by academics (at least in a quick reading) that their previous level of accomplishment was dreadful. This may have been another reason why the report did not receive much attention within the schools.

It is also fair to observe that the profession did not take on, as a priority, the disciplinary association's statement of continuing responsibilities to the improvement of precollegiate education. Here, as is the case with the general academic-schools relationship, there is more than enough fault to go around. No disciplinary body can force its members to reorient their priorities. The APSA did in fact accomplish a good deal. It sponsored or helped bring into being several important university centers in curriculum development and materials; a number of useful monographs on new concepts and approaches; and prototype courses that led to significant and venturesome new texts in American Political Behavior and Comparative Political Systems. These were organized around principles of structured inquiry and logical analysis in the service of decision-making,* and are generally considered to be exemplary in terms both of disciplinary standards and pedagogical strength.

Many of these materials and approaches are still widely used, and many of the young political scientists who began to participate in these processes are today leaders in political education at the different levels. However, it cannot be said that there has been a clear shift upward in the quality of instruction. Quite the contrary. Within the last few years, People for the American Way, a nonpartisan constitutional liberties organization, sponsored another review by distinguished political scientists and school teachers of U.S. government and civics texts. If anything, this assessment was more despairing than that in 1971.[33] It reported that texts were bigger, broader, more attractive, and well-balanced. It also reported that they were bland, uninteresting, lifeless, and cognitively unstimulating.

> The encyclopedic nature of these texts may be their greatest failing. Readers are led to conclude that what is most important to learn about government is facts, facts, and more facts. . . . What is missing, in a word, is controversy. . . . Eighty percent of the civics books and half of the government books minimize conflict and compromise. The dynamic sense of government and politics . . . is lost. The vitality of political involvement . . . is neglected. . . . The crucial role of participation is not high-

---

*They can be seen as a part of the second wave of the New Social Studies, in which the relevant subjectmatter, having been analyzed as to its inherent conceptual organization and hierarchy, is then reconfigured for instruction (section 5.3.2).

lighted. . . . If students are led to believe that the work of democracy is done, that no problems remain unsolved, they will see no need for their involvement. As one reviewer put it: 'If there are no injustices to right and no villains to defeat, it is hard to get excited.' (pp. i–ii)

The diagnosis is clear—and consistent over many decades. But the lack of a point of purchase from which to go beyond exhortation—to reform teacher preparation or curriculum making (if that is the answer)—is as evident as ever.

6.3   Conceptualization and Socialization in Political Education

The era of the New Social Studies marked the confluence in the 1960s and early 1970s of a period of intense public interest in the improvement of schools, the involvement of academics in precollegiate education in a new spirit, and the impact of a new 'master idea' on the intellectual scene. In social studies, no such confluence of influences has ever been seen other than in the correspondence of the 'descriptive sociology' pattern of the committee of 1916 with the Cardinal Principles of 1918. The new spirit of academic involvement was, not to seek courses or time in the curriculum (as, for example, in the 'electives' trend of the late 1930s and the 1940s), but to rethink the nature of instruction at the level of specific content and classroom interaction. The emergent 'master idea,' succeeding social evolutionism, structural-functionalism, and behavioralism, was cognitivism.

Cognitivism in political science was clearly reflected in the popularity of political socialization research, which investigated broad aspects of the development—normally along the dimension of age, but not necessarily—of how young people arrive at attitudes and concepts. The other facet of cognitivism, the conceptualizing of the structure of disciplines, was not easily adaptable to political science. Beyond a certain level of analysis, some of the central ideas and concepts of the field are not reducible: Authority, Legitimacy, Rights, and so on, can be glossed in many vocabularies, and many instances can be given, but they do not display neat dimensions and clearcut attributes. They are images and icons; they are simultaneously philosophical primes (like 'causation' in history) and overly determined symbols that cannot completely be 'unpacked.' There is also the fact, on a more pragmatic level, that political science has very ancient distinct traditions—such as political theory, jurisprudence, institutional description—and humanistic as well as social scientific aspects, and these are not convertible into each other.*

---

*This separation of traditions is reflected at the level of disciplinary self-description. American Government, American Politics, Political Science are all familiar enough labels in education, each with its own set of implications as to the essential subjectmatter. It is not clear where the field most directly touches on educational philosophy. Amy Gutmann, herself a political scientist, writes (*Democratic Education*, p. 15): "Most political scientists who write about education subsume it under the concept of political socialization," a judgment that I believe many of her colleagues would reject. Gutmann's own book is about political theory and education.

Particularly with regard to citizenship in the schools, the structure-of-the-discipline approach never dominated, as it did for a time some of the other disciplines in relation to their own distinctive subjectmatters. Bruner himself said that the goal of education should be a dual one, personal development (in schools, largely intellective in nature) and effective citizenship.*[34] In New Social Studies materials and curricula, however, education for citizenship was hardly ever confronted as a subject: it was at best a byproduct or understood as an unanalyzable goal.

Leaving aside the fact that citizenship per se was not the focus of interest in political science during this era, we can still identify some approaches typical of New Social Studies thinking. One was the attempt to correlate bodies of knowledge, so as to show how separate ways of looking at the same phenomena are really facets of each other—the translatability of organized knowledge. Fenton's interrelating of the concepts and materials of history and political science[35] is an example, although many historians believed that history cannot be analyzed into a 'structure' of concepts and generalizations.†

Another approach was to regard any single discipline as a subset of a broader framework, an idea of 'sizing down' or 'sizing up' that today might be called holographic. Thus, politics is a subsystem of the study of society, as are economics, sociology, and so forth. This approach was implicitly exemplified in the general approach of Taba to curriculum, especially in the middle grades, and is clearly compatible with the ideal of a 'fused' social studies field.‡

Comparative government was considered a subfield compatible with the notion of analyzing systems into their component parts, so as to see commonalities and uniqueness. The Fenton and Penna text followed this path, with particular attention also paid to historical backgrounds of given systems.

Perhaps the most straightforwardly analytical approach, separating out dimensions or facets of a delimited subject, was taken in the American Political Behavior materials, which emphasized key concepts such as socialization, status, role, leadership, decision-making—going back and forth from these as generic in any system to their specific manifestation in the American context.

The fact that these descriptions of NSS curriculum projects sound very much like any systematic, analytical approach to the exposition of a social studies subject is perhaps itself an indication that the New Social Studies approach did

*Bruner can in some ways be seen as Dewey, reversed. That is, Dewey held the same goals; but while Dewey believed that personal engagement developed, through education and other avenues, into an understanding of intellectual structure, Bruner believed that grasping the structure of a subject contributed strongly to personal development.

†Assessments by social studies professionals in the 1970s tended to show that civics and government New Social Studies materials were used more frequently by teachers trained in political science than in history. It may be that the former found these materials intrinsically more compatible with their own teaching orientations. But it could also be that on the average those trained in political science were younger (and fewer) and thus tended to be more venturesome, more prone to adopt new method.

‡For a political scientist's skeptical view of this approach, see p. 134.

not go very deep into political science. For one thing, these materials were developed rather late in the New Social Studies period. By then it was already apparent that the explicit interrelating of concepts across several disciplines at once—that is, the laying out of corresponding terminology, the demonstration that the same generalization can arise from many different kinds of instances or fields—was laborious to produce, to teach, and to learn.*

Concurrently with the curriculum projects here cited, several important thinkers concentrated on developing the formal analysis of values—often, or usually, civic and political values. This, of course, *was* directly relevant to civics, and remains a significant approach in that area today.† The work in values analysis was compatible in tone with the more empirically oriented work of the day, in the sense that it assumed that concepts in one culture or system can be related to alternative or corresponding concepts in others. But such an approach is commonplace in the study of ethics or analytic philosophy, which may be the more natural 'host' to the values analysis aspect of social studies than any kind of cognitivism.   On the other hand, the careful and sophisticated, ethically neutral, approach of Shaver or Oliver and Newmann fitted the times in being orderly and social in character—delineating comparative systems and dimensions of values, both in time and in space, and acquainting the student with a wide range of actual examples before moving to a more abstract level. The values clarification approach also communicated one very crucial concept unifying at least one approach to social studies: that is, the fundamental difference between fact and value.‡

Critics of the values analysis approach could grant this, and still believe (as many did) that the intellectual/analytical approach to values was largely backward: first should come the affective commitment to particular values, then could come the study of 'valuing.' That is, of course, fundamentally inimical to the Brunerian ideal, which would hold that 'political theory,' for example, can meaningfully engage ten-year-olds as well as political science majors or political philosophers. The dilemma—of commitment permitting breadth of view, or breadth of view as the basis for commitment—is an eternal one in education. Ultimately the clarification of values and valuing may lead to a *narrowing*, not a broadening, of possible choices (or even of the 'zone of tolerance' of the

---

*We refer here not to charges on the part of some that the whole enterprise was artificial and unsuitable for the schools, and perhaps more interesting to academics than to students or their teachers, but to a simpler consideration. Concept learning is by definition systematic: the 'concept' does not arise until the entire critical set (of dimensions, attributes, and so on) has been exposed. This takes time and concentration, not always available in the classroom, where other forms of learning by inference, more gradual, probably fuzzier, may be more feasible. A criticism of highly structured exposition in the schools is that if you do not go the whole way, you end up with less than nothing—for example, a partially formed concept that is distorted or misleading.

†For example, the Harvard Public Issues Series of the late 1960s (section 5.3.3).

‡The approach is ethically neutral only up to a point; that is, it assumes the value of rationality and tolerance.

choices of others), agreed upon for the sake of societal stability.* That is, for any sociopolitical system, only some alternatives are tolerable. The empirical study of individual and collective decision-making, in both its factual and value-laden aspects, is a contemporary feature of the field of political science. It would be wrong to suggest that the 'goal' of that field is to achieve the ideal balance. However, a revival of strong interest in political theory, based more on modern than on classical experience (for example, John Rawls, Michael Walzer, Alasdair MacIntyre) may make some progress toward that end.

6.3.1   Socialization

We now turn to the other main cognitive orientation, in this general period, within political science—political socialization. The field within political science developed in close conjunction with a corresponding subfield in social psychology. In the discipline of political science itself, in terms of the quantity of empirical research, 'political psychology' rapidly became the leading substantive field, by far, in the 1950 to 1970 period, especially among younger political scientists.[37] The 1971 APSA report (see p. 187) recommends that students in school understand the social psychological sources of their own attitudes and beliefs. Such a consideration would not have appeared twenty years earlier.

The research field has been organized around two central questions: first, what is the developmental pattern (in principle, lifelong) of knowledge about and attitudes toward politics; and, second, where are the sources of such knowledge and attitudes—where do they come from and how are they maintained or changed?[38]

A rough summary of what the research has shown, in the context of this country especially, is that basic orientations and affiliations with respect to politics—identification with and overall trust in the system, respect for leaders, national and even party loyalty, a basically liberal or conservative penchant—are attained early in life, are bred in the bone, at least among children who grow up where political awareness is a feature of the home situation. Thus by the early grades of primary school, certain stable if simplistic dispositions are set: this is a great country, its leaders care about us, the wars we fight are just wars, and so on. A little later, in the upper elementary grades or in middle school, attitudes become more differentiated, more knowledge-based (at least in the sense of children being able to cite more features of politics in connection with their beliefs), and more unstable. There is a degree of separation from the home, and teachers and peers may have a stronger influence. Basic commitments and orientations continue undisturbed, but children at these ages may now say that not all presidents are equally successful, or that the police sometimes make

---

*On this point, Sidney Hook has recently discussed, very cogently, a confusion between moral relativism and 'empirical relativism,' a confusion that he sees in Allan Bloom.[36]

mistakes, or that some groups are 'different.' The knowledge of political concepts like democracy, liberty, or rights, grows in terms of appropriateness of reference—students now offer definitions or summaries of what is meant by such terms—but it is very shallow, often just formula language or paraphrase.

This growing cognitive awareness, even if superficial, continues so that, for example, around grade 7 or 8 students seem to become interested in sociopolitical ideas. Some researchers distinguish between 'attitudes' and 'conceptualizations,' holding that the former are affectively based while the latter involve images and examples; however, both can be seen as broad dispositions. The instability arises both from new 'input' and from the degree of questioning the student may demonstrate. Early in high school, students often reveal concerns with the ideal versus the real, and show an awareness of and sharp dislike for 'hypocrisy': whether or not this develops seems quite dependent on peer interaction and on how the students themselves are treated.

Older adolescents, into university age, continue to refine their principles on the basis of new factual knowledge. Some continue to be especially sensitive to contradictions between what ought to be and what is. The sense of political 'efficacy' is formed at this age; that is, whether or not a person feels that she or he can make a difference in the political realm, either directly or with others.[39]

By their mid-twenties, many young adults seem to reach a plateau, where they are either interested in politics or relatively indifferent, are concerned with personal goals such as jobs and marriage, are no longer angrily disillusioned (if they ever were) though far from credulous, and often have reverted in some of their attitudes to those of their own origins and traditions, though perhaps in a more reasoned way. Studies of the adult population generally show that many to most adults are not greatly interested and not very active (though interest and activity may increase in the later years). It has often been noted that not only are politics, other than electoral politics, not very salient to a very large proportion of adults in the United States, but that those who focus on issues tend to do so in isolated frameworks, not related to historical experience, other issues, or longterm considerations.

Researchers have also found[40] that adults seek consensus and dislike controversy; they approve in the abstract of democratic procedures with regard to conflict, but tend to dislike those who use them. Attitudes toward political parties and social groups are fairly stable, often showing very little accurate knowledge of relevant issues and interests. Thus, while it is highly oversimplified, one can view both early childhood and adulthood as fairly stable periods, with a strong affective or subcognitive basis; in between, the school-age years show more interest and relatively more cognitive activity.

Note especially that there seems to be a fairly narrow period, perhaps in the middle-school years, when children seem open to the uptake of new knowledge and to temporary independence, at least, from prior 'setting' influences. As is always the case, it is not necessarily that schooling *produces* this, but that children at this age—who are demonstrating qualitatively new kinds of cognitive capacities, who are out in the world enough to be gaining information from new sources, whose linguistic abilities bring them into contact with others, and who may be psychologically insulated to some degree from their parents—are at an age when important new knowledge-based attitudes could be formed and tried out.

It is thus possible, ironically, that grade 9 is quite the wrong place for civics. (Recall that its existence here in part depended on 'catching' developing minds at the last possible moment before most of them would leave school; section 4.4.) From a cognitive developmental point of view, earlier would be more promising. Furthermore, instruction at grade 9 *leads* nowhere: students then begin a series of required courses and field-specific electives, and do not have the chance to inquire deeply about political matters (for example, in a grade 12 government or problems course) or engage in political activities (such as community service or civic 'internships') until the end of high school, if then.

Worse, the predominant style of instruction about politics in the middle grades is dry and distancing: the facts and dates of American history and the structure of different levels of government, combined—even more disastrously—with messages from teachers and textbooks that play down or camouflage conflict, seek 'coverage' rather than commitment or participation, and cut off the expression of opinion. This is not malfeasance by the schools; it reflects the passion for mastery of material, the passing of graded competency tests, and the like. Sears says: "It is worth noting that the school seems *most* cautious, and most dedicated to minimizing exposure to partisanship and conflict, in those years that seem . . . to be crucial for the development of partisan commitments."[41] It also reflects the proper reluctance of schools at this age to seem to be engaging in a too ideological or normative a way in 'political socialization' directly. That is, schools know they are one—but only one—arena for this aspect of socialization, and do not wish to appear to preempt others such as parents, community organizations, or political action groups.

6.3.2 EDUCATIONAL DEMOCRACY

The characteristics of schools as one of the arenas, of the school as a *setting* for political education, have concerned a number of thinkers. Many have looked at whether or not schools themselves are authoritarian or democratic, whether teachers 'model' democratic behavior in their treatment of their students, whether true discussion of issues is permitted, and many other such factors. In general, the answer is mixed. 'Classroom climate' has often been shown to breed cynicism—although it does not follow that *factual* learning is then reduced. A strong position is that *only* 'democratic' schools can instill a commitment to active, rational discussion, productive contention, and debate that lead in turn to a deep and sophisticated commitment to democratic political behavior. This is the view of, for example, Engle and Ochoa.[42] A review by Hepburn[43] is less clearcut on this matter, but does show, as do many other sources, that students at this age are easily 'turned off' by hypocritical, condescending instruction—or well-meaning blandness. It is not clear whether the variable of *engagement* is important—whether, for example, effective political instruction needs something more than teacher talk and text-reading. Some recommend games and simulations or group discussion and debate; others show the desirability of a student voice in school government; others favor cooperative learning (that is, in non-teacher-dominated student groups) of political material and concepts.* As Torney-Purta points out,[44] using concepts from cognitive theory, *exposure* to contrary evidence or opinions that differ from one's own has little effect, by itself. A ritualistic citation, sometimes found in texts, of "others, however, believe that . . ." has little salience, since students at this age have a great capacity to assimilate such cognitive input to their existing frameworks or to hold in mind comfortably quite contradictory facts or principles.

Some thoughtful commentators have made a very strong case for the negative effect of sheer *redundancy* in the whole sweep of schooling, especially when it is combined with hypocritical or stultifying instruction. Students are introduced to the basic facts and values of the American system from the earliest grades, in celebrations of holidays and the American way; to state and national history about grades 4 and 5; to some discussion of other societies (all too often, with a chauvinistic tune carrying the culture-fair words) in grades 6 to 8; often, to Civics at grade 9; U.S. History again at grade 11; Government at 12; and so on. How many times can a student answer a low-level factual test or recitation question on why Americans had to break from England, or what principles are laid out in the Declaration of Independence, before she stops thinking about the material?† There is compelling evidence that a redundancy-bred nescience is often the result.[45]

There are problems, however, with putting too much weight on this explanation. For one thing, other educational systems impose even more official civic redundancy on students, or so most observers believe. For another, the source of 'redundancy' *within* schooling may be minuscule compared to that delivered by the extended family, the church, the workplace, the media, and many other outside sources. This may mean not only that it is unfair to blame the schools, but that genuine attempts within school to deliver a challenging and sophisticated 'product' may be seriously undercut by other influences.

6.3.3   WHAT THE SCHOOLS CAN ACCOMPLISH

This brings us to the question that we said was the second major concern of political socialization research: What are the sources of political information

---

*Cooperative learning need not, of course, lead to consensus, but can be the avenue for quite conflictual debate, sometimes with 'reporting back' to the class and some resolution offered.

†Even this is not the crux of the matter. Students can be led more deeply into history or more challengingly into political science theory while still a certain core of iconic facts or concepts remain formulaic and buffered from examination.

and attitudes, and what are their relative weights? Specifically, what effects does schooling, per se, have? We offer here as examples only two pieces of evidence, both dealing with the schools. First, a large crossnational study conducted in 1971 in eight European democracies and the United States,[46] involving hundreds of schools and thousands of students, showed that American students ranked about midway in factual and basic conceptual knowledge, compared to all the countries; that *in all countries* a strong emphasis in schools on simple patriotic rituals and exhortations in the early adolescent years seemed to have counter-productive effects, being associated with lesser knowledge and commitment; and that American students scored *low* on attitudes toward democratic partici-pation and procedures (such as respect for minority rights and dissent). Such data suggest that American schools do a fair job in factual areas, but a relatively poor one in the creation of *either* interested and committed, or committed and critical, citizens.

Again, this does not mean that such a pattern is the fault of the schools; after all, as we have pointed out, attitudes arise from more sources than 'facts.' In many ways the most interesting aspect of the IAEEA study is that in *none* of the Western countries were the schools very successful with regard to all four goals tested in the study: knowledge, support for democratic values, allegiance to the national government, and interest in personal participation. By now, this should not be a surprising result. Schools in democratic societies pursue multiple, perhaps quite incompatible, goals. The IAEEA study and others show that, if anything, 'interest in participation' is *negatively* associated with allegiance to the government, and that in some countries that scored high in tested knowledge, cynicism and alienation were quite evident. The study also reported that knowledge scores were not strongly associated with the number of courses taken that dealt with government, national history, and the like.

These results once again suggest that the schools cannot, themselves, count for a great deal in helping students to reach the various goals, and that other influences are of great importance. As Ralph Tyler[47] puts it: "If civic education is to be made more effective, it will be necessary for the school to re-examine contemporary conditions, to identify the kind of contributions that it is capable of making, and to encourage and support efforts of other community institu-tions."

In their large and well-analyzed study in the 1960s, Jennings, Niemi, and Langton[48] found that the high-school curriculum had strikingly little effect on citizenship outcomes. There was, first, no major difference between students who had taken American Government courses and those who had more topical Problems courses. In either case, for the study population as a whole, the number of courses taken was associated only slightly with level of knowledge, attention to political content in the media, engaging in political discourse, feelings of political efficacy, espousing a participative (rather than a loyalty) orientation, and showing more civic tolerance. It did appear that taking more courses increased the level of trust in the political process—up to a point (taking *many* courses was *negatively* correlated with trust, to a slight degree). The authors comment, "The increments are so minuscule as to raise serious questions about the utility of investing in government courses in the senior high schools, at least as these courses are presently constituted" (p. 191). The number of history courses taken showed even less effect. Even worse, perhaps, most of the 'incremental knowledge' appeared to be recent, and to come from students who were currently taking relevant courses. These authors report that similar findings have resulted in studies in other Western democracies (the IAEEA studies, above), and they suggest a version of the redundancy hypothesis: "Students not taking civics courses are probably exposed to these other sources in approximately the same doses as those enrolled in the courses" (p. 193)—and thus score almost as well.

The redundancy notion and related ones generally suggest that in the realm of civic knowledge and attitude there is an enormous *adaption* effect in education: that is, that everyone knows 'the agenda' before it is formally stated, the same material is presented over and over, the students know it anyhow, and those who learn a great deal merely happen to learn it in school or learn it *through* schooling but not because *of* schooling. Leming points to this concern[49] when he writes: "The interesting thing in the well over 100 experimental studies [of curriculum effects on student values] was that in the *traditional* [control group] classes not a single case was identified where... the traditional text, curriculum, and method of instruction [had] a measurable impact on student values" (emphasis added).

In the study by Jennings and colleagues, which used probability sampling of segments of the high-school-student population, there was one hopeful finding. The civics curriculum turned out to be a substantial source of political knowledge for blacks. It is reassuring that minority group students gain new knowledge, even if the majority group is 'saturated.' Blacks who had taken more courses also showed more of a resulting sense of political efficacy. Unfortunately, the *kind* of civic attitudes that the blacks demonstrated were those of 'the good' rather than the active or critical citizen: the general picture was that of a relatively 'depoliticized' group, especially among blacks from higher status families. The authors comment: "While the civics curriculum has little impact upon the white student's view of the good citizen role, it appears to inculcate in blacks the role expectation that a good citizen is above all a loyal citizen rather than an active one" (p. 202). There are at least two possibilities here—that blacks in general were relatively more indoctrinated, in the bad sense of the term, than whites (at a time in our history when the civil rights movement was at its height) through schooling, or that most of the effects in the study came from higher-status blacks who indeed, through schooling, became more 'like' the majority group, while lower-status blacks remained alienated. Neither interpretation is reassuring.

In this tradition of research there are many such studies of the effects of schooling on citizenship, some using large probability samples and many dimensions of inquiry, some small in size and quite ad hoc. The results are mixed. However, there appears to be *no* research of any impressive technical quality that shows a strongly *positive* relationship. This does not mean that civics education is not leading students toward adequate citizenship in practice, but it strongly suggests that there is something the matter with the way the specific educational goals and behaviors are defined. The body of research touched on here is important because it does separate out different *aspects* of political education and it does establish quite firmly that different *kinds* of education occur at different ages: basic affiliations and attachments, in childhood; the development of concepts and images and general knowledge 'bundles,' in later childhood and early adolescence; and a decision to participate in the political process or to remain relatively remote, in young adulthood. From these broad considerations, we suggested above that grade 9 may be too late for the kind of approach Civics generally employs. Training in citizenship (in the sense of explicit behavior) through Civics is not something the schools do well. It is also quite possible that the grade 12 Government or Problems course (besides being for some quite redundant) is ineffective with regard to knowledge, skills, and motivations relevant to participation, though it may in some cases be intellectually enriching or challenging.

Having suggested all this, we still would point out that *in principle* the sequence Civics, History, Government is a rational one, given what is known of the stages of political learning. Parker and Jarolimek[50] provide a very useful, cautionary, and realistic point: "The *absence* [emphasis added] of social studies from the curriculum would mean that what is virtually the only structured source of direct citizenship education would be missing. For the younger students, this would remove a direct program of citizenship education just when the foundation of the citizenship identity is being crystallized. For older students, this would remove a direct program of citizenship education just when partisan affiliations are being examined and general civic knowledge acquired." In other words, things could be worse.

Moreover, even if the particular goals of 'citizenship' are contradictorily or unrealistically conceived, social studies may provide other, related things that can only be beneficial. Students themselves can be quite clear on this. A recent survey of graduating seniors in four quite diverse communities across the country[51] again showed that the extent of coursework in government, history, and so forth, seemed to bear little relationship to citizenship attitudes. More interestingly, students did not seem to conceive of 'citizenship' as having much to do with *either* factual knowledge *or* with participation in politics, nor did they see citizenship as a central or defining thread in social studies. Instead, for these students, interpersonal morality (cooperativeness, tolerance, and the like) and wise decision-making (strictly speaking, good judgment that permits such) were the crux. To them, 'citizenship' did not seem to be a very political matter. In a related study by the same investigators,[52] teacher educators and methodology teachers seemed to put the importance of the skills of thinking and analysis ahead of either knowledge per se or actual participation. They, too, seemed to converge on effective and ethical decision-making as a prime goal. Regardless of what others outside the schools may wish, most would agree that if those within the schools—teachers and students—could accomplish just this, much good would result. Note that such an accomplishment might well involve reasoning *with* democratic values[53] as opposed to either value indoctrination or a laborious attention to values clarification. It implies a core of unexamined assumptions, but a considerable degree of 'practice' with democratic principles and procedures. This would reassure those like Leming, who believe that it is illusory to suppose that students in school are in fact able and free to make important participatory decisions, and that to pretend otherwise breeds cynicism or anomie.

Gutmann[54] again summarizes many of these considerations.

> Empirical studies measure the results of history and civics courses as they are, not as they might be . . . and only some, not all, of the results that are relevant to the concern for fostering democratic virtue. Only a small minority of high-school history or civics teachers take as one of their major goals to challenge their students to think critically about history or politics . . . to *reason*, collectively and critically, about politics. . . . The ability is so essential to democratic education that one might question whether civics courses that succeeded in increasing political trust, efficacy, and knowledge but failed to increase the ability of students to reason about politics were indirectly repressive. How can a civics course legitimately teach teenagers to trust their government more without also teaching them to think about what kind of government is worth trusting?

She cites testimony (from Diane Ravitch) that such intellectually challenging courses are not a "utopian fantasy," and makes the point made in somewhat different terms by Parker and Jarolimek: "However students have been socialized outside of school, there should be room within school for them to develop the capacity to discuss and defend their political commitments with people who do not share them . . . schools that fail to cultivate this capacity do not foster democratic virtue" (p. 107).

6.4   A Future for Political Education*

In many respects, political science is now in a good position, in terms of its intellectual orientation and in terms of its cultural reputation, to cooperate

*Many of the topics and considerations covered in the present chapter, together with recommendations for theory, research, and practice in education, are treated also by Russell F. Farnen.[55] His book contains a useful comparison, 1976–86, of goals and practices in the schools of various countries, and reviews a huge literature. In general, Farnen finds an inherently multidisciplinary framework offered by policy analysis or policy science heuristically powerful in dealing with citizenship and related topics—a conclusion compatible with that reached by the present author, in his treatment of decision-making (section 6.4).

fruitfully with the schools. Its 'slots' in the curriculum are secure (although we have suggested that Civics may not be effectively presented at grade 9). A perhaps extreme fascination in the 1950s and 1960s for small, discrete behavioral studies of political processes, which inevitably led to rampant empiricism and technique-fondling, has receded.

Similarly, a certain obsessive trendiness with regard to the study of political socialization has passed. At one extreme, that specialty tended toward over-drawn models of necessary developmental stages of political and moral thinking, which might logically call for carefully calibrated indoctrination or intervention at precise points in order to effect particular attitudes, knowledge structures, civic commitments—all of that being impossible to achieve, as well as undemocratic. At another extreme, the study of political socialization became so complex, in trying to handle the interaction of human development and cognition, sociological structures and variables, social psychological dynamics, and cultural setting factors over time, that it had the potential to subsume all political science, perhaps all social science, within some vast net of concepts about the relationship between the individual and society.

Instead, there have recently been a number of intellectual developments that are hopeful. The discipline is once again interested in the study of the state in ways going beyond the nation-state, and in institutions that are of political consequence without being strictly governmental. The appearance and persistence of additional instances of democratic government and culture, since the immediate postwar period, enriches the field from which analyses can be drawn, as does the apparent movement toward forms of democracy in nondemocratic societies. Enriching the fields of political science, economics, social psychology, and sociology, at least—in fact, adumbrating a general field of 'decision science'—is a body of 'public choice theory' and powerful research findings about collective decision-making in various kinds of collectivities and institutions, ranging from corporations to governmental agencies to voluntary groups to international negotiations.* Additional experience has, by now, accumulated in such matters as presidential versus legislative dominance, national/state relationships, the avoidance of nuclear disaster, and the reform of party politics. That means, not that political life has become easy or safe, but that the theoretical frameworks may have become more ample and true to life.

There are, in the society, signals of troubled, interesting times ahead (section 18.0). No doubt it is just as well that the citizenry no longer seems as complacent as it did a few decades ago, that there has been some abatement of the view that citizenship involves judging whether or not 'the system' works—for me and mine. At the same time, this view *is* held by a significant portion of the society, and a lack of a strong faith in politics, government, and a broader range of civic life (social institutions, legal structures, cultural norms of human interaction) is widespread. The most useful development within the field of political science,

*Herbert Simon, James March, Kenneth Arrow, James Buchanan, Mancur Olson, among others.

with regard to public education, may be the development of the empirical science of collective decision-making, because it tells us that people in general do not try to 'solve' problems but to mitigate or go around them, and that people in general do not seek perfect happiness but a reasonably stable compromise among 'goods.' The next most important development (in this writer's opinion) may be a renewed interest, as yet shadowy, in intermediate levels and forms of group action, participation, governance, allegiance, and the like: in the state house and local government, in social networks and non-single-issue groups, or in how persuasion and influence work, for good or bad, in communities. There seems to be some agreement to look, neither at purely behavioral processes nor at formal institutional structures, but at a range and density of politics that mediates between the extremes of leadership or oligopoly, on the one hand, and of atomistic experience, such as individual self-aggrandizement or alienation, on the other.

If some of these developments persist, it would help democratic education. Newmann has pointed recently[56] to the insufficiency of educating for either "supportive" or "instrumental" participation, but calls rather for socially productive human interaction, involving a kind of cooperative self-determination. Walzer[57] recommends something similar: the idea that modern 'citizenship' is some blend of orderly argument and compromise reached through pragmatic experience, sufficient to the demands of the situation, together with a degree of reflection on first principles and philosophical reasoning on how, ideally, to deal with value conflicts. This view partially counters the emphasis of advocates of 'strong democracy'—those who insist on full, fairly direct democratic participation, such as Benjamin Barber.[58] Thinkers such as Walzer want to see, not some citizens conducting the practical business of politics and others reflecting upon the ideal, but citizens in general doing some of both.

Gutmann, in her recent and brilliant book, comes down on the same side of what might be called negotiated realism, and insists that the matter of political education remains inescapable. "A more robust democratic politics . . . would render the concerns of democratic education not less but more important. Just as we need a more democratic politics to further democratic education, so we need a more democratic education to further democratic politics. If we value either, we must pursue both" (p. 18). R. Freeman Butts, eminent in the educational world and espousing a set of values and priorities quite different from Gutmann's, nevertheless in his 1989 book[59] quotes Gutmann to this point:

> 'Political education' has moral primacy over other purposes of public education in a democratic society. . . . The most devastating criticism we can level at . . . schools, therefore, is not that they fail to give equally talented children an equal chance to earn the same income or to pursue professional occupations, but that they fail to give all (educable) children an education adequate to take advantage of their political status as citizens.

There are significant numbers in our society who simply do not agree, for whom socialization or vocational preparedness or academic achievement is the overwhelming goal (section 15). This disagreement on overriding purposes is why Welter[60] wrote: "The idea of education is powerful in the United States today without being persuasive." But even those who do not give primacy to political education give it some importance, as do those in official control of the enterprise of education. For these strategic reasons, together with the more thoughtful reasons of philosophers and political theorists, it would be disastrous to assert that 'civics' is no longer an issue.

'Civics' needs to be reinvented, in a practical, thoughtful, realistic way. Political science cannot do the job alone.[61] Those within political science who care about public education at the precollegiate level have sometimes seemed to recommend giving up on the whole enterprise, because the discipline cannot make a permanent, effective commitment to take responsibility for it. This is unrealistic, and unfair. Others within political science (and neighboring disciplines) will always distance themselves from the problem, observing that 'civics' is fuzzy, nonspecifiable, normative in tone, and generally suspect. In this view, civics is not political science (or history, or sociology)—and thus must be lesser. The legitimacy of democratic education, however, cannot derive from any single source or goal, academic or other.

The solution does not lie finally in the improvement of teachers or texts, though both would be helpful. There are reasons why, as a group, teachers are ineffectual and at cross-purposes with regard to civics (and government) instruction; these reasons have to do with the reality of conflicting, and morally and cognitively stressful, expectations on the part of those with stakes in the matter. The back-to-basics reforms so widely recommended in this era offer no panacea; the 'basics' referred to are a necessary but not sufficient set of fundamentals for political education. Furthermore, the emphasis on the tangible *achievement* of specific knowledge, as in test scores, raises deep questions about equity and the balancing of interests in public education. To be blunt, 'back to basics' will be an advance only if it works well for most students, not simply those who find one set of 'basics' compatible and easily attained. As Sidney Hook points out (see p. 192), relativism is a necessary condition of viable democracy.

Most of the calls for reform of public education in the 1980s (section 1) reiterate the need for education in the service of citizenship. Almost all professional educators agree. Within social studies, in 1979 the NCSS reaffirmed that citizenship was the central aim of the entire field.[62]

There is still pervasive disagreement on what should be accomplished in education with regard to citizenship and politics, and recently there has been a tone almost of panic in recognizing this. People in the field today see the confusion acutely, but do not recognize the longstanding nature of it. To some degree, the fading away of the New Social Studies brought this perpetual conflict back into play by default. The conflict was sharpened in the 1980s, by the renewed attention of groups outside education to citizenship as one of the major, if not the major, goal of education generally.

But the civics/politics issue contains all the tensions in social studies, in sharpened form: emphasis on content versus emphasis on process; history versus social studies versus social science; a curriculum aimed at a rich description of reality versus one that provides opportunities for students to act politically; 'high culture' versus technical or instrumental goals. Various groups involved with citizenship and with the schools disagree even among themselves.* To repeat once again: the *source* of conflicts about what civics education (and the social studies generally) should be is quite clear. It is a multiplicity of and incompatibility among goals. Turner puts it clearly in discussing 'the textbook problem,' which is now more than fifty years old. "If all texts fail in some degree despite the good will of political scientists, the interest of the APSA, and massive expenditures of developmental money, it seems logical to assume that the fault may be with the goals themselves."[63]

It is important not to ascribe goal conflicts that impact *upon* the schools *to* the schools, as if they originate there. To do so is continually to overemphasize a set of constants, and underattend to what does change. Politics and governance are a universal aspect of social life, and students are heavily influenced by many factors outside education. Remy[64] makes the point that citizenship education is a matter of giving students cognitive understanding of what they already know anyhow. The Newmann-Oliver approach to the cognitive analysis of values in society depends on the notion that students must first be able to describe their own system realistically before they can move on to comparisons and the weighing of alternatives. Such comments refer to the constants in education, the making conscious of what is latent. But it is also well to remember that citizenship education in the schools seems to have a *differential* effect at the extremes: if important knowledge and useful concepts are provided to the culturally disadvantaged, they appear to benefit more than do those whose knowledge is already present, albeit tacitly. (The corollary is that if those who are already enculturated in such matters are taught the obvious, especially in an authoritarian way, boredom and cynicism ensue.)†

---

*For example, in an era when political scientists subscribed, at least officially, to the notion that they had a special responsibility for and authority in civic education in the schools, the executive secretary of the APSA and his political scientist wife stated sharply that the view that high-school students should learn to be good citizens through the educational process showed a distorted view of how citizens are in fact developed, how the political world works, and what political science as a field is all about. Evron and Jeane Kirkpatrick, cited in Turner, "Political Education," p. 126.

†Some recent results of NAEP testing in civics (National Assessment of Educational Progress; see section 14.3) support the claim that civics instruction in the schools may be having different effects on different groups of students. Scores from 1988 showed a decline in achievement for seventeen-year-olds compared to 1976, but a modest increase for thirteen-year-olds. Among the latter, scores changed for the better for minority students, while scores for students from "advantaged urban communities" appeared to decline. The 1988 results come several years after some schools, at least, gave renewed attention to the 'basics' of American history and government. As suggested in section 6.3.3, such an emphasis might simply produce boredom (owing to redundancy of instruction) or cynicism among majority students, increasing across the grades, but a better grasp of test-relevant facts and concepts among minority students, especially at a younger age.[65]

We should be suspicious of any idea that conflicts among goals and fundamental assumptions can be solved simply by the right balancing of material. It is always helpful, within reason, to see a topic in broad perspective. But such a perspective can fail in focus. Today, for example, there is the clear message among many educators that, not only is 'global education' necessary *for* effective citizenship (in a kind of defensive reasoning—that is, those who know little about the present world cannot operate in it), but also the message that today's citizen must be a citizen *of* the world. That may well be true, but as yet such citizenship is unspecifiable on the concrete level. How does a global citizen gather the necessary information, globally? To which forms and levels of fealty does she subscribe, and what happens in cases of conflict? How does a citizen participate 'at a distance'?* How will all the potential citizens of the world have effective access to the process? It is not that such questions cannot be answered; indeed, raising them is the first step. But we also know that since before 1900 commentators on citizenship have been emphasizing the local/national balance; since 1950 or so the national/supranational balance. Simply moving the target or enlarging the framework does not solve the problems of focus.

Not only is political education thought to be essential for citizenship, it may also be essential for social studies. By this we mean that there is no curriculum area in the schools where it is so starkly clear that there *must* be both factual knowledge and the development of critical reasoning. In this subjectmatter, unless mere totem-worship or reflexive negativism is to result, both must occur or the facts are inert and the reasoning mere formalism. A student who likes a subject can recall enormous numbers of events and personages in history, or master a set of place names from geography that will win contests, or read two hundred ethnographies—all without ever getting 'the point'—that is, without drawing any productive kinds of inferences or evolving workable conceptual frameworks for such knowledge. There are, after all, students who memorize the value of *pi* to thirty places, or learn the entire Mendeleyev table, and such feats have a certain cultural value. But in civics this level of knowledge is of little consequence.

Political education is at the core of social studies in a special sense: not that it is intrinsically the most valuable knowledge, but that it is a fulcrum, a test point, around which other subjectmatters vary. Historians and geographers, for example, may argue that in these school fields there should be *relatively* more factual learning for the sake of citizenship, while anthropologists may argue that the mastery of culturally specific detail is *less* important than understanding conceptually what forms societal participation may take. For economics, the centrality of decision-making will be almost the sine qua non. For history, the mark of a truly educated person is always to seek out historical knowledge as part of the intellectual armamentarium when decisions are needed.

For political education, any extreme deviation from a synthesis of facts *and*

---

*A nice formulation here is that the citizen will think globally but act locally—René Dubos's phrase.

attitude, socialization *and* countersocialization, sociology *and* history, and the like, is counterproductive. Fortunately, since civic education is intrinsically multidisciplinary, it makes a practical focus for all social studies. At any moment, many of the key concepts of the several disciplines converge on this school subject: in economics, the allocation of scarce resources; in sociology, the concepts of interest group and social stratification; in anthropology, the fact that universally 'citizenship' is closely related to socialization (enculturation), but is always somewhat distinct from this, as a function of the political system.* In history, the rapidly expanding material of social history, using a wide range of nontraditional sources and materials, results in a knowledge of the biographies and experiences and situations of 'ordinary' citizens, in a multitude of eras and places, which can instruct and inspire the young.

For all these reasons, it seems unlikely that to give up on political education in the school curriculum would unify the field. Quite the contrary. Social studies needs political education as truly as political education requires social studies.

---

*For example, for the young in a new, developing country, it may be essentially nation-building: the training of elites to run the system. For citizens of a nondemocratic society it might involve periodic forced demonstrations of affiliation; for example, where failure to vote (generally for a single candidate or party) is penalized. Recent cultural anthropology also offers much new knowledge of a range of 'native' legal systems that have rich implications for enlarging the concept of the state.

7.0 Economics

7.1 Economics and Citizenship
7.2 Economics and the Problem of Realism

Economics was twice rebuffed as an equal partner in the social studies curriculum, in 1893 and again in 1916. Despite this, it became an important subjectmatter in the 1920s and 1930s, and after about 1950 set out to win a major role in the school curriculum. This it has succeeded in doing, thanks to organizational ability on the part of its proponents and to a continuing demand in society for its inclusion. In an important sense, the subjectmatter economics has ridden on the crest of that demand, even as it altered from era to era—from the desire for knowledge of political economy, to an interest in economics within 'community civics,' to an emphasis in the 1920s on business economics, to an altered emphasis in the 1930s on 'economic efficiency' and reforms. There has also been a widespread interest in 'personal' economics (consumer or household economics, and the like) and, most notably in recent years, a demand for the teaching of free-enterprise economics or economics in relation to global systems and interdependency. While economics scholars and curriculum experts have in many cases resisted giving any of these particular emphases pride of place in the courses they design—generally preferring that mainstream economics coexist with such specialized emphases in the curriculum—the field has on the whole benefited from the wide scope and constancy of interest and pressure from outside.

Tryon[1] reports that prior to 1900 the focus of economics in the college preparatory academies was Political Economy: in this context, a quite abstract, moralizing, and 'disciplining' study of the formal interrelationships of production, distribution, consumption, and exchange. Apparently there was little interest in economic history or in another aspect of 'political economy,' the relationship between governmental forms and economic systems: presumably this would have brought Marx, rather than Adam Smith, into consideration.* For whatever reasons, the highly rarefied nature of economics teaching at the end of the century caused it to be kept out of the 1893 NEA compromise (unlike

---

*This is not an inference of Tryon's.

the study of government). It was assumed that much economics could be taught through History.

In another demonstration of the rapidity of change in the frame of reference of the social studies within twenty-five years or so, the 1916 NEA committee also kept the study of economics out of the center of the curriculum, but on different grounds. The 1916 reformers wanted to make economics an important part of Community Civics, in close linkage with sociology and economic geography. By this time, the term Economics was the customary course title in the schools; curiously enough, it denoted a *less* systematic study, a more problem-oriented approach in the general progressive spirit, than had Political Economy. (This would remain true up to about 1950.) From 1920 on, the emphasis tended to center on the activities of making a living (and related matters), together with attention to the problems of industrial democracy. Thus a well-known text by L. C. Marshall, an academic economist deeply involved with the schools,[2] was described as "a new type of economics for the senior high school. Instead of economic theory it presents the distinguishing features of industrial life and discusses them as important community activities." Other texts of the day spoke of drawing lessons from 'everyday' experiences as workers and consumers. By the mid-1920s it was estimated that about 40 percent of the high schools offered Economics, with perhaps 5 percent of high-school students enrolled.[3] This indicates that—while many more students were taking the strongly sociological Civics, which included some economics—Economics had nevertheless established itself in terms of course recognition to a greater extent than Sociology.

In a treatment of Economics in the schools, Armento[4] speaks of a consistent tension between personal economics and "citizenship economics (analytical, social science education)." Normally one regards the latter term as divisible into two: economic decision-making as part of citizenship, and analytical or 'pure' economics. What Armento means is that for many years economic study, like the study of government, was *justified* for the sake of citizenship. A logical underpinning for such an enterprise is the central place that neoclassical economics gives to rational, individual decision-making, and to a balancing of individual self-interest and the pursuit of public goods, both of which involve enlightened, or at least informed, citizens.*

In the schools of the 1930s, the personal economics emphasis seemed to be dominant, with much attention to 'thrift education,' economic competence in the personal (often occupational) sphere, and economic 'skills' for living. This emphasis is often evident today in the schools when 'economic literacy' is invoked, although equally often, in the 1980s, economics for citizenship is implied.

---

*Armento might justly point out that economic decision-making as part of economic citizenship requires analytical knowledge. For example, one stimulus for the midcentury growth of economics in the schools was the passage of the 1946 Employment Act, which suggested that government would be heavily involved in influencing the direction of the economy—which in turn should require increased economic knowledge on the part of citizens.

Beginning in 1949, a group of economists, educators, and others from business, labor, and government (convened originally by the Committee for Economic Development) began to organize a disciplinary-based 'pure economics' curriculum for the schools. This effort was to result in the Joint Council on Economic Education (JCEE), now headquartered in New York. Early in the process, the central topic was identified as 'the economic problem'—that is, scarcity. Students were to "see factors in the economy in relation to a unifying structure;"[5] in addition, they were to be enabled to participate "in those activities in a democratic society which affect the common welfare." Ben Lewis,[6] a high-status academic economist, in 1962 agreed on 'the economic problem' as the focus and on the immensity of private wants relative to limited economic resources, but put a decided emphasis on "good economics and straight economics . . . explicitly in the service of citizenship" (p. 107). He held that it was *public* economic issues (his emphasis) that "urgently demand the presence of economics . . . within the school curriculum" (p. 110), and invoked again the term 'political economy' to refer to a "manmade set of arrangements instituted, maintained, and modified by society to guide, induce, and compel the economic behavior of individuals and the ordering of resources in patterns that reflect society's desires" (p. 120). Tactfully, but with an evident cautionary tone, Lewis raised in his essay the notion that school Economics should not simply be the college course, but should emphasize 'understanding' in a sense beyond the purely academic.

In large part, since the 1950s, economics in the schools has been organized by interest groups maintaining a certain distance from both the schools and the disciplinary association, though they have brought pressure on the former and have sought the endorsement of the latter. Unlike other social science disciplines, which have alternated between periods of interest in and neglect of the school curriculum, the economics groups have worked assiduously for some forty years, with notable results. The very reference to 'groups' and the use of the pronoun 'they' indicate that the significant actors can be identified. Some have tried to steer a course between an overemphasis on consumer and business behavior, on the one hand, and highly formal, mathematized theoretical approaches, on the other hand. One sector has furthered practical economics, such as consumer or business economics, often for non-college-bound students, while another has furthered the cause of 'free enterprise' economics, generally in terms of state- or district-mandated 'coverage' within existing courses. Another sector, represented by the JCEE, has worked for the inclusion across the curriculum of economic concepts and understanding, often within history; a subset of this pure-economics group, together with those not connected to the JCEE, has emphasized a grade 12 elective course, with great success. (See section 3.1, where it is shown that Economics has become part of the typical high school curriculum.) Finally, another group, of which the leading organization is the Foundation for Teaching Economics (San Francisco), has tended to fit its efforts into a broad civics framework early in high school or in the middle grades. They tend to quote such statements as that by Alfred Marshall, "Economics is a study of mankind in the ordinary business of life," as a general educational rationale, though they agree on the centrality of such concepts as supply and demand, trade-offs, marginal analysis, associated costs and benefits, and short-term and long-term effects.

A perhaps curious pattern here is that it is those economics groups furthest separated from the discipline that tend to seek concentrated time in the curriculum—for example, a part-course on consumer behavior, banking, and other 'practical economics,' or a unified series of presentations on the virtues of the market economy as opposed to other systems, in either case around the junior high school level. They see the need to communicate a finite, bounded subjectmatter clearly, forcefully, and at the optimum grade level. The pure economics advocates, on the other hand (over and above their interest in a solid grade 12 elective for its own sake), have traditionally preferred an 'infused' approach over a number of grade levels. The reasons for this are several. First, it is difficult to expect that the number of well-trained Economics teachers would ever equal the number of History or Government teachers in the schools. Second, historical understanding presumably demands a good deal of economics knowledge and repays attention to economic factors, especially in the context of U.S. History. Third (a reason that generally goes unstated), providing appropriate exposure in almost every grade to 'legitimate' economic concepts counteracts or dilutes concentrated units of special-purpose or ideological economic instruction. Fourth, the subjectmatter is viewed as hierarchically organized and conceptually complex, so that it should be built up a little at a time in a 'spiraling' fashion. For example, it is assumed that young children can learn from participating in experimental 'markets' in the classroom before they can understand distributed markets in general; or, it is argued that 'scarcity' is conceptually a simpler concept than 'goods' (in particular public goods), so that the one should be introduced well before the other.*

A gradual infusion of economics topics across grade levels also serves to protect economics in the schools from the popular challenge that it is an arcane subject, too difficult for most students, or a subject that appears to yield faulty predictions—in either case, not very helpful in personal or citizenship-related decision-making. To these challenges economists can respond that students hold economic concepts and principles anyhow, and might as well learn sound ones; and that there is more to economic understanding than prediction. There does seem to be general agreement, however, that in order to teach quantitative

---

*This is a particularly interesting example of the predominance of 'common-sense' wisdom in curriculum design. A cognitive-developmental psychologist might well argue that a positive entity is earlier understood than a negative one, while other psychologists (and economists) might hold that children experience want or need earlier than they do a resource or a good. Research has not been done to clarify the point, largely because one's own common sense is imputed to all.

economics and/or macroeconomic behavior and systems, an elective course at a high grade-level is needed, especially for those going on to college.*

The well-ordered structure of economics as taught in the schools—for example, the general notion that 'scarcity' precedes 'opportunity cost,' which in turn precedes 'trade-off'—is reminiscent of the New Social Studies, but the relationship of economics to the schools as a system has been distinctive. In effect, an interest group representing 'real' economics has set out to impact upon that system. Whenever a school district feels itself on shaky ground in Economics, there is a corps of economics engineers available. This, of course, was far from the approach of the New Social Studies, which emphasized the development of new materials, not an actual intervention within the school. Even history, which has had the largest impact on schools over the century, has never used this research-and-development approach, preferring to exert its influence through commissions and curriculum committees and teacher education at the preservice level. There are, to be sure, local History Teaching Alliances, which join teachers and academic scholars on a voluntary, not necessarily long-term, basis, and which tend to seek incremental improvement—the infusion of new material or content, for example, into existing courses or teaching styles. (Geography as a field for the schools is currently following such a pattern.) The cumulative effect of the activities of such networks may be great, but they do not depend on the commitment of a school or system and do not normally create or maintain structures in the schools. Alliances of this sort may be seen as ad hoc *projects*, chiefly benefiting individuals. Only Economics has mounted *programs* of intervention and change, and created the network to sustain them long-range.

The signal success of the JCEE owes to the fact that it was founded as a broad coalition of interests (including, for example, both business and labor); that it gives teachers and schools tangible and sustained help in developing economics programs, rather than depending on the eventual attainment of a cadre of already trained teachers; that it does so recognizing the existing structure of the curriculum and system, for example, by the infusion approach, from the elementary level forward; and that in devising effective ways to meet a demand for economics it helps structure or even create that demand. Its DEEP program (Developmental Economic Education Program) involves state economics councils in all 50 states, providing curriculum guidance, materials, and 'networking' help, and some 300 campus-based centers providing in-service training, summer workshops, trained teacher aides for the classroom, help with testing and evaluation, and so on. Because of this elaborate infrastructure, DEEP programs are now in place in more than 1,900 districts with some 16 million students, more that one-third the total enrollment in U.S. schools.† The height-

---

*Advanced Placement tests for both micro- and macro-economics have now been instituted. The argument with regard to macroeconomics is not so much that younger students cannot understand the basic concepts, as that economics instruction never reaches this topic, except for some coverage of business cycles, unless there is a senior course.

†In principle, a district makes a commitment on behalf of all its students, across schools and appropriate grade levels.

ening or management of 'demand' for economics results directly from the very availability of such support, which makes all the difference in curricular innovation or enrichment, and from the fact that local business councils provide substantial external funding for at least the early phases of new programs. School districts tend to emulate each other, and the availability of start-up funding is an added incentive. Once having invested deeply in economic education across the grades, it becomes more likely that a school system will also adopt senior high school Economics course to complete the sequence. There is no question that, because of DEEP and the efforts of other economics groups, more external funds and entrepreneurial effort have been devoted to economics in the school to than any other subject.

The JCEE sponsors a research-oriented *Journal of Economic Education* and provides for a continuing review of its work, from a professional point of view, by the education committee of the American Economic Association. Its Master Curriculum series and Framework for Teaching Economics address scope and sequence for economics in the schools, provide a syllabus for such infusion approaches as economics in U.S. History, and also form a standard for commercial texts to follow. The JCEE's Test of Economic Understanding (more recently, Test of Economic Literacy) exerts a similar content-defining influence, and also provides a means of measuring educational growth. This last aspect is particularly important in justifying the entire effort, since a clear difference in test scores obtained before a DEEP program begins and those obtained subsequently (or preinstruction and postinstruction scores from successive generations of students) are compelling indicators of accomplishment. Once again, only Economics has a test of this kind in the schools.*

Table 7-1 shows the content structure of one current form of the test—reflecting in turn the underlying organization of the Master Curriculum in the DEEP approach. The columns represent increasing levels of understanding ("evaluation" means the ability to make reasoned decision or policy judgments). The four main 'rows' show how many items in each broad field of economics are included on the test; the table entries themselves show the assignment of questions by cognitive level and topic. The content for this test is entirely at the high school level.[7] In 1986 achievement tests based on this curriculum were administered nationally to more than 8,000 grade 10, 11, and 12 students, serving as a kind of economics 'report card,' a national diagnostic indicator. The students could be grouped into those taking an Economics semester course, those taking a personal finance or consumer economics course, and those taking a social studies course where economics content, if any, occurred via 'infusion.' It made relatively little difference in obtained scores, into which group these students fell. In general, students were found to have a better grasp of

*In several fields—history, government/political science, and now economics—scholars have worked through the College Entrance Examination Board to write advanced placement tests, but these do not describe the content of typical achievement in the subject; they are oriented toward college placement, not high school mastery. Thus, only Economics can say, Here is what the student should know *through coursework*—and here is a test to measure that.

Table 7-1 Economic Concepts in the Test of Economic Literacy (Form B), Assigned to Cognitive Levels

Concepts	Cognitive levels*					Total	%
	I	II	III	IV	V		
Fundamental	6	4	1	0	1	12	26.1
Scarcity		2				2	
Opportunity cost/trade-offs			1			2	
Productivity		2				2	
Economic systems	1					1	
Economic inst./incentives	4					4	
Exchange, money, interdependence	1					1	
Microeconomic	1	3	6	1	2	13	28.3
Markets and prices			1			1	
Supply and demand			1	2		1	4
Competition/structure			3			3	
Income distribution	1	1				2	
Market failures		1				1	
Role of government				1	1	2	
Macroeconomic	1	5	1	6	1	14	30.4
Gross national product	1	1				2	
Aggregate supply		1				1	
Aggregate demand		1		1		2	
Unemployment				1		1	
Inflation/deflation				2		2	
Monetary policy		1	1		1	3	
Fiscal policy		1		2		3	
International	0	2	2	3	0	7	15.2
Comp. advantage/trade barriers			1	2		3	
Balance of payments/exchange rates			1	1		2	
Growth/stability		2				2	
Total questions	8	14	10	10	4	46	
Percentage	17.4	30.4	21.7	21.7	8.7		100.00

*I = knowledge; II = comprehension; III = application; IV= analysis; V = evaluation; Total = number of items.

†Arabic numbers represent the number of items testing for the concepts at that level.

SOURCE: William B. Walstad and John C. Soper, "What Is High School Economics? TEL Revision and Pretest Findings," *Journal of Economic Education* 19 (Winter 1988): 28.

fundamental concepts and microeconomics than of macro- or international economics. However, several of the fundamental concepts of the field—scarcity, productivity, opportunity cost—were poorly understood.

After further test development, the test was readministered to some 8,000 students, and modest but reliable differences were found across groups of students.* Obtained scores varied with intelligence level, racial origin, region of the country, family income level. (Ultimately, of course, the purpose of instruction is to overcome or minimize such differences.) Scores also reflected the kind of courses taken by the students: those taking Economics courses scored higher than those taking social studies or practical economics, *in that order*. Once again, students had more difficulty with international and macroeconomic items (such as balance of payments and comparative economic growth; inflation, monetary, and fiscal policy). There are several questions of interpretation that further use of this test and the gathering of other data may illuminate. First, the effect of recency in testing for achievement of social studies knowledge has often been noted (see section 6.3.3). Following up students taking the test—retesting them later—would be useful, though difficult to control against further learning exposures.† Second, the effects of cumulative background through the curriculum, across grade levels, are unknown. Do those taking social studies courses score higher than those taking practical economics because of the infusion of fundamental economic concepts in a number of their courses; or because such students have tended to take more 'academic' courses, or to be of higher native intelligence; or because learning 'consumer economics' in some way acts against broad economic learning? (Interactions of such factors are, of course, likely.)

In data from related studies, the investigators[8] found evidence that History and Government teachers in high school taught only certain clusters of concepts, omitting others. If this can be confirmed, instruction either in the infusion courses or in separate Economics courses could presumably be adjusted (although here, as elsewhere, student knowledge of particular content may come from beyond the classroom). Good studies of how specific knowledge is gained through infusion, from grade level to grade level, are extremely difficult to contemplate; detailed studies of Economics instruction per se are far more likely. Moreover, trends in educational policy toward achievement testing generally will, other things equal, conduce to separate courses, whose 'output' may be easier to measure (section 3.2.1).

Students taking Economics courses were more positive toward the field than other students. This might simply mean that students would always be more positive toward any social studies field were all courses to be purified as to content. The infusion strategy of economics and of such content areas as legal education has tended to rest on the assumption that by this approach students may like the material more and do better, at least up to about grade 12. Currently, some hold that History has been muddied or weakened in schools by

---

*Such test development sharpens up the questions and eliminates those that do not discriminate: that is, those that virtually no students, or virtually all students, answer correctly. Thus, the 'validity' of the test rests on using items that do show the effect of instruction. Since cross-sectional tests are of comparatively little interest (who is to say what the level of knowledge 'ought' to be or where such knowledge may come from?), such 'buying' of validity is unavoidable for an instrument suitable for pre- and posttesting.

†The JCEE plans to do this, insofar as possible.

the inclusion of nonhistorical material. If only 'pure' history were taught, it is conceivable that *some* students would like it more, and *some* would like it less. Further, if teaching toward basic economic concept understanding in the lower grades in History were minimized, would students' understanding of economic history be furthered or hindered? Looking at course and enrollment patterns and statistics over the past thirty years, one can suggest that the infusion strategy on the part of JCEE and other groups was relatively more effective earlier, before so many states and districts put separate economics courses firmly in place in the curriculum. In other words, the presence of courses drives out a significant commitment to infusion.

Another recent study by the JCEE has turned up interesting descriptive findings about the status of the field of school economics. The survey[9] showed that most students taking Economics courses at grade 12 have had very little concentrated economics instruction previously, even within other courses. Unlike their teachers, Economics students put practical goals, such as making money, high on their list of priorities in taking the course; and like teachers, rated 'understanding other economic systems' low as a goal. Students in Economics courses had SAT scores roughly comparable to those of other seniors, but tended to come from families of higher educational attainment. Despite the efforts of DEEP since the mid-1970s, most economics teachers had little formal training in economics or economics teaching (50 percent had taken 6 hours or less of course work), and almost all of that training had been on an in-service basis. Most believed that the typical level of preparation was inadequate. (Other data show that there is a small cadre of teachers in the schools with the equivalent of a college minor in the subject, virtually all of them teaching Economics.)* Most teachers had been in the system for fifteen years or so, and had taught other social studies previously. (It is not known whether moving into Economics teaching was viewed as a reward or a punishment.) Economics teachers were white and male, more so than their students.

Other studies by those associated with the JCEE[10] have shown that the content taught by Economics teachers, as opposed to those teaching social studies or consumer economics, is quite different. As suggested in the foregoing, in many respects consumer economics teachers are less like Economics teachers than are social studies teachers of various kinds. Even Economics teachers, however, often do not teach what seem to the expert to be key concepts: trade-offs, opportunity cost, even scarcity. The most reasonable explanation is that teachers do not teach what they themselves do not understand.†[11]

Surveys of teachers and state and district data appear to show that, at the

---

*In recent years, the number of economics bachelor's degrees has climbed sharply, but from what is known of graduates' first jobs it is not likely that many will go into precollegiate teaching.

†Ethical avoidance of ill-mastered topics may not be the whole story. Soper and Walstad, "The Reality of High School Economics," wondered how it is that even Economics teachers report teaching 'supply and demand' more often than 'scarcity,' since the former would seem to depend on the latter concept.

postelementary level, separate courses are growing in prevalence, relative to infusion approaches. At the same time, mandated requirements for free-enterprise instruction are growing rapidly, in terms of what is stated on the books, but these are often met by indirect means—for example, isolated coverage or coverage by emphasis of the merits of free enterprise, rather than organized lesson or course sequences.* The JCEE estimates that about twenty-seven states have free-enterprise mandates on the books (often in combination with requirements for more disciplinary-based instruction).

It would be unwise to assume that courses in 'mainstream' Economics are the wave of the future. Across the country as a whole, and taking all grade levels into account, there is considerable evidence that 'personal' or practical economics may be the most common subjectmatter. In a 1979 study of social studies textbook publishing,[12] the most favorable market conditions for expansion—for textbook sales, workbooks, and the like—were in economics, but the potential for consumer economics and for free enterprise economics was rated higher than that for disciplinary Economics. The publishers also reported that within elementary Social Studies books, private enterprise and a normative description of the U.S. system was the major content focus.

Large high schools, of course, offer levels or tracks within economics. Kokomo High School, for example, in 1988 offers Economics, Consumer Economics, and Advanced Placement Economics. The first of these is a course "designed to provide the layman with a citizen's understanding of the forces that shape our economic lives . . . problems of inflation, unemployment, economic growth, international trade, the banking system, free enterprise,† and the basics of investing." Consumer Economics deals with "the real world of money [*sic*] for each consumer . . . job and family . . . skills for everyday living." AP Economics surveys the rudiments of microeconomics, but emphasizes macro concepts from national income to international trade in preparation for the College Board Macroeconomics Exam.

In summary, those associated with the JCEE, having achieved a remarkable degree of penetration of the curriculum by infusion, seem now to be emphasizing the separate senior course, seem to be seeking depth rather than breadth.‡ There are some principled doubts about this trend, even within the academic world (see below, section 7.2). In addition, the trend may be risky, in that Economics is already relatively stronger in the curriculum *as a course* than in terms of

---

*There are conspicuous exceptions. In some states, lengthy exposition of comparative economic systems with a free-enterprise emphasis, or the formal explanation of a pure market economy, are serious business. If this takes half a semester, for example, it may make the rest of a course (in Social Studies or Economics or Civics, for example) hard to design. Texas high schools require a semester of "economics with emphasis on the free enterprise system and its benefits." A Texas high school need not offer an Economics elective.

†Note how this is included in passing.

‡That is, depth as measured by university-based disciplinary standards, or more precisely, in terms of what preparation would lead logically to university-level coverage.

enrollments (as compared, say, to Government).[13] At the extreme, a 'good' school would offer Economics for reasons of prestige, but most of its students would learn 'economics' in other courses or out of school. This imbalance would of course change if states moved toward requiring Economics for graduation (as is the case, for example, in California and New York). It takes little prescience to see that, were a severe economic crisis to affect America, the academically oriented high school course now making progress in the schools might be changed to concentrate on problems and social reforms, at the expense of explanatory concepts or lifelong individual decision-making.

The general approach of other economics groups enjoying academic support avoids such a risk, in that they are more focused on the upper elementary and middle school levels, often—as has been mentioned—within a broad Civics or Social Studies framework. There is also more interest in such groups in the developmental *stages* of economic understanding, and in devising a variety of instructional means, including games, simulations, mini-economies, and the like, for classroom use.

7.1   Economics and Citizenship

The Foundation for Teaching Economics (FTE), a California-based organization with considerable business and civic support, focuses on grades 7 to 10, and takes a more variegated approach to its promotion of economics in the curriculum. Working often in cooperation with other groups (including the JCEE), it develops materials suitable for these grades, has published a text, worked on films about economic life, and collaborated with *USA Today* to produce a classroom newspaper. The FTE takes a particular interest in developmental aspects of learning, and thus has sponsored or used research bearing on stages of learning, hierarchies of concepts, the growth of value systems in children, and so on. As mentioned earlier, the FTE is comfortable with a framework for inclusion of economics of a broad Civics design, and is currently working with the Constitutional Rights Foundation, especially in California, to create a 'fused' (rather than infused) government-and-economics course for grade 9.[14]

Thus, although the FTE subscribes to a different rhetoric, in effect it is repeating one of the central ideas of the 1916 committee: in essence, the conviction is that 'civics' will not work for adolescents unless information about the structure of government and the legal system is closely combined with 'real-life,' largely economic, knowledge.* A number of teachers, especially those trained in history or government, find the FTE approach less imperialistic, which is to say interventional, than that of the JCEE, and far less committed to a disciplinary model, which tends to limit impact of the subjectmatter to the

---

*California requires a high-school-economics course for graduation, but does not specify the grade level; presumably a well-developed Civics/Economics course at grade 9 would be acceptable.

already crowded last years of high school. If "complexity and unreality" are "the two great barriers to vitalizing economic education"[15]—that is, if many students and teachers report that the subjectmatter as promoted by the JCEE seems intrinsically difficult and remote from immediate concerns—then the FTE approach is promising. On the other hand, it may be that, without some special rationale such as the possibility of a reformed Civics in the schools, efforts such as those of the FTE will have only local, sporadic effect. The availability of a test appropriate for economics learning at these grade levels may help to justify the effort to those governing the schools.[*]

The specter of "complexity and unreality" in Economics in the schools is in fact widely perceived. As Armento points out, there is continually the danger, which was experienced in the New Social Studies, of laying out a neatly articulated structure of concepts and definitions before students, who then proceed to memorize them. To be sure, the materials developed by the JCEE and the FTE and other such groups are various and challenging. There are workbooks and games that bring in a wide range of everyday experience and nonobvious examples; there are simulations that can use computers in the classroom; there are exercises in arranging, plotting, and analyzing data that involve sustained group work.[†] On the other hand, there is probably no more time taken in Economics classes to allow or probe for inquiry and reflection than in other subjects; decision-making, so important in principle in economics, is often taken to be something that the student will be able to do, as a citizen, once she has 'learned economics,' rather than while she is learning it.

The developmental-cognitive approach, as pioneered by researchers associated with the FTE (and others), is in a sense assumed in the JCEE framework, in that 'spiraling' is the normal approach in any infusion strategy. But various analyses of actual curriculum guides reveal oddities, and a tendency to repeat propositions and definitions with more sophisticated language but with little true increase in cognitive complexity.[16] An excellent discussion of these and related problems is given in a special issue of *Theory and Practice*.[17] Here many of the fundamental themes of social studies education—teaching for skills rather than facts, teacher versus student activity, exposure to a range of examples rather than one prototypical instance, deductive logic versus inductive inferences, and so on—are reported in fascinating detail.

---

[*]The JCEE has a *Test of Economic Knowledge* for the middle school, which may prove appropriate.

[†]A particular strength of economics in the curriculum today is its emphasis on quantitative data and 'social statistics.' In principle, such an emphasis could be achieved in social and demographic history and in sociology, and in a rather different form it is a feature of much work in geography. One observer's generalization would be that, especially in the middle grades, economics materials and projects have a particular immediacy, a real-life saliency, that tends to be lacking elsewhere. Work by Marilyn Kourilsky and others in developing classroom projects involving mini-societies or token economies seems particularly promising, in that it leaves room for the appearance of actual economic behavior that does not fit the theoretical models of the field—for example, 'markets' that do not clear at the end of the class, or the nonoccurrence of 'optimization.'

7.2   Economics and the Problem of Realism

There is also inevitably the problem—given limited instructional time, the imperative of testable mastery of content, and the tendency of schools to avoid sustained discussion of controversial issues—that the exposition of a 'positive' (that is, theoretically orderly, factually supported) economics can become 'normative' economics, by default. Leming[18] points out the central goal in schooling of perpetuation of the system, which calls for a degree of conscious awareness of and devotion to the virtues of, for example, the modern mixed market economic system or the assumption of self-interest in economic motivation. "Enlightened allegiance" (Durkheim's phrase) is probably necessary for constructive decision-making, and is perhaps a desirable standard for instruction, on the grounds that students will be exposed to unorthodox notions, from the Right or the Left, from many sources outside the schools. However, many economists point out that in precollegiate education virtually the entire range of economic history and political economy is omitted, being inadequately handled in History texts and hardly present in Economics, which does not even offer much of a real description of the working of 'alternative' economic systems. The rather bland neoclassical-plus-a-little-Keynes model taught (at best) in the schools does not, in the view of some, ever get at, for example, the nature of capitalism.

Helburn, for example,[19] concludes that economic growth, in the economic history sections of U.S. History texts, is largely attributed to technological advances, with the role of the accumulation and control of capital stated but not really analyzed. Similarly, restructuring today of the world economy, new forms of core and periphery, new forms of labor markets cannot adequately be conveyed because the basic elements of economic history and systems are lacking. (As noted above, the JCEE test data confirm that international economics is not well grasped by students.) In another paper, Helburn says that the authors of even the best economics texts "attribute much of the confusion in discussions of economic problems to a failure to distinguish between analysis (what *is* happening) and value judgments (what *ought to be* happening)—a distinction between positive and normative economics that they obviously want teachers and students to learn. They create the impression that economic analysis is value-free and actually *does* explain what *is* happening in the real world."[20] Helburn is, of course, describing the 'unreality' problem, about which many economists worry.

'Unreality' is not specific to Economics, in the school social studies curriculum. However, since the subject has become an important part of the modal curriculum, the criticisms of highly abstract unrealism, pseudomathematization, downplaying of institutional factors, ignoring of economic history, and excessive formalism, as voiced by a number of professional economic leaders,[21] should be taken seriously. Thoughtful persons have often argued over the years that there is, perhaps paradoxically, a greater need for realistic (rather than theoretically powerful) models at the precollegiate level than at the university level, since most students will not take much more (or any) work in a given field. No one expects high school students to do econometric analysis, but they should have a grasp of some of the structural anomalies and problems of empirical economics, in the United States and other systems. Moreover, the place of Economics in the curriculum is today argued for by those who are concerned about American economic competitiveness, international interdependency, and the like. If economics in the schools fails to educate students about the hard trade-offs involved in achieving 'productivity' within a society, or even that mature developed societies may not need to achieve productivity growth in all sectors forever (but can conceivably enjoy a desirable standard of living within a larger set of economic relationships), this pragmatic expectation of the field will not be met, and the discipline of Economics may be discredited.

A nice example of how external expectations condition the actual teaching of economics is provided by a description of Japanese economics education,[22] especially since some present-day concern for the improvement of economic education in this country seems to be directed at the desire to emulate the Japanese. In the heavily tracked national curriculum of Japan, according to this source, economics is taught in a more functional than formal style, with considerable attention to national goals and strategies and the ideologies and practices of competing economies in the world and in close association with political learning. Students receive their required economics instruction within a grade-9 civics course and a grade-10 'contemporary society' course; thereafter, as an elective, 'politics-economics' is the accepted term. Japanese teachers typically have little economics background, but teach to a highly elaborated syllabus, where stepwise exposition and memorization of material is chiefly the goal. Observers have commented that economic analysis, per se, does not fit the Japanese mode of teaching. Whatever the reason, the important American triad of scarcity, opportunity costs, and trade-offs are treated as rather primitive concepts, covered lightly in social studies at grade 5 or 6.

In grades 9 and 10 in Japan, unlike the United States, the concept of the national economic system seems largely absent; the Japanese have a private enterprise system, but appear not to teach ideological allegiance to it.* On the other hand, the Japanese seem to give more attention to macroeconomic performance and to the attendant controversies about planning, constraints of the business cycle, government input, and the like. The Japanese also pay more attention, by a considerable amount, to the concepts of international economics—balance of payments, exchange rates, and so forth. While few would draw proposals for reform of American school economics from one international comparison, this may suggest that the particular combination, in American schools, of heavily ideological/normative education in the middle grades with

*It may be, of course, that such systems-maintenance work is done elsewhere, or pervasively in society.

highly formal/conceptual course work at the highest grades leads to what, in effect, is an 'excluded middle' of rich realism.

There is reason to believe that there may be movement toward a new richness of description and empiricism within the discipline. The solution to the omission of economic history is not readily apparent, except to suggest that it be covered in much greater depth in World History. But in formal or quantitative economics, trends toward 'experimental economics' and 'behavioral economics' could have an important impact in the schools. The discipline of economics offers a curious, and important, challenge to this writer's general model of the progression of 'master ideas,' affecting all the social science fields across time (section 18.3.1). That is, in the terms of that model, economics, societally the most highly valued of the social sciences (with the possible exception of history in its humanistic aspect), has not moved beyond a structural, prebehaviorist, mathematical-deductive phase. Many have called, for many years, for a more eclectic, more empirical field; some would rely to a greater degree on experimental data, at the micro level; and many have expressed concern that economics, in the words of one prominent economist, is a way of "doing math while maintaining the credible pretense of relevance by labeling the variables." Recent research on the experimental characteristics of small-scale, controlled, simulated or actual mini-markets or exchange systems; demonstrations of initially random, but soon fixed, paths of development of small systems, or the rapid 'capture' of initially free systems by one element; the study of 'satisficing' and partial solutions in economic motivation and behavior, rather than optimization; the convergence of economics with other disciplines in the study of contextually specific decision-making, at the individual, group, and collective level, as opposed to the aggregation of atomistic choices in situations of perfect information and weighing of choices—all of these and other very significant developments in the field* have the property of being, in principle, quite comprehensible to precollegiate students of a wide age range.

In fact, these new approaches could be of special interest to them, since the students in some sense could produce or replicate such phenomena directly. Moreover, an integration of some aspects of economics, psychology, and political science is clearly implied—under the general rubric of 'decision theory' or 'organizational behavior'—and this might be of value in the school curriculum. It is true that none of these developments offer much, yet, beyond the 'micro' level of analysis. Nor does it solve the question of renewed attention to large-scale institutional and historical factors. (As suggested above, the solution here probably does not lie with economists, but with historians.) But any movement anywhere in the social studies curriculum—in course placement, in content emphasis, in approach—toward a better balance of logical and empirical elements will be welcomed, by many if not by all.

---

*I refer, among others, to Herbert Simon, Maurice Allais, or Charles Plott.

8.0 Geography

8.1 The Test Score Scare

Geography in the schools shows a situation almost opposite to that of Economics. Whatever economics has been in the curriculum of the schools at a given time,* it has enjoyed a reasonable relationship, in its intellectual patterning, to the disciplinary or university field; with geography, the correspondence has never been close. When the discipline of economics wished to alter the nature of school economics, it was able to do so without much trouble (particularly with regard to the high school elective); when geography tried to do so, little happened. Whereas economics as a field was the basis for school economics, in that sense preexisting its schools aspect, in effect 'human geography' in schools predated the university discipline. Although it is roughly accurate to say that many parents and taxpayers have little understanding of what 'real' economics is, but are willing to accept that whatever courses are in the schools must be what economics is, most laypersons have a distinct sense, *from* exposure to it in the schools, of what geography is—and might be surprised to know that much of the discipline disagrees with the lay conception. Where, in 1893 and 1916 at least, those designing the school economics curriculum rebuffed the discipline, university geography rebuffed the schools. Finally, if today a problem with the Economics course in the social studies curriculum may be a tendency for it to be taught in too formal a fashion, remote from everyday experience, with Geography a problem may be that it is not formal, abstract, and autonomous enough.[†]

Most Americans, when asked What is social studies, will reply history, government—and of course some geography. That is due partly to the temporal primacy of the subject of geography in American education, which goes back to the early nineteenth century, and to the fact that, whatever the general curriculum pattern of upper elementary grades over time, some 'geography' has been taught at virtually every grade. Not only was American History localized to grade 5 fairly early, but it has often been taught as combined history and

---

*That is, formal, systematic economics, under that label.

[†]In structuring this comparison by referring only to 'pure' economics, I have not, in one way, played fair. One could argue that 'school geography' is to geography as consumer economics is to economics: a quite distinct enterprise. In other respects, the comparison holds.

geography, essentially as the story of American exploration and growth from the Atlantic to the Pacific. To some, geography has been but the 'material aspect' of history.[1] Otherwise, geography has often been seen, in the primary schools, as an 'enabling' subject, a set of skills involving place-naming and the locating of historical events in space, together with the general orientation that Canada lies to the north, Mexico to the south.

In the history-geography partnership, at first geography was, if anything, the dominant strain[2] in conveying the process of Americanization (perhaps because in the early 1800s in America there appeared to be less 'past' to understand, while space seemed vast and mysterious). School books prior to the Civil War were heavily geographical, with lists of place names and locations to be memorized or located on maps (albeit, in many cases, with historical significance). There was clearly a heavy strain of environmental determinism, whether of manifest destiny (the inevitability of occupying the continent) or of the burdens and dangers of exploration and settlement. These primary school readers, in most cases, arguably made more of a connected story of geographical expansion than of historical process; in other words, historical figures and happenings broke into the exposition of 'geography,' rather than geography providing coordinates for history.[3] It should be remarked, again (see section 4.4.1), that the 'expanding environments' format for primary education has obvious roots far back into the nineteenth-century schools. Not only was there the underlying assumption that the development of a person's life in some sense corresponded to the movement from awareness of the immediate circle and surroundings to a broader frame of reference—that is, that a child functioned in a small environment relative to that of an adult—but also (at least prior to the 1970s or so) that growth and maturing of an individual American would stand in some contributing relationship to nation-building.*

This relationship altered appreciably with the 1893 reform. The reorienting of the school curriculum, undertaken through the auspices of the NEA and instigated by the needs of the 'new' universities (see section 4.2.2), took account of the fact that geography was now one of the 'Moderns' at the college level. However, university geography then was overwhelmingly physical geography, not perhaps very distinguished in terms of geoscience but still a distinctly natural science owing considerably to nineteenth century fascination with large-scale historical causation, geopolitical determinism, geology and archaeology, teleological evolutionism, the rediscovery of the classical world, and so on. Geographers and historians could agree that geography did not belong with the social and human sciences, except insofar as physical factors, such as climate or topographical features, jumped the natural-social barrier and impacted upon the social and human realm. 'Cause,' in other words, proceeded from the natural

---

*With reference to the deeply ingrained expanding environments model for early education, Rugg, p. 59, quotes Guyot, a Swiss-American follower of Pestalozzi. Guyot's reader in the 1880s would downplay memorization by "taking the child about his home locality first, then on journeys farther and farther from home.... Physical, scenic, commercial, and historic units or types are chosen for these journeys.... Maps are not used before, but after a region has been thus traveled over with picture and text."

to the social.[4] Since the New History was spearheading a deeper look at causation *within* the social realm, it is understandable that geography faded in its importance, becoming subsumed in the now more richly historical curriculum of the schools.

Nevertheless, in 1916 the NEA committee, which saw a vital place for geography in a community civics framework (a kind of economic geography was clearly foreshadowed), again offered the university discipline the chance to participate in the curriculum revision process. Once again, disciplinary leaders made it clear that geography was not a social science, and had little it wished to offer.[5] During the 1920s and 1930s, as students stayed in school longer, completing more grades, as some attempt to 'fuse' social studies following the 1916 model proceeded, and as the vocational aspect of the 1918 Cardinal Principles' reorientation of the schools became more entrenched, Geography gradually reappeared in the school curriculum;[6] but it was largely in the form of Commercial Geography—what a merchant needed to know to move goods to market, or raw materials to manufacture, or what a salesman should know to conduct his work. Such teaching tended to occur at about grades 6 or 7, where geography has remained most prevalent.*

Elsewhere, the 1916 design included geography in close association with the study of European History about grade 10—but not as a separate academic course. In a famous school curriculum, that of Gary, Indiana, about 1912, geography was taught in the upper primary grades in a form that both exemplified the history-geography relationship and foreshadowed the 1916 community civics emphasis: this curriculum offered, for example, a course called The City: A Healthful Place in Which to Live.[8] As for physical geography, during the period of approximately 1890 to 1930 or so, it came to be contained within the General Science curriculum; in the earlier part of the period, it probably was the core of General Science.

The hegemony of physical geography in the universities began to recede during the 1920s and 1930s, reflecting a generally growing orientation toward the social sciences within the university—in community and regional studies (sociology), field work (anthropology), regional economics and public administration, and so on—and the emergence of a generally more empirical, structural-functionalist attitude. The case of university geography is atypical in that it was not a matter of an established *social science* discipline showing a movement from evolutionism to empiricism, but rather that a new *kind* of professional and research geography emerged to participate in the social science endeavor.[†]

---

*The College Board discontinued its high school geography test in 1934. While grade 7 Geography is no longer Commercial Geography, it remains true that in grades 6 to 10 non-college-bound students are often tracked into Geography as a kind of basic skills course, perhaps helpful in understanding history or in reading the newspaper, while college-bound students are directed into World History, hemisphere studies, and the like.[7]

†There were, in fact, several distinct academic/professional associations, each with very small membership. When the Association of American Geographers was reorganized in 1949 as a more pluralistic association, incorporating the American Society of Professional Geographers, the new *combined* membership was only about 1,000.[9]

There was also a division in practice between private or Eastern universities, which had offered physical geography within their natural science faculties, and midwestern or public universities, which opted for the social science model. This difference carries some legacy up to the present. Harvard's President Conant, in the late 1940s, said firmly that geography was not a university-level discipline (he meant that the discipline that was emerging was not for Harvard). In the 1980s, the closing of geography departments at Columbia, Northwestern, and Chicago, for example, seemed to reflect the failure of social science geography fully to take shape there *and*, simultaneously, the gradual absorption of the subjectmatter of physical geography into earth science, geophysics, and related departments. Though geography showed impressive growth after 1950, it remains by far the smallest of the academic fields (table 16.1) Like anthropology, geography's growth in recent years has been largely on the applied side, reflecting new kinds of professional occupations.*

University geography differentiated out over the decades, with little direct effect on the nature of the school subject. After World War II, an area studies and regional emphasis emerged; in the 1950s the behavioralist influence was seen, with some important developments in perceptual and ecological theory, as well as an emphasis on the behavior of persons living in 'subjective landscapes'; also in the 1950s a new domestic importance was assigned to geography, with the growth of urban and suburban systems, metropolitan planning, national highway and building projects, and the dependence of much economic activity on 'location' as a systematic concept. The predominance of regional/areal analysis in these years† did prove important for the school curriculum, but indirectly. That is, several lines of cross-field affinity were established based on the regional model. One, which tended to be domestic in focus, combined elements of geography, economics, and sociology—as in regional planning.‡ The other, which tended to operate on the transnational level, combined aspects of geography, anthropology, and history (along with economics and international politics and some humanistic disciplines) into such enterprises as area studies, economic anthropology, demographic history, human biology, and cognate fields. The schools showed the influence of the latter combination of disciplines in their concern, beginning around 1950, for hemisphere and world studies, world cultures, and the general concept of cultures. This tendency was interrupted to some extent by the New Social Studies, but has reemerged in the current emphasis on broad World Studies or Global Education. To the extent

---

*Unlike anthropology, which had the good fortune or perhaps genius to establish itself from the beginning (in the United States) as an inherently multiform 'field'—simultaneously physical, cultural, linguistic, archeological—geography gradually came to accept itself as a multifaceted field, involving physical, social, and human science facets.

†I omit a discussion of the significant differences between the terms, in geography; see Preston James[10] and p. 226, below.

‡The development in the 1970s of what its practitioners see as a separate field, Regional Science, reflects this combination of interests.

that high schools today include Geography, it is due to the growth in the 1950s of World Studies and World Geography—which in fact included, at one time or another, a substantial amount of anthropology, international relations, areal history, and development economics. The former configuration—the intersection of geography, economics, and sociology—never took shape to any degree in the schools.*

The general claim here, however, is that geography in the schools, quite divorced from the university discipline, drifted along on broader currents, rather than finding its own channel. Given the overall level of disciplinary flux during the postwar period, *had sociology and/or anthropology been fully present in the schools* at the time that geography was searching, the history of American social studies might have been quite different. One may simply suggest that a pattern of truly multidisciplinary study of systems and subsystems—both in relation to nation-states and with respect to the world as a whole—might have emerged. (Such a period of fused subjectmatter—long envisioned by some in social studies, but not seriously sought since the 1920s—would more likely have emerged in the schools rather than at the university level, where departmental barriers are greater.)

Leaving aside this tantalizing possibility, the separation between school geography and the very small and fissiparous university field, together with the failure of geography to command a course slot at the high school level, meant that geography in the schools continued to be shadowy: sometimes a hand-maiden to history, always an important dimension of early elementary instruction, a vague though interesting presence in the middle school. This last is not meant dismissively. Grade 7 Geography can be excellent, and can (and does) teach things that students should know. But it is *school* geography, a place-finding, map-reading, world-orienting subjectmatter that bears little direct relationship to the disciplinary field, in the way that History or Government or Economics does. This does not make it of intrinsically poor quality, but it does mean that it lacks a reliable academic base of support, or standard for definition. Students who enter the university are often surprised to find that geography is a department and a major there;[12] from what they know of the subject in primary and middle school, they do not think of it as having academic depth. The field of geography is so small (and the separation of the school subject from the discipline so marked) that very few teachers major in it. It would not be feasible at present for school authorities or the discipline to insist that geography teachers have majored in the field. Finally, when—as today—external demands arise for improvement in 'geographical literacy' (see below), the academic discipline can neither defend the school subject nor, given its long-enduring

*As one indicator of this failure, the political scientist Norton E. Long, in the 1962 ACLS-NCSS volume,[11] speaks scornfully of geography texts that contain "banal imbecilities on the causes of graft and slums in the cities"; the context suggests that he found this actual subjectmatter inconceivable for Geography. In the same volume, the geographer Preston James makes it quite clear that Geography might indeed have things to say about such matters.

distance from the schools, protest too haughtily that what the public conceives of as geographical competence is not necessarily the whole of the subjectmatter.*

A curious feature of the field in the schools is that, in a sense, its exposition on the elementary level tends to be more 'formal' or conceptually abstract than it is subsequently (excepting, of course, the fine Geography electives that some high schools do offer). That is, there is more concern in the early grades for what maps are *about*,† for 'occupied space,' for 'spatial relationships,' than is common again until the level of a college major or graduate degree.‡ This is another example of the tension in the curriculum between the structure of the discipline and the direct description of the 'field' behind it.

With the New Social Studies in the schools, and in geography as a field in the 1960s, an increasing quantitative emphasis and the development of new techniques (for example, the beginning of satellite mapping) was associated with a shift on the theoretical level from regional analysis to systematic description of spatial distribution and interrelationships. A certain sizing-up, with increasing abstractness, is involved. Put crudely, the field had moved first from an emphasis on areas, differentiating out units of particular interest, to an emphasis on regions, which were thought of as formal, synthetic segments of the earth's surface defined by relative homogeneity of particular features. Areas tend to be analyzed down from traditional, perhaps politically established, entities, while regions are analyzed up, to express distributive patterns, often of population in relation to resources. The region is a formal geographic generalization, always arbitrary in that it summarizes only some variables, and also 'abstract' in the sense that it is socially constructed. A rough test (for a nongeographer) is that areas lend themselves to proper names ('the Ruhr'), whereas regions lend themselves to generic label ('savanna'). But in practice, even among some geographers, 'region' just meant a large area, or several areas conglomerated. Thus, in a second transition, some in the field became more interested in the variables themselves, or special topics or dimensions, within a complex system, potentially within one world system. (An analogy: those in population genetics who look at demes or particular populations are interested in different questions from those who analyze gene flow through several systems or levels of 'systems.')

The High School Geography Project of the 1960s, which resulted in the course "Geography in an Urban Age," brought together professional geographers and teachers to develop and deploy new materials suitable for a more sophisticated

---

*This does not mean that the disciplinarians do not care about school geography; but it is not accidental that the 'improvement' of geography generally counts heavily upon the commitment of the National Geographic Society.

†The phrase in this sense is used by Winston, "Teaching and Learning," p. 47.

‡One could argue that the same is true of History, where the basic conceptualization of the notion that time 'runs,' or the various kinds and degrees of causation, seem to be the crux of the matter to elementary teachers . . . and graduate historiography seminars.

form of school geography. It wanted to move school geography beyond a focus on tightly derived 'areas' or the 'trash-can' approach to regions,[13] which involved trying to define an arbitrary 'system' by making a census of everything in it. One of the HSGP progenitors described the overall model as follows:[14]

> We build from the city to systems of cities, using central place theory. . . . We then move to the inhabited parts of the globe that are not highly urbanized . . . then to those parts of the world which are not inhabited, but cover a lot of the earth's surface. We finally end with . . . a single globe, as part of a single, interacting system.

Others, within the NSS, found this a bit grandiose, and pointed out that the "yearning for totality" (McNee's own term) did not itself ensure a systems-analysis achievement. Morrissett said:

> [Geography and history] have never claimed a theoretical body of knowledge in the same sense as those possessed by the natural, physical, and social sciences. The HSGP is making use of those limited bodies of theory which it shares with other disciplines—particularly location theory, which it shares with economics, and cultural anthropology. . . . One searches . . . in vain for a substantive concept to identify with history or geography, as 'culture' is related to anthropology, 'power' to political science, and 'scarcity' to economics.[15]

As imprecise as this claim may be (the four-fold discipline of anthropology, for example, puts 'culture' at the very *center* of only certain of its subfields), it expresses the common perception among social scientists that geography had no central unified structure.

Be that as it might, the HSGP (and related NSS-style projects) marked the only major instance in which the discipline and the schools, in geography, attempted something new together. It emphasized what professional geographers do, the methods and nature of geographical inquiry. Especially in the context of projects (in and out of the classroom) it focused on 'topics' in the field (and the associated methodologies), rather than the analysis of specific regions.

Inevitably, in so doing, it acted counter to the natural alliance that had grown up, regional-cultural in essence, in Area Studies and World Culture study in the schools. The HSGP was a bit of a stretch, compared to earlier geography in schools, but was indubitably challenging intellectually. Some students and teachers, at least, liked to ponder abstract conceptions (such as the notion that a 'location' on the face of the earth can be a geometric point, a set of topographical coordinates, a measurement datum along some dimension—temperature, physicochemical, botanical, and so on—a named entity, the locus of human values, a part of an areal structure, and almost infinitely more). Others never quite got the message.

HSGP materials were widely admired—but little used. Insofar as the dimensional or topical approach influenced texts (which it did, to this day), it tended to reintroduce natural and environmental aspects into school geography, in a curious way reviving earlier notions of the physical/human divide. That is, this was a much more powerful human geography, in part because it used a new level of conceptualization in ecological research, a larger notion of the environmental 'habitat,' and the idea of global systems—with 'man in the system.' (Concurrently, in terms of its intellectual orientation, the discipline of geography deepened its ties to the historical, population, and evolutionary sciences.)*

Not the least interesting of the accomplishments of the era was cognitive-developmental research on geographic learning at the early grades. Dewey had pointed out that young students come to instruction with ideas and concepts already formed: "We must discover what there is lying within the child's present sphere of experience which deserves to be called geographical. . . . To the child . . . geography is not, and cannot be, what it is to the one who writes the scientific treatise on geography. *The latter has had exactly the experience which it is the problem of instruction to induce.*"[16] Research by Crabtree, among others, combined naturalistic with semiexperimental methods in laying out some of the ways in which young children think about space, correlate perceptions gained through different senses, make and test inferences, and learn concepts from finding their way around. In one research project, for example, Crabtree showed how leading children through a neighborhood, with the children referring to maps and photographs, can lead to a sharp increase, through the correlation of direct experience and symbolic frames of reference, in the level of conceptualization. Crabtree's work[17] was among the best research done in the social studies on the comprehension of specific material at a specific age—that is, domain-specific learning, a research approach much in vogue today.

Among other implications, such research reminds us that, while the expanding environments approach may be logical and practical in the primary grades, it does not mean that children can only attend to and understand the very near, then the medium-range, then the far, and so on. In fact, across a wide range of 'dimensions' (near-far, familiar-remote, concrete-abstract) children have complicated and rich mental 'schemata'—which in important respects happen to be wrong. This, too, is important for those who deliver instruction to recognize. However, unless *teachers* can be enabled to learn in their preteaching education to use for their own purposes what researchers know about domain-specific and age-specific learning (and especially how these interact) there is little hope for instruction in the classroom to become more powerful in cognitive terms.

The best teachers learn some of these principles and practices through experience; others will simply follow the text, and tradition. In a now-familiar pattern, as the effects of the New Social Studies receded, geography in the schools was left as it had been in the 1950s: an introduction to basic concepts in primary grades, a heavy dose of place-learning and area study in the middle school (often ancillary to history), the possibility in grade 9 or 10 of a course

---

*Thus, as we have suggested above, filling out an implicit structure as a three-fold discipline: natural, social, and human.

related to, or a denatured version of, World History (or Area Studies, which by the late 1970s was becoming an outmoded fashion in the disciplines)—and the occasional high school elective in Geography per se.*

One thing blocking the development of the last—besides the rarity of trained teachers—was the lack of a clear model on the college level. Not only were geography departments small and somewhat at risk in the university, but there seems to be no established pattern of an *integrated* introductory course, spanning and explaining the principal subfields of geography, as there is in anthropology and psychology, for example. The predominance of physical geography as the first college course, together with the fact that some states require *physical* geography as part of a Social Studies certification, is surely a factor in the finding that a good 40 percent of elementary teachers (virtually all of whom cover considerable geographical material) have little or no coursework in the field, and that teachers at higher levels believe that physical geography is really the center of the subjectmatter. School history teachers who have had any geography course work are much more likely to have had it in physical geography rather than economic or regional geography.[†] In a 1965 national survey of grade 12 teachers, only 6 percent reported having taken geography courses, while 100 percent had taken U.S. History, and over 50 percent World History.[19] In the high school, teachers *of Geography* reported feeling far more capable of teaching history.

Today, in a typical large and 'good' high school one might find a World Geography course at grade 9 or 10, still emphasizing 'skills' and area descriptions,[‡] together with an advanced course at grade 11 or 12—still emphasizing the same aspects.[§] Little, anywhere, about economic and population geography, settlement geography, location theory, or ecological systems. And little, curiously, that stems from new techniques such as remote sensing, satellite observation, computer information systems, methods of mapping and representation—all things that ought to interest some high-school students, and could be of great value in other subject fields.[‖] There seems to be little that deals with new research in human spatial and ecological perception, which is also a bridge to

---

*"Occasional" is not too strong a term. Such courses seem to be the property of rare, individual teachers. Short and Matlock[18] have shown that while the likelihood of a high school elective course in Sociology, Economics, and Psychology is a direct function of the size of the school, the presence of an Advanced Geography course is not.

[†]None of this is meant to imply that teachers should not have any background in physical geography. Quite the contrary; but they should have something besides that, at least so long as Geography is offered in Social Studies.

[‡]Thus, from a curriculum guide, "Students will study map reading, the location of various areas of the world, physical features and their influences on man's activities, and political and cultural characteristics of people of six continents."

[§]"Tools to be used will include atlases, gazetteers, and globes. Cause-effect relationships between geographic features and cultural outcomes will be stressed worldwide."

[‖]One of the great strengths of Geography is that maps and related artifacts are beautiful. The new high-altitude photographs, with high resolving power over large terrains, are not only beautiful as pictorial representations but have fascinating map- and model-like qualities.

other social studies. Nor is there much recognition of historical geography, for example the significance of 'public spaces' in social history. There is much promise, in other words, not only from 'systems'-level geography—which could easily be carried too far toward the abstract and the distributed aspects of occupied space—but from an enriched approach to place-specific aspects: what is 'situated' in the social and human, as well as the spatial, world. Unfortunately, with reference to either tradition, while school geography once seemed to be ahead of the disciplinary field—in terms of social study and 'human geography'—it now seems to be lagging behind it.

Some of that lag may be accounted for by a certain caution (or conflict) brought about by demands placed on geography in the schools in the 1980s. On one side, there are those who see geography as a central element in global education. Here, the question is whether the field should follow the world-systems approach or ally itself with other disciplines in some form of regional/areal study; or even whether those outside the schools, who are horrified by the geographical 'illiteracy' of students and its implication for economic competitiveness, will insist on an expanded form of place-recognition drill. (Instead of learning the 50 state capitals, students would now know 150 national capitals.) On the other side, there is, especially in the primary and middle school, a renewed interest in the history-geography affinity (see below). In either case, interestingly, the underlying rationale external to the schools seems to be a renewed concern for *citizenship*—but this itself is full of traps. The knowledge and skills suitable for global citizenship should of course build on, and not be incompatible with, those needed for American citizenship; but the priorities, within a limited range and duration of schooling, could be quite different.

8.1   The Test Score Scare

The results of recent surveys and national tests of geographic knowledge have produced very disturbing results. As is repeatedly emphasized in this volume (for example, section 3.2), such results may be quite spurious—but then again, they may not be: the trouble is, it is hard to tell. Tests of place-name recognition knowledge are easy to write, administer, and score. It does appear shocking, on the face of it, that the *New York Times* found that in 1950 the great majority of college students knew where the Amazon flowed, while in 1985 only 25 percent did.[20] But some historical perspective on knowledge scores is essential. It is almost impossible to know whether students or the public today have 'lost' some items of knowledge while gaining other such items; the extent to which sources of knowledge other than schools and colleges (for example, television news, travel, military service) may be involved; whether one can make fair comparisons between 'college students' today and in 1950.* In its original report, the

---

*For example, which colleges did the 1950 *Times* test cover? In fact, the 1985 scores were obtained from a North Carolina survey and then compared to the Times's previous national results, a methodologically doubtful procedure.

Times did not have the prescience to warn that in thirty-five years things would be truly dreadful. Instead, its 1950 article began "American college students know shockingly little about the geography of this country. They know even less about the world. American or world geography is a forgotten subject in our institutions of higher learning." In 1964, Hofstadter[21] reported with some sense of urgency that about 15 percent of Los Angeles grade 8 students could not locate the Atlantic Ocean on a map. All that can be concluded is that the state of knowledge has clearly been reprehensible in all recent times.

Geographic education specialists, however, suspect that the level of place-name knowledge has declined; and if so, they are right to worry about it. Former Secretary of Education William Bennett[22] seems to blame the poor achievement by students on ignorance on the part of teachers who have been education majors—but this simply displaces the problem. If a weakness in place knowledge is real, which it probably is, means exist for direct improvement of this particular situation. For example, computer-assisted drill 'works,' and grade-level achievement tests can verify it. Furthermore, such drill procedures have the important side-benefit of quickly revealing which students do *not* need it, so that instructional time and effort are not wasted. There is no mystery to improving such knowledge, as there is none in drilling students on dates and names in history.

But this seems to be not quite the solution desired, either in the educational field or among interested critics and observers. At least some experienced geography educators,[23] while calling geographical literacy "appalling," hasten to say: "Ability to locate words in a dictionary does not make a person literate. . . . An atlas is sometimes misperceived as a dictionary of geography. It is rather an alphabet of geography, and only deep knowledge of geography can make it into a basic dictionary. Thus geographical literacy is attained only when people understand why places are where they are, what these places are like, and how they relate to these people and to other places. What appear to be measures of . . . literacy are indeed complex."

Some of the critics would certainly agree. Others, like E. D. Hirsch,[24] whose 'list' of necessary items of our common cultural heritage includes 700 or so geographical entries, insist that such a comment misses the issue: it is not that 'literacy' is nothing *but* 'item' knowledge, but that true literacy cannot be built without it. Here recommendations diverge. The National Geographic Society is investing heavily in maps and materials, television specials, and other graphics and media-oriented campaigns. What this will mean for school instruction is unclear. (In principle, place learning need not occur *in* school at all, as learning the alphabet need not.) The society is also cooperating with the professional, education-based Geographic Education National Implementation Project (GENIP), whose main approach initially is the building of teacher alliances and local schools-university-business networks.* GENIP is using as an organizing model a *Fundamental Themes of Geography* statement recently developed by

---

*GENIP plans subsequently to work on improving materials, teacher education and certification, and the public image of geography.

the National Council for Geographic Education and the Association of American Geographers.[25] The five themes are: Location: Position on the Earth's Surface; Place: Physical and Human Characteristics; Relationships within Places: Humans and Environments; Movement: Humans Interacting on the Earth; and Regions: How They Form and Change.

A great virtue of this scheme is that it is concise and clear. Another is that it is discipline-centered, in the sense that the first three themes especially are specific to geography. Thus the tendency in schools for geography to be seen as primarily the basis for studying and interpreting other subjects is countered. A possible weakness, reflecting what may be ineffective use of the discipline as the most capacious resource for school geography, is that the guidelines statement is not very venturesome, in terms of intellectual frontiers: note the absence of the word 'space' and of concepts involving interrelationships *of* 'places' and 'locations,' rather than relationships, movement, and the like *within* them. Perhaps a more serious problem is that local teaching alliances and the dissemination of materials, while enriching to those who can participate (and respectful of the autonomy of teachers and schools), reach relatively few teachers, and do not reach those deeply—in comparison with sustained 'hands-on' developmental intervention programs in officially committed schools (as with the DEEP program of the economists); and do not attempt a deepening of subject knowledge *and* pedagogy among all or many of those becoming teachers or a deliberate altering of current texts, most of which do not reach GENIP's current standards.*

The other prevalent recommendation in the field is to link geography even more loosely with history. A geography professor is quoted[26] in a newspaper interview as saying that educators have overlooked the fact that geography provides an essential framework for other fields of study. "How can you understand Civil War battles unless you know where they were fought and why they were fought where they were fought?" Geography does indeed supply such a framework. But the history-geography nexus has been obvious in the schools since the mid-1800s. Some carry the point so far that geography becomes essentially a tributary to history. Quite in contrast, the American Federation of Teachers' recent report, *Education for Democracy*,[27] recommends an explicit core of history and geography—"with history providing the perspective for considered judgment and geography confronting students with the hard realities that shape so many political, economic, and social decisions." Such reasoning seems to give to history a unique role, a rather exposed position, and to lay an impossible burden, that of imparting 'reality,' on geography.†

*However, it should be pointed out that GENIP leaders plan to focus on the preservice geographic education of teachers, and that the guidelines were drafted to be as clearcut and accessible as possible to the general public.

†The latter burden has been urged on geography before, for example, by Charles Merriam, *Civic Education*, who wrote that through geography students could "obtain more objective consideration of the qualities and skills of people of the earth, than through the agency of history. Whatever faults geography may have, it has not generally been found as a propagandist, except in mild form" (p. 95), but (p. 120) "seems to have acquired a degree of impartiality which makes it a safe agency of instruction." Merriam doubted that history could be the sole provider of judgment. Even Merriam, however, did not feel that geography could be the sole medium for the consideration of reality.

Much depends on the spirit of integration, of course. The new California curriculum framework links history and geography across the grade levels. "Throughout this curriculum, the importance of the variables of time and place, when and where, history and geography, is stressed repeatedly." (However, when one looks at the detail of the topics to be covered, course by course, specific geographic learning seems to fade out.) A prominent geographic educator, Christopher Salter, says: "All events, as has been said so many times, occur at the intersection of space and time." Another eminent geographer, Donald Meinig, views history and geography as "bound together by the very nature of things."* But such truths still ignore the fact—and it is a very important fact—that 'time' within geography (as a discipline) is by no means always *historical* time, nor are the 'events' that geography touches upon all historical events. Further, there are structural and synchronic aspects of the field that go far beyond a simple place/ time grid. If all these aspects—if all but geography related to history and historical geography—are to be omitted, politics and economics and sociology can be omitted also (the more easily, in fact, since their 'events' are historical in nature and thus could be 'handled' by history). Finally, reopening an absolute division between history/geography and the natural world (in both its physical and biological aspects) would seem to some to be a needless retrogression in twentieth-century science.

Both the GENIP and the Backler or California approach face some decisions about strategy and feasibility. Those facing GENIP have been briefly outlined. With regard to the latter, one may simply suggest that implementation necessitates that text publishers be induced (as the state of California intends) to use a history-and-geography grid throughout the curriculum, and the vast majority of teachers be educated far more deeply in the two fields, taught correlatively. Unfortunately, it is not easy to see where the geographic improvement of teacher education is going to take place, given the size, interests, and goals of the discipline of geography. It does not bode well that geographers believe that the quality of geographical exposition in history texts now is "marginal to unacceptable."† Since history in the schools has traditionally been hospitable to such material, it is hard to explain why it should be so poor, after all these decades of collaboration. Since history is by far the dominant force and presence in the schools, with by far the widest base of support in the universities, textbook publishing, and the other relevant sectors, it may be the responsibility of history to bring this special relationship up to the necessary standard. If that is not acceptable to others, others will need to bestir themselves to improve the situation.

---

*All quotations are from pp. 2–3 of Alan Backler,[28] a highly experienced educator, who makes perhaps the best succinct case for the sufficiency of a history/geography tandem for the essence of social studies in schools.

†As Backler, p. 4, admits.

9.0 Sociology and Anthropology

9.1 Sociology

9.2 Anthropology

In this section we discuss two fields together, not in consequence of their once-frequent association in the American university structure, but because—in the context of the social studies—both seemed to promise, at one time or another, to occupy a place at the center of the curriculum. Neither succeeded. Today, Sociology is a high-school elective of some popularity, but it is hard to identify the broad influence elsewhere in the curriculum that it was intended to have. Anthropology, in contrast, is a common element in World Cultures and World Study courses at several grade levels, but as a separate course of study is largely absent.

9.1 Sociology

The discipline of sociology had an important shaping effect on the schools from mid- to late nineteenth century, then again around the 1916–18 reform period, and finally during the 1930s. Thereafter, the interests of the discipline and the school field touched upon each other in the New Social Studies era, but otherwise have not much coincided.

Sociology's early influence derived from the enormous notability of the Englishman Herbert Spencer and his followers in American intellectual life for several decades. It was Spencer, writing in 1859 on modern education[1] from his belief in social evolution and inherent progress in modern life, who suggested the kind of 'descriptive sociology' (a phrase used by Spencer) that was later evident in the 1916 committee rationale.

The modern intelligence, Spencer believed, could take stock of history and geography in their relation to the industrial revolution and large-scale society and, through education, make the necessary decisions to move society efficiently along its largely preordained path.* Spencer's sociology text, *Principles of Sociology*, appearing first in 1877 and in many revised editions thereafter, established the full-scale study of society in its modern complexity as a scholarly discipline, brought into being in part because of the necessity to deal with what the English thought of as 'the social problem'—a modern industrial class-based society with its potential for conflict. Spencer and his American disciple, William Graham Sumner, thought social reform largely futile: the role of leaders was to help the society gradually adapt to 'circumstances.'

Other early sociological founders, notably Lester Ward and Albion Small (the latter the founder of the sociology department at the University of Chicago, in 1892), took a more sanguine view of society's evolution, in line with scientific progressivism and the turn-of-the-century sacred dogma of progress. This was the founding line especially of midwestern American sociology, a number of whose main figures were sons of Protestant ministers. The community study, the activities of sociologists and social workers in civic life, the reform of municipal government, and the improvement of public education, not only for the young but for adults moving off the farms and for immigrants—all were intended to serve the purposes of social betterment. This spirit is clear in the community civics program of Dunn, adopted by the 1916 committee (section 4.4).†

This tradition was prominent well into the 1920s. The social meliorist aspect of early sociology is an important strain in American intellectual history as regards the schools. A related, but distinctly different, tradition in sociology grew up a little later, reaching its fullest influence in the 1920s and 1930s. This was the strong positivism of sociologists who believed that the accumulation of 'scientific' knowledge provided in effect an entirely new basis for social decision-making by experts or leaders. George Lundberg, for example,[2] called on sociologists to "grind out and publish systematically related and significant 'if . . . then' propositions." It was their business to "determine reliably the immediate and remote costs and consequences of alternate possible courses of action, and to make these known to the public." Lundberg believed, despite his reference to "the public," that sociologists were essentially engineers, designers, cost accountants. Their clients were managers and governments. The scientists were to be strictly neutral, were not to factor in value aspects (that was the concern of policymakers), and were not responsible for society's use of knowledge thus established. This is the positivism of Auguste Comte, which depended on knowledge arrived at through an intense, deductive rationalism. This Enlightenment positivism, in scientific sociology, had a greater influence initially on

---

*At least in terms of English society, Spencer was elitist as regards education: a 'modern' education was a necessity for society's leaders, not for the masses.

†Dewey, because of his association with the University of Chicago and with the idea of the school as a community, is sometimes associated with this tradition of sociology. His intellectual allegiances, however, are more with G. H. Mead and the social interactionism of early social psychology.

the Eastern sociological establishment than on the Midwestern meliorists.* In the school *curriculum*, the spirit of the 1916 reform was largely that of the meliorists. In school *management*, through the social efficiency and scientific management movements, the strong positivist influence played a part. It is natural that those outside the social sciences and education who came to deplore the latter approach to educational policy tended to assume that students must be studying an ultrascientific form of sociology in the classroom.

In 1896, Small had written: "Sociology knows no means for the amelioration or reform of society more radical than those of which teachers hold the leverage."[3] And Ward believed that the task of the schools, as of the end of the century, was to reallocate cultural capital, as other reformers wished to reallocate real wealth in society.[4] By the time of the 1916 committee, sociology was predominantly committed to intervention and progressive reform (in part through the schools) rather than a Spencerian 'adaptation to circumstances' through a dynamic historical, that is, evolutionist, process, at the level of the entire society. The prominent sociologist Ross Lee Finney, speaking for an American Sociological Society committee in 1920, saluted the 1916 design for the schools, in particular Community Civics and Problems of Democracy, with their strong sociological elements.[5] He wrote, in an internally contradictory statement, that the 1916 report was "significant not only because of the radical innovation it recommends, but also because of . . . the consensus of opinion of all the committees at work on the problem, including that of the American Historical Association, whose program the schools have been following for the last twenty-five years."[†]

Thus, at least one main stream of sociology was fully reflected in and compatible with the progressive compromise of 1916. As for anthropology, it too was established on the American university scene by then, largely thanks to Franz Boas at Columbia. But in its nineteenth-century English origin (not that of Boas), anthropology was largely oriented toward the problem of Empire, and was thus the study of external societies. Boas himself, as part of his thorough refounding of the discipline in America, was deeply antievolutionist in his thinking, and was committed to an adequate description of social life in its various aspects, not to scientific 'reform.' In addition, anthropology was—then and at all times—a much smaller discipline than sociology. For all these reasons, anthropology had no program for progressive social revision through the schools. Moreover, it entailed research skills and fieldwork that could not be a part of the school curriculum. The ethnographies and culture-and-personality

*It is hard to draw a firm line. Sumner himself was located at Yale, in the heart of the Eastern establishment. The influence of the meliorist sociologists on public policy is clear, for example, in the relation between Chicago-style sociology and the governing of Chicago, and in the way in which states used the 'Wisconsin idea,' pioneered by La Follette, of drawing on state university experts in social fields for advice ranging from tax codes to public health. These sociologists, however, unlike those of the Lundberg school, were specialist-advocates, not disinterested technicians.

†The AHA, of course, supported the 1916 report because it did not find it all that radical.

studies that became well known to educated readers in the 1920s and 1930s indeed had far-reaching implications for the nonuniversality of many aspects of 'human nature' and, for example, the enculturation of the young, but implied no overt agenda for schooling in America. Therefore, with the exception of a few anthropologists in the late 1930s who were interested in urban life and American studies, such as Jules Henry, anthropologists did not pay much attention to public education, and vice versa, until after World War II.*

From the viewpoint of about 1920, then, one might expect sociology to sweep through the social studies curriculum in succeeding decades—perhaps even to supplant history as the core subjectmatter. Insofar as a sociological focus or emphasis was strong (together with economics, geography, and government) in the grade 9 Community Civics course; and insofar as the Problems of Democracy course at grade 12 generally was a social problems course, the influence of sociology no doubt did grow throughout the 1930s. In addition, applied sociological techniques—the beginnings of scientific surveys, the improvement of community studies, and so on—were certainly of relevance to some school courses and teachers in the New Deal era, bringing an accessible enrichment of empirical knowledge.

However, the ease of adopting a modicum of 'descriptive sociology' in the schools was also a weakness, since this could be managed within other courses, including U.S. History, but primarily Civics and POD. By the 1930s, moreover, the widespread public unease about social reconstruction (see section 4.7) tended to keep sociological subjectmatter hidden or contained within other labels. Finally, in the universities, by the 1930s at any rate, the dominant structural-functional model of sociology was incompatible with the earlier interest in the profession in community study and reform. The intellectual program of sociology became the study of society as a self-reproducing system, and many in the discipline believed this focus of study to be too difficult for precollegiate education (see below). The empirical description of American society became a task shared by many disciplines, social reform a task of none (except for the professional field of social work).[†]

For these reasons, separate courses in Sociology did not become common, and enrollments (therefore) were not impressive until the 1960s. At the same time, many of post-1916 school courses were, in effect, Social Problems courses drawing heavily on descriptive sociology. Tryon[6] points out that Sociology courses in the high school were present by about 1910 and grew in number sharply until about 1920; but he also shows that this was part of a general increase

---

*An irony, of course, is that while those in sociology felt the need to repudiate Spencerian evolutionism in favor of structural-functional analysis, those in anthropology (and social science in general) have been comfortable enough with the notion of societal-level 'evolution'—that is, complex systematic change through internal historical processes and through the diffusion of influences across cultures, in a loosely Darwinian, fundamentally non-Spencerian form.

†This is not to deny that many sociologists were frustrated, throughout the midcentury development of the field, by this separation of theory from practice and the rejection of reform.

in size and proliferation of subjectmatters offered in the high schools, and that enrollments did not support the growing number of (elective) courses. The largest enrollments in Sociology tended to be in the upper Midwest, which probably reflects the continuing emphasis on social meliorism and Chicago-style sociology. As of 1930, Tryon found that decreases in Sociology enrollments were a function of schools' adding POD courses, as one would expect. His explanation for a cessation of growth, as of about 1930, sounds familiar: "The lack of teachers prepared to teach the subject; the contention among college people that the subject was too difficult for high-school pupils; the general lack of understanding among school boards and school administrators as to the true nature of the subject; the overcrowded condition of the high-school curriculum when sociology sought admittance thereto; and especially since 1920, the fact that sociology had to dwell in the same house in which community civics and problems of American democracy lived" (p. 386).

Tryon's analysis of the prevalent topics in sociology courses over the years showed that Social Problems was always the typical focus. Texts were normally organized in chapters with "Problems of . . ." as the guiding format. However, the problems changed from decade to decade: immigration, heredity and race, poverty, sanitation and health, liquor, 'defectives' in the 1920s; internal migration (that is, from the farm), industrial relations, unemployment in the 1930s. A fuller history of 'problems' by era is given in Angell.[7] Angell's analysis suggests that in any era 'problems' in school sociology are likely to be problems facing society, or problems confronting particular persons or small groups. Rarely is there attention to the structural problems of different units or subsystems in relation to each other *within* the society. An obvious example would be that racial unrest is a problem 'for' society, and discrimination is a problem 'for' a member of a minority group. Institutionalized or structural racial inequity is seldom analyzed as a property—that is, a 'problem' *of* the system.

This is a familiar dilemma: 'real' sociology was too abstract for high school students, while 'school' sociology was already covered in other courses. Elective enrollments have depended heavily on the 'problems' focus of courses, even though the discipline has wished it otherwise.* In the also-familiar pattern, the discipline attempted in the 1960s to shift the focus from the study of problems to the study of 'domains'—that is, the structure of the discipline and its central conceptions and procedures. An even more puristic goal was set in the 1962 ACLS-NCSS volume, in which the author of the Sociology chapter, Gresham Sykes, pleaded for a *functional* treatment of sociological topics, going further by holding that a "functional analysis *of society* is essentially equivalent to socio-

---

*By about 1960, careful surveys of high-school course offerings[8] showed that as an elective course POD was definitely on the wane in grade 12, typically being replaced by students' taking paired semester courses in Sociology and Economics—with enrollment about twice that for Psychology. See also Turner, "Political Education," 53. Some of these Sociology courses, but by no means all, would have been patterned after the college introductory course.

logical analysis"—in other words, the true business of sociology is the formal study of the system itself. Sykes pointed to barriers that make "difficult the widespread adoption of sociology as a separate course"—these barriers involving "taboo" subjects and "emotion-laden issues"—but concluded that it was "possible and desirable that sociology should be made available as an avenue of study *for the academically talented*."[9]

A more schools-adapted approach, following the notion that the fundamental logic of a discipline (if not a grasp of all the specialized methodology) was accessible to students at any age, was exemplified in the New Social Studies era. The American Sociological Association, between 1964 and 1971, sponsored a major curriculum project for the schools, Sociological Resources for the Social Studies, which resulted in a text and associated materials called *Inquiries in Sociology*.* This was to promote informed curiosity in social processes and structures among students, while encouraging them to analyze and think— inquire—like sociologists. The overall approach was to divide the content into thirty or so broad topics or subfields, offer lengthy excerpts from the sociological literature, and then encourage students to draw generalizations appropriate to, and using terminology of, the field. To an outsider, it is notable that the SRSS did not attempt to cover the various 'branches' of the current discipline, unlike contemporaneous projects in economics and geography. That is, the main emphasis was on socialization (the social psychological tradition), institutions and social stratification (the functional systems approach), and social change (which touched to some extent on problems and social action). There was relatively little or no attention to survey research, demography, 'critical' sociology, or symbolic interactionism other than as an aspect of socialization.

The fact that a complete description of the field was not attempted was compatible with the intention that the materials would lend themselves to infusion into courses other than Sociology electives in high school. To an outsider, again, the inductive emphasis seems restricted to the end-of-unit questions and exercises, not to the spirit of the 'episodes' themselves. That is, it is not so much the research itself or the quoted text that demonstrates 'inquiry' but the student's own groping for the right sociological gloss—as guided by the textbook. After the presentation of a long, richly textured excerpt from W. F. Whyte's *Street Corner Society*, for example, the 'prompts' in the text elicit generalizations about social class and neighborhood-based reference groups that seem simplistic in comparison.† In Reichenbach's terms, all the inductive procedures seem to bear on interpretation or 'justification,' not description or

---

*The history of the project is discussed in Switzer and in Haas. One interesting aspect is that, toward the end of this period, the SRSS group and the High School Geography Project sponsored a joint project book, *Experiences in Inquiry*, which represented a combined approach to both urban and rural topics that seems attractive today.[10]

†This is, of course, a common charge against sociology and the social sciences in general, to which the present writer does not subscribe: that the generalizations and concepts are merely commonsense notions dressed up in specialized language.

'discovery.' Such an emphasis, in the classroom, can easily seem like 'cooked' inquiry, and can be highly manipulative when the teacher doggedly follows it through to a predetermined end.* Switzer[11] refers to this problem in saying that it was "convergent inquiry" that was employed: "the outcome is still conditioned by the structure of the discipline being studied." This overdetermined procedure is quite different in spirit from the kind of critical inquiry or reflection recommended by Dewey and others.

The receding of the NSS projects in the schools[12] did not mean a dying-out of sociology from the curriculum. Unlike the economists, disciplinary experts did turn their attention away from the schools—largely because they were once again convinced that "the interrelationships of the various components of society requires a level of abstraction that cannot be mastered at the secondary school level."[13] But enrollments in elective courses took a decided upturn in the late 1960s and all through the 1970s (see figure 13-1). This is particularly noteworthy in that the number of B.A.s and M.A.s in sociology from the university was concurrently falling—this at a time when the average educational background of school teachers was rising, so that if anything the shortage of qualified teachers would be felt even more acutely (table 16-1). Part of the explanation for the upturn in enrollments might be the virtual disappearance of POD and multidisciplinary Civics courses, which had considerable sociology content; students with interests of this kind would need to seek elsewhere. To a far greater extent, however, the answer lies in the continued appeal among high school students of the study of social problems.

Even with too small a pool of trained teachers, it appears that 'good' high schools will offer Sociology electives—as they do Psychology electives. (The likening of these two subjects is appropriate, since, unlike Economics, neither Sociology nor Psychology is aided by mandating.) Recent surveys[14] reveal that typically a school offering the Sociology elective has one sociology teacher, with the equivalent of a minor in the field. The leading texts today are essentially college-market texts, expository in nature, with little overt emphasis on 'problems' of society or on the nature of sociological inquiry at the research level; but it is not known whether *teachers* tend to emphasize social problems and applied aspects of sociology, offer an introduction to the field, or give special attention to some topic. Especially interesting is the finding that Sociology is heavily localized to high schools whose students are 'average blue collar' by family origin. A supplementary small survey more recently[15] suggested that those taking introductory courses in the subject in college did slightly better when they had taken high school Sociology (with grade point average controlled), but the differences were small and rather inconsistent.

Putting together such evidence, as well as anecdotal testimony, it appears likely that high school Sociology is actually taught as a predominantly applied

---

*Alternatively, as has often been noticed in classroom use of inquiry-related materials, if the teacher uses only the expository sections, avoiding the 'inquiry' apparatus, his true concern—coverage of the material, or what will be on the test—becomes only too apparent.

subject, revolving around topics of particular interest to adolescents: family, occupation, sex roles, and the like.* That is, legitimately enough, because students are interested in their own relationships to the social environment, and Sociology comes as close as any elective to satisfying that need. In this regard, Sociology's appeal is probably rather like that of Psychology. 'Relevance' is easier to attain in the schools than a direct examination of 'problems'— individual or societal. Teachers can respect community mores, in other words, by not delving deeply into sensitive areas and by not modelling or encouraging critical or iconoclastic behavior—but they can still teach what immediately interests their students.

Unlike Psychology, however, high-school Sociology *may* appeal especially† to those who do not go on, at least directly, to liberal-arts programs in universities and colleges. A largely applied emphasis, though it is unlike that of college introductory courses, is not incompatible with the professional field today: currently, in the American Sociological Association, the largest membership sections are those in medical sociology and the sociology of sex roles.

If these suppositions about why and how Sociology is taught in high school are for the most part correct, it may reflect a process by which, given the relative failure of the sociology curriculum project in the New Social Studies era, the assumption that 'true' sociology is too abstract and difficult for precollegiate students becomes self-validating. On the positive side (in the view of some), it would also show that the goal of the reformers of 1916—for students to think socially, to be curious about social phenomena—is still expressed in the high schools.

There is also, of course, a basis for sociological curiosity and information in the 'expanding environments' framework for the early grades, which in principle is meant to offer a kind of graduated *tour d'horizon* of social life, starting from material having to do with the student's own family and her agemates to the introduction of information about social roles played by adults, occupational roles and statuses, and the like. Ravitch has criticized much of the approach of social studies in grades 1 to 4, or so, as "tot sociology." However, it is known that very little instruction about specific concepts and phenomena takes place in the classroom at this level (since there is little sustained attention to *any* social studies content), and there is no research to suggest that any sociological orientation or sensitization that may take place there is related to later learning.

9.2 Anthropology

Anthropology, a much smaller field than sociology, has had a rather similar trajectory in the schools, but much compressed in time and scope. In the same

---

*Even in an 'academic' high school the course description may read something like the following: "Emphasis is placed on self-awareness and how to cope actively in society."

†There is no clear evidence.

way that the first two or three decades of the century were 'sociological' in terms of the tone of public discussion of American society and its progress, so was the period after World War II an era of réclame for cultural anthropology, which was suddenly found essential for knowledge of foreign societies, emerging nations, culture 'areas,' esoteric languages—all within the context of the enlarged global responsibilities of the United States. Not only was there a demand for such specialized knowledge for national purposes, but the universities enrolled mature students (thanks to the G.I. bill) who had served abroad and sometimes married foreigners.

This was the era in which many research universities began separate anthropology departments, or enlarged them into departments that reflected the 'fourfold' nature of the field. In part this reflected the considerable intellectual prestige accorded European structuralism, in ethnology, linguistics, and related fields. But also, by 1950 American cultural anthropology had accumulated enough ethnographic research findings for there to be at least a minimal depth of knowledge of most of the world's cultures, and considerably more about some. Thus the founding, for example, of the Human Relations Area File at Yale could imply a rational program of worldwide cultural comparison: an empirical approach to determining the frequency, distribution, and the co-occurrence of cultural 'traits' within and across societies.

With the emergence of the notion, following World War II, that America would assume a special responsibility—welcome or onerous—vis-à-vis the rest of the world, with the onset of new nations and movements of people, with the outbreak of postcolonial wars affecting the interests of Western nations, and finally with the growth and maturity of anthropology itself (table 16-1), some of those who thought about the school curriculum came, for the first time, to imagine that, as history served as the medium for an infinite number and instances of temporal comparison, so might anthropology serve as an integrative medium for comparison across peoples and cultures. The comparative idea affected many social science disciplines during the postwar decades, especially the basic notion that there was an 'inside' and 'outside' viewpoint on any social phenomenon, and that each could act as a corrective lens for the other. The very act of orderly comparison, in any discipline, was seen as a hallmark of social scientific epistemology.*

In education, a particular benefit from comparison, when properly done, was that in and of itself it enlarged the theoretical frame of reference and thus acted against the stupidity (leaving aside the immorality) of ethnocentrism. The anthropologist Paul Bohannan has described this attitude of mind as the "anthropological squint": that is, by learning to be a fieldworker (or participant observer), even in one's own culture, one realizes that any set of manmade things do not have to be as they are. Thus anthropology was inherently attractive to

---

*Even in fields that had thought of themselves as dealing with universals; in social and developmental psychology, for example, the culture-comparison approach became acceptable.

those who had worried about the inculcating aspect of education. Even more fundamental, at a deep level, was the ontological appeal of anthropology: what more important goal, after all, can there be in education than to convey what being human is about, and what all who are human share? Finally, for curriculum-making, anthropology's distinctive central idea of culture formed useful bridges to other subjects, appropriate for the times.

To be sure, these factors and perceptions amounted more to a program for anthropology than a reality in the school curriculum. Prior to about 1960, anthropology in the school curriculum amounted to the relatively infrequent inclusion of the subject as a high school elective—in the 'better' schools—and to participation in vague kinds of 'multicultural' instruction, involving world areas or culture regions, often in conjunction with history and geography, in the middle grades. The relative newness of the field in universities, on any sizable scale, meant that virtually no teachers had more than an introductory course in the discipline; in particular, elementary level teachers would have little experience with anything more complex than Sunday-supplement materials. Dynneson[16] points out that each Anthropology course or unit in the 1950s and early 1960s was inevitably a curriculum experiment, since publishers as yet had no market for texts.

However, the cross-cultural comparative method, intrinsic to anthropology, and the etic/emic double-lens notion of sociocultural anthropology, helped make Anthropology the success story of the New Social Studies.* An Anthropology Curriculum Project was founded at the University of Georgia. Over the years it developed grade-specific materials for anthropology teaching, especially in primary and middle schools, but it has been underfunded and the materials are not nationally well known. The American Anthropological Association (AAA) sponsored, with NSF funds, the Anthropology Curriculum Study Project (ACSP), directed by Malcolm Collier, which produced a one-semester high school course and text, *Patterns in Human History*.[17] This project used the comparison-grid approach, involving an array of communities around the world analyzed for their communalities and differences. It ranged from ancient man to tribal, peasant, and urban communities of the present, focusing centrally on the unifying concept of 'role.'

Perhaps the best-known project was that of the Educational Development Center, under the direction of Peter Dow, which produced a variety of printed material, ethnographic film, and so on, suitable for grade 5 or 6 under the title *Man: A Course of Study*.†[18] MACOS looked primarily at one community, an Eskimo village, and explicitly asked, What is human about all humans? (By

---

*It helped, of course, that there was no earlier failed legacy of involvement of the field in the schools. The promise was fresh.

†This project was notable, among other things, for the participation of Jerome Bruner, the spokesman of the Woods Hole movement (section 5.3), and for including elements of human biology and comparative social behavior, that is, across species, in its purview.

studying one community it contrasted in its tight ethnographic focus, and its essentialist central question, to the more comparative ACSP.) MACOS was pathbreaking in its use of anthropological film—unnarrated, without sound, and using insofar as possible an unedited style: the methodological point was to force students to understand that 'seeing' a culture depended on conscious attention to the frame of observation. But MACOS ran into trouble with some parents and school authorities—for example, for showing the abandonment of the elderly ill.

Both the ACSP and MACOS materials are still used, and considered of high quality. Localized strong objection to the MACOS materials did not appear to undercut anthropology itself in the schools.[19] Gearing, however,[20] raises a deeper caution about any 'Mankind curriculum,' by which a student is encouraged to enter vicariously into the experience of other peoples in search of what is distinctively human. "The anthropological message competes most directly at this juncture and many others with aspects of the (particular) cultural transmission processes of the society. . . . A Mankind curriculum is 'out in front' of the culture, anticipating and perhaps generating cultural change."

There are problems also with the comparative approach, with courses that inventory social variation. Hanvey[21] points out:

> Teachers . . . respond to what they perceive as the 'relativistic' aspect of anthropological writing. . . . They respond sympathetically to the 'accepting' quality of anthropology, its willingness to take other people on their own terms. . . . But to the anthropologist, respect for other cultures is so *axiomatic* that he cannot imagine wasting time on it. The anthropologist wants to 'understand,' but in theoretical terms, and that is quite different from what teachers want. (Emphasis added)

No doubt this is an overstatement of a difference in attitude, since teachers also want to 'understand,' and have their students 'understand,' in conceptually extended ways. It does point to a problem with the NSS approach, and all discipline-oriented approaches in social studies. It would be helpful if disciplinary scholars would consider that the task of teachers in the school curriculum is to bring into awareness for students precisely those principles and concepts that become 'axiomatic' at a later stage of understanding.

Relative to a pre-1960 baseline, anthropology in the schools was the social science field that the NSS benefited most. That is, it went from a promised to a real presence in the curriculum. Further, what remains today is not different in kind from what the NSS pursued—as is the case to some extent with the other fields. This is partly due to the fact that the central enterprise of sociocultural anthropology is obviously adaptable to the curriculum in principle (even allowing for the cautions raised by Gearing and by Hanvey), while the other constituent fields of anthropology have simply been ignored.* On the other hand,

---

*With the exception of occasional teaching about prehistory and archaeology in connection with history.

Dynneson points out that anthropology is largely a component within other instruction, an ingredient in the larger study of Psychology or Sociology or World Cultures. Teachers continue to have very little background in the field; the number of university degrees in the field has been declining since the 1970s; and anthropology is far down in publishers' rating of likely textbook markets.[22] Many anthropology electives use college texts. Jane White, in a study of teaching about other cultures in the elementary schools in Maryland, concluded that such teaching (not specifically anthropological in emphasis) seemed to convey, in general, their 'quaintness' (and by implication their trivial value).[23] The Council on Anthropology and Education, founded in 1969 and now a unit of the AAA, is interested primarily in education as a cultural enterprise, rather than on anthropology in the curriculum.

Future possibilities for anthropology and for sociology in the schools could be quite different. In the foregoing, with regard to sociology, we commented that the schools and the discipline may fundamentally agree that the essence of the discipline, as expressed at the university level, is not the focus of school sociology; rather, that for various reasons, a continued emphasis on problem-centered and applied sociology may mean that the schools are involved with particular *subfields*, those of most saliency to students. The same could be true for anthropology, especially since today most university graduates in anthropology go into applied work of one special kind or another. But here (and I believe in the case of geography as well), it seems unlikely that the technical and applied fields of these disciplines can have any special importance in the schools. That is, it is hard to imagine that the *focus of instruction* in the future would be salvage archaeology or satellite cartography or computational linguistics or transportation network planning—to take examples from the two fields.

In anthropology, various developments have occurred to make the fundamental unity of the field, in the Boasian model, honored more in spirit than in practice. As Hymes has pointed out[24] students are no longer trained in the four fields, though they may have to demonstrate ceremonial familiarity with the traditions and basic principles of all of them. Linguistics in some of its aspects has become an autonomous field. Biological anthropology and human biology have drawn closer to evolutionary biology and neurobiology; archeology to physical chemistry and related sciences. However, in every case there is a crucial residuum. That is, a comprehensive linguistics must always be partly an anthropological research field, and the underlying question of biological anthropology and of archaeology remains: what is cultural, what somatic or physiological, what historical, evolutionary, or diachronic in nature? Senior figures like Hymes or Stocking[25] return to the conviction that, in the latter's words, there can be no end to a "unified discourse about the development and diversity of humankind in all its aspects and in the broadest temporal framework." It may be true that anthropology, with specialization and the closing of the 'ethnographic frontier,'* is becoming a *metadiscipline*—an attitude of mind, a level of

---

*Never closed, of course, since domestic studies and comparative studies are always feasible.

analysis. If so, it is hard to conceive that precollegiate education has no place for that attitude and that level.

Teaching about World History and World Cultures almost demands such a framework (section 12.4). Furthermore, the depth and richness of the connection between anthropology and history is ever more evident. The cultural studies of Clifford Geertz and others are simultaneously studies of history, politics, and culture. Political anthropology—for example, studies of African states and legal systems—is a codisciplinary field. Modern studies of religion in society connect directly to the history of existing peoples and the role that religion and other 'symbol systems' play in not only the ethnographic present but in historical change. The study of *mentalités* has reached archeology; much can now be known—or hypothesized—not only about culture as captured in material artifacts but about vanished symbolic and mental structures. Cognitive anthropology studies collective memory and historically specific symbols. The insistence, originally, by Boas (and the other great founders) that cultures and societies are historically *contingent*—that is, not brought into being by some supraorganic evolutionary determinist process, but representing a path taken among many possible ones—is deeply compatible with the historical enterprise.

The pertinence of archaeology and prehistory to the testing of schemes and taxonomies established by the historical and political sciences—for example, 'levels of civilization' as described by Childe or Wittfogel or Toynbee—has long been recognized, as it has been in the study of the epochs of mankind—the Neolithic leading to the agricultural, and so on.[26] Oliver put the general point well:[27]

> Anthropologists have been preoccupied with very long-range cumulative change, as exemplified in such formulations as cultural evolution and diffusionism. Time devoted to these matters [in the school curriculum] would have the advantage of broadening generalizations beyond the scope ordinarily permitted by conventional courses in history. For example, an objective examination of the causes and sequences of cultural change would provide a context for contrasting and evaluating the various theories *of* history underlying so many competing political ideologies.

By definition, customarily, anthropology has a far greater time-depth than sociology. However, the present writer's suggestion that certain subfields of sociology are 'natural' to schools, while it is the anthropological *stance* that is valuable, may be fundamentally an illustration of a common fallacy: that sociology looks internally, at the workings of our own society (or another society of a comparable stage of development), largely in a contemporary focus, while anthropology ranges more widely in space and time. This in turn can lead to the assumption that anthropology is 'safer' than sociology: anthropological studies are curious, instructive, revealing—but sociology cuts close to the bone of our own society and life. Thus, the argument runs, we will always need sociology in the schools to illuminate family styles and sex roles and division of occupational labor in our own culture—but it will have to stay away from class or deviance. Given the MACOS controversy and, on the other side, Gearing's comment (above), this is clearly a too-facile model.

Sociology also has an overall attitude or commitment: to social data explained in social terms. This commitment—to a level of reality above that of individual experience, of factors external to individuals operating on them—is as deeply threatening to some as is the secular humanism or indiscriminate relativism ascribed by some to anthropology. Many Europeans have also noted that American sociology, even American social science, denies conflict as a pervasive aspect of social life, preferring to focus instead on consensus and on the structures that hold together differing interests and identifications.* In the end, sociology's commitment to objective empirical description of processes and structures within a society makes it invaluable to that society. For example, the entire enterprise of 'social mathematics' † has keen relevance to all in the schools. Data gained from successive censuses, sample surveys, and other such studies form invaluable indicators of widespread and fundamental processes over decades, so that one can see one's own society in flux.‡

Furthermore, sociology too has a certain breadth temporally and across societies. As anthropology does not simply study the exotic, so sociology does study others comparatively—modern social structures and institutions, occupational hierarchies, social stratification processes, leader/group relationships, and much else. Beyond this, the entire Weberian tradition in sociology is deeply historical in nature, both with regard to the evolution and adaptation of social institutions and to the ideologies and other meanings held by the members of a society across time. Thanks to figures such as Robert Merton, the history of science and of some other traditions of intellectual history have become in part a sociological undertaking. Finally, new work in historical sociology, social history and community studies, and demographically based history§ shows an increasing convergence of the historical and the social sciences that may well be

---

*I refer here to work by Serge Moscovici and Ralf Dahrendorf, among others. Curiously enough, this imbalance is reversed in history, where it can be argued that the American form of social history has emphasized conflict and the special interests and experience of particular groups, more than the European form.

†A phrase used by Michael Hartoonian, in the broad sense of quantitative coverage of qualitatively salient topics and phenomena.

‡For instance, the results of the longitudinal General Social Survey, which has been conducted now on a national sample for over twenty years, are so reliable statistically that a change of one percentage point on a particular measure of attitudes or behaviors is taken by some investigators as prima facie evidence of a significant change on the national level. Beyond this, social indicators and demographic parameters are crucial in our modern society in the very definition of 'problems' to be examined in pedagogical or other terms. For example, the elderly poor become a social 'problem' when the elderly become numerous in the age structure. Teenage crime is more 'a problem' when the male adolescent cohort is large.

§I refer here to the work of Charles Tilly, Bernard Bailyn, Peter Laslett, and Natalie Zemon Davis, among many others.

the most important intellectual movement of the later twentieth-century in American (and British) scholarship.

Thus we should be careful not to close off areas of disciplinary sociology and anthropology to the schools prematurely. The fact that in each case the central theoretical enterprise of the fields—respectively, structural-functional analysis and ethnology—could not be easily accommodated in the American schools may have been an accident of timing, both for the schools and for the disciplines. There is much in these fields that is accessible today, regardless of the status of elective courses in the curriculum. Put bluntly, sociology and anthropology are a secondary, modern core of social study. Without their considerable presence in the schools we do not have a truly comprehensive curriculum.

10.0   Psychology

By and large, the importance of psychology is that it has studied educational process. Whether psychology has been studied *in* the educational process, at the precollegiate level, is open to question.

Although psychology courses in high school have been known since before 1900,* and have in recent years been probably the fastest-growing elective in terms of enrollments, it has at all times been difficult to know in what they consisted. The location of psychology within Social Studies is also ambiguous, with numerous problems of definition. Psychology is commonly considered by a school system as one of its social studies, but it is sometimes classified as a science course or a nonacademic course. (This means that statistics on course frequency and enrollments are to some extent unreliable. For example, some believe that Psychology was more apt to be located in the science department of schools in the 1960s, which alone would inflate its rate of growth as a social study subsequently.) No states require Psychology in the high school curriculum, but many states have legislative language that calls for 'psychological' topics to be covered somewhere: this could be in a Social Studies course in junior high school, or in a Health and Hygiene or General Biology unit.

The influence of psychologists on curriculum design and planning, pedagogical studies, testing and evaluation, guidance and vocational counseling—in other words, the entire educational psychology and psychometrics enterprise—has been noted by educational historians as being of unusual force in the United States and England. Clearly, the nature of public education in this country was affected by the doctrines of faculty psychology and mental discipline in the later 1800s; by the Herbartian notion of student learning, correlated across subject-matters, 'recapitulating' the history of cultural epochs; by the supposed disproof of 'mental discipline' effects by Thorndike and other learning theorists in the 1920s and 1930s; by Dewey's emphasis on experience-based learning; by G. Stanley Hall's formulation of adolescence as a special developmental stage; by Piaget and Jerome Bruner and the cognitive revolution; and today by those promulgating concepts of multifaceted rather than general intelligence.†

On the other hand, there has been obvious at all eras a negative reaction among educationalists to the influence of psychologists: for example, in the widespread dislike of, and refusal to adopt, strict behavioral or 'mechanistic'

---

*The 1893 NEA committee report gives a count of courses so named.
†I refer to the work of Howard Gardner and Robert Sternberg, among others.

249

principles from the learning research of Watson or Skinner, or a resistance to psychodynamic ideas. Furthermore, some outside the schools have very much disliked the emphasis on life adjustment and personal growth through education that is evident in the 1918 Cardinal Principles, which they may ascribe, probably unfairly, to the influence of psychologists.

Most teachers, in their education and preservice training, take some work in educational and developmental psychology, as part of their pedagogical preparation; this has been typical of the approach of the education school and education major, and has been reinforced by state certification requirements. Thus, virtually all elementary-level teachers have some background of this kind, but Psychology as a subject is absent from the curriculum before high school. Guidance counselors in high school are far more likely to have some background in psychology, required for certification, than those who actually teach Psychology. Most teachers of Psychology have a social studies background (history or government or general social studies, seldom sociology or economics or the elective majors). Yet psychology is the forgotten discipline in the pages of *Social Education*, and those who belong to the psychology special interest group in NCSS report that sessions on psychology at NCSS meetings are hard to arrange and not well attended.

Correspondingly, although the educational psychology, testing and assessment, and counseling divisions of the American Psychological Association are huge, there has been little sustained attention on the part of the Association to the place or nature of psychology in the precollegiate curriculum.* About 1970, rather late in the history of New Social Studies curriculum projects, some distinguished psychologists (together with behaviorally oriented sociologists and anthropologists) developed Human Behavior courses and materials, but the materials, though of good quality in terms of academic psychology, were not widely disseminated. According to Bare,[1] the project stopped when National Science Foundation funding lapsed.

Without putting undue interpretation on this, one may generally observe that the ambiguous status of psychology in the schools is probably an oblique result of the fact that as a research and university field psychology has enjoyed the lion's share of students and federal and corporate research support, within the social/behavioral sciences, from about 1950 to date (table 16-1). The prestige of the academic theoretical enterprise, which has generally been regarded as the most 'scientific' of the various fields, and the size of the field in terms of degrees

---

*There is currently a precollegiate committee and a newsletter for teachers in the schools—of which it is safe to say most Psychology teachers are unaware. There is also concern for standards of professional behavior, as regards counseling students, administering vocational tests, and the like. Otherwise the association involvement is minimal. One reason for this is that many applied psychologists who work in education-related fields are licensed by their states, which may preempt association involvement; this does not apply to school teachers, however, since they do not have separate legal-professional status. The association is concerned about the certification of poorly trained persons to teach psychology, and equally concerned about psychology teaching performed by those without any certification, but is currently able to do little more than deplore the situation.

awarded and jobs filled in both the research and the applied sectors have meant that the *teaching* of psychology at any educational level has had little attention (compared, for example, to research and preprofessional *training*). Relatedly, there has been a prevalent attitude in the research-dominated academic field that psychology was not a fit topic for young people. For example, in the 1930s— an era when learning theory and measurement theory were thought by many within and outside of the field to be attaining physics-like power—the introductory college course was customarily not open to freshmen, on the grounds that they lacked sufficient maturity to understand the material.[2] This attitude is not simply an intellectually snobbish one: the very extent and sequencing of the many courses in the many fields of psychology, stretching up from undergraduate to master's-level to doctoral-level and beyond, tends to suggest to some that the whole enterprise is a high-powered, technical one that should not be entered into until the university.

Nevertheless, the growth of the Psychology elective in the schools has been strong since the 1950s—even without a New Social Studies acceleration—and has continued to date. Just as sociology was the dominant mode of thinking, in the general American culture, about human and social life earlier in the century, so psychology was the 'new wave' of the midcentury. Freud, Skinner, Carl Rogers, and a few other figures in academic or lay psychology altered conventional wisdom, and this must have had some effects in the classroom. Psychology in the schools today has enrollments only a little less than those for Economics and Sociology (and Economics is often mandated).[*] Many high-school teachers believe that Psychology is the most popular elective: this may reflect the fact that during the last decade it has certainly been the fastest-growing elective, and that *in some districts* it may indeed be the most popular elective course.[†] It would not be a great surprise were the next National Center for Educational Statistics enrollment study (full-scale national studies are done only every decade or so) to show Psychology ahead of all subjects in high school except History and Government.

The reason for this popularity is student interest. In all kinds of institutions of higher education, students enroll in freshman introductory courses in psychology in great numbers. In high school today, many or most students at the grade level where Psychology is taught are working part-time and in other ways are emancipated from the degree of parental caution about the field that is said to have existed some years ago. (It was noted after World War II that psychology enrollments under the G.I. Bill zoomed, and that the prewar attitude that psychology was a somewhat dangerous subjectmatter had become obsolete.) All

---

[*]Figure 13-1. It should be noted that Sociology enrollments include a range of kinds of courses, and that the enrollment shown for Geography includes many students taking World Cultures and related courses.

[†]See Heed, section 2.2.1. The status of Psychology probably varies more across the country than is the case for other grade 10 to 12 subjects. In Kansas, for example, Psychology was 'ahead' of Economics or Sociology by 1975.[3]

recent careful studies[4] agree that high-school students seek to learn about matters of direct personal concern: emotions, social behavior, mental health and illness, love and marriage, drugs and alcohol, and related topics.

This is not *exactly* what they study. There seems to be a factor in the system that produces a balanced dimorphism of courses: a set of academic, survey-of-the-field courses (essentially like the college introductory course) and a set of courses built around personal adjustment. *Within* the latter set there is a balanced compromise between what the schools think such a course should be and what students might ideally like.

With regard to the first distinction, we have noted elsewhere (section 2.4) that the course title Social Psychology serves in some high schools to indicate the presence of an academically oriented course (that is, not a life-adjustment or personal-interests course). Such a course will limit itself to social and personality psychology, motivation, human (but not very much animal) learning, child development, abnormal behavior (but not psychopathology in all its aspects): in other words, 'general psychology' without an experimental or physiological or mathematical emphasis, and without undue attention to deviance or therapy or other possibly touchy areas. By contrast, in some schools, the Psychology course does survey the major 'scientific' aspects of psychology—including most of the research fields omitted from a Social Psychology rubric. In such courses, there is then a tendency to downplay social psychology, personality measurement, abnormal psychology, and related topics, and all 'problems of living' material, in favor of a university-like first course. Thus, the 'academic' elective comes in two forms, the latter being more research-oriented.

In personal adjustment courses, which appear to be more common than the academic courses in the nation as a whole, the rationale is two-for-the-price-of-one. Thus, from the syllabus of a large and affluent high school: "Special instructional emphasis will be placed on understanding personal adjustment *as opposed to* the science of psychology as a discipline. [But] topic areas will *include* personality development, human growth and development, motivation and learning, mental health and mental illness, and social behavior" (emphasis added). We note also that the 1977 publishers' 'futures' study[5] listed *both* Psychology and Personal Adjustment together, near the top of the list just below Consumer Economics, Private Enterprise, and Principles of Economics. In section 7.0 we discussed how the system (or different mandates across states) tends to separate out incompatible economics elements into separate courses or grade levels. With regard to Psychology, where a mandate basis for differentiation does not exist, we suggest that there has emerged a kind of stable compromise: it will be shaded in one direction or another, but in essence it will be a shapely compromise, with something for everyone. The economics of publishing, in a school field structured in this way, make it likely that texts will become larger and more inclusive, rather than distinctly of one variety or another. It is also observed by those in the field that Psychology courses use, in addition to a text, many other materials, such as *Scientific American* reprints. And it is, of course, common for teachers of an elective in a broad field with many established subdisciplines to use a comprehensive textbook—but only selected chapters.

Evidence for such a grand compromise comes from Stahl and Matiya, who report the fascinating finding (supported by other studies) that teachers with psychology backgrounds, teachers with social studies backgrounds, and teachers trained in guidance *all teach pretty much the same course.* Teachers whose own courses have been in humanistic psychology and those whose training, if any, has been in 'scientific' psychology *teach much the same way.* There is, in other words, a disseminated conventional wisdom about what a high school Psychology course should be. For example, while students do not rate personality theory at the top of their list of interests, that topic is commonly taught by any teacher. Conversely, students rank love, marriage, and the family high in interest—but these receive little instructional attention. Such a situation must be based on education lore and on widespread agreement about what students need and can master (in concert with some tacit consensus on what 'the field' is about).

Such a central tendency has also been seen in Sociology, where a compromise between a broad survey of the field and attention to social problems obtains. *It seems to be typical of high school electives*, when mandates do not act against the process.* If this is true, it suggests again the inapplicability of the Wesley dictum, that the social studies are the social sciences simplified for pedagogical purposes. It also suggests that the assumption by professional groups outside the schools, that instructional improvement and higher test scores will perforce occur if teachers all have subject majors or are 'certified' in the school field, is untenable without other factors being taken into account. The 'conventional wisdom' may indeed be wisdom. School subjects, perhaps some more than others, cannot simply be cut to the pattern of the discipline. In the case of relatively popular electives like Psychology or Sociology, teachers may quite actively 'market' their courses to maintain demand. The reputation of the individual teacher is of critical importance to the longterm success of the courses in the curriculum.

In the particular case of Psychology, it is not even clear what content pattern would be the exemplar, since it is an extremely complex field with many separate research traditions. In recent years, many psychological researchers have left the APA, taking up membership in other more specialized or more exclusively research-oriented organizations. On the other hand, there are large subfields of psychology that represent combined aspects of research and practice (educational, clinical, and occupational psychology being examples). Whose 'field' would the schools follow? Beyond this practical question, it is obvious that school courses have to reflect the several goals of public education, which include both intellectual and personal adjustment ends and an orientation to

---

*Or where (like geography) the subjectmatter is not also present in the curriculum in other forms at other levels, so that a high-school course would consist in what was not covered elsewhere.

adult life beyond the requirements of further education.* For example, neither social psychology nor personality psychology is today a flourishing research field in psychology, in the sense of possessing powerful new theories or receiving substantial grant funds. Yet it would be unlikely for the school to remove them from the syllabus for this reason. Conversely, neuropsychology is a flourishing field, but it would be nearly impossible for the schools to teach it.

Within the mainstream of strictly psychological research—that is, not shading over into biology or biophysics—the dominant attention today is to cognition, with particular attention to the structure of thought in particular 'domains,' themselves highly structured objects or ecologies of thought. One might think that this had particular relevance for classroom instruction, in the sense of being subjectmatter for student learning. However, for various good reasons, school subjects have always resisted being carried too far toward a principle of recursive subjectmatter. That is, while it is by no means impossible to teach children about child development, or students about studying, or citizens about citizenry, this can only be carried so far. Finally, considering schooling as a complex social institution, it is understandable why Psychology must (in the conventional view) take up topics of special interest to students—without going so far as to take special responsibility for students' needs and personal problems.

At a very fundamental level, society has been ambivalent about psychology as a field and about the extent to which human nature and human behavior should be studied. Almost everyone agrees that it should, but many dislike and reject some of the results of that study.† The schools *may* have reached a viable entente. For the social studies in general, Psychology in the school curriculum may be such a synthetic subject that it will continue to receive very little attention from social studies and curriculum professionals. For example, Psychology is the one subject in this branch of the curriculum that appears to have little to say about citizenship, in its sociocivic aspect. Is it not possible, however, that what Psychology teaches about intergroup relations and social cognition (that is, the understanding of others by both objective and empathic means) is highly relevant to the larger goals of civic understanding? With this field in the schools, we have above all others a case where what is taught, and with what slant or tone, has little counterpart outside the school. This may be the school subject of which it is most accurate to say that what is taught in the classroom is what is contained in the textbook. Unless Psychology becomes more closely related to the social studies, this is unlikely to change.

---

*Both William James and John Dewey, two of America's greatest thinkers and both psychologists (among other things), believed that schools must enlarge and shape the spirit (as in character development) as well as the mind.

†For example, that 'personality' may be a useless concept; or that much of social behavior may be biologically based.

11.0   Historical Study

11.1   At the Focus: American History

Previous chapters of this volume* have established in some detail that at every stage of the development of the social studies the field of history has been at the center, and has always enjoyed the status of *primus—inter alia*, not *inter pares*. As Robinson and Kirman[1] indicate in their chapter title, History in the schools moved, over the decades, from monopoly to dominance. The claim or suggestion that at some point history was displaced by 'social studies' is true only in this limited sense. Moreover, as we have seen (sections 4.2–4.6), not only did the discipline of history take the lead, in the early decades, in designing a modern curriculum for the public schools, but the terms of readjustment in the relative positions of history and the 'allied subjects' were also worked out primarily by historians. These adjustments over time had a layering effect in the curriculum, where, for example, the 1899 solution persisted in most schools long after the 1916 committee put forth its new plan and after some schools began to adopt it.†

As one authority puts it:[2] "From its beginning, the [American Historical] Association took an active interest in shaping the curriculum in . . . schools as

*See also section 13.0.

†Even today, traditional independent high schools of a certain size and age tend to offer the quatrain history sequence: Ancient, Medieval, Modern European, English, as well as American and now World History.

well as in colleges. . . . The historians involved in these activities were among the most able and prominent in their profession. Such was not the case with other social science professional associations formed during the 1880s and in the following decades. . . . By the time the 1915 and 1916 reports were issued, history was firmly established as the major component of the elementary and secondary curriculum."

The fact that history has enjoyed enormous prestige in the curriculum, and deserves great credit for modernizing that curriculum (and school History within it), does not mean, to be sure, that it has had an unlimited authority or that the curriculum pattern followed exactly what the historians set in motion. There was, all agree, a strong 'sociological' current in the society at the time of the 1916 recommendations, a faith in the rational solution of societal problems by the social sciences acting together, a focus on not only the present but the future— which was to be planned, to some extent, without undue reference to (though without a rejection of) history. Some of the 'new historians' of the age, notably James Harvey Robinson and Charles Beard, shared this view of an expanding and self-revising society, with the professional and scholarly fields cooperating. It is true that, as schools proved slow to change their curricula, some people such as Harold Rugg saw history as a dead hand, a retardant force. The distinguished political scientist Charles Merriam, in his book for the 1934 AHA Commission,[3] wrote: "The tendency of history to serve as a medium of class or other form of propaganda, then, and the difficulty in employing history as a preparation for the great adventure of reorganization,* makes its position as the center of the new orientation exceedingly questionable in anything like its present form." Note, however, that Merriam acknowledged that history *was* the center; he was more hostile to the *kind* of history than to history itself.

Nevertheless, there was a degree of antihistory sentiment among the other fields in the 1920s and 1930s. But, as Morrissett says, other disciplines never devoted the talent or the energy to effecting change in the schools that historians did. Thus, when after 1934 or so the historians withdrew from that role, then-present practice tended to perseverate. The changes that ensued, in the period up to the 1950s, owed more to the influence of the newly 'professionalized' nondisciplinary educationalists than to efforts by other disciplines. In addition, as the high school elective courses, made to disciplinary lasts, began to take shape and become accepted, any conflict over history's dominance became mitigated: History could reign in the *required* portion of the curriculum, without governing the entire pattern.

The dominance of history at times made it an easy target for various reformers who did not understand that curriculum change is a slow and complexly negotiated matter, or who did not know that history itself was undergoing major changes, in incorporating the protosocial history of the (first) New History. There is also the difficult question of style or tone. Kliebard is correct[4] in

*I.e., of society.

pointing out: "Even when the name of a subject like history remained intact, the subject itself frequently took on a new character in line with the demands of the citizenship aim as the Cardinal Principles report had recommended." Keels[5] takes a longer-term, more institutional view.

> [Historians] were seen as the appropriate advisors for all of the social studies. But this changed, and paradoxically, it was in their most profound influence that the roots of this change were embedded. The insistence of the historians that the social studies should be taught by specialists was the beginning of a strict subject as discipline orientation in secondary social studies. . . . As the social sciences were increasingly breaking down into specialized fields, historians came to be seen less and less as speaking for all of the social sciences. They came to be seen as subject area advisors for only history. . . . In fact, historians themselves began to reject the idea that history was a social *science*.*

Thus, historians ushered in change to the school curriculum in the early decades, but did not, after the 1930s, stay for the end of the party—which they would have found disorderly. But they were never driven away from it, as Gifford,[8] for one, wrongly asserts. In the 1960s and 1970s, for example, as historian Hazel Hertzberg in the Gifford volume (and elsewhere) makes clear,[9] "Civics and Problems of Democracy, not History, were the chief social studies casualties." Much evidence accumulated in the present volume indicates that changes in the shape of the History curve in figure 13-1 should be viewed as follows. All other subjects *added together* have never equaled History in enrollments; except perhaps today, as the result of growth in mandated courses and a few elective subjects. The decline in the 1930s was the result primarily of the growth of POD courses, which probably reached their height about 1940. The relative flatness of the curve in the 1940–60 period reflects the growth of Government and Geography in the curriculum, counterbalanced by the waning of POD. In the 1960s, as Hertzberg says, Government and Geography seemed to lose out as the New Social Studies took some effect and as 'relevance' became the marching order. The resurgence of Political Science, together with the marked growth of Economics, Sociology, and Psychology (over a somewhat longer period), have probably cost History some enrollments it might otherwise have had in the 1970s and into the 1980s.

The continued pride of place for History in the secondary school, especially

*Emphasis added. The notion of scholarship in history as impartial but not objective—nonscientific—is discussed by Van Tassel.[6] The trend toward viewing history, within the profession, as deeply humanistic, as not possessing a 'logic' like that of the social sciences, is evident in the AHA commission report (the Wesley report) of 1944[7] (without any lessening of support *for* social studies in the schools), in the Bestor critique of 1955, and in some of the criticisms of the New Social Studies era. Keels says that, generally speaking in the early decades of the century, "Historians were more concerned with showing that history was *not* philosophy than that it *was* social science" (emphasis in original).

recently when subject majors for teachers have become more and more the norm (even master's degrees; table 4-3) is even more remarkable given the steep drop in university 'output' in history, which began shortly after 1970 (table 16-1). Hertzberg[10] shows that the proportion of history bachelor's degrees *relative to the social sciences* (excluding the field of history) dropped rapidly beginning about 1968. With reference to table 16-1, the other fields could not have shown growth in the school curriculum without an increase in trained teachers. However, History could continue to lead, even with a declining number of potential teachers in the same period.

History B.A.'s have been dropping relative to *all* bachelor's degrees since 1970 or so. The overall pattern since the early 1970s and continuing into the early 1980s is that all the social sciences (with the distinct exception of economics) and most of the humanities have declined in university course enrollments, majors, and degrees. History's declines have been the most severe of all the principal humanities fields;[11] relative to the social sciences also, history's decline has been among the most marked. There is some evidence beginning about 1986 that most of these fields, including history, are showing an upward reversal, as yet modest. While such declines in the size of fields would not be directly felt in the schools,* any proposal sharply to *increase* cadres of school teachers in these hard-hit fields meets an immediate challenge as to feasibility.†

11.1.1   HISTORY IN THE EARLY GRADES

If there is no evidence that History has suffered, in terms of its general status in the curriculum, from grades 4 or 5 upward, there is a much more confusing situation in the early grades. Tryon analyzes how the trend toward 'fusion' of subjectmatter in the *upper* primary grades, in the 1920s and 1930s, or in the then-new junior high schools, did not wipe out the dominance of History.[12] The picture changed back and forth over the decades, as follows.

Up to about 1890, American history was rare in the primary grades (that is, the 'grade school'), and very rare in the early primary ones. 'The national story' was told in a number of celebratory ways, such as school observances and holidays, and specifically within 'general history' (that is, of the Western World).‡ Between about 1895 and 1910, thanks to the history-led revisions of the curriculum and to the rapid expansion and improvement of the schools, Ameri-

---

*Highly trained teachers tend, after a few years, to stay in the school system. Moreover, junior high and high school enrollments have been dropping (figure 4-1), so that a high level of replacement of teachers has not been needed (i.e., some attrition could be allowed).

†As those who recommend a sharp increase in science and foreign language courses in the schools have to meet obvious challenges in this regard, so, too, do those who wish to see new historic levels of enrollments in, for example, World History.

‡Cartwright[13] quotes school officials in this period as protesting that "pupils in the lower grades, *where history has never been taught*, are eagerly seeking to know something of their country's history."

can History became normally present in the primary grades. What most adults today would regard as serious study began about grade 4, but units of instruction in earlier grades were also common. Tryon says (p. 196) that content can be known "with considerable exactness"—as follows:

Grade 1: Indian and pioneer life; stories, biographies connected with U.S. history

Grade 2: Material from some phase of American history; material relating to Old World history; fairy tales, myths, legends

Grade 3: Stories of great Americans; Hebrew life and heroes

Grade 4: Roman History

Grade 5: United States History (often oral and focused on biography)

Grade 6: U.S. History "with text in hands of pupils"; English History

Tryon concludes (p. 201): "During the second decade of the present century history in the elementary grades was under the almost complete domination of the report of the Committee of Eight of the American Historical Association, published in 1909." As of about 1927, Tryon (p. 215) found the sharp break to be between grade 3 and grade 4, in terms of minutes of instruction, number of schools offering history, and the like. The average number of minutes of history instruction in grade 1 was 17 per week; in grade 6, 97.*

According to Tryon (pp. 435ff and 451ff), in the upper-elementary grades, including the first cycle of U.S. History at grades 4 and 5, up to about 1910, textbooks used a strict chronological order: material prior to 1789 was ordered separately for each of the colonies; that covering the Revolutionary War, by year; and that after 1789, by presidential administration. From about 1920 on, Tryon reports that the biographical method become the common pattern in grades 4 and 5. Since he does not say otherwise, we may assume that grades 1 to 3 remained more or less as outlined above. Beginning in the 1930s the 'expanding environments' approach to the primary grades became common; in the 1940s, the rule. This incorporated state history (often) at grade 4, U.S. History at grade 5 (as the rule), and World Cultures (incorporating much history) at grade 7 (almost as much the rule)—fitting the rest of the 'expanding' subject matter into and around those fixed points.

Despite this, the expanding environments approach has been viewed by many as nonhistorical in nature. Ravitch has recently made the emphatic claim that the earliest years of the public school curriculum have been the most disastrous in terms of a moving away from rich historical instruction.[14] If the expanding environments scheme is taken *by definition* to be nonhistorical,† then there is

---

*In 1978, NSF studies (section 2.1) found that the average number of minutes per week for *social studies* generally was, for K–3, about 100; for 4–6, about 180. Especially in the early grades, where history has always been the main fare (together with geography related to history), it is very hard to see a 'golden age' of history instruction in the data from that period.

†Assuming that *chronological* is taken as defining history; in fact, historians and others did not so take it during the period in question—see the discussion of presentism, below.

little doubt that more instructional time carried the label 'History' prior to the mid- to late-1930s than later. However, the number of minutes of instruction in grades 1 to 3 is very small (then and now) and the quality of the instructional content open to serious question (then and now) as regards subjectmatter exposition generally, in contrast to teaching of basic skills. This very doubt as to the presence of much of any content is what prompted the AHA Committee of Eight (1909) to recommend more, and more serious, history beginning about grade 4. As with the Committee of Seven (1899) on the secondary level, the AHA group said, less Roman, less Hebrew, less legend—and more American history, please. That recommendation was largely followed in the schools. The fact that these historians did not, in 1909, call for a reconstruction of a grades 1–3 pattern cannot be taken to mean that pattern was seen as ideal—or even acceptable. The widespread belief, among historians and others today, that children in the early primary grades could benefit from more exposure to history may be perfectly correct. It does not mean that some cultural cataclysm occurred some decades ago in the school curriculum.

In every era, at each level of schooling, it has been the *how* of history instruction, not the *how much* (with the possible exception, as we have seen, of grades 1–3), that has been the main point of issue, within the history teaching profession (and the field of historiography) and among critics and admirers of history from outside the field. We organize much of the rest of this chapter around discussion of these controversies, in a rough progression from least disputed to most contentious.*

11.1.2   GOING BEYOND THE FACTS

What has been almost beyond debate, in the field of history and in the schools, is the idea that History should be more than the learning of 'mere' facts—names, dates, and events. The past is infinitely large, and infinitely factual. History is not simply an arrangement of 'entries' in some vast encyclopedia of the past, but a selection, an interpretation, and an explanation of some of them. The idea that 'data' are always preliminary to, and broader than, orderly investigation is true of all scholarly disciplines. Rote memorization of enormous arrays of facts is not in itself admired in any field. The controversy enters in two respects. First, *some* facts have to be mastered, both to provide a common frame of meaning for communication among those in the field, between them and those to whom they wish to communicate, and among nonspecialists (to the extent that they under-

---

*In the following treatment of the history of the academic field, we draw throughout especially on Robinson and Kirman, "From Monopoly to Dominance"; Kammen, *The Past Before Us*; Van Tassel, "Trials of Clio"; and Downey.[15] The discussion centers primarily on instruction in national history, which means primarily American history. Only the best and biggest high schools teach English, French, Russian, and other national history. Questions having to do with world history and American history in that context are taken up in section 12.0.

stand or can draw upon that field), and to undergird generalizations, inferences, and explanation.* There is the sense, further, *in the historical sciences generally*, that a richer factual and denotative base may be needed than in other fields, simply because these deal with particularities and nonrepeating events; the data are unique instances that will not come around again. Thus, in relatively nongeneralizing and nonpredictive sciences, and in systematizing fields, lots of facts are expected: natural history or systematic biology, for example, or archaeology or geology where 'the record' must always be consulted and can never be too rich.[16]

Second, some of those who condemn recent education for failures to provide knowledge-in-common make it clear that they are arguing from what they consider unacceptable performance on factual tests, and are willing to provide lists of such facts, in history and geography, for example, that should be known to all. The most well-known of such critics recently has been E. D. Hirsch, Jr., who has had the courage to develop his own lists.[†] The layperson's expression of a similar demand for considerable factual knowledge is captured in a remark by the American political writer Theodore H. White: "dates nail down history." He intended this as self-evident, a cultural given. Others would take it as a historian's unwitting self-indictment: is "pinning down" history like pinning down butterflies—which preserves but kills them?[‡]

All of this seems so obvious—knowing some facts is necessary; knowing a plethora, a trivial pursuit—that it is puzzling that so many looking at the schools for so long have fulminated against 'mere fact-learning.' The historian authors of the 1893 Committee of Ten report said:[18] "The result which is popularly supposed to be gained from history, and which most teachers aim to reach, is the

---

*The sufficiency of 'facts' varies, intuitively speaking, in these two respects. For the sake of communication and the frame of reference, chronological or descriptive history can always accommodate more facts. It is never obvious what detail or instance will make the picture come into best perspective. For the construction of generalizations and logical inferences, enough is enough. A generalization with too many instances becomes a catalog, and thus not a generalization. A logical argument needs only some crucial examples, especially some negative evidence, to prove or disprove (in the scientific sense of 'prove'). Thus when Brinton argued that 'revolution' is not a coherent unitary concept, he needed only show that several revolutions did not fit a single model.

†It takes courage, since the lists of others, with similar motivations, in the past—for example, the superintendent of schools in Winnetka, Illinois, in the 1920s—inevitably seem quaint today. See section 5.6.

‡On 'coverage' as stultifying, see Thornton.[17] In this study, 'Mr. Carson' at 'Taylor High' believed in the inquiry approach, but found that parents and students complained that he went too slowly through the material and did not 'cover' enough in his course. On the other hand, the conviction on the part of some educators that students dislike memorizing facts should be looked at with some skepticism. Young children enjoy memorizing the names of state capitals or rulers' dates, and parents are pleased to take this as evidence of learning. Older students appear to learn the names and batting averages of baseball players with enjoyment; still older students seem to benefit from learning the opus numbers and key signatures of a huge number of musical compositions. What psychologists call incidental learning typically involves factual bits of information that sometimes have seemingly permanent significance for the individual. They are 'incidental' only to the observer. People like to memorize things they like to memorize. They may not like to do so when required by a teacher or a test.

acquirement of a body of useful facts. In our judgment this is in itself the most difficult and the least important outcome of historical study" (p. 168). They warned against recitation by students: "It is better to omit history altogether than to teach it . . . by setting pupils painfully to reproduce the words of a text-book. . . . The first duty of the teacher is to emphasize the essential points . . . to show, if possible, what is the main thing worth remembering." The teacher should point out what should be ignored, and open-book work is recommended, with the teacher "constantly framing questions which will require for an answer a knowledge of the necessary facts"—together with the habit of looking up others. The teacher should make the material interesting by "frequent cross-references" to other history and to literature: "Here is the place where the teacher's superior knowledge and training tells"—in "stirring up the minds of the pupils" (pp. 189–90).

The historians of the 1899 Committee of Seven[19] remarked that "matter has been placed in the books because it has been the fashion of previous history to put such and such topics in. . . . So our textbook makers have supposed that only dead history is good history and the deader the history the better. . . . Some books seemed to think that this present end of our national history was hardly worth mentioning." Textbooks are "mere jumbles of things."

The historians of the 1934 AHA Commission, writing nearly twenty years after the 1916 revision—which was intended, among other things, to make history come alive by not neglecting "this present end of our national history"— still felt it necessary to concentrate on this very point,[20] albeit in a more constructive tone. "If by knowing history one means the ability to recall dates, names, and specific events. . . . Americans in general do not know this kind of history.*. . . If the objective of history is to develop understanding and insight, the emphasis will have to be placed upon wide and critical reading, upon the interpretation of data, upon the synthesizing of diverse accounts, and upon the understanding of relationships. *These too can be taught.* . . . A test which measures these outcomes is a good instrument, even though the specific contributing factors have been forgotten" (emphasis added).

That students can be *taught* to go beyond the facts was a cardinal value of the New Social Studies. A possibly extreme view was that of the historian Edwin Fenton, a key figure in the whole NSS movement.[21] "A student who learns facts and generalizations about the past without becoming involved in the process of inquiry—and most students in American schools do exactly this—does not study history." The view is extreme relative, for example, to that of historian Arthur Bestor, whose 1953 denunciation of the schools rested in part on their failure, owing to progressive education, to teach facts that stuck with the students.†

---

*Wesley refers here to young adults; see section 14.1.

†On inquiry as the heart of history, see Robinson and Kirman, "From Monopoly to Dominance," p. 20, on Collingwood's and others' views. Thornton, "Curriculum Consonance," pp. 314–16, shows how in a strongly 'academic' high school the *students* seem to resist the teacher's attempts to promote inquiry. Also see section 17.3.

The viewing-with-alarm is typical of all eras. Gagnon, recommending a more richly contextualized American History,[22] warns that "relentless mentioning without pointing up central questions of drama and significance is confusing and soporific. . . . Larger contexts are missing, as are the ideas, the contrasts, and the comparisons that might awaken students." And the Bradley Commission,[23] recommending more history in the precollegiate curriculum, comments that "such study must reach well beyond the acquisition of useful information."

Given such a unanimity of goals, why is it that condemnation of the results is always with us? Note that two, rather different, general avenues are suggested for 'going beyond the facts.' One is that the *student* be guided or encouraged toward a higher level of intellective process than the noting and mastering of facts. This is the view of the New Social Studies, and indeed of all those who are concerned with higher-order thinking and the critical or reflective habit of mind.* For Engle and Ochoa[25] an 'event' in history has to have a structure, a context, a significance to stand out from the myriad of other candidates, and it is the students who have to *construct* this salience. To do so they have to understand how dimensions or relationships may interact in forming an 'event'; the part played by scientific evidence in relation to culturally assigned value; and how an event can be defined by its contemporaneous properties or by its consequences. They have to know something, in other words, about the 'problem of knowledge.' Whether or not one emphasizes the understanding *of* historical method and significance—weighing of evidence, the cycles of consensus and revision, and so forth—or whether one emphasizes the analysis of factors *in* historical action, the main problem with pursuing such goals has always been that teachers find them time-consuming, difficult to implement in the classroom structure, and hard to reward externally.[26]

The other general avenue for going beyond the facts, implicit in some of the quotations above and in much comment on teaching, is that the *teacher* should go beyond the facts, and do so in a way that students cannot miss observing. That is to say, the teacher should display, and model, skepticism toward received wisdom, an attitude of picking and choosing from the text what is important, a questioning bent, and an appreciation of how others—historically or culturally 'other'—would see things differently. This kind of demonstrated venturesomeness, a kind of dramatistic attribute in teaching, is often seen among 'good' teachers.[†] Although it may not produce a lot of in-class 'higher-order' activity

---

*For example, Laville and Rosenzweig hold that "If history education were to achieve no more than the stimulation of students' questioning abilities, it would be accomplishing a great deal." Note that questioning (in an intellectually responsible way) was not on balance a strength of the New Social Studies, which was aimed more at analysis and logical mapping. The idea, in the NSS terms of reference, that history 'lacked structure,' meant that the reflective and questioning aspects of higher-order thinking were overlooked.[24]

†Note that as 'teacher behavior' it gets coded, in observational studies, in the same category as many undesirable behaviors, such as reading the text aloud, droning on, and so on. This is one example of how the *origin* of activity in the classroom is not a sufficient description of the entire pattern or tone; see section 18.3.4.

among students, it can profoundly affect the way they question and comment in class and the way they read and reflect. Anecdotal evidence suggests that adults remember the teacher's own attitude towards her material, her own relationship to her subject, long after they have forgotten most of the facts she imparts.*

Thus there are at least two often recommended ways for making history something more than a "mere jumble of facts." Each approach, however, runs against the reality that the textbook, which is (necessarily) fact-based, does have to be 'covered.' More important, tests call for factual or discrete, formal responses. Even supposedly enlightened tests, for example those that call for fill-in answers rather than checking off the right answer, may still demand a modern form of written recitation: the student must provide quickly recognizable phrases, as tokens of knowledge. The problem that tests do not easily tap deeper forms of knowledge is confronted by the recent California framework, which means to provide deep historical study at nearly every grade level. Thus the California Assessment Program Staff[27] comment: "Perhaps our greatest challenge is designing an assessment to match the bold new History-Social Science Framework. To support this curriculum, teachers will be encouraged to use a full range of technology and oral, written, and performance measures, including mock trials, debates, simulations, and field trips."

As difficult as it is for teachers and school-based curriculum experts to develop such measures for internal testing and evaluation, it is harder to design and implement such measures for external achievement or diagnostic testing across districts or states or the nation. As long as such measures perform summative or gate-keeping functions, as perhaps they must, the temptation to spend most class time teaching to these tests will remain. An implication in the California staff's statement is that to enable schools to provide richer and more thoughtful history instruction over the long haul, *teachers*—working with the designers of national objective tests—must generate more suitable measures of students' understanding. It will be important for those who educate prospective teachers, and hire them, to help them do so.

In short, the oversimple (but correct) answer to the question of why poor practices persist is that to some degree their results—easily measured factual knowledge—are valued. Teachers know this. They are sympathetic to students who ask, in one way or another, Will this be on the test? Things have not changed much since the Lynds' Middletown study,[28] where a high school history teacher explained:

> In class discussion I try to bring out minor points, two ways of looking at a
> thing and all that, but in examinations I try to emphasize important
> principles and group the main facts that they have to remember around

---

*The potency of this 'dramatistic,' ostensive dimension in teaching is conveyed nicely in Wineburg and Wilson, "Models of Wisdom," 55–58 especially. The epistemological theory seems to involve a form of mimesis; the student, by empathetically assuming an appetitive but critical stance toward a subject, as modeled from the teacher, begins to learn as the teacher learns.

them. I always ask simple fact questions in examinations. They get all
mixed up and confused if we ask questions where they have to think, and
write all over the place.

11.1.3   DEPTH AND REPETITION

If boring facts produce bored students,[29] the repetition of material is especially
deadening to some. This is a particular problem for American History, which is
customarily taught in three year-long cycles, at grades 5, 8, and 11. This pattern
in part reflects the concern by some educators that 'the past' accumulates
rapidly, so that to teach about it requires more and more instructional time.
Since this specific logic is not evident in the university—where specialized
courses come into the curriculum, not more and more survey courses—the
concern seems to be that every graduating school student should have been
'exposed' to all American (and now, in principle, world) history. Most practitioners have come to recognize the impossibility of this enterprise, but laypersons
may not.

A more fundamental reason for the three cycles is the assumption that
important material must be gone over more than once to be understood and
retained; it is also generally assumed that students have quite different cognitive
abilities at different ages, so that different *aspects* of history are attended to at
different times. The cycle or spiral approach—moving over the same terrain,
deeper and deeper each time—has a foundation in European pedagogy of the
nineteenth-century. Problems in this approach were apparent early. Charles
and Mary Beard in 1921[30] remarked: "To put it bluntly we do not assume that our
children obtain permanent possessions from their study of history in the lower
grades. If mathematicians followed the same method, high school texts on
algebra and geometry would include the multiplication table and fractions."

Of course, history is not mathematics, with a neat sequence of elements. A
problem has been whether to divide the material into historical periods, and if
so how to allocate it, or to emphasize a particular kind of material in each
sweep—for example, political history first, then social history, then perhaps
'thinking historically' about specific themes or problems bearing on the present
or near-future. (Some other choices are discussed in what follows.) All schemes
have their problems. Covering the precolonial, colonial, and constitutional
periods at grade 5, for example, seems to put the most remote and in some ways
most difficult subjectmatter (for example, that dealing with political philosophy)
at the youngest age. In an earlier day it also meant that students who left school
after grade 6 or 8 only 'had' history up to a certain date. Nevertheless, the 1909
Committee of Eight[31] proposed "*One distinct* portion of the country's history to
be presented *fully* and *finally*," avoiding "recurrence in successive years of
subject matter that has once been outlined. . . . It has been an error to strive for
a hurried survey of the whole field; we have repeated and enlarged the picture

in successive years, but the charm of surprise and novelty has been lost if pupils have failed to appreciate the value of further elaboration. . . ."*

The 1944 AHA Commission saw the problem as far more complex. As usual Wesley put it forthrightly:[32]

> The truth, which is even more difficult for the brilliant than the mediocre to comprehend, is that at any one level much may be taught, less will be learned, and a great deal will be subsequently forgotten. Educational realism demands that any subject be taught and taught again until the cumulative effect becomes significant and enduring [p. 12]. . . . [However,] the blunt truth of the situation is that courses in American history are often outright duplications of one another. This repetition is particularly obvious at the senior high school level. . . . It lessens or destroys the interest of most pupils. . . . It promotes superficial and shallow results, for the pupils . . . unwarrantedly assume that they already know and understand the materials. . . . [It] may also *interfere seriously with retention* [pp. 68–69]. . . . Repetitive courses are likely to be catalogic and unvaried in content and emphasis. . . . The selection of fewer topics would enable both writers and teachers to give them enough attention to develop their significance. The treatment can thus be graduated from simple narrative, through descriptive accounts, and on into interpretation and synthesis [p. 69]. (emphasis added)

Trying to combine considerations of content, tone or approach, and developmental learning, the 1934 commission recommended a *topical-chronological* method. As to tone or style, the progression was narrative, descriptive, expository/interpretive, critical/reflective/historiographic. The allocation of content to historical periods was, for the middle grades, primarily How the People Lived, with a concentration on the period up to about 1776 (but not with a terminus there of such concerns); for the junior high school, primarily The Building of the Nation, starting about 1650 and tailing off to some extent after 1900; for the senior high school, A Democratic Nation in a World Setting, reviewing the 'civic career' of democracy evenly from precolonial times to about 1865, with greater attention then to recent history and America in the world. Distinctly different pedagogical approaches are suggested across grade levels: in the early grades the teacher is the primary source of 'narrative'; later, texts and teachers together are the origin for description, exposition, and interpretation; eventually, students themselves must primarily do the critical and reflective work, concerning themselves, among other things, with the adequacy of narration and description and interpretation in history.

---

*In fact, even today, negative comments from students tend to emphasize that they are bored by 'the same old stuff,' which they assume they 'know.' International comparisons recently have seemed to show that American students were quite confident that they 'knew' American history when test scores did not bear them out. This could be because they recognized material that they had never mastered.

Joseph Strayer, in the history chapter of the 1962 ACLS-NCSS volume,[33] substantially agreed with the 1943 position, but located the reasons more within the nature of the material than in consideration of learning capacities or student interests. The colonial and the early national periods (to 1861) were suitable for grades 5 and 8; industrialization and the emergence of the United States as a world power should be left to grade 11. Precolonial and early colonial history was likely to benefit from much geography and a kind of historical anthropology (the origins and ways of life of settler groups and groups in conflict, early sectionalism, and so on); the approach to the Revolutionary War should be taught as "combined politico-economic topic"; politics was the focus of the early national period; the Civil War should be taught, not as the "great legend of our history" but as "one of the clearest examples of the impact that a war can have on the structure of a society" (p. 30); the closing decades of the century would be most easily integrated by a focus on the history of technology, together with the study of reactions to technological change (agrarianism, the labor movement, and the like). This period might involve "large blocks of material from the fields of economics and sociology" (p. 31). The twentieth-century needed special attention to foreign policy, recent European history, and international affairs. It is hard for a nonspecialist to know whether such schemes, which correlate topics with periods with developmental cognitive capacity, represent professional lore or the assumption of some design fixed in nature.

There is a third main model for how to handle the three cycles. It involves the idea of cutting into an essentially chronological treatment with special exposure to, and analysis of, general topics or recurrent themes that have particular salience to students of different ages, or that arise at particular points in national history. Most texts do this, with exhibits and appendices and special boxed material; most teachers do it, not only to catch and retain students' attention, but to share, as the 1893 recommenders foresaw, their own interests and specially developed knowledge with their students. Or it may simply be for the sake of feasibility. Much of the material that falls within the category of basic civic knowledge is handled this way. For example, it is difficult to teach about the enlarging of the electorate or the shifting balance of rights and obligations surrounding civil disobedience or press freedom in any other way. One introduces the topic at an appropriate chronological point, but then carries it forward as a sustained topic, often extending to the present. How and when this is done is closely tied to considerations about chronological organization, presentism, or 'postholed' history, discussed below.

In practice, most schools and texts adopt a modified chronological-forward scheme, with the *center* of the frame of attention on the precolonial, colonial, and early national period in grade 5, the nineteenth-century up to about Reconstruction in grade 8, and the modern period in grade 11. There is much review at the beginning of each cycle, especially in the middle cycle. There is much prefiguring and recapitulation in any design, at least in the syllabus if not as taught. Inevitably, the grade 8 (or thereabouts) presentation is the most difficult to contain within such a scheme, since an inadequate mastery of earlier periods must be compensated for, in order to move on successfully, and present-day or recent events can hardly be avoided.* Thus, many junior-high-school courses do indeed cover virtually the entire sweep, in order and more or less evenhandedly. Not surprisingly, great pressure is felt. The description of an excellent California junior high American History course says: "Some of our history teachers have majors in American history. Evidence has shown that they have difficulty deleting historical data . . . since they consider everything important . . . in order to meet the time span requirements of the mandated course. Some of our history teachers do not have a major in history and have experienced difficulty in determining what is essential. They have problems covering the American Experience from Colonial Times to the Present."

In grade 8 and grade 11, as teachers introduce new units of material with review sessions of what they expect was covered (if not learned) before, an interesting effect of the 'priming' of factual memory is often seen. That is, at first in a given class, the students appear to remember almost nothing, but dates and names and slogans start to jog memories in the group as a whole, and the level of complexity at which students contribute—the quality or depth of their responses—clearly increases as the session goes on. By contrast, texts can hardly prompt or prime such processes, but begin each new section with little casting-backward, and thus no running start. Teachers often ask a class to organize their memories before the next class: they preview the new material and warn that they expect the students to think back to what they have already studied. The implication of this kind of dynamic process is not just pedagogical. That is, there should be concern not just for what a student has learned but how she is going to retrieve it. For example, the results of multiple choice or fill-in-the-blanks tests might be different if the test items were presented in chronological or thematic order. Adults 'telling history' inevitably start at the beginning or at the end, even when they intend to focus on something in between. The claim is not that memory itself is necessarily structured this way, but that the *discourse* of 're-membering' is (even when we talk to ourselves).

The U.S. History grade-8 syllabus in Albuquerque states: "Fifth grade U.S. history includes a heavier emphasis on the pre-constitution period and is more concerned with legend and ideas reflecting core values. High school U.S. History spends . . . more time with the twentieth century, and is more concerned with analysis of issues and themes. The eighth grade course, then, provides the 'big picture' of history and the basic familiarity." The Indianapolis grade-11 U.S. History syllabus lays out seven rather thorough units of review, one to two weeks long each, from European Empires to the Frontier, and begins new (that is, nonreview) coverage only in the late fall, with the Spanish-American War. (Such a depth of review is perhaps unusual.) In Kokomo, grade-11 U.S. History reviews up to 1900 in six weeks, and then is a course in twentieth-century

---

*Many observers, however, have illustrated the tyranny of 'coverage' by reporting, for example, that in an American History class the day after some remarkable national event the class will take up the next chapter in the text, with no reference made to the happening and its historical context or implications.

American history. The advanced placement course, however, goes deeply into documents and monographic reading over all periods.

One is led to suspect that, in most districts, knowledge testing of the sort that assesses civics-relevant dates and names and principles of 'the national career' would show better levels of knowledge if it were administered earlier, perhaps about grade 9, rather than in connection with applying to college or certifying the right to graduate. Putting the same point in another way: many students may have a historical time-sense, a sense of a period or a large-scale process (for example, urbanization), that does not lend itself to testing. When students complain about over-familiarization they may in fact be complaining about the lack of versatility in testing for the several *kinds* of historical understanding that they have encountered. We may also suppose that those who justify the three cycles of national history *entirely* on the grounds that the subject is so deep that it takes three levels of exposition for students to 'get it'—as if 'it' will not 'take' until there have been three exposures—have a needlessly mystical view of what occurs, perhaps on the order of a fairy tale where a promise is not binding until it is sworn three times.

11.2   How History Happens

There has always been widespread agreement that history *as written*—that is, when the historian has ended her research, satisfied whatever curiosity she began with, and wishes now to communicate with others—tends naturally to involve chronologically organized narrative. Among many authorities involved with school history who could be cited to this effect, here are two.[34] Henry Johnson (1940): "History is the intellectual form in which a civilization renders account to itself of its past." Lester Stephens: "[History is] a mental construction of the past based on evidence which has been carefully subjected to tests of validity and then critically and systematically ordered and interpreted to present a story of man's interaction with other men in a society." Whether one *learns and remembers* history this way is quite another matter.

As we have seen, the strictly chronological march through what is known of the past was a matter of mental discipline in the nineteenth-century. Some have seen this as related to notions of teleological determinism *in* history, but that is not entirely logical: the *scala natura*, the evolutionary chain, the great chains of being, and similar series can be traced as easily backward as forward, down as well as up. Probably the underlying assumption has been that one thing in history does truly lead to another, even if in a very weak causal sense. It is the overriding interest in capturing in some natural way change in history (and nonchange—that is, continuity) that led most historians to protest, in Tryon's words, that those who attacked school history for the stultifying effect of "strict adherence to the exact order of events," around the turn of the century, were directing their tirades against a "has been" situation (p. 179). Chronology was a means to an end. The historians of the 1893 NEA report had commented that a start-to-finish chronological organization per se was not needed: "If this process is at any point interrupted the child is left with the feeling that the world stops where his study has ceased." Tryon himself simply says that the "chronological approach and the *logical* approach are one and the same thing in history" (p. 437ff, emphasis added).*

Some historians around 1900 made much of the idea that history should be *taught* backward. The general notion was that people, including young students, are interested not only in What happened next? but in, Before that? ... and before *that*? The highly influential learning psychologist E. L. Thorndike, rejecting Herbartian culture-epoch recapitulationism, wrote:[35]

> The pupil actually begins with knowledge of the present condition of his own immediate environment plus a variable and chaotic acquaintance, through talk and books, with facts located vaguely in other places and earlier times. ... The educational value of finding the causes of what is, and then the causes of these causes, is so very much superior to the spurious reasoning which comes from explaining a record already known, or pretending to prophesy what the wisest men of the past would not prophesy, that the arrangement *of the first part* of the course in history in the inverse temporal order, *leaving the chronicle till later*, deserves serious consideration.†

School historians, for their part, pointed out that beginnings are dull and conjectural; far better to jump *in medias res*. Of course, teaching history backward no more means beginning every exposition with the actual present or some psychologically established present interest and working undeviatingly in reverse than chronological history forward means beginning each topic with 1492 or 1066. In practice, school historians started with a known, clear event or institution or state of affairs, and asked what preceded it. The preceding process might well be entered by means of some backward temporal leap, but then be told forward. This method is common enough in monographic history today, or in introducing special topics in history texts. It is also a characteristic method in legal history, which specifically rejects the spurious-prophecy fallacy by beginning with, say, a court decision and then looking at what decisions and cases preceded it. It is the common procedure of stylistic analysis, in art, music, and architectural history, where examples from widely separated eras may coexist in

---

*Tryon goes on to observe, in passing, that the problem with Community Civics, beginning around 1910, was that it was inherently multidisciplinary, hence could follow no single organizational logic. Some historians have always believed that the 'synthetic' approach to civic knowledge was a disaster, a pointless rejection of what could quite easily be conveyed through History. The inventors of Community Civics, however, believed that the 'situation' of the present should be confronted, in all its chaotic complexity, before beginning the study of history which might illuminate it. They did not look, that is, for a *single* presentational logic.

†Once again we have evidence of the remote background to an expanding environments format for early-grades instruction.

the 'museum present'—and where what is being sought is not really chronological ordering but illumination of the continual process, at any given period, of
going beyond the conventional. It is, in short, the functional/dynamic approach.

The eminent English historian Collingwood went further, in holding that a
historical 'problem' could not be identified except in terms of its subsequent
solution; and that there had to have been a rational process involved in the
solution, otherwise these two would never be paired conceptually. Thus it was
entirely logical to work backward from an event to an earlier, more complex
situation. To James Harvey Robinson, the central question was How did we get
this way?—with much "left out as irrelevant or unimportant." The historian
Louis Mink has a particularly interesting conception of how historical thinking
works both forward and backward in order to provide a distinctive kind of
adequate explanatory context. Mink reasons that 'historical perspective' is "at
least in part a claim that for the historical understanding of an event one must
know its consequences as well as its antecedents; that the historian must look
before and after. . . . Not infrequently we ask 'and then what happened?' not
merely out of curiosity but in order to understand what we have already been
told." The problem, of course, is whether what happened then truly *explains*
what happened before.[36]

Neither the backward approach (however modified that may be in practice)
nor the functional approach is equivalent to a commitment to presentism in
history instruction. Presentism reflects a judgment about what historical knowledge is *for*, ordinarily in terms of personal or social action.* Thus Dewey's
laboratory school had an early-grades curriculum filled with rich history (and
geography), but the selection of material tried to make connection to the child's
present experience, as it unfolded, and it was finally in the service of ethical
conduct by living members of society in the present. The goal was rational and
moral decision-making. This goal for history is present today in the curriculum
philosophy of many educators, for example, Shirley Engle or J. F. Butts, as well
as philosophers such as Richard Rorty. Similarly, being a historian does not
mean *not* being interested in the present.[†]

11.2.1   THE SAKE OF THE PRESENT

The 1916 committee was largely interested in a present *purpose* for history:[38]
"The past becomes educational to [children] only as it is related to the present."

---

*In this discussion, 'presentism' is used in this proactive sense. It should be distinguished from
Whiggism, which involves the recasting of the frame of reference for the interpretation of the past
in terms of the experienced present, a procedure that is by definition historically insensitive.

†Thus, Diane Ravitch: "My continued interest in contemporary issues made me a historian; there was
simply no other intelligent way to understand the origins of our present institutions, problems, and
ideas."[37]

It admitted, however, that the "history of a thing may add to its present interest": railroads, for example, became more noteworthy to students once they knew something about road and river transportation in the earlier years of the nation. A Detroit superintendent went so far as to say, "The future is of more consequence to the average individual than either the past or present."[39] Wesley, however, writing in 1944, said (p. 23):

> The historian believes that knowledge of the past will help us to understand the present, but he knows that his primary job is to explain the past.... History is only a guide, not a dictator ... it can suggest but cannot command.... Immediate concern with the present is reserved for the teachers of politics, sociology, and economics, and *much historical knowledge is useful only after* they have done their work.... Values and ideals ... are implied in the study of history, but they are made explicit through courses in religion, literature, and civics.

There seems to be here another vote for attention to present factors, especially those involved in civic activity, before delving deeply into the study of history, and a downplaying of any commanding relevance of history to present decisions.

This seems somewhat different from Ravitch's position, for example. However, it turns out that, while Ravitch may have turned to history as the only intelligent way to address problems of the present, a very long detour is involved. "History is above all the retelling of what happened in the past," with emphasis on telling a coherent story. According to Ravitch, internal disorder in the field of history has crowded out the idea of the sustained narrative. Further, the new (that is, restored) approach "must break through the present-mindedness of today's adolescents."[40] This appears to be a 180-degree turn, in its calculation of benefits to education, from the spirit of the New History of seventy-five years ago, one of whose progenitors, James Harvey Robinson, said: "No one questions the inalienable right of the historian to interest himself in any phase of the past that he chooses. It is only to be wished that greater numbers of historians had greater skill in hitting upon those phases of the past which serve *us* best in understanding the most vital problems of the present."[41]

One might think that the Wesley committee would recommend, as some have, that a meaningful study of history should wait until the later years of schooling.* But the 1944 AHA commission, as we have seen, recommended history from the early grades. The solution to any apparent paradox is that they also recommended the study of civics and the social environment from the early years.

Hardly anyone holds to an extreme position, claiming either that history has *no* application to the present or that it should be taught *only* for such utility. The 1916 committee, for example, proved influential in a different recommendation:

---

*Some English researchers of developmental abilities suggest that true appreciation of chronology in history is not possible until midadolescence; see section 11.3.1.

that chronological presentation be a framework for, and frequently interrupted by, intensive analysis of particular situations, problems, and so on, using nonhistorical methods as appropriate. Such episodes correlate facts and approaches 'from other disciplines, in a temporally located but synchronic frame of reference. They interrupt, but do not destroy, chronology in history. They are, however, fundamentally non-narrative in nature; a different kind of explanation is involved.* Once again, Robinson gave the justification: "While events can be dealt with chronologically, conditions have to be presented topically if they are to become clear . . . the medieval church, castle, monastery, and farm have to be described in *typical* forms" (p. 42, emphasis added).

   This is no matter of present relevance, but one form of the structural understanding of a relatively static aspect of the past: continuity, seen, as it were, from inside. What is sought, for some historians in their concern with education, is history-mindedness, a sense of period or era or of social patterns specific to that time. It is the appreciation that things were once fundamentally different, but 'normal' in their own time and place.† What is implied, for the doing of history, is the importation of, or correlation with, other methods and nonhistorical logic. Strayer (quoted above) held that certain periods in American history lent themselves, for example, to a codisciplinary focus: history cum economics, or demography, or politics. Cremin makes a more general point:[42]

   Any history is always the history of something in particular, and the explanatory categories the historian uses in writing about that something in particular are almost invariably drawn from other domains—from politics or philosophy or psychology or economics. . . . As soon as the historian attempts to go beyond mere chronicle . . . he must perforce reach beyond the events themselves to some set of laws, principles, or generalizations . . . [which] almost always come from outside the discipline of history.

This consideration, of course, is the essence of the contribution made by historians, around 1900, to the invention of 'social studies.' Not all agree with Cremin, however, about the importance of explanatory categories external to the construction of history, preferring to think of a sufficiency and shapeliness of the historical material itself. Barzun, for example:[43]

   Let me say once again what recognized, acknowledged historians have always understood to be genuine: it is a narrative that sets forth a chain of motive, action, result. The sequence in time—chronology—must be clear. Dates are important *solely* for this purpose of orientation in the stream of

---

*A point made by the early *Annales* historians of the mid-century, with regard to the description of long-lasting structures or processes of long duration.

†It also is the tone captured when history (often popular history or historical fiction) is written in the historical present tense. John Poster (cited in Downey and Levstik, "Teaching and Learning History," 337) says that historical time requires a "sense of existing in the past as well as the present, a feeling of being in history rather than standing apart from it."

motives, actions, results. The chain need not be long . . . but it must be *thick*, for the motives and action, being those of many individuals, are always tangled, and the results cannot be understood unless a full view of that preceding tangle is given.

Such a view, of course, does not forbid the use of principles from other fields to contribute to the historical treatment. For example, some believe that psycho-history is a means of contributing to the understanding of motives and actions in their tangled thickness. But it does eliminate the notion of categories or organizing ideas superior or prior to the historical material itself.

In the era of the New Social Studies, as would be expected, there was particular emphasis on the richness of synchronic understanding within history. One purpose was to allow for, or draw on, memory structures other than those organized narratively. A date should trigger off, in the student's mind, a whole set of events and circumstances so that an entire historical period can be reviewed. One danger of such an approach (for which historians correctly condemn other social scientists) is that of attending to periods and topics where evidence exists and omitting everything in between. This is a weakness often found in intellectual history, but it is not limited to that field. Much narrative history of any kind is likely to have to follow this strategy anyhow. The effect of 'postholing'—of stopping to look deeply into the structure of special periods or situations—can be to accentuate the problem. (It is not a necessary danger, of course: the point of demographic analysis, for example, is that, within limits, missing 'data' points can be interpolated from known data with considerable reliability.) For historical education, decisions on how to handle thin evidence will depend, once again, on the goal. To what degree is it best to look where the light is, to understand what is most evident? Other things equal, is not what is closer to the present better illuminated?

Axtell, in criticizing the organization of texts, says: "The task of explaining the Age of Discovery [in the New World] is made largely impossible by the way we divide our survey courses at Reconstruction. . . . Not only is this pedagogical nonsense but it smacks of egregious whiggism as well: the closer we get to the present, the more important events become."[44] The executive secretary of the Organization of American Historians, however, argues: "Since the United States is such an enormous world power and since this development is almost exclusively a 20th-century phenomenon, it makes sense for instructors and textbook authors to reconsider collapsing some of the detail and material on less important 19th-century presidents and events or trends that no longer help us understand the significance of the country's impact on the rest of the world."[*]

In his critique of Bruner and the New Social Studies, Krug focused on a tendency toward a present bias.[46] Bruner had written that "we are bound to

---

[*]She goes on to say that there are, to be sure, other considerations, for example in concentrating on the constitutional era.[45]

move toward instruction in the sciences of behavior and away from the study of history," partly because social science must aim to describe the "human condition" rather than the "particularities . . . of history," and because the "records before (the last few centuries) are minimal, while the records after are relatively rich." Historians must condemn such an attitude. But it is well to remember that Bruner was emphasizing an *instructional* strategy: that is, in encouraging students to reach generalizations and abstractions, narrative treatment of 'thin' historical periods was not useful. Since Bruner wrote, as he would no doubt be the first to admit, the social sciences have for the most part taken a historical turn, each in its own terms, with the result that more is available for use by historians than was true in the heyday of behavioral positivism. It is likely, however, that any 'functional' approach to history in education will encounter some of these problems.

Thus historians themselves disagree over chronology versus 'postholing' and present-orientation, but these positions are relatively stable: that is, each is evident at each stage of the social studies. Thus, while there is no consensus, there may be compromise that need not be renegotiated often. This is in fact seen in U.S. History texts, where a kind of subnarrative style is adopted. The organization is primarily chronological-forward, but much material is separated out for topical or analytic treatment; and in chapter-end exercises students are asked to relate recent coverage either to earlier periods or to aspects of the present. The relative coverage of periods and episodes in American History is quite consistent from book to book, despite urging by historians to alter this pattern. This stability of relative emphasis is largely a competitive market phenomenon. As has previously been pointed out, history texts are not necessarily *used* according to this pattern: in having to 'cover' everything, they have become reference books, at least to some teachers and students. To break out of the format of the textbook, some teachers may spend more time on topics or periods that interest them especially, and thus build up in richness what texts only mention in passing. Other teachers, especially those concerned with coverage, take a 'snapshot' approach so that the past becomes a series of 'how it was' vignettes in a picture album. This jettisons much of the material in the text. In either case, the teacher can insist that the student will be *tested* on the material in the text, which means that the student should take the relative emphases of that coverage as a rough guide for study.

Generally speaking, a chronological-cum-topical approach involves more recency of material (and emphasis) than the strictly chronological, owing to the 'flash-forward' nature of much topical treatment. Publishers' own surveys of teachers reassure them that the desired pattern is a concentration on Civil War and slavery, the American Revolution, and colonial growth. Reconstruction, the Federalist period, Jacksonianism, industrialization and Progressivism, and particularly recent American history (Vietnam, Watergate, the civil rights movement, and others) are far behind. Clearly, a strong tendency toward orientation to present problems is missing *in texts*. Less clearly, there seems to be a narrative tropism to the great heroic episodes and the life-and-death crises of the national story (cf. Strayer, cited above, on the Civil War's becoming a 'legend'). Persistent issues and tension in American society are omitted.* A comparison of grade-8 and grade-11 texts shows little difference in this regard. To the extent that tendencies such as this become self-perpetuating, the national 'story well told' is *already* complete, shapely, and apprehensible. To that extent, the specific benefit promised from conventional, narrative history—truly to *explain*—tends to become moot. What is there left to explain?

11.2.2 HISTORY AND THE CULTURAL PURPOSE

The goal of explanation of human activity in humanly sensible terms involves the recognition that 'objectivity' in history is, in Beard's phrase, "that noble dream." Historians will generally point out that history is never 'true,' indeed is never true *enough*.[†] David Fischer has cited many errors and weakness, not only in history but related fields as well.[48] Objectivity in social science, generally, is always ephemeral, and historians have as good a record as any scholarly field in admitting this. The political scientist Norton Long[49] wrote: "The danger of history as presently taught is that the plausible common sense of the historian's narrative is accepted as valid social science generalization." The sense of such a comment is obscure, since the validity of social science generalization is never final and since 'narrative' explanation is fundamentally different in nature from scientific generalization. The mere fact that historians disagree on the content and sufficiency of specific explanations can itself be taken to indicate that truth is never final, or that particular events have multiple meanings, depending on the frame of reference. This is not to take such disagreement lightly. Thus, Norman Hampson[50] writes despairingly of George Rudé's as opposed to Simon Schama's interpretation of the French Revolution: "With the best will in the world it is difficult to see how they can both be right, and the reader is faced with the question of what to make of the situation when two serious professional historians study the same events and arrive at such incompatible conclusions." The almost ritualized disclaimer in texts—"Historians disagree"—is taken by students as a kind of good manners in scholarship. But some historians would take such disagreement seriously, and hope that it would lead students to serious inquiry about *how* such disagreement arises.

---

*In a study of Connecticut history teachers in high schools and colleges, it was found that both groups tended to apportion time similarly, as regarded historical periods and episodes in American history. But college teachers gave more emphasis to certain problematical *topics*: especially, immigration and minority history and experience. In the latter, college teachers spent more time on the black slave experience and on American Indian life and history, while high-school teachers gave more attention to the civil rights movement of the 1960s.[47]

†Thus, Donald Warren, "Political Education," states that much issue-specific, thematic research now completed by social historians has "raised doubts about the traditional account of the American past," leading us to question, "Is the history *true enough* to cast a broad, inclusive net?"

   The much more important issue raised by historians and nonhistorians is that history systematically oversimplifies or distorts: that the traditional explanation is not credible—or should not be. Thus Axtell's complaint is that texts on the exploration of North America cover the English, but not the French, Spanish, Dutch, and other activity. Kaestle[51] explains the fact that most persons responding to a *New York Times* test item on the development of religious toleration in the British colonies chose 'the wrong' answer: "The correct answer . . . seems to assume a curriculum of inquiry . . . not just popular tradition." Kaestle means that students as presently educated will not have thought deeply enough to know that the popular assumption in part conveyed through school history *has* to be wrong. Contradicting Ravitch, whom he quotes as saying that "history frees us from the apparent inevitability of the status quo," Kaestle says that "most history as taught in the schools does the reverse."

   Ultimately, the issue is an ethical one: whether history, especially national history, is intolerably biased and chauvinistic. Thus, in connection with the 1992 quincentenary, some have wondered whether '1492' will stand only for the year in which Isabella sent Columbus sailing or also for the year in which she drove the Jews violently out of Spain. And American historians recently have discussed the persuasive myth of 'exceptionalism' in American history, by which the United States is seen at all periods as developing essentially free from external influences.* The revised California framework, announced in 1988, attempts to alternate the teaching of U.S. with non-U.S. History throughout the curriculum (section 12.1). If well implemented, this will not automatically solve the problem of bias, but it should help keep in students' minds a broader frame of reference.

   Merriam wrote, in his 1934 AHA commission volume, "History has proved an effective carrier of the traditions of the special group seeking its services, the medium for memories of the special culture seeking political independence."† Ernest May[52] has cited strikingly racist explanations in connection with Reconstruction in the 1930 American History text by Morison and Commager, "widely and not unreasonably regarded as the best United States history survey ever written." Commager, for his part, has written against the "one bias, one prejudice, one obsession so pervasive and so powerful that it deserves special consideration: nationalism."[53] Gagnon[54] wrote with dismay on textbook treatment of America as constantly newborn or free from taint: "All is darkness and light, and America is born of light. The only legacy to us from medieval times is their disappearance. . . . All the texts . . . pay almost no attention to the outside world. . . . They create the impression that modern industrialization was mainly an American product and that we did it all by ourselves."

---

*This tendency, if true, is shared by Europeans, perhaps even instigated by them as in Goethe's salute "Amerika, Du hast es besser!"

†*Civic Education*, 89. Merriam referred not only to groups winning power but to groups already exercising it: specifically, French chauvinism as a tendency deliberately reinforced in the post-1884 period in the interest of national commitment.

Such examples of weakness and error in texts are easy to find. It is not surprising that history books, meant to tell a national story, do so in an ethnocentric way. Or that texts oversimplify intellectual complexity.* Texts are in multiple jeopardy. Somehow they are to contain all possibly relevant facts, constantly warn against Manicheanism and exceptionalism in history, provide guidance for student inquiry—and much else. As Gagnon points out (p. 63), even the constant adjuration in texts that students 'draw lessons from history' can be of ambiguous benefit. "The 'lessons' of 1914 were wrong for the 1930s. . . . What European diplomats *failed* to do in 1914, what the Big Four *failed* to do in Paris, shaped the lives of all of us, more directly than much of what takes up space in our history books" (emphasis added).

Fortunately, good teaching can powerfully supervene. For example, many U.S. History teachers not only present two or more sides of a controversy or a conflictual set of events but make students work from original documents reflecting such disparate viewpoints, stage debates in which students must on the basis of careful preparation take the role of 'the enemy' or 'the other,' and in many additional ways bring home to students the recognition that the point of view matters.† However, as has been argued before in this volume, while both teachers and students may find such an approach deeply rewarding, there are few external rewards. Many teachers, referring for example to statewide testing that occurs (let us say) in March, report something like the following: Up to March, I cover the book; then, I *teach*.

11.2.3   History as past politics

At each stage of reform in social studies, there seems to have been the assumption that moving beyond political history or the recounting of actions of great men (great, of course, because they are seen as affecting the course of history) would in itself counteract chauvinistic, class, and cultural bias. Some have gone so far as to believe that a more social history would empower those whom conventional history had ignored, as if their heirs in the present could then act on their behalf. Merriam, as quoted above, pointed to the converse of such a notion, in that revisionist history, for example, could be as biased as the history written by the prior victors. It may be that political history is always tutelary in its demonstration that power is *not* distributed equally, and that at any age those

---

*For example, a team of astute analysts of history texts, Beck and colleagues comment that for grade 5 history "the goal of history instruction at this early level should be to build understanding of major historical periods upon which later exposures to history content can build." This can be read as saying that learning about history requires a cognitive framework of 'periods.' It can also be read as saying that the concept of what constitutes a 'period' is a given—as indeed it is, generally, prior to advanced courses in the university.[55]

†Impressive accounts of such teaching in the U.S. are given, for example in Rogers, et al., *Portraits*; Wineburg and Wilson, "Models of Wisdom."

in power not only tend to control decisions that affect others but the record of such decisions and consequences.*

Krug has been quoted (section 5.3.1) as questioning Bruner's faith, underlying much of the New Social Studies, that humankind progresses in rationality—so that the window of attention in history has only to open on modern times for students to see how far we have come. However, much the same faith was apparent in the New History of the early twentieth-century. Carl Becker[56] implied that if every man were his own historian—an argument for inquiry and independent analysis of the evidence rather than credulity about authority—everyman might thus enter into history more fully. There is certainly some cogency to the idea that those who have been written out of history have a hard time drawing useful lessons from it. But the notion that an individual or group must be historically literate to count for anything in the course of history is doubtful.†

These disputes get conflated with disputes about the nature of human agency in history, whether 'great men' affect the course of the world more than anonymous persons or groups, the extent to which history is determined by nonhuman forces, the degree to which the past is seen as episodes of change or the persistence of established patterns, and the definition of the public and private spheres.[57] With regard to the influence of famous male persons, Thomas Carlyle said, "The history of the world is the biography of great men." Fernand Braudel said that a qualitative change in the world between about 1400 and 1700 "was maintained over long periods by the initiative of groups of men, not individuals (the exceptions prove the rule)." Hegel believed that the forces of history were ultimately impersonal, but that they were worked out by humans, both heroes and victims. Ecological historians explain that the 'heroes' of European imperialism were, by definition, all those who occupied new territory to their biological advantage.[58]

At the heart of the matter, perhaps, is the definition of events, event structure or complexes, and 'movements' in history. Social history *tends* to deal with the latter, with structural aspects of continuity or change, with longer historical time, although it can of course deal with the anonymous single life or how typical life events occur (as in diary history or personal history). French social historians have distinguished among events, *conjonctures* (middle-range structures), and processes of *la longue durée*. A useful criterion may be whether or not individuals in such processes would have had the sense of significant ongoing change. Social history can encompass both alterations over centuries in *mental-*

---

*Many have pointed out that while history written about and by formerly dispossessed groups permanently alters and enriches the record, there tends to be a generational pattern by which younger scholars find the emphases and interpretations of the pioneer scholars sadly deficient. In the American field, this is certainly evident in black history, women's history, and labor history.

†One of the central tenets of some social history is that anonymous persons *did* count, perhaps more than those who became famous in history. For a discussion of 'consensus history' of the 1950s, which tended to play down the knowledge-is-power idea, see Van Tassel, "Trials of Clio," 6.

ités and letters home from a soldier in battle. Inevitably, textbooks find it easier to arrange events in meaningful order than to capture movements or *mentalités*. Kammen[59] observes: "An emphasis on events tends to put people into the foreground, whereas an emphasis on structures and series calls our attention to large socioeconomic forces." And Bernard Bailyn says:[60] "the problem of relating latent events, especially those detected and expressed in quantities, to events that register in the awareness of contemporaries . . . is, I believe, becoming the central methodological problem of modern historiography." (Bailyn here refers to what others might call dynamic patterned change—for example, shifts in family size and structure.) By definition, a *chronicle* involves a connected narrative of events whose causal relationships are assumed to be nonproblematical: that is, if one thing led to another it was at least partly determinative, and involved human agency or intent. Generally speaking, texts and courses in the schools of this country have shown far more interest in middle-range social history—for example, the history of the family or of a socioeconomic nexus like slavery—than in long-duration history.

Three reasons for this are quite apparent. First, topics having to do with human groups, their structures and stories, are thought to be intrinsically more interesting to students than a description of very slow change—for example, in the circumstances of material life or in the population structure. Second, the United States, owing to its relative recency, is better outfitted with parish records, local population registers, architectural or agricultural censuses, and the like, suitable to the middle-range, rather than with evidence, spanning centuries, of impersonal processes. (This is changing, with the success of New World social archaeology, which makes North American prehistory accessible.) Finally, it is widely assumed that an understanding of temporal processes on the epochal scale is inherently more difficult, cognitively, than the understanding of processes across generations or a few lifetimes.

Certainly the New History wanted to go beyond experiences or manifest events to a deeper level of structure. In particular, the accounts of great men were to be downplayed, not out of concern over bias and the perpetuation of unequal power relations but out of concern over superficiality in historical explanation. An explanation, in this view, was more than a chronicle, but a statement about what essentially, tellingly, sufficiently connected events.[61] Hazel Hertzberg discovered a talk given to Wisconsin teachers in 1891 in which one of the most influential of American historians, Frederick Jackson Turner, spoke as follows:

> The focal point of modern interest is the fourth estate, the great mass of the people. . . . Far oftener than has yet been shown have . . . underlying economic facts affecting breadwinners of the nation been the secret of the nation's rise and fall. . . . It is not surprising that the predominant historical study is coming to be the study of past social conditions. . . . History is past literature, it is past politics, it is past religion, it is past economics.[62]

Tryon reported that texts about 1920 were largely devoted to political (and military) happenings and individual biography.[63] He predicted that "oblivion" was near for the biographical method. This was especially interesting, in that Tryon's citation of an authority who had been uncritically followed—that is, one who had overemphasized biography—was John Dewey. Dewey had said, in connection with his own school and as a general comment, that children liked to hear about others' lives, and that this made for vital and concrete episodes in history instruction. (Dewey also, of course, found that the *end* of learning was the attainment of abstract and generalizable concepts; biography was a natural starting point.)[64]

Robinson and colleagues agreed.[65] "That work of history should begin with elementary studies in biography... needs no argument. The interest of the pupil is thus stimulated and he is prepared to take up *more serious study* when the time comes" (emphasis added). Robinson and Dewey believed that one began with biography; it was vicarious experience, and study should be experientially based. They then assumed that the processual, well beyond individual action, would follow. Wesley, however,[66] said firmly that "History is the record of human decisions, as well as the record of human experience. . . . History is made by men and not by blind forces beyond human control. . . . We must discuss great men as well as great events; we must think of what might have been as well as what was." It is a confusing judgment: it is not clear whether the decisions that *count* are made by rare individuals (which is not only possibly tautological but seemingly contrary to Wesley's conviction that citizenship is learned through the study of history), or whether 'what is' is determined by multiple decisions, in which rare individuals occasionally dominate. Earlier, writing in 1934, Merriam[67] questioned the biographical approach as being not truly biographical, but stereotypical. He remarked (with particular reference to Lincoln) that heroes in history are stripped, for the sake of conventional pieties, of their venturesomeness, their ingenuity, their "radical and unconventional nature." He cautioned against this kind of biographical "narration as a variation of story telling." In principle, the biographical method could be accommodated safely were students to have access to exemplary or representative biographies and event narrations; that is, to ordinary persons acting purposefully, for example as citizens, with discernible effects on their times. In practice, few texts manage convincingly the task of trying to present the moderately consequential person.*

Since the schools are charged with helping to enculturate the young, and since

---

*However, in middle school especially, students are encouraged to write biographies of specific individuals for which they must do some version of original research. The latter requirement tends to mean that they write about someone of local or personal significance, not someone of 'historic' proportions. The importance of such activities is that it involves both foreground and background: to write a life, the student must understand the times. If the experience is not judged in those terms, the student may simply display her own imperfect conception of how individuals act in time and on others.

history preserves collective 'memory,' it is natural that there should be a desire to emphasize, in school history, the national story, the American memory. The overriding purpose, especially in the earlier years of schooling, is to ensure cultural coherence and stability by providing common knowledge. Without that, group identity may come to count, so the argument goes, for more than the national culture.[68] (There is possibly a misunderstanding here about the concept of culture; on this matter see section 18.4.) In terms of the present discussion, there is also a deep skepticism, on the part of some, about the conception of history as collective memory, shared and rehearsed by story telling. After all, children are warned, Don't tell stories. 'Stories' are fiction. 'It's only a story' means it isn't true. Similarly, memory is unstable, misleading, inaccurate, and easily edited and revised.[*]

The concern here is less that about chauvinism or bias than about fundamental intellectual indolence. Much may depend, for education, on distinctions among stories, legends, and myths. When Merriam cautioned against "narration as story-telling," he did not mean that 'stories well told' were not appropriate in the instruction of young children, but that the perpetuation of unrealism was to be avoided. Herodotus, of course, said that since the past did not recur, and constantly receded, the purpose of history was to "preserve the memory of the past." Does this provide for revision, in the interest of preservation? Or does constant narration simply deepen the rigidity of memory—as it becomes impossible to recount a bedtime story to a child in a new way?

In this regard, an idealist approach to history suggests that 'meaning' is not a problem, or rather that meaning inheres in the sequence of events themselves. As a recent anonymous writer[69] puts it: "If historical perspectives are incredibly complex for children to take hold of, they can seem over-simple to the adult. . . . History . . . can too easily become 'the history' . . . can assume the rightness of the single narrative and the obvious explanation. Liberation from the present runs the danger of imprisonment in the past." Those who advocate, with some urgency, a return to political history and narration and an eschewing of specialized analytical study appear to believe that the meaning of the past is fixed. Gertrude Himmelfarb, one of the most distinguished of these advocates, is quoted as saying, "The issue should not be what historians happen to believe, but what contemporaries in the past believed, as they experienced reality."[70] The ethical principle here is admirable, but surely *how* those in the past believed is the problem that historians set out to solve. Are the answers they come up with happenstance, as Himmelfarb suggests, then cross-checked against what past

---

[*]On the second point, at least, the evidence from psychological research is clear: memory is an ongoing construct, constantly revised in content and structure, not a palimpsest whose earlier layers can be discerned. The riposte to this could be that *collective* memory, being by definition transpersonal, is less easily distorted. Since personal memory tends to rigidify over time, erasing earlier constructs, history is precisely the means to edit it and keep it true.

actors experienced?* How could the latter be seen directly, without intervening interpretation?

11.2.4   HISTORY AS NARRATION

The conjoining of emphasis on story-telling (that is, narrative), as a method, with priority to the importance of collective memory, as a goal, varies in education with age and grade level. While collective memory is of signal importance, to some commentators, at all ages, everyone understands that story-telling is particularly recommended for pedagogical purposes at the early grades. A forceful proponent of this view, and thus a forceful critic of the expanding environments model for the early grades, is Kieran Egan.[71]

Egan holds[†] that what young children care about most is stories, and that the frame of reference young children bring to stories is a kind of moral and affective valuation: what is good, bad; safe, dangerous; familiar, unknown. If the latter is true (and there is no doubt that children do use such polar judgmental categories in dealing with a wide range of experience), the assumption on the part of progressive educators that children understand their immediate social environment in *social* terms may not be true—hence, would not be grounds for starting instruction there. In fact, Egan says, children are fascinated with the nonreal but not the hypothetical: that is, with witches and dragons so long as they can deal with them emotionally (that is, as bad but not dangerous), but not with 'downtown' or 'on the West Coast' or 'in other countries.' Egan concludes that the story form is what holds the attention, and that the story must take a binary form; it must, for example, lead to a happy or good outcome or a sad or bad one. Early history instruction must tell such stories, and the stories will necessarily be legends—that is, simplified versions, tending toward the archetypal and the universal dualities. He holds that such legends need not breed a taste for unreality; quite the contrary. For example, "Initiating children to scientific understanding might *begin* with establishing the binary distinction between science and non-science. . . . Stories of the dramatic victories of reason over superstition, of observation over received dogma . . . would thus be central to the *earliest* stage of science instruction"(emphasis added).

There are several things possibly wrong with Egan's position. For one thing, the appeal to an early and basic rational/nonrational distinction in the teaching of young children is inconsistent with the rest of the argument, since children can hardly 'begin' from such a conception if they do not achieve it until later, once

---

*The superficiality of 'experience' in and of the moment is suggested in the popular phrase, 'That was an *experience*—which invariably means that the speaker cannot really make sense of what happened. To the extent, of course, that actors in the past were articulate about their experience, their accounts must be taken seriously; but such accounts are not prima facie 'true,' and they tend to be preserved from atypical sources, so that what people in general believe is not known.

†Egan's position has been refined, and somewhat narrowed, over the years.

they have gone beyond primitive emotive oppositions.* Egan does not seem to realize that teachers using an expanding environments format do not so much *depend* on the child's social understanding as elicit and refine it. Egan also seems to overlook another early-developmental opposition—familiar versus unfamiliar—and the notion that young children play with and test their early dualisms while using them: this is, of course, *curiosity* at work.

An astute critic, Stephen Thornton,[72] pointed out that Egan put a great deal of emphasis on discrediting views held by Dewey and by Piaget (on the limits of children's logical understanding), views that were not in fact held by Dewey and which had generally been found wanting in Piaget—a criticism Egan largely accepted. Thornton's most important criticism was that of a confusion of categories on Egan's part: the fact that children have emotively based reactions *to* educational (and other) experience and content does not mean that they use only those emotive 'primes' in *thinking about* such content. In other words, emotive 'knowing' may be an inherently defective notion.[†]

Nevertheless, there is something intuitively appealing about Egan's position, and about his recommendation that literature, legend, and emotively organized narrative be used in early history instruction. (This had, of course, been the normal approach to the teaching of classical history, Hebrew legends, and the like in the early grades in nineteenth-century schools.) It would be hard to insist that bland, remote, chronologically straitened 'history' texts must automatically prevail over imaginative, historically relevant literature in the early grades. (However, the books that children are asked to confront are more likely to be basal—that is, normed by grade level—'readers,' which may contain historical material but are not in any sense texts.) Underlying Egan's position, of course, is the conviction that by the use of literary and emotively sharpened material with young children, they will come to love and respect history. There is also the assumption that young children base their historical understanding on a mechanism of empathy with those in the stories and some kind of intuition of causal relationships as exemplified by the actions of others.

The latter position is highly doubtful. Young children do display empathy relative to those actually present—a hurt child, a happy parent—but that is entirely different from empathic understanding through the symbolic representation of others in stories. The same is true for understanding of others' motivations: for example, the complicated or nonconscious causal reasoning by 'actors' in history. For every research study that shows remarkable sensitivity or understanding in children, there is another that shows gross distortion or peculiar inferences. (Think of the bizarre lessons that young children draw from stories, let alone actual happenings.) One review of the literature,[73] for example,

---

*It is also questionable from the point of view both of the philosophy and the history of science.

†Dewey, curiously, made a parallel argument in his book, *Art as Experience*, pointing out that 'aesthetic experience' quickly moves beyond the mere experiencing of affect. Though it might imply a different mode of feeling, knowing more does not mean feeling less.

holds: "young children have difficulty differentiating between fantasy and reality, between fact and fiction, and between the physical and mental. . . . [T]hough children are eager for the new, they seldom see its relation to the old. An additional point, worthy of careful observation in any attempt to teach young children, is the limited ability of children to learn from verbal explanations." Another such review[74] concludes that "Children virtually never form an internal representation of the story which is identical to the explicit content of the story, and furthermore, children of different ages may form different interpretations." Engle and Ochoa[75] develop a similar argument in pointing out that social perspectivism—the ability to take the role or point of view of another—develops slowly, and that "Relying exclusively on language, whether oral or written, is not likely to be helpful unless it is tied closely to the children's immediate or recent experiences." Thus, Egan's sketch of how young children move from what they recognize or enjoy toward understanding is probably defective.

There is a tendency in all reasoning about the instruction of young children, be it that of Egan or Dewey or another, to assume that the more that children 'know' in the general area of instruction, the more will be learned. This should not be taken uncritically for granted. Cognitive research, including recent schema theory,[76] suggests that 'domains' of knowledge are quite narrow, and strongly dependent (in the current lingo) on the mental 'operations' that will be called for. Knowing how to multiply does not mean knowing how to divide; there is a missing step, which must be grasped before the logical connection is clear. Memory and reasoning are also modality-dependent: what one knows from books is different from what one knows from class discussion, at least until one accomplishes a later synthesis; and this is true with regard to the modality in which knowledge is used as well as possessed. Constructing a narrative account for others is different from possessing facts in a form elicitable by short-answer tests. Paraphrasing is different from repeating, and so on. It is likely that children's comprehension of personal or family history is different *in nature* from the comprehension of 'local history,' and then 'national history,' and so forth. And myths are different from legends, and legends from stories.*

It might also be well, in this regard, to point out that school learning is built partially on *non*knowing: on needing to go further. A good teacher's apothegm is: Always leave them puzzled. History is, among other things, a forum for inquiry—in this sense, inquiry driven by puzzlement, the fallibility and ambiguity of evidence, the nonknowability of the past.

None of this suggests that the use of literature, stylistically heightened narrative, and the like, is inappropriate for history instruction. In California, and elsewhere, the movement toward 'reading through the curriculum,' which uses literature in conjunction with other subjectmatters (latterly, mathematics and natural science) seems to produce impressive results. To an observer, however,

---

*On the first of these differences, see the classic on the retention and transmission of oral epics, A. B. Lord's *A Singer of Tales*.

they seem particularly fine in the middle grades, where students understand literary genres and types of explanation and can take advantage of the richness of discourse that results from such understanding. In a middle school, the student may be reading a fictional account of 'an ordinary hero,' and may be writing a biography of an ancestor based on research in family documents. Such activity is, of course, a form of research training toward the end that Carl Becker anticipated.[77] It certainly involves mastering chronology and period time-sense, a geographical setting, the relationship of events to a life-span, the relation of 'events' to 'experience,' the relation of one life to the experience of the cohort, interviewing as well as reading, perhaps the use of kinds of language different from one's own (for example, nineteenth-century versus twentieth-century English; regional variation; diary or epistolary language; and the like). The difference between early elementary and middle school grades, of course, is that in the latter the student no longer is only 'told' biographies and stories, but in some sense works on history herself.

History (and social studies) in the early grades need not be a choice between Story Hour or Field Trip. Many good teachers using an expanding environments format constantly invoke historical (and cross-cultural) similarities and comparisons. Conversely, Dewey's Laboratory School used history and geography as the organizing threads across the grades. Biographies and myths were excellent for the younger children; thereafter children would look, through history, at inventions, exploration and discovery, the formation of governments—and all the other typical content of these grades.* The recent recommendations for K through 6 of the Bradley Commission, looking at history in the schools, are much like the pattern of the Dewey school—and not that unlike the modal 'expanding environments' format.†

On grounds similar to those discussed here, an outside observer, reviewing social studies,[78] writes:

> proposals calling for replacing most of the current primary grades social studies curriculum with a curriculum that would emphasize history and related literature are certainly feasible from the perspective of developmental and educational psychology, *probably just as feasible* as the expanding communities approach. It should be noted, however, that the same is true of other reform suggestions, such as those calling for comparative study of world cultures and customs [p. 401]. . . . Students [come to instruction with] misconceptions about social phenomena just as they

---

*A fine account of the Dewey curriculum is contained in Kliebard, *Struggle*, 75ff. Dewey was clear, however, that myths were "a very excellent thing" when regarded simply as stories, but that "it is self-deception to suppose that . . . by some inner affinity to the child's nature, he is being morally introduced into the civilization from which the myth sprung, and is receiving a sort of spiritual baptism through 'literature.'" Kliebard, 68.

†Bradley Commission, *Building a History Curriculum*. We refer specifically to Pattern B, which resembles the new California framework, combining historical, literary, and biographical material within a loose here-to-there, now-to-then pattern.

do about natural phenomena. . . . Children's misconceptions about social phenomena may be easier to correct than their misperceptions about natural phenomena because they tend to be implicit expectations based on oversimplified notions of morality or the omnipotence and benevolence of authority figures rather than explicit beliefs based on personal observations [pp. 402–03; Brophy refers to the way children 'see' the sun circling the earth; in general here, he has in mind science teaching based on deliberate eliciting of erroneous 'schemata,' and then engineering appropriate conceptual revision].

Still . . . the conceptual change research on science teaching has shown that students often do not even become aware of conflict between their currently held misconceptions and the scientifically correct conceptions being taught in the curriculum unless these conflicts are confronted directly. . . . Curricula should be developed so as not only to explicate key concepts clearly but also to contrast these key concepts with anticipated misconceptions [p. 403]. . . . Second . . . curriculum developers should avoid including content that would create or reinforce such misconceptions. . . . I agree with Ravitch (1987) that well-chosen biographies and engaging accounts of historical events can make the study of history more concrete and interesting to elementary students; however, I do not share her enthusiasm for infusing myth and lore into the curriculum. . . . There is value in studying myth and lore as literature . . . [or] as part of culture studies. . . . To the extent that myth and lore are included in the social studies curriculum, it is important to be sure that, as Ravitch intends, they are presented as *fictions that tell us something about the culture under study* [p. 403].

11.2.5   HISTORY AND COLLECTIVE MEMORY

One problem with myths and stories is that they have 'plots' that always come out right. Many believe that history can have a story-line—but not a plot.* For one thing, there are no denouements in history, only temporary resolutions and reconciliations. History is always open-ended. More important is that students need to learn that actions and movements in history have no necessary outcomes; it is all provisional. As Wineburg and Wilson, two researchers in the forefront of study on how teachers become 'wise practitioners'—that is, experts—in a particular subject, put it: "The making of history is a dynamic process. What happened in the past wasn't fated or meant to be." They give an excellent detailed illustration of fine teaching and learning, in this case involving sustained classroom debate on Loyalists versus Revolutionaries in early America, in which the students gradually come to realize that:

*This distinction, which is related to one made by E. M. Forster about fiction and myth, has been discussed by Lee M. Benson.⁷⁹

Tories were not the villains depicted in the textbooks, but ordinary people who saw their world differently from their rebel neighbor. . . . At the end of the debate, one girl stared at the ceiling, dazed. "You know," she muttered to no one in particular, "we could've all been like Canada." The realization that, had the loyalists prevailed, Queen Elizabeth would appear on our stamps as well as those of our northern neighbors, does not come easily to adolescents who grow up in an era when America, not Britain, is the dominant world power.[80]

Plots and fictions, in history, have a compelling veridicality in both personal and collective experience.* Brophy (above) refers to the fact that students can answer correctly, on a test, that the earth revolves around the sun—while continuing to experience the sun circling the earth. There is, possibly, a realm of collective knowledge in history that is impervious to alteration. It consists of icons and symbols, and illusory connections between them, that form part of the national memory. Recently, Michael Frisch[81] has called his methodologically modest, but compelling, investigation of what students 'know' and where that comes from "empirical iconography."

For fifteen years or so Frisch has been asking his college introductory U.S. History survey students, at the beginning of the year course, to generate lists of names from American history. Year after year the students write down virtually the same names in virtually the same order. The lists across the years always begin with Washington and Lincoln, move on down through Madison and Revere and Monroe, and trail off with Andrew Johnson and Cornwallis and Lewis & Clark (sometimes Lewison Clark). Of particular interest is the appearance of names, in virtually the same list position, of only pseudohistorical, or historical by courtesy, figures with strong iconic significance: Betsy Ross, John Smith, Daniel Boone, and the like. The generated lists consist of something more than what psychologists call 'clang' (automatized) responses. Benjamin Franklin, for example, always appears very high on the list, except when Frisch instructs students to omit "presidents, generals, statesmen, etc."; students apparently know that one of Franklin's genuinely historical roles was as minister to France.

Frisch's analysis is detailed; only his overall interpretation can be touched on here. He interprets these stable data as the stuff of legend, as tapping into the popular culture, rather than school learning. At the most, students might have been exposed to some of what they 'know' here, in grade-5 American History; but the point is, they have been exposed to it over and over from stories, media presentations, conversation, and from a constant reiteration of what is barely true and questionably significant.† The students know figures of an "almost

---

*As in general do experiences that have causal or deterministic qualities. There are many visual illusions, for example, where one body seems to impart motion (or direction, etc.) to another. Knowing it is not so does little to change the perception on the part of the observer.

†The 1944 AHA commission's test of general knowledge revealed that adults 'knew' that Thomas Jefferson drafted the Constitution. Wesley, *American History*, 8.

exclusively political and military cast, focused on epochal events," the figures reflecting the "civil religion." It is a kind of "cultural imprinting" at the national level: it appears (the evidence is thus far slight) not to vary with the region of origin of the student, or to have much to do with the amount of history taken in school. Frisch says that it reflects the "presumption of newness" at the core of the American myth (cf. American exceptionalism, discussed above), and that in these understandings "myth must be understood as the driving force behind history" (p. 1,143).

On one level, the results show that, as so many suggest, something is wrong with the condition of history in the United States: "The almost childish character of the revealed pantheon seems quite consistent with the diagnosis that we are producing generations for whom a meaningful national history in even some of its richness and complexity is not an accessible resource" (p. 1,150). But what these high-school-educated students carry around in their heads, this culturally common and well-structured American Memory, is *unlikely to have been learned in school.* What has happened to what *is* taught there? Frisch suggests:

> Beneath the huffing and puffing about historical studies lies a fear not dissimilar to that propelling the 'Americanization' efforts that so dominated education and politics in the United states in the early years of the twentieth-century, fueled by a terror of immigrant cultures and concern for the future of the Anglo-Saxon race and heritage. . . . The point of education is not individual but national . . . education and indoctrination— cultural and political—seem almost indistinguishable [p. 1,153].

This analysis, paradoxically, may itself ascribe too much force to the educational enterprise. Frisch seems to be saying that schools simply stamp in lay knowledge. Given the power of cultural symbols, however, all that is needed is for people to talk to each other in society in order for shared memory to be affirmed and recreated. What one learns in school drops away—or if it does produce genuinely curious, reality-respectful habits of mind, goes underground. (Presumably, a request from a professor to generate a list of names will prompt iconic memory; a request to write a paragraph on the causes of the Civil War would yield some attempt at explanation.) The editor of the journal in which Frisch's article appears, David Thelen, comments[82] (p. 1,120): "Memory, private and individual as much as collective and cultural, is constructed, not reproduced. . . . This construction is not made in isolation, but in conversations with others that occur in the contexts of community, broader politics, and social dynamics." He also suggests, quoting Eric Hobsbawm, that the "invention of tradition" is characteristic of modern developed nations confronted with rapid social and technological change (p. 1,126).

If results such as Frisch's are repeated in other studies, the attribution of poor historical knowledge in the population to a supposed 'severing' of American memory cannot be sustained, nor can the situation be improved by a return in the schools to 'our national story.' School history would then be all the more important, but for corrective reasons. As Frisch puts it: "Appreciating the powerful grip of collective cultural memory becomes a necessary first step if we are to help our students to understand the real people and processes of history, to locate its reality in their lives, and to discover the power and uses of historical imagination in the present" (p. 1,155).

11.3   Teaching and Learning in History

The very prominence of History in the schools over the decades and the importance assigned to the subject by virtually all parties, professional and lay, guarantee that the level of contention about history—its purposes in an educational framework, its essential nature as a subject, its 'logic' internally or pedagogically imposed—will result in patterns of teaching far different from those suggested for the elective subjects discussed in previous sections. For school subjects such as Psychology and Sociology, and to some extent Economics, there appears to be an understood agreement to deal with the subjectmatter in one of two or three ways: in a problem-oriented or normatively oriented fashion, or in a survey of the various subfields, a kind of preliminary outline of the discipline. For all the reasons presented in this discussion, that is not possible in history.

Although most teachers of history tend to be trained in that field, the special interests of those not so trained may matter a good deal.* Wilson and Wineburg, in their work on teachers as expert practitioners,[83] have given a nice demonstration of particular 'instructional decision making' for teaching American History, as supplied by teachers trained in political science, anthropology, and history. One teacher believed that what happened and why it happened amounted to the same thing—that is, that an integrated narrative supplied both—while another believed that history provided the facts and other disciplines an understanding of the causes. One teacher was an environmental determinist; others believed that a single event had multiple causes and multiple levels of meaning. One teacher taught the Industrial Revolution as a paradigm for all 'revolutions,' political and economic. Some were resolutely presentist; others emphasized the 'drama of the past.' The authors make the point that certain of the teachers had passed the National Teachers Examination in history with flying colors. "Does this mean that Fred *knows* history? Hardly." They also point out, acutely, that the teachers least trained in the field were using their own disciplinary lenses to *teach themselves* the subjectmatter, to organize history for themselves as teachers—which is why a test, for teachers, of factual knowledge in a teaching field does not necessarily show that the teacher has learned what is appropriate (or thought so by the profession) in instructional approach.

Such a demonstration gives some support to the belief among some historians that, even when history is taught in the curriculum, it may be taught in a

*In contrast, possibly, to the case in Psychology (section 10.0).

disciplinarily skewed way.* So long as schools cannot perfectly calculate how many teachers, trained in this or that way, will be needed in the system for so many courses in a given year, there will be problems with the general idea that teaching would be 'better' if everyone had more academic coursework. The coursework may be orthogonal to the subjectmatter. On the other hand, the Wilson and Wineburg case may be relatively rare: it will tend to happen only in a school whose teaching staff includes those highly trained in the various elective fields. Many studies and much observation tends to show almost the opposite: that in most schools, the 'disciplinary lens' is not the predominant influence on actual instruction. For example, Thornton, in a long and careful piece of curriculum ethnography,[84] looked at different teachers teaching the same 'unit' in U.S. History. He found, as many have, that the intended curriculum was not the curriculum delivered. This applied both to types of content and pedagogical approach. One experienced teacher believed that essays gave students valuable practice in organizing their ideas—but did not assign them because he had not the time to correct them adequately. Another, new teacher found that his attempts to linger over special topics and themes were canceled by criticisms from parents and students for moving too slowly through the stated curriculum. Another teacher put great stress on probing and inquiry, on skepticism; the observer found that it was the teacher himself who did all the probing and skeptical appraisal.[†] Truly to teach for 'inquiry' is not only time-consuming and hazardous, in terms of a teacher's control of the classroom, but is also rejected or resisted by students, even in a 'good' high school. Thornton quotes students in one class as saying, "What he [the teacher] asks us on tests, he doesn't tell us during class," and its complement, "Many things he talks about in class aren't really on the test." Many teachers report feeling guilty about taking time for inquiry procedures, and about demanding work that will not be tested. On ethical grounds, it is hard to blame them.

An interesting approach to history teaching, based indirectly on Piaget, has been suggested by Elkind, who holds that it is cognitively more demanding for students to build knowledge from the raw materials, so to speak, than to analyze and categorize material presented to them—'demanding' in a good sense, at every age level. Thus, the constant differentiating of the materials of history into eras, reigns, periods, places, types of institutions, classes of events, and so on, lends itself to memorization, and bespeaks the endeavor by students to master a topology of knowledge that a teacher will accept. Conversely, working up from evidence to inference to the weighing of all the factors demands scanning, judgment, and the ability to look across categories. In Elkind's terms,[85] "Under-

---

*That is, owing to training in fields other than history.

†Elsewhere I have suggested that 'modeling' of this kind is not without its benefits. On the other hand, some teachers at the high school level, especially in History, seem to be something equivalent to the village anarchist: they seem to be giving a performance about iconoclasm, and showing off a rather stupid kind of cynicism. In one class I visited, the teacher ended the period with, "And what should you always remember?" The class responded chorally: "Never forget the economic motive."

standing concepts based on *similarities* requires logic and reasoning, whereas remembering facts about *differences* requires rote learning."

This position is not new: it is seen in the recommendation of the New Historians (at several stages of newness, actually) to provide students with the documents and with unreduced evidence; in Deweyan notions of encouraging students to find resources in near-at-hand experience; in the emphasis in the New Social Studies on helping students to 'think like' disciplinary scholars. It has the virtue of encouraging students to look for a wider range of evidence, which tends to be one of the advantages claimed for 'bottom-up' social history, and to not cover their trail in reasoning—that is, it preserves the evidentiary level from which higher reasoning proceeds. But it tends to confuse two stages of inquiry, the inductive and the deductive, the research and the interpretation. After all, as was charged against late-nineteenth-century 'scientific' historians, one can amass and organize huge amounts of evidence to prove a foregone conclusion. It also re-creates an error charged against the New Social Studies: the failure to realize that only an *expert* can reason appropriately, in a given field—and that to do it well, one has to know a good deal about the structure of that field. It ignores the reliance in humanistic scholarship on secondary sources and interpretations, and the self-correcting aspect of 'intertextuality.' If history as a field has an 'open' structure, if ultimately plausibility of interpretation is the test, it is precisely the rules of evidence and of reasoning that students, by definition, cannot handle (perhaps owing to cognitive developmental factors, as well as inexperience). Students also do not understand some of the rhetorical or discourse rules that historians use, the reliance on and meaning of phrases like "It must have been," or "On balance, then."*

Elkind, and others, have a point, however, about the power of individuation and personal saliency in encouraging true, and sustained, inquiry—prior to historical judgment. For example, he says (p. 436): "If you want to do some beginning historical work in the early grades, set children to uncovering their personal histories . . . the best way to lay the foundation for a true historical perspective—a foundation that can be elaborated in adolescence—is to build on children's spontaneous intuitions and interests in history."† Elkind goes on to regret that local history, for example, cannot be "packaged for national consumption." The doing of local history, oral history, and the like is of course one facet of recent social history; it is also implicit in the expanding environments

---

*Samuel Wineburg has pointed out (personal communication) how impressed high school students are when they read a personal account of some set of events that opens with the writer saying something like, "I didn't keep a diary, and some of the letters I sent home were lost, but to the best of my recollection. . . ." They take this as the admission of fallibility, and thus proof against bias. A more experienced reader takes it as a signal that: We're not going to be pedantic about facts here; *my* current view is . . .

†Sleeper's studies of adolescents' sense of personal history as distinct from impersonal suggest that a conception of how things might have been different develops in the former earlier than the latter. Epochal events within one person's own lifetime, for example, the assassination of a President or the outbreak of war, serve to connect the two aspects.[86]

scheme, which among other things originally placed state history before American History on the grounds that students would master what was personally relevant or immediate and thus understand national history more easily. (Especially as regards the American periods of settlement and discovery and nation-forming, this works much better for the state of Delaware than the state of Arizona; it is one reason why some states, such as Texas, stipulate that state history shall be taught later.) But there is no necessary reason why local history has to be a microcosm of national, or indeed, world history. In the United States, communications technology and the mobility of the population mean that local history does not feed into national history, as tributaries do to a river, but can coexist with it. Most historical evidence begins as 'local history,' in some sense, and all such material provides opportunities for careful comparison, for testing generalizations, for estimating variability around some central tendency.[87]

We suggested earlier (section 6.0) that it is also desirable for students to understand that civic membership and civic action are possible on a subnational level. Moreover, it is much easier for students to assess the validity of the local story or legend, by a visit to the courthouse or the local archive, than the validity of 'the national story.' The recent development of History Day, in many communities, draws on such possibilities. If, however, local history is to be important in the curriculum, it should not be just as a unit in grade 4. Clearly, the profitable use of primary sources is easier at later stages. Nor should it be restricted to material which is given the flavor of colorful minutiae, or the semireal. With regard to state history, Hoge and Crump[88] comment: "The backdrop of pioneer history is often left hanging in the past as the narrative leap-frogs through several hundred years into the present. Little treatment is given to entire periods of history." In so many ways, local history and social history intersect neatly: in industrialization, the move off the farm,* slavery and immigration, invention and technology, economic growth and regional economic systems. The current desire for a fuller, more serious, less skittish treatment of religion (and hostility to religion) in American life might well begin here, as it has had to in doing the history of ethnic groups.†

11.3.1   Developmental understanding

Only in the past twenty years or so has there been considerable attention to the presumably basic question of what students can (and cannot) understand, at

---

*And rural history itself; 'social history' is no longer taken to indicate largely urban matters.

†Hoge and Crump may be alluding to a somewhat different problem: local history as a storage facility for that which fails to reach national prominence, and thus is selected against in the national story. This, however, can be turned to pedagogical advantage. It is curious, to be sure, that most history involving Native Americans deals with local specimens, long since extinct or remnants trapped in a sociohistorical backwater. There is no early national history organized *around* an adequate account of the occupation of the continent, through time, by the Indian peoples. In saying this, I do not mean to denigrate historical scholarship on particular groups or episodes, but to suggest that such study can petrify them.

different ages and stages of cognitive capacity, about history. As has been suggested, posing these questions usefully, in terms of research, is not easy, since it makes all the difference whether one is interested in the nature or the logic of history as a finished narrative, something to read and understand, or history as a discovery process; chronological history or history as a set of (limited) generalizations to be tested; history as an agreed-upon story or history as a record that will always be frustratingly incomplete.

On the particular matter of the understanding of time by people of different ages, there is now a considerable literature.[89] Much research remains to be done. Suffice it to say here that it is now clear that what once, in the 1950s and 1960s, seemed to be an emphasis on the limitations on possible understanding of 'time,' owing to an excessive reliance on Piagetian and other forms of stage theory in which cognitive abilities appear in strict sequence (especially with regard to the physical universe), has been replaced with a general understanding that young children do understand quite a bit about historical time: the difference between present, past, and future; the one-way flow of historical time; and so forth. They are better with the ordinal than the ratio scale: in other words, they can order events on a timeline, but *how* long ago the seventeenth century was, as opposed to the Spanish-American War or the Crusades, remains vague. They understand that effects do not follow immediately upon causes, in history, and that an abrupt 'cause' can be associated with a gradual 'effect,' or vice versa. There is great difficulty with the idea that certain kinds of processes inherently take longer, or move more quickly or slowly, than others (for example, that 'revolutions' tend to be shorter than 'wars'—and how exceptions prove the rule). Cultural frames for time are hard to understand in school-age children: periods named after persons or prototypical events—for instance, the Jacksonian period, late Victorian; the way we say the sixteenth century but Italians say the cinquecento; the idea that there are 'dead spaces' in history where nothing much went on. The whole notion of *rates of change* in history is difficult, in terms of either inherent dynamics or multiple levels of process, as in Braudel's distinctions (see page 279). Finally, most of us tend to accept history as pastness; but we also think of 'history' as what was important—what made a difference; and these are rather different concepts.*

At the other end of the age spectrum, as regards education, Peel, Hallam, and other researchers in England saw things even more negatively, for those aged eighteen or so, than those who depended reasoned from Piagetian research, typically with children aged about six to twelve. Their research[91] seemed to show that even young adults cannot understand the causal implications of textlike material, miss some of the evidentiary qualifications in such material, and so on. The choice, for their experimental material, of rather densely packed, expository, textlike material was unfortunate: in texts, much is presented in an arbitrary

---

*Perhaps counterintuitively, older children seem to adopt the latter sense, although they are also able to divide up 'pastness' more finely than younger children.[90] The answer may be that older children understand that history is not just a record of the past, but an explanation of what mattered.

order, much 'explanation' is omitted, and many conventions of implicature are deeply ambiguous even to the experienced reader. What Hallam and colleagues may have shown is that textbooks are hard to comprehend.*

Or they may have simply been showing what is the fact of the matter. It takes a certain maturity to understand, genuinely, that things are always in flux; and, especially, that while at any moment nothing is finally determined, the pathways by which history can proceed are not infinite but have been constrained by prior circumstances. The paradox that history helps us to understand the present, but that history conveys no exact lessons for present choice, is something that has bothered the finest minds.

Thus, Hoge and Crump[92] are unduly apologetic when they remark: "The available evidence indicates that formal thinking ability in history is achieved somewhat later than in other areas of the curriculum. If this is indeed true, how do we account for such a result? It seems doubtful that we would be able to argue that the nature of history is more abstract than advanced mathematics or ideas in science." Why doubtful? What can be more abstract than a discipline whose special reasoning requires continual judgment about indefinite matters? From number and set theory in mathematics, one can in principle generate the most advanced propositions. There is nothing like this that generates History. Hoge and Crump give their own answer:

> Formal reasoning in history requires command of a broad range of relatively ill-defined and disputed ideas, concepts, and theories. To deal with the degree of tentativeness and conjecture involved in formal history requires a mature level of knowledge and higher-level thinking ability. Only at the very fringes of research knowledge do science and mathematics deal with such disputed ideas. . . . [Additionally] human beings, by their very nature, cannot easily grasp the passing of time. . . . History deals with lengths of time which, because they cannot be directly experienced, must be defined *by the discipline itself.* History must not only describe and interpret the past, it also is responsible for conveying the *meaning* of time.†

Given all this, it is perhaps no wonder that some historians, like G. R. Elton, suggested that history should not be in the precollegiate curriculum. This is hardly the conclusion that most would draw. It is troubling, however, that a 'return to the narrative,' a dependence on 'a story well told,' is being urged so widely for younger children, when most researchers and historiographers seem to agree that historical narrative itself requires the most sophisticated and mature abilities for comprehension. To repeat once more: the fact that history as an intellectual activity ends with the constructing of narrative need not mean

---

*Conversely, pure chronicles are also hard to understand, for other reasons, including the oddity of delaying the outcome of a story whose ending is clearly predetermined.

†Emphasis added. It is unfortunate that these authors use the term 'formal,' since in cognitive-developmental research this has a meaning contrary to what they intend, referring to decontextualized basic 'operations' that apply generally.

that is where students should begin. The emphasis on 'story' may be quite appropriate for grade 5 History, since that often includes, in practice, the use of literary materials, which are not strictly speaking historical narratives. But even here there is a confusion. One group of researchers into how textbooks convey meaning[93] say, in regard to grade 5 History, "Because history is narrative in nature, the major elements for such understanding are the causes of events, events themselves, and the consequences of events. To the extent that history is narrative, a key to understanding lies in the learner's appreciation of a causal chain of events." Such a view seems to say that grade 5 historical narrative lays out exactly what must be understood in order to comprehend it, which is circular; and it says that learners must have the capacities that many other researchers say they do not have.

At present, grade-5 History tends to emphasize the early political history of the United States, with considerable attention to the texture of experienced social life 'back then' and to the geography of exploration and nation-building. There are many good reasons why it should, having to do with a framework for civic understanding and with what interests children about social life. Grade-11 History, thanks to the efforts of historian-dominated commissions and other reforms, is still political history but has been 'stretched' to include attention to economics, cultural change, social movements, and other processes. The problem with this is that, although it makes for a more complex and socially aware History course, many students have had little exposure to the fields and approaches from which this fuller material is drawn. The 1916 committee's intention to develop a fused Community Civics course about grade 9 may not have been an ideal attempt, but it was meant to provide this kind of background for the high school History course.

Currently, grade-8 History is the most ill-formed and ambiguous of the history cycles: it is both political and social, it tries to center in the nineteenth century but must look backward and forward in coverage, it uses a relentless, through-written textbook narrative without the charm of grade 5 accounts or the depth of the special grade 11 units. Its inevitable superficiality leads students to believe, later, that they have 'had this stuff.' Given Cremin's comments (p. 273) on how a well-developed *interpretation* of history, as contained finally in a narrative, depends on knowledge from and organized by other fields, and given the likelihood that students do not comprehend such a narrative until they know a good deal about human motivation and action, social structures, and the ways of the world, it might ideally make sense to reserve full narrative history until grade 11—making sure that students, between grade 5 and grade 11, had the chance to learn about these other matters. To achieve that, Economics, Sociology, Political Science, and related subjectmatters would have to be investigated prior to grade 12.*

Throughout the twentieth-century history of public education, the needs and

---

*Wesley (see p. 272) recommended something like this. If such a solution is not feasible, the second-best solution might be to organize grade 8 History solidly on topical chronological lines, still reserving the full narrative approach for grade 11.

interests of history have often been set apart from those of the other social studies. However, it appears that the conflicts and tensions *within* history are those *between* history and the social studies—or even of social studies in general. These lines of cleavage go very deep: the one-society frame of reference versus the comparative approach; the national level of explanation versus a deeper, more pyramidal picture; a focus on events versus one on processes and structures; a configural versus an analytic approach; a particularistic versus a generalizing model; cause located in the actions of humans versus nonhuman agencies; cause located in the actions of individuals versus supra-individual social mechanisms; teaching to the needs of the student as opposed to the norms of organized scholarship; education for a common cultural understanding or for helping each individual follow her or his own preferred path; school subjects versus subjects aimed at the transition to higher education; a present or problem orientation versus one that assumes that much understanding gained through education has little direct relevance; a fused versus disciplinary approach; a curriculum built around the armature of one or two subjectmatters, with other material threaded through it, or a neat division of fields; facts versus inference. Reviewing the list, one sees that most of these tensions and choices affect all the fields,* and touch on all the major controversies in pedagogy for the social studies. Even the obvious exception—the role of chronology in history—is not an issue exclusively for that field. One must conclude that the overriding debate cannot be history versus the other social studies. Both confront the same choices.

How both can confront them productively is a question of special importance in dealing with the study of the world. In a sense, when a curriculum dealing primarily with one nation is the focus, all the choices—as difficult as they are—are somewhat constrained. Only one entity, after all, *must* be studied. (It may be desirable, for various reasons, to study English history or Soviet economics, but because that is relevant to the principal end.) When one nation is the focus, one can, in principle, always go more deeply into history *and* into nonhistorical detail.

The same is true, of course, of world study in a surveying or *cataloging* approach. Separate ethnographies, histories of particular world areas or epochs, and other ad hoc studies can accommodate an infinite amount of factual detail. In this approach, world study is simply the set of such narrower studies. An inherently *comparative* approach, on the other hand, assumes a sufficiency of factual evidence. Testing whether patterns and structures and event complexes are essentially the same or different, organizing them into a table along two or more essential dimensions, or summarizing them in a few descriptive generalization, assumes that beyond a certain level more facts are unlikely to count for much (until they force a revision of the framework). An intermediate position is that knowledge about the world should be *systematic*, but within a feasible perimeter: the nineteenth and twentieth centuries, for example, or the Western world.

---

*For example, political science and economics are concerned with the question of explanation mostly at the national level; social psychology and sociology differ on the matter of individual action; and so on.

12.0   World Studies

Those three attitudes—the cataloging, the comparative, and the systematic (p. 297)—correspond respectively to a typological (or ethnological) world history, a structural/functional world-study approach, and an approach based on present relevance. The first assumes that we study the world because it is there; the second, that we study the world because we cannot understand any single segment of it without understanding it, to some degree, in general; the third, that there is much we must know about the world for the sake of our own course in it. All are essentially 'etic' approaches, in that they center on how *we* understand *them* (or *it*).* How (or even whether) other nations should write their own national histories or describe their own societies is not for us to determine (although of course the disciplines have much to suggest about such matters).

The agenda for world history as elaborated by historians (and others) in American social studies has reflected largely the third attitude: what Americans need to know about the rest of the world in order to understand their own situation. Initially, this somewhat opportunistic approach was a reaction against the sweeping, deterministic, large-brush history of the European nineteenth century, where the Idea of History—possibly the defining Idea of the post-Enlightenment—saturated most intellectual endeavors. It was, to some extent, the rational appeal of the philosophes and of Enlightenment-bred positivism, the absence of a sense of long organic development in social institutions, that attracted turn-of-the-century social scientists in America, and caused them—including the New Historians—to turn away from German idealism, historical materialism, Spencerian evolutionism, and the trend in intellectual history toward the historicizing of knowledge. This was certainly part of the 1893 NEA and 1908 AHA efforts (section 4.2)—along with a reaction against the amateur-

---

*An ethnological approach in principle moves beyond this distinction, to show how 'inside' and 'outside' descriptions relate to and complement each other. School curricula, however, do not reach the level of culture theory, in this sense, but at best reach the level of categorizing types of social organization, historical traditions, and so on, from a fixed vantage point.

ishness of much previous ancient and classical history writing. Then, too, the increasing involvement of the United States in its own hemisphere and the emphasis on the image of the western frontier tended to move the framing of attention from a European-centered focus (ranging from Mesopotamia and the Near East to the eastern United States, as a kind of western annex to Europe) to something more nearly trans-Atlantic in focus.

12.1   The World History Problem

When there is added to this the spirit of Progressivism, and the role of public education in that enterprise, it is natural enough to see that early calls for 'world' history—America-Plus would be a more accurate description—were skewed toward the Atlantic fulcrum and toward the present. To a much lesser degree, there has been some interest in comparison as a way to sharpen the 'essential' aspect of the United States as an object of study. This is a blend of the first and the third attitudes. By studying in depth the history and culture of one other society (perhaps chosen as having a particular impact upon one's own) one seeks a contrastive understanding of one's own society. Furthermore, the mastery of one other society's history and culture in principle demonstrates the ability to appreciate any other society, as by analogy the mastery of any foreign language brings a certain metalinguistic awareness.*

The 1916 NEA report[1] sounds what appears to be an enlightened call for the study of other nations as an antidote to domestic chauvinism.

> One of the conscious purposes of instruction . . . should be the cultivation of a sympathetic understanding of such nations and peoples, of an intelligent appreciation of their contributions to civilization, and of a just attitude toward them. . . . This 'Study of nations' . . . instead of focusing attention upon the past, would start frankly with the present of typical modern nations . . . and would use history in explanation of these nations and of clearly defined problems of supreme social importance at the present time. . . . It would help to a truer understanding and appreciation of the foreigners who come to our shores . . . and it would lead us to be more helpful in our relations with backward peoples.

The rationale is highly presentist, and appears to counteract national chauvinism by substituting a strict national utilitarianism. This is not surprising, since the same document has said, very clearly, that the "life history of any nation" is to occupy and use the land and to establish a form of government which will provide the "elements of welfare."

Nor is it surprising that, in the end, the committee recommended nothing

---

*Such an approach is apparent, for example, in the New Trier curriculum during the 1960s and 1970s (section 5.4).

beyond European History as such, together with a sampling of recent history with regard to nations whose actions currently impinged on the United States. Sometime in the 1920s two patterns began to appear: the European-plus-contemporary pattern, following the 1916 recommendation and usually called European History (the 'plus' being understood), and a more culturally conservative pattern among schools that did not like the 1916 reform but could not, as many independent schools did, stick to the 1909 pattern of Ancient, Medieval, European (plus English) History (section 11.0, n 1). The compromise in this pattern was to collapse a three-year non-American history sequence into one: this was normally called World History.

Tryon,[2] writing about 1935, remarks that the idea of a World History course as such "seems to have been one of the many aftermaths of the World War. It has never been recommended by a committee of national scope on which there were any historians."* As we have mentioned (section 2.3), most analysts point to a growth in the number of World History courses beginning especially after World War II and lasting through to today, and associated with interest in area studies, hemisphere studies, and 'world cultures.' That is, to oversimplify, schools believed that they needed some course along these lines, and sometimes found World History easier to fashion than something newer or more multidisciplinary. Further, for reasons having to do with cultural prestige, they found it difficult to offer anything that *omitted* 'history.' Peet[3] points out that the number of courses always was disproportionate to the size of enrollments. In Gross's large 1977 survey of school offerings and enrollments,[4] the percentage of secondary schools offering American History per se was 53, while the percentage of schools offering World History was 51, a trivial difference: however, enrollment in the former was more than twice as great.

Some kind of Contemporary Civilization orientation—to use the title of the famous Columbia College course initiated about 1919—was implicit in the aims of the New History. Van Tassel[5] points out that the emphasis by Robinson and Beard on making the present explicable by history meant that all the lost causes and dead ends would be pruned away in favor of "moving western European man on in his steady progression towards democratic and industrial civilization"—in other words, Butterfield's Whiggism, and an approach that still gave European civilization the central place.

---

*Curiously enough, in an instance of educationalists acting to preserve a high-culture legacy, it was the administrators, according to Tryon, who attempted to preserve "that which was good," in this case World History, when so many new subjects were "clamoring for a hearing." Because the historians did not approve, few textbooks were written. An observer in 1927 (quoted in Tryon) wrote: "It cannot be said that the high schools have really caught the idea of the new world history. Both the courses and the textbooks remain in nearly all cases overwhelmingly European in content and point of view, while the reasons for introducing them are in many cases utterly reactionary . . . rather than any recognition of a World Community or of the need for a new world history. Such . . . practice is simply a reversion to the old 'general history' so vigorously attacked a generation ago" (p. 222). What texts there were, were heavy on Greek and Roman, 'Progress in Democracy,' and Imperialism (the last in connection with the 'cause' of World War I, so Bosnia took on an unusual prominence in the world).

By the time of the 1944 AHA investigation into history, Wesley was saying that the student "must have an understanding of geography, economics, sociology, government, and *particularly world history* if Americans are to approach an understanding of their own history." The rationale is the same—self-referred need—but the Atlantic focus has broadened. "It was not very important for our ancestors in the eighteenth century to know the history of the Far East; it is of greatest importance for us. . . . It seems clear that the intensive study of American history should be *supplemented* by a *survey* of the history of the *more important* foreign countries.[6]

For Strayer, in the 1962 ACLS-NCSS study, Western Civilization itself was an impracticably wide goal. "If a student realizes that the human race accomplished some rather remarkable things before 1800 [sic] he does not need a complete survey of ancient and medieval history. What he does need are a few landmarks, points of reference. . . . It is better to whet the appetite than to sate it." Strayer argued that specialized history courses, while admirable, were off the point: the ideal blend might be for students to "learn something about one early civilization and about at least one nonEuropean civilization," plus a "fairly detailed study of the nineteenth and twentieth centuries" in survey form.[7] Gagnon, writing in 1988,[8] sees what is needed in a much enlarged form, compared to Wesley or Strayer, and is not satisfied with some arbitrary balancing of this much special-locus history, that much survey. He makes the point that "We must widen our focus. American history is what has happened to us and why, *no matter where it happened*"—a classic example being the European dynamics of World War I and its sequelae. Gagnon's emphasis, however, is still squarely on what we need to know. He simply believes that we need to know a great deal more than American historians tended to believe in previous decades.

There was, of course, Toynbee's monumental history of civilization in the 1930s, but many historians (and others) found this an overly Hegelian and empyrean synthesis. Another broad synthesis was done by McNeill,[9] less evolutionary-deterministic in tone than Toynbee, and taking pains to go very far beyond Strayer's bland concession that some remarkable things happened in non-Western civilization prior to 1800. McNeill's is a kind of stretched Western Civilization approach in that it shifts focus from the Western to the universal scale, showing that equivalently dense history *could* be written for any major region (aside from various problems with the record). McNeill chooses to foreground the West against the world, as Gagnon chooses to foreground the United States against the West. In a concise chapter on 'the problem' of World History,[10] McNeill acknowledges that a Eurocentric vision of the past is in principle unsatisfactory. Europe was a backwater before 1450, and its primacy in the world has in some respects been taken over by others since 1950. Further, writing a world history that attempted to capture what men and women perceived and believed in their lifetimes (cf. Himmelfarb, p. 282) would lead to cacophony. Moreover, much large-scale change—even political, social, and economic, let alone climatic or demographic—is visible only in retrospect and from a wide angle of vision. Most important, "World history is not the sum of national histories, and not even of civilizational histories," though he admits that peoples of the world want and will produce both, and that these are valid. Though McNeill does not say so, there is little evidence that he would be satisfied with a Braudel-style approach, with those few individuals and events permitted to mark the landscape being mere "sparks in a cosmic flux."

McNeill's reasonably argued case for what should *not* be approaches to World History poses problems for the schools. For a variety of reasons, to be touched on below, middle-school courses, typically at grades 6 or 7, called World Cultures or Hemisphere Studies are a mélange of history, map and globe geography, cultural anthropology, international relations, and current events. This need not be a bad thing, but the goals of such courses are often confusing, as is the constant realignment of coverage.* Teachers of these courses at this level are more likely to have general Social Studies certification than elsewhere (section 16.0). Courses called World History or World Geography at grade 7 and grade 10 tend to be more recognizable as to the source of their content and principle of organization, and the teachers are somewhat more likely to have a subject major preparation. However, especially at grade 7, these courses also draw on many fields; moreover, especially at grade 10, they follow a Western Civilization—plus current 'hotspots'—organization. (During the 1970s, Africa was 'in': today, the Middle East is 'in' and Africa is 'out.' Latin America seems to be always coming and going.)

In some high schools, one can see a clearcut distinction between a 'history' and 'cultures' approach at grade 10. The former will have a Western focus, by implication dealing with societies that have 'a history,' while the latter will deal with the "history, culture, and current problems of the nonWestern world." The course titles convey the distinction: World History versus World Civilizations. But in a smaller school, or one that does not adopt this convention, a course entitled World History may also have a strong cultural aspect *within* its historical framework. Almost by definition, such a world history course has a less thoroughly political nature than a national history course. In a consolidated (that is, large rural) high school observed in the Perrone study,[11] one World History class looked like this: "Students went over a work sheet on the Dark and Middle Ages they had completed earlier and then heard a lecture that spanned the Vikings, the reasons why Constantinople was a good location for a capital, the difference between the Greek Orthodox religion and those of the Western world [*sic*], and the characteristics of Gothic church architecture." This is a case where the label World History does not seem to impart any special clarity of organization.

Many high-school teachers report that World History texts are written at 'grade-12 level' and are hard for tenth-graders to read. That is one reason why

---

*A sixth-grade teacher said, "Latin America has been in and out of my syllabus so many times I always have to ask at the beginning of the year."

some states, such as New Mexico, are moving toward World History taught in the last year of high school. In this case, students probably do not labor under the impediment of believing that they have 'had' the material before, as in high-school American History. Instead, the material seems complex and strange, especially when organized in parallel chronological chapters (sometimes within an ancient/modern pattern, or one that is organized by some scheme of 'stage of civilization' or development). Many try to hold together the breadth of material by a threading-through of worldwide comparisons at selected moments: for instance, at the time of Christ, or 1000 A.D. Almost all texts try to provide cross-cutting strands or themes: technology, the arts, religion.

Despite these various organizational devices, however, most World History texts are examples of the 1899 pattern with a Western Civilization overlay. Publishers' data from 1984[12] showed that World History teachers expected to spend most time in the course on modern Europe and contemporary world history—in essence, the recent background to current events, defined as impor-tant by American perceptions. Beyond this, they spent considerable time on a chronological forward coverage of ancient and classical civilizations and medie-val Europe, and then turned to particular regions of interest. Comparatively little time was spent on the Renaissance and Reformation or on the European epoch of empire and revolution. The kind of correlation called for by Strayer or Gagnon, in which aspects of world history particularly relevant to the various periods of U.S. History would be presented in an orderly fashion, a kind of World History Background to U.S. History, is not a strong option in texts (although some teachers report that they bring this organization into play in class).

The World/American alternation of focus may increase in popularity if states follow the proposed California Framework for History and Social Studies. In this pattern, the variety of subject matter now taught in grades 6 and 7 would be constrained by providing two years of World History—with another year (as in present practice) at grade 10. The interdigitating of world and U.S. history is reasonable, in terms of chronological alignment.*

Grade 6	Ancient Civilization to About 500 A.D.
Grade 7	Medieval and Modern European History, to About 1789
Grade 8	U.S. History, from About 1776 to 1914
Grade 10	Modern World History
Grade 11	Recent and Contemporary U.S. History

Special attention is to be given throughout the world history sequence to the development of democratic philosophy, traditions, and forms of governance around the world; and geography is to be a major element. Thus, the pattern of

*Many teachers, however, find the back-and-forth procedure confusing for students, and the chronological alignment inadequate. The basic problem in realization of the scheme may be the separateness of the individual courses and lack of year-to-year carryover.

1899 is to be recaptured, but with a tighter relationship to the history of this society. Conceivably, the links now apparent in grade-10 World Geography (when that is taught) to economic and social structures and holistic cultural descriptions will suffer, since in the California format a largely political and intellectual history seems to be anticipated. One question that arises, as noted above, is whether presently trained teachers can handle the material. In addition, the linear view of time, the focus on what Americans need to know about their own history, and—most acute, to some—the lack of any framework for the study of *problems affecting the world itself*, that is, the 'world system' in its economically, socially, and ecologically interrelated complexity, will bother some historians—and many others.

The California design comes tantalizingly within reach of what ideally might be the perfect solution: a sequence of three or four years of world history in which, at the appropriate times and without special spotlighting, U.S. history emerges as an embedded figure, a resident image of particular force, within the world design. In this way, if it were done well, the American story would carry its own narrative integrity, as in Italian painting the central figures and the historical meaning of the Flight into Egypt make their way (to those familiar with the story) across the canvas with only the subtlest pictorial guidance. Such a treatment of one history within a comprehensive history would be an example of the second possibility for the study of the world, as suggested at the beginning of this chapter: seeing one segment take shape within a larger composition. That this can be done is evident in some works of world history, such as McNeill's *Rise of the West*, and in many monographs that deal with one dimension of history, for example, exploration and colonization in which early America is embedded. That it is seldom if ever done in schools is probably due to the conviction among all parties that the national history should receive 'framed' attention, other material being carefully cropped out.

It is not yet possible to look to the university for guidance, since the same ambiguities and frustrations exist there. The universities seem to have abandoned an area studies framework for world study without having yet found any single common pattern to put in its place. A prospective teacher will certainly be able to take one survey course, either in Western Civilization or in World History. The former appears to be losing strength in terms of academic fashion, but is still very strong in the liberal arts colleges. It is not yet clear what the latter will be. It is often a survey of selected national or areal histories, which orients the history major toward a rather deep sequence of specialized histories— Africa, Far Eastern, Latin America, and so on, sometimes cut by earlier and later periodization. This is of little use to the prospective history teacher, who has time for only one or two courses in addition to American History; conversely, the history major who has taken three or four courses in the specialized fields, or a distribution across them, may not want to teach a one-year high-school course that follows a superficial survey approach or a Western Civilization one.* With

---

*A teacher thus prepared may not be very good at the necessary synthesis and simplification.

university enrollments dropping in history for a number of years, (see table 16.1), it is hard to see how the schools will staff more extensive (or intellectually deeper) World History courses if they move to institute them.

Any essentially political and ideological world history* poses the problem of imposing our own categories on others' histories. This is not simply a matter of intellectual ethics, but one of practicality or adequacy of description. As many have pointed out, the very concepts we use—for instance, of nation-state and political process—do not apply well to the authority traditions of central African peoples, or nonsecular, sometimes transnational, societies. The political boundaries and labels we are comfortable with—such as the Near and the Middle East, the Dark Ages—are not recognizable *as historical realities* to many of the present-day peoples with whom we have to deal.† Even the maps we use in textbooks and in the classroom are problematical: do we show the Falklands or the Malvinas? In any case, many of the world's peoples are engaged in political and economic action that decisively ignores (or denies) the history that texts, accurately enough, contain.

The enormity of the task of constructing a world history that does reach into the sociopolitical present, the multiple present, and the interactive multiple present of other societies inevitably has a restraining effect on much curriculum thinking. Can the schools, with any degree of rigor and responsibility, really do much more than teach about one society—in some combination of basic factual knowledge and unifying values of citizenship? There are more than one hundred and fifty nations today whose history ought to be understood—but why by Americans? Does not the possible fading of America as a singular hegemonic world power, or at least the obsolescence of the First-Second-Third World schema, imply that much that goes on in the world is not our affair? Is anything really possible other than a watchful awareness of what impinges upon the United States? That attitude, a mixture of practicability and ethical prioritizing, is seen as early as 1966 in this comment from the Council for Basic Education, the back-to-basics organization founded to further Arthur Bestor's ideas for reform (see section 5.1.1 and in reaction to the One World thinking in some sectors of social studies): "At the heart of the desire for reform of the social studies* is the conviction that an understanding of citizenship and the values of democracy, and an understanding of the peoples of other nations, are not directly teachable matters but are products of knowledge—ordered geographical knowledge, knowledge of the history of one's own country and of the world, knowledge of how government functions."[14]

Here it would seem that, from within a national vantage point, one can study

---

*Ideological in terms not of specific bias but of reliance upon a Rankean kind of accounting for intellectual or philosophical patterns and currents across peoples and eras—i.e., using terms such as 'spirit of the Age' or *Weltanschauung* or 'national culture.'

†The most forceful expression of this view, with regard to scholarship on this part of the world, in recent years is Edward Said, *Orientalism*. See also Bernard Lewis.[13]

‡I.e., the CBE's desire.

the past of others but not their present attitudes and actions. Few other statements could so clearly emphasize the special purpose assigned by some to 'social studies' as an exclusively precollegiate-level enterprise. Students are to master the basics. These basics may include world history and descriptive geography. There is no occasion for them to inquire into such fields as cultural anthropology or comparative government or economics. This can be justified on the grounds of practicability. There may be a need in the society for persons who understand Thai culture or worker participation in factory-level decision-making in Yugoslavia. But there is no need for the schools to produce them. In the same way that covering, within World History, some hundred or more national political experiences is pointless, so is a huge ethnology of others' ways of life.

Other aspects of the CBE statement, however, imply that much of what is done in social studies in the middle school and junior high school is actively wrongheaded: for example, world-regional geography (with its 'situated' knowledge of economic and social activities) or hemispheric history (with its multinational, culture-area emphasis). It is true, much middle-school teaching in general is aimed at a transnational social perspectivism, the attempt—without going beyond the state as the principal actor in world affairs—at least to establish variation of behaviors, attitudes, and goals as a fact of life among the world's societies taken together. (For example, a long and interesting list of what human geography may attempt, at this level, is contained in Winston;[15] here, grade 7 Geography is overtly intended to act against portraying the home country and people therein as inherently the most fortunate and advanced; suggesting that the discovery, or even exploration, of a place does not occur until Westerners arrive; implying that the world centers on North America and Europe by using maps aligned this way; selecting the most exotic aspects of a foreign culture for special attention; the use of such concepts as 'modern' or 'developed' in a facile and uncritical fashion.) What the CBE statement ignores is the possibility that true perspective on social reality is gained *only* from a thorough knowledge of another culture or period, or comparative study at a systematic level. '*Autres temps, autres moeurs*' is a slogan, not a form of understanding. Bohannan makes the argument for a noncataloging ethnological approach[16] when he emphasizes that culture has a historical facet: "If you try to make World History the sum of its parts, it is so complicated that it probably cannot be done at all. But if you make it the story of the development of culture pattern, it is fairly easy."

It is the limitation of an ethnocentric categorical framework *together with* a resolutely past orientation to the experience of others* that will bother those who are concerned with a broader framework or with what they claim to be a qualitative shift in the situation of the world. The world is moving on, and real-world agenda are forming. What about Europe 1992, they will say? What about the Islamic revival, from North Africa to Southeast Asia? What about 'global

*Though for the sake of a fuller understanding of our present and future, curiously enough.

interdependency' in social and economic terms? What about linked activities across national boundaries that go on through nongovernmental means, whether multinational corporations or citizen action toward environmental improvement? What of the North-South concerns and cooperation that are so evident in the Eurasian world, so missing institutionally in the Western Hemisphere?

12.2   Global Systems and Global Studies

The farthest contrast to World History as the context for domestic study* is the proposed analysis of the world as a global *system*, an interactive dynamic whole. This concept, common enough among some sociologists, economists, and political scientists (and some, by and large not cultural, anthropologists), claims a higher level of analysis than the comparativists, in these disciplines, of the 1950s and 1960s, or those who have been interested in areas and regions.† The claim is an assertion about *actuality*, not simply a desirable form of analysis. That is, the first part of the argument says that communication patterns have truly changed, so that people are globally linked; that trade flows and currency exchanges and stockmarkets now operate at a new level of mutual impact; that investments, profits, and taxes are not all contained within the same national or regional framework; that the movements of people in very large numbers across boundaries is highly significant, both socially and biologically; that technology and productivity must spill over national barriers; that labor and consumer markets can be dissociated (in ways different from the imperial pattern); and so on. The claim is that these amount to qualitative differences, major shifts in the history of the world comparable to such large developments as the nation-state, modernization, or the demographic transition. (Whether such developments are of the permanence or importance claimed is of course a task, ultimately, for 'world historians.')

There are others who are as yet uncommitted as to the extent of such dimensions of change, but who are nevertheless concerned with some of the same phenomena in a more limited context of present global *interdependency*. They are not sure that 'the system' has shifted to a radically new level of integration, but they believe that the old categories and dimensions of experienced life are breaking down.

Persons in either group may now be interested in the concept of 'global citizenship,' on philosophical or on pragmatic grounds. This is particularly interesting for the curriculum of American schools, because it does not correspond to any neat division between historians and social scientists. World historians who go beyond a Western Civilization approach may be engaged in considering whether modernization theory or demographic transition theory is 'true,' or to what extent. So may sociologists of the Weberian tradition, or

---

*Which almost everyone would agree is at all times legitimate, if not the ne plus ultra.

†See section 8.0, on 'culture regions' in geography and related fields.

economists trying to discern what might come after the neoclassical synthesis. Soon after 1900 both historians and other social scientists were concerned about developing a curriculum for effective American citizenship; it was not the case that historians, ipso facto, had one view of citizenship and sociologists and economists another. So it may be today, but with a major limitation to the analogy: scholars of any discipline may put these changes in the world at the forefront of their study, and may be interested in the concept of 'global citizenship,' but hardly anyone has more than the sketchiest notion of what that might amount to.

Moreover, one can be interested in a metaphorical or superadded notion of 'global citizenship,' as something over and above primary citizenship but not canceling it. This is important, since recent discussions of global studies in the schools have been denounced as inherently unpatriotic. Similarly, one can be interested in the notion of 'a good citizen' in global terms, while not taking seriously the idea of a radically new historical dimension in human organization. This would describe cultural and biological anthropologists who desire cross-cultural knowledge and respect but not assimilation; those concerned with mutual security and new forms of international (but not supranational) cooperation; those who desire a richer knowledge on the part of all the world's peoples of international relations; social psychologists concerned with reducing inter-group hostility and tension, without disturbing the definition of 'group'; and many others.

In summary, the concept of global *system* is largely an analytical construct of the kind that is familiar to social scientists generally—with historians likely to be less interested in it than others. If it proves generally useful—as it already has, for example, to some geographers and some ecologists—it will become an accepted concept. The reality of *particular* dimensions or degrees of global interdependency will be largely a matter of empirical investigation, requiring the efforts of all the disciplines, certainly with historians much involved. There is, for example, a distinct Whiggism, and perhaps disciplinary bias or selectivity of the evidence, in all claims along the lines of 'the pace of social change today is (obviously) much faster than ever before in human history.' And the image of global *citizenship* is as yet a philosophical or practical vision, with little theoretical and no empirical force.

Finally, with regard to the school curriculum, Global Studies can mean something as conventional (educationally speaking) as a fused anthropology-geography unit for grade 6 or extra attention in U.S. History to international politics. It can mean something as extensive as a magnet high school in which each subjectmatter is deliberately turned away from the micro level or the domestic range of reference to at least a comparative, if not a worldwide, scope.

There are such schools, just as there are some states putting special emphasis on non-American material of all kinds. In each case, there may be a certain trendiness involved, a response to national concern about America left behind in the world. One high school visited recently adopted a Global Study curricu-

lum because it was the only way that the principal could see to persuade the
school board to permit a school to be organized around the several social studies.
The school is a great success, one of the most sought-after of the system's magnet
schools. It enjoys a close cooperation with nearby universities and an active
World Affairs Council chapter, and offers superb teaching. The school curriculum involves world-oriented study for all four years; U.S. History at grade 11 is
angled toward America-world relationships. Students must take one foreign
language for four years, and may take even more foreign language. (The order
of popularity of languages is Spanish, French, Chinese, Japanese.) It does give
one pause to learn that, less than ten years ago, the same school was an arts
magnet school. What will it be ten years hence?

It is important to realize that many courses in U.S. History at grade 11 are
organized around recent and current events and trends, with U.S. circumstances
examined in relation to trends and events elsewhere. Thus, if what is desired in
global studies is a general awareness of broad factors involved in America's
future course in the world, there is in principle no reason why U.S. History
cannot provide this.

A comparative study of national history textbooks might show whether other
modern Western societies, less blessed or afflicted with an attitude of 'exceptionalism' or more continually involved with other nations in their national histories,
do not organize every period of that history in a framework of international
relations, at least as nearby nations are concerned. Some studies of comparative
education have found all history texts in modern European schools intensely
chauvinistic; for example, studies cited in Nelson.[17] But this does not mean that
attention to other nations has been missing—quite the contrary. However,
factual knowledge about other nations, learned in the context of studying the
national history, may not transfer to awareness or interest on the part of the
student in current developments in the world generally. On this phenomenon,
Torney-Purta has provided data drawn from Western European societies.[18]

A problem may be that if earlier American History courses have not done so,
such contexting may be difficult to introduce at this level. In a very large urban
high school, two grade 11 U.S. History courses were visited in the same day. In
one, during the review period at the beginning of class, the students seemed to
remember nothing about U.S. foreign policy: not the Monroe Doctrine, not the
Open Door policy, not how the United States acquired Alaska. The grasp of
chronological placement was very shaky. (The teacher pleaded that World War
I could be 'placed' in terms of presidents by remembering Woodrow Wilson's
initials.) The class came to life only when, unexpectedly, a discussion broke out
about where city water came from, and when the main reservoir had been
constructed—and once more, when the teacher discussed how the United States
'got' Puerto Rico, which was of personal interest to a number of the students. In
the other class, also grade 11, also U.S. History, in the same school, the students
were preparing for a mock U.N. Security Council field trip at a nearby university.
In this class there was heated discussion, sustained over fifteen or twenty

minutes, about how nations manage to dispossess themselves of seized or occupied territory. Extremely sophisticated concepts were apparent, having to do with retributive justice, the noncitizen status of inhabitants of such territory, and the question of nations dealing diplomatically with shadow governments. Many of the students were doubtful that 'punishment' and 'paying-back' made sense between nations. One student suggested that a nation cannot 'lie' when it recognizes another, since the act of recognition carries a force independent of intention or sincerity.

A sharper contrast could hardly be imagined. The first class was 'learning' about American foreign policy historically, but seemed to have little basis for the study of current issues. The second class seemed to understand such issues well, but with no particular historical frame of reference. Most observers would find the second class far better, from the point of view of involvement of the students, level of reasoning, and so on. But (on the basis of one observation) it is not clear that, had the students in the second class taken a factual test, *they* would have known much about the Monroe Doctrine or how we acquired Alaska. Presumably, the task for World History must be to organize the subjectmatter so that students understand major events and significant dates and processes with reference to each other across national lines, so that some sense of histories-within-history is gained. The minimal task for Global Studies, correspondingly, would be to give current issues, events, and problems some analytical framework that goes beyond the idea of one nation 'having' a problem caused by another—but without ignoring the aspect of national decision-making.

Thinking about who is affected by 'problems'—one, two, some, most, all nations—and whether one nation causes problems for others (as opposed to sharing problems with them) may be a useful way to organize global studies in the curriculum. A foreign policy focus, political or economic, may fit well into an advanced national history format. International politics may suggest a regional systems approach, peace studies a dyadic emphasis—for example, with the study of the national histories and cultures of two nations, or the comparative study of binational relations. Some problems, such as environmental, seem to require a regional-to-world progression. A recent survey of high school teachers in one state(table 12-1) yielded opinions about where—at what grade level and in what course framework—'problems' could be taught.[19]

These data suggest that multinational problems, especially those with an ecological component, are thought of as appropriate for courses with 'world' in the title—*except* where national sovereignty and security interests are involved. The latter move out of a 'world' framework and into a 'U.S.' framework, even though decisions on the part of more than one nation are clearly involved and despite the fact that, logically, one can argue that the best way to study such problems is to remove them, for study purposes, from a national frame of reference.* Such inferences are, of course, complicated by the possibility that the

*A similar argument would apply to the study of 'racism' as a global issue.

Table 12-1 Virginia Teachers' Assessment of When Selected Global Issues Should Be Taught

Issues	World History (grade 9)	World History (grade 10)	U.S. History (grade 11)	U.S. Government (grade 12)
Ecological imbalance/ environmental concerns	70%	23%	31%	50%
World resource allocation	82%	35%	26%	38%
Population growth	76%	46%	40%	47%
Hunger/poverty	74%	46%	41%	48%
Nuclear proliferation	31%	60%	68%	71%
Global human rights	57%	76%	36%	52%
Increasing militarism, revolution, and limited wars	31%	22%	78%	68%
Racism	35%	46%	78%	63%

SOURCE: Dan B. Fleming, "Foreign Policy Issues in Social Studies Textbooks," in Volker R. Berghahn and Hanna Schissler, eds., *Perceptions of History* (Oxford: Berg Publishers, 1987).

teachers, in such a survey, are actually assessing the lack of cognitive demand of the various topics, and relating that to grade levels—thus, nuclear proliferation, for example, ends up in U.S. Government because that is the course taught at grade 12. It is also obvious that questions of patriotism and political sensitivity enter in to the question of curriculum placement. Certain topics that bear on the question of for whom are problems 'problems'—and who cause problems for whom—are most safely discussed in 'U.S.' courses.†

At present, perhaps at any juncture, the systems approach to world study concerns an image or conception of the world, not a tight description of it. The dominant image is that of a unified system made up of a number of subsystems: regional geography or international economics, with its attention to trading zones, functional markets, and so on, are examples. Area studies is another model, although in practice the description of inter-area connections has seldom been made. Beyond this is an as yet shadowy conception of a global society that has properties different from those of its particular parts. For global studies, the thinking here is roughly as follows.[20] The societies-in-isolation perspective, describing relatively closed societies, each with its own history and culture, is rejected as descriptively inadequate. (It is, however, one of the main approaches in the school curriculum—for example, in the selective 'world cultures' coverage of the middle school where anthropological evidence or some aspect of comparative sociology is included.) Next is the statist conception, geopolitical in

†In recent years, American administration officials have said that the schools should foster a national consensus in support of administration policies, and that much called global education was "pacificistic, capitulationist"; see Fleming, "Foreign Policy Issues," 117.

nature, consisting of separate polities with an 'interstate' system that links together and mediates conflicting and compatible national interests. The modern international state system now includes nations other than European ones. A historically earlier form reflected empires, with core-and-periphery relationships. In the schools, selected national histories (not only the domestic history but the histories of the most relevant allies or antagonists), analysis of their national economic systems, and a concern with concepts of citizenship express this model, and thus account for its conceptual preeminence.

There is, next, the world-economy, world-empire perspective, which has no special role for the concept of societies or polities, but focuses on social geography and modes of production and systems of exchange. In this conception, international economics becomes inadequate to describe a complexly linked world system; so does international relations, on the side of politics. There is the tendency to assume a dominant mode of production and hegemonic cycles, in which one core state holds sway for a time (for example, the Netherlands, Great Britain, the United States) and then a period of transition ensues. The implication is that world empires tended to precede world economies, in that political/military control preceded core-periphery economic patterns, but of course the two are associated. By about 1900, a European-centered world economy is described. This view is not explicated in the schools as such, but nevertheless plays an important role. World History clearly describes hegemonic cycles and shifts. The emphasis on 'the American century' or on the U.S.-Soviet relationship in the decades after 1950, as described in coverage of international politics and U.S. History, reflects—and conveys—this image. It is also clearly foreseen in the invention of social studies (and the insistence on the inclusion of some world history) about 1920. And it is implicitly emphasized today, in the concern for educational reform, among those who point to the obsolescence of First and Second World models, the rise of a unified Europe, and the Pacific Basin. Those critical of the notion can claim, with considerable logic, that the geopolitical, statist conception (the second conception outlined here) describes everything that the world-economy model attempts to describe, except perhaps very slow, large-scale change such as that attended to by world history and historical sociology. It is on the basis of such 'neorealist' reasoning (which is also a preference for present empirical knowledge in preference to more speculative modeling) that some who are concerned with the curriculum recommend a continued emphasis on a 'stretched' national history and economics.

Finally, at the most abstract level, there is the growing interest in a global society model. Such a model holds that *actual* interdependence across societies and nations exceeds what is currently recognized, as do human interests and allegiances: in Lee Anderson's language, the contemporary world is a "panhuman society in an early stage of historical development." Many social scientists—historical demographers, historical sociologists, anthropologists interested in patterns of human radiation and diffusion, economic historians, and a number of others—would point out that this process of integration began centuries ago, at least, and is a continuous one. Those who foresee a liminal shift may point to presumptive ecological 'limits to growth' or to a homogenization of culture worldwide as qualitatively different limiting factors, to human problems that cannot be solved by one or a small set of nations, and to the need for a form of governance that expresses supranational goals. It is here that the concept of 'global citizenship' takes on a more than trivial status (that is, involving more than respect and good behavior among those who deal in or with other societies), implying the need to work socially for interests that transcend national goals. In the schools, with particular reference to social studies, a global citizenship conception is sometimes promoted as a logical extension of national citizenship, insofar as that implies the necessary partial subordination of personal, group, and now strictly national interests. Such a view is evident in, for example, Merriam's view of citizenship in the 1930s. The difficulty here is the evidence that 'citizenship' is not well constructed as an image or described as a set of activities and relationships on the national level (section 6.3.3); so long as this is perceived as a problem—for example, so long as students' scores on tests of civic knowledge and attitudes are considered to be poor—the wider conception of citizenship can hardly make progress in the schools.

12.3   Global Citizenship

For the sake of clarity, it seems important that those using the concept of 'global citizenship' try to indicate whether they are using it in a fairly strict sense, as implying actions and attitudes reflecting some degree of supranational law or universal political philosophy (as yet uncodified), or in a looser metaphorical sense, as when someone who shows a spirit of cooperation within an organizational structure is said to be a 'good citizen.' This would be prudent as well, since much of the criticism of 'global education' on the part of American political figures ascribes a deficiency in national loyalty to those who, for example, want to take global effects into account in decision-making bearing on national policy—for example, the consideration of eventual worldwide 'clean-up' costs in industrial policy, or decisions against protective trade barriers on the grounds that they will harm developing countries' export interests. Those who cite the apothegm of René Dubos, To think globally while acting locally, may have in mind working within this framework, or they may have in mind a people-to-people advocacy that will actually limit national degrees of freedom (for example, the 'Green' parties advocating environmental responsibility, or those seeking to persuade their own governments to respect the Universal Declaration of Human Rights). Those who are interested in and highly value cultural pluralism—the multiplicity of social-cultural forms around the world—may wish to act strongly in behalf of the cultural interests and integrity of other peoples while finding supranational mechanisms quite repugnant, in that they limit the freedom of such societies to develop and act according to their own needs. (An example here would be international denunciations by environmental 'good citizens' of the 'cropping' of wild animals, which some societies find to be in their own economic interest.)

In social studies curriculum thinking, an appeal to multicultural study across societies is often linked to respect for multicultural, multiethnic variation within a society. Thus, for example, on the West Coast the study of particular southeast Asian languages and cultures may be recommended on the grounds that, given recent immigration patterns among school-age children, a wider scope of sociocultural curiosity and knowledge in schooling can be built on interest in and commitment to one's own heritage. This may be an excellent idea on many grounds. But it may also lead toward a model of extended cultural identity (on analogy, for example, to pan-Islam or various episodes of irredentism) and cultural action that would imply a cantonal organization of the larger society; and this would by no means necessarily move nations toward a truly 'global' order.

Here, the aspect of political sensitivity inherent in public education, and social studies, is hardly surprising. Historical perspective is useful on all sides in considering the development of global studies. There has always been a tension between knowing about the world as a means of ethnocentric security and as a framework for less culture-bound understanding. Much of the impetus behind social studies curriculum planning in the earlier decades of the century is traceable to a fear, for society, of immigration and the importing of foreign values.* Much of the growth of area studies and world culture studies in the schools beginning after World War II reflected a quite conservative concern for the national security, coexisting with a desire on the part of others for 'international understanding' and One World goals.[21] Efforts today by the World Affairs Council and the Foreign Policy Association, which emphasize the infusion of relevant materials into (primarily) the history curriculum, continue to balance these two attitudes. The discourse of the field changes, as images in society change. The fact that today some forty states have mandated an infusion of 'global education' or 'global studies,' or that New York State requires a two-year high school course sequence,† may *depend* quite directly on a perception of détente as regards American-Soviet relations. The basic *justification*, however, remains that of educational realism and self-interest: as regards the latter, that Americans' lack of knowledge about the world and its people works to the disadvantage of the nation; as regards the former, that as Merriam said in 1934,[22] "The economic and cultural ties which bind the peoples of the earth into a single web are no less real than are the forces of internal evolution."‡

*Theodore Roosevelt, in 1915, told the Knights of Columbus that, "The man who is a good American is the man who is an American and nothing else." Quoted in Michael Kazin, 19.

†The New York curriculum includes two years of study, at grades 9 and 10, of "major areas of the world," focused primarily on contemporary sociocultural and sociopolitical aspects but with historical background.

‡Or, to select just one of many such developments, that rapid urban growth is now localized in the Third World, so the historical relationship between 'modernization' and urbanization no longer holds.

If anything, social studies authorities need to resist unrealistic demands on the part of national leaders and the business community to study 'global' change without a framework for adequate socioeconomic study within the domestic context. This, in turn, raises the question of whether the curriculum should be mostly history—and if so, how to bring attention to contemporary issues and ongoing social change into the historical framework. The consideration of educational realism also amounts to a judgment about whether 'neorealism' or the statist-based description provides an adequate description of how human affairs are conducted. Is there a realistic grounding for the idea of the "global character of human experience"—a conception that need not refer to a person's own immediate perception, but rather to the consequences of others' perceptions and actions, along with one's own? If so, the conceptual clarification or development of the notion of 'global citizenship' might become moot, insofar as the schools are concerned.*

The idea that 'global citizenship' really depends upon such an assessment might persuade some who are still trying to define it to adopt a provisionally open attitude. It is not like Pascal's wager, where the possible costs of being a nonbeliever (in the case described by Pascal, in God), if nonbelief is proven wrong, outweigh the intellectual costs of being, erroneously, a believer. On one side are those who believe that democratic education involves the study of societies that are democratic in their civic culture. In that view, global education takes attention away from the educated reinforcement of democratic values. The recent American Federation of Teachers report[23] thus faults the global education movement for detracting from American students' "ability to understand the role and meaning of democracy in world history." On the other side are those who see *aspects* of the democratic tradition—for example, the inalienability of human rights or some form of the consent of the governed—in most nontotalitarian civic cultures (for example, in democratic socialism) and believe that democracy, largely Western in origin, is increasingly a trend or an option over much of the world. For either side, citizenship could be something to reserve unto ourselves or to export to others. Both calculations are inherently matters of national policy—isolation versus activism abroad—as well as personal conviction. The first level of inquiry in the *study* of extended citizenship might well be a more ethically and politically neutral one: whether parliamentary or presidential democracy works better for some societies, what citizenship means for Jews and dissidents in the Soviet Union, or the role that organized international opinion can play in theocratic societies.

Although this writer is in general a skeptic about technological determinism as it affects education,† there is in developed societies today—and, in principle, in lesser-developed societies—a means for easing into global citizenship in an informal and low-risk way. Thanks to electronic means of communication and

---

*That is, reality will break in soon enough. and Economics will become international, Sociology a matter of world systems, and the like. This would still leave room, as has been noted, for a largely utilitarian extension of a workable definition of enlightened, effective primary citizenship.

†Witness the teaching machine or instructional television.

to the possibility of distributed databases or materials displayed at many terminuses, students can indeed interact with each other and learn from and with each other across national boundaries. They can penetrate others' cultures, to some extent, without the culture shock of going to live within them. Instead of American students doing a classroom research project on Saudi life, and vice versa, Americans and Saudis can collaborate in joint or reciprocal inquiry, and do so in a way that negotiates the terms of the research as it develops, rather than mechanically applying research formulas developed elsewhere. To some extent, problems of translation and cultural meaning can be overcome, in part by building in non-real-time procedures that permit mutual construing apart from or alongside the main interaction.* Age-appropriate projects—the analysis of shared social problems, such as crime or pollution, or the construction of a mapping system that 'works' for both Canadians and Australians—can be pursued over the course of a semester, with a permanent record made of each phase of the project. Such examples merely touch the surface of the possibilities. If corporations would, in their own interest, fund such links (which are not very expensive) and if school systems would, for educational reasons, permit them, radically new forms of cooperative, intercultural, distributed, interactive learning could take shape. Not only might this have a very significant effect on pedagogy (replacing book learning-about with interactive mutual learning), but it would go far toward a form of global participation on which 'citizenship' might or might not be built.†

12.4   The Centrality of Culture

The strong attraction toward global studies in recent years, on the part of both educators and national groups, poses a challenge both to historians and to the other social studies disciplines. There is the sense that the real-world agenda must elicit educational change. History, it seems, never quite connects to the present, and uses categories of human and social action that may not capture the emerging situation. The nonhistorical social sciences seem to offer primarily some form of systems theory, which tends to be too abstract to be fully adequate; or they assume the necessary expansion of present forms of disciplinary analysis—which have been constructed so as to pertain primarily to our own society and perhaps similar ones. (Such an expansion of focus will be difficult enough at the university level.)

Scholars at present offer rather modest, partial solutions to this dilemma, whatever their disciplinary background. Van Tassel notes that "when historians have dropped westernization as an integrating theme for world history, the

---

*That is, a separate 'channel' for interpretation, expert judgment, or other gloss or commentary.
†Research in these kinds of networks as "rich learning environments" is being conducted, among other places, at the Interactive Technology Laboratory, University of California, San Diego, by Hugh Mehan and his colleagues.[24]

course has often become an unrelated parallel series of histories of world cultures"[25]; he suggests that 'modernization' might become the unifying theme. Many, however, find that modernization theory is essentially a rationalized description of westernization. McNeill[26] suggests cumulative technology and the growth in size of human institutions as universal processes of signal importance, which is no doubt true but does not capture possible processes now under way involving devolution and fragmentation. Peter Stearns[27] suggests that social history could become the dominant element in world history if it would focus less on a narrative constructed to contain events and build itself instead on "long-term processes of change, on pattern and process in history, on the complexity of social change." How this illuminates the agenda of the present, however, remains unclear.

Others suggest that selecting a thematic area of present concern to many in our society—the role of women in history, the nature of the family, the ongoing urbanization of the globe and the structures of urban life (including 'peasant urbanites'), or the life-history experience of age cohorts across national boundaries—can revivify world studies, partly by bridging the interests of historians and other scholars. This may be true, to an important extent, but in the view of others it leaves the 'definition of the situation' or 'the context of the situation' (to use conceptions suggested by W. I. Thomas and Bronislaw Malinowski, respectively) to what is real to scholars, that is, to what is being 'worked on.'

Whatever new forms of research and scholarship may be needed to deal with social description and analysis on the global level, the trend across the established disciplines, I would suggest, is that of the *semiotic turn*, or *social cognitivism*.[*] This seems to be the emerging master idea that links together historical sociology, human geography, world history and national history, political theory and political anthropology, and many related fields.[†] In national history, there seems to be a confluence of quantitative social history and specialized or local history with political history, via the study of the historical consciousness involved in ideology and cultural identity. On the level of history broader than the national, there is renewed attention, thanks to such scholars as Clifford Geertz and Victor Turner, to the reality of the culture region or cultural ecology. Historians such as Natalie Zemon Davis and Robert Darnton write like anthropologists, and sociologists like Charles Tilly write like historians. Intellectual history (except perhaps in the history of science) tends toward the description of mental attitudes and structures broadly held in societies of many different kinds and eras. In the postquantitative period of the social sciences, Geertz's 'thick description' joins 'the comparative method' as the cynosure of scholarly work. This sketch of tendencies in social thought conflates many traditions and

---

[*]Note that Saussure's definition of semiology (in the *Course in General Linguistics*) was a "science which will study the life of signs *in the midst of social life*" (emphasis added).

[†]The emergence of this 'master idea' may be one aspect of a suggestion made previously (section 9.0), that the subfields of the discipline of anthropology were in the process of merging with their cross-disciplinary affines—anthropology itself evolving into a metadiscipline.

movements. But few would deny the renewed prominence of Culture Theory in the various disciplines of the social and human sciences. For the schools, some years hence, a sense of culture as a truly permeating force, a meaningful presence, in history and in social structure (for example, of *civic culture* as the deeper structure beyond the ascribed or experienced aspects of citizenship) may prove a unifying influence for the curriculum and—for a time—a central focus for social studies.

PART IV

Conflicts and Concerns

13.0   History and Its "Allied Subjects"

"History and its allied subjects" was a familiar phrase in educational writing around the turn of the century, at the time when historians led the campaign for sound public schools beyond the grammar-school level.* At that time, Civil Government was established as a satellite subject to history, requiring to some extent separate treatment. Economics and Sociology, on the other hand, were considered to be subjectmatters that could be handled within a more modern and commodious form of history.

Within twenty or thirty years the sense of an alliance across fields was considered outdated, even provocative, on all sides. Nonhistorians found it condescending; historians found it a snare. Thus Gifford observes: "While this alliance was beneficial in the sense that history was supported as an eminently practical subject, it was dangerous."[1] In this view, by 1916 the horse was out of the barn and history had lost its monopoly. Its allied subjects thus became rivals; the issue thus centered on history *versus* the other fields. In some quarters, that debate continues today.

One can be fully sympathetic with the widely stated desire, today or at any era, for there to be more history and better history in the schools, while rejecting the sometimes associated view that 'social studies' has driven history out of the curriculum. Although there are deeper aspects to the debate than this, to be discussed at several points in what follows, the factual claim that history has been replaced by social studies is based on a semantic misunderstanding or is ill-informed.

Thus, Gifford (p. 10) refers to Ravitch's contention that the "public schools, with their social objectives . . . have largely eliminated history." Lasch[2] refers to history's having been "subsumed" under social studies. Writing in 1988, a university dean[3] charges that the "study of literature has now given way [in the schools] to what is known as 'language arts' while history and government courses have been abolished in favor of social studies." One may regret, with these commentators, that schools tend to refer to congeries of subjectmatters using neologistic or jargonish terms,† while pointing out that other levels of education do likewise, and, more important, emphasizing that history courses

---

*The phrase appears, without comment, in the 1916 NEA committee report.

†Although the term 'social studies' has a perfectly respectable history; section 2.4.

321

have not been abolished or internally destroyed by some social studies phage. Moreover, Gifford somewhat misrepresents Ravitch, who for the most part holds that, for a variety of reasons, history over the years has been watered down or wrongly oriented in its presentation.

The specific charge, of a takeover of the curriculum, should have been disposed of long ago. Edgar B. Wesley, the director of the joint Committee on American History in Schools and Colleges,[4] and his research colleagues looked into the matter with great care. His report (pp. 36, 56–57 especially) makes the point that history, other than the catechismal recitation of names and dates, did not become fully established in the graded grammar schools until late in the nineteenth century. Then, "formal attention to American history has continued in the middle grades," and has been added in the junior high schools. "The rise of the high school witnessed the introduction of an additional course in American history. The feeling that this additional course was needed for citizenship training, the influence of the academies and colleges, and additional legislation, particularly in the 1920s and 1930s, served to make the American history course in the senior high school a standardized offering" (pp. 36–37). He then points out that "Prior to 1920 one-semester courses in American history were rather frequent, but by 1934 nearly nine-tenths of the courses in both junior and senior high schools were a full year in length" (p. 38). Citing data up through 1940, Wesley reports: "The evidence is overwhelming that American history is taught in the vast majority of schools in three cycles, and it is certain that nearly all the pupils enrolled in the schools study it" (p. 39). Wesley considered with some care the fact that

> There is a widespread notion that history, particularly American history, is being squeezed out of the curriculum . . . the assumed cause of this assumed calamity is the mere existence of the field of the social studies. . . . The elimination of English history, the merging of ancient and medieval history, and the subsequent substitution of a one-year course in world history for the two-year cycle in European history do seem to imply lessened attention to the subjects. The loss is more apparent than real, however, for few students elected the two-year cycle in European history, whereas world history has become a requirement in many schools. . . . American history has made steady gains . . . in time allotment and in absolute and relative enrollment. . . . Furthermore, American history is receiving not only more formal recognition, but also more attention within other subjects. Numerous topics and units in economics, sociology, government, modern problems, and other subjects draw heavily from history. . . . One may question the accuracy and adequacy of the history learned by this indirect method, but no on can deny that large elements of modern and contemporary history are involved in the study of these topics. (pp. 59–60)

There has been no net change since the 1944 study. Empirical inquiries cited

Table 13-1 Comparison of Social Studies Offerings Versus Exposures During Grades 10–12 for High School Seniors

Course	Percent Attending School Offering Course	Percent Who Have Taken Course
American History	98	98
World History	80	53
American Government	62	43
Economics	65	30
American Problems	42	27

in the present volume up through about 1980 confirm that U.S. History is the lodestar of the social studies curriculum. Study groups and researchers looking into the place of Civics, Government, and law-related education in the curriculum have all made the point that American History is the one subject in the schools in which the percentage of those *taking* the courses is virtually the same as the percentage of those schools offering the courses, or the percentage of those students attending schools that offer them—and this in the face of requirements in most states for the study of other subjects as well. Data from Jennings and his colleagues show very nicely the position of both American and World History, and the difference between them (table 13-1).[5]

An especially revealing analysis of 'exposure' to history generally in the high schools over time is provided in figure 13-1. These data pool together history—

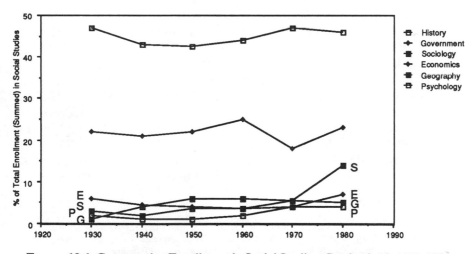

FIGURE 13-1 Comparative Enrollment in Social Studies: Grades 9–12, 1930–1980

SOURCE: Adapted, with thanks, from geographer David Hill, University of Colorado.[6]

that is, the aggregate of American, European, World, and specialized history in the curriculum; they are based on national-level data, where inherent problems in course labeling will almost certainly undercount history rather than overcount it, relative to disciplines more circumscribed in the schools; and they are stabilized, as data, by being expressed as percentages of all enrollments totaled, so that the varying number of those taking social studies courses generally, in any mixture or pattern, over the years is not a factor.

Clearly, history courses have maintained their preeminence at all times, throughout various shifts and trends. The apparently inverse relationship between the strength of History and Government since 1960 is probably not a direct trade-off, but actually represents separate dynamic processes. The principal factor for the broad dip and recovery in the history curve is probably the relative decline of non-American history (that is, European, ancient, and so on) in the earlier decades, and the relative growth of World History and Western Civilization, in the later decades.*

Most recently, in the 1980s back-to-basics movement, the ambiguity about what are basics (at what school level? in the curriculum generally? within each broad area?) has been intensified by the implication on the part of some that those in charge of public education have been pulling back from their commitment to history as a fundamental subjectmatter in education. Such charges take a rather complex form: *n* states do not require a course in history; or, once did but no longer do so; or, still do so but in a different form; or, do not do so at such-and-such a level; or, require it at a certain level, but not for graduation in every case; and so on. Such charges are hard to evaluate definitively. Moreover, as we showed in section 3.1, there are different kinds, degrees, and levels of mandates and other requirements. A state that permits its department of education to set standards may well end up with a more consistent and rigorous pattern of requirements than a state with loosely drafted language 'on the books.' In general, the absence of explicit positive sanctions should not be interpreted as evidence that anything goes.

At least one direct comparison over time can be made. As part of the 1944 joint history inquiry,[8] the committee reviewed the educational law and established practices of all the states. It found that of the then 48 states, 46 required American history (by law or by action of the state department of education) in both elementary and high school; one additional state required it in high school only. One state had no formal requirements.

The American Bar Association study[9] in the late 1970s found that of the 48 states, 43 prescribed *by statute* the history of the United States. In 1989 we again

---

*In this regard, the historian Hazel Hertzberg, also in Gifford,[7] states that the New Social Studies era cut into the strength in the curriculum of Government and Civics, not History, a conclusion that this figure would reinforce. It should be pointed out that rapid growth of Psychology in the 1960s and Sociology in the 1970s may be misleading, in that many Psychology courses were not social study in nature, and many Sociology courses have been oriented toward current issues and problems.

surveyed the 50 states and the District of Columbia.* Using the same criteria as those of the 1944 study, we found that 3 states had no stated requirements; 46 states required American history courses at secondary *or at all* levels; one state required it in the middle school only; one state required it at an unspecified level. Two of the three (out of 51) entities that did not require a U.S. history course are the most recently admitted states of Hawaii and Alaska; a temporal factor, some secular trend in educational law, may be involved. It would be hard to see a decline in official standards, based on these data.

All of the discussion above in this section deals with the status of history between grades 4 or 5 and 12, where 'courses' can be identified. For the early grades, where 'courses' are not recognized, this leaves open the question of a possible decline in history. Wesley recognized this in 1944 (p. 36):

> The Committee of Eight of the American Historical Association in its report of 1909 recommended that some elements of American history should be taught in every grade of the elementary schools. Indian life, stories of national heroes, special celebrations, biographical studies.... It is certain that the recommendations of this committee were based upon fairly widespread practice and did not initiate an entirely new movement.... Although the historical elements introduced in the primary grades have remained there, they have become more informal and less overtly historical.

Wesley refers here to a mixed pattern for grades 1–3 also documented carefully by Tryon[10] in 1934.

Sometime in the 1870s or 1880s (section 11.1), the 'elements' of American history and its European background became the core of instruction in the earliest grades, replacing geography. The myths-holidays-heroes approach subsequently coexisted with an early form of an expanding environments approach—organizing instruction from the present toward the past, from the immediate surround to the larger social world—supposedly reflecting the native capacities and interests of young children.† Wesley's comment refers to the general belief that the expanding environments scheme gained in prevalence throughout most of the twentieth century; this is certainly suggested by a study of elementary methods texts, and there is no reason to doubt something similar in practice in the classroom. His comment also implies an even broader pattern, also widely noted in actual implementation of the classwork in the early grades: to begin units of instruction with contemporary or near-at-hand phenomena,

---

*The present author, with the staff of the National Commission on Social Studies in the Schools and with the cooperation of the Council of State Social Studies Supervisors. See also table 3-1, and its discussion.

†Although Paul R. Hanna is generally credited with the working out of this approach, its presence in spirit has been traced by many back to 1900 or before. A full exposition of the Hanna approach is given in his 1956 publication, but the scheme was under development by the 1940s.[11]

and then to jump to contrastive statements or phenomena. That is, most teachers do something like the following: "Today we use the car to go to the supermarket—but in your grandparents day . . . and in some countries in the world . . ." Finally, Wesley refers to there being much *informal* citation of historical material, with reference as appropriate to national figures, holidays, and historically founded customs but little chronological history and little sustained narrative. It is in order to attempt to clarify this unstable mixture that the new California framework emphasizes history in the early grades as "the story well told." In summary, it is not clear that instruction in the earliest grades has ever been 'truly historical.' Many believe that it could and some that it should be.

If the share of the curriculum is not the heart of the matter in the long-standing low-grade irritation (which sometimes erupts into something more hectic) between those who are proponents of history and those who espouse the other social studies, there are many other levels at which the struggle goes on. At the furthest extreme are those who on principle are hostile to the social sciences, or to history. These extremes may be interesting from the point of view of cultural history or epistemology, but there is little that can usefully be said about them in the context of reform or improvement of the schools. While a few educational figures who commanded the airwaves in the 1920s or 1930s, such as Harold Rugg or David Snedden, denounced the historical enterprise as the residuum of an outmoded 'high cultural' legacy or as an intrinsically antiprogressive influence, such strident voices—like those viewing the social sciences as the source of all positive knowledge about humankind and society—are today very faint, if heard at all.

Hardly anyone has seriously proposed that history not be at the center of the school social studies curriculum. While an argument in principle can easily be constructed for the notion that anthropology or political theory or sociology might be a synthesizing subject matter capable of occupying the central position in the curriculum, no group has ever spent time or effort developing the case. Quite the contrary: many geographers and economists working in the schools have *preferred* that their subjects be interwoven with history rather than stand alone in separate courses. Those developing instruction in 'law-related studies' during the 1960s and 1970s also believed that the history curriculum was broad enough, practically and intellectually, to contain it.

This preference on the part of 'allied subjects' is not simply a pragmatic one, but reflects either the overriding concern on the part of most educators about citizenship or the unique cultural prestige that the study of history commands. By most definitions of culture or society, the person who knows no history is deracinated, unenculturated, asocial. Further, most adults, in our own society at least, see the accessibility of history as one element in freedom. To be ignorant in sociology or geography or economics means perhaps being a fool; you may send your goods to the wrong market, or spend too much on life insurance and not enough on investments. But being ignorant of history means being a knave, a person who threatens the body social by misunderstanding the choices and the responsibilities of citizenship.*

It is, of course, the case that there was a time when school teachers, insofar as they were educated in substantive fields at all, were educated in history. That is no longer true (see table 16-1). Given the emergence and growth in the universities of the other disciplinary fields, it would be impossible today to staff the schools with history-trained persons only, or to forbid those with other backgrounds to become teachers. This does not necessarily mean that many, even most teachers, especially at certain levels, should not have a solid background in history. One could well argue that most elementary-level teachers should be well trained in that field. It is when we consider *how* to improve world history today, for example, together with the global studies, international economics or politics, and so on, that the hard choices come in the preparation of teachers in the future. Simply returning to history, *tout court*, is not a possible choice.

If we put aside the extreme views, we can perhaps come closer to isolating the real source of problems. If history has always been, and still is, the core of the curriculum, the universally respected discipline (in more than one sense), why the unease, and why the shrillness of the dispute? Put crassly, it is because the schools are viewed as defective. The national test scores are discouraging. In the context of social studies in the public schools, this poses a painful question. If 'kids' today test out as ignorant on factual knowledge—in what century did the Civil War occur? where is Mexico?—what have the History teachers been doing all this time? Some blame might be laid to the teachers of Government or Geography, but hardly the bulk of it. History teachers 'teach' the Civil War, and the Mexican-American War and the Treaty of Guadalupe Hidalgo, and the Constitution and the Federalist Papers and the amendments, and the creation of NATO and SEATO and all the rest, and do so several times over. The texts contain all the facts. The teachers help write the tests, sometimes the texts. Why is it that so much history is taught, and so little learned?

To some extent, history teaching is the victim of its own dominance. If the problem of achievement is a general one, affecting all of education, historians may come in, unfairly, for much of the blame. If social studies is boring, as has often been charged, or if social studies try to teach too much too thinly, the problem is not with history alone. (There is some apparent validity to these charges; see section 17.0.)

But some historian teachers, historical specialists, and educational philosophers have specific intramural complaints—which those complained against

---

*There is a less benign facet of this distinction, in that some may believe that in the more 'scientific' fields, such as sociology or economics, knowledge is indeed differential power and should thus not be widely shared. Knowledge of history, by contrast, yields no such advantage since 'history' is a view of the past that must be culturally agreed upon to have any force in the world.

turn back with vigor on the aggressors. The historians' argument runs roughly as follows. True history is dynamic, configured, dramatic, dense, while social science and its relatives in the schools are formalist, analytical, abstract, bloodless. History is actual, in that the past happened; sociology is virtual, in that it describes relationships and structures that are arbitrarily defined. Social studies have bought into the 'inquiry' mode for teaching and learning, which emphasizes how to approach and manipulate a subject rather than how to grasp the real stuff.* Social studies also tend to value problem-solving and other utilitarian, rather than intellectual, aims. Or (alternately) they teach relativism of judgment rather than deepening and sustaining the shared memory of a society. The social studies have been associated with a fascination for 'process' in thinking, and for seeking to instill skills rather than knowledge. Thus, owing to the particular pattern of development of social studies in the schools, or to an unwarranted vogue for the social scientific attitude in the general culture, or, in a more blameworthy fashion, to the educational professionals who value process over content, method over matter—in fine, for one or more of these reasons, there has been something wrong in *how* history (and other 'basic' intellectual subjects) has been taught.[12]

No one critic believes all the elements of this set of charges (or the corresponding elements in rebuttal). For one thing, they are internally inconsistent.[†] Each dichotomy is a false one; but none is *entirely* false. Discussion of them, to one extent or another, occupies much of the fourth main part of this book. It is also true that history as a school subject and a discipline contains within itself all the tensions and polarized tendencies that are contained within history and the social studies taken together, a theme developed above (p. 297). Finally, it is perhaps true that the scholarly fields are changing, through the dynamics of their own intellectual momentum and through their participation in a changing world, in ways that will eventually make some of the choices obsolete, or at least less forced. This possibility is explored in part V.

First, however, it may be useful to look more closely at the charges, brought in the first instance by laypersons, that objective external indicators such as national test scores show that the schools, and social studies, are now failing. If this matter can be substantiated or laid to rest (or simply clarified), it will be helpful in considering, more deeply, curriculum change and related matters.

---

*This is one aspect of the critiques by Diane Ravitch and others.

†But the passion with which some critics argue some of them is striking. Thus, for example, Finn and Ravitch:[13] "Everything that is worth learning that is commonly found under the rubric of 'social studies' can be taught and learned *as* history, but *only* if it is taught and learned in an essentially chronological framework can the student emerge with a sense of how he and his society came to be what they are" (emphasis added).

14.0   Test Scores and Interpretation

14.1   Knowledge and Attitudes
14.2   What Is Due to Education
14.3   National Assessment
14.4   Looking Behind the Scores

All broad-gauge knowledge testing suffers from technical inadequacies and from problems of interpretation. Knowledge tests (that is, 'achievement' tests, though they may not represent any deliberate achievement) that are written ad hoc or de novo—for example, sponsored by an educational organization, a committee of concerned academics, a national newspaper, or an advocacy group—may not only be carelessly constructed, in the wording and sequencing of items, but are often administered to some adventitious sample of students, whether on a local or regional or national level. The result will then reflect in a biased way the characteristics of those who took the test. Broadly administered tests that do use a representative or carefully defined population may still reflect a structure of knowledge, a set of knowledge items, that does not correspond well to actual educational curricula or processes. That is, the 'fit' of the items to what is actually taught, let alone learned, in any particular setting or cumulatively in one location, may be very poor.*

Even if the results of general-purpose testing are reliable, in the sense that the same test if readministered would yield similar results, they may pose the *compared to that?* problem: there are no comparable results from similar groups in past years, or from meaningfully different groups, to which the new results can be related.

There are even more difficult problems than reliability and representativeness. Tests that do use equivalent sampling over time—for example, on a representative national basis every decade or so—may have problems in item

---

*When tests are prepared and administered at the level of the classroom or school or district, in principle the test items can be related to what is taught there. In principle, also, the scores of one student can be made sense of in terms of some knowledge of that student's background, abilities, and so on. But these 'local' tests have problems of their own. For discussion of school achievement testing, see also section 3.2.

construction: that is, they may utilize some questions that are the *same* or very similar to questions in prior testing, mixed with *modified* items (to take account, for example, of changes in terminology or cultural salience) and new questions. Probably more important, they, like other broad-gauge tests, do not show where 'knowledge' (as reflected in test answers) comes from. Tests of school-age persons, for example, seldom can show that a specific piece of information was gained in school, or in school together with other venues, or initially in school and reinforced elsewhere, or vice versa.*

This ambiguity means that changes in the apparent level or pattern of 'knowledge' between test waves may be attributed to (for example) changes in the curriculum, changes in teaching, the appearance of new knowledge sources (like television versus outside reading), changes in the culture that may affect motivation for learning, or specific factors like a war or a depression. Tests such as SAT and ACT tests, which involve comparable items tested frequently in comparable populations and are administered annually, avoid many of these problems; but then problems with the specific items become more acute—for example, whether a test in successive years uses the very same question or a formally equivalent one, whether the questions are valid 'knowledge items' or reflect knowledge on a more generic level, and so on. As is well known, those who develop standardized tests for education attempt to construct items that do not so much test for specific facts—since students can always be trained to respond correctly to a finite set of such items; that is, learn the test—but serve as indicators of areas of knowledge, kinds of concepts, and the like. Since in such tests quite a broad substantive knowledge area may be sampled using only one or two items, in any given year the 'validity' of an item may count considerably in the score.

All of these problems are to some degree unavoidable. (There are broader issues also: for example, how useful in later life is the knowledge being tested for?) The inherent problems do not mean that tests are useless or that testing is immoral. Here we simply touch on these various aspects of 'knowledge tests' in connection with inferences and recommendations that are made, on the basis of such tests, for reforms in schools.

14.1   Knowledge and Attitudes

In 1987, using a special wave of data gathered (in 1986) with researchers from the National Assessment of Educational Progress (see below) eliciting factual knowledge in history,[†] Ravitch and Finn found the level of knowledge among

---

*Pre- and posttesting within a school classroom or grade can plausibly show that students did not possess, for example, place-name knowledge at one point—and did later. This may argue for the impact of specific instruction, though it cannot prove it. But general-purpose knowledge tests seldom involve this kind of local, before/after check.

†More factually specific and more nearly limited to U.S. history than the typical ongoing NAEP data; thus this study falls into the category of special-purpose national testing.

eleventh graders highly unsatisfactory.[1] Students were inconsistent in their grasp of historical periods and sequences, and in general did not seem to have a mastery of a meaningful chronological historical sequence.   They were particularly shaky, it seemed to the authors, on the important concepts in constitutional history and their implications. The authors emphasized, insightfully, that students can 'possess' certain facts, in terms of recognizing names and slogans, without knowing the fairly elementary concepts—checks and balances, division of powers, and the like—that would permit one to draw reasonable inferences about later history and constitutional questions today.

The problem of students knowing some 'facts' but missing the central points, and of seeming to know some periods and episodes in fairly great detail while having a curiously blank understanding of others, is something that has been noticed in NAEP (and other) national results. It is disturbing to those who believe that everyone schooled in the United States should have a well-configured common heritage of facts, concepts, and principles. However, this is not new. In 1905 the American Political Science Association[2] reported on a test given to 238 students in ten universities, prior to their taking college courses in government.   These were, of course, students from highly 'academic' high schools or academies.   Very few entering freshmen could state what the Constitution provided in regard to the establishment of federal courts; how members of Congress were "chosen"; how the Constitution could be amended; what was meant by "township government" in New England.

In 1920 the secretary of the College Entrance Examination Board[3] found that over 50 percent of college applicants failed the American history test.

In 1944 the joint Committee on American History in Schools and Colleges wrote their own test. Wesley, as usual, put the test in a reasonable context.[4] "Any useful, practicable, and reasonable standard of achievement in American history must be derived, not from what a group of enthusiasts think should be the standard, but from the records of what selected groups actually achieve" (p. 3). The test involved 65 multiple-choice items (shown, together with scores from 'selected groups' in the appendix), administered to 1,332 high school seniors in 22 schools (in 22 states) thought to be representative of all high schools; to students in military academies; to 'representative' social studies teachers; and to adults selected from various civic groups and (by random selection) from *Who's Who in America*. The results were on the whole discouraging. Some 70 percent of those taken from *Who's Who* believed that Thomas Jefferson helped write the Constitution.   On the whole, students were better at 'facts' than at simple inferences or at items requiring familiarity with actual political processes. In terms of average performance on all the questions, military students knew a little more than high school students and about as much as typical adults. *Who's Who* respondents and social studies teachers (not all of whom were history teachers) knew considerably more. Those who had taken more history or who were 'superior' high-school students scored a very little bit better than the group as a whole.

Wesley concluded. "At any one level much may be taught, less will be learned, and a great deal will subsequently be forgotten. . . . Even the best instruction will not make high school students perform at the level of their teachers or of persons listed in *Who's Who in America*. This is true, not because instruction is poor or content ill-chosen, but because the human being learns slowly and forgets quickly." In a forceful summary bearing on educational issues surrounding knowledge attainment (then as now), the Wesley report said:

> The Committee does not believe that it is possible to prescribe *the* magic formula by which teachers can fix *the* content of American history in the minds of their pupils for all time. . . . Americans must repeatedly be exposed to their own history in school, in college, and in adult life if they are to know it and use it. The Committee is also convinced that material in American history must be interesting, timely, and pertinent, that the education of the teacher must be improved, and that the student must have understanding of geography, economics, sociology, government, and particularly world history if Americans are to approach an understanding of their own history. Passing a law ordering Americans to know their history, prescribing a unit of American history for all high school and college students, liquidating professors of education, or abolishing objective tests are not solutions to the problem. (pp. 12–13)

In 1976, the *New York Times*, at the instigation of a group of eminent historians, paid for a survey at 194 college campuses of freshmen's knowledge of American history and history-based attitudes toward civic life. The results were compared, descriptively, to a 1943 *New York Times* survey on 36 campuses, with the *Times* pointing out that the questions were not necessarily comparable (though the 1943 test was said to have been much more factual in orientation), and the sampling of students also not comparable.* With all these provisos, the *Times* suggested that overall the level of performance was about the same.[5]

This is an interesting conclusion. The *Times* had concluded editorially in 1943 that students showed a "striking ignorance" of American history; this conclusion was said to have "led to an increase in the required American history courses in high school."† In 1976, although not pleased with the results, the *Times*'s front-page lead was: "A nationwide test . . . shows that (students) generally know the high points of American history but that their knowledge of the details and the context of these epochal events does not run deep. The survey contradicts the widely held view of young Americans as profoundly ignorant of their country's past, but it discloses that they lack the kind of detailed information that historians say they must have to understand either the past or the present."

The *Times* in 1976 discussed the recent trend away from "fact teaching" and

---

*The 1943 test had been a fill-in-the-blanks test, while the 1976 one was multiple choice. The latter method would presumably, other things being equal, lead to better performance in 1976, even correcting for guessing.

†The Times offered no evidence to support that claim.

toward "concept teaching" and "inquiry methods" (citing Fenton's efforts, see section 5.3), and concluded that in the test as a whole it was unclear whether such an approach helped or hindered. Edward Fiske, an experienced education writer, reported that authorities were not sure that more than a minority of students had in fact been exposed to the new approaches, and that some believed that what that amounted to was a change from students being drilled in 'facts' to being drilled on 'terms.' All told, the *Times* report on history knowledge suggests that such test-based comparisons from era to era are almost impossible to evaluate, even on the most facile level: Are things pretty good or pretty bad? Internal evidence in several of the articles on May 3 and 4 suggests that the newspaper and the historians who organized the survey expected the 1976 results to be unequivocally poorer than those from 1943, and, had they been so, they would have been attributed to recent pedagogy and/or the fact that the "nature of student bodies has changed in the last three decades."

A special analysis of the test scores in terms of the college freshmen's intended majors revealed that prospective history majors got 58 percent correct, while math, science, and social science majors got 53 percent correct. Education majors stood at 46 percent correct.* Those who presumably cared more about history knew more—but not by much.

In a special treatment of questions bearing on students' *attitudes* toward the American experience, the *Times* reported that students found materialism, opportunity, and democracy characteristic of "their national heritage," with violence and justice ranked about equally in the midrange, and inequality, repression, and immorality considered uncharacteristic. (The mid-1970s, of course, are considered to be an era of considerable student alienation and rebellion.) Black students downrated the positives more than they upgraded the negatives.

It is difficult to see any good solution to the problem of comparing 'objective' knowledge test results over time, at least with regard to drawing meaningful conclusions about 'the state of history,' for example, in the schools nationally. However, repeated cycles of very large testing projects like the NAEP can be useful, especially when several waves of results are looked at longitudinally. The reason for this is that, by careful item selection and analysis, obsolete items can be removed and roughly comparable items substituted with a fair degree of assurance that the average difficulty of the test cycles has been comparable. (This is, of course, circular, in that through pretesting and other means each item can be assured to be substantively appropriate and of medium difficulty.) If the timeliness and the approximate difficulty of the test items nationally can be controlled, then *subnational* differences appearing on a particular test or over a series of tests become presumptively significant. For the *national* pattern of scores, one could be reasonably convinced that a consistent pattern of improve-

---

*Compare the 1944 joint committee survey's results, reported by Wesley, from social studies teachers—who, however, had been teaching for some years.

ment or decline over several waves meant something about performance in the school-age population, but the reasons for such trends are still obscure. At any rate, this kind of repeated comparable testing is the best that can be achieved.*

The problem with ad hoc national tests such as the Ravitch-Finn 1987 or the Wesley 1944 or the *New York Times* 1943 and 1976 tests, no matter how interesting the purpose of the test and the selection and construction of items, is that the results are essentially uninterpretable. In a recent documentary study, Whittington attempted to reanalyze all the national objective history tests where data were available on the wording of each question and the scores for that question.[6] Whittington realized that:

> The [Ravitch-Finn] study provides no indication whether 17-year-olds know any more or less than anyone else living in the United States today. It also does not suggest how much 17-year-olds know compared to 17-year-olds in the past. Its validity rests solely on the authors' judgment that the questions on the test *all* represent *basic* information about history, geography, and literature that *all* students should be exposed to and have permanently ingrained in their memory and on their assertion that to "pass" the test, students needed to answer 60 percent of its questions correctly. (Emphases in the original)

In comparing the test items across the analyzable tests, Whittington shows that in every case relatively more items are taken from then-recent history, with correspondingly less weight placed on early U.S. history. This means, intuitively, that there will be a certain emphasis on 'the present' (and on the prior history that illuminates it) that shifts from era to era. In terms of test validity, it means that the indisputable essentials of U.S. history become captured in fewer and fewer, and remoter and remoter, items for which exact comparisons can be made. After a point, that is, this set of core items becomes so small and so canonical that the items cease to be indicators of knowledge and become the essentials themselves—names, dates, places, key concepts that the culture insists are nonnegotiable. At this point, there are easier and cheaper ways to assure that such 'knowledge' is mastered than broad-scale, expensive national tests.

Comparing across the analyzable tests, Whittington concludes that the Wesley 1944 test had 'harder' items than roughly similar tests from the 1960s and the Ravitch-Finn 1987 test. These latter tests were apparently equally difficult: that is, on most items about 60 percent of the respondents got the correct answer, whereas in the Wesley test 35 percent correct was the most typical result. This obviously cannot be taken to mean that students' performance has declined. Wesley and his colleagues did not, on balance, view 35 percent correct as a national scandal; Ravitch and Finn viewed 60 percent as bad news. Whittington's study can only create cautions in the minds of those trying to interpret such

*Without dropping the basic assumption that the test items *sample* desirable *kinds* of knowledge, and moving to tests which simply ask for a specific, finite, set of performances on the part of those tested.

tests—cautions that appear to be important to keep in mind in debating and establishing policy for the future. Even where test items and data are still available, reanalysis proves hardly feasible. The testmakers and analysts were not prescient. The data do not provide the answers to the questions we wish to ask, let alone the questions investigators two decades from now may wish to ask. Some stones are not worth lifting.*

14.2 What Is Due to Education

An elaborate, cautious, and methodologically sophisticated study of the level of knowledge in the U.S. population at different ages in different periods was published in 1975 by survey researchers Herbert H. Hyman, Charles R. Wright, and John Shelton Reed.[8] By assembling and reanalyzing the responses to a multitude of knowledge items originally included in surveys conducted in many populations over the period 1949 to 1971—involving, *in toto*, some 80,000 people, broken into groups ranging from those who had been enrolled in school or college at about 1910 to those most recently enrolled—the researchers were able to approach a definitive answer to several related questions, all of which lead to one generalization: every U.S. generation in the century showed that formal schooling had positive lifelong effects. The more schooling, the more knowledge—especially of formal 'academic' material, even allowing for length of time after completion of education. The better-educated did not forget relatively more than the less educated; conversely, the greater real-world knowledge (for example, of current events, which could not have been learned in school) displayed by the better-educated was in part 'primed' by staying in formal education longer, not by native intelligence. There was no evidence that being educated up to a given grade level at one point in the century counted for more subsequently than the comparable exposure at another: that is, no evidence that the greater inclusiveness of public education over the decades attenuated educational effects (at any point in later life), or that the range of ability in schools, over time, had a direct effect, or that any dominant style of

---

*These rather negative conclusions are not altered by a recent report from the National Assessment of Educational Progress of scores obtained, in a regularly scheduled wave (1988) of U.S. history testing, from a subsample of grade 11 students using some of the same items administered in the Ravitch and Finn study in 1986. Little change in the level of factual knowledge was apparent, in either direction. The Ravitch-Finn results were reported in 1987. Even with the considerable amount of publicity paid to their report, one would hardly expect major improvement in a year or two; had better scores been obtained, one would still need evidence that teaching styles or syllabuses or textbooks had indeed altered to begin to believe that school history had changed for the better, and would want to see such scores continue in future years. The overall U.S. history results from 1988 NAEP testing of students at grades 4, 8, and 12 (the national sample) are interpreted by the project as showing that American students have considerable factual knowledge, but in most cases lack the ability to interpret and think deeply about historical information and ideas. This is the same conclusion drawn from 'knowledge' tests in previous decades. It is difficult to imagine that any other conclusion will ever be drawn.[7]

teaching or 'culture of the schools' mattered consistently. Nor could lifelong knowledge be attributed differentially, across eras, to learning taking place outside the schools (for example, by military service or the entry of women into the workplace).

It is a unique study, worthy of very careful attention. As soon as one thinks of a possible flaw (in the admittedly complex and inferentially traced argument), the authors demonstrate that that factor cannot have made a significant difference.* All in all, the Hyman study is perhaps the best empirical evidence against the idea that there was once a Golden Age in the schools when real teaching and learning took place, when the curriculum was rigorous, and when the motivation for lifelong learning was ordinarily bred.† Nor was it ever the case, within the period covered by Hyman and associates, that 'in school' learning was crucial, compared to learning outside (or vice versa), or that there was a sharply defined minimum (or maximum) of school-learning needed for living in society.

The authors conclude, rather, that the "better educated have wider and deeper knowledge not only of bookish facts but also of many aspects of the contemporary world; that the differences [in level of schooling] override obstructions and endure despite aging, and characterize individuals who represent *several* generations and *several* historical periods in the functioning of the schools" (pp. 58–59, emphasis added).

The large number of surveys over the years upon which the Hyman study drew tended to use knowledge items involving public affairs (current events, names of foreign leaders and world figures)—which by definition would tend to be period-specific—and 'academic knowledge' in various content areas, especially history, government, geography, authors of classics in literature, and basic scientific data.‡ The latter kind of knowledge would tend not to 'date.' (A limitation on the study is that concepts were not tapped: there were no items on the nature of relativity, how fluoridation works, or what freedom of speech really means theoretically.) In certain civics-related areas of 'academic' knowledge— know five cabinet positions, understand the electoral college, recognize the Bunker Hill war—the data tables for the early 1960s, later 1960s, and early 1970s show essentially the same pattern. At each era, people ages 49–60 in the population know more than people aged 25–39, for example (consistent either

---

*The study could not, however, deal with factors logically *prior to* schooling: that, for example, the 'value-added' effects *of* schooling may apply only so long as natively intelligent or 'educationally motivated' students go to them. This would be a rather trivial conclusion, in any case. Furthermore, since the study included those in school in the late 1960s, when schools had become quite inclusive, any model for how schools have recently collapsed in educational quality would have to select factors specific to the 1970s or 1980s.

†The study makes it clear that 'academic' mastery in the humanities (broadly construed) *is* partly cumulative, so that the more one learns the better equipped she is to learn more and remember much of what is learned—but such a pattern was provided to those seeking it in the 1940s and 1950s as well as the 1920s and 1930s.

‡The planet nearest the sun; diabetes not contagious.

with additional education or more exposure to learning generally, the latter being more plausible).   In *each* age range, those with higher educational attainment know more, on average, than those with lesser attainment (that is, those who are college graduates know more, factually, than those with only elementary school education). This finding is as expected. But it offers no support for those who might assume that the typical 60-year-old person in 1970 who completed eighth grade about 1925 knew more (in 1970) than a 40-year-old who completed eighth grade about 1945, for whatever reason (better schools in 1925, a more intelligent or academically motivated school population, a greater incentive for lifetime learning in the 1930s than in the 1920s, etc.).

With regard to civics-related knowledge covered in schools, there are data from the Purdue Youth Opinion Poll on civics knowledge and attitudes from the 1940s to the 1970s. Elam[9] compares some results of the 1951 Purdue study of high school seniors (that is, the class of 1952) with data obtained for 1983, in both cases involving a similar number of students sampled nationally.* On nine more or less comparable factual items, the level of knowledge in 1983 was no worse, possibly a bit better, than that in 1951. In comparing attitudes across the two cohorts toward basic civil liberties and freedoms guaranteed by the Bill of Rights (where at least the questions are strictly comparable), Elam found a mixed result. The 1983 students "agreed more closely with the founding Fathers" than the 1951 students on principles such as freedom of public speech and assembly, but were less 'correct' in their expressed attitudes on police searches without a warrant, denying legal counsel to criminals, and accepting constraints on religious freedom. In 1951, relating 'correctness' of attitudes, as judged by Purdue political scientists, to the level of factual knowledge (presumably within the group, not within individuals), it had been found that the better-informed held more prodemocratic and anticommunist attitudes. However, those who had taken civics and government courses were *not* more 'correct' in their attitudes; the effect of taking such specific courses seemed to be to polarize attitudes, causing some to hold positive attitudes strongly and others to adopt antidemocratic views. Such a relationship was not tested in 1983, but other studies besides the 1951 Purdue study have found that knowledge of the mechanics and form of government are not positively related to holding democratic or liberal views (see section 6.3.3).

Recently, a study by political scientists of the American public's factual knowledge about civics and government[10] related the level of current knowledge among adults (as gathered in a telephone survey) to the results of polls conducted between 1945 and 1957. The authors of the study found the public in 1989 "marginally better informed than 40 years ago," in the words of one of the investigators, "and not nearly as much as one would expect, given the increases in formal education." The interpretation is interesting, considering that others

---

*This study falls into the category of a series of comparable testing 'waves' over time, but there are so many methodological difficulties that the results should have no more than 'snapshot' status.

recently have charged that the schools in the past several decades have been doing a noticeably poorer job of imparting basic information about American history and civics. It is hardly necessary to point out that the level of information in the adult public, at any point in time, is not directly determined by what was learned in school. It is also possible that schools did a better job in the past *for a relatively smaller population of students* than they have done recently for a higher proportion of school-age persons now enrolled in school. How this would affect the results of national polling is unclear. (This possibility, however, is not given much support in the various studies summarized in this chapter.)

None of these ad hoc studies over the years, conducted for different purposes, can prove much of anything about the *quality* of history and civics knowledge gained in education over the years, or disprove the hypothesis that such knowledge was deeper, more coherent, more culturally important at some eras than at others. Taken together, the studies clearly demonstrate only one thing: *that the level of achievement in the recently schooled or the educated public has always been inadequate, compared to an ideal standard.* Unless and until such a standard can be determined that will suit all critics and hold over a considerable period of time, it will be difficult to blame one or another set of shocking test scores on the performance of the schools in a particular set of circumstances. Ideal standards, even something approaching an ideal, are valuable to try to agree on, and there is nothing to say that standards for the schools should not alter over time, as cultural and societal needs change and evolve. Those who would absolve the schools from blame, on the grounds of unrealistic or shifting expectations, are as shortsighted as those who believe that the Golden Age of public education was the moment when they were educated (or, often, the generation just before that, to which their mentors wistfully allude). We now have some insight, however, into why the schools have always disappointed the public and why, in Hofstadter's terms, the 'educational diatribe' has been a constant feature of American life. With the steady growth of testing for educational achievement, apparent since the 1920s and at full flood today (section 3.2), diatribes typically appeal to, and argue from, test scores. Whatever *they* may mean.

14.3   National Assessment

The National Assessment of Educational Progress is a very large national survey of knowledge, learning skills, and attitudes (especially in the area of civics), conducted since 1969 by the Educational Commission of the States and recently under the auspices of the Educational Testing Service, Princeton. In each wave of testing, which covers a particular broad curriculum area, staggered so that each broad area is tested every few years, results are obtained from 50,000 or more nine-, thirteen-, and seventeen-year-olds in school and from a sample of adults in the mid-twenties to early thirties. To a considerable extent, the NAEP repeats questions in each wave of testing, so that some direct indication of change in level of knowledge is possible. Like other broad-scale testing, the knowledge displayed by the respondents cannot be attributed directly to schooling. (That attribution is perhaps reasonable for scientific facts, for example, but less so for reading comprehension and related skills or for attitudes toward citizenship, both of which are strongly affected by out-of-school learning and practice.)

In the first social studies assessment, administered in 1971–72, there was, of course, no prior baseline to compare results to, but some interesting patterns in the data were nevertheless observed. In general, what the test-makers regarded as important *skills* (obtaining and interpreting information) and *attitudes* (e.g., the worth of the individual, or First Amendment rights) were more stable and higher-scoring than *factual* knowledge. At age nine geographic knowledge was stronger (in terms of this test's items) than historical; thereafter the order of factual knowledge tended to be political, historical, economic, geographical. Insofar as it could be determined, out-of-school knowledge played an important past in the results, especially with regard to skills and attitudes. The combined Social Studies NAEP has never been repeated; thus there can be no direct estimate of change in students' competence over time.*

Citizenship/civics has been tested repeatedly, in 1970, 1976, 1981, and 1988. A very rough summary of the 1970 results would be as follows: factual knowledge of government, civic processes, rights and duties, and social complexity increased across the tested ages. In some formal specifics, seventeen-year-olds knew more than adult, but adults were more in touch with procedural aspects than students. The factual knowledge seemed shallow, showing competence with terms rather than with concepts. Political-social attitudes seemed to be more nearly fixed at the younger ages than factual knowledge, with increasing sophistication being largely verbal.

In the 1976 data, discouraging trends, for the most part, were seen in the data from ages thirteen and seventeen. Both factual knowledge and 'correct' attitudes showed generally lower scores than in 1970, although the later results showed better scores for racial understanding and international issues bearing on world peace. Social studies educators were discouraged, in that political knowledge and attitudes showed a steeper drop than that shown in other curriculum areas in NAEP testing across this period. Mehlinger[12] concluded that high-school students "tend to be unaware of sociocultural forces associated with political behavior. They are largely ignorant of the relationship of social

---

*The reasons for failure to repeat social studies testing are obscure. The NAEP was, of course, intended to track domains of knowledge over time. As mentioned above, a special history testing occurred in 1986, and citizenship attitudes/civics knowledge testing has been repeated several times; see below. Although NAEP officials acknowledge that social studies are part of the 'core' curriculum, they appear to have difficulty, perhaps related to outside pressures, in deciding exactly what subjectmatters lie at the core and what prominence to give, in this broad area, to inquiry, reasoning, and decision-making skills. Butts alludes to this problem.[11]

class to differences in influence and power among different groups of citizens. And they are unfamiliar with the informal political processes that characterize such governmental organizations as state legislatures, city councils, and Congress."

In general, in 1976 scores for knowledge declined more than scores for attitudes. Furthermore, there was no evidence on a national scale for increased participation or personal involvement (such as is possible for students) in political matters or affairs—discouraging, given the Twenty-sixth Amendment, which in 1971 had given eighteen-year-olds the vote. Knowledge and positive attitudes were quite strongly related to the educational level of the parents, suggesting the importance of factors beyond the school. On the other hand, those who reported having taken courses in which active discussion and deliberation were emphasized (and perhaps training in fact-finding and evaluation) tended to score better.* Tentatively, it appeared that the kind of classroom interaction and style of teaching and learning in this area of curriculum might be important, especially in depth of factual knowledge and inference from facts (as opposed to basic attitudes).†

The period from 1969 to 1976 was a highly volatile time in American civic life, from the winding down of Vietnam to Watergate. Various studies and polls showed that the degree of trust in political institutions and leaders in American life declined throughout the period. The voting rate fell. A growing cynicism toward the media as a source of reliable information was measured. Observers of the NAEP trends could point to these factors as contributing to the decline. Others suggested that the movement (in some schools) to a more analytical, conceptual approach to social studies in the late 1960s and early 1970s might have caused a drop in understanding. (If so, this would have been opposite to the intention of the New Social Studies educators, who aimed to bring about a more deeply thoughtful, logically connected set of understandings, rather than superficial, largely terminological, knowledge.) Some took heart in the trend toward greater knowledge of legal rights and the necessity to protect such rights among the accused, and an apparent growth in racial sensitivity. Butts, however,[13] remarks that credit for the first, at least, of these trends might have to be shared between law-related education programs and television police shows.

In 1981–82 the NAEP assessment again focused on citizenship and civics knowledge, adding more social studies 'content' to the battery of questions (that is, specific knowledge in history and government) without altering many of the questions administered in the first two waves of citizenship testing. There was

---

*Neither relationship should be viewed as causal in a simple way. That is, for example, students from more politically/socially aware backgrounds may have been tracked into classes with more participation and discussion, and may have been more generally motivated to read and discuss political matters widely.

†This finding tends to go against those studies that have found that explicit instruction in politics and civics is counterproductive; section 6.3.3. It becomes important to separate *amount* of instruction or class time from the *style* of such educational exposure.

also an attempt to probe more deeply into information-gathering and communication skills as part of the learning process (and as part of participation in society generally). Educational critics and reformers associated with the 1980s 'back to basics' movement questioned this alteration in the design of the NAEP,[14] believing that it reflected the testers' overvaluation of independent thinking, which might be regarded as moral relativism. Be that as it may, the 1982 results showed an increase in scores for ages thirteen and seventeen, especially in those items testing factual or low-level conceptual knowledge. The gains were small, but like several other testing indicators scores, they were turning up at the end of the 1970s and beginning of the 1980s—just at the time when concerned reform groups were viewing schooling, definitely including social studies, as being on a downward slide.*

The relatively sharp decline in NAEP citizenship/civics scores in the 1970s should not be overinterpreted. Nor should the smaller upturn in more recent years. The 1988 results are inconclusive (see p. 203). On the other hand, the NAEP scores for various subject and educational skills areas have shown very complex patterns since 1969, and a great deal of regional variation. There is no one area on the national level that shows steady decline; even most reading measures, after a period of decline, have recovered somewhat.[15] NAEP results have been useful in the schools, in that—since the broad objectives in each of the tested areas have been made public, together with many of the repeating test items—schools and districts have been able to ask themselves how well their curricula and their own internal assessment procedures match those of the NAEP, and perhaps make some limited inferences about their own frameworks for judging educational performance. That is, they can see how NAEP defines reading-related skills or math performance and judge how they, as schools or districts, measure their own aims and accomplishments. They should not, however, take NAEP *scores*, reported nationally or regionally, and assume that these scores pertain specifically to them.

Much the same is true of trends in the Scholastic Aptitude Test and related tests, and in their interpretation. Overall trends in scores (for example, national or regional) can be indicators against which more specific sets of scores (for example, in districts) can be evaluated. In the words of Stedman and Kaestle,[16] "Standardized tests reveal national trends, and the problems are a national concern. But the solutions must be largely local."† Stedman and Kaestle review recent trends in knowledge and skills tests at various levels of schooling (achievement tests) and for college admission, and conclude: "The big decline is over. It ended sometime in the late 1970s. . . . the National Commission on

---

*For some evidence from about this period on political knowledge and attitudes among the U.S. school-age population compared to those of other developed countries, see section 6.3.3.

†However, see section 2.2.2, where it is argued that local solutions are becoming less feasible. A disquieting recent proposal is to make NAEP scores available on a state-by-state basis, which could lead to invidious comparisons and 'solutions' at the level of the individual state.

Excellence in Education, with its dire warnings of a nation at risk in 1983, was about five years too late" (p. 204).

14.4   Looking Behind the Scores

The technical interpretation of standardized test scores is extremely difficult. There have been many elaborate analyses of changes in test-taking populations (especially important in college entrance tests), changes in the curriculum and teaching approaches, attitudes towards education (for example, supposedly pervasive teacher-student hostility in the 1960s or 1970s), and many other factors.

There is fairly general agreement that some *portion* of test score declines in the 1960s and early 1970s was due to the increased heterogeneity of the school population, but that only a fraction of the decline can be so attributed. The phrase 'increased heterogeneity' can be used as a euphemism indicating the presence of more lower-class, poor, black, or Hispanic students, or students with 'nonacademic' motivations in the schools. It is not a totally rebarbative usage: one of the central responsibilities of U.S. public education has been precisely to bring such students into school and provide them with a coherent and useful education, and it is important to be continually clear about how 'inclusive' the schools really are.

With regard to tests, however, the concept has an even broader, and more technically neutral meaning. Tests employ a relatively few items, of which only some really discriminate among levels of competence. The selection of items, with regard to the perceived curriculum and the obtained distributions of scores, and the 'norming' of tests generally, is always post hoc, and each item on each test carries with it the weight of many psychometric, and broader educational, decisions. That is, test items are a very narrow sample of a very broad reality— cognitive, educational, social, cultural, and so on. *Any* increase in the number of distinct patterns of and in the educational experience—whether owing to the kinds of students, teachers, schools, backgrounds, motivations, expectations as to progress through the grades and the curriculum, access to school-related resources, out-of-school experience and learning, classroom 'climate,' or a host of other factors—*can* affect scores from even very broad-gauge tests, not so much in their mean level as in their stability and in the orderliness of trends over time. It is a very complex and 'noisy' system to be tracked by a few test items.

One particular argument offered for test score declines, that of the 1983 National Commission on Excellence in Education (which held that the "curricular smorgasbord" or a "homogenized, diluted" curriculum accounted for the scores), is internally inconsistent and difficult to evaluate. Other things being equal, a "homogenized" curriculum would stabilize test scores, though the average difficulty of the test items might be driven down over time. A true "smorgasbord" might have few obvious effects in the short run, since the variety of educational experiences would tend to cancel each other out.

What may be especially true of social studies is the presence, perhaps growing, of a wide range of *patterned* variation in the educational process and experience—and a pattern that is not detected.* The argument among some educators that grade-level achievement tests, for example, do not 'capture' the true spirit of conceptual understanding, the facts-cum-attitudes teaching said to be typical of social studies, may miss a deeper reality: that there may be an unusual degree of relatively stable but disjunctive procedures in the entire social studies enterprise. Thus, with regard to Civics, even under the same course labels and using the same textbooks, some classes may be consistently aimed at factual or descriptive knowledge, others at 'correct' attitudes, still others at understanding broad concepts (such as constitutional principles) within the chronological developmental story of history. There may be elaborate 'tracking' of students across or within sections, according to supposed ability and kind of motivation. Some teachers may consciously select one manageable and compatible set of goals, while others try to meet inherently conflicting ones. Some may approach Civics with enthusiasm and a deep range of knowledge; others may dislike the whole business, or fake it.

It is not that other branches of the curriculum do not show variation, change over time, experimentation, inevitable failure in meeting goals. But some believe that the social studies are *committed* to the perpetuation of multiple conflicting patterns. In mathematics, long division precedes analytic geometry, which precedes calculus. In social studies, geography may 'precede' history, follow it, or be interwoven with it. The three exposures to American history may repeat the same material three times, or divide it up chronologically. Some teachers teach for mastery of facts, others for critical thinking. Civics instruction, we know, is patterned in several different ways.

Educational researchers, in explaining test scores, have repeatedly demonstrated something quite obvious, but important. Scores depend very directly on actually 'delivered' instruction on specific subject matters (or cognitive procedures) that the tests actually test. (This does not of course imply the converse, that everything that is valuable in the classroom can or should be tested.) To take one example, a sophisticated analysis of math achievement in the U.S. schools considered and rejected the importance of many external variables, like family and sociological background, the mix of students, class size, the preparation of teachers, even the globally judged 'quality of teaching,' concluding instead that the most powerful factor was *curriculum intensity*—that is, time on test-relevant tasks, with clearly specified objectives and opportunity for practice and feedback. This study also found that the schools were powerful "distributors of opportunity to learn"—and that, for whatever sets of reasons, some students devoted actual instructional and practice time to the pertinent tasks, while others simply did not.[17]

If it were well understood, almost any amount of patterned variation in social

---

*A detected pattern of variation can be accounted for in test score analysis: by size of the school, level of expenditure, et al.

studies—which may be defensible on many grounds—could be taken account of in testing schemes. To the extent that it is ill-understood and undocumented (as to its extent and nature), and to the further extent that it is concealed or unconsciously 'denied' by those in the schools (not excluding the students, at some level), so does it become a serious problem in judging the actual outcomes of schooling and the true achievements of students. This will affect not only the interpretation of test scores but the understanding and appreciation of social studies in general. If this is the case, then optimism about (for example) civics scores turning upward, or the recognition that the Commission on Excellence was in some respects behind the times, is facile and of little ultimate consequence. In succeeding sections we consider some of the evidence that social studies may be so ambiguously understood and so thoroughly multiple in approach that the favorite charge of critics—that social studies is muddled, unclear as to its purposes, unstable as to its procedures—may be justified.

15.0 Goals and Expectations of the Schools

15.1 Public Expectations
15.2 Students' Views
15.3 Teachers' Dilemmas

Observers and students of American education will generate any number of sets of descriptors for the multiple goals and purposes of public education. At a minimum, and stated simply, the schools have always pursued for their students the goals of Cultural Continuity, Intellectual Orientation, Reflective Thinking, Technical Capacity, and Personal Adjustment—variably blended at different levels of education and in different eras.

Of these, Cultural Continuity and Technical Capacity are virtually cultural universals: all schools enculturate students and prepare them for somewhat differentiated adult roles. In a culturally homogeneous society, the process of Personal Adjustment in the young may occur conterminously in schools and the larger society, so that schools have no special role. However, in the United States today some suggest that the society as a whole is so fractionated that family, neighborhood, and community are diminished entities, and thus that the schools no longer can 'adjust' students to life, beyond some minimum.[1] For American education, some have denied that Technical Capacity is an important purpose, decrying 'vocationalism' as a threat to other purposes or, recently, suggesting that the occupational and technocratic needs of the society alter so rapidly that schools cannot effectively prepare students for adult life in this regard. Indeed, American schools can be viewed as keeping a very high proportion of the young *out* of adult society, in particular the occupational realm, for as long as possible. Finally, while few have thought Reflective Thinking to be a trivial or inappropriate educational goal, its unique character vis-à-vis the more widely accepted Intellectual Orientation has been unclear. Some intellectuals and men and women of affairs alike believe that Reflective Thinking is something done by philosophically minded persons, later in life and on their own initiative.

In discussions of the curriculum per se, Personal Adjustment and Technical Capacity are often omitted from consideration, on the grounds that they are nonintellective in nature. This is unfortunate, since a close look at the actual

345

curriculum—meaning what is taught in the classroom as well as how courses and units are organized and labeled—reveals that facts and concepts relevant to the former are a substantial part of elementary education, while only a narrow definition of 'the curriculum' in secondary schooling implies that subject matter learning has no technical purpose. That it does is evident, for example, in recent calls for increased foreign language education, where the explicit rationale includes more effective marketing of goods abroad and a better basis for international cooperation.

A recent selection of broad goals "that underlie universal public education in a free society" has been given by the American Association for the Advancement of Science, in connection with a large study of science education.[2] Their stated criteria are Knowledge for its own sake, Illumination of human meaning, Improved success in individual work and the economy, Increased social responsibility, and Enhancement of the experience of youth. We see here, as conceived by American scientists, a familiar configuration, except that Cultural Continuity per se is missing. Though missing explicitly, it is presumably not excluded from the 'illumination of human meaning' or from 'increased social responsibility'— but with a more universalistic emphasis than is often the case. (Closer analysis of the full AAAS text reveals that Reflective Thinking is included in the first goal, especially, and to some degree in the second.)

In social studies as a branch of the curriculum, Reflective Thinking has been the subject of endless discussion and of perplexed debate, not only in regard to its relationship to intellectual orientation but also its relationship to Cultural Continuity. In the former relationship, a special period of attention was the era of the New Social Studies; in the latter relationship, the discussion centers in citizenship. Social studies has also been concerned with Technical Capacity over its entire history, with regard to both the spirit of 1916, with its emphasis on practical modern competence, and Social Science electives such as economics, sociology, and geography—subjects that train students, especially in applied areas, for occupations and roles that did not exist in earlier times (for example, econometrician, survey researcher, computer cartographer).*

The distinguished educational researcher, John Goodlad, has written about many of these goals and distinctions, and has gone on to point out that different *sectors* attend to different *aspects* of public education. He writes:[4]

> We have, it seems, extraordinary faith in education and grandiose expectations for schools. We expect schools to teach the fundamentals, expose students to the world's knowledge, socialize them into our ways of governing and conducting economic affairs, develop their thinking talents, and 'civilize' them even when we as parents frequently feel unable to do so.

---

*There have been elaborate analyses of the various approaches or traditions within the social studies, which generally tend to collapse technical capacity into other categories. Two of the most detailed, thoughtful, and best known are Barr, Barth and Shermis, and Morrissett and Haas.[3]

Yet successive waves of disaffection for schooling concentrate almost exclusively on the small piece of academic shorelines we measure with achievement tests. When push comes to shove, is all the rest of the terrain of schooling irrelevant or insignificant? (p. 468)

For a majority of people (i.e., nonparents and parents whose children are not in school), whether schools are satisfying places for the students who attend them is largely irrelevant or of passing concern. . . . They want schools to contribute to an efficient work force, provide employees who can read, graduate a steady stream of qualified applicants to universities, keep pace with schools in countries where we sell or hope to sell goods, and so on. . . . A drop in scores calls for a hard-nosed dose of discipline and fundamentals in schools (p. 468)

Parents, that large but nevertheless minority group, may share some of these perspectives . . . but most are interested in quite different things when it comes to the specific schools their children attend. They respond cognitively to public opinion polls on schooling and tend to give the schools low marks, but they respond both cognitively and affectively (and more positively, usually) to their own children's schools. What a relief it is for a parent to be able to say to friends and relatives, 'Terry just loves school.' When matters come down to the relationship of child and family to the local school—down to what matters each day—the rise or fall of SAT scores becomes irrelevant (p. 469).

Goodlad's Study of Schooling, involving in-depth study of over a thousand classrooms and published in 1983, made some headway in sorting out the expectations and assumptions of different groups. The research revealed, for example, that parents, on the average, viewed decision-making in their schools as proceeding in this order: superintendent, board, principal, teachers. Parents would prefer this order: principal, teachers, superintendent, and board—and express the desire to prevent higher-level administrators from 'passing the buck.'* Goodlad admits, however, that "we have no thermometers comparable to achievement tests for measuring clients' satisfaction with their schools." Furthermore, it is not always clear what decision-making addresses. Superintendents and school boards

may be remarkably uninformed about conditions in the local schools but attuned to newspaper reports of declining SAT scores nationwide. . . . the message they often transmit to teachers is 'back to basics and more discipline.' The tap is be given a few more turns—regardless of whether the pipes are frozen, leaking, rusted, or have been carried off by vandals. . . . it is a message teachers hear and to which they tend to respond— in ways that assure relatively little change in their classrooms. (p. 469)

*And, presumably, from simply invoking national trends or professional practices to justify their own preferences.

The implication of Goodlad's last comment needs careful consideration. There is a large body of educational and sociological research showing that 'the system'—like all systems—is impervious to reform and slow to change. The general implication tends to be that teachers and others in the schools protect their own territories and practices. This may be true, descriptively, on the side of the functioning of 'the system.' But Goodlad also says that teachers attend to calls for change. There is a great deal of evidence that teachers (and others in the schools) *do* continually reassess what they are doing and what is being said about the schools, and that locally they come to a rather stable accommodation between their professional conduct and the nature and desires of the community. Thus it is possible that, at a given moment, external pressures on the system are widely registered but that only local modifications are forthcoming—the national picture altering slowly, and more at the level of rhetoric than of practices. If this is an accurate description, it may result from a pattern of input that is so diverse and contradictory that the system cannot track and respond to it. It raises further the possibility that those most directly involved in the actual process of education—teachers and students—may experience signs of confusion, strain, and conflict and, eventually, a kind of numbing or alienation from that process itself.

15.1   Public Expectations

Partly reflecting the tendency toward local accommodation, and perhaps owing to the general respecting of local control of the schools (an attribute changing quite rapidly today; section 3.0), there is very little empirical evidence about what different groups (and sectors and regions) expect of schools. The data from polls and surveys that do exist are of very approximate validity, because of the shallowness and variability of the questioning.* Another common problem is that respondents are not tallied as to all their possible roles and interests: a person can be both a taxpayer and a parent, a teacher and a parent, and so on.

Bearing that in mind, Gallup Polls over recent years show similarities and lines of cleavage of opinion that are worth noting. When asked in 1984[5] to rate the importance of certain educational goals, both the U.S. public and teachers showed a mixture of *kinds* of goals, the former more so than the latter.† For the public the highest-ranked goals were as follows: to develop the ability to speak and write correctly; to develop standards of what is right and wrong; to develop

---

*For example, polls that ask, Which of the following purposes of public education are important? will produce results different from, and not comparable to, results gained from asking, Rank the following purposes from 1 to 5. The same is true when what is being surveyed are courses, problems of the schools, and the like.

†N.B.: the respondents were rating specifically worded statements put to them, not generating the goals.

an understanding about different kinds of jobs and careers; to develop skills needed to get jobs (for those not planning to go to college); to develop the ability to use mathematics for everyday problems; to encourage respect for law and order. Skills, moral training, and career preparation tended to be near the top (interwoven as to rank). The development of motivation for learning and other broad intellective goals tended to receive midlevel rankings. Goals concerning life adjustment (for example, to help students overcome personal problems) and what might be called adult realism (e.g., to develop the ability to live in a complex and changing world) tended to be next. Goals pertaining to particular areas of the curriculum, be they social studies, the arts, or science and technology, came close to the end. (No doubt this last, low ranking reflected in part the narrowness of the stated goals, including the fact that these goal statements might not, for example, be as applicable to elementary education as some of the higher-ranked ones.)

Teachers, in the same poll, ranked basic learning skills high, as well as goals relevant to developing intrinsic intellectual motivation. In comparison with the public, they downranked career goals, aspects of life adjustment, and aspects of moral training sharply. Teachers ranked math *skills* as highly as the public, but ranked mastery of specific subject matters—science, computers, social studies—much lower than parents; that is, relatively speaking, teachers valued broad approaches to content more highly than factual mastery.

These are typical results. A Gallup poll in 1986, asking a rather different question—Why do you want your children to get an education?—showed consideration of careers and financial security first, with broad considerations of specific knowledge, active and morally desirable participation in society, and life adjustment far down the list.[6] A very similar question, asked by Gallup in 1972,[7] had produced comparable results, although considerations of a happy and productive life were nearer the top ranks than in 1986. (Much polling throughout the 1980s on general attitudes in society has shown an intense emphasis on disposable income and status attainment.)

Teachers, based on these and similar results, are skittish about instrumental goals for education (for example, career, keeping up with technological change), moral inculcation, and specific content teaching. They agree with 'the public' that basic skills are crucial, but they value an orientation toward lifelong learning and broad learning motivation more highly than parents.

When asked about essential *subjects* at the high school level—again quite a different kind of question—there are Gallup data from 1979 to 1987. For those going on to college, the public generally expect every student to study math, English, U.S. history and government, and science, with foreign language far down the list, and music and art at the bottom, along with vocational training. For the non-college-bound, the order is about the same, except that science drops sharply, foreign language drops even more, and vocational and business education rise to near the top. Although the questioning frameworks are very different, from both kinds of surveys—goals for education versus essential subjects in high school—the salience of the college/noncollege distinction in affecting results is evident.

When the public and teachers are asked the still different question Where do we go from here? (that is, what changes should we make), very interesting differences between the public and teacher become apparent—as well as striking examples of how question frameworks affect responses. Recall that in most polls, both the public and teachers agreed that basic learning skills were of paramount importance in education. When asked[8] in 1980 whether *more* attention should be given to 'the basics' (here, the three R's), the public agreed and the profession disagreed. School administrators disagreed even more than teachers, while college, junior college, and vocational college administrators *and teachers* at this level agreed with the public—more basics were needed. Such differences across educational levels and between teachers and administrators in the system at different levels are important to keep in mind. It is perhaps not surprising that higher education teachers and administrators want students to come out of the public schools better prepared in 'the basics,' while school administrators particularly, and school teachers also, either feel that enough is being done or that more is not possible. It would be interesting to know whether by now school educators have been affected by external criticism to the extent of feeling forced to agree that more 'basics' are needed. Anecdotal evidence would suggest that high-school educators will be more susceptible to shifting in this direction, since it is teachers and administrators at the lower grades that really confront the problem (if a problem it is). With regard to basic skills, each level in education expects those below to do a better job.

In the same polling study, it appeared in 1980 that educators in general (at all levels) were more in favor of learning about foreign nations and cultures than the public generally. It may be that here, unlike the case with 'the basics,' school personnel are more at one with recent calls among American corporate and civic leaders for broader international knowledge—for the sake of economic competitiveness and America's place in the world—than is the public at large. The analysis of who wants what changes from the schools, and on what grounds, in this area is complicated.*

In the matter of increased rigor in and mastery of basic learning skills, not only do the public and teachers tend to disagree about where we go from here, they sharply disagree on how we take such steps. The NEA/Gallup data from 1987,[9] which result from a poll on *how* to "ensure that students learn the basics," show that the public believes in 'accountability' far more than do teachers. The public believes in more tests at more levels, and in promotion and graduation being denied if performance does not meet a specified standard. Stated more cautiously, the public believes in going further in that direction. Moreover, since

---

*Former President Reagan and former Secretary of Education William J. Bennett, who must be counted as civic leaders, have suggested that a global education emphasis in the curriculum is undesirable, on nationalistic grounds.

there have been local revolts against some of the actual implementing of 'accountability,' there is the question of whether the public puts its faith in accountability for the system as a whole or for each local arena. The Goodlad data show that 'the public' favors a good deal of local adaptation and a voice in the process, and does not want national solutions arbitrarily imposed. The NEA/Gallup data on these and other aspects of quality of education suggest that the public seeks 'standards,' believing that standard-setting itself will be salutary, while professional educators want a more differentiated approach involving various and flexible mechanisms.

The most recent such study available[10] shows that teachers continue to value learning skills, orientation, and attitudes more than factual knowledge, relative to the general public; to resist do-or-die testing for promotion and graduation; and to seek higher-order thinking in their students. The same data show a sharp increase, compared to 1984, of teacher discouragement and professional frustration, and a resentment of the 'accountability' movement. Already-divergent goals show signs of further divergence.

We suggested above, and many assume, that the goals and program of the early grades in public education may enjoy more of a consensus than is true at higher levels. One should be cautious about uncritically accepting such a notion. For one thing, just as the education that children get in the early grades influences and constrains the educational process subsequently, so the needs and priorities of the higher levels are propagated downward from the universities to (or in conjunction with) the schools of education, the high schools, middle schools, and the early elementary level. The basic skills controversy at the elementary level cannot be resolved without reference to the question, To what end, to whose benefit? Does the health of the scientific research establishment require broad math mastery among K–4 students, or a deeper kind of mastery among some students later? To fulfill their role, do the vocational colleges and the universities with professional schools require literacy or specialized knowledge? And if many of those who do now go on to higher education do not do so directly after high school (see p. 154) what intellectual competencies are needed for young adults during the transition?

Slagle's 1959 study[11] used a rather nice adaptation of a forced choice method to ask both educators and noneducators about 'the task' of elementary schools.* Here, unlike studies looking across the several levels of schooling, the public and educators (administrators and teachers) agreed that the teaching of the three R's was the crucial task. Then came developing the "desire for knowledge," followed by the instilling of social skills—chiefly the ability to work with others. Lower on the list were such goals as critical thinking, ethical behavior, citizenship

*The sample size was large, but sampling was apparently not random or stratified, so doubt must obtain about representativeness of the result. Also, 1959 was in a period when there was much post-Sputnik concern about basic skills and rigor in the national interest, which no doubt affected the rankings.

and patriotism, emotional stability, and physical development. Developing a "fund of knowledge" was low-ranked, as was vocational training (not surprising in the elementary context). Only on one dimension was there a sharp disjunction of ranking: noneducators were considerably more in favor of "early identification and training" (that is, of intellectual capacity) than educators.

The last result may seem counterintuitive, but it is fairly typical. By and large it is educators in the schools who strive to achieve the actual implementation, to the extent possible, of the same education for all students. They tend to believe that rigid accountability measures—such as test scores, promotion/nonpromotion, and the like—magnify inevitable person-to-person differences in achievement, while failing to measure many of the important aspects of schooling that most students experience together.*

Some educators, such as testing psychologists, have principled and reasonable commitments to such measures. Even among professional school administrators, there has long been a 'scientific management' purpose analogous to industrial efficiency goals among factory managers. It is also true that 1959 was at the beginning of a laudable era of federal attention to improving the early identification of gifted children and children with learning problems of various kinds. In general, as some of what Goodlad has indicated (above) suggests, it is the parents who are 'practical,' in the sense of wanting their children to receive the *appropriate* kind of personal attention, before the common needs of the group or, through the educational process, the general goods of society are met.

The Slagle data showed clear attitude differences in the public by class and age. Upper occupational-class respondents supported goals reflecting the desire to learn and critical thinking more than those in lower-status occupations; the latter ranked patriotism and moral behavior relatively higher. Younger respondents—as early as 1959—put more emphasis on 'world citizenship,' as well as developing the inquiring mind. In general, the higher the level of education in the public, the more their attitudes were like those of educators. Beyond college level, however, this altered, and public respondents' attitudes shifted toward such goals as the inquiring mind and aesthetic appreciation. The overall similarity between public and teachers as a function of education no doubt reflects, basically, the sharply rising levels of education in the general public *and among teachers* in the middle decades of the century. It is not surprising that the more schooling people in the society receive, the more alike they become in their attitudes toward education. But only up to a point: beyond that point, attitudes that are specific to those with graduate-level or professional education come into play.

If different sectors of the society want and expect different things from the schools (and at different levels in the schools), and if educators in a given district

---

*Specifically, the argument would run, the goal, shared by educators and the public, of instilling a "desire for knowledge" is not well served by elaborate grading distinctions and other indicia that freeze many students into self-estimates and externally imposed categories that act against this.

reach a political accommodation with perceived pressures and expectations expressed outside,* then national polls may be intrinsically an uninformative or even misleading procedure. Far more important would be carefully stratified local or regional surveys, ethnographic enquiries, and detailed studies of local media, school finance referenda, specific power and pressure groups, and the like. With the exception of the last two of these, such studies are rare. They should be strongly recommended at the level of states and regions, especially before educational authorities at the state or district level decide to bring their areas into line with supposed national practices concerning, for example, the curriculum or teacher preparation and certification. This is not to say that local public opinion should dictate what schools should be like; but it needs to be taken into account, and cannot be if it is believed that 'the public' generally holds uniform views on education.

15.2   Students' Views

One group that is seldom surveyed as to their expectations and goals in education is students themselves.† Data gathered in Albuquerque as part of a thorough self-study of the social studies in 1984[13] showed that middle-school educators considered social studies essential, while primary- and high-school educators found it important; parents split between the two descriptions, while students predominantly considered it important, not essential. There was some evidence that grade 5 students were more inclined to 'essential,' which might be an attitude in some sense borrowed from their teachers or may indicate that students become somewhat 'turned off' at later grades. Close to 40 percent of the students at the higher grades accepted the rating, "a good idea, but not essential"; this was a less-positive endorsement than that of any group of educators or parents.

In Albuquerque the various groups were asked for their relative rankings of *goals* for social studies: citizenship, factual and methodological mastery, reflective inquiry, participation in public life, personal development, and the like. The reported data are quantitatively almost impossible to evaluate, since most rankings tended to fall about the middle.‡ Thus the following generalizations are based on qualitative analysis, and do not use the terminology of the self-study document. Elementary level teachers and administrators rated personal devel-

---

*A view shared by most of those who have studied episodes of local agitation or struggles for control.[12]

†More likely, there are such surveys, done within school systems but not widely reported. For a discussion of students' attitudes toward social studies, see sections 17.3 and 18.4.

‡Recall that, in general, particular subjectmatter areas are not highly ranked in goals surveys, nor are social studies believed to deal crucially with either 'basic skills' or vocational preparation, the two (somewhat conflicting) overriding goals assigned to schools.

opment first (a 'basic skills' choice was not an option in the questionnaire). Elementary- and middle-school teachers rated an understanding of American and world citizenship quite high. High-school teachers rated world citizenship high, along with the capacity for social examination (that is, factually based critical awareness), and gave high ranking also to American citizenship and involvement with public issues. Parents rated American citizenship at the top, together with social examination, but ranked involvement with public issues rather low; world citizenship was intermediate. High school students ranked world citizenship and American citizenship at the top, with social examination next and public issues at the bottom.

These comparative rankings can only be suggestive; if they proved reliable in Albuquerque or elsewhere, they might be more than that. It is not surprising that only at the elementary school level was personal development the highest goal (of those available for choice). It is also not a surprise that both teachers and students appear to value world citizenship more highly than the general run of parents. There may be an attitude dependency here: high-school students become interested in world citizenship because their teachers are; later they may revert to relative lack of interest, although age trends argue against that. The fact that teachers rate attention to public issues rather more highly than either parents or students do may simply mean that teachers take the informed awareness of *specific* issues as diagnostic indicators of having achieved knowl-edge-cum-interest among their students, a sign that teaching about a specific topic has 'taken.' All groups seem to value the more general habit of mind that might be called social awareness or social examination as important; this presumably includes at least a modicum of critical or reflective thinking.

Particularly interesting in these results is the fact that all levels of teachers, parents, and students care little for mastery of social science *methods*; all groups also rate the attainment of a wide range of social studies *facts* at the bottom—*except for high-school students* themselves. We have pointed out that the structure of questioning about goals and purposes tends to cause all subjectmat-ters, as congeries of specific knowledge, to be relatively downgraded, probably as a function of averaging.* Albuquerque's is a system with solid high-school electives and a significant college-going school population, but it does not stress advanced placement courses or social *science* approaches. That may explain the lack of interest in disciplinary/methodological commitment. But it is widely held that a problem with social studies generally is that there is too much teaching of facts, largely from the textbooks, and not enough emphasis on reflection and inquiry and 'going beyond the facts.' These results raise the possibility that this is not a safe assumption, and that high-school students value 'facts' more highly than supposed. (It is as likely, however, that the Albuquerque high-school program happens to blend the 'social examination' orientation and a moderate

*That is, some respondents will care deeply about English, others about social studies, etc., and a canceling process occurs.

level of factual learning in an effective way, so that students do not experience a factual overload.)

15.3   Teachers' Dilemmas

In summarizing this section, we remark again that those who teach and are otherwise engaged in social studies in the schools face a set of multiple, and, to some extent, conflicting expectations, norms, and ideal goals. In general, social studies receives wide but shallow support. Its distinctive and intrinsic concerns fall midway in the societal scale of values and concerns.*

However, since the explicit desires of different sectors cannot fully be met—since academics and professionals want one thing, parents and the public another, commerce and industry another—an uneasy compromise must obtain. This is true of all branches of the curriculum; it may be especially difficult in social studies, simply because of its relatively middling level of support. Society may be more willing to leave, provisionally, basic literacy and numeracy to 'the experts' (so long as test scores look acceptable). They would rarely if ever suggest removing these subjects from the curriculum. At the other extreme, science and foreign languages are not, for whatever reasons, demanded to any *great* extent of the schools, That is, society seems willing to have these subjects in the curriculum but not in fact 'delivered' to all students, so that here, too, within bounds, the experts are left alone to deal with them. In social studies, we may have the one broad area of the curriculum in which everyone accepts its being there, but without knowing what form it should take.

There is another interpretation of the perhaps special ambivalence about social studies. That is, that the specific aspects that *social studies educators* take as desiderata for their subjects are not highly valued by anyone—except themselves. Two sets of concepts and associated values that have been held to be central to social studies are citizenship education and the instillation of habits of reflective and critical thinking. But these, for the most part, do not seem to be goals that are actively and concretely and convincingly sought—at least not very widely. The two cases are quite different in nature. Virtually all historians, social philosophers, and commissions of enquiry see civic virtue and civic learning as absolutely central to schooling. Anthropologists and other students of education concur that some aspect of citizenship is central to any system of education. Thus, this goal may be taken as a constant: if the schools were to *stop* seeking it, its absence would be immediately felt—and corrected. The telling question then becomes, Do social studies pursue this goal in a distinctive and coherent fashion? (See section 6.0.) With regard to reflective and critical thinking, this appears to be desired by all to some limited extent—though not at the expense of 'facts.' The questions then arise: is it valued (or valuable) enough

*Except for the importance given American history, which commands a higher cultural value.

to justify the importance put upon it in social studies, and, if so, is it being actively pursued, as opposed to simply honored rhetorically (section 17.0)?

Teaching (and learning) and the support of education generally are highly moral undertakings. Teachers who must deal with goal conflicts imposed on (and interiorized by) them, or who sense that they are victims of or contributors to hypocrisy in an enterprise as important as theirs, are undercut as teachers. If they feel a sense of malaise in these matters, so may students.

16.0 Preparation of Teachers

To cover, with reasonable brevity, the academic and professional preparation of teachers in the schools is in some ways even more difficult than to describe the courses in the curriculum, and for similar reasons. There are layers of law and regulation bearing on what preparation teachers must have for certification,* and then more layers of choice and decision that affect hiring, retention, promotion, and other aspects. There are, moreover, fine points and exceptions: 'grandfather' clauses for teachers already in the system, rules about state reciprocity and transferability, procedures for emergency hiring and other exceptional circumstances. In this section we deal only with entry-level preparation of teachers possessing bachelor's degrees, and with the rough patterns of such preparation.†

Requirements for all levels of teacher education involve academic subject preparation and pedagogical courses, together with some form of supervised practice teaching. With the gradually increasing level of education in the general population over the course of time, with professionalization, and recently with the emphasis on accountability of the schools all such requirements have gradually tightened up. (A market effect can also be seen from time to time. During the Great Depression, requirements increased rapidly, since many educated persons were out of work. Currently, in fields such as science, on the other hand, where for salary and other reasons teachers are hard to find, some requirements may be waived.) During the 1980s the stipulated requirements increased more notably on the side of academic preparation than in pedagogy and practice teaching.[2] Along with an overall tightening of requirements, however, new forms of certification are being explored, such as alternative certification for mature persons or others with specialized backgrounds other

---

*I use this term in a generic sense, making no distinctions here between certification, licensure, and related terms.

†Although education authorities and agencies have to be consulted for thorough analysis, a useful summary of current certification rules state by state is the annual series of reports compiled (currently) by Mary Paxton Burks, on which the present description of the specifics on certification is based.[1]

357

than education, and teacher proficiency tests for entering teachers. If such innovations proceed, the question of tightening or loosening present requirements may become moot.

With regard to academic—that is, subjectmatter—preparation at the elementary level (usually K–6, but there are many modifications and complications across states), the great preponderance of states stipulate a breadth of general education, expressed often in such terms as "broad teaching fields": what is wanted are generalists who know a lot about teaching children. Most states include a phrase like "the subject matter of social studies" in their description of what background the teacher should have. About six states* require a specific proportion of academic courses in one branch of knowledge: that is, they seek breadth built around some core.† Thus a few states stipulate, for example, 18 hours spread across three of the following: history, geography, economics, political science, or social-cultural anthropology; or that there must be a *particular* distribution: so many course hours in geography, U.S. history, government, economics.

The more typical pattern, true of about fourteen states, requires that *all* elementary teachers must have taken some work in specific fields—or that those being certified in 'social studies' must have. The ranking of fields required will not be a surprise. Ten states require background in American History; five in American History or Government (or formal coursework covering the U.S. and state constitutions); four in American Government; four in U.S. Geography; three in state history; one in Economics; one in Indian Studies. Considering these twenty states together, the rank order of requirements is U.S. history, U.S. government, geography, state history. The other states' requirements are too vague or complicated to summarize. However, there is no state that requires academic work in a social studies field other than history or history/government that fails to require them.

At the middle- and junior-high-school levels, it is quite common for a teacher to have multiple certification in quite disparate fields: for example, social studies and math, or language arts and physical education. The more credentials, especially when diversified, the more chances to be hired. It is not uncommon at the high-school level to possess credentials as a history and a German teacher, say; but the academic double major that is implied requires more investment in credit hours.‡

At the junior-high and high-school levels, the authority of the comprehensive

---

*The specifics in this section refer to requirements as of about 1988.

†It should be made clear that whether a teacher was an education or an academic subject major is not an issue here: education majors still take departmental courses, and academic majors must still take methodology courses; double majors are possible; etc.

‡The 1977 NSF study[3] reported that only 24 percent of junior high school teachers *taught* only social studies, but it is not clear what this implied about certification, nor is it clear whether or not the other teachers taught academic courses in addition to social studies.

university is apparent.* By the high-school level, university 'majors' correspond more exactly to specific teaching fields in the schools: an economics teacher tends to have an economics major.† In some states with only one or two leading state universities, or where there are few or no schools of education save at the flagship university, state educational authorities simply specify that certification as a teacher is earned by meeting that university's own degree requirements in education: that is, that university's pattern of requirements, distribution of courses, and so on, applies.

At these levels, a teacher may have a Social Studies or an academic field certification; in either case, methodology courses will ordinarily be required, and in either case a much more detailed and fuller set of academic requirements will obtain than in the primary grades. For 'field' certifications, a teacher may be required to have completed 60 or 72 semester hours of academic work, perhaps with at least 27 semester hours in each of two fields, with a certain number of these being upper-division work. Both concentration and distribution may be sought: for example, a major and one or more 'subject minors.' Some states will honor three or four such subject minors. Different fields may require different preparation. For example, in one state, for a 'behavioral science' certification, one needs 39 hours in some combination of psychology, anthropology, and sociology (27 plus 6 plus 6), while one needs only 27 hours to be an economics or history or geography teacher. In another state, history teaching requires 30 hours, other fields only 20; the stated reason is the "breadth" of history as a field. In several states, within an academic major, there are distribution requirements for fields within the discipline: for example, for both micro- and macroeconomics, and comparative economic systems and 'personal economics.' (Such specificity generally means that the state wants solid academic preparation, but also has specific emphases written into state law.)

Within Social Studies certification per se, about seven states have very loose requirements—for example, "48 semester hours in social studies." This means that in those states one could *in principle* teach social studies without having taken any history, for example.‡ A systematic 1980 study[4] found that of all secondary social studies teachers 49 percent had been prepared in history, 16

---

*In most states the formal requirements tend to be the same, even though junior-high-school teachers may not teach the same 'subjects,' at least nominally, as high school teachers.

†The fabled pattern of history being taught by the football coach has never been quantified. It certainly has been true in some schools. It is certainly less true today, for legal among other reasons. In fact, the pendulum has swung so far that in some states with tightly specified rules and/or where a teachers' union is strong, a government teacher can refuse to teach U.S. History—and get away with it.

‡This means little. Such a teacher could teach Social Studies, but few Social Studies courses are offered in high schools. Few universities will grant an undergraduate degree in this area to someone who has taken no history. The more likely case would be someone teaching Civics without much or any background in history.

percent in general social studies, 5 percent in political science, and 3 percent in geography. This may leave some background unexplained. Perrone and associates[5] in their large-scale observational study of high schools across quite different milieux reported that "teachers appear for the most part to be teaching in areas in which they completed college university [sic] majors," but that this was somewhat *less* true of social studies. "In the social sciences, there are more people teaching in what were either minor fields in college or composite social science majors.... those teaching in minor fields tended, it appeared, to be even more tied to the textbooks than were those with more extensive academic backgrounds." Such a finding agrees with a general survey of sociology in the schools,[6] in which it was found that a minor or several courses in sociology was the norm, rather than an undergraduate major.

Such findings raise two important points. First, the status of a subject as required or elective has a direct effect on patterns of preparation. For example, Sociology has higher enrollments in high schools than does Economics, overall, but Economics is a required course in a number of states (table 3-1)—and more economics teachers have economics majors than is the case correspondingly with sociology. An implication is that economics teachers can insist on teaching Economics to a greater degree than sociologists vis-à-vis Sociology.* Second, a trend toward 'improving' the academic background of prospective teachers by encouraging double majors or complicated distributions of courses in different fields within the social sciences may be counterproductive, in and of itself. Any such pattern must fit the reality of what courses are to be taught, and to what end. For example, if all were to agree that at every grade in every school a History course should be the sine qua non, it might make sense to require the typical high school teacher to have at least a history minor along with her or his preferred major. Conversely, if one believes that the ultimate goal for social studies in the schools is to teach subject-based courses but to provide teachers with a diversity of preparation—that is, to make sure that each economics teacher, for example, had a good grounding in political science and some exposure to economic anthropology—then quite a different pattern would obtain.

An additional seven states are vague about social studies background, but require *any* teacher to have taken some U.S. history or history/government, state/U.S. history, or Indian studies, in that order. (This pattern seems to be a holdover from the days when primary and higher-level teaching requirements were treated the same.) In those seventeen or so states where specific subject preparation *is* specified, U.S. history is invariably included, and generally leads the list in terms of the number of semester hours stipulated. There is, at this level, however, less of a *preponderance* of number of hours of history required, relative

---

*Psychology (section 10.0) is an intermediate case: it has about as much total enrollment as sociology and is generally not required. Its teachers in the schools have had relatively more diverse subject majors than sociology, but less than economics. A problem in this field is that psychology has many distinct subfields and traditions, can be taught as different *kinds* of courses in the schools—for example, a health versus a social science orientation—and thus lends itself, logically, to different kinds of preparation.

to other academic areas: that is, looking across all the states where distributions of subject preparation are stipulated, history does not lead by so large a margin as in primary school requirements. After history, the order of requirements stipulated for Social Studies preparation is, approximately, government/political science and geography (about equally strong), economics, and anthropology or sociology trailing behind. It is not surprising that economics is stronger at this level than at the elementary; the fact that geography is often specified reflects its course frequency at the junior-high-school level.

At the elementary level, history requirements essentially mean American history. At the higher levels, for Social Studies certification, history background is likely to be some U.S. and some European or Western civilization; 'world history' is as yet uncommon as a component of preparation. Background in world or non-Western history is never acceptable without American and European. By contrast, where the certification is in History, a considerable catholicity of subfields is permitted, reflecting what the history department of a 'good' university would offer. Asian history, African history, and the like are acceptable—though never without American history.

In summary, in secondary public education a more academic background is required of teachers, even those with Social Studies certification or with Education majors. As one would expect, there is more variegation of permissible backgrounds, and where a specific academic field certification obtains there is no deliberate effort, as there is at the elementary level, to build in cross-field breadth (that is, to make sure that an Economics teacher is well prepared in government)—though, as we have seen, such a pattern may appear, especially in the less-required fields. Overall, U.S. history is still the most commonly required course area. It is technically true, as has been feared by some of those who believe that history is the (threatened) core of social studies, that in a number of states one could teach Social Studies or even History without much preparation in history—but such a situation is, today, relatively uncommon. When it happens, it is likely to be because of special factors rather than deliberate or endemic looseness of the regulations.

16.1   After Certification

A few other general observations may be in order. The supposed problem of the high-school football coach's teaching U.S. history is not due to his having been 'prepared' in physical education *rather* than history. The problem is more subtle. A high-school curriculum expert recently noticed[*] that in a particular school all the social studies teachers were men—it is well established that nationally most social studies teachers are men[†]—and, furthermore, that they all had their study

---

[*]Personal communication.

[†]Between 60 and 75 percent at the junior high level and above; *The Status of Pre-College Science, Mathematics, and Social Studies Educational Practices in U.S. Schools*, 1978, 139ff.

halls or 'prep' or free periods at the end of the school day. During this time, they were in fact preparing in one way or another to coach after-school sports. This simply illustrates the difference between a teacher's formal training and his (or her) *interests*, the latter of which may be as important as the former.

This principle cuts both ways. It has often been established, within a given setting (for example, within one high school), that those teachers who are relatively less well prepared, academically speaking, in a given subject area teach as effectively (in terms of students' ratings or tested achievement) as teachers who are formally better prepared; even more interesting, that teachers with very different backgrounds will teach in essentially the same way (over and above considerations of using the same text, etc.).* This is probably not true to any great degree within the larger and older fields such as history or government, but rather in the smaller, elective, fields. If so, just as the 'climate of the school' is often observed to have pervasive, homogenizing effects, it may also be that the 'image of the field' acts as a controlling factor: that is, that teachers in some subjectmatters tend to have a mental model of what should be taught, and how it should be taught—beyond what any school syllabus or selection of texts may impose. Such a phenomenon may be temporally specific: anthropology teachers may teach 'anthropology' of the 1960s in the 1960s, and so on. However, when you add to this the very common observation by researchers and supervisors that teachers teach, in school, as they were taught in college,† the outcomes of teacher education at the university level can be seen to go far beyond the simple question of, How much geography (or whatever subject) did this teacher 'take'? More background may not mean better teaching—even with all other factors held equal.‡

These considerations, of course, get at the broader questions of what makes a 'good' teacher. In the early primary grades, it is generally assumed, a judicious breadth of subjectmatter background is appropriate precisely because one teacher teaches everything, a few minutes at a time; she is a specialist in *teaching* (or 'in children'). Thus, at the education school, the elementary teacher in training takes mostly methodology courses. Depth here involves training in kindergarten methodology, as distinct from second-grade methodology—not in social studies as against art. For high school, on the other hand, it is assumed that the teacher needs to know a subject deeply in order to lead the interested student

---

*See for example, the case with Psychology; section 10.0.

†A similar-sounding apothegm is that teachers tend to teach as they were themselves taught *in school*; it is a rather different argument, usually referring to methodology and interactional approach, rather than handling of the subjectmatter.

‡At an excellent junior high school in California, whose program was built around the integration of language-related and social studies subjects, I noted that the older teachers were trained in 'social studies,' the younger ones in the subjects. This division was deplored by the teachers themselves, not just because it tended to create two cadres of teachers but because the younger teachers, by virtue of their more specialized training, were found to have more difficulty in grasping the 'writing-across-the-curriculum' notion.

into its inner essence and variety so that the student vows never to stop learning it. *How* to teach is relatively unimportant; high-school teachers-in-training receive very little serious methodology. In the middle grades, the common image is that a good teacher knows both children, in their developmental and sociocultural variety, and subjectmatters, plural, since a teacher here needs to introduce many subjectmatters and develop many kinds of intellectual skills, hoping to catch and spur children's interests as they emerge, unpredictably. (Hence the emphasis on fused subjectmatter, on following each child's bent, and so on.) Most middle- or junior-high-school teachers may have had only an hour or two of instruction in college on how to teach history, or geography, probably within a semester course (or less) on 'social studies methodology' in the department or school of education. Supervised practice teaching is not a neat answer: the teacher in training will be graded, for the most part, on the degree of poise and confidence shown or on the mastery of techniques for gaining attention and controlling a classroom, not a deep knowledge either of children or of the subject.

All this should be a matter of some concern. It has been pointed out[7] that teaching as a profession lacks the concept of clinical training or internship. A medical student intending to go into dermatology goes on rounds where she sees a lot of skin diseases, and sees them treated (and, incidentally, discovers whether she likes the field). A pre-lawyer interns for a summer with a lawyer who specializes in tort law. But no teacher is instructed in exactly how to teach grade-5 American History, and how to make it build on grade-4 state History—and how to make it an educational experience not only appropriate for eleven-year-olds but different in essence from what the same students will receive in U.S. History six years later.

Those who condemn a supposed fascination on the part of pedagogy specialists with 'process,' on the grounds that 'content' must always be more important (see p. 366), or who deplore (often with good reason) the superficiality and superstitious behavior typical of methodology courses, may aggravate one of two reciprocal tendencies: that of teachers' reading the text to students, and referring all questions there, or that of teachers' doing what their admired grade 15 professors did, because that 'is the way it is done.' Those who care deeply about history, for example, may be concerned by the fact that school teachers have a rule of thumb that a student can 'understand a time line' by about grade 4, although some researchers have held that there is a cognitive incapacity to grasp 'chronology' well into adolescence.

That particular matter is highly controversial (see section 11.3.1). On the general point, however, Mehlinger comments:[8] "Rarely, if ever, will prospective high school history teachers be given specific help in dealing with subject-specific tasks [such] as helping students understand historical causation, problems associated with periodization, or nationalism, although these are the kinds of teaching tasks they will face as first-year teachers." Mehlinger goes on to point out that the separation between education and arts and sciences extends to in-service education for teachers: when (and only when) there is external funding for a teaching institute does Arts and Sciences cooperation become the rule. "It appears that we cooperate if we are bribed to do so." The point is that teacher education requirements—whether in course hours *or* exposure to methodology—cannot be simply shibboleths. In and of themselves, they make no distinctive difference. It is how they fit together, and what the requirements are *for* that matters.

16.2 Preparation for What?

One aspect of this question will involve the demographics of teacher education, and the relationship between the liberal arts university as a whole and the school of education. Given some of the questions raised in the foregoing, what is the long-range significance of the fact that the master's degree is becoming the norm in the preparation of teachers (table 4-3)? Toward what end is this additional education? If it should be true that the quality of American teachers has declined in recent years in terms of their 'native' ability intellectually,[9] does additional education compensate for this? Or does it deflect some teachers into elite positions, leaving the others perhaps worse off? Will a content-versus-process cleavage open wider in this pattern, with teachers without master's degrees being restricted to handling 'process' only? If, on the other hand, there are few essential differences between teachers with the two levels of preparation in terms of quality of performance, is the trend toward master's degrees economically justifiable?* And what of the trend toward relatively more 'subject' degrees than education degrees—at a time when only elementary education shows the potential for growth? Will this improve early education, or prove irrelevant to it?

Only rarely is attention given to supply-demand dynamics of preparation across the various social science fields (table 16-1). Currently, economics is clearly providing 'supply.' Would this justify relatively more 'investment' in economics in the high school? Not if those with economics degrees are bid out of teaching. Will the widespread demand for more and better history in the school be undercut by the long decline of history degrees? If, for example, the enterprise of World History needs to be enlarged in the schools by an order of magnitude, where will the teachers come from, and will the universities train them toward the specific competence that the schools envision? Similarly, will the overall recent decline in the total number of social science (and humanities)

---

*One version of this question is, If it should be true that teachers with more advanced preparation still perform poorly, by the criterion of students' achievement scores, should not the university as a whole be putting its energies into changing the precollegiate system in responsible ways, rather than gathering more tuitions and granting more degrees? A prior question is, Should not they be doing less, better?

Table 16-1 Number of Degrees Awarded by U.S. Universities in Social Science Fields, 1949/50–1985/86

	Anthropology			Economics			Geography			Sociology		
	B.A.	M.A.	Ph.D.	B.A.	M.A.	Ph.D.	B.A.	M.A.	Ph.D.	B.A.	M.A.	Ph.D.
1986	2,625	742	343	21,602	1,937	789	3,100	562	134	12,271	965	504
1980	3,330	868	358	17,863	1,821	677	3,273	562	119	18,881	1,341	583
1975	5,609	993	386	14,046	2,127	815	3,950	721	212	31,488	2,112	693
1970	3,711	664	215	17,197	1,988	794	2,163	463	145	30,436	1,813	534
1960	250	80	70	7,453	708	237	973	206	68	7,147	440	161
1950	—	—	—	14,568	921	200	—	—	—	7,870	552	98

	History			Political Science			Psychology		
	B.A.	M.A.	Ph.D.	B.A.	M.A.	Ph.D.	B.A.	M.A.	Ph.D.
1986	16,413	1,959	497	26,439	1,704	439	40,521	8,293	3,088
1980	19,301	2,367	712	25,457	1,938	535	41,962	7,806	2,768
1975	31,470	4,226	1,117	29,126	2,333	680	50,988	7,066	2,442
1970	43,386	5,049	1,038	25,713	2,105	525	37,880	4,431	1,782
1960	14,737	1,794	342	6,596	722	201	8,111	1,406	641
1950	13,542	1,801	275	6,336	710	127	9,569	1,316	283

SOURCES: U.S. Dept. of Education, National Center for Education Statistics, *Digest of Education Statistics 1988*, tables 203, 205, 206; Michael F. Doran, "The Supply and Demand of Doctorates in Geography," *The Professional Geographer* 30 (February 1978); National Academy of Sciences and Social Science Research Council, *The Behavioral and Social Sciences Survey* (Englewood Cliffs, N.J.: Prentice-Hall, 1970): *Anthropology*, pp. 107–110, *Geography*, p. 109. The numbers for 1950, in the smaller fields, are only approximate.

bachelor's and master's degrees, a process under way since the mid-1970s, mean that there will be intrinsically less 'play' in the system for social studies reform? For example, if there is an irreducible demand for persons with conceptual and explanatory abilities—as social science communicators or managers of one kind or another—those with teaching ability might be attracted away from teaching, at least at precollegiate levels.*

Clarification on the proper, or at least recognized, goals of schooling and of social studies within that larger system should be prior to calls for 'reform.' The chairman of the National Endowment for the Humanities[10] says, "The culprit is 'process'—the belief that we can teach our children *how* to think without troubling them to learn anything worth thinking about." Former Secretary of Education William J. Bennett agrees, and further points out that elementary education majors show map and place-finding skills as poor as those decried in students. "Can we really expect these students to handle geography effectively when they begin teaching?"[11] (Bennett appears to endorse the recommendations of the Holmes Group, to do away with undergraduate education degrees, thus forcing elementary teachers to acquire subject preparation.) On the other hand, Perrone and his colleagues comment,[12] with regard to *high school* teachers, "Academic strength did not necessarily translate into high-quality teaching. It is in the area of pedagogical skills . . . that teachers appear to need the most assistance."† None of this debate is new. Back in 1945, the Harvard Red Book report[13] noted: "Too many children have learned too little about too much. The fault has probably been as much with school authorities and with those responsible for college-entrance requirements as it has been with teachers. . . . Courses have commonly been planned only for the needs of prospective college teachers or research scholars. . . . All alike must recognize more clearly the limitations inherent in a succession of broad surveys; all must encourage intensive as well as extensive study."

The idea that a concentration on 'process' is downright negative in its consequences in the classroom led to the action in 1987 by the state of Texas to impose a *maximum* of 18 credit hours in teacher-education courses—including not only methodology but practice teaching—in what may be offered toward certification. (Prospective teachers may take more than this number of 'process' courses, but they will not count toward certification.) The Texas action caused some educators to propose to the National Council for Accreditation of Teacher Education the revocation of accreditation of schools of education that acceded to such a policy.[14]

---

*The social sciences have always been heavily teaching-oriented fields, like the humanities. In recent years, for example, about 30 percent of all nonprofessional higher degrees in the United States have been awarded in the social sciences; these fields together draw about 4 percent of federal funds for basic research.

†It is, of course, quite possible that the best-prepared teachers academically do need pedagogical help, while the best-prepared teachers pedagogically need more academic preparation. But it would be impossible to conduct good research following this hypothesis without its being agreed what educational 'competency' or outcomes are in fact expected at each level.

The separation between the broad academic world and the world of education, including the teaching of teachers in the university, to which Mehlinger and the Harvard report, and many others, allude, is natural enough; after all, it *is* a goal of colleges to meet the needs of college teachers and researchers. But it continues to cause problems. Each wave of reform calls for the academic improvement of teachers, seemingly by some hypodermic principle: the more subject courses taken, the more the dosage of knowledge delivered. More than this, part of the problem is structural, having to do with the noncorrespondence of curricula at different levels. Here is a recent example of how a state mandate appears unrealizable. In one state the legislature mandated that the high schools move rapidly toward required World History courses. The education school of the state university consulted with the history department to design appropriate courses for prospective teachers, but found that the department did not in fact teach 'world history.' The department's view was that students from the education school were welcome to take the sequence of Western Civilization, African history, Asian history, twentieth-century Latin American history, and so on. For the education school, this was not only unfeasible for most students, but would violate the intent of the state mandate, which called for a broad *synthesized* survey course to be taught in the schools. Academic protocol and degree-granting rules, as well as financial considerations, make it difficult, if not impossible, for the school of education to offer such a course itself.

Virtually everyone, on all sides of the continuing debate, can agree with the Harvard committee's claim that too many students learn too little about too much. This opens room for exploration. Any *lengthening of the course* of teacher education, whether by doing away with an undergraduate education major or by going to a five- or six-year program, might serve to improve matters, in everyone's view—*if* both academic and pedagogical skills were thus strengthened, as needed. There might then be room for both additional academic course work and a longer 'practicum' involving neophyte teachers in actual classrooms. (This, however, certainly implies much more supervision of practice teaching by subject specialists, themselves very well trained, and that is hard to foresee in a time of tight budgets in the schools and in the schools of education.)

Of crucial importance may be the *timing* of additional education for teachers. For example, in some states there is movement toward a teacher's obtaining a bachelor's degree with a subject major and then working as a teacher with provisional certification for a few years, during which time deeper pedagogical skills are acquired with supervision and school-based coursework. Permanent certification would depend on the teacher's earning a master's degree (again in a subject field) within a certain period of time, say five years. Such a pattern provides time for the sharpening of skills, both academic and pedagogical, and a series of checkpoints for verifying such gradual improvement.*

---

*It is also rather reminiscent of a pattern of seventy or eighty years ago in the (then rare) high schools or academies, where experienced schoolteachers went to the university for disciplinary education, often returning to the schools afterwards. Others did not so return, and became college teachers—which many believe made them better teachers of teachers subsequently.

17.0 Higher-Order Thinking

'Higher-order thinking' has been a shining goal of the social studies since their inception about 1916—and even before that, as historians around the turn of the century urged moving beyond memorization and recitation. The ability on the part of students to 'go beyond the facts' or 'beyond the information given' is taken to be a requirement for intelligent citizenship, an ability central to a successful and rewarding personal life, and an aspect of good scholarship whether by students, amateurs, or professionals. These are all transcendent goals of schooling.

The last of these goals also has special relevance to social studies. Knowledge in these fields is often considered to be loosely structured and nonhierarchical in nature. Unlike math or science, the question with social studies (and social science, relative to other fields of knowledge) is not how far the student 'gets' (in the sense of working one's way up to advanced calculus or biochemistry) but how thoughtfully he thinks about the domain, how deeply she understands. Thinking deeply and thinking well has been a concern for educators devoted to 'high culture,' for life-adjustment proponents, and for disciplinary advocates—all of whom, on other issues, may sharply disagree. It is the goal of Arthur Bestor and John Dewey—and Charles Beard, Jerome Bruner, and almost everyone who has written carefully and provocatively about schooling.

They may well disagree, however, as to priorities and balance. Thoughtfulness about the civic culture and the political process should lead to a more enlightened form of participation; but 'critical thinking'—the ability to look beneath the surface of things, to see contradictions and paradoxes—may lead to a distancing of the person from that process, an observer's stance, or even the diminution of commitment to action.* Similarly, the analytical or model-

---

*For reasons mentioned in section 6.3, having to do with very early and deep affective and attitudinal orientation to the sociopolitical system within which social development occurs, this distancing seldom leads to disloyalty; and if it does, that is more attributable to something like a conversion of faith, not to what is learned in school.

building ability sought by academics, the ability to think theoretically, may be of relatively little priority to those who most value educated and productive workers and consumers.

Nevertheless, the rough consensus-in-principle among most interested parties on what constitutes high-quality learning and thinking in social studies means that, to the extent this has proven chimerical in realization, a heavy indictment of schooling as presently managed is implied. In social studies and in math and science, most observers find most classrooms, at every level, to be places where reflection, debate, and creative discussion seldom occur.[1] It should be recalled, however, that factual knowledge and job-related skills tend to be the highest-rated goals for the schools among parents (section 15.0), so the 'indictment' may not be shared significantly by them.

What is meant, and sought, in the phrase 'higher-order thinking'? A convenient gloss, that of going beyond the facts or the stated information, is not very helpful. Everyone in ordinary life does so all the time, at any age. Common observation and many lines of naturalistic and experimental research, the latest of which is 'schema theory,' show that learners come into the situation with cognitive frameworks in place that lead them to make inferences, about any material, that go far beyond what is given and, at the same time, to discard much information that is present. Ignoring relevant facts, miscategorizing information, and jumping to conclusions have been amply documented on the part of novice learners.[2] Then too, going beyond the facts means restructuring them, combining them with other information, subordinating some and giving special place to others. These are inevitable operations of almost any learner or conscious observer.* Simply exposing the learner to a sequence or selection of material—a particular set of examples, a set of events in a temporal or spatial order—will dispose the learner to a particular conclusion or generalization, as every experienced teacher knows. That is why curriculum design, at its 'delivery' level, involves *guided* discovery, and sometimes the deliberate restructuring of experience so as to counteract erroneous or automatic thinking.

Mere sequencing or packaging of material, no matter how ingenious, is not sufficient, since each student unpredictably discards or ignores much that is offered. Students, taken together, arrive at various conclusions, some of which may be creative but wrong. Speaking of the teaching process, Lauren Resnick remarks:[4] "It is not enough just to focus on making an excellent presentation, because you cannot assume that your elegant explanation will be heard and understood in its entirety. In fact, you can be 99 percent sure that no child in your classroom will get it the way you said it. Most children will get some portion of what you said but not all of it, a few will get it totally garbled, and a few will go beyond what you said."

---

*Developmental-cognitive researchers, however, demonstrate that *how* this occurs varies markedly across domains of knowledge. See, for example, the work on "multiple intelligences" of Howard Gardner and his associates.[3]

You know it when you see it. The phrase, referring to higher-order thinking, is common enough in descriptions of the actual process of the *construction of knowledge* by learners or by learners and teachers together. Teachers in the younger grades may use the technique of the interrupted story, where the teacher stops before the end of the recounting and asks, What do you think happened then? This encourages the students to think ahead; it exposes them to other students extrapolating from what is known along different paths; and it gives the teacher some insight into how the presentation is understood thus far (which may well require repair). A related technique is the open-ended dilemma: here the teacher asks students to suggest ways in which a problem could be solved. In the middle school and later, challenge questioning is seen: the teacher will ask not only What happened next? or How would we solve this? but, more important, *Why* do you think so? This challenges the student to marshal the relevant evidence, to appeal to some generalization about social behavior, to cite some causal model—and most of all it allows students to hear each other doing so. These and many other approaches to eliciting but at the same time guiding discovery may seem the essence of teaching, but they are not the norm, in part because they are time-consuming and frustrating. An experienced teacher writes,[5]

> As teachers, we tried to be as Socratic as possible, accepting but challenging all ideas, answering questions with questions. Anyone who is experienced at classroom questioning knows how demanding that style can be. I struggle with it even today after 20 years, trying to find the patience to wait, trying to listen to each response closely so my next question is framed by the student's response. That kind of patience and concentration required for inquiry teaching may have forced many teachers who tried inquiry methods to abandon them.

Guided discovery learning, of course, is not simply a matter of moment-to-moment transactions. Curriculum planning and lesson plans are crucial, or the right moments never occur. In social studies, Hilda Taba's work in the 1960s focused on the teaching *strategy*:

> [A] matrix of cognition, curriculum, learners, and teacher. . . . The teacher acted as a cognitive guide and led student thinking through a sequence of cognitive processes, extending, lifting, and distributing thought as needed, until not just a few students, but the group of learners had succeeded at the sense-making task at hand, whether the discovery of a central idea (e.g., interdependence) or the construction of a key generalization (e.g., the actions of a people are influenced by the values they hold).[6]

Working at the level of an entire series of lessons or a semester, some teachers set a broad 'focus question' or a general proposition to which much or all of the discussion, reading, reflection, and so on should be related, and which the students must answer or confront to some degree at the end of the process: for example, "The American Revolution was inevitable," or "All social groups denigrate others." This is quite different from simply drawing out 'concepts' from ongoing material; generalizations and key questions are broader than arrived-at concepts, and require judgment. The expectation is not that the students will come to the 'right' answer or formulation, but that they will engage in high-quality (that is, higher-order) work, whatever the outcome. They are being asked to inquire about something complex in a way that amounts to something, to arrive at an outcome that is shaped by thought, to search and re-search. This is Quintilian's adjuration: To teach students so that they may no longer need to be taught. In all of these approaches, attention is given particularly to the teacher-student (and student-teacher) transaction and to the partly public nature of the enterprise, a point we will return to later.

Such a description of discovery and inquiry is inadequate without some consideration of how the process begins and where it is supposed to lead. The inquiry-discovery process is inherently oriented toward a building up and restructuring of 'information,' toward assimilation, mental model-building, toward thought that grows richer and more complex—but this is not the only kind of mental procedure called for among those interested in higher-order thinking. The world is said to be divided into 'lumpers' and 'splitters,' those who put things together and those who separate them out. What has been sketched thus far is primarily the 'lumping' aspect; it is summarized neatly by a distinguished cognitive researcher[7] as follows:

- Higher order thinking is nonalgorithmic. That is, the path of action is not fully specified in advance.
- Higher order thinking tends to be complex. The total path is not 'visible' (mentally speaking) from any single vantage point.
- Higher order thinking often yields multiple solutions, each with costs and benefits, rather than unique solutions.
- Higher order thinking involves nuanced judgment.
- Higher order thinking involves the application of multiple criteria, which sometimes conflict with each other.
- Higher order thinking often involves uncertainty. Not everything that bears on the task is known.
- Higher order thinking involves self-regulation of the thinking process. We do not recognize higher order thinking in an individual when someone else 'calls the play' at every step.
- Higher order thinking involves imposing meaning, finding structure in apparent disorder.
- Higher order thinking is effortful. There is considerable mental work involved.

The list puts considerable emphasis on synthesis, on combining and recombining—hence 'higher order.'

In the literature of the social studies, however, much emphasis has also been put on another aspect of *critical thinking*. And much attention has also been paid to the goal of inquiry, in *decision-making* and *problem-solving*. Schools, after all, are supposed to further the critical faculty and help people learn to make wise choices. The relationship among the three elements—critical thinking, inquiry, and decision-making—is treated by different writers in very different ways, to the point that a differential definition of one such way will seem to another analyst to describe a different one exactly.* In principle, of course, the three aspects are interrelated at every point. The young child, for example, decides or acts upon a problem when he pauses or directs attention to reflect critically upon the information before him, because it seems incomplete or paradoxical or, as stated, uninteresting or interesting—thus beginning a period of inquiry that may ultimately lead to the reduction of confusion, a decision, the solution of a problem, or further inquiry. That this is not simply a pious hope is attested by those who observe such sequences in observational studies of 'microlearning.' Unhappily, most observe, in most classrooms, something quite different: a deadening process of ingesting 'information' and displaying it on tests, in which the information itself is forgotten and problem-solving and inquiry are left to be pursued elsewhere, if at all.

Part of the definition problem is that the *entire* inquiry-discovery process tends, especially by those outside the schools, to be associated with the intellective or—in the social studies context—the 'social science' tradition or perspective, and thus is assumed not to apply to the domain of values or to the pragmatic goal of the realization of each person's potential in the conduct of life. A thorough, if necessarily complicated, summary of these supposedly distinct traditions in social studies is provided by Barr, Barth, and Shermis,[8] among others. Within the tradition of 'inquiry,' some differentiate between reflective inquiry and analytic or social-science inquiry, the first tending toward philosophy and judgment and to making sense of inadequate knowledge from many fields, the latter tending toward bounded thinking, the setting aside of evidence that cannot be treated by a model, and the generating of additional information within one frame of reference. (This, in turn, leads directly into controversies about social 'science' and other epistemology, about whether the distinctive aspect of the social sciences is the class of phenomena they address or the methodologies by which they proceed, and other difficult problems.[9])

To say that schools need both kinds of 'inquiry' is not very helpful to curriculum designers and teachers. Engle and Ochoa, for example,[10] say that *if* one learns to think best by engaging in the formal procedures of the disciplines, then being presented with the conclusions reached by scholars is not sufficient. But *if* development of the critical capacity is the goal, then not only is training in the disciplinary methods not the answer, but the "expository mode in which most social studies instruction is carried on is wholly self-defeating." Bruner, in his apologia for the New Social Studies, which he helped to found,[11] admitted

*See Brophy's definition (and footnote), p. 376.

that a kind of rational structuralism had been an unexamined assumption: "that everyone who came to these curricula in the schools already had been the beneficiary of the middle-class hidden curricula that taught them analytic skills and launched them in the traditionally intellectual use of mind." Even here, Bruner seemed to be saying that social scientific analysis *is* the intellectual tradition, while of course it is only a part of it, and that only some are socialized to value rationality and intellect. An insightful, if brief, suggestion for how to think of the reflective and the analytical aspects of 'inquiry' as joined, in social studies, is offered by Helburn.[12] For the school curriculum, much depends on whether students should be led through the actual steps or logic of discovery within specific fields or frameworks or whether, other things being equal, time and effort are better spent on learning how to use the fruits of organized knowledge in a responsible, critical, appreciative, confident way in a messy, decision-laden world.

17.1   Critical Thinking

To return to the distinction between splitting and lumping, analyzing and configuring, if inquiry is the center of the intellective process then 'critical thinking' is the occasion or the goad, and 'problem-solving' is the summation or goal. Critical thinking involves knowing when to pause to explore a paradox, how to be skeptical about factual claims, and how to remain curious even when the answers are not forthcoming. To Engle and Ochoa, encouraging critical thinking is part of the schools' duty to provide countersocialization, that is, to help students learn not to be credulous. Curiosity and openness to experience are implied, insofar as premature categorization is to be avoided. Whitehead[13] remarked, "In the Garden of Eden Adam saw the animals before he named them; in the traditional system [of education], children named the animals before they saw them." Critical thinking reveals where evidence is missing or contradictory; it should prompt one to find or clarify it.

The consensus is that critical thinking is a habit of mind, encouraged or repressed through experience, perhaps temperamental to some degree, and certainly not taught as a unitary skill in school.[14] Critical thinking about things in general, especially about subjects where one is a novice, is mere captious skepticism or a nugatory addiction. It is not limited to value claims or policy statements. Cornbleth says (p. 14), "It is generative as well as evaluative and appropriate to the range of ideas and events we encounter, including our own ideas and experiences . . . [and] anticipation of future consequences of alternative actions." It is also recursive (p. 18): "As one question is explored, for example, others may be raised and pursued while the initial question is put 'on hold' or abandoned altogether." It is not linear, and is not logical (except in post hoc reconstruction). In rough terms, critical thinking is noncategorical thinking, a breaking out of a format. "Most people tend to resist modifying existing schemata or creating new ones.... Critical thinking can be seen as an invitation to schema tuning and restructuring by questioning, not blindly accepting and assimilating, ideas we encounter" (p. 44).

By and large, education is structured so as to encourage critical thinking *only insofar as it leads to inquiry*. A student may get praise the first time she interrupts the class to ask, But how do we know this? Eventually, she will be challenged with, You tell *us*, or, Be quiet! There is one major aspect of the curriculum where these ground rules may be waived. In educating for 'informed, enlightened citizenship' and for participation in the political process, many philosophers and educators hold, that there is a limit to inquiry, since certain prime assumptions and values are not to be questioned. Furthermore, all that is relevant cannot be known before formal decisions are taken.* This reasoning holds only where decisions are formally required at a particular moment, as part of the system (since part of reflective decision-making in many situations of less than perfect knowledge is the decision not to decide, or the 'satisficing' procedure of making do with limited information and merely an adequate outcome). Thus it can be argued that in citizenship, schools encourage a moderate form of attention to the *quality* or *veridicality* of the information at hand, for example, the believability of campaign literature and political news, and then, in some sense, put special emphasis on the act of choosing *as opposed to* further study.†

This, however, can be seen as an example of how critical thinking in practice is adjusted to a particular domain. We vote because it can make a difference, and the difference can matter to us. We make economic decisions in a condition of less than perfect information. But we can never know enough history or 'prove' a sociological generalization to the point that additional evidence is irrelevant, and here education emphasizes the step from critical thinking to sustained inquiry. The inquiry itself, as has been suggested, may be of different kinds. Reflection is different from research. Productive thinking, that is, generating new hypotheses, is appropriate for some purposes,‡ while weighing existing evidence is appropriate for others. Thus the kind of critical thinking we display is closely tied to the kind of decisions or problems we confront. Dewey's summary of 'reflective thinking' serves as well as any:[17] "Active, persistent, and careful consideration of any belief or supposed form of knowledge in the light of the grounds that support it and the further conclusions to which it tends constitutes reflective thought." Note that the "further conclusions" clause leads

---

*This is evident, for example, in arguments against nonvoting: that there is always *some* difference between the candidates, that one vote *can* swing an election, and so on.

†In an unusual piece of research, Guyton estimates the importance of the 'paths' leading from critical thinking to political participation, suggesting that the key links are in the way that engaging in critical thinking enhances one's sense of personal efficacy—that she can make a difference—and thus the decision to participate. Such reasoning is supported in much of the political socialization literature, as summarized by Sears.[15]

‡The Harvard Public Issues project of the 1960s was oriented toward an intervening stage in this process: the critical evaluation of the quality and dependability of public discourse.[16]

on either to further inquiry or to decision, to 'splitting' or 'lumping,' or both. As Toulmin has pointed out, the coupling between reflective thinking and decision-making, the trial-and-error or approximation process, is often assessed in terms of 'personal logic'—in other words, is partly a matter of individual criteria and taste.

17.2   Problems and Decisions

For obvious (and nonobvious) reasons, schools do not emphasize the link between inquiry and decision-making/problem-solving, the way they do the link between critical thinking and inquiry. Even in the special realm touched on above, the student of voting age who does not vote does not fail Government. One reason is practical; as Beard commented,[18] "No scheme of education can foresee all the important choices of the coming years and provide . . . correct reactions for each situation in which a decision must be made." Another reason is ethical and political: schools cannot be launching platforms for social action, other than that which—as in community service programs—can be construed as practical learning. It would be more accurate to say that schools do not emphasize this link except insofar as the classroom contains (in two senses of the term) the problem.

When teachers stimulate and guide sustained classroom activities in 'prob-lem-solving' they often give attention, actually, to problem-*finding*, that is, problem definition. They want the student to spot the weakness in the argument, or ask the trenchant skeptical question.* Problem-finding is closely tied to critical thinking and reflection on the *individual* level; customarily, one or two students find and state the problem. Insofar as the class then works on the problem, it does so as a group (in whole or part).† The classroom as a prototype of problem situations in life is peculiar, in that, normally, a problem or question is put to a natural group from outside. (Even so, the first step in problem-solving in a 'natural group' is often a sharpening, a redefinition, of the problem by a specially analytical or expert member.) On the other hand, the classroom *is* a prototype problem-solving situation in that the solution is supposed to be 'real'—it is supposed to be perceived by the participants as adequate or better, it is supposed to satisfy them in the sense that they see the process as finished, and it is not supposed to be preordained by the teacher. One of the difficulties for the teacher is that she must learn to prepare for the process, but not intervene.[19] The solution to an empirical question found by the students through

---

*Of course, the teacher may do this work, as in focus questioning above, or the text may state 'the problem' to be addressed.

†This occurs for the most part in public, as a matter of equity and to ensure that the participants stick to the task. Analytical problem-solving as done by individuals in 'seatwork' is entirely different, in that it involves finding the 'right' solution and reporting it to the teacher (who already knows it).

cooperative research; the ending of a serious debate, in which a range of evidence is offered and weighed; the fuller description of a phenomenon merely touched on in the text—all of these have to meet criteria of adequacy or sufficiency as recognized by the students.

In this sense, 'problem-solving' as conducted in classrooms exactly corresponds to what the social studies founders of around 1916 had in mind, in their Progressive faith that the American society was a pragmatic problem-solving society in which knowledge mattered, and that knowledge was in part a social construction to be judged by realistic societal standards. Problem-solving thus is judged by its ecological validity, even in the classroom. Again, definitions vary and must be looked at carefully. For example, I am here making clear what I mean by 'problem-solving' in insisting that it must meet the ecological validity test. However, Brophy, in an excellent analysis, regards as 'problem-solving' something I would call analytic sufficiency:[20] "Problem solving implies seeking explanations for observed phenomena or addressing relatively well-formed and noncontroversial questions that can be resolved by evidence alone (without having to take into account values and without necessarily carrying the process through to some kind of action based on the obtained solution to the problem).'*

Problem-oriented, sustained group effort in the classroom has many benefits, social and intellectual. It respects and utilizes the heterogeneity of the students in the classroom, perhaps mirroring the heterogeneity of sociocivic life and often producing a richer range of generalizations, induction, trial-and-error procedures, and validity checks and standards than any one or two students would generate. This consideration was important in Taba's thinking for the first six grades.[21] The claim specifically includes the assertion that brighter or more intellectually oriented students do not generate more and inherently better contributions to the work in progress, except insofar as they may know more facts that help define the problem. This general claim is fairly well supported by research on group problem-solving in non-well-structured domains. This does not mean that 'content' is less important than the 'process,' but rather that pooled content and strategies lead to better solutions.

Resnick points out[22] that the social setting provides means for skilled thinkers to model effective strategies for others. "Through observing others, students can become aware of mental processes that might otherwise remain entirely implicit." But this is less important than the chance for those in the group to

---

*This is not, I believe, what Dewey and Beard and Robinson had in mind, although they also valued such procedures. The crux of the matter lies in the reference to 'evidence.' Whitehead, *Science and the Modern World*, p. 187, comments: "It is easy enough to find a theory, logically harmonious *and with important applications in the region of fact*, provided that you are content to disregard half your evidence" (emphasis added). The hallmark of a tight theory is that it is clear as to what kind of facts it explains, and thus what range of application. The problem for social studies is well-known to all who accept the notion that social knowledge is messy, contaminated with the values and assumptions of the observers, and otherwise provisional and partial in nature. Were it not so, 'higher-order thinking' would not be claimed to be so important.

critique and shape each other's work, and to exercise a kind of division of labor. "The public setting also lends social status and validation to what can perhaps be best called the *disposition* to higher order thinking. . . . . Engaging in higher order thinking with others seems likely to teach students that they have the ability, the permission, and even the obligation to engage in a kind of critical analysis that does not always accept problem formulations as presented or that may challenge an accepted position" (emphasis in original). It is a way, among other things, to build communities that decide things jointly, or at least to acquaint people with that form of activity—which includes much uncertainty and some conflict along the way, and the reaching of less-than-perfect solutions. Following the notion of ecological validity, it is also a way in which young people learn that, while the active teacher/passive listener dyad is *not* typical of much problem-oriented social interaction, the presence of a leader and/or a judge of the results is. (Within the classroom, the teacher must organize, provide for, sustain, and validate the process and serve as the final arbiter of when the task is done.)

Brophy makes important sense in pointing out that all these procedures converge to show the centrality of rich teacher-student interaction in almost every dimension: in individual work, homework, the use of the text, cooperative projects, structured debates, assessment of students, and the like. This consideration provides the link to the even larger issue of how to achieve richly patterned, serious classrooms (see section 18.3.4).* We emphasize group effort here because it expresses important goals in social studies and the schools, *in certain respects* tying school experience to life, as called for in the Cardinal Principles of 1918, the Harvard 1945 report, and many other programs. The caution comes in estimating how much group-based problem-solving, learning, or decision-making actually occurs in life—as opposed, for example, to models of distributed collective decision-making, which in theory may depend more on individuals' abilities to engage in critical thinking. (An entire body of sociological and political theory ties together these levels of atomistic and collective decisions, of which group processes are one mediating part.)

17.3   Thoughtfulness in the Classroom

Most observers report relatively little evidence in classrooms for concerted work on higher-order thinking. There is no doubt that this is true as a generalization—

*There is a kind of dramatistic analysis of schooling, familiar enough in principle to ethnomethodologists in sociology and to some applied linguists, but as yet little done in the classroom: that is, the kind of 'performances' that teachers give—for good and ill—and the kind of work they are seen to accomplish. College professors play different roles (using these terms in a strong sense) from those played by school teachers, who may (or may not) do relatively more guiding, stimulating, cajoling, modeling, nurturing, forgiving. Certainly there are important teacher behaviors seen in a middle school classroom—for example, calming an overactive child by stroking his shoulder—that are virtually never seen in college.

and that it has always been true in this and other public education systems. There are significant departures from the norm, however.[23] There is also, possibly, a problem in the observation methods that tend to show little *other than* routine work in classrooms.

What seems like business as usual in the classroom can coexist with, or contain within it, exciting intellectual and social experience in the lives of individual children. Synthesis of material and deep reflection are primarily private events. They take place unpredictably and in idiosyncratic ways. Thus, an observational scheme that shows that the teacher does most of the talking fails to capture what it is that is being talked about and how that talk is being done, and how reacted to. Many experienced teachers report having the entire year in their heads, either prospectively or retrospectively, as they conduct a class. They may use certain terms and concepts, or running jokes, for example, as markers to tie together the whole sequence of instruction. Some contretemps that occurred in October can be invoked in May. Much of this 'marking' of shared experience originates with the students or the events of a particular classroom, and is only understood there. Observers will miss the significance of what is going on. A focus on the dramatistic aspects of the classroom, as suggested above, needs to capture these nuances and markers, and it needs to try to capture the entire pattern: what the students do *in relation to* what the teacher does, and how all this is organized within the class hour and within a series of class hours.*

Particularly important is to understand all the *kinds* of instructional interaction, how these are sequenced or balanced, and what the participants want to accomplish. Many experienced observers conceive, for example, of a classroom in terms of a continual negotiation between teacher and students; and this has special relevance to emphasis, or lack of emphasis, on 'higher-order thinking.' No teacher teaches for high-order understanding all the time. Even when a cooperative project or sustained class discussion is under way, the teacher sets limits and goals that the students understand. There may be an understanding that a certain amount of group project work can take place if students have kept up with text coverage, or if they show attention to the lecturing segment. There may also be a perverting of the inquiry process, in which in effect the teacher predetermines what happens, and how. Vincent Rogers, for example, writes:[24]

> We know little about . . . genuine student inquiry. A careful examination . . . reveals that the kinds of questions raised, the problems studied, the discoveries or generalizations arrived at, are rarely the children's. We try valiantly; we smile, entreat, and cajole. Some of the students are caught up in it some of the time—perhaps an unusually challenging topic catches their fancy, or perhaps an unusually dynamic teacher draws them out through the force of his or her personality. More often than not, however, we end up with something Vincent Glennon has

---

*Work of this kind, although not 'dramatistic' in approach, is beginning to be done (section 18.3.4).

described as 'sneaky-telling.' We know where we're going; we know what the questions should be, what the 'big ideas' are, and what conclusions one should come away with if one follows the teacher's manual.

Some students, at every educational level, learn how to indicate that they are playing the game by the rules; in graduate school, for example, that one has 'an original mind' and yet 'knows the stuff.' Many who have studied 'the Socratic method' carefully have demonstrated the way in which the mentor who answers the student's question with a question poses just the right question that will lead on to the desired conclusion.

Some students, when questioned about their attitudes toward school, show that they are aware of the precooked nature of much class discussion—especially in Civics—and find this kind of procedure 'phony.' In classrooms, one does pick up, sometimes, the faint aroma of performing seals.* There is nothing strange about teachers wanting to reach a good conclusion. But it limits true inquiry. As Theodore Sizer has put it:[25] "A lot of us are teachers because we like to tell the truth, not because we want to help kids find the truth on their own." On the larger issue of 'negotiation' in the classroom, Ponder has written:[26]

> In classrooms, it is essential that teachers gain and maintain the coopera-
> tion of students in order to accomplish instruction. . . . Academic tasks are
> defined by formalized exchanges of students' performance for grades, by
> students deciding, in other words, what must be done to get the grade they
> want. To make these decisions, students often actively use strategies that
> reduce the ambiguity inherent in academic tasks and lower the risk. . . . *In*
> problem-solving lessons, in which teachers intend for students to use sets
> of incomplete information to generate their own conclusions, many stu-
> dents ask repeatedly for more explicit information about procedures and
> content . . . until the lesson becomes not one of problem solving but of
> applying a set of procedures learned previously. . . . The students indeed
> engaged in 'critical thinking' and 'decision making.' However, those
> cognitive processes were not used to engage the *content* of the curriculum
> but to establish the academic task. (Emphasis added)

Correspondingly, teachers may use inquiry strategies to implement their own goals; thus they, and not the students, control this resource. On the other hand, when hypothetical discussion or free-ranging debate is allowed to run, the students may reach 'the end' of the process before (or after) the teacher.

Thus, before insisting on higher-order thinking efforts in the classroom, we need to remember that there are inherent limits to what is possible; and that what is done in public and what occurs privately, in one person's mind, are quite different. For the latter reason, a rich, various, unpredictable mixture of tasks and talk may be more important than a conscious striving after 'inquiry.'

---

*In Lorenz Hart's immortal words. This is not specific to education, of course. Similar patterns have been seen in psychotherapy or in the confessional.

There are, no doubt, aspects of 'higher-order thinking' that have not been included in social studies contexts, but could and perhaps should be. One is the possibility of awareness, in the instructional setting, of aspects of discourse. Why are texts dry and full of facts, and how can one rise above this? How is historical narrative different from sociological exposition? What makes a good debate in civics, and what are the understood limits? Some teachers and some students would find it possible to raise such aspects to greater consciousness, to make them objects of study. To some extent, the writing-through-the-curriculum movement may do this (for example in helping to establish what makes a good history report, as opposed to an English theme).*

Another area of higher-order understanding in the social studies classroom could be attention to how, and to what extent, qualitative material and judgments can be handled quantitatively, and vice versa. What are tables of data for, how should they be organized and used, and how can they be summarized in words? How is a 'preponderance of evidence' established in history, and how do exceptions prove a rule? What are the basic rules of inference in the various disciplines? What is a good measure of central tendency? What is the basic notion of probability, and how does one relate probability to utility or value? How did the field of statistics turn from the collection of data useful for the business of the state into a form of mathematics?[28] What is variability, what is error in observation, and what is a statistical sample? What are principles of graphics that communicate well, and how can presentations of data seriously mislead? These matters are raised, not to suggest that 'quantitative literacy' should be handled entirely within social studies, but because some aspects of it must be if the goal of perspicacious decision-making in modern society is taken seriously.†

The importance of thinking about higher-order classroom work as embedded in a larger description and a more complex enterprise is illustrated by very interesting work, on a detailed scale, in classroom research by Newmann and colleagues.[30] These researchers, observing social studies teachers over a fairly sustained period, in a few demographically diverse schools, arrived at a description of a *thoughtful* classroom, essentially one in which mindless or chaotic activity structures are minimal. Thoughtfulness of (and in) such classrooms consisted of some combination of sustained examination of a few topics, rather

---

*That discourse quality makes a real difference, in and of itself, in social studies in the classroom is demonstrated quite disturbingly by the anthropologist Jane White, who studied the 'tone' of social studies instruction in early elementary grades, as distinct from the tone in which reading instruction was conducted. In brief, she found that the latter sounded like serious business, while the former had the ring of forced jollity, of trivial pursuit. One can understand why this should be so; but, understanding how it occurs could serve to alter the situation.[27]

†A joint committee of the American Statistical Association and the National Council of Teachers of Mathematics is currently concerned with extending the scope of statistics, broadly construed, in the curriculum so that it is not considered simply the bailiwick of the math department. For an excellent discussion of this topic, see a paper by Hartoonian.[29] It should be noted that in some schools such practice is in fact part of the social studies curriculum.

than superficial coverage of many; substantive coherence and continuity; time for students to think and respond; challenging questions or tasks set by the teacher; thoughtful behavior by the teacher; and students who offered explanations and reasons for their conclusions.*

Even limiting their report to classrooms whose thoughtfulness was proven (in their terms), Newmann and colleagues found considerable variation in the *patterning* of elements. In general, demarcated 'inquiry' procedures were not very common: not much time was devoted to group projects, free-ranging discussion that might generate fresh ideas from students, sustained Socratic questioning, and the like. Most of the observed thoughtfulness was attributable to the teacher's own behavior and the activities she set in motion: that is, to her own thoughtfulness of exposition and handling of questions, to respect for serious, task-oriented interaction between teacher and students, to the planning of the lesson, and to the use of written tasks demanding information gathering and weighing of evidence. In these high school classrooms, group-centered and student-paced work was not common, nor did the teachers seem to be seeking student approval and enthusiasm as much as actual engagement. Overall, one key seemed to be taking time to arrive at depth of discussion—rather than either the wide coverage of a range of material or the setting-up of sophisticated 'performances' by individuals.

Especially interesting, in these results, was the fact that students found teacher-led discussion and questioning challenging, more so than either group tasks or individual processing of material (for example, forming concepts from examples or outlining a chapter). The description of what ongoing or public activity was found demanding sounds like the conduct of a lively seminar, or a serious spontaneous discussion where some know more than others but the others are not dealt out. Individually reflective and inferential work seemed to occur in the written aspect of the class. In this study, a kind of teacher-led but probing quality is described that is somewhat different from what has been described in other classes specifically devoted to higher-order thinking tasks.†

In the schools studied (which had 'good' social studies departments) many students found social studies—for example, U.S. History—*more* cognitively challenging than science or math or English, precisely because the material did *not* deal with well-defined problems and unique solutions. Another group of

---

*That thoughtfulness in and of the classroom is a very different kind of conception from 'higher-order thinking' as an individual (or shared) intellective process is obvious by comparing these characteristics of the Newmann et al. classrooms with those attributes listed by Resnick, p. 371 above.

†The latter often come out of middle school classes, where more free-form, student-centered activities are typical in the higher-order enterprise. It makes sense that at these grades a teacher may want to do relatively more diagnostic listening to students and more setting the stage for peer-oriented involvement. In high school, a deeper penetration of the particular subject matter is sought. Here the teacher has special knowledge to share, provided the students are willing to pay attention. This dimension of discourse is interesting, in that it suggests that, in schooling, an older student provisionally cedes social control to an adult that he might otherwise reserve for himself—for example, in meeting that same adult in the street or on a social occasion.

students found science or math inherently more demanding on the opposite grounds. It is not surprising that tastes or cognitive styles differ. What is noteworthy is that, in these classes, few perceived social studies as intrinsically boring or mindless. Here, social studies was conceptually difficult—making inferences and justifying one's conclusions were hard work. As the Newmann 1988 report put it (p. V7), "Social studies apparently becomes difficult *only* when the teacher makes [the students] work or intellectually play with the material." Comparing studies such as this one, which focused on the top of the range, so to speak, of teachers and classrooms, with what is typically reported about social studies classrooms, one is led to the general hypothesis that social studies may become interesting *only* when it becomes challenging; or that students are bored with social studies *when* it is taught from the book by teachers who do not probe and insist on active involvement in the intellective process. Students in the classes observed by the Newmann team do find this kind of challenge difficult. In another situation, they might try to negotiate the level of task difficulty downward, perhaps with disastrous consequences—ennui on all sides.* Finally, in the Newmann study, the typical ability level within the classroom was not a factor in the level of thoughtfulness arrived at. This is to say that, so far as could be determined, these classes were not aimed at, or facilitated by, the most 'able' students.

Taking all of these, admittedly suggestive, findings into account, one cannot help but be struck by an irony. In the early grades, according to Jane White (and others), students and teachers alike regard social studies as not serious business. In the high school, social studies seems to work, for teacher and students, only when it is taken seriously indeed. Is it surprising that, in between, much social studies seems dutiful but dumb? Or that many students never quite get the hang of social studies?

The need in the earliest grades is not necessarily to teach more social studies, or even more content-filled social studies. One can perfectly well argue that reading and computation and the development of desirable school and social attitudes should take precedence. But certainly making social studies a silly business, revolving around the Pilgrims at Thanksgiving and wearing funny hats and studying quaint children in foreign lands, could be avoided, even given the fact that few early-grades teachers have much of any background in social studies fields. The problem is all-pervasive. Social studies in the early grades is known as 'afternoon time': that is, the subjectmatter that is taken up after lunch or close to dismissal, when the serious work is over. One teacher told me that she was sorry I was visiting in the afternoon: "We do academics in the morning when the children are fresh." Social studies is also known in the elementary school as 'bump time': the subjectmatter that gets dropped if there is an extra assembly or an early closing or some other interfering event.

---

*That is, for example, if the teacher were under pressure to accomplish 'coverage,' or were in doubt about the propriety of discussion of civic matters.

The labor-intensive, demanding, time-consuming nature of all forms of instruction, at any grade level, involving 'going beyond the facts' or 'coverage' is a formidable barrier to progress. The failure to pursue it is a source of guilt, or at least unease, on the part of many teachers, for reasons outlined at the beginning of this chapter. That much can be accomplished is evident from research studies and observation of classrooms where students are engaged in the study of history or geography or the other subjects with a degree of curiosity and involvement that makes a mockery out of the notion that social studies is inherently boring. The fact that most external assessment ignores social studies understanding in favor of tapping factual 'knowledge' may be the greatest single deterrent to progress.

17.4   Analysis of the Text

Given these considerations, some suggest that a means for improvement lies in the quality of the texts. This is doubtful. Here, in the typical discussion, 'quality' means quality of exposition, explanation, encouragement of thinking, and so on. The quality of texts can indeed be improved quite directly in terms of essential content (and, for that matter, nonessential). Academicians can effect this by insisting that the 'facts' in a text be accurate, up to date, unbiased—that is, by invoking expert authority. Few textbook adoption committees will choose a text that those in the disciplinary field clearly label a bad book. Teachers can also effect change, by serving on adoption committees or documenting that what they are supposed to teach (in terms of the state requirements or the district syllabus) is ill-served by a book. It may be that teachers can have more influence on the 'delivered curriculum' by this means than by arguing or defending principles of pedagogy within their departments or schools or systems. On the other hand, to believe that improving textbooks *directly* improves instruction (and learning) is largely fantasy.

A legacy of the New Social Studies era was, most observers agree, an upgrading of texts, on the average. Texts became more analytical, better organized, more cognitively demanding, better sequenced, less ideological in tone—at least to some degree. They have, without question, become more capacious, with bigger (and sometimes better) graphics, a better integration of tabular or specialized material, and more attention, throughout the main body of the text and at the ends of chapters, to suggestions for further reading, questions for reflection, and other inquiry-oriented apparatus. Why, some wonder, should they not continue to improve, perhaps to the point where they call higher-order thinking into being in the minds of students?

We have commented elsewhere on how texts inevitably follow the market and the trends in content, and how a tendency toward a national curriculum in social studies tends to make all texts alike.[31] It is also true that textbooks are sitting ducks for criticism. They are always out of date, and never good enough.

The most effective, and most responsible, way that academic scholars can help to improve public schooling (barring a sweeping revision of the relationship between schools of education and the rest of the university) is to exert a measure of quality control over texts by constructive criticism—specifically, by reviewing them and holding them to a reasonable professional standard *as scholarly entities or resources.*

The emphasis is important. Texts are resources for teachers and students, are aids to study, are reference compendia. How they are used, and to what ends, are decisions to be made by teachers and others involved in 'delivering' the curriculum. If a rich, challenging, variegated, flexible teacher-student relationship and classroom interaction are at the heart of successful education in the schools (as we believe they are), those who wish to promote this must be careful not to assume that textbooks can do the work of the teacher or the student.

This tendency is evident with regard to 'higher-order thinking' in social studies, where many believe that if the *books* were of a higher order, cognitively speaking, a better education would ensue. This is like saying that well-edited orchestra parts will result in better performances by the orchestra: they may help, but the conductor and the players have something to do with it. Much commentary about textbooks asks that they be structured in a way that 'maps onto' what is supposed to be the cognitive process. They are supposed to display an extraordinary level of metacognitive awareness, so as to provide topic sentences and summary sentences just when needed, arrive at generalizations just when the student is prepared to appreciate them, exhibit interesting offbeat supplemental information (in boxes or specially screened pages) when students are bored, cross-reference elaborately, distinguish between factual propositions and general assertions, and so on.

This is impossible to achieve. One has the impression that textbooks are to be like advertising broadsides, with arrows in the shape of hands pointing out *MAIN STATEMENT*, red shading indicating opinions or causal reasoning, and an eye-actuated cassette recording that speaks up when the student reads too fast or skips a connection. In social studies, broadly speaking, texts should be used as reference material, as secondary or tertiary summaries, as lesson or study organizers. Oddly enough, one sees them used this way relatively more in earlier and middle grades than in high school (except in 'good' classes where it is understood that there is something more important than coverage). This is not, on reflection, so surprising. In a mathematics classroom, when a student is completing a worksheet at her desk, looking in the book can constitute cheating—or at least the failure to have the algorithm firmly in mind. In much of social studies, referring to the book to pin down a date or a datum constitutes intelligent procedure.

Some expectations of texts are repeating the fallacies of the New Social Studies: texts are supposed to state the conclusion and give explicit directions on how to get there, in terms any reader can follow. Beck, for example, criticizes history texts for failing to give an "explanation of why A caused B, and B led to

C."[32] But isn't this what students should *arrive at*—and tentatively, having read the facts and considered the chain of causation from many perspectives and in the light of many instances? If all the steps and procedures are in the text, is this not simply a more analytical way of presenting the students with predigested material?

In another criticism, Beck indicates that texts should not move from explanation to narration without indicating that they are doing so. Should not students learn that texts do combine both modes, and understand how they shift from one to the other? A grade 6 or 7 world geography book is criticized[33] for discussing the Soviet Union's size by reporting that in the north the Soviet Union "touches the Arctic Circle," while in the south "farmers can grow oranges and melons all year long." Beck comments, correctly, that much knowledge and many inferences are needed to convert this information into a mental representation of the size of the Soviet Union. But should not the student, in the context of the class, be marshaling precisely that knowledge—correlating past knowledge or seeking knowledge that is needed—and making the appropriate inferences, perhaps guided by the teacher or using reference books? Finally, Beck and coauthors[34] deplore the way a text cites the many different kinds of 'deserts' there are without clearly emphasizing the prototype case: that a 'desert' is hot, arid. But many geographers would say that this begs the question: not all deserts *are* hot and arid, or not all of the time. Certainly there is more to the concept *desert* than hot and arid. Is it not better for students to construct a prototype, out of a range of examples—some better than others—than be handed it at the outset?

Much of the work of Beck and her colleagues is extremely well taken, in showing how confusing and misleading texts can be—in fact, how they may fail to prevent novice learners from wrong inferences, too-rapid conclusions, and so on. But some comment on textbooks, whether focused on cognitive structure, reading level or clarity, factual immaculacy, or some other attributes, manages to suggest that at the limit a 'good' text is the secret to a 'good' education. If that were true, the schools would be easier to reform than many have thought.

PART V

Conclusion:
After a Century of
Social Studies

18.0   After a Century
of Social Studies

As one looks back over the history of social studies in the schools, reform in the mid-1980s and reform in the mid-1910s seem paired or aligned. Together these episodes bracket what may be a complete cycle of experimentation and development. The NEA committee of 1916 marked the beginning of 'social studies' as a federation of subjectmatters organized around, but going beyond, history. It was preceded by more than two decades of trial and error within the curriculum of social study in the schools. 'Social studies' would not have been ushered in had the field of history been satisfied with its own solution to what should be taught. Today, reviewing seventy-five years or so of cohabitation, some would like to usher social studies out, and set out once again to modify the study of history in the schools so as to make it not only the necessary center of the curriculum but sufficient unto itself. This program within history, as exemplified by the work of the Bradley Commission and others, will probably continue for some time.

For others—including some historians—the recognition that some substantial, broadly selected study of society and human experience, contemporary and historical, is needed in the schools has never wavered over the entire period. But the principles of selection have changed markedly over time. The 1916 effort was embedded in an era of hopefulness, during which, as the Cardinal Principles of 1918 show, the schools were expected to carry forward, express, and to some extent realize the progress of society—a progress that was not considered inevitable, strictly speaking, but was seen as deeply rooted and irreversibly under way. The mid- and later 1980s, by contrast, are anxious times in America. A long period of demographic and economic expansion that marked the entire midcentury has slowed. For the first time much of the public expects the coming generation to be less well-off, in economic and social terms, than they themselves have been. In the larger world, the American century seems to be drawing to a close, as new nations become powerful and as technological and political change threatens American productivity and its hegemony in the world economy.

This does not suggest, to most, that history and social studies are no longer important—quite the contrary. But it does suggest, as was true in the complementary case seventy-five years ago, that they may need to change—in content, approach, or tone. For one thing, at the most obvious level, we know (though they did not) that in 1916 the entire educational system was beginning an enormous growth in size and complexity, riding upon an unparalleled expansion of the national population and economy. Today, part of the tone of lowered expectations reflects an apparent leveling off of these large processes. Choices become more difficult. The assimilation and acculturation of immigrant children into the schools today (figure 4-2), for example, will take place in a different context of the possible.

18.1   The Era Ahead

The trends and changes that come to define eras in a national history are far deeper than what can be counted or measured. Many social historians and social scientists today perceive distinctive new social and cultural patterns forming. James Coleman, for example, comments that "school as we conceive of it implies family as we conceive of it. Yet family as we conceive of it no longer corresponds to family as it now exists."[1] Coleman believes, as do many, that 'social capital' for the young is located differently today, in terms of the relationships among family, community, and nation, than was true in the past, and takes very different forms. Some historians and economists alike believe that we are living beyond our means as individuals and as a nation, and are in danger of becoming a highly developed colonial society, dependent on others' capital and markets. Others predict growing intergenerational conflict as, in Frank Levy's terms, dreams and dollars fail to go hand in hand. The 'good jobs, bad jobs' issue arises, and with it the possibility of increased class and ethnic strain. Between the late 1970s and today, the family income of those in the wealthiest fifth of the population rose and that of the poorest fifth fell. Those in between maintained their level of family income by virtue of more persons working harder. The current business expansion is the first since the 1930s in which the average working American has not experienced an increase in real wages. Consumption at the expense of investment, and accumulating debt, may lay a heavy burden on the young as they live their lives.

The economic prospect is not the only focus for anxiety. Polls show a steady decline over a number of years in confidence in societal institutions and mechanisms*; curiously, a general satisfaction with 'how things are going' coexists with widespread disapproval of specific policies and goals. What will the nation be like if it truly begins not to believe in progress, but believes that things cannot be made better? What will a nation stand and strive for if it believes that environmental degradation is inevitable, that political corruption is endemic, that corporate greed and welfare cheating are inevitable, that an acceptance of civic squalor is the sign of a realist? Where does this anxiety lead, in other words? To willingness to work out new rules of the game, in the national and international sphere—or to a massive denial that any change is needed? The history of England since 1870 or so, for example, does not reassure one that such realities of change, when *relative* decline is involved, are easily faced.

18.1.1   THE DILEMMA OF THE SCHOOLS

Much, obviously, will depend on invention and ingenuity on the part of individuals, a sense of comity among groups, and a commonality of cultural images and goals. In all of these arenas, the public schools have been held to be crucial: the Cardinal Principles of 1918 express that belief, for example. The very success of public education, which *is* a success simply in terms of educating more of the young to a higher level than any other modern nation has accomplished, has also led to a ratcheting-up of the basic dilemma: the conflict between excellence and equity. Some find this better stated as a paradox contained in the single term 'excellence,' since by definition not all can 'excel.'

Others, this writer included, see the problem as involving three terms: excellence, equity, and efficiency. Excellence and equity can be balanced and traded off in any number of ways—but some ways may be more efficient than others, in terms of the broadest consideration of society's welfare. For example, some believe, since schools have become so heterogeneous in their inclusiveness (a mark of 'success') and since the pace of technical change in the working world has become so rapid and the international system so complex, that academic knowledge—the achievement of basic knowledge and intellective skills—has become the *only* possible unifying purpose. Others would point to the probable irrelevance and obsolescence of knowledge and even skills, and argue that good citizenship, learned partly in school, must override all other goals. The further consideration is what knowledge and citizenship are *for: how much* of each is

---

*The difficulties encountered in the 1990 census have been interpreted by experts in such terms.

needed, and in what blend? That some notion of 'efficiency' (a term, in the context of education, that has been roundly and properly disliked) continues to operate is suggested, for example, by evidence that shows that elderly taxpayers are willing to help pay school costs—even when their own grandchildren are not in the schools they help to support—so long as those schools are seen as 'good,' that is, doing a reasonably successful job.

Simply saying 'Excellence for All' does not make it come right. Some take the slogan to demonstrate hypocrisy on the part of those who are fundamentally elitist, as if they really want fully to educate only those who are easily educable but do not dare to say so. This is not fair to those, of any political persuasion or social standing, who have genuinely believed in a common, public, general education. But, as Christopher Lasch puts it:[2]

> If they really wanted to make a case for general education of
> everybody . . . they would fall back, as Arthur Bestor did, on the need for
> intelligent citizens—for people who, whatever the nature of their jobs,
> understand the complexities of modern life and can make intelligent
> political choices. The failure to mount this kind of argument these days
> strengthens the suspicion that excellence, as an educational slogan, has
> come to be more and more closely identified with an implicitly techno-
> cratic conception of the social order.

The technocratic conviction is not the same as elitism. But in social studies it has been an article of faith that a perfectly efficient 'meritocratic' sifting and sorting would cancel, or at least undercut, democracy in education.

All such considerations involve deep intuitive calculations and commitments to the feasible versus the ideal. As a French saying expresses it, wanting the best can sometimes work against achieving the good. Institutions such as schools should do what they do best, as well as they can. On the other hand, they should attempt to do whatever they can, as best they can. These dimensions of value and choice are evident even within the last two decades, in education. The 'back to basics' movement of the 1970s worked toward assuring that minimum standards would be met on the part of and for all participants. The negative consequence is that minimum standards tend to become all that can be achieved—or worse, in an imperfect world, approximated.* The 'excellence' movement of the 1980s has tended to argue that it is not an adequate level of tangible 'outcome,' for example in terms of test scores, that is important, but a commitment among all concerned to learning and success. This puts the goal further in the future, and leaves the paths uncharted. What if the commitment is in practice extended only to those already committed?

---

*Furthermore, polls in the 1970s suggested that what 'the basics' were was unclear to many citizens. Though reports of declining test scores had kicked off a demand for reform, in the media and elsewhere, and though most parents and other adults agreed that reading, writing, and arithmetic were basic, others interpreted the move as a return to the values of schooling in an earlier day: respect for teachers, good behavior at school, and moral fibre.

In 1960, in *The Process of Education*, Jerome Bruner, on behalf of his Woods Hole colleagues, urged a more deeply intellective substance for the classroom and a higher level of cognitive demand. Not only *could* all disciplinary knowledge be conveyed to school students in an intellectually respectable fashion, there was the implication that that was the only form it which it *should* be conveyed—or so many of Bruner's colleagues believed. In 1971, Bruner voiced a poignant change.[3] He said that the reform movement in which he had participated had assumed that:

> Learning was what students wanted to do. . . . Their motivation was taken for granted. [We] also accepted that everybody who came to these curricula in the schools already had been the beneficiary of the middle-class hidden curricula that taught them analytic skills and launched them in the traditional intellectual use of mind. (p. 19)

By 1970, Bruner said, American education had

> failed to respond to changing social needs, lagging behind rather than leading. . . . My work on early education and social class, for example, had convinced me that the educational system was, in effect, our way of maintaining a class system—a group at the bottom. It crippled the capacity of children in the lowest socioeconomic quarter of the population." (p. 20)

In 1988, the chief education writer of the *New York Times* reported that there was a public perception of an "inherent conflict between excellence and equal opportunity." Fred Hechinger quotes a self-described conservative school principal: "I can put 25 honors students in a class, and people say it's too many. I can put 35 in a remedial ninth-grade English class, and nobody gives a damn." Another education official is quoted: "The ground has shifted from helping the needy to helping those who score well." In the *Times* at the end of the year, a curriculum coordinator is quoted as follows: "The real criticism is the way tracking has been handled. The strongest teachers should be working with the weakest students." Another authority remarks: "Tracking is a red herring. . . . [You can always track] simply by ignoring half the class."[4]

Writing in 1983, a former U.S. commissioner of education, Harold Howe II, wrote that then-new calls for reform were conspicuous for not facing the heterogeneity of the school population and the attendant differences in cultural attitudes and cognitive styles. He wrote: "Clearly there is little remaining commitment to the idea that separate but unequal schools are unacceptable."[5] The comment is not extreme. Many in and outside the schools are willing simply to write off the public education systems of the larger, older cities, where the drop-out rate is enormous and it is unsafe to attend school (either to teach or to learn). This, too, may reflect an efficiency calculation, rather than racism or selfishness: such schools are hopeless, it is a matter of realism . . .

There is concomitantly, however, a denial of the social *process* involved.

Many such 'realists' do not see that almost all systems have deeply divisive problems related to class and race *to some degree*. The efficiency rule tends to be dichotomous: a school system is either, in a common enough parlance, 'a going concern' or it is 'educationally bankrupt' or 'in receivership.' The distinguished Swedish educational leader Torsten Husén comments: [6] "An elite *can* be cultivated within a comprehensive educational system. Whether or not the elite produced within such a system is *worth its price* is another question" (p. 460). (Latter emphasis added: Husén goes on to point out that highly selective systems also pay a heavy price, accounted for differently.) Looking at the educational results of several more or less inclusive national systems, Husén concludes that educational opportunity does not result in equality of 'life chances.' He argues, on the contrary, that such differences have become more marked, owing in part to the inevitable reliance on credentials and formal qualifications. "Formal education in our technological society exists to impart competencies and is, therefore, *creating* difference. The school...cannot at once serve as an equalizer and as an instrument that establishes, reinforces, and legitimatize differences" (p. 461).*

Such tensions are always with us. John Goodlad comments that, in education as elsewhere, "A democratic society depends for its existence and renewal on the blending of self-interests and the public welfare," and goes on to remind us that "the common school was created by those who did not need it, for those who would not be formally educated otherwise."[7] The educational historians Thomas James and David Tyack catch the perspective very well:[8]

> Consider the phases in the proposals for reform that we have examined. In conservative times—in the 1890s, the 1950s, and the 1980s, for example—the keynotes of 'reform' have typically been a focus on the talents (often justified by outdoing the Russians or outperforming the Japanese), calls for greater emphasis on the basics and greater stress on academics in general, and concern about incoherence in the curriculum and a lack of discipline. The editorials and articles on public education in popular magazines of the 1950s might be reprinted today without any substantial change and be fashionable once again. By contrast, in more liberal eras—the progressive decades, the 1930s, the 1960s, or the early 1970s—attention shifted to the 'disadvantaged' and to broadening the functions of schooling. In times of liberal reform, people worry less about consistency and more about overcoming past rigidity. Calls for change in both kinds of periods reflect the anxieties and aspirations of the time and an image of

---

*Emphasis in original. Even this may overestimate the concrete effects of schooling in matching competencies to function in society. A number of studies in recent years appear to show that educational attainment per se makes a difference in the level of entry or first jobs, but decreasingly thereafter. As persons make their ways in life in our society, there may be a general 'reversion to type': that is, that people from poor origins of various kinds do not generally do well in life. If this is so, then inclusive education is turning out exceptions, partially or temporarily, that prove the rule.

the preferred future. Seen in the long perspective of history, reformers seem to wear blinders, to see only part of what constitutes a healthy education system—a system in which the persisting reality is that such values as equity, excellence, and liberty are always in tension.

The printed record certainly bears out this latter generalization. In the 1930s the American historian James Truslow Adams spoke of schools, not only as a vehicle for democratic inclusion but as a way of proving to students that the American blessing was that errors and failures can fall away: history can start fresh every morning, was his phrase. In 1954, the historian David Potter[9] said that our character and morale *rested* on the assumption of abundance and unlimited economic growth. As the physical frontier closed, an endless frontier of education and knowledge opened. For a time it appeared to many, not so much that the experience of growth and abundance underlay the improvement of education, as that education brought about the abundance. Thus as economic growth began to slow, education was regarded as the engine for reversing or overriding that slowing—an assumption prevalent today, mixed perhaps with some anxiety about how many scholars and scientists and managers the nation needs (and, if there is a limit, what to do with the rest of the educated). If the growth curve continues to flatten,* the schools may be blamed for letting us down. When one adds to this the century-long tendency for the understood goal of education to alter from providing as much education as each person needed—for her or his role in life—to as much education as each person might enjoy or humanly benefit from, the management of decline in public education (if that occurs) becomes tricky business.†

At some level, the excellence/equity/efficiency problem is understood by all. Exquisitely fine social distinctions and differentiations are conveyed in ordinary language. Everyone understands (or believes she does) when a teacher or a parent refers to 'a good school' or that someone received 'a good education.' You can walk into a school building cold and in five minutes know whether this is a good school. A bit more observation will tell you whether that good school would have been good under any leadership or any kind of community support, or whether it is good in tough circumstances. The question of 'efficiency' enters when you see to what extent the instruction is tracked. Even at very early grades, tracking is common and pervasive, although few schools at any level offer completely differentiated or completely common courses. It is the fact that schools operate relative to their particular social environment, and that tracking further separates out and patterns different goals and procedures within schools, that makes national-level survey and polling data—and achievement scores of

---

*Some economic theory associated with William Baumol holds that leadership in productivity passes from one developed nation to another, in long phases, as economies 'converge.'

†An excellent discussion of such issues is contained in articles by Michael J. Bakalis, entitled "American Education and the Meaning of Scarcity."[10]

various kinds on that level—relatively meaningless. Such data conceal *clusters* of relationships between what is sought and how it is sought that vary enormously. In most national data, this is 'noise' in the system. But for those in the system, it is the essential reality.

Through the accretion of procedures and norms in American public education, through the increasing rationalization of institutions and professions, and through the layering effect of waves of reform and adjustment, there is less room, less play, left in the system than used to be the case. True local control may be a thing of the past. The curriculum is full. For social studies, it is unreasonable to think that more time in the day or more days in the year can enlarge the pie to be shared; besides, the science, foreign language, and arts advocates all want more. The accumulation of legislatively and bureaucratically stipulated mandates and the widespread use of knowledge tests that are superficially easy for governors and education departments to use for comparisons mean that reformers of the schools are discounted—except for the politically imperative change, which is thus not 'reform'—unless those reformers can suggest trade-offs, adjustments within the overall system. This means that calls for reform now run less the risk of possibly getting what they want (which has always been dangerous), and more the risk of simply contributing to school-bashing—that habit of bitter condemnation that educational historians describe.

Many in the social studies, over the years, have assumed, realistically enough, that progress would be gradual, and that as much time as was needed would be available. Reading through the pages of *Social Education*, the journal of the leading social studies organization, in the 1960s, for example, one sees that those describing the elephant all through this decade found it remarkably similar to the pachyderm that had evolved by 1916—but never ceased to doubt that change was finally imminent. There were arguments, throughout, that appealed to historical necessity: change is occurring in life in general, hence the schools must inevitably change. There were arguments that appealed to the attraction of the new thing: 'behavioral science' has been invented (that is, some configuration of psychology, sociology, anthropology, and contiguous fields), and this alone must precipitate change in the curriculum. One recognizes also an argument according to the dynamic of internal stages, as follows: One begins, in the curriculum, with civic-political instruction. But because all societies do this (for good or ill), one moves from indoctrination to education, that is, to disciplined inquiry and academic preparation. But because not all need this and only this (and because this framework itself changes through time), eventually the schools address 'higher thinking' and judgment of a more secular, nonspecialized, kind.* Despite

---

*Over the years there was some disagreement as to the exact strategy. By one line of reasoning, one ought to be able to move from the first to the third before all possible disciplines are represented in the schools. By another argument, one *must* go through the second stage, as imperfect as that may be, since people cannot confront their experience intelligibly without some disciplined framework.

these expectations and this logic, fundamental change has still not occurred (see section 5.6).

18.2   Expectations of the Social Studies

The tone of the 1980s, in social studies, is different, and perhaps new. Put bluntly, some believe that time has run out—leaving social studies still in a muddle. Careless disassembly, throwing the baby out with the bath water, seems a possibility. As two commentators have put it:[11]

> Retrenchment could set in motion the haphazard process of incremental-ism, only in reverse: Educators could initiate an equally haphazard decrementalism by peeling away parts of the system with little sense of purpose. The economics of scarcity could stimulate factionalism and bitter competition among the various interest groups in education. As loyalty to the common goal of public schooling erodes, parents who have the opportunity could choose exit from rather than improvement of public schools, leaving the public system to become a place of last resort.

The necessity to confront the strong likelihood of trade-offs, rather than something more for everyone, is especially relevant to the long-standing tension between history and the other social studies. There are important issues here, which should be discussed on their merits. Currently the quality of debate suffers from shrillness on the part of some historians. (In the 1930s, the reverse seems to have been the case.) Arguing that 'the problem' of insufficient excellence in that branch of the curriculum known as social studies is due to the ruination of history by social studies runs up against several compelling objections.

After seventy-five years of contention about *nothing but history* versus *history and the social studies*, the debate is beginning to seem endless. If it were not seriously intended and morally motivated, it would be comical. History in the schools has been by far the leading subject at all times, and in virtually all curricula. Far more things called by other labels in the curriculum have been in fact history than the other way round. Most teachers have been trained in that subject. Although legislation and custom have wrought changes to history in the school curriculum, nowhere has it been dethroned. Moreover, the texts have tracked the wishes of historians, and changed their emphases and approaches accordingly. Whatever their limitations, the texts for many years have been full of more facts, useful references, reasonable suggestions for further study, and so on, than even the best student can make use of. In sum, the contention that students have not had access to a detailed and comprehensible history is, at best, mysterious. If achievement scores are disappointing, it is not for lack of trying— on all sides. The information that students do not know is, alas, what is taught. Thus historians (and teachers of government, insofar as they have taught the testable basics of government) cannot denounce poor performance on the part of students without opening themselves to the challenge, What have you been doing all these years? If it is not working, why have even more of the same?

There is a good answer to that challenge: it is that 'the same' is not what is wanted. The books *are* dry and crammed with minutiae: most textbooks, in any subject, are so. Some teachers do drone on, reading the book aloud. Knowledge-item tests do drive teaching and learning toward minimal levels of 'comprehension' and 'retention.' No one wants simply more of these. From 1893 onward, historians at all times have been in the forefront, to their credit, of those concerned with better, not just more, history. The problem is that historians, like others, have disagreed on how to achieve this. Historians disagree about the sufficiency, even the appropriateness, of full-bodied narrative versus a presentation of 'facts' essentially for reference versus an approach that challenges the students to make their own mental models of events and how and why they happened. They disagree about chronology versus history-mindedness, and about whether causal reasoning should proceed from effect to cause, or from cause to effect. (Such disagreements are not peculiar to history, but are typical of social studies in general. The proposition about reality that is imparted by history and anthropology, among other fields, *that things do not have to be just one way* still leaves open most of the hard choices about what to study, and how.)

In addition, there has been a broad shift in the human sciences in thinking about historical determination. The historians around 1900 who concerned themselves with school history assumed that the past was determined (although in complex ways); the educational challenge was to select and illuminate what would apply to the near future, the present being always out of focus. Today, many assume that the past was probabilistic, as the future will be. No specially relevant lessons can be drawn; instead, broad generalizations can be tested in the light of what is known of the past, and thus can gain plausibility for (but not causal efficacy in) the future. This epistemological shift, which is partial and complicated in nature, by no means reduces the importance of the field of history. To the contrary, most of the human sciences have become more historical in nature and in interest. This means that the relevance of the local, the situated, the particularistic increases, and the dream of a universal rationalism recedes. Contemporary thinking in these fields rejects Descartes's judgment that "History is like foreign travel; it broadens the mind but it does not deepen it." Thus history is as important as ever on the intellectual scene, if not more so.

Some of the debate is not really about knowledge of history, but is an argument about civic affiliation and national loyalty. Some historians have argued that only the 'story well told' will compel belief, since mere knowledge of how our system of government and politics work is of a lesser order, and can be used for selfish rather than civic-minded decisions. The fundamental question of normative rather than descriptive learning is an ethical question. But all systems, even (or especially) tyrannical or totalitarian ones, seek 'the story well told' in education, and seek to create a binding national memory. We dislike the use of history to serve ideological ends, but recognize that it should so do and will so do to some degree. Belief, however, cannot be compelled, and some studies by historians (section 11.2.5) suggest that the mythic and iconic interfere with effective conviction. When students complain that the civics aspects of the national history are boring, they appear to resent being condescended to and filled with pabulum. There is no good evidence to suggest that Americans today are by conviction less patriotic or less willing to put national needs ahead of their own than seventy-five years ago. Nor is there any good evidence for a Golden Age of knowledge of American history, now lost. To try to link two doubtful propositions is bound to be of doubtful validity.

The tensions within history are the tensions between history and the nonhistorical social studies, and the tensions within these fields in general. Over the years, some historians have looked at the charge that social studies had driven history out, and have rejected it (section 13.0). For all the historians who see the 1916 solution as an attack on history, there are social scientists who see it as a preemptive undercutting of the development of their own fields in the schools. Both are true, to a limited extent. The creation of the multidisciplinary Civics course or the Problems of Democracy course was an attempt to go beyond history—but not so far beyond that every social science would have to be taught.

Some tensions have finally to be faced. In the coming years we will need an accepted frame for instruction in our schools. This frame must contain history and other fields. The problems of society in each era cannot be permitted to alter the basic curriculum rapidly, or we will have a system that in fact does not bring knowledge to bear on problems but is always setting off in new directions to try to find what could have been useful today. The wastefulness of such procedures is clear, for example, when one looks at the excellent materials on energy and its control and use that were developed in the 1970s. They are impressive. But using them effectively demanded that there be *already* in place a curriculum that covered the economics of scarcity, international relations, the history of the Middle East, and issues of fiscal policy and public choice—together, of course, with some knowledge of how Americans have faced such crises before, and what the rules are for public choice. The whole idea of a curriculum is to provide both 'strands' and 'slots': a set of background knowledge that automatically bears on the issue of the time, and a place for the connection to be made. The attempt to add Energy Studies quickly into the social studies curriculum was doomed to be too little, too late. Some teachers were able to use some of the materials a few times; then they went on the shelf.

The fact that some deep tensions in social studies in the schools have always been with us should not be taken as a sign of necessary internal disorder, a metabolic incompatibility. 'Social studies' since 1916 could prove to have been a seventy-five-year misunderstanding; if so, it would have to be reconstructed. But education moves slowly, so as to prevent the search for the ideal from driving out the existing good. The quarrel between the Ancients and the Moderns lasted at least from the time of Francis Bacon to the time of Herder, in the context of both university and lay learning. Eventually a solution was found.

A more plausible interpretation, I believe, is that social studies has suffered bad timing.* The solution of 1916 assumed some kind of 'general sociology' growing up in the curriculum and adding a tincture of descriptive realism to the existing core. But shifts in the national agenda during the depression and the world war meant that the Problems of Democracy course never settled into a stable replicable form. Thus, by 1934, national commissions were envisaging a kind of League-of-Nations approach to the curriculum, in which all the disciplines would be represented. They failed to consider how a range of kinds of teachers would be educated and attracted to the schools, and in fact the growth of the disciplines was not yet of a magnitude where that would have been possible. After World War II, the general education movement, as exemplified by the 1945 Harvard report, held great attraction, but for the schools at least was out of step with the huge expansion of industry, commerce, vocationalism, technical development, and change on a national scale involving urbanization and internal migration. Each of these three models was reasonable enough; each failed to 'take.' The last major innovation, the New Social Studies, *was* well-timed. A drive for educational excellence was on the national agenda, and even the smaller disciplines, such as geography and anthropology, were now mature in terms of institutional support, the recruitment of students and teachers, and agreement on the major subfields. But while the reforms of 1916 were carried forward on the crest of a sea change of educational expansion and progressivism and the fundamentally centrist agenda of twentieth-century nation-building, the reforms of the 1960s were swamped by an even greater expansion of the educational system, a resulting aggravation of the problem of excellence versus equity, and an intergenerational hostility and cultural hostility that made 'relevance' supremely important to some students and acutely distasteful to some of their elders.

All these models for social studies are still with us. Social realism, disciplinary enlightenment, a shared core content, and the ability to think analytically—all are still goals in the curriculum. Movement toward them has never ceased at the level of course designs, text writing, or the preparation of teachers. This leads, as has been suggested in this book, to an uneasy coexistence, a grudging toleration of different, to some extent incompatible, approaches. One can see this situation as a sign of failure. I see it as a sign of limited (because mixed) success.

Much the same has been true of the history of the social sciences in the university and of their impact in society. The very rapid growth of these fields between the 1930s and the 1970s led some to interpret the cessation of growth that followed as a crash or repudiation. The growth in question began from a tiny baseline, so that those who participated in it had the sense that epochal change

---

*As, for example, has biology in the schools where by the time it was ready to be taught it had fundamentally changed.

was under way. The field of the philosophy of science was in the same years heavily affected by considerations of the social construction of reality, of the partial and relative nature of knowledge; and this led some in both the humanities and the natural sciences to say that we had entered a social scientific age. But the public, other intellectuals, and the decision-makers have remained ambivalent. To them, the social sciences are only one way of knowing—which of course is correct. Social knowledge has not proven more effective in its application or its 'engineering' power than other forms of curiosity-driven knowledge. Moreover, the cultural assumption that 'science' is the prime exemplar of rational procedures is called into question by the recognition that *all* thought derives from particular points of view and special interests. Still, many find 'actual' knowledge, however modest, preferable to the 'virtual' knowledge that social inquiry stands for, and are wary of the idea that what we know is mutable.* The idea that historical process is contingent, that reality is multiple, that philosophical indeterminacy can coexist with a pragmatic system of judgment,† and the observation that social scientists seem actively to reject consensus on the intellectual categories with which they work—all of these habits and characteristics make people uneasy about social study, and students of society uneasy about their own work.

The public's support for social study has always been limited. There are no satisfactory measures, but it appears that the public is willing to support social study and humanistic study about equally—which is to say, not nearly so well as biomedical research or materials engineering.‡

Schools accept the limitations placed on social studies, as they do those on other parts of the curriculum. They must be cautious about proposals for sweeping reforms. They will know, for example, that to accede to the desire for history to be once again the only significant field ('handling' geography, economics, civics, and other ancillary material) is too high a risk, for history and the schools. Twenty-five years from now, if students' knowledge of the facts of history and civics were to be as poor as it is today—and was in 1943 and in 1908— it would be too late ingenuously to propose that something was needed besides history: that was the solution bruited around 1900.

Ultimately, the curriculum is not itself the problem. Or, rather, the curriculum is an effective point of purchase on education only in times of cultural stability

---

*Social scientists, by and large, are comfortable with the idea that what we know is mutable, and what is immutable we cannot know. Many others are not.

†As argued today, for example, by Richard Rorty.

‡There are innumerable instances of this strictly limited endorsement. One nice example is that of British sociologists of sport, who in the late 1970s and early 1980s could not gain public research funding, since, after all, the sociology of sport sounds like trivial business. This changed rapidly after the British soccer riots—except that research funds came then with a scolding, to the effect that sociologists ought long since to have stopped doing research on abstract matters of no consequence and gotten busy investigating real life.

and political consensus, in which goals for the schools are not at issue. When people become dissatisfied with levels of achievement, on any grounds, the impulse is to change the curriculum. If students are not learning, teach them something else. This has the effect of confusing what is actually taught with what is officially taught, and it also confuses possible problems with what is taught with problems of how learning can be improved.

There are indeed many problems with how to capture and represent knowledge and how to produce learning among students that have virtually nothing to do with the curriculum. A curriculum is a negotiated agreement that tries to accommodate many interests, not simply to propitiate outside forces but to educate a broad range of persons with different interests, needs, and abilities. No school fails to open its door in the fall because a curriculum has not been agreed on: a solution is always found, a solution whose modifications, from year to year, are essentially ethical. Wittgenstein said that ethical decisions tend toward the aesthetic; they may also tend toward the practicable. The fact that the social studies curriculum is close to being full, partly because entities accumulate and partly because a national model is being approached, does not mean that it will not change over time—simply that there is less room than before for accommodating additional elements.

Those outside the schools who wish to propose curriculum change have, many believe, the responsibility to sketch an overall plan for content and instruction, a so-called scope and sequence. Only by doing so can those with schools to run understand the relative importance that the reformers allot to the different bodies of knowledge, and their theory of what leads to what in the experience of the student. However, in practice, those concerned with reform seldom want an entirely new configuration, but have things to propose or delete at the margin. This is all the more prudent today, when room for maneuver is limited. Even more useful would be for reformers to examine existing elements within their particular competence, and suggest improvement or change there. The benchmark would be, in this approach, not so much whether one field or subfield is more important than another intrinsically, but whether a particular content area or approach can be effectively improved, relative to established standards and values in that field and to the *likely* feasibility of institutional change in that area or approach. Some parameters are obvious to those proposing reform. For example, if World History is to be widely taught in a form beyond that of America-Plus (section 12.1), the university courses that prospective teachers will need to take will have to be more nearly in place than is presently the case.

18.2.1   INCREMENTAL STEPS

In that spirit, and in the light of the discussion of parts of the curriculum in this volume, we comment here on some things that seem to be problems that could be fixed, or emphases that could probably be shifted. The most obdurate deficiency is in civics education. This is the one area where, after seventy-five years of trying, one is tempted to say, Enough.

It is not citizenship as a fundamental goal of education that has failed, but instruction in civics. Any educational system must address the goal of citizenship in a diacritical fashion. That is, citizenship is not just a *function* of schooling (like bringing the young together in a safe place, keeping them out of the work force prematurely, or providing a means for nest-leaving), but a *goal* the progress to which can be measured, where value-added considerations apply. Being a functioning American means knowing certain specific things about this system, about the democratic idea, about the role of law and electoral ratification, about cooperation and disobedience, about the harm in this system that bigotry and disenfranchisement bring. Educational ethics does not require that all possible positions and values be created, only that those that commonly exist be represented. Other systems will need other principles and other content.

The specific choice of what is taught in civics has always been criticized as being idealized and hypocritical, or banal and conceptually uninteresting. In the 1920s and 1930s the American Political Science Association worried about the latter. In the 1940s the Harvard report found civics to be without a philosophical foundation, while ten years earlier Charles Merriam had found it socially unrealistic. Teachers feel forced to jump through two hoops: to teach babyish lessons that insult the intelligence of their students, or to guide students through independent and critical thinking that, like the 'cooked' experiments of chemistry, always lead to the right answer. The Mandarin democracy preferred by Whiggish elements, at the founding of the nation and steadily thereafter, is different from the civic republicanism of Tocqueville, which is different again from the image of politics as the mediator between enlightened self-interests. Research seems to indicate, over and over again, that merely spotlighting certain principles and issues in the classroom breeds cynicism, because it reveals to the most credulous student the gap between the ideal and the real.

However, this is not at all to say that the experience and climate of public schooling does not contribute importantly to the gradual forming of responsible citizenship. Schools are relatively benign places, compared to some other arenas, and the very bringing together of different kinds of young people, the studying together of the facts and principles of our system, and the goodwill that tends to exist between students and teachers (again, relative to other milieux) may be the important part of the process. Citizenship became a focal *content* for social studies, a kind of residual core subjectmatter, only about the 1950s, when citizenship faded out as the central business of schools in general. Before then, educators worried about those who were excluded from schooling, and thus susceptible to alienation; after this point, they worried about those included who became alienated by being instructed.

The content of civics instruction consists of certain basic principles and a modicum of relevant information about the realities of life, former and current, and how these express or limit those principles. Knowledge in the social studies, generally, does not involve the notion of 'critical periods'—moments at which basic concepts must be mastered or become inaccessible. But the political socialization literature shows that positive attitudes toward sociopolitical responsibility and system affiliation must develop quite young. History can provide a model for such thinking, in the sense that it can show others acting as citizens, for better or worse, in circumstances that were crucial or where specific judgments can be shown to have had effects. More advanced history can refine and to some extent correct these understandings. But the sense of political efficacy that schooling is supposed to create in individuals probably can only be achieved with a richer kind of *social learning*, by which the young move from affiliation and basic knowledge of the system to actual involvement in it.

The Civics course about grade 9 was intended to bring in richer understanding of aspects of civic behavior by focusing on circumstances of the times and on real systems in which people operate, typically beginning with the local and working toward the national. It was this potential blend of economics, political behavior, public administration, and descriptive sociology that was never achieved. By contrast, the Problems course at grade 12 was put in place, fairly widely, but was undercut because the middle stage—the apprehension of the real processes within society that surround democratic decision-making—was missing.

If a fairly concentrated dose of social veridicality cannot be delivered by the end of the middle school, further recitation of the basic attitudes and fundamental principles should be dispensed with. It is counterproductive. It abuses the ethical trust between teacher and student, which rests on the attempt by the teacher to abjure fairy stories and add knowledge to existing foundations, not just repeat the obvious. This latter endeavor need not, probably cannot, involve one synthetic course. The great benefit that the development of law-related studies in the 1960s and 1970s brought was that fairly concrete procedural knowledge could be conveyed within a number of courses in the curriculum— 'procedural' meaning that principles were related to actual practices, that things that were tacit could be made clear. Legal education can mediate between transcendent principles and constitutional design on the one hand, and a close description of how things work on the other. Each course in history and the social studies can bring in more of this mediating knowledge. If that has been done, but only if, a 'capstone' course is still a good idea for the final year. (I return to this point below.)

Any social studies course can deal in some way with what is on the horizon, but only if those outside the schools make an attempt to state forthrightly and concretely what they would like young adults to know, for the coming decades. In Europe, for example, the question of specific rights and duties as a framework for the European community—i.e., concretely, what 'European citizenship' may involve—is now on the agenda, in quite a practical way. For Americans, there are similar, if perhaps not so pressing, questions about responsible citizenship in a transnational context, ranging from how Americans working in transnational corporations must behave to how the 'global commons' can be preserved. A knowledge of riverboat protocol is no longer so appropriate as it was in the mid-1800s. Knowledge of what Chernobyl's fallout can mean in terms of citizen and governmental action is of considerable importance. There is probably a need for some group of leaders, managers, and scholars to meet every ten or twenty years to consider those social trends and national needs that seem to demand attention within the schools. This would be a statement of the de facto oncoming situation and, in addition, a sketch of what citizenship, in a given age, would need to address: What rate of voting, in our system, is necessary or ideal? What are the purposes of foreign language mastery (other than personal benefit), and who should possess it? How should national law deal with international terrorism? Without such an enterprise from time to time, imperfect as it may be, outsiders can hardly fault the schools for failing to 'flesh out' the concepts of citizenship, or for being behind the times in terms of relevant content. At least such a census could help to determine what should be accepted as indicators that progress is being made.

While there is obvious duplication of geographic content in a number of courses in the middle school, there is nothing intrinsically wrong with this. As with history, one can never know too much about spatial particulars. Whether those in the field want geography in the schools to be an 'organizer' for other subjects* or to be more of a connected and to some extent hierarchically arranged set of concepts depends on some estimate of feasibility, on whether 'infusion' ultimately amounts to more than separate 'units' or courses. It may well do so, since geographical learning of the kind prevalent in school is always to some extent 'incidental,' meaning that it occurs in close connection with other dimensions of knowledge. It is hard to see, however, how—without special units of instructional time and without well-prepared texts and teachers—the fundamental concepts of geographical *systems* (section 8.0) can be communicated. Perhaps even more important, modern geography bridges the natural and social sciences and the humanities in a way that may be of keen importance in the modern world. The very nature of distinctions among the natural, the social, and the distinctively human (in the sense of the capturing of individual experience in intelligible terms) is at the heart, not just of contemporary geography but also of modern social theory. There is more to occupied space than location.

If geography seems to some to underestimate its own reach, economics in the schools is the best example of a field that has pursued its own interests in a single-minded fashion. In doing so, it may have achieved, more than any other field, what is good without attempting what is ideal. That is, those aspects of institutional economics that were called for around 1916, the promise of behavioral economics based on quasi-experimental research first developed in the 1960s, and recent theoretical work on collective decision-making in real situations have never truly been part of economics in the schools. The first of these

---

*This is not to be dismissed. Some of our most productive historians today, like Bernard Bailyn, credit historical geography with opening up new fields of scholarship for them.

was probably blocked in the 1916 compromise, because it opened the door to 'political economy.' (Insofar as it required the development of microeconomics as a field, it was also premature.) With regard to the second and third aspects, eventually they may still become part of the mainstream subjectmatter. On the other hand, little progress has been made in recent years to make sure that economic history is well covered, either in History or Economics. Similarly, many have commented that the history of science and technology, in its connection to economic development and growth, is heavily emphasized in covering the nineteenth century, industrialization, and empire—but not twentieth-century economic systems, the changing nature of war, or the information revolution. It is not that neoclassical mainstream economics is inadequate, or too difficult for students, but perhaps that too much related material has been allowed to slip away—material that is itself well studied and fairly easy to organize for instruction.

18.2.2　A MISSING SECONDARY CORE

Those who examine the social studies curriculum over the decades, without much prior acquaintance with it, may find its most surprising feature to be the absence of a general descriptive sociology. It is clear why history and some aspects of government and politics are present, uninterruptedly, in the curriculum: they are the first core of social studies, from the point of view of cultural prestige and intellectual stability. But where is the expected second core, the subjects that invented and use the distinctively *social* descriptive language that describes not only who we are and where we have been but who the various *we* of the world are, and what constitutes the contemporary situation? Through what means do we examine our own sociocivic culture, the way we live now, and—because internal comparisons are touchy—the ways that others live, through some extension outward of the sociological description to a cross-cultural framework?

Beard spoke of this genre of knowledge as representing the "conditioning realities." Rather than thinking of sets of subjectmatters as the primary and secondary cores, largely in terms of their priority or recency in the intellectual landscape and in education, it would be more sensible to think of a core and surround: that is, with the later-established subjects *conditioning* the selection and significance of the contents of the inner core. Such a model would hold at any era and in any locale. It would also accord with Lawrence Cremin's notion that history, at least, 'borrows' analytical concepts from adjacent fields.

The curious absence of an adequate social description would come as a surprise to all the thoughtful scholars and educationalists of the turn of the century, and to those who know American intellectual and cultural history well enough to know that the Progressive movement itself assumed some kind of lively, casually empirical, quotidian sociological description. Educated laypersons may also be surprised. While it is not true, as some intellectuals have claimed, that from a scholarly and scientific point of view the midcentury has seen a domination by sociological thinking,* the 'sociological imagination' has been evident, and the methods of sociologists—polls, surveys, and so on—have had an enormous effect on the conduct of affairs and on what might be called civic literacy. Here we deliberately use the term 'sociology' as something roughly equivalent with 'social science' because, while this is a crude usage, even quite sophisticated people think that, fundamentally, sociology and social science are the same enterprise. (No one uses, say, 'politics' or 'economics' in such a synecdochic fashion.)

The reasons why a general sociology never took shape in the schools are, essentially, that the discipline itself changed direction soon after the twentieth-century expansion of public education began, so that the aim of empirical description of society altered; and that the subjectmatter of sociology, for schools, is always a sensitive one. The kind of community-based sociology, involving close and sustained fieldwork and participant-observation, that was the style of those sociologists who so influenced the background of the 1916 reform (section 9.1), went relatively out of fashion by the 1930s, as a more analytical and functional approach came in. This meant, among other things, that sociologically trained teachers could not 'do' sociological studies with their students in their own community: or rather, they could (and sometimes did) do that, but it wasn't Sociology. The sensitive nature of socially realistic study in schools is known to all, at some level of awareness. In the same way that one wing of social studies tends to avoid the study of religion and philosophical values, so does the other wing manage to avoid studying class, social conflict, and ethnic strife.

This is not just a rhetorical generalization. The fact is, social studies and sociology textbooks do *not* confront conflict directly, except to allude to it in the context of pointing out that American society has always survived internal conflict in the past, and better than some societies. Ethnic diversity is shown to be present, but not described in any detail. A sociology textbook will explain concepts such as occupational status, social mobility, family of origin, even 'social stratification,' but it will not normally take the term 'class' and demystify it, to show how it may mean nothing more than these specialized concepts, in some contexts, but then again can mean something more—a hypothesis about the motivation for and perpetuation of one aspect of social structure. It is as if, by analogy, 'scarcity' in economics had to be shied away from.

It is not just because some American history is too rosy and chauvinistic that some believe that social studies has amounted to nothing but a course in Americanism; it is because a facet of social description is missing. It is missing, first of all, on the empirical level. Most students do not, I believe, leave high school with the attitude that social study can provide evidence bearing on the

*An English observer, Peter Scott, claims that "We are all social scientists now." He overstates.[12]

dreams and interests and intuitions of human beings. They do not understand survey results over time as a meaningful social indicator, rather as snapshots used for a policy argument. They do not understand population dynamics and how they shape the quality and character of life, or what is involved in controversies about share of national income, the poor as victimized, or racism as institutionalized. They do not know their own relationship to the media that affect them. It is not that they do not have the *correct* answers on these matters, but that they do not appreciate the power that social data and empirical reference points give (to some) in the sociocivic conversation. They do not know that the social studies have analogues, on the one hand, to libraries in the humanities or, on the other hand, to tables of constants and tolerance calculations in the physical and engineering fields. James Madison said: "Knowledge will forever govern ignorance. And a people who mean to be their own Governors must arm themselves with the power which knowledge gives." This kind of rough-and-ready empirical familiarity with present-day life has been widely thought to be a necessary goal of social studies, and in fact of education. A grasp of the conditioning realities branches both to social understanding and informed decision-making—or so it has been assumed.

It is not that sociology and anthropology must be given separate courses or a fixed amount of time in the curriculum. History can do a great deal to teach a sense of objective relativism—that is, the simple fact that circumstances and setting make a difference in human experience. In addition, 'social' history of recent decades adds the kind of depth of evidence of broad-scaled or representative events and structures that can amount to the sociological attitude.* The development of microeconomics, human geography, the study of political behavior—all of these help to get across the idea that, while history makes men, so does the world make men in history. With regard to anthropology, which first studied societies 'without history' (in European terms), we have pointed out that anthropology today is comfortable with the notion that cultures are, if not historically determined, historically contingent.

In discussing what world studies have to be, most come to the conviction that, since neither parallel sequential histories nor a full taxonomy of traits and customs can be achieved, some flexible confluence of geography, economics, anthropology, and comparative sociology is still needed, over and above the historical perspective. Global studies should ideally involve three partly parallel, partly hierarchical approaches. First is a bottom-up description of the actual interconnectedness of specific structures. This is the social scientific attitude, essentially an extended form of structural analysis, going beyond area studies and case-by-case cultural inventories. It can meaningfully consider whether some level of transformation, integrating subsystems into larger working systems, is occurring. (It should not assume that such is the case.)

Second is a level of policy-framing, a relating of current developments and

---

*The greatest founders of European sociology, most obviously Max Weber, came out of history-laden backgrounds, and wanted primarily to test historicism as a broad 'modern' epoch formed.

events to social and political choice, within particular societies and as regards choices one nation makes that concern or affect others. This extends the tradition of international relations, in that while it is neorealist or geopolitical in character, it raises the *possibility* that, on the world level, things are not a zero-sum game where one society's progress is another's setback. Note that this possibility can apply either to certain *dimensions* that concern special interests, such as protection of the environment or scientific cooperation, where interrelatedness leads to relatively greater order, a positive sum, in one particular sector; or to a *general* positive-sum thinking involving supranational organization or action.* Third, there is the goal of an adequate historical-descriptive picture, as part of general ethnological study. Some things are worth studying because they exist, and have cultural value, and because they exemplify what we cannot study only in the abstract: language, history, culture, social organization. Here it is important *not* to invent new approaches, or assume that established traditions and disciplines are obsolete. Women's studies, ethnohistory, environmental economics, and so on are all legitimate and exciting approaches. But traditional courses, especially in precollegiate education, can often yield the most challenging questions and the most illuminating angles.

This brings us back to a difficult problem. Teachers can accommodate, in fact they welcome, new material and new slants. A good teacher has in her armamentarium all kinds of insights and fresh ways of thinking, to use as needed, when the discussion reaches that point, or when students make known their own interests and needs—some of which are bound to be new in every new classroom. But teachers cannot synthesize all the material they deal with from all angles of vision. Only geniuses can do so. On a less exalted level, few persons can attain 'the sociological attitude' or Bohannon's 'anthropological squint' without studying or at least reading deeply in those disciplines.

18.3   How Progress Can Be Made

The reformers of 1916 assumed that teachers trained in this secondary core would appear in the schools (at least teachers trained in general sociology—presumably since the intellectual temper of the times would filter into the teaching profession). Those who served on broad national commissions in the 1930s and 1940s assumed that all the disciplines, now solidly represented in the universities, would be taught in the curriculum. Neither set of circumstances proved true. Today it is believed by some that the sheer necessity of a global frame of reference for social studies, combined with the recognition that the problems that have to be faced by the generation now being educated are inherently multidisciplinary, will somehow guarantee that things will change: that universities will train, and schools will hire, the right mixture of educated

---

*In other words, world studies should attempt to raise objectively a question of theoretical ecology: whether greater degrees of order or bounded energy in one system suck energy from, and thus impose disorder upon, adjacent areas.

persons for a curriculum suitable for the coming century. Based on past experience, this is doubtful. So is the opposite alternative. The 'infusion' of all the best modern thinking into the minds of teachers, and the fusion of such thinking there, does not generally happen spontaneously. Why should we expect teachers to synthesize knowledge across entire bodies of knowledge, covering a huge expanse of time and space, when university scholars and men and women of affairs do not? Most of us are magpies, not Minervas. Geniuses are rare in every walk of life.

There are three plausible grounds for some hope. First, in the revision of textbooks; second, in the gradual convergence of the disciplines themselves to new patterns; and third, in the recognition that the middle grades are traditionally and intrinsically more permeable, more flexible in organization and tone, than the grades of the senior high school, where required courses and disciplinary electives take up all the available time.

The first is easily described, though not easily accomplished. As argued in section 17.4, if scholars are willing to accept the responsibility (and the degree of attention to the realities of schools that is implied), they are probably in a position to establish workable quality control over textbooks that few school systems or public groups will question. This would be a far more substantial contribution to precollegiate public education in the nation as a whole than almost any amount of energy spent on inservice workshops, 'refresher courses,' and similar teacher-professor contacts, which must inevitably be limited and local in effect (although ethically admirable, and important to the individuals involved). The practice of seriously reviewing school texts would substantially change things if: (a) it were done in a gracious and beneficent spirit, recognizing that texts for schools are not works of original or deep scholarship; (b) it were done in a practical fashion, keeping bad, out-of-date, and intellectually dishonest books out of the schools, rather than promoting masterpieces; and (c) if scholars would see to it that *co*disciplinary expositions, where two or three related subdisciplinary bodies of knowledge are brought to bear on the topics at hand, were effectively realized. In this way, students would be saved from trendy materials bearing the magical label of 'multidisciplinary,' while being shown that scholars and theorists do deal with topics that cut across disciplinary traditions, and do read and talk to each other. If serious reviewing could be accepted as a responsibility, and if those who pass judgments on books were willing to appear before text adoption committees, teacher professional bodies, and so on to explain those judgments, much could be accomplished. To assume, however, that this would solve all problems of instruction would be a foolish mistake.

18.3.1   MOVEMENT IN THE DISCIPLINES

The second locus of promise is that the human science disciplines are currently in a phase, neither of topical differentiation and division of labor nor of methodological efflorescence in the service of such specialization, but a period of cross-talk and convergence of interests.*

In most of the disciplines, the drift from structure to culture is marked. 'Civic culture,' for example, is a more meaningful notion than it has been in previous decades. Political anthropology, cultural geography, economic demography, and many other fields now combine the static and the dynamic, the local and the universal, in their approaches to human affairs. All of these, and cognate fields, represent a recognition of cultural integrity and diversity, and, moreover, a model in which 'culture' is not contained within distinct geographical boundaries or shared historical experiences. Cultures leak, in other words, and affect each other. This large trend is hopeful for the sake of world study in the schools, and for the sake of a social studies that integrates human perceptions and attitudes with objective description. As Sidney Hook has put it:[13]

> Every student needs to be informed, not only of significant facts and theories about nature, society, and the human psyche, but also of the conflict of values and ideals in our time, of the great maps of life, the paths to salvation or damnation, under which human beings are enrolled. He or she must learn how to uncover the inescapable presence of values in every policy, how to relate them to their causes and consequences and costs in other values, and the difference between arbitrary and reasonable value judgments.

This general movement to bring together the analytical and the interpretive, the configurational and the processual—a movement that provides room for the humanities and the social sciences to cooperate—is generally thought of as the semiotic turn, or the cognitivization of objective analysis. As such, it is the most recent of the succession of 'master ideas'—sea changes in the intellectual spirit—sketched in at various points in this book. That succession, crudely summarized from about the 1880s onward, runs as follows:

- social evolutionism: in the schools, represented by the centrality of traditional history and civil government
- structural-functionalism: the New History, political science, and in some respects community civics
- empirical positivism: Merriam's division of labor across the social science disciplines; behavioral political science
- cognitivism: the New Social Studies, with its logic of the disciplines
- the semiotic turn: legal study and constitutionalism, the return to citizenship, history as a story well told, culture theory in the various disciplines

Further off, on the horizon, I believe there is forming a new master idea, which represents an important interpenetration of biological, cosmological, and social

*This is a description of processes under way, not a judgment of good or bad in intellectual history.

thinking. This is a kind of running together of evolution and history, which in a deep way expresses, at several levels, the Darwinian notion of random variation with selective retention. In evolutionary terms, it is not deterministic, but stochastic. Evolution in the human realm (which means that natural and social realm that human beings inhabit simultaneously) does not so much unroll as meander. Historical process and cultural inertia close off paths not taken, but leave the future relatively open. Nature itself now has its own evolutionary history rather than merely a fixed physical structure. On its side, society is not a fixed order but an adaptive process. Both the actual and the virtual change over time. This is no longer a Newtonian world.

This is not news to some anthropologists or to some historians.* But it is beginning to be prefigured in an evolutionary-stochastic economics; it is already present in the convergence of historical demography, prehistory, archaeology, historical sociology, and the biosocial sciences such as primatology, human population genetics, and social biology. It goes far beyond nineteenth-century models of historicism and national or ethnic character. It transcends questions of diffusion versus independent multiple invention, or uniformitarianism. As usual, students seem not to be taken aback by such sweeping notions, but to take very large and long-term, sometimes cosmological, factors in stride. As Whitehead predicted in 1925,[15] the realization that even natural law is local and partial in action, and that probabilistic thinking works, has changed the world.

Historical evolutionism and culture theory work well together, in fact entail each other.† For the schools, this might mean, in twenty or thirty years, that the attempt to confront world study was not a chimera. (If so, the relative failure of sociology to take root in the schools in order for citizens to deal adequately with domestic society would become less serious, because that need would have been superseded.) But twenty or thirty or more years means a lot of ill-educated students. And the world study program may well turn out to be just a fatter photo album, ethnocentrically selected and arranged.

Given the disciplinary structure of training of teachers, how can judicious codisciplinarity and the convergence of fields on new frontiers (temporal as well as spatial) be introduced into the curriculum? One possibility is that the disciplinary pattern of education in the universities will alter. The social sciences have developed a number of powerful methodologies and focal questions by staying apart from each other, by staying distinctive. Modern biology is no older than the social sciences, and the biological sciences have gone through even more sweeping change of paradigms and master ideas. Yet students in these

---

*Or to the founder of theoretical sociology, Max Weber, who pointed out that transhistorical or universal generalizations in the social realm are ultimately weak. "For the knowledge of historical phenomena in their concreteness the most general laws, because they are devoid of content, are also the least valuable. . . . In the cultural sciences, the knowledge of the universal or general is never valuable in itself."[14]

†Unless a vogue for 'culture' is simply a Panglossian 'reading' of one's own perceived reality, or a self-validating mutual recital of 'shared meanings.'

sciences study a whole set of related fields, at least to some level, and a good part of chemistry as well. As theoretical continuity develops in the social science disciplines, it may become difficult or impossible for someone with a sociology major never to study economics. The advantage of this would be not so much in the added content that a student would know, but in the prevention of the development of theories and models that are radically incompatible with other knowledge.

18.3.2   THE SENIOR COURSE

We might also recall that the reformers of 1916 (and others since) placed special importance on the grade-12 'capstone' course in social studies. This was a brilliant and moving idea.* The senior course was to provide a chance, finally, for historical understanding to be brought to bear on present circumstances, and for disciplinary knowledge to illuminate a real-life situation or set of problems. It was understood that the relevant disciplinary knowledge was likely to be plural, since problems demanding choices do not come in disciplinary wrappings. It was also wagered that by the last year touchy or controversial issues could be discussed, especially those that recur, in changing form, in American life. The course was intended to show students that their education amounted to something: the ability to make life real for themselves, and to participate fully in it. Personal and citizenly efficacy would go hand in hand.

It is a fine vision still. If there were such a culminating framework in place, many conflicts over how particular subjectmatter comes into and leaves the curriculum would be solved. The problem of Holocaust Studies might be lessened, for example, if the nature of prejudice, ethnic repression, and genocide were examined periodically in such a frame. Ecological aspects of global change could be accommodated, whatever the specific crisis, within a general approach. Such a standing frame would help to keep unstructured, trendy, or trivial stuff *out* of the curriculum: the POD course was not to be a rap session. One can imagine the teachers of such a course telling their students that its great virtue was that the topic of that year would be obsolete in short order—but that the ability to bring knowledge toward generic application would not be. It also would provide a way to bring up to date students' familiarity with data series, with new legislative and regulatory law, and with the ramifications of current events. It would permit national traumas to be ventilated and perhaps assuaged.

The intended significance of such a course perhaps lay even deeper than this. One function of public schooling is to knit together social interaction and experience. This is clearly so in the early grades, where learning about others, about differences and similarities, about dealing with nonfamilial (in fact

---

*The customary course title, Problems of American Democracy, was perhaps a strategic error; see section 4.7.

nonpersonal) authority occurs for children in groups. As groups move through school, they help to construct each others' biographies, they live in history together. The capstone course, at grade 12, surely was intended to catch this sense of shared experience, to celebrate differences and similarities, and to capture the essence of a cohort, which some sociologists and historians believe to be of lifelong significance. The possibility that such an emphasis on the cohort or the era might create a certain oscillation in the system—by heightening a Class of '89 reality, a Class of '90 reality, and so on—would be offset by the perspectives instilled by the prior study of history and the other social studies. If such a course were to analyze current issues and problems, texts as such would not be available, and higher-order thinking would have to be attempted.

The reasons why the twelfth-grade capstone course never became what it was meant to be are fairly clear. The course demanded much preparation, and probably team-teaching. Some parents did not want students seriously discussing problems and policies of society.* In eras when vocationalism was strong, some students found it a waste of time; when the academic motive was ascendent, other students preferred to take advanced elective work. Beyond this, it implies a homogeneous student group and a dominant educational purpose subscribed to by most or all participants. It is impossible for the educational system to 'track' its students in prior years and then expect them to believe that they can, at the end, contribute jointly and with equal dignity to such a course. Most important of all, in many schools, it will be impossible for students to bring a plural, discipline-based set of knowledges to a focus if they have missed the rudimentary concepts of some of the social studies; as, without practice along the line, it will be impossible for them to produce historical-mindedness and critical thinking on cue. Thus a Current Issues course in grade 12 may be desirable, but it can be only one option suitable for some students (together with AP courses, supervised community service, remedial skill work required for graduation, studying computer science or accountancy at a local community college or trade school, or dropping out, in some cases to enter the world of work).†

It will be pointed out that these limitations apply generally throughout the high school years. That is why the middle grades are important. They still provide some room for maneuver in and enrichment of the curriculum, though not by the addition of separate courses. This is the third basis for hope.

18.3.3 THE MIDDLE GRADES

One aspect of the importance of the middle grades (here, the upper elementary through junior high school years) is well summarized by a historian and a psychologist, writing jointly:[16]

*Indeed, such a course does provide the possibility of thought-control. And advocates of 'strong' democracy, such as Rousseau, sometimes minimize the need for, even the appropriateness of, group discussion and debate prior to democratic decision-making, on the ground that the powerful use this to coerce the weak.

†The increasing extent of course mandates and graduation requirements actually reduces these options in many cases.

We maintain a generally undemanding common curriculum in the middle schools, in the hope of reaping social benefits from a school system that does not sort children according to academic performance.* Then we track within the comprehensive high school—but on the basis of a middle school preparation that is often too weak to permit high-level study, even for the most able students. Thus, an important first step toward raising educational standards is to raise the level of instruction and performance in the middle school. . . . [One way, they point out, is to track earlier and more pervasively.] The harder but preferable path is a nontracked middle school curriculum that sets high intellectual standards in a core program required of *all* students—even those who have effectively been denied, up to now, the stimuli of high expectations and challenging programs.

The potential of the middle grades is that of flexibility and fluidity—in terms of content, pedagogy, and child development.† In these years, children are open and curious and able to entertain hypothetical and abstract notions. They know enough about the world to make talking with them—for the purpose of forming and trying out ideas—easier: not a small matter for teachers. They are in the midst of major cognitive and linguistic developmental changes, toward a more flexible competency in handling language and managing the rules of discourse; they are becoming aware that things said differently shift their meaning, for example, that textbooks are not stories; they can paraphrase and talk about talk. They are certainly making inferences beyond what is given as fact, and are relatively willing to make their inferences public so that they can be shaped: in other words, higher-order thinking is already under way but has not yet been stylized into academic discourse, philosophical disputation, political debate, social intercourse, and all the other grown-up registers and routines. Because of the formal nature of later disciplinarily oriented learning, and the highly constrained nature of 'higher-order thinking' there, it is probably true that if in these years children are not encouraged to do truly reflective thinking, to combine ideas in creative ways, to puzzle genuinely and idiosyncratically over conceptual problems and inconsistencies, they will not be likely to do so—with regard to intellectual material, at least—for some years if ever. Socially, at least in the younger years, students are still connected to home and community, while being to some extent out of the nest. They are intensely curious about others, and are not yet locked into stereotyping by gender and ingroup/outgroup.

For these and related reasons, the possibility of 'fused' study and of 'spiraling' are real. With regard to the latter, children have not yet reached the point at which most school content is somewhat familiar: meaning that it is either old hat or carries with it the conviction, arrived at through experience, that the learner is hopeless at it. Spiraling here can mean truly going deeper and getting tighter;

---

*The authors fail to point out here that most children are 'tracked,' in one way or another, with regard to their progress in the basic academic skills, chiefly reading and numeracy, very early.

†This theme, and the interrelation of these aspects, is well presented in a recent report from the Carnegie Council on Adolescent Development.[17]

later, it often means simply quick review. With regard to the former, children do not yet expect that academic work will be divided into fields and procedures appropriate to fields. Thus the dense correlation of history and geography, each serving as a ground for the other, seems natural, as does finding a long unit on the fundamental concepts of sociology or anthropology in the middle of a history or world cultures class. The student will accept learning about market crashes and their causes and results, without worrying that too much time spent on 1873 will mean that they will do poorly on the American History test at the end of the semester. Here it is possible for teachers and students to decide to wander down a byway of special interest to them, or to play for a while with exotic terms and concepts from a new field; later, it may not be feasible or ethical to do so, as 'coverage' becomes imperative.*

The middle-grades are currently the focus for much research, by psychologists and others, that is of potentially great importance to the schools. One body of research deals, roughly speaking, with *social cognition*: that is, the ways in which people (developmentally and otherwise) conceptualize social processes and relationships, and achieve a sense of the otherness of others, the range of social perspectives that individuals bring to everyday or intellective topics, how social motivations interact with subjectmatters, how attitudes toward conceptual material develop, and so on. Social study per se depends directly on understanding the perspective of another, and on understanding that things are not self-evident.†

The other crucial line of research is that of cognition in specific subject domains: basically, the idea, for example, that people understand history differently from math. (And that the doubling-back process, the refocusing of the old by the assimilation of the new, varies across fields. This, of course, is part of the spiraling idea, which is actually a sort of artichoke model in which one gets to the essentials last.) Such research naturally enough involves the middle grades. Earlier, children may not know enough fundamental content and may not be able to work with it, mentally and linguistically, in enough diverse ways to make them very rewarding subjects (at least in nonhierarchically organized fields); later on, their ways of dealing with specific kinds of material are set (at least temporarily), and difficult to break down and refigure.

Most cognitive scientists concerned with education today agree, whatever their theoretical backgrounds, that the general area of domain-specific learning and understanding is the most important research area of all. Unfortunately, the

---

*In 1948, Fred Hoyle wrote: "Once a photograph of the Earth, taken from the *outside*, is available... a new idea as powerful as any in history will be let loose." This is the kind of idea, new in the world, that can be taken up productively in the middle grades, perhaps better so than in high-school courses.

†Nothing sinister is implied here, simply that social thinking is not done by people who see nothing below the surface or who find life quite unproblematical. No matter how radically divergent they may be in other respects, social thinkers invariably believe that 'reality' must be scrutinized, worked on, to make sense; that there is no such thing as immaculate perception.

close study of cognition in the area of mathematics, for example, goes back only thirty or forty years, and it is only beginning in history (and in the other fields of the social studies to a much lesser extent). Quick progress cannot be expected—but any real progress is likely to be valuable. The other strong caveat, besides warning against expecting rapid breakthroughs, is that research on domain-specific thinking tends to look at the mental (and related) operations of individuals, and in tightly controlled experimental settings. As has always been the case in applying research on individuals to education, there is a huge gap between these procedures and the reality of children learning in groups in a very complicated and hard-to-analyze situation. In classrooms, researchers cannot—and teachers cannot—be expected to get inside the kids' heads at the precise moment to see concepts being put together, syllogisms created, inferences drawn. There is some promise in cognitive sociology and anthropology for bridging this gap, but that promise is as yet weak, partly because it is undervalued in the research world. The point as regards the middle grades is that any advance, probably involving multidisciplinary research teams, toward a more realistic sketch of students interacting with teachers, teachers representing knowledge in various ways, the actual use of materials, the pacing of learning, and so on, will probably happen here.

Some will object that the emphasis in the middle grades on combining of subjectmatters, on spiraling forward and back, and on encouraging speculation and reflection holds back the specific progress that some students could be making along certain specific lines of content. A very complex set of judgments is involved here. Obviously, if one wants children to learn lists of names and dates, or memorize log tables, they might as well start young. But such learning has serious limitations, in almost any field. Studies of cooperative learning and, more generally, learning that takes place more or less in public in the classroom do not show that able students are harmed or held back.* Much learning, of course, has to take place within one person's head, particularly the synthesis of knowledge. But almost anything learned is better learned if one participates with or simply observes others in approaching it from many other angles and perspectives (including the perspectives provided by other knowledge). No student is so gifted that she apprehends all the ways in which a datum or a concept can be approached, or how it will fit into other mental structures. This is why the richness and relative flexibility of content and pedagogy in the middle grades can be so rewarding. Part of learning for very able students, after all, is to learn what to do on their own, when they have finished the lesson or figured out the answer. A student who cannot decide how to use a pocket of free time in the classroom is not truly a capable student. And for students of any ability, part of the game is to know where you are facile, where you have to be cautious,

---

*A good summary is given by Robert Slavin.[18] A caution is that studies of cooperative learning have not looked at long sequences and episodes of learning, but at limited situations that may benefit from novelty. Cooperative learning may need to occur in contrast to other aspects in order to be effective.

what helps you forge ahead quickly, and where you have to be content with minimal competence, or faking it. It is impossible for a learner to learn how to learn without observing others doing the same.

Finally, a nontrivial reason why the curriculum of the middle grades should be kept dense but malleable is that some teachers thrive on it. It is hard for some (fortunately not for all) to engage in the limited conversation, year after year, that adults can have with younger children. It is hard for some to teach the same formal material, organized in the same way, again and again, in high school. Some teachers welcome the chance, in middle grades, to introduce new material, to use special units, to respond to current issues and problems in society—without having to bill themselves as specialists in Energy Studies or Central America, and without having to press the district for permission to create a new course, adopt special textbooks, and the like. If such teachers thrive on the relative intellective and social freedom that these grades can permit, that must also benefit students, parents, and the community.

Nothing in what is said here should imply that the middle grades should be unstructured or that any and all content should simply be stumbled upon or glanced at. Quite the contrary. Here, as elsewhere in the process, rigorous selection is needed. A concentration on less can be more valuable than a forced march through more. It is simply that here a more flexible matching of content to the interests and abilities of students can take place. The wisest short advice on pedagogy and the curriculum ever offered may be Whitehead's recommendation to be ruthlessly concrete in deciding what to study, but then to deal with that material *in every possible combination*. Only such an approach does justice to the interrelationship of content and the reality of paths to understanding.

The other widely perceived problem with keeping the middle grades rich and variegated is downward pressure from higher levels of education for unequivocally higher levels of achievement of basic skills. Colleges and high schools do not want to teach reading and writing remedially: therefore the middle schools had better make sure the job is done properly. One consideration here is that reading and writing, like thinking, have to involve some object: children need to read and write *about* something. Reading and writing (like thinking) about something can be a strength of the middle school, as more kinds of things get studied, read, and written about. This is why the writing-across-the-curriculum movement has found its natural place, and seems to be accomplishing much, in the middle grades.

A further consideration involves the standard or definition of competence in basic skills such as reading. The societal level and distribution of 'literacy' changes enormously over time, and generally upward.[19] We expect more and more literacy in the population, and always find present levels inadequate. Further, because from the point of view of cognitive and educational researchers reading and related skills are so mysterious, so hard to understand scientifically, we all tend to think of learning 'reading' as difficult and risky for children. This may be a whopping fallacy. In terms of the basic processes, of knowing what marks on the page call for in the way of focused attention and of sight-sound 'decoding,' most children learn and learn easily, apart, of course, from the problem of neurologically based reading disability. But many of the problems with reading and basic comprehension are created *in* schools, in the early grades, in ways that make it impossible for the middle school to do the job later. Most children start out acquiring reading skills (or refining them, since many of the most basic skills are picked up outside school) quite well. Then, by grade 3 or so, some become identified as nonverbal, or culturally deprived, or 'learning-disabled.' Children so classify themselves. Social shaming occurs, and a complex set of tracks open up that will debar many children from a richly verbal, referential world in the school. By the time they reach grades 4 or 5, many children are reading about things that are of no meaning to them; and here drill will not help, nor will 'more content.' By grade 6 or 7, because their deficiencies are so accentuated by the importance of literacy skills in school, many students have come to think of the school as not a nurturing place for growth but a prison.

Such a sketch does not do justice to the difficulty of the problem. But the well-meaning call for reform—*at least* we can provide basic literacy for all our children in school—is in part only a restatement of the problem, not a solution. It is equivalent to saying, If we spend $100 on each child we provide equal opportunity. There are features of early schooling in our society that militate against schools being able to teach reading, per se, effectively. Many have been struck by how in other societies (for example, Japan) a mother works intimately with the very young child, holding him on her lap, tracing the characters with him, shaping the corresponding sounds—and producing a child for whom literacy is not a problem. How such a result can be achieved in our society is unclear. But basic skills boot camp in middle school provides no satisfactory solution.

18.3.4   WHEN SOCIAL STUDIES WORKS

We have given special attention to the middle grades and special endorsement to Whitehead's recommendation, because together they form much of the basis for this writer's attempt to make sense of social studies. There must be a principled selection of rich but representative content to be included in the curriculum, and there must be a reasonable multiplicity of approaches to and framing of that content, taking account of pedagogy, the institutional features of schools, the goals of society, and the ability of learners. I have no better short summary to suggest than that the social studies must instill *socially realistic thinking*.

'Social realism' carries with it some rather debased literary or political connotations.* Let us try to approach socially realistic thinking in a somewhat broader frame. A number of years ago, when the social study of language was

---

*I am tempted to suggest another term, *colloquial realism*, to mean how people together deal with the world. Beard spoke in a more external mode, of the "conditioning realities."

first in the program of linguistics (one should say, first again, since it had been the normal frame of reference in most periods prior to the 1950s), Dell Hymes, a linguist, anthropologist, and educator, suggested that there might be three dimensions, which tended to be levels, in the social study of language.[20] One could ask that students of language (or linguistics as a field) be *socially aware*. This would mean, for example, that it be granted that people speak differently from each other, that most nations include more than one linguistic group, or that in every context, ranging from social intercourse to legal procedures or science, language matters. Social awareness would involve acknowledging the pervasiveness of linguistic variation.

One could then propose that students (and users) of language be *socially realistic*. This would entail some attempt to discover why and how variation occurs. Is such variation random or patterned (or when is it the one, when the other)? What are the purposes to which language is put that cause it to alter, according to the topic or discourse, the intention of the speakers and listeners, the history and circumstances of communities of language users, and other motivational, social, and situational factors? In considering why language varies, one is obliged, in order to be 'realistic,' not to accept uncritically assertions like 'One can only really think in one's native language,' or, 'The meaning of speech lies in the intentions of the speaker' (or the intentions of the hearer, or in the intervening ether), or 'Bilingualism in a society tends to drive its members apart.' A socially realistic sociolinguistics thus involves a degree of disciplined inquiry, a certain amount of knowing what you are talking about combined with curiosity about looking further—all this without any irritable reaching after conclusions.

The third level of the social study of language, Hymes suggested, involved thinking of language as *socially constitutive*. That is, to think of linguistic behavior as that which continually creates and re-creates society, of verbally construed concepts as having practical force in the world, of the rules of the game that we use to handle language as determining to some extent the way we know. Obviously, this aspect of language can never be absolutely or exclusively or 'essentially' true. But it is broadly characteristic of much thinking in the social and human sciences—it is the semiotic idea—and much of social *science* per se depends upon some such notions at the theoretical and model-building level.*

The burden of this book as a whole is that 'social studies' is not realized merely by schools undertaking to create a degree of social awareness. Most people come to this without schools; some, educated or not, never get the idea. At the other extreme, 'social studies' need not demand the commitment of students to the idea that social processes and structures and concepts are the first and foremost aspect of reality, or that the work of the world is first and foremost social and political and only then aesthetic, scientific, philosophical, commercial. One of

---

*For example: Let us define 'opportunity cost' as . . . ; or, We may distinguish between class and caste in the following terms . . .

the failures of the New Social Studies was that it seemed to be asking for some commitment to the constitutive power of social concepts—a commitment that may be required of graduate students and theorists, but only provisionally, even there.

Specifically, the study of social science electives in high school *may but need not* require such a commitment. One can study any subject seriously, and come to understand its rules and terminology deeply, without believing that the world is a text, or that science makes the world, or that history is destiny, or that the only physical causation that counts is at the subatomic level. Moreover, by relatively undisciplined paths, a student can stumble onto a principle, a book, an insight, a style of thinking that will change his life or cause her willingly to profess. Conversely, in the early grades, the goal of social awareness may indeed make it desirable to highlight facts and words and phenomena, to orient children earlier to possibilities for social study that lie ahead. But the early grades have other crucial intellective and social goals in public education. So do the high school grades, where meeting tests of sufficient understanding of the subjects that society calls essential (with or without deep personal commitment) is a matter of considerable moment. Again, the middle school years are of particular importance, in that social realism cannot exist without (and must follow from) social awareness; and can in turn lead on to a deeper belief in the social construction of reality—but need not do so.*

From 'social studies' in the schools we want students to regard the social world and understand that to do so means to look through and beyond—that it is not objectively given, and that to think it so is not social thinking. Outside a high school in Boston in late 1988 I encountered a tenth-grader who was reading the news section of the daily *New York Times*. He commented that he generally glanced at the headline and the first paragraph of each story, to see what it was all about, and then turned to the end to read the story more or less backward. He did this, he said, because he couldn't really understand why what was happening was happening without knowing what had occurred before, and without some commentary about why it was happening this way. I have no reason to think this student exceptionally brilliant, but there is much reason to think him thoughtful and well educated. This is the student everyone wants in social studies. He knows that 'what is happening' is incomprehensible without a formal frame of reference, which comes very largely, in world affairs, from social and cultural (and economic and political . . .) conceptions. He knows when he must teach himself history backwards. He knows that 'data' are meaningless unless they

---

*The most interesting dependency here is that the effective study of 'civics' (whatever it is called, in its cross-disciplinary complexity) *must* by democratic theory involve socially realistic understanding before the next stage can be reached, but also *must* lead on to the next stage. Understanding about citizenship, no matter how sophisticated, is not sufficient in itself. But training in active citizenship, which is the extreme case of knowledge and attitudes 'constituting' society, is not ethical unless it corresponds to the truth.

refer to something beyond themselves. He knows, at the same time, that things do not happen in general, but only in particular, as located in time and in space. He seeks 'content' by reading the newspaper, and he uses the 'process' that works for him. He is well on the way to being an educated person, perhaps on a lifelong basis.

This is why the temptation to polarize matters, to insist on chronological history only, or place-name geography only, or the minimum of facts and the maximum of higher-order thinking, or the taskmaster teacher or the nurturant teacher, is so destructive. Above all else, the schools must offer richness, variety, and alternatives, rich discourse, and rewards for curiosity. Those who know nothing specific, know nothing. Those who know only the specific, still know nothing. The usual verbal solution is to say that, of course, content and process must go together, or that both the diachronic and the synchronic are needed. This is to say a very great nothing. I doubt that skill-learning and content-learning actually co-occur, but suspect that they alternate and only complement each other at certain junctures. I doubt that the formal structure of any social entity or phenomenon can be examined at the very same moment, and in the very same mental mode, that the developmental or historical aspects are in focus. A course or a semester or a curriculum that is all of piece, all foreground or all background, fades quickly from sight. In particular, 'higher-order thinking' is not simply a unitary alternative to memorizing facts. Facts can only be memorized when they are organized along some dimension and internally connected. 'Inquiry' can be reflective and value-laden, as in philosophy and theology; elaborative, exegetical, exfoliating, as in literary and aesthetic study and connoisseurship; logical and analytical, as in the disciplined inquiry that seeks for further discovery; or critical, in the sense of seeking the unique standpoint or first principles, as in law, political theory, or logical philosophy.*

The Whitehead dictum means that even the sound advice of 'less is more' cannot be taken too far. To do so can impose a grid or schematic on what has to remain messy and odd and hard to grasp. Some subjectmatters *need* conceptual outlining to keep them away from the level of the endless list; I have suggested that geography tends to be in this category. Other subjectmatters need richness and diversity of examples; I have suggested that economics in the schools could use more of this. Textbooks cannot do everything—cannot present all possibly useful information in perfectly organized and sequenced fashion. Nor can teachers alone.

18.4   A Plea for Pluralism

In the social studies curriculum, there need be, and can be, no hard choice between the story hour and the field trip. History should not be a known terrain

---

*Think of the different sorts of books indicated by titles such as *A Reflection on . . . ; An Inquiry into . . . ; A Critique of. . . .*

through which guided tours are conducted. Conversely, one cannot do fieldwork all one's life or hang out in museums looking at fabulous things. Again, the solution may not be to do both simultaneously, but to do them seriatim. The most brilliantly guided tour, explicitly for the purpose of learning (as with that form of the Grand Tour in the nineteenth century in which young men who would manage the Empire were led through Europe by their university tutors), can only take one so far before one gets off the bus and sets out on one's own.

At times we may face a Hobson's choice, between a recklessly blended soup of content, unpalatable because mysteriously composed, or a grazing menu, little tastes in quick succession, which is unnourishing. When terms like 'boring,' 'mindless,' 'muddle' are used in judging the social studies, it is not obvious where the problem really lies. Students do complain about lack of variety in social studies,[21] but they also complain about lack of continuity, across the extent of a year or across grades. Looking at the relevant studies, taken together, seems to show a rather complex interrelationship among the difficulty of the subject, the intrinsic interest of the subject, and its importance—a point to be taken up below.

That social studies classrooms need not be experienced as boring or mindless, and that a consistent going-beyond-the-facts can be achieved, has recently been demonstrated by Susan Stodolsky and her colleagues. Her research and the resulting book[22] have carried even further the work of Newmann and colleagues (section 17.3), which found that 'thoughtfulness' in the classroom was still very much a matter of the teacher's intentions and control. Stodolsky has provided a lead for the many observers of social studies in the schools who could not entirely believe the reiterated findings of experienced researchers such as Stake and Easley, Goodlad, or Perrone and colleagues, who consistently found classrooms to be teacher-dominated and one-note in tone (section 17.0).

In brief, it appears to be seriously misleading to look only at the dimension of who takes the initiative in the classroom and who tends to do the public performance. Teachers inevitably shape and control the class, providing sequence, timing, pace, and the like. But in this they are sensitive indeed—good teachers—to cues and responses from the students, so that matters are in fact codetermined. And teachers also, while directing the interaction, manage to create a great deal of variety, of *kinds* of activity, so that simply to code 'teacher control' does not mean that only one sort of thing is occurring. Similarly, to code 'teacher talking' does not mean that the teacher is talking in only one way.

One reason for the difference in results may be that Stodolsky and her team stayed in some thirteen schools in the greater Chicago area for some weeks, observing fifth-grade math and social studies classrooms contrastively. Thus, they came to understand the school culture more deeply than do those who make briefer visits. This meant that they could observe and record more subtle activity and interaction more accurately. More important, they used a detailed protocol for such observation and recording, which involved simultaneous dimensions such as the unit of activity, the time it took, the pace and tone, who initiated it, how it was introduced and concluded, who took the leading roles, what all others were doing, what the focus content was, what parallel content was involved, and in what form students were participating—catching the teacher's eye, trying or preparing to speak, avoiding contact, asking a question for clarification, seeking 'rule' guidance, helping to orient another student, consulting the index of the book, taking notes, and the like. Thus, to the extent feasible, they had a record of an entire grid of activity made possible by considering together all the actors, the setting, the time markers—and the various dimensions that quickly emerge from the interactions of all these.

They found a great deal more student involvement than most researchers do, provided one defines involvement in plural ways, and they found it much more in social studies than in math. They also found far more questioning, venturing, discussing, and stating of opinions in social studies than in math classes. (This latter finding is not unusual, but the former is.) Social studies instruction was not 'well-defined,' in the sense of proceeding in a set pedagogical way through a set sequence of steps; math was. Within the Chicago area, fifth graders were studying mostly history, and American history, but there were other subjects involved as well; the specific content varied greatly across classes. There was far more switching from content unit to content unit than in math, more abrupt changes in approach and tone, and more likelihood of departing from the lesson plan. There was far more group work in social studies than in math, where—other than teacher talk—seat work was the norm. Only social studies involved student reports and other task-oriented talk (other than answering teacher questions) in class.

It is not surprising that social studies showed, quite consistently, a more complex and various activity structure—more kinds of things going on in one class period. What is interesting is that *all* teachers 'did' social studies more or less the same way, even those teachers who were observed to teach math quite differently. There appeared a rather dense *patterning* of activity among teachers, over and above their individual styles: that is, whether they were better trained in social studies or better trained in math, were 'traditional' teachers or less traditional ones, or—other things being equal—talked more or invited more student comment and questioning.* This was not a rigid kind of patterning, as it sometimes is in the very early grades, with tiny episodes orchestrated down to the moment by the teacher. The social studies classes were in fact often rather stochastic in organization: one thing would lead to an unexpected next thing, which would then tend onward to a third thing. To repeat, in the public part of the class the teacher held the reins, but loosely.

There was, moreover, student-paced group work that had its own dynamics and rules, where the teacher was absent, judging only the product or bringing such work to a halt. This is not quite accurate: Stodolsky and her colleagues observed students asking for a good deal of instruction about *how* to get into and

---

*In other words, 'traditional' teachers did not stop being traditional in social studies—but they were *more* traditional in math.

out of such group time, *how* to behave while in it, and *how* the outcome would be judged. In general, in social studies, students asked for information about the management of affairs much more than in math. It was clear that an important aspect of social studies was to agree, not only between the students and the teachers, but among the students, on how things were to occur. There was also in social studies a more gradual and consensual approach to the formation of concepts, where it was not so much that a student 'got it' as how it was gotten and how expressed.

A few rather traditional, math-like social studies classes were seen, with whole-class instruction originating from the teacher and with all students responding, in principle, in the same way: reciting or reading aloud in a set order, taking notes, doing units of seatwork, and so on. These tended to be seen in classes where the topics were chronological history and geographical drill. Stodolsky writes: "There does seem to be a tendency for topics dealing with culture and society, civics, and psychology to appear in group-work or mixed format classes. The social studies curricula . . . are also distinctive in their strong emphasis on group problem solving and higher mental process objectives. . . . Peer-work groups have a high proportion of more complex intellectual goals" (p. 69). However, she points out that, even in 'traditional' classrooms, social studies students used reference materials and developed similar research skills, and felt freer to ask for clarification or in other ways to break into the presentation, than in math. In general, the Stodolsky study did not find the pervasive commitment to 'lower-order' intellective procedures and goals that some other observers have, perhaps by focusing too much on teacher behavior and not enough on student response (and indeed on the complexity of the setting and the using of time).

18.4.1   PATTERNING IN SOCIAL STUDIES

None of this means that social studies is inherently richer than math, or that group work is better than listening to the teacher. What is important is that there is a consistent interaction between what is being studied and how it is being taught and learned. The *same* teacher does more things more flexibly, and in a sense more thoughtfully, in social studies than in math. Conversely, the same students pay *more* attention to the teacher's own exposition of content in math than in social studies. Why? Because it is understood that in math if you miss a step the teacher will not catch your eye nor help you individually; and you cannot work it out with another child (because group work is not part of the class); and there is no reference book you can go to. That is the nature of math.

Some may see this as another indicator that math is 'serious business' in school, while social studies is looser and less do-or-die. This doesn't go very far: there are exams in social studies, too. Some might be disturbed that in social studies the teacher spends relatively more of her or his 'on' time giving the instructions, doing the stage management, and explaining rather mundane aspects of the material. Others will be interested to see that students' involvement increases, and that they begin to initiate more follow-up activities of their own, when questioning is allowed, when the answer is not just given but explained, when there is a fuzzy conceptual point to be sharpened up—in other words, when social studies is allowed to be messy and to some degree consensually or cooperatively done. Finally, this kind of patterning and variety in social studies is characteristic of the upper-elementary and middle-school grades, not the earliest grades and not higher grades, where another mix of activities and style of interaction may be appropriate.

While recommending careful attention to the substance of Stodolsky's book, which has important methodological implications besides, we want to comment here only on the broad implications of what has been reported. At least in these schools and in this grade, social studies has quite a special aspect. It involves a lot of different kinds of work—reading, paying attention to teacher explanations, reciting, working in groups. You can ask for clarification in social studies, and to some extent criticize the adequacy of the solution others have found. You have to learn how to use tools and helpful materials. The answer doesn't pop up at one moment. Sometimes the teacher will feel that the answer the class came up with isn't really 'right' but is pretty good anyhow, or is 'right' but not interesting. There can be periods of intense attention mixed with periods of contemplation. Some kinds of information come most efficiently from an authority, and would be stupid to ignore for that reason. Other information requires seeking for it in ways not entirely obvious. Sometimes group opinion is important, sometimes it is irrelevant.

This complexity probably depends upon a relative lack of accountability pressure: in schools and subjects where *only* factual mastery is tested for, classes are not like this. In more complex and multiform situations, it is not entirely clear who the 'good student' is: One who memorizes quickly what the teacher imparts? One who has little factual knowledge to contribute to a group, but who can keep others working toward the right goal? One who tests poorly but is good at research skills and can write a good report? For one thing, this kind of setting permits a student who simply doesn't much like social studies—and why should everyone like social studies, any more than everyone likes math?—to find some way to be at least moderately involved some of the time. Social studies may offer more routes to learning, perhaps more routes to teaching, than some other subjects do.

Neither students nor teachers may all *like* this patterned complexity, but there is no reason to think that they do not *perceive* it. We find here some support for a proposition put forward by Newmann and others: that social studies is most involving and works best (in quite concrete terms, such as the actual time spent by students paying attention and doing what is called for) when it is rather demanding, rather flexible, and rather conceptually oriented. (As Stodolsky points out, there is no evidence at all that this prevents the mastery of at least some facts—while there is considerable evidence that straight drill does.)

We also see, I believe, that in social studies the relationship between demandingness, interest, and valuation (and accomplishment) may be quite complicated. Students can find the more conceptually challenging aspects of social studies demanding, and still find social studies 'boring.' Most commentators have assumed that difficulty and interest go together, perhaps in a U-shaped fashion: that is, if it is too cut-and-dried or too 'easy,' students will not be interested, while if it is too hard they will also deal themselves out. This may be true, along a single dimension. But it is also possible that some students dislike the inherent variety and complexity of social studies (while others value it). It is a myth that all students like to participate, be called on, be expected to work with peers, and so forth. Beyond these factors, and interacting with personality and preferences, there may be a cost-benefit calculation. It is quite possible that some students come to find social studies 'boring' simply because, for most, the field is *inconsequential*. Generally speaking (there are exceptions), you won't be held back a grade if you don't do very well, and you won't be considered a dunce, or not be hired, if you know only a few dates in history.

Some would address this possible combination of complexity and inconsequentiality—it is a hypothesis—by making social studies simpler and more fateful: going back to rote learning and hard factual tests. There is very little evidence to suggest that this would work, for most students. A kind of stable learning could be engineered, but it would not appeal to most students or indeed to most others. As for making it fateful, it is not really feasible to deny someone her citizenship or other avenues for social participation in society on the grounds that she failed to be good at civics or sociology.

It would seem far more promising to face up to the complexity and tensions of social studies and make them a virtue, rather than something to be hidden or apologized for. There is a considerable bad faith contaminating social studies in the schools. Teachers signal to students that this is strange territory, stranger than English or math, and that they aren't quite sure how it should be done. Citizenship is important, but what is it? Facts must be learned, but isn't 'thinking' more important? Students signal back that they already perceived this, that they don't benefit much from being signaled that there is a problem— and that it's not their job to solve it. To the extent that this tone pervades, social studies must seem an inauthentic and confusing business.*

*The question of the extent to which multiple expectations and a kind of collusional, rather than principled, mixture of patterns within a part of the curriculum afflicts other fields is an important one. There is probably a fundamental difference between 'essential' subjects, such as English and math, and the so-called enrichment fields, such as social studies and science. In the former, external expectations may be fewer or less inconsistent, and the differentiations may be those of tracking or 'high literacy' (of which higher-order thinking is sometimes a part) versus minimal competence. In the latter, the issue may be which version of social studies is *real*—for example, real psychology, or solid sociology, or history taught in the 'modern' manner. (History, lying on both sides of this divide, may show both dimensions of difference; and, as has been pointed out, American History may be quite distinct from elective history.) My suspicion is that in 'science,' which is like social studies in that no student has to take it in quite the extent or fixed order that a student must take language arts or math, a great deal of 'signaling' goes on between teachers and students about the fact that science is 'hard'—real science, anyhow—and if the science course you're taking isn't very hard, let's call it science anyway.

How can those outside the schools preserve and defend, within limits, and help make a virtue of the diversity and tensions within social studies?

18.4.2 PROTECTING DIVERSITY

That tension and diversity are reflections of the world we live in, and must be recognized in order to face the difficult times ahead. Adaptation in society becomes impossible if we seek to limit freedom to invent and explore new social forms and attitudes, to rethink our own experience, to let some knowledge languish and other knowledge bloom. Our society possesses ways in which to winnow newness and retain what is valuable; one of these is democratic education. History and the social studies matter in society today; the former always has, and the latter have become established in part to make it matter better, to fit the present situation as exactly as possible. We still lack an adequate understanding of sociocultural diversity, in its institutional and formal aspects as well as its human aspects, and this means that as yet we fail to achieve "a decent respect for the opinions of mankind." This phrase from the Declaration of Independence referred initially to the opinions of other peoples. The opinions of other peoples count even more today, as the world becomes more highly interconnected. The social studies cannot be courses in Americanism. The phrase must also be taken to refer to the opinions of all who live within our own society—even those who believe that history is bunk, and the social sciences a mere language game. The minimal goal for social studies here must be to make it socially realistic—not for the sake of the development of social studies per se, but for the sake of the people we are and the problems we face.

Accountability as a juggernaut should be resisted. Taken too far, it prevents adaptation in the curriculum and through education. It closes off serendipity in the learning and lives of children in school, and it makes teaching a mere delivery of services. It aggravates the tension between excellence and equity. It is a further stage of the scientific management principle for schools, and if taken too far it cuts against professionalism in education. It does not matter that one form of accountability is a kind of high-culture, rather than commercial-sounding, form. To teach the old verities and test for them endlessly is boring education and inefficient besides, since the job can be done more quickly and less expensively in other ways. The back-to-basics movement, like all such schemes that involve too severe a form of management by objectives, works against both humanistic and social studies. Accountability closes paths by which experts outside the schools can sift and evaluate new knowledge and incorporate it into instruction. For example, academics can have an effect, working with teachers, in improving textbooks when textbook adoption cycles take place every five or seven years. It is unlikely that they could play such a role in a system where official textbook selection took place at the beginning of each year or, at the other extreme, where it required a change in education law to adopt a new text.

'Accountability' is disastrous only when it becomes a single standard. Obviously, the schools have to account for what they do to many publics. Rigid accountability takes away this sense of responsibility from teachers, who currently feel policed and infantilized in their relationship with the management system above and around them, but feel that they are both free and responsible in the classroom. Rigid accountability makes all efforts to bring teachers and subjectmatter specialists together pointless. In general, school-university partnerships, while immensely valuable to a few (on both sides), can have only small-scale and transitory effects. They may, indeed, widen the gap between the have and have-not systems. Professors who wish to improve schooling should direct their attention to the quality of texts, the success of the schools and departments of education in the university, and should insist that, as tests are more and more used, they be developed to test fairly what is said to be taught. We know how to test for basic skills (or think we do). But we say we teach young people to think. Within limits, tests can be directed toward this claim, and this end. They should be.

The close connection between curriculum mandates and tests needs very careful consideration by those outside the schools, since it is those outside the schools who send the message of concern and disappointment that drives the mandating and testing process. As Denis Doyle puts it:[23] "If there are national achievement tests, can a national curriculum be far behind? Indeed, in this scheme of things, we are backing into a national curriculum ... we will not choose a national curriculum so much as a national curriculum will choose us."

In the opposite direction, there are many specific forms of accountability that experts—academic and others—need to feel *toward* the school. The schools need to be protected against baseless criticism. When tests reveal that the population doesn't know very much, the schools of today should not have to take all the blame. The legal profession understands that the law will not work if the educated do not understand. Political scientists need to protect the schools from being blamed for low voter rates. And those fields of the social sciences that take schools as the object of their study—the history, sociology, anthropology of education, for example—have a responsibility to state clearly how schools work and what they are like over time, and why.

Teachers and others in education should be released from a feeling of guilt (which sometimes takes the form of massive denial) about the patterned diversity of social studies. Expectations for social studies are inherently divergent along a number of dimensions: academic knowledge and citizenship, the mastery of facts and the ability to use them in thinking, the particular and the generic, the configural and the analytic. This acceptance of the inevitable is the beginning of progress, especially in social studies where, after all, almost the root proposition is that *people disagree*—and in ways that matter to other people. The notion that the students should not experience diversity and conflict in the classroom and the curriculum tries to make school into some isle of the blessed. Most students prefer their own messy environments. They would certainly prefer not to share the anxiety and moral scrupulosity that is imposed on teachers by those who would prefer a simpler reality.

Among those who do so are thoughtful and well-intentioned people who believe that reform can be achieved by specifying a core set of knowledge, in any branch of the curriculum, which when learned by all will form the basis for cultural coherence, now and into the future. The recommendation sounds attractive on two grounds: it is inclusive (in its best form) in intention, and it specifies—and thus makes possible discussion of—what selection among content is intended. There should be more such specification. When those who make curricula compare such lists, considerable consensus results.

The underlying assumption, however, that an agreed-upon core and canon will produce better education and greater cultural integrity is, beyond a certain stage of self-evidence, doubtful. Many of the objections are obvious. Wisdom may be immutable, but it goes in and out of fashion. Lists date. Knowing facts and concepts means little without knowing how to connect them. 'Knowing' facts and concepts can prevent further learning and discussion by turning them into ends in themselves: icons and badges of membership in a mandarin caste. If adults who specify what the young should know cannot deliver the rewards they promise to the young, they are indulging in a nostalgia for their own lives and are celebrating their own success.

An even more serious problem is that the great books or cardinal doctrines or essential facts approach does not work. We know this in our lives as adults: most of what we learn we forget, and we discover that we believe something different from what we believed previously. Listing out what must constitute the core in itself accomplishes little. If we look at the essential items recommended for American schooling by E. D. Hirsch, Jr., and compare it to what is in textbooks, we see that the texts contain virtually everything on Hirsch's list (and far more besides). This, then, is another example of the fact that what is taught is not what is learned, not permanently at least.*

Most educators in fact welcome such listings, if proffered modestly. Hirsch's list frightens educators not because it implies radical rethinking and institutional change, but because it promises more of the same slogging through facts and names and mastered, tested 'content'—to very little effect. Newmann points out many of the educational problems with the approach.[25]

> It is extraordinarily difficult, virtually impossible, I believe, to begin with a list of unrelated pieces of information and then, *after* the fragments have been selected, to weave them into a meaningful message. . . . Hirsch's list still poses the enormous difficulties of contriving an integration among items chosen initially not for their contribution to an integrated message,

---

*A nice analysis of the backwards reasoning that produces such lists, as if they will in and of themselves guarantee education, is provided by James Hoetker,[24] who points out a peculiar form of reasoning from complex effect to singular cause. "Hemingway didn't spell well; therefore, spelling was not in the Oak Park schools' curriculum."

but for their frequency of use. . . . It may be useful to remind ourselves how the 'culturally literate' learned this information. . . . They learned it as a result of, but not as the major reasons for, studying authentic messages that contained the information. . . . The research on schemata and our own experience in teaching and curriculum development indicates that specific background information is most efficiently learned when it is embedded in messages that have important human purposes *other* than teaching the information itself.

Those who press Hirsch's point insist that it is exactly these messages that they want schools to convey. That is why they put 'cultural coherence' as the goal, even beyond good education. This soon runs up against the possibility that cultural coherence is defined by those who already have it; and this then becomes a form of domination that acts against, not only adaptation in society, but democratic procedure.

There is a further consideration, and one that illustrates the importance of social studies in modern education. A serious misunderstanding of the concept of 'culture' is involved. A culture is not a set of entities, physical or mental, possessed in toto by all its members. I and my fellows in a culture do not know all the same things, and only those. I do not truly 'belong' to my culture, nor does it 'belong' to me. Only part of my life is cultural, and only part of a culture is contained in a living person, or even a large set of living persons. Every person belongs to several cultures, and thus every culture contains some persons who see themselves more centrally within an adjacent culture. Cultures overlap and leak, and persons move within and across them.

These abstract propositions are easily exemplified. I look at the names carved into stone at the cornice of the library downtown. One or two of them mean nothing to me. My godson, who is a baseball fanatic, has sworn on all that is sacred to him, that 'Willie Mays' means nothing to him. I and my friends, most of whom read and talk a very great deal, every once in a while use a word that the speaker says is in his working vocabulary but that others cannot recall ever seeing or hearing. Does my godson not belong to 'my' culture, or I to his? Do I not 'belong' to my language community if my friend knows a word I do not? Should I worry that the work of the unknown eminence on the library frieze has dropped off the edge of my culture and drifted, lost, into another? 'A shared culture' does not mean a total reduplication of experience across all members— or anything approaching that. Within a culture, certain groups know relatively more of some things, and relatively less of others.

The question of domination comes up, inevitably, in these regards. Many of those who wish to share their culture genuinely wish to do so for altruistic and benign reasons. They argue that all must know a certain number of things for their own sake, in order to get along in the world. This is particularly problematic when those who define what needs to be shared are also those who determine how others get along. Very few concrete facts and concepts truly have to be known by all (except those entities that all human beings must possess, which is a level beyond culture). What is often meant, in practice, is that it is convenient and better for *us* if others know what we know. *Our* conversation flows more smoothly.* There is a philosophical problem here. 'The human conversation' becomes a monologue. The intent is fine. But cultural bullying, like moral bullying, is always for others' good. In social studies, the conversation must be more general, and had better be colloquial.

The best of the shared-culture reformers believe that pluralism is a necessary part of democratic education. They really know, too, that students do not learn by prescription, and that, while they can be caused to master a fixed array of things (in fact, may quite enjoy it, at times), education does not begin until they connect and make sense of the things they know. Reformers like Hirsch are not well served by their admirers. In April 1989, the former assistant secretary of education said, "Anyone living in a Western culture has greater need of knowing the corpus of violin music than sitar music."[26] This principle, stated in this extreme form, excludes people who might wish to study ethnomusicology or South Asian culture, some of those whose religion is not Western, and those who are basically unmusical and can't tell the sitar from the violin. For starters. In June 1989, a Bangladeshi student who had come to New York City eight years earlier was first in her class at the Washington Irving High School. She will attend a local college because her parents speak only Bengali, and she needs to live at home.[27] She will, of course, need to take time off for remedial mastery of the corpus of violin music. Whose country is this, anyway?

We face difficult times. The management of contraction and perhaps of relative economic decline in our society will not be easy in the schools, which historically could rise above certain tensions so long as they could show that they were educating more children to higher levels. The schools have done a decent job. As David Tyack and Elizabeth Hansot put it:[28]

> It is useful to compare schooling not only with its own high ideals but with the performance of other social agencies. And in that light, there is much room for pride. What other major social institution displays *less* bias with respect to race, sex, or class than do public schools? What other institution does *more* to promote equal dignity among groups or equal opportunity for all? What other public institution is *more* responsive to public influence than are the public schools? And where else can citizens find a better forum for debating the shape of a common future?

---

*Some years ago, a child from a polyglot family in the American west was enrolled for the first time in the public schools. She came home after the first day assigned to special (remedial) English. This puzzled the parents, who believed that this six-year-old child spoke English well for her age. It turned out that the new children had been given a group test in their homeroom, where it was determined by oral means who in the class understood Spanish. Those who did were assumed to be deficient in English; the working theory was that the presence of one language must mean the absence of another. (Here, incidentally, is a good example of why social studies should at least achieve the socially realistic level.)

Future-mindedness is as characteristic of this century as history-mindedness was of the previous century, in the West. Just as some in the nineteenth century saw all change as evidence of inexorable progress, so some in the late twentieth century see all change as evidence of decay and catastrophe. American exceptionalism no longer serves the purposes it once did. Nostalgia and mythic reconstruction do not make the future credible. The nation can continue to be great without being supreme in the world. In part, Americans have an advantage, in possessing a pragmatic tolerance of what the world has to offer and a healthy curiosity. As a distinguished historian has recently remarked: [29]

> What the rediscovery of Greece accomplished for learned men in the Renaissance, what the rediscovery of Aristotle meant for the medieval church, only faintly hints at what is to be gained from gazing at the modern world and its artifacts in new ways.

A cautious but confident approach to the future has been a feature of American education in general, and the social studies especially. It is why the New History came in, and why the social studies were invented. It is why enlightened citizenship is still a goal, on a broader—but not less vital—level. Given a modicum of social thinking and a due respect for diversity of content and method in education, there is no reason why the schools cannot prove the wisdom of the words of Thomas Jefferson, carved on his memorial: "Laws and institutions must go hand in hand with the progress of the human mind."

Notes

1.0 A Nation at Risk?

1. National Commission on Excellence in Education, *A Nation at Risk: The Imperative for Educational Reform* (Washington: Government Printing Office, 1983). A similar warning came from the Task Force on Education for Economic Growth, Education Commission of the States, *Action for Excellence: A Comprehensive Plan to Improve Our Nation's Schools* (Denver: ECS, 1983). Secretary Bell's comment is quoted in David Hill, "Reform in the 80s: Fixing the System from the Top Down," *Teacher Magazine* (September/October 1989):50.
2. For example, the Kettering Commission. National Commission on the Reform of Secondary Education, *The Reform of Secondary Education* (New York: McGraw-Hill, 1973).
3. Ernest L. Boyer, *High School: A Report on Secondary Education in America* (New York: Harper and Row, 1983); John I. Goodlad, *A Place Called School: Prospects for the Future* (New York: McGraw-Hill, 1983); Theodore R. Sizer, *Horace's Compromise: The Dilemma of the American High School* (Boston: Houghton Mifflin, 1984).
4. Excellent treatments of this era of corporate trusteeship over education and civic activity are contained in Richard Hofstadter, *Anti-Intellectualism in American Life* (New York: Knopf, 1964), and Rush Welting, *Popular Education and Democratic Thought in America* (New York: Columbia University Press, 1962).
5. An exception here was the report of the Twentieth Century Fund, calling for English and more English: "The most important objective of elementary and secondary education in the United States is the development of literacy in the English language."

Twentieth Century Fund Task Force on Federal Elementary and Secondary Education Policy, *Making the Grade* (New York: Twentieth Century Fund, 1983).
6. Educational Testing Service, *ETS Policy Notes* (Princeton: ETS, March 1989).
7. American Association for the Advancement of Science, *Project 2061: Science for All Americans* (Washington, D.C.: AAAS, 1989). Going even further than those commissions and panels that predicted a shift in the knowledge needed for occupational success and the economic security of the society, the AAAS ventured that "The terms and circumstances of *human existence* can be expected to change radically during the next human lifespans" (emphasis added).
8. Task Force on International Education, National Governors' Association, *America in Transition: The International Frontier* (Washington, D.C.: National Governors' Association, 1989). For the assistant secretary's views, see Chester E. Finn, Jr., in *The American Spectator* (May 1988). The governors, of course, did not specify that education *begin* with global awareness, only that it be arrived at.
9. The 1982 baseline data are provided in Educational Testing Service Policy Information Center, *What Americans Study* (Princeton: ETS, 1989). Indeed, by 1987 high school graduates nationally had increased their number of semesters of science and math to between five and six.
10. William B. Walstad and John C. Soper, *A Report Card on the Economic Literacy of U.S. High School Students* (New York: Joint Council on Economic Education, 1988).

11. Diane Ravitch and Chester E. Finn, Jr., *What Do our 17-Year-Olds Know?* (New York: Harper & Row, 1989); Gilbert M. Grosvenor, "Geography Has Been Losing Ground in Our Schools," *National Geographic* (August 1984); Grosvenor, "The Case for Geography Education," *Educational Leadership* 47 (November 1989).

12. Finn, *American Spectator*.

2.0 Organization or the Curriculum

1. National Commission on Excellence in Education, *A Nation at Risk: The Imperative for Educational Reform* (Washington: GPO, 1983).

2. *The Status of Pre-College Science, Mathematics and Social Studies Educational Practices in U.S. Schools: An Overview and Summaries of Three Studies.* (Washington: National Science Foundation, [Document SE 78-71] 1978), 14.

3. Lynn Fontana, *Perspectives on the Social Studies* (Bloomington, Ind.: Agency for Instructional Television [Research Report 78. ERIC Document 249 965], 1980).

4. Noted also in Karen B. Wiley with Jeanne Race, *The Study of Pre-College Science, Mathematics, and Social Science Education: 1955–1975, Volume III: Social Science Education* (Washington: National Science Foundation, [Document SE 78-73] 1978), section 1.

5. Irving Morrissett, "Status of Social Studies: The Mid-1980s," *Social Education* 50 (April/May 1986):86.

6. Wayne L. Herman, Jr., "Development in Scope and Sequence. A Survey of School Districts," *Social Education* 52 (September 1988).

7. Thomas Heed, "Social Studies Disciplines Taught in Bergen County Public High Schools 1985–86" (Report to New Jersey Department of Higher Education, No. 86-990780-1599, 1986, mimeographed).

8. *History–Social Science Framework for California Public Schools* (Sacramento: California State Department of Education, 1988).

9. A recent compilation of graduation requirements is given in William H. Clune with Paula White and Janice Patterson, *The Implementation and Effects of High School Graduation Requirements: First Steps Toward Curriculum Reform* (Center for Policy Research in Education, [CPRE Research Report Series RR-011], 1989). Available from the Publications Office, CPRE, Rutgers, the State University of New Jersey.

10. Edgar Bruce Wesley, *Teaching the Social Studies: Theory and Practice* (Boston: Heath, 1937).

11. Stanley P. Wronski, "Edgar Bruce Wesley (1891–1980): His Contribution to the Past, Present and Future of the Social Studies," *Journal of Thought* 17 (Fall 1982).

12. For example, Herbert M. Kliebard, *The Struggle for the American Curriculum, 1893–1958* (New York: Routledge & Kegan Paul, 1987), 125.

13. Rolla M. Tryon, *The Social Sciences as School Subjects*, part XI of the American Historical Association Report of the Commission on the Social Studies (New York: Scribner's, 1935), 401. Tryon notes wryly that in the first three decades of this century, 'social studies' might mean a coordination of subject-matters each maintaining its identity, or an expression meaning exactly the opposite: "namely... a body of integrated material in which all subjects lost their identity." He also cites examples in these decades of "social studies" indicating a sort of serial introduction to the basic terminology and concepts of the social sciences "other than history."

14. Alan Backler, *Teaching Geography in American History* (Bloomington, IN: Indiana University Social Studies Development Center, 1988), 5.

3.0 Curriculum Control

1. An authoritative comprehensive history is Lawrence A. Cremin, *American Education: The Colonial Experience 1607–1783; American Education: The National Experience 1783–1876* (New York: Harper and Row, 1970, 1982).
2. Arthur E. Wise, *Legislated Learning: The Bureaucratization of the American Classroom* (Berkeley and Los Angeles: University of California Press, 1979).
3. *Digest of Educational Statistics* (Washington: U.S. Department of Education, National Center for Education Statistics [Document CS88-600], 1988), fig. 11.
4. *Mandate for Change: The Impact of Law on Educational Innovation* (Chicago: American Bar Association Special Committee on Youth Education for Citizenship, 1979).
5. *Essential Goals and Objectives for Social Studies Education in Michigan (K–12)* (Lansing: Michigan State Board of Education, 1987).
6. Steven L. Miller, *Economic Education for Citizenship* (Bloomington, IN: Social Studies Development Center [Indiana University] and Foundation for Teaching Economics [San Francisco], 1988), 18.
7. Irving Morrissett, "Status of Social Studies: The Mid-1980s," *Social Education* 50 (April/May 1986), 304.
8. *Excellence in Social Studies Education: The Foundation of Active Citizenship* (Quincy: Commonwealth of Massachusetts, Department of Education, 1988).
9. Hazel Whitman Hertzberg, *Social Studies Reform, 1880–1980*, a Project SPAN Report (Boulder, CO: Social Science Education Consortium, 1981), chap. 2, 3; Richard Hofstadter, *Anti-Intellectualism in American Life* (New York: Knopf, 1964), pt. IV; Kliebard, *Struggle*, chap. 4.
10. Walter P. Metzger, "The Spectre of 'Professionalism,'" *Educational Researcher* 16 (August–September 1987).

4.0 Description of the Curriculum

1. Jeri Ridings Nowakowski, "On Educational Evaluation: A Conversation with Ralph Tyler," *Educational Leadership* 40 (May 1983).
2. Herbert M. Kliebard, *The Struggle for the American Curriculum, 1893–1958* (New York: Routledge & Kegan Paul, 1987).
3. O. L. Davis, Jr., "Understanding the History of the Social Studies," in Howard D. Mehlinger and O. L. Davis, Jr., eds., *The Social Studies: 80th Yearbook of the National Society for the Study of Education* (Chicago: NSSE, 1981).
4. Hazel Whitman Hertzberg, *Social Studies Reform, 1880–1980*, a Project SPAN Report (Boulder, CO; Social Science Education Consortium, 1981).
5. James S. Coleman, "Families and Schools," *Educational Researcher* 16 (August-September 1987).
6. U.S. Department of Education, Center for Education Statistics, *Who Drops Out of High School? Findings from High School and Beyond.* Contractor Report CS 87-397c (Washington, 1987).
7. U.S. Department of Commerce, Bureau of the Census, *Detailed Population Characteristics: United States Summary* (Washington, 1983), table 260.
8. Hazel W. Hertzberg, *Social Studies Reform*, 4.
9. Rolla M. Tryon, *The Social Sciences as School Subjects*, part XI of the American Historical Association *Report of the Commission on the Social Studies* (New York: Scribner's, 1935), 131ff; Thomas S. Peet, "A Selective History of Social Studies Scope and Sequence Patterns, 1916 to 1984" (Ph.D. diss., Ohio State University, 1984), 101ff.

10. A short treatment is Dorothy Ross, "The Development of the Social Sciences," in Alexandra Oleson and John Voss, eds., *The Organization of Knowledge in Modern America, 1860–1920* (Baltimore: Johns Hopkins University Press, 1979). An excellent longer treatment on the social sciences in the late nineteenth century is Thomas Haskell, *The Emergence of Professional Social Science: The American Social Science Associations and the Nineteenth Century Crisis of Authority* (Urbana: University of Illinois Press, 1977).

11. Richard Hofstadter, *Anti-Intellectualism in American Life* (New York: Knopf, 1964), 326, makes this corrective point clearly.

12. Hertzberg, *Social Studies Reform*, 5.

13. National Education Association, *Report of the Committee on Secondary Social Studies* (Washington: GPO, 1893), 167.

14. Tryon, *The Social Sciences as School Subjects*, 12.

15. American Historical Association, *The Study of History in Schools* (New York: Macmillan, 1899).

16. American Historical Association Committee of Eight, *The Study of History in the Elementary Schools* (New York: Scribner's, 1909).

17. Peet, "A Selective History," 126.

18. Tyron, *The Social Sciences as School Subjects*, 26.

19. For example, by Edward L. Thorndike, *Educational Psychology* (New York: Columbia University Teachers College, 1913), in terms of 'transfer' of learning as reflected in test scores.

20. For a good treatment of Hall's influence in the schools, see Merle Curti, *The Social Ideas of American Educators* (New York: Scribner's, 1935), chap. 12.

21. See, especially, Michael Lybarger, "The Political Context of the Social Studies: Creating a Constituency for Municipal Reform," *Theory and Research in Social Education* 8 (Fall 1980); and Lawrence A. Cremin, *The Transformation of the School: Progressivism in American Education, 1876–1957* (New York: Vintage Books, 1964).

22. Ascribed to Adolph Meyer. William James used a similar phrase.

23. Stephen Toulmin, "The Recovery of Practical Philosophy," *American Scholar* 57 (Summer 1988). The papers of Dewey are being prepared by John J. McDermott, and intellectual biographies are said to be under preparation by Richard Rorty and by Lawrence Cremin.

24. George S. Counts, *Dare the School Build a New Social Order?* (New York: John Day, 1932); David Snedden, *Sociological Determination of Objectives in Education* (Philadelphia: J.B. Lippincott, 1921).

25. Quoted in Edward A. Krug, *The Shaping of the American High School* (Madison: University of Wisconsin Press, 1972), 370.

26. Kieran Egan, "Reply to Thornton, 'Social Studies Misunderstood,'" *Theory and Research in Social Education* 12 (Summer 1984): 66. Ravitch, a sharp critic of the excesses of progressive education, treats Dewey insightfully: Diane Ravitch, *The Troubled Crusade* (New York: Basic Books, 1983), 78–79 passim.

27. Cremin, *The Transformation of the School*, p. 136.

28. Arthur W. Dunn, *The Teaching of Community Civics* (Washington: U.S. Department of the Interior, Bureau of Education [Bulletin No. 17], 1915).

29. National Education Association, *Social Studies in Secondary Education: A Six-Year Program Adapted to the 6-3-3 and the 8-4 Plans of Organization* (Washington: U.S. Department of the Interior, Bureau of Education [Bulletin No. 28], 1916, 52–53.

30. John Dewey, *Democracy and Education* (New York: Free Press, 1966), 214.

31. [NEA] Commission on the Reorganization of Secondary Education, *Cardinal Principles of Secondary Education* (Washington: U.S. Department of the Interior, Bureau of Education [Bulle-

tin No. 35], 1918).

32. Patricia Albjerg Graham, "Schools: Cacophony About Practice, Silence About Purpose," *Daedalus* 112 (Fall 1984).

33. Thomas James and David Tyack, "Learning from Past Efforts to Reform the High Schools," *Phi Delta Kappan* 64 (February 1983): 403.

34. Kliebard, *The Struggle*, 112ff.

35. NEA, *Social Studies in Secondary Education*, 27.

36. William A. Smith, *Secondary Education in the United States* (New York: Macmillan, 1936), 61.

37. Hertzberg, *Social Studies Reform*, 129.

38. Peet, "A Selective History," 49.

39. Tryon, *The Social Sciences as School Subjects*, 29ff.

40. Tryon, *The Social Sciences as School Subjects*, 230ff.

41. Peet, "A Selective History," 55. Peet's dissertation is invaluable in pulling together most or all known curriculum surveys from the different eras. He notes, correctly, that there is seldom any direct comparability across surveys and that inferences must be cautious.

42. Described in Peet, "A Selective History," 60.

43. Edgar B. Wesley, *American History in Schools and Colleges* (New York: Macmillan, 1944).

44. James and Tyack, "Learning from Past Efforts," 401, 403.

45. Robert S. Lynd and Helen M. Lynd, *Middletown: A Study in Contemporary American Culture* (New York: Harcourt, Brace, 1929).

46. Graham, "Schools: Cacophony," 33.

47. David Tyack and Elizabeth Hansot, *Managers of Virtue: Public School Leadership in America, 1820–1980* (New York: Basic Books, 1982), 249ff.

48. Marvin Lazerson, "Introduction," in Marvin Lazerson, ed., *American Education in the Twentieth Century: A Documentary History* (New York: Teachers College Press, 1987).

49. Nowakowski, "On Educational Evaluation: A Conversation with Ralph Tyler" in *Educational Leadership*.

50. *Time*, November 20, 1937.

51. Lester H. Gulick, *Education for American Life* (New York: McGraw-Hill, 1938).

52. *Education of All American Youth* (Washington: Educational Policies Commission, National Education Association, and American Association of School Administrators, 1944). The study was widely reported several years before this publication, and was preceded by preliminary reports.

53. *What the High Schools Ought to Teach* (Washington: American Council on Education, 1940).

54. *What the High Schools Ought to Teach*, 31.

55. Wilford M. Aiken, *The Story of the Eight-Year Study* (New York: Harper, 1942).

56. An excellent account of the disputes over the content of the POD course over these two decades is given in H. Wells Singleton, "Problems of Democracy: The Revisionist Plan for Social Studies Education," *Theory and Practice in Social Education* 8 (Fall 1980).

57. Hertzberg, *Social Studies Reform*, 31; Peet, "A Selective History," 150–64. The latter treatment is excellent, in its coverage of the many deep lines of cleavage within history and between history and the other fields. Peet also points out that some of the conflict was structural, in the sense that more traditional academic high schools tended to follow an 8-4 grade pattern, and the 1899 history scheme, while others had moved to a 6-3-3 grade format.

58. Hertzberg, *Social Studies Reform*, 37.

59. Harold O. Rugg, "A Unified Social Science Curriculum," *The Historical Outlook* 14 (December 1923): 394.

60. The commission issued many numbered volumes of its report. These range from Tryon's 1935 history of the school subjects from the nineteenth century forward, to separate volumes on civics and geography as school subjects, to rather technical works on tests, pedagogy, and the preparation

of teachers. A valuable work was Pierce's, which surveyed the organized groups outside the schools that attempted to effect 'citizenship training.' Charles A. Beard, *A Charter for the Social Sciences in the Schools* (New York: Scribner's, 1932); *Conclusions and Recommendations of the Commission on the Social Studies* (New York: Scribner's, 1934); Charles E. Merriam, *Civic Education in the United States* (New York: Scribner's, 1934); Isaiah Bowman, *Geography in Relation to the Social Sciences* (New York: Scribner's, 1934); Leon C. Marshall and Rachel Marshall Goetz, *Curriculum-Making in the Social Studies: A Social Process Approach* (New York: Scribner's, 1946); Bessie L. Pierce, *Citizen's Organizations and the Civic Training of Youth* (New York: Scribner's, 1933).

61. Kliebard, *The Struggle*, p. 236. The Bode quote is from Boyd H. Bode, *Progressive Education at the Crossroads* (New York: Norton, 1938), 94. The Dewey quote is from John Dewey, *Experience and Education* (New York: Macmillan, 1938).

62. James A. Michener, ed., *The Future of the Social Studies: Proposals for an Experimental Social Studies Curriculum* (Cambridge, MA: National Council for the Social Studies, 1939).

63. Herbert M. Kliebard, "Three Currents of American Curriculum Thought," in *Current Thought on Curriculum*, 1985 ASCD Yearbook (Alexandria, VA: Association for Supervision and Curriculum Development, 1985).

64. Among them, Kliebard, *The Struggle*, 258ff; Ravitch, *Troubled Crusade*, 78–80.

65. Lazerson, "Introduction," 27.

66. Harvard University Committee on the Objectives of General Education in a Free Society, *General Education in a Free Society* (Cambridge, MA: Harvard University Press, 1945). The report was often known as the "Red Book."

67. Ravitch, *The Troubled Crusade*, chap. 3, describes the mood insightfully, as does Carl F. Kaestle, "School Reform and the Public Mood," *American Heritage* (February 1990).

5.0   How the Curriculum took Shape: 1950 to the Present

1. Robert L. Hampel, *The Last Little Citadel* (Boston: Houghton Mifflin, 1986), 137.

2. Thomas James and David Tyack, "Learning from Past Efforts to Reform the High Schools," Phi Delta Kappan 64 (February 1983): 401.

3. James B. Conant, *The American High School Today* (New York: McGraw-Hill, 1959).

4. Michael Young, *The Rise of Meritocracy* (Harmondsworth, England: Penguin Books [1958] 1961).

5. Marvin Lazerson, "Introduction," in Marvin Lazerson, ed., *American Education in the Twentieth Century: A Documentary History* (New York: Teachers College Press, 1987), 37.

6. For example, Graham, "Schools: Cacophony about Practice: Silence About Purpose," *Daedalus* 112 (Fall 1984), 47ff.

7. Lazerson, "Introduction," 41. Perhaps not quite so, given the bitter debates over the nature of the common schools in the Jacksonian and Horace Mann period; but these debates had smaller carrying-power beyond local communities.

8. Graham, "Schools: Cacophony," 48.

9. James and Tyack, "Learning from Past Efforts," 405.

10. Arthur E. Bestor, *Educational Wastelands: The Retreat from Learning in Our Public Schools* (Urbana: University of Illinois Press, 1953).

11. Hazel Whitman Hertzberg, *Social Studies Reform, 1880–1980*, a Project

SPAN Report (Boulder, CO; Social Science Education Consortium, 1981), 92–93.

12. Ravitch, *The Troubled Crusade*, 75–76; Allan Bloom, *The Closing of the American Mind* (New York: Simon and Schuster, 1987).

13. Bernard Berelson, et al., *The Social Studies and the Social Sciences* (New York: Harcourt, Brace & World, 1962).

14. John D. Haas, *The Era of the New Social Studies* (Boulder, CO: ERIC Clearinghouse for Social Studies, and Social Science Education Consortium, 1977).

15. Jerome Bruner, *The Process of Education* (Cambridge, MA: Harvard University Press, 1960).

16. For a succinct sketch of several forms of structuralism in this era, including European anthropological structuralism, see Howard Gardner, *The Quest for Mind* (Chicago: University of Chicago Press, 1981).

17. Alfred North Whitehead, *Science and the Modern World* (New York: Free Press, [1925] 1967).

18. Jerome S. Bruner, "The Process of Education Revisited," *Phi Delta Kappan* 53 (September 1971).

19. C. Benjamin Cox, Emily S. Girault, and Lawrence Metcalf, "Review of Research in Social Studies: 1965," *Social Education* 32 (May 1966): 348.

20. Quoted in Irving Morrissett, ed., *Concepts and Structure in the New Social Science Curricula* (W. Lafayette, IN: Social Science Education Consortium, 1966), 64.

21. Personal communication, C. Frederick Risinger.

22. Morrissett, *Concepts and Structures,* xv.

23. Mary Jane Nickelson Turner, "Political Education in the United States: History, Status, Critical Analysis, and an Alternative Model" (Ph.D. diss., University of Colorado, 1978): 136.

24. David L. Lowenthal, *The Past Is a Foreign Country* (Cambridge: Cambridge University Press, 1985).

25. Susan S. Stodolsky, *The Subject Matters* (Chicago: University of Chicago Press, 1988), 10, 34.

26. Taken from Morrissett, *Concepts and Structures*, 25, 31.

27. Karen B. Wiley with Jeanne Race, *The Study of Pre-College Science, Mathematics and Social Science Education: 1955–1975, Volume III: Social Science Education* (Washington: National Science Foundation, 1978) Document SE 78–73), section 1, 312ff.

28. Thomas J. Switzer, "Teacher Preparation in Sociology and Adoption of *Inquires in Sociology*," *Social Education* 41 (January 1977): 68.

29. Gerald W. Marker, "Why Schools Abandon 'New Social Studies' Materials," *Theory and Research in Social Education* 7 (Winter 1980).

30. David Elkind, "Child Development and the Social Science Curriculums of the Elementary School," *Social Education* 45 (October 1981): 437.

31. Fred M. Newmann, "The Analysis of Public Controversy–New Focus on Social Studies," *The School Review* 73 (Winter 1965): 414.

32. Mark M. Krug, "Bruner's New Social Studies: A Critique," *Social Education* 32 (October 1966): 401.

33. Fred M. Newmann with Donald W. Oliver, *Clarifying Public Controversy: An Approach to Teaching Social Studies* (Boston: Little, Brown, 1970); Donald Oliver and James P. Shaver, *Teaching Public Issues in the High School* (Boston: Houghton Mifflin, 1968).

34. James P. Shaver and A. Guy Larkins, *Decision-Making in a Democracy* (Boston: Houghton Mifflin, 1968).

35. Carleton W. Washburne, "Building a Fact Course in History and Geography," in Harold O. Rugg, *The Social Studies in the Elementary and Secondary School, 22nd Yearbook of the National Society for the Study of Education*, pt. II (Bloomington, IL: Public School Publishing, 1923).

36. Mary A. Hepburn, "I Get Déjà Vu

442 Notes

When I Read You, Mr. Hirsch" (Paper delivered at the Annual Meeting of the Social Science Education Consortium, Binghamton, NY, July 23, 1988).

37. Edwin Fenton, *Introduction to the Behavioral Sciences: An Inquiry Approach* (New York: Holt, Rinehart and Winston, 1969); *Sociological Resources for the Social Sciences, Inquiries in Sociology* (Boston: Allyn and Bacon, 1972).

38. Edwin Fenton, *A New History of the United States: An Inquiry Approach* (New York: Holt, Rinehart and Winston, 1969).

39. *Chronicle of Higher Education,* March 15, 1989, p. A2; *Education Week,* August 2, 1989, p. 3.

40. For example, for the state of Kansas, John Guenther and Patricia Hansen, "Organizational Change in the Social Studies: Mini-Course Subject Options," *Educational Leadership* 35 (October 1977).

41. Thomas S. Peet, "A Selective History of Social Studies and Sequence Patterns, 1916 to 1984 " (Ph.D. diss., Ohio State University, 1984), 65ff.

42. Richard E. Gross, "The Status of the Social Studies in the Public Schools of the United States," *Social Education* 41 (March 1977).

43. Wiley, *The Study of Pre-College Science.*

44. Douglas P. Superka, Sharryl Hawke, and Irving Morrissett, "The Current and Future Status of the Social Studies," *Social Education* 44 (May 1980).

45. Michael J. Elliott and Kerry J. Kennedy, "Australian Impressions of Social Studies Theory and Practice in Secondary Schools in the United States," *Social Education* 43 (April 1979).

46. James P. Shaver, O. L. Davis, Jr., and Suzanne W. Helburn, "An Interpretive Report on the Status of Pre-College Social Studies Education Based on Three NSF-Funded Studies," National Council for the Social Studies, 1978. A summary is contained in *Social Education* 43 (February 1979).

47. John I. Goodlad, *A Place Called School* (New York: McGraw-Hill, 1983); Vito Perrone and Associates, *Portraits of High Schools* (Princeton: Carnegie Foundation for the Advancement of Teaching, 1985); Larry Cuban, *How Teachers Taught: Constancy and Change in American Classrooms* (New York: Longman, 1984).

48. John I. Goodlad, "A Study of Schooling," *Phi Delta Kappan* 64 (March 1983).

49. Donald O. Schneider and Ronald L. Van Sickle, "The Status of the Social Studies: The Publishers' Perspective," *Social Education* 43 (October 1979).

50. Wayne L. Herman, Jr., "What Should Be Taught Where?" *Social Education* 47 (February 1983). In a Delphi study the results are fed back to the respondents in iterated stages, so that the emerging pattern of the data is made known to them and they are asked for finer judgments or forced choices.

51. For example, E. D. Hirsch, Jr., *Cultural Literacy: What Every American Needs to Know* (Boston: Houghton Mifflin, 1987); Diane Ravitch, "No Trivial Pursuit," *Phi Delta Kappan* 69 (April 1988).

6.0 Political Study

1. Merrill D. Peterson, "The University and the Larger Community," ACLS Occasional Paper No. 6 (New York: American Council of Learned Societies, 1988).

2. Susan S. Stodolsky, *The Subject Matters* (Chicago: University of Chicago Press, 1988).

3. Lawrence A. Cremin, *American Education: The Colonial Experience*

1607–1783 (New York: Harper and Row, 1970); Carl F. Kaestle, *The Evolution of an Urban School System: New York City, 1750–1850* (Cambridge: Harvard University Press, 1974); J. Freeman Butts, *The Civic Mission in Educational Reform* (Stanford, CA: The Hoover Institution Press, 1989); Rush Welter, *Popular Education and Democratic Thought in America* (New York: Columbia University Press, 1962); Amy Gutmann, *Democratic Education* (Princeton, N.J.: Princeton University Press, 1987); Donald Warren, "Political Education in a Pluralistic Society" (Paper delivered at the Annual Seminar, Atlantic Education Committee, The Atlantic Treaty Association, Airlie, VA, April 13–16, 1986).

4. John J. Patrick, "Continuing Challenges in Citizenship Education," *Educational Leadership* 38 (October 1980): 36.

5. Gutmann, *Democratic Education*, 36.

6. Mary Jane Nickelson Turner, "Political Education in the United States: History, Status, Critical Analysis, and an Alternative Model" (Ph.D. diss., University of Colorado, 1978), 19–20.

7. Paul Gagnon, "Why Study History?", *The Atlantic Monthly* (November 1988): 51.

8. Fred M. Newmann, *Clarifying Public Controversy: An Approach to Teaching Social Studies* (Boston: Little, Brown, 1970); "Political Participation: An Analytic Review and Proposal," in Derek Heater and Judith A. Gillespie, eds., *Political Education in Flux* (London: Sage Publications, 1981).

9. Shirley H. Engle and Anna S. Ochoa, *Education for Democratic Citizenship: Decision-Making in the Social Studies* (New York: Teachers College Press, 1988).

10. James S. Leming, "Paradox and Promise in Citizenship Education," in William T. Callahan, Jr., ed., *Citizenship for the 21st Century* (Bloomington, IN: Foundation for Teaching Economics and Social Studies Development Center, forthcoming).

11. Robert D. Hess and Judith V. Torney, *The Development of Political Attitudes in Children* (Garden City, N.Y.: Anchor Books, 1968), 248.

12. Warren, "Political Education," 7.

13. Welter, *Popular Education*.

14. Turner, "Political Education."

15. I thank Patricia Thévenet for calling this to my attention.

16. James L. Barth and S. Samuel Shermis, "Nineteenth Century Origins of the Social Studies Movement: Understanding the Continuity Between Older and Contemporary Civic and U.S. History Textbooks," *Theory and Research in Social Education* 8 (Fall 1980).

17. Earle Rugg, "How the Current Courses Came To Be What They Are," in Harold Rugg, ed., *22nd Yearbook of the National Society for the Study of Education. Part II* (Bloomington, IL: Public School Publishing Co., 1923).

18. Michael Kazin, *New York Times Book Review*, July 2, 1989, p. 1.

19. Arthur W. Dunn, *The Community and the Citizen* (Boston: D.C. Heath, 1914)

20. Rolla M. Tryon, *The Social Sciences as School Subjects*, part XI of the American Historical Association Report of the Commission on the Social Studies (New York: Scribner's, 1935), 290.

21. Charles A. Beard, *A Charter for the Social Sciences in the Schools* (New York: Scribner's, 1932), 46–47.

22. H. Wells Singleton, "Problems of Democracy: The Revisionist Plan for Social Studies Education," *Theory and Practice in Social Education* 8 (Fall 1980).

23. Charles E. Merriam, *Civic Education in the United States* (New York: Scribner's, 1934).

24. Turner, "Political Education," 21ff.

25. Turner, 32ff.

26. Joseph Schumpeter, *Capitalism, Socialism and Democracy* (New York: Harper and Row, 1956).

27. Robert Dahl, *Preface to Democratic Theory* (Chicago: University of Chicago Press, 1956).

28. V. O. Key, Jr., *Public Opinion and American Democracy* (New York: Knopf, 1961), 537.

29. Summarized in David O. Sears, "Political Behavior," in Gardner Lindzey and Elliot Aronson, eds., *The Handbook of Social Psychology. Volume Five: Applied Social Psychology*, 2nd edition (Reading, MA: Addison-Wesley, 1969).

30. Quoted in Turner "Political Education," 83.

31. Turner, 88ff.

32. American Political Science Association, Committee on Pre-Collegiate Education, "Political Education in the Public Schools: The Challenge for Political Science," *PS* 4 (Summer 1971).

33. *We The People: A Review of U.S. Government and Civics Textbooks* (Washington: People for the American Way, 1987).

34. Jerome Bruner, *The Process of Education* (Cambridge, MA: Harvard University Press, 1960), 8.

35. Edwin Fenton and Anthony Penna, *Comparative Political Systems* (New York: Holt, Rinehart and Winston, 1973).

36. Sidney Hook, "*The Closing of the American Mind*: An Intellectual Best-Seller Revisited," *American Scholar* 58 (Winter 1989).

37. Heinz Eulau and James G. March, eds., *Political Science* [National Academy of Sciences and Social Science Research Council Survey of the Behavioral and Social Sciences] (Englewood Cliffs, NJ: Prentice-Hall, 1969), 82.

38. Some comprehensive or basic sources for a review of the literature are Hess and Torney, *Political Attitudes in Children*; Sears, "Political Behavior"; David Easton and Jack Dennis, "The Child's Image of Government," *Annals of the American Academy of Political and Social Science* 361 (September 1965); and M. Kent Jennings, Richard G. Niemi, with Kenneth P. Langton, "Effects of the High School Civics Curriculum," in M. Kent Jennings and Richard G. Niemi, *The Political Character of Adolescence: The Influence of Families and Schools* (Princeton: Princeton University Press, 1974).

39. Lee Ehman, "The American School in the Political Socialization Process," *Review of Educational Research* 50 (Spring 1980).

40. Samuel A. Stouffer, *Communism, Conformity, and Civil Liberties* (New York: Doubleday, 1953); Herbert McClosky, "Consensus and Ideology in American Politics," *American Political Science Review* 58 (June 1964).

41. Sears, "Political Behavior," 441.

42. Engle and Ochoa, *Education for Democratic Citizenship*, chap. 9.

43. Mary A. Hepburn, ed., *Democratic Education in Schools and Classrooms* (Washington: National Council for the Social Studies [Bulletin No. 70], 1983), chap. 2 especially.

44. Judith Torney-Purta, "Political Socialization," in William T. Callahan, Jr., ed., *Citizenship for the 21st Century* (Bloomington, IN: Foundation for Teaching Economics and Social Studies Development Center, forthcoming).

45. For example, Jennings, Niemi, and Langton, "Effects of the High School," 190ff. Richard Remy, cited in Turner, "Political Education," 106, has written on the redundancy *between* history and government or civics courses.

46. For the International Association for the Evaluation of Education Achievement. See Judith Torney, A. N. Oppenheim, and Russell F. Farnen, *Civic Education in Ten Countries: An Empirical Study* (New York: Wiley, 1975).

47. Ralph W. Tyler, "The U.S. vs the World: A Comparison of Educational Performance," *Phi Delta Kappan* 62 (January 1981): 24.

48. Jennings, Niemi, and Langton, "Effects of the High School."

49. Leming, "Paradox and Promise," 81.

50. Walter Parker and John Jarolimek, *Citizenship and the Critical Role of the Social Studies* (Washington: National Council for the Social Studies [Bulletin No. 72], 1984), 28.

51. Thomas L. Dynneson, Richard E. Gross, and James A. Nickel, "An Exploratory Survey of Four Groups of 1987 Graduating Seniors' Perceptions

of (1) The Quality of a Good Citizen, (2) The Sources of Citizenship Influence, (3) The Contributions of Social Studies Courses and Programs of Study to Citizenship Development, (4) Student Preferred Citizenship Approaches, (5) Teacher Preferred Citizenship Approaches, (6) Citizenship Approaches and Elementary Students, (7) Citizenship Approaches and Secondary Students." Report of The Citizenship Development Study Project (Stanford, CA: Stanford University, Center for Educational Research at Stanford, 1989 [89-CERAS-06] and 1990, forthcoming). In general, the project authors recommend that teaching democratic values should be paramount in elementary education, and that community participation, law-related education, and higher-order cognitive skills should dominate in secondary education.

52. "An Exploratory Survey of CUFA Members' Opinions and Practices Pertaining to Citizenship Education in the Social Studies, 1985–86" (Stanford, CA: Stanford University, Center for Educational Research at Stanford, 1988 [88-CERAS-18]).

53. Alan L. Lockwood and David E. Harris, *Reasoning with Democratic Values: Ethical Problems in U.S. History* (New York: Teachers College Press, 1985).

54. Gutmann, *Democratic Education*, 106.

55. Russell F. Farnen, *Integrating Political Science, Education, and Public Policy: International Perspectives on Decision Making, Systems Theory, and Socialization Research* (Frankfurt-am-Main: Verlag Peter Lang, forthcoming).

56. Newmann, "Political Participation."

57. Michael Walzer, *Spheres of Justice* (New York: Basic Books, 1983).

58. Benjamin Barber, *Strong Democracy: Participatory Politics for a New Age* (Berkeley: University of California Press, 1984).

59. Butts, *The Civic Mission*, 44.

60. Welter, *Popular Education*, 334.

61. For a wide-ranging coverage of several disciplinary approaches currently, see Richard E. Gross and Thomas L. Dynesson, eds., *Social Science Perspectives on Citizenship* (New York: Teachers College Press, forthcoming).

62. "Revising the NCSS Social Studies Curriculum Guidelines," *Social Education* 43 (April 1979).

63. Turner (p. 228) holds that some goals are unreachable. Whether or not this is true, they are certainly mutually irreconcilable, at least to some degree.

64. Richard C. Remy, "Criteria for Judging Citizenship Education Programs," *Educational Leadership* 38 (October 1980).

65. National Assessment of Educational Progress, *The Civics Report Card* (Washington: U.S. Department of Education ([Report No. 19-C-01], 1990).

7.0 Economics

1. Rolla M. Tryon, *The Social Sciences as School Subjects*, part XI of the American Historical Association Report of the Commission on the Social Studies (New York: Scribner's, 1935), 334ff.

2. Leon C. Marshall and L. S. Lyon, *Our Economic Organization* (New York: Macmillan, 1921). Publisher's promotion statement.

3. Thomas S. Peet, "A Selective History of Social Studies Scope and Sequence Patterns, 1916 to 1984" (Ph.D. diss., Ohio State University, 1984), 55.

4. Beverly J. Armento, "Promoting Economic Literacy," in Stanley P. Wronski and Donald H. Bragaw, eds., *Social Studies and Social Sciences: A Fifty-Year Perspective* (Washington: National Council for the Social Studies [Bulletin No. 78], 1986), 100.

5. Armento, 100.

6. Ben W. Lewis, "Economics," in Bernard Berelson, et al., *The Social Studies and the Social Sciences* (New York: Harcourt, Brace & World, 1962).

7. This discussion of the TEL is based

largely on articles in the *Journal of Economic Education* 19 (Winter 1988), especially papers by William Walstad and John Soper, and Soper and Walstad, and "Comments" by W. Lee Hansen and Phillip Saunders.

8. John C. Soper and William B. Walstad, "What's High School Economics? Posttest Knowledge, Attitudes, and Course Content," *Journal of Economic Education* 19 (Winter 1988).

9. William J. Baumol and Robert J. Highsmith, "Variables Affecting Success in Economic Education: Preliminary Findings from a New Data Base," *AEA Papers and Proceedings* 78 (1988).

10. John C. Soper and William B. Walstad, "The Reality of High School Economics: The Teachers' Perspective," *Journal of Private Enterprise*, Fall 1988.

11. William Walstad and Michael Watts, "The Current Status of Economics in the K–12 Curriculum," in Mark C. Schug, ed., *Economics in the School Curriculum, K–12* (Washington: National Educational Association, 1985).

12. Donald O. Schneider and Ronald L. Van Sickle, "The Status of the Social Studies: The Publishers' Perspective," *Social Education* 43 (October 1979). Such information is rare, being hard to get from publishers.

13. Walstad and Watts, "The Current Status," 143.

14. Steven L. Miller, *Economic Education for Citizenship* (Bloomington, IN: Social Studies Development Center [Indiana University] and Foundation for Teaching Economics [San Francisco], 1988).

15. Quoted in Armento, "Promoting Economic Literacy," 106.

16. Beverly J. Armento, "A Study of the Basic Concepts Presented in DEEP Curriculum Guides, Grades 7–12," *Journal of Economic Education* 14 (Summer 1983).

17. Steven L. Miller, guest ed., "Developing Economic Literacy," Special Issue, *Theory into Practice* 26 (Summer 1987).

18. James S. Leming, "On the Normative Foundations of Economic Education," *Theory and Research in Social Education* 15 (Spring 1987).

19. Suzanne W. Helburn, "Two Traditions in Economics: Implications for Teaching U.S. and World History" (Paper delivered at the Annual Meeting of the Social Science Education Consortium, Binghamton, NY, July 22, 1988).

20. Suzanne W. Helburn, "Economics and Economics Education: The Selective Use of Discipline Structures in Economics Curricula," in Steve Hodkinson and David J. Whitehead, eds., *Economic Education: Research and Development Issues* (London: Longman, 1986), 19. Emphases in the original.

21. For example, in a conference proceedings issue of the *Journal of Economic Education* 18 (Spring 1987), assessing the JCEE framework. See especially the papers by Robert Heilbroner, Barbara Bergman, James Galbraith, and Lester Thurow.

22. J. Lucien Ellington and Tadahisa Uozumi, "Economic Education in Japanese and American Secondary Schools" *Theory and Research in Social Education* 26 (Spring 1988).

8.0 Geography

1. For example, Paul A. Gagnon, "On *Education for Democracy*: A Reply [to Fernekes]," *Social Education* 51 (October 1987).

2. Earle Rugg, "How the Current Courses Came to Be What They Are," in Harold Rugg, ed., *22nd Yearbook of the National Society for the Study of Education, Part II* (Bloomington, IL: Public School Publishing Co., 1923).

3. Rolla M. Tryon, *The Social Sciences as School Subjects,* part XI of the American Historical Association Report of the Commission on the Social Studies (New York: Scribner's, 1935), 119ff.

4. Preston C. James and Geoffrey J.

Martin, "The Concept of Occupied Space," in Preston C. James and Geoffrey J. Martin, *All Possible Worlds: A History of Geographical Ideas* (New York: John Wiley, 1981).

5. Michael Libbee and Joseph Stoltman, "Geography Within the Social Studies Curriculum," in Salvatore J. Natoli, ed., *Strengthening Geography in the Social Studies* (Washington: National Council for the Social Studies [Bulletin No. 81], 1988).

6. Tryon, 231ff.

7. Barbara J. Winston, "Teaching and Learning in Geography," in Stanley P. Wronski and Donald H. Bragaw, eds., *Social Studies and Social Sciences: A Fifty-Year Perspective* (Washington: National Council for the Social Studies [Bulletin No. 78], 1986).

8. Lawrence A. Cremin, *The Transformation of the School* (New York: Vintage Books, 1964), 156.

9. Saul B. Cohen, "A Question of Boundaries: the Response of Learned Societies to Interdisciplinary Scholarship," in *Learned Societies and the Evolution of the Disciplines* (New York: American Council of Learned Societies [Occasional Paper No. 5], 1988).

10. Preston E. James, "Geography," in Bernard Berelson et al., *The Social Studies and the Social Sciences* (New York: Harcourt, Brace & World, 1962).

11. Norton E. Long, "Political Science," in Berelson et al., *The Social Studies and the Social Sciences*.

12. David Hill and Lisa A. LaPrairie, "Geography in American Education," in Gary L. Gaile and Cort J. Willmott, eds., *Geography in America* (Columbus, OH: Merrill, 1989).

13. See James and Martin, "Occupied Space," 372.

14. Robert McNee, "An Approach to Understanding the Current Structure of Geography," in Irving Morrissett, ed., *Concepts and Structure in the New Social Science Curricula* (West Lafayette, IN: Social Science Education Consortium, 1966), 62.

15. Irving Morrissett, *Concepts and Structure*, 7–9.

16. John Dewey, "The Psychological Aspect of the School Curriculum," *Educational Review* 13 (April 1897): 361. The emphasized (in the original) sentence is the gist of a problem with the New Social Studies approach (section 5.3.3).

17. For example, Charlotte Crabtree, "Inquiry Approaches to Learning Concepts and Generalizations in Social Studies," *Social Education* 32 (October 1966); and, concerning Crabtree's work, Marion J. Rice and Russell L. Cobb, *What Can Children Learn in Geography: A Review of the Research* (Boulder, CO: Social Science Education Consortium, 1978).

18. Alvin P. Short and Donald T. Matlock, "Sociology Programs in U.S. High Schools: Current Findings with a National Sample," *Teaching Sociology* 9 (April 1982).

19. Hill and LaPrairie, "Status of Geography"; Joseph M. Cirrincione and Richard T. Farrell, "The Status of Geography in Middle/Junior and Senior High Schools," in Natoli, *Strengthening Geography*.

20. *New York Times*, January 15, 1985, p. C1.

21. Richard Hofstadter, *Anti-Intellectualism in American Life* (New York: Knopf, 1964), 304.

22. William J. Bennett, *First Lessons: A Report on Elementary Education in America* (Washington: U.S. Department of Education, 1986).

23. Salvatore J. Natoli and Charles F. Gritzner, "Modern Geography," in Natoli, *Strengthening Geography*, 2.

24. E. D. Hirsch, Jr., *Cultural Literacy: What Every American Needs to Know* (Boston: Houghton Mifflin, 1987).

25. Joint Committee on Geographic Education of the National Council for Geographic Education and Association of American Geographers, *Guidelines for Geographic Education: Elementary and Secondary Schools* (Washington: AAG [ERIC document ED 252 453], 1984).

26. *Richmond Times Dispatch*, October 23, 1988.

27. Education for Democracy Project, *Education for Democracy: A Statement of Principles* (Washington: American Federation of Teachers, 1987).

28. Alan Backler, *Teaching Geography in American History* (Bloomington, IN: Indiana University Social Studies Development Center, 1988).

9.0   Sociology and Anthropology

1. Herbert Spencer, *Education* (New York: A. L. Burt, 1859).

2. George Lundberg, *Can Science Save Us?* (London: Longmans, 1947). Lundberg's views were well known by the 1930s.

3. Quoted in Lawrence A. Cremin, *The Transformation of the School*, (New York: Vintage, 1964), p. 99.

4. See Herbert M. Kliebard, *The Struggle for the American Curriculum, 1893–1958* (New York: Routledge & Kegan Paul, 1987), 260ff, for a treatment of Ward's anti-Spencerian, that is, anti–social Darwinist, views.

5. Lawrence J. Rhoades, *A History of the American Sociological Association 1905–1980* (Washington: ASA, 1981), 9.

6. Rolla M. Tryon, *The Social Sciences as School Subjects*, part XI of the American Historical Association Report of the Commission on the Social Studies (New York: Scribner's, 1935), 376ff.

7. Robert C. Angell, "Reflections on the Project, Sociological Resources for the Social Studies," *The American Sociologist* 16 (February 1981).

8. Willis D. Moreland, "Curriculum Trends in the Social Studies," *Social Education* 28 (February 1962).

9. Gresham M. Sykes, "Sociology," in Berelson, *The Social Studies and the Social Sciences*, (New York: Harcourt, Brace & World, 1962), 161 (emphasis added throughout).

10. Thomas J. Switzer, "Teaching Sociology in K–12 Classrooms," in Wronski and Bragaw, *Social Studies and Social Sciences*; John D. Haas, *The Era of the New Social Studies* (Boulder, CO: ERIC Clearinghouse for Social Studies/Social Science Education, and Social Science Education Consortium, 1977); *Experiences in Inquiry* (Boston: Allyn & Bacon, 1974).

11. "Teaching Sociology," p. 130.

12. As widely documented; see section 5.3.2. With regard to the SRSS materials, see Thomas J. Switzer, "Teacher Preparation in Sociology and Adoption of *Inquiries in Sociology*," *Social Education* 58 (January 1977).

13. Switzer, "Teaching Sociology," 125, characterizing the view of the profession.

14. For example, Short and Matlock, "Sociology Programs."

15. Donald T. Matlock and Alvin P. Short, "The Impact of High School Sociology: Some Preliminary Test Results from the College Introductory Course," *Teaching Sociology* 10 (July 1983).

16. Thomas Dynneson, "The Status of Pre-Collegiate Anthropology: Progress or Peril?" *Anthropology and Education Quarterly* 12 (Winter 1981).

17. Anthropology Curriculum Study Project, *Patterns in Human History* (New York: Macmillan, 1971).

18. Education Development Center, *Man: A Course of Study* (Washington: Curriculum Development Associates, 1970).

19. Dynneson, "The Status of Pre-Collegiate Anthropology." For one thing, such objections did not eventuate in many places that used MACOS.

20. Frederick O. Gearing, "Anthropology and Education," in John J. Honigmann, *Handbook of Social and Cultural Anthropology* (Chicago: Rand McNally, 1973), 1,243.

21. Robert Hanvey, "Anthropology in the High Schools: The Representation of a

Discipline," in Irving Morrissett, *Concepts and Structure in the New Social Sciences Curricula* (W. Lafayette, IN: Social Science Education Consortium, 1966), 102.

22. Donald O. Schneider and Ronald L. Van Sickle, "The Status of the Social Studies: The Publisher's Perspective," *Social Education* 43 (October 1979).

23. Jane J. White, "An Ethnographic Study of the Construction of Knowledge About Different Cultures in an Elementary School" (Ph.D. diss., University of Pennsylvania, 1980).

24. Dell Hymes, "The Use of Anthropology: Critical, Political, Personal," in Dell H. Hymes, ed., *Reinventing Anthropology* (New York: Pantheon Books, 1972).

25. George W. Stocking, Jr., "Guardians of the Sacred Bundle. The AAA and the Representation of Holistic Anthropology," in *Learned Societies and the Evolution of the Disciplines* (New York: American Council of Learned Societies [Occasional Paper No. 5], 1988).

26. William H. McNeill, *The Rise of the West: A History of the Human Community* (Chicago: University of Chicago Press, 1963).

27. Douglas Oliver, "Cultural Anthropology," in Berelson, *The Social Studies and the Social Sciences*, (New York: Harcourt, Brace & World, 1962) 137 (emphasis added).

10.0   Psychology

1. John K. Bare, "Teaching Psychology in High Schools" in Wronski and Bragaw, eds., *Social Studies and Social Sciences: A Fifty-Year Perspective* (Washington: National Council for the Social Studies [Bulletin No. 78], 1986).

2. Bare, p. 186.

3. Thomas Heed, "Social Studies Disciplines Taught in Bergen County Public High Schools 1985–86" (Report to New Jersey Department of Higher Education, No. 86-990780-1599, mimeographed); John Guenther and Patricia Hansen, "Organizational

Change in the Social Studies: Mini-Course Subject Options," *Educational Leadership* 35 (October 1977).

4. E.g., Robert J. Stahl and James C. Matiya, "Teaching Psychology in the High School: Does Area of Certification Transfer Into Different Types of Teachers and Courses?" *Theory and Research in Social Education* 9 (Summer 1981).

5. Donald O. Schneider and Ronald L. Van Sickle, "The Status of the Social Studies: The Publishers' Perspective," *Social Education* 43 (October 1979).

11.0   Historical Study

1. Paul Robinson and Joseph M. Kirman, "From Monopoly to Dominance," in Wronski and Bragaw, *Social Studies and Social Sciences.*

2. Irving Morrissett, "The Needs of the Future and the Constraints of the Past," in Howard D. Mehlinger and O.L. Davis, Jr., eds., *The Social Studies: Eightieth Yearbook of the National Society for the Study of Education* (Chicago, NSSE, 1981), 46.

3. Merriam, *Civic Education*, 91.

4. Herbert M. Kliebard, *The Struggle for*

the American Curriculum, 1893–1958 (New York: Routledge & Kegan Paul, 1987), 125.

5. Oliver M. Keels, Jr., "The Collegiate Influence on the Early Social Studies Curriculum: A Reassessment of the Role of Historians," *Theory and Research in Social Education* 8 (Fall 1980): 123–24.

6. David D. Van Tassel, "Trials of Clio," in Wronski and Bragaw, *Social Studies and Social Sciences: A Fifty-Year Perspective*, 2.

7. Edgar B. Wesley, *American History in Schools and Colleges* (New York: Macmillan, 1944).

8. Bernard R. Gifford, "Introduction: Thinking About History Teaching and Learning," in Bernard R. Gifford, ed., *History in the Schools: What Shall We Teach?* (New York: Macmillan, 1988), 10.

9. Hazel Whitman Hertzberg, "Are Method and Content Enemies?", in Gifford, 36; see also her more quantitative coverage, "The Teaching of History," in Michael Kammen, ed., *The Past Before Us* (Ithaca, NY: Cornell University Press, 1980).

10. Hertzberg, "The Teaching of History," 488.

11. *Speaking for the Humanities* (New York: American Council of Learned Societies [ACLS Occasional Paper No. 7], 1989), appendix.

12. Rolla M. Tryon, *The Social Sciences as School Subjects*, part XI of the American Historical Association Report for the Commission on the Social Studies (New York: Scribner's, 1935), 214 and 231ff. Tryon, a professor of history at the University of Chicago, assembled for the 1934 AHA commission the most complete statistics on courses, patterns, enrollments, etc., at all grade levels that could be achieved. Many questions still go unanswered, and there are many ambiguities in his data, but there is no more authoritative source on social studies up to the early 1930s.

13. William H. Cartwright, Jr., "A History of the Teaching of American History" (Ph.D. diss., University of Minnesota, 1950), 70 (emphasis added).

14. Diane Ravitch, "From History to Social Studies: Dilemmas and Problems," in Chester E. Finn, Jr., Diane Ravitch, and P. Holley Roberts, eds., *Challenge to the Humanities* (New York: Holmes and Meier, 1985).

15. Matthew T. Downey, ed., *History in the Schools* (Washington: National Council for the Social Studies [Bulletin No. 74], 1985).

16. On nonreductive particularism, see Michael Kammen, "Introduction," in Kammen, *The Past Before Us*, 37; Mark M. Krug, "Bruner's New Social Studies: A Critique," *Social Education* 32 (October 1966): 400.

17. Stephen J. Thornton, "Curriculum Consonance in United States History Classrooms," *Journal of Curriculum and Supervision* 3 (Summer 1988): 313.

18. National Education Association, *Report of the Committee on Secondary Social Studies* (Washington: GPO, 1893).

19. American Historical Association, *The Study of History in Schools* (New York: Macmillan, 1899). The quotations are given in Tryon, *The Social Sciences as School Subjects*, 188–189.

20. Wesley, *American History*, 1–2.

21. Edwin Fenton, "A Structure of History," in Irving Morrissett, *Concepts and Structure in the New Social Sciences* (W. Lafayette, IN: Social Science Education Consortium, 1966), p. 51.

22. Paul Gagnon, "Why Study History?" *The Atlantic Monthly* (November 1988).

23. Bradley Commission on History in the Schools, *Building a History Curriculum: Guidelines for Teaching History in Schools* (Washington: Educational Excellence Network, 1988).

24. Christian Laville and Linda W. Rosenzweig, "Teaching and Learning History: Developmental Dimensions," in Linda W. Rosenzweig, ed., *Developmental Perspectives on the Social Studies* (Washington: National Council for the Social Studies [Bulletin No. 66], 1982), 62.

25. Shirley H. Engle and Anna S. Ochoa, *Education for Democratic Citizenship: Decision-Making in the Social Studies* (New York: Teachers College Press, 1988), 19.

26. This is not to say that many teachers do not work this way. See, for example: Vincent Rogers, Arthur D. Roberts, and Thomas P. Weinland, eds., *Teaching Social Studies: Portraits from the Classroom* (Washington: National Council for the Social Studies [Bulletin No. 82], 1988); Kevin O'Reilly, "Thinking, Viewing, and Deciding: Strategies in United States History," in Rogers et al.; Samuel S. Wineburg

and Suzanne M. Wilson, "Models of Wisdom in the Teaching of History," *Phi Delta Kappan* 70 (September 1988).

27. In a statement quoted in *Educational Leadership* 46 (April 1989): 6.
28. Robert S. Lynd and Helen M. Lynd, *Middletown: A Study in Contemporary American Culture* (New York: Harcourt, Brace, 1929), 199.
29. As shown in History by many studies; see, for example, Douglas P. Superka, Sharryl Hawke, and Irving Morrissett, "The Current and Future Status of the Social Studies," *Social Education* 44 (May 1980).
30. Charles A. Beard and Mary R. Beard, *History of the United States* (New York: Macmillan, 1921).
31. American Historical Association Committee of Eight, *The Study of History in the Elementary Schools* (New York: Scribner's, 1909), 6.
32. Wesley, *American History.*
33. Joseph Strayer, "History," in Berelson, *The Social Studies and the Social Sciences.*
34. Quoted in John D. Hogue and Claudia Crump, *Teaching History in the Elementary School* (Bloomington, IN: Indiana University Social Studies Development Center, 1988), 1.
35. Quoted in Tryon, *The Social Sciences as School Subjects,* 441 (emphasis added).
36. R. G. Collingwood, *An Essay on Metaphysics* (Oxford: Oxford University Press, 1940); Robinson is quoted in Van Tassel, "Trials of Clio"; Mink is quoted in Matthew T. Downey and Linda S. Levstik, "Teaching and Learning History: The Research Base," *Social Education* 52 (September 1988).
37. Diane Ravitch, *The Schools We Deserve* (New York: Basic Books, 1985).
38. National Education Association, *Social Studies in Secondary Education: A Six-Year Program Adapted to the 6-3-3 and the 8-4 Plans of Organization* (Washington: U.S. Department of the Interior, Bureau of Education [Bulletin No. 28], 1916), 33.
39. A. S. Barr, "The Social Studies Program of the Detroit Public Schools," in

Harold O. Rugg, ed., *22nd Yearbook of the National Society for the Study of Education* (Bloomington, IL: Public School Publishing Co., 1923), 156.
40. Diane Ravitch, "The Revival of History: Problems and Progress" (Paper delivered at the Annual Meeting of the American Educational Research Association, Washington, April 24, 1987) 6.
41. Quoted in NEA, *Social Studies in Secondary Education* (1916), emphasis in quotation.
42. Lawrence A. Cremin, *Traditions of American Education* (New York: Basic Books, 1977), 162.
43. Cited in Suzanne M. Wilson and Samuel S. Wineburg, "Peering at History Through Different Lenses: The Role of Disciplinary Perspectives in Teaching History," *Teachers College Record* 89 (Summer 1988): 538 (emphasis added).
44. James Axtell, "Europeans, Indians, and the Age of Discovery in American History Textbooks," *American Historical Review* 92 (June 1987): 630.
45. Joan Hoff-Wilson, "Preface," in *Looking at History: A Review of Major U.S. History Textbooks* (Washington: People for the American Way, 1986).
46. Krug, "Bruner's New Social Studies," 405–46.
47. William H. Streich, Kenneth Poppe, and Ellis B. Page, "American Literature, Chronological American History, Topical American History and the Bentee: A Study to Determine What to Teach" (1978).
48. David H. Fischer, *Historians' Fallacies: Toward a Logic of Historical Thought* (New York: Harper & Row, 1970).
49. Long, "Political Science," in Berelson, *The Social Studies and the Social Sciences* (New York: Harcourt, Brace & World, 1962), 102.
50. Norman Hampson, *New York Review,* April 13, 1989, p. 11.
51. Carl F. Kaestle, "Comments on a paper delivered by Diane Ravitch, 'The Erosion of History in American Schools.'" (Paper delivered at the National Academy of Education Fall

Meeting, Cambridge, Mass., 1986), 7.

52. Ernest R. May, "The Dangerous Usefulness of History," in Gifford, *History in the Schools*, 233.

53. Henry Steele Commager and Raymond H. Muessig, *The Study and Teaching of History* (Columbus, OH: Merrill, 1980), 51.

54. Gagnon, "Why Study History?," 47.

55. Isabel L. Beck, Margaret G. McKeown, and Erika W. Gromoll, "Learning from Social Studies Texts," *Cognition and Instruction* 6, no. 2 (1989): 132.

56. Carl C. Becker, *Everyman His Own Historian* (New York: Crofts, 1935).

57. On the last of these, see especially Mary K. T. Tetrault, "Integrating Women's History: The Case of United States History High School Textbooks," *The History Teacher* 19 (February 1986).

58. For example, Alfred W. Crosby, *Ecological Imperialism* (Cambridge: Cambridge University Press, 1986).

59. Michael Kammen, "The Historian's Voice and the State of the Discipline in the United States," in Kammen, ed., *The Past Before Us*, 38.

60. Quoted in Kammen, 38.

61. A good exposition is James Harvey Robinson, *The New History: Essays Illustrating the Modern Historical Outlook* (Springfield, MA: Walden, 1912 [1958]), pp. 70–100 especially.

62. The full quotation is given in Hazel W. Hertzberg, "Frederick Jackson Turner on 'The Significance of History' for Teachers," *Social Education* 51 (October 1987).

63. Tryon, *The Social Sciences as School Subjects*, 192–93.

64. John Dewey, *Democracy and Education* (New York: Free Press, [1916] 1944), 251.

65. NEA *Report of the Committee on Secondary Social Studies*, 177ff.

66. Wesley, *American History*, 22.

67. Merriam, *Civic Education*, 90ff.

68. Lynne V. Cheney, *The American Memory: A Report on the Humanities in the Nation's Public Schools* (Washington: National Endowment for the Humanities, 1987); Hirsch, *Cultural Literacy*.

69. "The Dangers and Importance of Historical Conversion," *Times* (of London) *Higher Education Supplement*, January 3, 1986, p. 12.

70. Quoted in *The Chronicle of Higher Education*, January 11, 1989, p. A4.

71. Kieran Egan, "What Children Know Best," *Social Education* 43 (February 1979).

72. Stephen J. Thornton, "Social Studies Misunderstood," *Theory and Research in Social Education* 12 (Spring 1984).

73. Hoge and Crump, *Teaching History in the Elementary School*, 7–8.

74. Royal Grueneich, "Issues in the Developmental Study of How Children Use Intention and Consequence Information to Make Moral Evaluation," *Child Development* 53 (February 1982): 41. James Leming, "Paradox and Promise," refers to such considerations in arguing why overt political bias is not the problem with slanted or prettified instructional material—i.e., children don't 'get the point' anyhow.

75. Engle and Ochoa, *Education for Democratic Citizenship*, 83ff.

76. A good introduction is provided by Lauren B. Resnick, *Education and Learning To Think* (Washington: National Academy [of Sciences] Press, 1987).

77. Becker, *Everyman*.

78. Jere Brophy, "Teaching Social Studies for Understanding and Higher Order Applications," *Elementary School Journal* 90 (March 1990). This long paper by a research psychologist is an exceptionally thoughtful and realistic appraisal of the social studies field, with special reference to the earlier grades.

79. Lee M. Benson, "Causation and the American Civil War," in Benson, *Toward the Scientific Study of History* (Philadelphia: Lippincott, 1972), 81–82.

80. Wineburg and Wilson, "Models of Wisdom," 53–54.

81. Michael Frisch. "American History and the Structures of Collective

Memory: A Modest Exercise in Empirical Iconography," *The Journal of American History* 75 (March 1989).

82. David Thelen, "Memory and American History," *The Journal of American History* 75 (March 1989).

83. Wilson and Wineburg, "Peering at History."

84. Thornton, "Curriculum Consonance."

85. David Elkind, "Child Development and the Social Science Curriculum of the Elementary School," *Social Education* 45 (October 1981): 438. In general, developmental research supports the notion that younger children find contrast easier to comprehend than similarity.

86. Martin Sleeper, "The Uses of History in Adolescence," *Youth and Society* 4 (March 1973).

87. On 'microhistory' in this spirit, see Kammen, *The Past Before Us*, 42ff.

88. Hoge and Crump, *Teaching History in the Elementary School*, 12.

89. Among the best research summaries are: Linda S. Levstik, "Teaching History: A Definitional and Developmental Dilemma," in Virginia A. Atwood, *Elementary School Social Studies: Research as A Guide to Practice* (Washington: National Council for the Social

Studies [Bulletin No. 79], 1986); Stephen J. Thornton and Ronald Vukelich, "Effects of Children's Understanding of Time Concepts on Historical Understanding," *Theory and Research in Social Education* 16 (Winter 1988); Hoge and Crump, *Teaching History in the Elementary School*; Douglas D. Alder and Matthew T. Downey, "Problem Areas in the History Curriculum," in Downey, *History in the Schools*; Richard K. Jantz and Kenneth Klawitter, "Early Childhood/Elementary Social Studies: A Review of Recent Research," in William B. Stanley, ed., *Review of Research in Social Studies Education 1976–1983* (Washington: National Council for the Social Studies [Bulletin No. 75], 1985).

90. Matthew T. Downey and Linda S. Levstik, "Teaching and Learning History: The Research Base," *Social Education* 52 (September 1988): 340.

91. For example, R. N. Hallam, "Logical Thinking in History," *Educational Review* 19 (June 1967).

92. Hoge and Crump, *Teaching History in the Elementary School*, 119.

93. Beck et al., "Learning from Social Studies Texts," 132.

12.0   World Studies

1. NEA, *Social Studies in Secondary Education* (1916) 38–40.

2. Rolla M. Tryon, *The Social Sciences as School Subjects*, part XI of the American Historical Association Report of the Commission on the Social Studies (New York; Scribner's, 1935), 221ff.

3. Thomas S. Peet, "A Selective History of Social Studies Scope and Sequence Patterns, 1916 to 1984" (Ph.D. diss., Ohio State University, 1984), 65–69 et passim.

4. Richard E. Gross, "The Status of the Social Studies in the Public Schools of the United States," *Social Education* 41 (March 1977): 194.

5. David D. Van Tassel, "Trials of Clio,"

in Wronski and Bragaw, eds., *Social Studies and Social Sciences: A Fifty-Year Perspective* (Washington: National Council for the Social Studies [Bulletin No. 78], 1986).

6. Edgar B. Wesley, *American History in Schools and Colleges* (New York: Macmillan, 1944), 13, 16, 22 (emphasis added).

7. Joseph Strayer, "History," in Bernard Berelson et al., *The Social Studies and the Social Sciences* (New York: Harcourt, Brace & World, 1962), 35.

8. Paul Gagnon, "Why Study History?" *The Atlantic Monthly* (November 1988): 63 (emphasis added).

9. William H. McNeill, *The Rise of the*

West: A History of the Human Community (Chicago: University of Chicago Press, 1963).

10. William H. McNeill, "Pursuit of Power: Criteria of Global Relevance," in Bernard R. Gifford, ed., *History in the Schools: What Shall We Teach?* (Macmillan, 1988).

11. Vito Perrone and Associates, *Portraits of High Schools* (Princeton: Carnegie Foundation for the Advancement of Teaching, 1985), chap. 6.

12. Hazel W. Hertzberg, personal communication.

13. Edward W. Said, *Orientalism* (New York: Vintage Books, 1979); Bernard Lewis, "The Map of the Middle East: A Guide for the Perplexed," *American Scholar* 58 (Winter 1989).

14. Mortimer B. Smith, *A Decade of Comment on Education 1956–1966* (Washington: Council for Basic Education, 1966).

15. Barbara J. Winston, "Teaching and Learning in Geography," in Stanley P. Wronski and Donald H. Bragaw, eds., *Social Studies and Social Sciences: A Fifty-Year Perspective* (Washington: (National Council for the Social Studies [Bulletin No. 78], 1986, 53–54.

16. Paul Bohannon, "Why Anthropology? What Can Students—and Teachers— Expect?" Paper delivered at meetings of the Association of Teachers in Anthropology in Two-Year Colleges, San Diego, Spring 1987.

17. Murry R. Nelson, "Social Studies: Something Old, Something New, and All Borrowed," *Theory and Research in Social Education* 8 (Fall 1980): 58.

18. Judith Torney, A. N. Oppenheim, and Russell F. Farnen, *Civic Education in Ten Countries: An Empirical Study* (New York: Wiley, 1975).

19. Dan B. Fleming, "Foreign Policy Issues in Social Studies Textbooks in the U.S.A.," in Volker R. Berghahn and Hanna Schissler, eds., *Perceptions of History* (Oxford: Berg Publishers, 1987), 117.

20. In this sketch I draw heavily on Lee F. Anderson, "Alternative Paradigms in Teaching About the Social Structure of the World" (Paper delivered at the Annual Meeting of the Social Science Education Consortium, Binghamton, NY, July 22, 1988).

21. On the tension between such movements, in social studies in the schools, see the chapters by Stanley Wronski, Murry Nelson, and Augene Wilson in Virginia A. Atwood, ed., *Historical Foundations of Social Studies Education,* Special Topic Edition of the *Journal of Thought* 17 (Fall 1982).

22. Charles E. Merriam, *Civic Education in the United States* (New York: Scribner's, 1934), 51.

23. *Education for Democracy: A Statement of Principles: Guidelines for Strengthening the Teaching of Democratic Values* (Washington: American Federation of Teachers, 1987).

24. Hugh Mehan, "Microcomputers in Classrooms: Educational Technology or Social Practice," *Anthropology & Education Quarterly* 20 (March 1989); M. M. Riel, "The Intercultural Learning Network," *The Computing Teacher Journal* 14 no. 7 (1987).

25. David D. Van Tassel, "Trials of Clio," in Wronski and Bragaw, *Social Studies and Social Sciences: A Fifty-Year Perspective,* (Washington: National Council for the Social Studies [Bulletin No. 78], 1986), 5.

26. McNeill, "Pursuit of Power.

27. Quoted in *The Chronicle of Higher Education,* January 16, 1985, p. 99.

13.0   History and Its "Allied Subjects"

1. Bernard R. Gifford, "Introduction: Thinking About History Teaching and Learning," in Bernard R. Gifford, ed., *History in the Schools: What Shall We Teach?* (New York: Macmillan, 1988), 10.

2. Christopher Lasch, "'Excellence' in Education: Old Refrain or New Departure?" *Issues in Education* 3 (Summer 1985).

3. Susan Resneck Parr, "Teaching the Humanities in the University," in *The Humanities in the University* (New York: American Council of Learned Societies [ACLS Occasional Paper No. 6], 1988): 11.

4. Sponsored by the American Historical Association, the Mississippi Valley Historical Association, and the National Council for the Social Studies. The report is Edgar B. Wesley, *American History in Schools and Colleges* (New York: Macmillan, 1944).

5. M. Kent Jennings, Richard G. Niemi, with Kenneth P. Langton, "Effects of the High School Curriculum," in M. Kent Jennings and Richard G. Niemi, *The Political Character of Adolescence: The Influence of Families and Schools* (Princeton: Princeton University Press, 1974), 185.

6. Sources: "A Trend Study of High School Offerings and Enrollments: 1972–73 and 1981–82" (Washington: National Center for Educational Statistics, Contractor Report, 1984); G. S.

Wright, "Subject Offerings and Enrollments in Public Secondary Schools, 1961–62." (Washington: GPO, 1965).

7. Hazel W. Hertzberg, "Are Method and Content Enemies?," in Gifford, *History in the Schools*, 36.

8. Edgar B. Wesley, *American History in Schools and Colleges* (New York: Macmillan, 1944), frontispiece.

9. *Mandate for Change: The Impact of Law on Educational Innovation* (Chicago: American Bar Association Special Committee on Youth Education for Citizenship, 1979).

10. Primarily in division two of his book. In the present volume, we consider the position of history in the early grades in section 11.1, as well as here.

11. Paul R. Hanna, "Society-Child-Curriculum," in Clarence W. Hunnicutt, *Education 2000 AD* (Syracuse: Syracuse University Press, 1956).

12. For example, Charlotte Crabtree, quoted in *Education Week*, December 1, 1988.

13. Chester E. Finn, Jr., Diane Ravitch, and Robert T. Fancher, eds., *Against Mediocrity: The Humanities in America's High Schools* (New York: Homes and Meier, 1984), 260.

14.0   Test Scores and Interpretations

1. Diane Ravitch and Chester Finn, Jr., *What Do Our 17-Year-Olds Know? A Report on the First National Assessment of History and Literature* (New York: Harper and Row, 1987).

2. W. A. Schafer, "What Do Students Know About American Government, Before Taking College Courses in Political Science?" *Proceedings of the American Political Science Association* 2, (1905): 207ff.

3. College Entrance Examination Board, *Annual Report of the Secretary* (The Board: New York, 1922).

4. Edgar B. Wesley, *American History in Schools and Colleges* (New York: Macmillan, 1944).

5. The 1943 *New York Times* results were

reported on April 4, 1943; the 1976 results on May 2, 3, and 4, 1976.

6. Dale Whittington, "What Did High School Students Know? The Report of an Attempt to Forge a Link Between Current Knowledge with That of the Past" (Research paper commissioned by the National Commission on Social Studies in the Schools, 1988).

7. National Assessment of Educational Progress, *The U.S. History Report Card* (Washington: U.S. Department of Education [Report No. 19-H-01], 1990.)

8. *Enduring Effects of Education* (Chicago: University of Chicago Press, 1975).

9. Stanley M. Elam, "Anti-Democratic

Attitudes of High School Seniors in the Orwell Years," *Phi Delta Kappan* 65 (January 1984).

10. As reported in the *New York Times*, May 28, 1989.

11. J. Freeman Butts, *The Civic Mission in Educational Reform* (Stanford, CA: Hoover Institution Press, 1989), 209.

12. Howard Mehlinger, "The NAEP Report on Changes in Political Knowledge and Attitudes, 1969–76," *Phi Delta Kappan* 59 (June 1978): 676.

13. Butts, *The Civic Mission in Educational Reform*, 198.

14. *Education for Democracy: A Statement of Principles: Guidelines for Strengthening the Teaching of Democratic Values* (Washington: American Federation of Teachers, 1987).

15. Ralph W. Tyler, "Dynamic Response In a Time of Decline," *Phi Delta Kappan* 63 (June 1982); George Miller, "The Challenge of Universal Literacy," *Science* 241 (September 9, 1988).

16. Lawrence C. Stedman and Carl F. Kaestle, "The Test Score Decline Is Over: Now What?" *Phi Delta Kappan* 66 (November 1985).

17. International Assessment for the Evaluation of Education Achievement, *The Underachieving Curriculum: Assessing U.S. School Mathematics From an International Perspective* (Champaign, IL: Stipes Publishing Co., 1987).

15.0   Goods and Expectations of the Schools

1. A version of this argument is made by James S. Coleman, "Families and Schools," *Educational Researcher* 16 (August–September 1987).

2. American Association for the Advancement of Science, *Project 2061: Science for All Americans* (Washington: AAAS, 1989).

3. Robert D. Barr, James L. Barth, and S. Samuel Shermis, *Defining the Social Studies* (Washington: National Council for the Social Studies [Bulletin No. 51], 1977); Irving Morrissett and John D. Haas, "Rationales, Goals, and Objectives in Social Studies," in Social Science Education Consortium, *The Current State of Social Studies: A Report of Project SPAN* (Boulder, SSEC, 1982).

4. John Goodlad, "A Study of Schooling: Some Findings and Hypotheses," *Phi Delta Kappan* 64 (March 1983).

5. "The Gallup Poll of Teachers' Attitudes Toward the Public Schools," *Phi Delta Kappan* 66 (January 1985), pt. 2.

6. Alec M. Gallup, "The 18th Annual Gallup Poll of the Public's Attitudes Toward the Public Schools," *Phi Delta Kappan* 68 (September 1986).

7. George H. Gallup, "The Fourth Annual Gallup Poll of the Public's Attitudes Toward the Public Schools," *Phi Delta Kappan* 54 (September 1972).

8. Stanley M. Elam and Pauline B. Gough, "Comparing Lay and Professional Opinions on Gallup Poll Questions," *Phi Delta Kappan* 61 (September 1980).

9. National Education Association, *NEA Research/Gallup Opinion Polls: Public and K–12 Teacher Members* (Washington: NEA, 1988).

10. Stanley M. Elam, "The Second Gallup/Phi Delta Kappa Poll of Teachers' Attitudes Toward the Public Schools," *Phi Delta Kappan* 70 (June 1989). Similar data on goals and morale appear in Carnegie Foundation for the Advancement of Teaching, *The Condition of Teaching: A State by State Analysis 1988* (Princeton, NJ: Carnegie Foundation for the Advancement of Teaching, 1988).

11. Allan T. Slagle, "What Is the Task of Our Schools?" *Elementary School Journal* 60 (December 1959).

12. Paul E. Peterson, *School Politics* (Chicago: University of Chicago Press, 1976).

13. Albuquerque Public Schools, *Social Studies Program: Evaluation* (Albuquerque N.M.: ERIC Document ED-258855, 1984).

16.0 Preparation of Teachers

1. Mary Paxton Burks, compiler, *Teachers, Counselors, Librarians, Administrators Requirements for Certification for Elementary Schools, Secondary Schools, Junior Colleges*, 50th ed. (Chicago: University of Chicago Press, 1985).
2. This and related trends are described succinctly in C. Emily Feistritzer, *The Condition of Teaching: A State by State Analysis, 1985* (Princeton: Carnegie Foundation for the Advancement of Teaching, 1985).
3. *The Status of Pre-College Science, Mathematics, and Social studies Educational Practices in U.S. Schools: An Overview and Summaries of Three Studies* (Washington: National Science Foundation [Document SE 78-71], 1978).
4. Lynn Fontana, *Perspectives on the Social Studies* (Bloomington, IN: Agency for Instructional Television [Research Report 78; also ERIC Document 249 965], 1980).
5. Vito Perrone and Associates, *Portraits of High Schools* (Princeton: Carnegie Foundation for the Advancement of Teaching, 1985), 649.
6. Alvin P. Short and Donald T. Matlock, "Sociology Programs in U.S. High Schools: Current Findings with a Na-tional Sample," *Teaching Sociology* 9 (April 1982).
7. For example, by Jean D. Grambs, *Schools, Scholars and Society* (Englewood Cliffs: Prentice-Hall, 1978), chap. 15 especially.
8. Howard D. Mehlinger, "Social Studies: Some Gulfs and Priorities," in Howard D. Mehlinger and O. L. Davis, Jr., eds., *The Social Studies: Eightieth Yearbook of the National Society for the Study of Education* (Chicago: NSSE, 1981), 258–59.
9. Some evidence on this rather complex matter is given in Feistritzer, *Condition of Teaching*, 71ff.
10. Lynne V. Cheney, *American Memory: A Report on the Humanities in the Nation's Public Schools* (Washington: National Endowment for the Humanities, 1987).
11. William J. Bennett, *First Lessons: A Report on Elementary Education in America* (Washington: U.S. Department of Education, 1986).
12. Perrone et al., *Portraits*, 649.
13. Harvard University Committee on the Objectives of General Education in a Free Society, *General Education in a Free Society* (Cambridge, Mass.: Harvard University Press, 1945), 147ff.
14. *Chronicle of Higher Education*, March 15, 1989, p. A21.

17.0 Higher-Order Thinking

1. John I. Goodlad, *A Place Called School* (New York: McGraw-Hill, 1983), chap. 4; Vito Perrone and associates, *Portraits of High Schools* (Princeton, N.J.: Carnegie Foundation for the Advancement of Teaching, 1985), 650 et passim; Karen B. Wiley (with Jeanne Race), *The Study of Pre-College Science, Mathematics, and Social Science Education: 1955–1975. Vol. III: Social Science Education* (Washington: National Science Foundation [Document SE 78-73] 1978), 245ff; Robert E. Stake and Jack A. Easley, Jr., *Case Studies in Science Education* (Washington: National Science Foundation, [Document 78-74] 1978). Volume I, *The Case Reports*.
2. In social studies, interesting examples are given in J. F. Voss, T. R. Greene, T. A. Post, and B. C. Penner, "Problem Solving Skill in Social Sciences," in Gordon Bower, ed., *The Psychology of Learning and Motivation*, vol. 17 (New York: Academic Press, 1983).
3. Howard Gardner, *Frames of Mind: The*

Theory of Multiple Intelligences (New York: Basic Books, 1983).

4. Ron Brandt, "On Learning Research: A Conversation with Lauren Resnick," *Educational Leadership* 46 (December 1988/January 1989): 15.

5. John Rossi, "Opening Mouths and Opening Minds: The American Experience Program," in Vincent Rogers, Arthur D. Roberts, and Thomas P. Weinland, eds., *Teaching Social Studies: Portraits from the Classroom* (Washington: National Council for the Social Studies [Bulletin No. 82], 1988), 71.

6. Discussed by Walter C. Parker, "Process and Content in Social Studies: Beyond the Dichotomy" (Paper presented at the Meeting of the College and University Faculty Assembly of the National Council for the Social Studies, Orlando, FL, November 1988), 25.

7. Lauren B. Resnick, *Education and Learning To Think* (Washington: National Academy [of Sciences] Press, 1987), 3.

8. Robert D. Barr, James L. Barth, and S. Samuel Shermis, *Defining the Social Studies* (Washington: National Council for the Social Studies [Bulletin No. 51], 1977), 67ff.

9. One careful treatment is that of Stephen Toulmin, *Human Understanding: The Collective Use and Evolution of Concepts* (Princeton, NJ: Princeton University Press, 1977).

10. Shirley H. Engle and Anna S. Ochoa, *Education for Democratic Citizenship: Decision-Making in the Social Sciences* (New York: Teachers College Press, 1988), 55.

11. Jerome S. Bruner, "*The Process of Education* Revisited," *Phi Delta Kappan* 53 (September 1971): 19.

12. "Comments of Suzanne W. Helburn," in Barr, Barth, and Shermis, *Defining the Social Studies*.

13. Alfred North Whitehead, *Science and the Modern World* (New York: Free Press, [1925] 1967), 198.

14. An excellent examination of the research literature is given by Catherine Cornbleth, "Critical Thinking and Cognitive Processes," in William B. Stanley, ed., *Review of Research in Social Studies Education 1976–1983* (Washington: National Council for the Social Studies [Bulletin No. 75], 1985).

15. Edith M. Guyton, "Critical Thinking and Political Participation: Development and Assessment," *Theory and Research in Social Education* 16 (Winter 1988); David O. Sears, "Political Behavior," in Gardner Lindzey and Elliot Aronson, eds., *The Handbook of Social Psychology, Vol. 5: Applied Social Psychology,* 2nd ed. (Reading, MA: Addison-Wesley, 1969).

16. Fred M. Newman with Donald W. Oliver, *Clarifying Public Controversy: An Approach to Teaching Social Studies* (Boston: Little, Brown, 1970); Donald W. Oliver and James P. Shaver, *Teaching Public Issues in the High School* (Boston, MA: Houghton Mifflin, 1968). Certain titles from the original 12-volume Public Issues Series, revised and updated, have recently been reissued by the Social Science Education Consortium, Boulder, CO.

17. Quoted in Guyton, "Critical Thinking and Political Participation," 29.

18. Charles A. Beard, A *Charter for the Social Sciences in the Schools* (New York: Scribner's, 1932), 95.

19. For example, 'Miss Jenkins' in Samuel S. Wineburg and Suzanne M. Wilson, "Models of Wisdom in the Teaching of History," *Phi Delta Kappan* 70 September 1988).

20. Jere Brophy, "Teaching Social Studies for Understanding and Higher Order Applications," *Elementary School Journal* 90 (March 1990): 375.

21. Hilda Taba and colleagues,*A Teacher's Handbook to Elementary Social Studies: An Inductive Approach,* 2nd ed. (Reading, MA: Addison-Wesley, 1971), 87.

22. Resnick, *Education and Learning to Think*, 40ff.

23. As described in some detail, for example, in Rogers, Roberts, and Weinland, *Teaching Social Studies*; Perrone et al., *Portraits of High Schools*.

24. Vincent Rogers, "What We Don't Know About The Teaching of Social Studies," *Phi Delta Kappan* 62 (May 1980): 597.
25. "Putting Ideas Into Practice: An Interview with Ted Sizer," *The Harvard Education Letter* 4 (July/August 1988).
26. Gerald Ponder, "Social Studies in the School: Questions of Expectations and Effects," in Howard D. Mehlinger and O. L. Davis, *The Social Studies: Eightieth Yearbook of the National Society for the Study of Education* (Chicago: NSSE, 1981).
27. Jane J. White, "An Ethnographic Study of the Construction of Knowledge About Different Cultures in an Elementary School" (Ph.D. diss., University of Pennsylvania, 1980).
28. J. Durbin, "Statistics and Statistical Science," *Journal of the Royal Statistical Society A* 150, part 3 (1987): 177–91.
29. H. Michael Hartoonian, "Social Mathematics," in Margaret A. Laughlin, H. Michael Hartoonian, and Norris M. Sanders, eds., *From Information to Decision Making* (Washington: National Council for the Social Studies [Bulletin No. 83, 1989).
30. Fred M. Newmann, "Higher Order Thinking in High School Social Studies: An Analysis of Classroom Teachers, Students and Leadership" (University of Wisconsin, National Center on Effective Secondary Schooling, 1988). Fred M. Newmann, "Qualities of Thoughtful Social Studies Classrooms: An Empirical Profile," *Journal of Curriculum Studies* (forthcoming).

Other relevant publications from this research include J. Onosko, "Comparing Teachers' Practices to Promote Students' Thinking," and R. B. Stevenson, "Engagement and Cognitive Challenge in Social Studies Curriculum: A Study of Student Perspective," both in *Journal of Curriculum Studies* (forthcoming); and J. Onosko, "Comparing Teachers' Thinking About Promoting Students' Thinking," *Theory and Research in Social Education* 17 (Summer, 1989). Newman and colleagues have recently completed research that appears to show that "thoughtfulness" in the classroom is indeed the result, in part, of teaching itself, independent of students' attitudes, backgrounds, intelligence, and so on. If valid, this would be one of the strongest demonstrations to date that teaching for thoughtfulness works.
31. The textbook adoption system is described in Harriet Tyson-Bernstein, A *Conspiracy of Good Intentions: America's Textbook Fiasco* (Washington: Council for Basic Education, 1988).
32. Isabel L. Beck, Margaret G. McKeown, and Erika W. Gromoll, "Learning from Social Studies Texts," *Cognition and Instruction* 6, no. 2 (1989): 132.
33. Beck et al., "Issues That May Affect Social Studies Learning: Examples from Four Commercial Programs" (University of Pittsburg, Learning Research and Development Center, 1988), 84.
34. Beck et al., "Learning from Social Studies Texts," 116.

18.0   After a Century of Social Studies

1. James S. Coleman, "Families and Schools," *Educational Researcher* 16 (August–September 1987): 32.
2. Christopher Lasch, "'Excellence' in Education: Old Refrain or New Departure?" *Issues in Education* 3 (Summer 1985): 6.
3. Jerome S. Bruner, *The Relevance of Education* (New York: Norton, 1971).
4. *New York Times*, January 4, 1988; December 21, 1988.
5. Harold Howe II, "Education Moves to Center Stage: An Overview of Recent Studies," *Phi Delta Kappan* 65 (November 1983): 172.
6. Torsten Husén, "Are Standards In U.S. Schools Really Lagging Behind Those in Other Countries?" *Phi Delta Kappan* 64 (March 1983).

7. John Goodlad, "A Study of Schooling: Some Findings and Hypotheses," *Phi Delta Kappan* 64 (March 1983): 52.
8. Thomas James and David Tyack, "Learning from Past Efforts to Reform the High Schools," *Phi Delta Kappan* 64 (February 1983): 406.
9. David Potter, *People of Plenty: Economic Abundance and the American Character* (Chicago: University of Chicago Press, 1954).
10. Michael J. Bakalis, "American Education and the Meaning of Scarcity," *Phi Delta Kappan* 63 (September 1981 [Part I], October 1981 [Part II]).
11. David Tyack and Elizabeth Hansot, "Hard Times, Hard Choices: The Case for Coherence in Public School Leadership," *Phi Delta Kappan* 63 (April 1982): 511.
12. Peter Scott, *Times [of London] Higher Education Supplement*, August 14, 1987.
13. Sidney Hook, "*The Closing of the American Mind*: An Intellectual Best-Seller Revisited," *American Scholar* 58 (Winter 1989): 134.
14. Max Weber, *On the Methodology of the Social Sciences* (Glencoe, IL: Free Press, 1949), 80.
15. Alfred North Whitehead, *Science and the Modern World* (New York: Free Press, [1925] 1967).
16. Daniel P. Resnick and Lauren B. Resnick, "Improving Educational Standards in American Schools, " *Phi Delta Kappan* 65 (November 1983): 180.
17. Carnegie Council on Adolescent Development, *Turning Points: Preparing American Youth for the 21st Century* (New York: Carnegie Corporation of New York, 1989).
18. Robert Slavin, *Cooperative Learning* (New York: Longman, 1983).
19. George Miller, "The Challenge of Universal Literacy," *Science* 241 (September 9, 1988); Anne M. Bussis, "'Burn It At The Casket': Research, Reading Instruction, and Children's Learning of the First R," *Phi Delta Kappan* 64 (December 1982).
20. Dell H. Hymes, *Foundations in Sociolinguistics* (Philadelphia, PA: University of Pennsylvania Press, 1974), chap. 10. Here I am departing to some extent from Hymes's scheme, especially with regard to language as "socially constitutive." Hymes would prefer "socially constituted and constituting" (personal communication, 1989).
21. As reported, for example, by Mark C. Schug, Robert J. Todd, and R. Beery, "Why Kids Don't Like Social Studies," *Social Education* 48 (May 1984).
22. Susan S. Stodolsky. *The Subject Matters: Classroom Activity in Math and Social Studies* (Chicago: University of Chicago Press, 1988).
23. Denis P. Doyle, "The Excellence Movement, Academic Standards, A Core Curriculum and Choice: How Do They Connect?" *Politics of Education Association Yearbook*, (1987): 23.
24. James Hoetker, "Re-Hirsching Some Questions About Curriculum," *The Clearing House* 62 (March 1989): 319.
25. Fred M. Newmann, "Another View of Cultural Literacy: Go For Depth" (Paper presented at the Association of American Publishers, Alexandria, VA, March 29, 1988), 6.
26. Chester E. Finn, quoted in the *New York Times*, April 12, 1989.
27. *New York Times*, June 10, 1989, p. 29.
28. Tyack and Hansot, "Hard Times, Hard Choices," 515.
29. Stephen R. Graubard, "The Agenda for the Humanities and Higher Education for the 21st Century" (New York: American Council for Learned Societies [Occasional Paper No. 8], 1989), 20.

Indexes

Subject Index

463

Name Index